PUBLIC ADMINISTRATION

PUBLIC ADMINISTRATION: ORGANIZATIONS, PEOPLE, AND PUBLIC POLICY

SAMUEL J. BERNSTEIN
Baruch College, City University of New York

PATRICK O'HARA
The Maxwell School, Syracuse University

Harper & Row, Publishers
New York, Hagerstown, Philadelphia, San Francisco, London

Sponsoring Editor: Dale Tharp
Project Editor: Rhonda Roth
Designer: Michel Craig
Production Manager: Marion A. Palen
Compositor: The Composing Room of Michigan, Inc.
Printer and Binder: Halliday Lithograph Corporation
Art Studio: J & R Technical Services Inc.

**PUBLIC ADMINISTRATION:
ORGANIZATIONS, PEOPLE, AND PUBLIC POLICY**

Library of Congress Cataloging in Publication Data

Bernstein, Samuel J
    Public administration.

    Includes index.
    1. Public administration. I. O'Hara, Patrick,
Date-   joint author. II. Title.
JF1351.B475   350   78-26531
ISBN 0-06-040649-6

For Deena and Janice;
And for Ariella, Chaim,
And Christopher;
Today is the day we repay
Yesterday's time lost.

CONTENTS

PREFACE

We anticipate that this book will have an eclectic audience: curious undergraduates probing for a major; juniors and seniors with social science backgrounds in fields other than public administration; graduate students beginning an intensive exploration of the field; and mid-careerists reentering academe to certify and enhance experience gained on the front lines of administration. The students will enter a field that, academically and practically, is equally eclectic. For instance, university economists and sociologists offer "theories" of bureaucratic behavior. At the same time, government economists help direct financial policy, and sociologists in the bureaucracy help shape human resource policy. Therefore, Part One underscores the multidisciplinary foundations of public administration as a field of academic study and as an applied craft.

After the overview provided by Part One, each of the book's subsequent parts highlights central features of public administration. Part Two stresses that the organizational form is a crucial determinant of administrative behavior and a major influence on public policy. We also emphasize, throughout Part Two, the tensions between the classical definition of bureaucracy, the operational reality, and ideological counterpoints to bureaucracy such as workplace democracy, and humanism. Capping this part is an extensive treatment of the open systems literature that draws upon the theoretical works of Parsons and Merton and case studies by Selznick and others. While some texts treat this literature briefly or not at all, we believe that constructs such as institutionalization and goal-displacement provide a powerful conceptual handle for grasping many of the activities of the public organization.

In Part Three, the focus is on individuals and groups in organizations. Theoretical and applied approaches to motivating the individual and the work group towards effective task performance are discussed. Subsequently we address the changing administrative framework for government's personnel system and subsume, under the rubric of conflict, the efforts of union and management, appointed and career executives, and professionals and administrative generalists to dominate personnel policy. Viewing these struggles in terms of competition for management authority in the public organization enables us to treat, in a coherent way, three topics that tend to be scattered about in most other texts.

In Part Four, the institutions and policy-making mechanisms of government are the central concern. We view, from a perspective of shared powers and administrative brokerage in a pluralist setting, administrative decision making, the budgetary process, and government finance. Government finance, particularly, is treated more extensively than in most other texts. This reflects our feeling that the financial pressure on government—from a lagging economy and rebellious taxpayers—will continue and that there will be a growing demand for financial problem solvers—budget analysts, bond specialists, and economic forecasters. By emphasizing finance, then, we hope to lay a groundwork for specializations that will become increasingly important in public administration education.

Part Five revolves around alternatives to incremental decision making that seek to loosen the hold of institutionalization and special interest politics on the policy process. Systems analysis, program evaluation, and computer applications are treated extensively. Thus, Part Five represents a major departure from most other texts. No other book devotes as much space or detail to introducing the framework, applications, tools, and techniques of systematic analysis to the beginning student. In part, this is because government's increased momentum towards more comprehensive analysis has become evident only recently in legislative and executive commitments to evaluative institutions such as the Congressional Budget Office. Moreover, conveying an elemental understanding of the highly quantitative techniques of systems analysis in a textbook presents pedagogical problems: The numbers tend to crowd out the underlying notions. By opting for a basically conceptual, although not numberless, approach, we hope to prepare the student for subsequent courses, or government assignments, where more sophisticated techniques will be imparted. Of course, teachers are free to expand upon the text presentation. Indeed, to give teachers more leeway in this regard, we worked in concepts that appear infrequently in other introductory texts. These include: Chapter 12's discussion of urban modeling, cost benefit analysis in Chapter 13's discussion of program evaluation, and research methodology in Chapter 13's discussion of evaluation design. In earlier sections, teachers can expand upon such topics as Arrow's Theorem (Chapter 8) and gaming (Chapter 7).

In addition to fashioning this book as a flexible tool for teachers, we have fashioned it as an easily accessible source for students. Case studies, illustrative vignettes, and graphic presentations appear throughout and are integrated into the text. The writing style is direct. Occasionally, light interludes are provided to help the students shoulder the information contained in this volume. Conversely, from time to time, we seek to raise fundamental questions in the students' minds. The central inquiry of the Mid-Book Case Study, for instance, concerns the ultimate responsibility for organizational acts. Such presentations are designed to generate understanding even as the "correct" answer eludes the students. More-over, we feel that it is good training for the student to come to grips with tough questions with elusive answers. As we note at several points, the integrity of our government institutions has been preserved by administrators—Elliot Richardson, William Ruckelshaus, Newton Minow—who asked fundamental questions about presidential directives.

At certain junctures throughout the book, we assume the perspective—that of the citizen, consumer, or line employee—through which most students view public and private organization. One reason for this approach is to acclimate the student to the managerial and societal perspectives used through most of the book. So, in Chapter 2, organizations are introduced "from below" with Kafka's "The Trial" providing the punctuation. In addition to making the text materials more accessible, the consumer/citizen perspective can show that organi-zations are not always "overtowering." In Chapter 14, a short primer on battling the government computer closes out the book by reminding students that they needn't feel outmatched by organizations. We wouldn't be surprised if this reminder pays real world dividends.

It is our belief that this text will be an effective teaching tool. It should successfully convey to the student the essential concepts, pro-cesses, and ideologies associated with public administration in the United States while accommodating a variety of teaching styles and perspectives. The extensive bibliographies at the end of each chapter should help students with term paper assignments and in subsequent courses. In addition, the book should come in handy to students in their present role as consumer/citizens and their future role as practicing administrators. If the book does serve these purposes, our efforts will have been well rewarded.

SAMUEL J. BERNSTEIN
PATRICK O'HARA

ACKNOWLEDGMENTS

This book, it seems, has claimed a three-year chunk of our lives. At times, its demands on our time and thoughts were continuous and, to our occasional despair, apparently perpetual. Happily, this was not so and *Public Administration: Organizations, People, and Public Policy* has progressed from idea to outline to manuscript to book. We have merely been part of this progression. Quite simply, there would be no book without the help of dozens of people. As a small repayment of an exceedingly large debt, we would like to take this opportunity to express our gratitude.

Working through ideas and concepts is not altogether unpleasant. Or so the pacific demeanor and healthy lifespan of the archetypical academic would seem to indicate. However, although books may be conceptualized in academic salons, they are written and produced in the pits. Again and again, sections of manuscript must be typed, proofread, Xeroxed, and edited. This is not possible without the help of indefatigable people who prove that substantive editorial advice need not be the exclusive preserve of academics. We were particularly lucky in receiving editorial assistance from a number of individuals who used their key vantage points of administrative assistant, graduate researcher, and secretary to develop astute perceptions of organizations in action. For sharing those perceptions with us and for producing this manuscript, we must thank Arline Landau, Dorothy Glass, Louise Attillia, Leslie Sanders, Nancy Donovan, Betty Hansel, Noreen Kelly, Christie Larbes, and Alan Zlotnik.

We are indebted also to our long-suffering colleagues who waded through the often turgid prose and disconnected thinking of the early drafts of this manuscript. This book is immeasurably better as a result of the contributions of Jesse Burkhead, Richard Campbell, Philip Cooper, Marc Holzer, Wilbur Rich, Norman Thomas, Frederick Thayer, John DeMarco, Ann Gregory, Edward R. Padgett, Lottie Feinberg, and Jeffrey Rinehart. Any errors of omission or commission appearing in the text are, of course, the sole responsibility of the authors.

We would be remiss if we did not thank Guthrie Birkhead, the Dean of the Maxwell School at Syracuse University, James D. Carroll, the Director of Maxwell's Public Administration Programs, and Samuel Thomas, Dean of the Graduate School of Business and Public Administration at Baruch College. Even as this project made demands on our time that competed with our institutional responsibilities, these gentlemen were understanding and supportive. The same can be said for our colleagues and students.

A colleague to whom we would like to express our special appreciation is Edwin A. Bock of the Maxwell School. Professor Bock guided us through the InterUniversity Case Series, a treasure of public administration reality that helped nourish this book. Ed Bock's commitment to preparing the student for the work-a-day world of public administration, will, we trust, be amply reflected in this book.

Finally, we must settle accounts with those whose association with this book was involuntary. For the better part of two years, our wives, Janice O'Hara and Deena Bernstein, shouldered a disproportionate share of our family responsibilities, yet continued to lend their support to this effort. In the final hectic stages of manuscript preparation, Janice O'Hara retyped most of the chapters. Our children, Christopher O'Hara and Chaim and Ariella Bernstein, have also suffered more than their share of fatherless days. To our families, then, we pledge to make up for lost time. Thus, we dedicate this book to them and to that end.

SAMUEL J. BERNSTEIN
PATRICK O'HARA

PUBLIC
ADMINISTRATION

PART ONE

OVERVIEW

CHAPTER 1

PUBLIC ADMINISTRATION: AN INTERDISCIPLINARY CROSSROAD

INTRODUCTION

Government accounts for one-third of this country's consumption and investment with a dollar amount in the neighborhood of one trillion. There are few of us who are not in daily contact with government and even fewer who do not feel the impact of government policies. News about government features presidents, governors, mayors, county executives, city council members, state legislators, representatives, senators, commissioners, cabinet secretaries, and various other spokespersons who speak on behalf of, or in opposition to, the policies of 80,000 national, state, county, and local government jurisdictions in the United States.

If one turns to the urban citizen's contact with public employees, the picture is rich in detail and complexity. The trip to work each morning can take one past police officers and sanitation workers on the streets, change booth operators, engineers, and conductors on a subway or commuter railroad. Sharing the trip, most likely, are teachers, clerks, economists, financial analysts, meat inspectors, chemists, nurses, social workers. All have one thing in common: they work for the government. Our traveler may have started the trip from a publicly sponsored housing development and, if unlucky, may be on the way to straighten out a problem with the meter maid, tax collector, motor vehicle cashier, or hearing officer. Rural dwellers, on the other hand, encounter government workers rarely seen within the city limits: agricultural experts, forest rangers, conservation specialists, and utility service personnel for the county.

This richness and complexity has had a considerable impact on the teaching and study of public administration. The subject is approached from a variety of angles. If teachers voted on a "central theory" of public administration, it is doubtful that any one proposition would receive majority support. However, this has not discouraged those searching for a definition of what is—and what is not—public administration.[1] The search presses on; the administration of government is becoming a greater force in the functioning of our society and ultimately in the way we live our lives.

In this introductory chapter we will trace the contributions of established social sciences to the study of public administration. A working definition of public administration will be given to help frame the broad objects of this book's attention: organizations, people, and public policy. Finally, we will present a summary of the book, showing how each section and chapter address a major dimension of public administration.

PUBLIC ADMINISTRATION: AN INTERSECTION OF THE SOCIAL SCIENCES

Public administration is a unique discipline. Textbooks and benchmark treatises on the subject have been written by political scientists, sociologists, economists, psychologists, and management scientists.[2] Except in works of fiction, such as Franz Kafka's *The Trial*, books on public administration were usually somewhat remote. This was understandable. Prior to 1926, when the Maxwell School of Syracuse University awarded the first master's level certificates, there were no degrees in public administration. It was not until the middle of this century that academic institutions awarded doctorate degrees to students of public administration. The number of recipients was small, however; and most graduates became administrators, not theoreticians. As a result, academic writings on the subject continued to flow primarily from other academic disciplines. Thus, these writings defined public administration, but through other disciplinary orientations. It remained unclear whether this new hybrid public administration would remain a part of more established disciplines such as political science and sociology. In the confusion, public administration sat, bigger than life, vaguely inscrutable, and without a true home in the traditional social sciences.

Public administration was, and remains today, an intersection of several disciplines. When law and political science diverged, each left a residue that became a part of the intersection of public administration. When bureaucratic organizations became aware of group behavior within, sociological explanations entered the intersection. Feeder roads ran off into psychology soon afterwards as public management sought more sophisticated methods of motivating employees. For administrative and analytical techniques, the crossroads of public administration was fed by management science and economics.

As each field of study entered the intersection it sought to set up blockades. No discipline, however, could erect one imposing enough to prevent others from barrelling through. Indeed, the public administration intersection is like a theoretical cloverleaf in perpetual motion. Competing theories abound. But none come close to shutting out the others. Economists, psychologists, and sociologists have all attempted to explain why employees act as they do. Political scientists, management scientists, and economists have focused on how public policy decisions are reached. Sociologists, political scientists, and economists have offered explanations on the nature of the modern state, in general, and the structure of the United States' government, in particular. Most provide very good descriptions; none provide reliable predictions. Thus, it may be possible to make this statement: Public administration is poly-theoretical on a descriptive level and atheoretical on a predictive level.

Many authors of public administration texts have recognized this diversity and have treated a particular aspect of administration, such as internal management and personnel management. Studies that have focused on specific areas of public administration have largely succeeded in avoiding credibility gaps.[3] Other works have attempted to subsume under a single paradigm the intersection of public administration and its multiple access roads.[4] Other scholars have attempted to describe all facets of public administration while remaining atheoretical.[5] Often, however, the theoretical and the purely descriptive approaches suffer the same fate: the complex nature and huge quantity of the information to be conveyed taxes and frustrates the beginning student. Before we describe how we plan to risk disaster, it is useful to detail what we accept and reject from other approaches.

Public Administration as Political Science and Law

Political science and law are the traditional avenues that lead to the study of public management. At one time the two fields were closely allied and a background in either discipline assured a position in government. Today, the commodity produced by law schools—technically competent, polished, value-neutral advocacy—is still in high demand by all sectors of the economy, including government. Political science, on the other hand, is often shunned by most nonacademic employers as esoteric philosophy that contemplates the relationship between government, as laid out in the Constitution of 1787, and the way society makes decisions today and will make them tomorrow.

As the study of law became more technical, and political science continued to focus on our government institutions through a historical perspective, both fields tended to treat government organization as a side issue. The world of the government attorney consisted of legislative law, departmental rules and regulations, and judicial review. It was a predictable blueprint and well-rewarded lawyers gained skill in its intricacies. Thus, administrative law books address the legal subsystem of government bureaucracy and little else.

If the lawyer's approach to public administration was too specialized and technical, the political scientist's approach was too theoretical and too committed to a rationalization of our traditional notions of government. Whereas law books placed too much emphasis on the legal subsystems of government bureaucracy, some political science/public administration texts told us too much about: (a) the Congress, (b) the President, (c) the Supreme Court and, it seems, every agency ever created by (a) or (b), as well as a random smattering of several hundred laws. Memorizing the whole text might have stood a future chief executive in good stead, but would have wasted about 90 percent of the time of a prospective agency budget officer. Those destined for state and local careers, approximately 80 percent of all government workers, were also ill-served by the emphasis on federal government often found in such texts.

It could also be said that political science let public administration escape by looking the other way when it left. In the 1940s, 1950s, and 1960s, political science became steeped in behavioral studies which analyzed voter profiles, voter responses to issues and candidate imagery, and demographic breakdowns of the electorate. Thus preoccupied, many political scientists failed to recognize that government organizations were successfully defying the President and Congress; that, in effect, a fourth branch of government had emerged in the United States. Similarly, many clung to the traditional notions of top-down democracy, using as evidence the fact that bureaucracy catered to constituencies and formulated policies that the legislature then certified as law. The opposing perspectives of Robert Dahl and C. Wright Mills, which we will consider in greater detail in Chapter 8, gave more attention to administrative power but sought primarily to determine major external influences on bureaucratic policy.

Neither law nor political science adequately explained the black organizational box that is the workaday world of the public administrator. Law offered specialized skills; political science combined a historical/formalistic perspective with explanations of and for the outside world. Neither field adequately explained to the future bureaucrat how to manage an organization when it eschewed the law, or thumbed its nose at institutional arrangements and invited private citizens to make policy.

This book will attempt such explanations. Administrative law and the formal structure of government, therefore, will be treated as two of many components of the administrative environment. The treatment, though, is neither encyclopedic nor representative of the core of the book.

Public Administration as Management

Business management, when applied to public administration, focused on administrative problems and technically inefficient organizational design. The solutions of business administration lay primarily in overhauling government machinery without tampering with the surrounding political environment. This was a mistake. Organizational blueprints in government were not drawn up by an engineer seeking to solve a problem; they were created in committee to deal with a number of related but discrete problems, many having political overtones. As a result, the field of management prescribed organizational forms to government only to see them rejected outright, either accepted in theory but disregarded in practice or instituted piecemeal over a period of decades. In government, reorganization plans have always led a perilous existence. The unlucky ones went to a shooting gallery of sorts where offended Congresspersons and enraged interest groups attempted to shoot the legs out from under the proposals.[6] To the embarrassment of the managerially inclined draftsman, who often disclaimed authorship, few reorganization plans went into effect without some key parts blown away.

Despite its failures, however, the management approach is an important one for government. Contrary to a belief that held sway in the United States for a number of years, our resources are not unlimited. When this book went to press, the American economy was in its second consecutive decade of economic sluggishness. As a result, many state and local governments felt the pinch of reduced tax revenues and skyrocketing service demands. Relief was available from the federal government, but there was growing concern about a balanced budget and fiscal responsibility in Washington, as well. The threat of reduced federal subsidy that sustains state and local government operations remains a real one.

It seems clear then that we will have to run government more efficiently. The knowledge and experience housed in our schools of management, in consulting firms, and in government service must be tapped. This is being done and our book reflects this tendency. For example, the creation of centralized executive and legislative units for the analysis of government programs and operations, the use of outside evaluators to judge the accomplishments of administrative programs, and the institutionalization of innovative management approaches that seek to outflank the existing bureaucracy are discussed in the text.

Management science, an outgrowth of the management approach, has also championed the use of new analytical and evaluative tools and techniques. The most sophisticated tool of twentieth-century management, of course, is the computer. While it is not the answer to all the government's problems, the computer, if properly used, can be a tremendous help because much of government's work is amenable to computerization. Astute government executives, therefore, are pushing for a greater data processing capacity and will likely get it. Whether the computer's potential will be fully exploited is questionable; but the likelihood that most future government managers will need at least a passing familiarity with computer techniques is not. Thus, we have devoted an entire chapter to the subject of computers and public administration.

It must be pointed out that while we emphasize analytical and evaluative approaches associated with management science, we do so with reservation. Many students who read this book undoubtedly will become government managers. Although the traditional notion conceives public administration as value-neutral, we know this not to be so. Much of public policy is made in government organizations and, of that, a considerable amount is rubber stamped by the legislature. Thus, many readers of this book will have an impact on public policy and, some, inevitably, will be major shapers of government activity. Since it is not our desire that these individuals become technocrats devoid of values, we will not ignore the pitfalls associated with technological zealotry.

Obviously when one suggests that the student carry certain values into the government bureaucracy, there has been a shift from teaching to preaching. In many learning situations, this shift would be considered improper. Fortunately, our government was overlaid with values two hundred years ago. The framers of the Bill of Rights, we are sure, would have preferred that administrators feel queasy when fatalities are perfunctorily factored into a cost-benefit equation. Similarly, an internalized warning system should sound when law enforcement officials are ordered to investigate prominent opponents of their political superiors. We do not believe that students should be taught to establish secret contact with the press upon entry into government service. However, if one must choose between polar opposites, we prefer "whistle-blowing" instruction to a "hear no evil, see no evil, speak no evil" pedagogy in our schools of public administration.

The field of management, thus, provides tools and techniques, particularly analytical ones, that have great value in public administration. However, a broader perspective on the part of government employees is also necessary to ensure that the tools do not mechanize one's thinking and that the techniques do not monopolize one's focus. One of the purposes of this book is to provide students with the tools, the techniques, and the perspective.

Public Administration as Economics

Economics is crucial to certain areas of public administration. In federal budgeting and finance, for instance, the whole of economics—theories, tools, and even jargon—underpins the process. This is due primarily to the economists' success in perfecting the art of large scale data analysis. Such analysis, in brief, consists of the periodic, societywide collection of information on income, consumption, savings, investment, and unemployment and measuring the effect of one or another economic policy over time. Economists, however, are not foolproof in their attempt to predict and trace the impact of public policies. Sometimes, the figures give the illusion that Policy A (e.g., tax cuts) will always bring Result A (e.g., increased employment). However, in economics, few such theories survive a decade. The value of macroeconomic analysis to national economic managers, thus, is its usefulness both as a guide in the formation of public programs and a monitoring device to determine whether the expected outcomes occur.

Whereas the full repertoire of economists usually has impact in government finance, their analytical tools have general applicability. Longitudinal studies of economic, physical, or social data relating to the target population or area of a government program are among the best ways to evaluate policy effectiveness. Although management scientists were in on the ground floor, economists laid the foundation for sophisticated data analysis and their books on the subject can be extremely informative to the future public administrator.[7] Similarly, economists have a penchant for "shadow costing"; that is, calculating costs where the task seems impossible. Such talent stands a public administrator in good stead when alternative programs for which real dollar amounts cannot easily be assigned to gauge value or merit are being considered.

When we treat budgeting and finance and delve into program evaluation, the economic perspective will be presented. However, we will strive to avoid what we believe are pedagogical traps in interweaving economics and public administration. One set of snares is the formulae and supply/demand curves that do as much to frighten beginning students as to enlighten them. Our forays into the mathematical will be brief and straightforward. Another pitfall in economics is the core maxim that individuals are motivated almost exclusively by self-interest. This book stresses that individual behavior in a public administration setting is the product of numerous stimuli. We encourage managers, therefore, to be prepared for the unexpected rather than the predictable. Public managers should never stand guilty of the charge that one economist hurled at his colleagues when he said, "Indeterminacy is to economists what garlic is to vampires. So they have replaced human beings, whose behavior must be studied if you want to discover what they are doing and are about to do, by robots programmed to respond exclusively to pecuniary stimuli."[8]

It is our view that the "robot hypothesis," which leads to rapid and often erroneous assumptions about the people that the public administrator manages, can be as dysfunctional to the public administrator as the hypnotic effect of modern technology. For instance, an approach to public administration that assumes that public employees are going to maximize their self-interests, and therefore must be watched closely lest they goof off leads to over-management, organizational tension, and a limited range of alternative solutions available to managers and acceptable to employees. The manager who believes in "economic man" may consider clients, legislators, and other organizations as predators. Such a mentality dictates that it is better to announce Monday morning policy changes at the close of business Friday night so that selfish clients cannot thwart the agency. Quite simply, we intend to nurture no such mindset.

Public Administration as Sociology

Sociology occupies the broadest boulevard leading into the intersection of public administration. Sociology pioneered the study of organizations and some of the earliest writing on the subject, such as those of Max Weber and Robert Michels, remain timely today. Overall, sociology's most important contribution to public administration is a generic framework of organizations. Students need not acquaint themselves with the full range of organizations from the Town Clerk to the Department of Defense. Rather, they should recognize that organizations—large or small, public or private—share similarities. For example, each organization has rules, whether public law or company regulation; but rules only play a part in controlling behavior. The gap is filled by informal rules and rulers in administration.

Such information on principles of organizational behavior provides more than a learning framework for students. It is also a guide for diagnosing real world situations in a variety of locales. Whatever organization he or she may work for, the student knows how to identify and classify certain activities independent of specific content. The manager who cast the dissenting vote in a committee decision dictates a memo to the file to guarantee absolution from anticipated disaster. Neither the issue nor the public or private character of the organization is likely to have an effect on this standard "cover your behind" response.

Sociologists also focused upon the relationship between organization and society.[9] The discovery that survival and other internal needs triggered independent organizational responses to the environment shook up traditional thinkers, particularly those in the political science/institutional school that considered the public organization lawbound except for psychotic episodes of corruption. From sociology also came the vital concept of open systems that linked studies of internal organization behavior and inquiries into the societal-organizational relationship.

Concepts from sociology provide descriptive frameworks. They have, however, the capacity to encompass everything and therefore, methodological purists would say, explain nothing. We concede somewhat to this argument on the philosophical plane, but reject it on pedagogical grounds. The purpose of this book is to provide an introduction to public administration. The sociological approach contributes significantly to this task. This is not the place to confuse the student with the intricacies of methodological debate. Unlike most authors of texts on public administration, we give the sociological approach more attention than the political science/institutional approach because we emphasize the generic in organization rather than the specific. We feel this approach is proper because the public administration student is destined to work in an organizational setting; as part of an organizational mission; and for a government jurisdiction. Training students to operate effectively within the organizational setting is probably the most enduring lesson that public administration education can impart. Indeed, most agencies do not trust book learning when it comes to their missions: most new employees are inexorably, if informally, debriefed, and then reprogrammed with the official philosophy. Thus, academic training in the formalities of budgeting or personnel management may fall by the wayside. However, the generic knowledge of the ins and outs of organizational life is not likely to be squelched and will help the employee cope more rapidly and successfully with the bureaucratic environment.

Public Administration as Psychology

Psychology is another primary thoroughfare feeding into the intersection of public administration. The thoroughfare is wide. Psychologists, like sociologists, began with a general theoretical search to find what moved people to act. Unlike economists, psychologists observed individuals up close in a variety of real life and experimental situations. The organization was the setting of many of these observations. When a closer look at human participation was desired, psychologists designed laboratory experiments to assimilate organizational situations.

Because organizations were willing to pay behavioral scientists to analyze their problems, psychology, of all the academic disciplines, has had the most opportunities to study organizations firsthand. Therefore, the studies of psychologists or behavioral scientists are prominent in the literature on organization theory. Their recommendations, moreover, have influenced management practice and have contributed to the understanding and practice of public administration. An extended discussion of the Human Relationists and the psychological humanists is thus provided. Despite the unresolved issues in behavioral science, we believe that the student will find the discussion illuminating.

Public Administration as Policy Science

When six or seven roads intersect, there is bound to be a collision; one or another vehicle is likely to plow into the open field creating a new road. Policy analysis, operations research, and systems analysis all have spun off the intersection of public administration. It is not yet clear whether these fields will remain adjuncts to the intersection, come under the dominance of their economic and management science forebearers, or become mainstream influences on public administration. (See Figure 1.1.)

At present, policy analysis and systems analysis appear to be mutually reinforcing adjuncts. Systems analysis aids in the creation of new programs and organizational units, the diagnosis of the ills of existing ones, and the comprehensible patterning of arrangements as complex as urban areas. Policy analysis charts the success of new or existing programs in negotiating the system in order to accomplish their goals.

Systems "thinking" is the subject of Chapter 12 of this book and is posed as an alternative to the stop-gap, reflexive managerial decision making often found in government. Although agency management can be besieged by a succession of internal and external crises that are handled as they arise one step at a time, we believe that government managers should be encouraged to dismantle their machines, on paper at least, to see how they work and if they can work more efficiently. Managers should also analyze the individuals, institutions, or geographical areas that they serve. Using systems thinking and systems tools, these assessments may be less overwhelming than expected initially.

Evaluation, or policy analysis, which deals with the criteria for judging the worth of government programs, is also allotted a chapter in this book. Again, we steer the student toward an analytical and managerial perspective. Our emphasis is on getting the biggest bang for the buck—providing, of course, that human values do not get lost in the explosion.

There are drawbacks, of course, with systems thinking and evaluative approaches. Although we stress the analytical approach, the first 10 chapters of the book detail the formidable obstacles, such as bureaucratic resistance and political commitments to the status quo, that stand in the way of a thoroughgoing evaluation of government activity. Nonetheless,

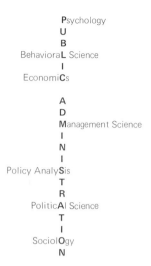

Figure 1.1   Public Administration and Its Intersecting Disciplines

government is becoming more receptive to analytical approaches, and we expect that graduates of public administration programs will increasingly become budget analysts, systems analysts, and communication specialists. We hope, therefore, the final chapters of this book prove useful to those who are today's students but tomorrow's managers.

A DEFINITION AND A SUMMARY

With due respect for those who counsel against one-sentence definitions of public administration, we shall, nonetheless, attempt one. We offer it as a guide but hesitate to designate it as *the* definition of public administration. *Public administration determines the way we live through people working in organizations that function and make decisions under rules reflecting past and present societal needs and values.*

Two key words, "organization" and "people," and the phrase "make decisions under rules reflecting past and present societal needs and values" (i.e., public policy making), are inextricably bound together and are the core components of this book. In the main, when there are large-scale, complex jobs to be done, society creates organizations to do them. Thus, organizations are the dominant elements in industrialized nations.

Organizations, however, are animated by people. The way people are managed determines how effective the organization is at its tasks. The agenda of tasks for the public organization is set by legislators, chief executives, and other government officials who act on behalf of society. This is the public policy input into administration. Public policy is not inviolate, however; it is subject to change by the people within organizations. Civil servants become policy makers because of a complex mix of beliefs: some stem from exposure to the bureaucratic organization and some derive from external sources. Thus, public policy outputs are the administratively edited version of legislative and executive inputs. What happens to us every day is determined by the public servant in the public organization as well as by the individuals we elect to public policy-making positions.

ORGANIZATIONS, PEOPLE, AND PUBLIC POLICY

Organizations   Organizations affect everyone. Students should be familiar with the impacts that large-scale organizations have on modern society. Therefore, Part Two of this book is devoted to the subject of organizations.

In Chapter 2 the genesis and essential characteristics of organizations are reviewed as well as Max Weber's classic formulation of bureaucracy. To introduce the student to organizations in a dramatic way, the works of Franz Kafka will be used to illustrate the apprehension that people may feel with respect to organization. In Chapter 3 the formal monocratic nature of leadership within organization is contrasted with the egalitarian mindset that flourishes in the United States and other countries. In this chapter, we will also note the nature and basis of the informal organization. The obedience experiments of Milgram, which shed considerable light on the operation and potential abuses of organizational authority, will be a central feature of the chapter and, we hope, student discussion. In Chapter 4 the organization will be viewed as an entity responding to and/or seeking to control its environment. The behavior of both "legitimate" and "illegitimate" organizations will also be discussed.

Organizations need people. Part III focuses upon the interplay between the people within organizations and the rules, particularly in government, that govern such interactions. Chapter 5 will view the theoretical approaches to worker motivation in organizations ranging from Taylor to the Human Relations movement and beyond. People as achieving and thinking animals—evaluating the organization's demands and deciding whether to obey—will be the primary focus. Chapter 6 will examine government personnel policies. The "Spoils System," and the "Merit System" will be viewed to highlight the continuing dichotomy between representative and value-neutral bureaucracy. The clash between the "political" and "career" public servant will be noted also.

Chapter 7 will treat the role of the public employee as it has become institutionalized in unions, professional associations, and benevolent societies. The politics of collective bargaining will also be discussed.

Public policy making Public organizations make decisions. At times, these decisions become public policy when promulgated by formally designated lawmakers and executives. In other instances, public organizations test the primacy of constraints imposed on them by laws and legislative and executive superiors. Part IV treats the interplay between the public organization and those who seek, formally or informally, to control it.

In Chapter 8, we will discuss the constitutional and legal constraints on public organizations. The widespread and substantial discretionary power of public administration vis à vis these constraints will be considered. We will also discuss the pluralist environment that surrounds administration and examine whether bureaucratic policy decisions are democratic or elitist. In Chapter 9 a focus on budgeting will illuminate the interplay among legislative rulemakers, executive supervisors, and government bureaucracy. The budget will be viewed as legislative supervision, presidential management, and one of the most concrete indicators of public policy. The centralization of legislative and executive budget activity and the recent planning and prioritizing budget approaches will be discussed. Chapter 10 will focus on public finance and related issues that affect the entire government apparatus, such as taxation and financial planning. Public goods theory will be highlighted, as will the macro-economic debates on the federal level and the efficiency-equality/public choice disputes that mark discussions of local finance.

NEW APPROACHES TO PUBLIC POLICY MAKING

In the book's final section, we will discuss some proposals (i.e., concepts, techniques, tools, and safeguards) for improving administrative performance and public policy making. In Chapter 11, a battery of proposed solutions to deficiencies of pluralist politics, incremental decision making, and administrative institutionalization will be covered. Topics discussed include administrative decentralization, public interest research groups, ombudsmen, and project management. Chapter 12 will address the systems approach to analysis. A framework for systems thinking, illustrations of management applications through the criminal justice system, and the analysis of policy fields through a review of urban modeling will be provided. In Chapter 13, program evaluation will be treated as an example of the use of systems thinking and analytical techniques in calculating the worth of alternative policies. The difficulties that arise between the evaluator and the organization will also be discussed. Chapter 14 will discuss the use of computers in public administration. Our focus will be their potential and government's failure to exploit fully that potential. A section on the abuse of electronic information systems will also be included.

APPROACHING THE MATERIALS

This book tries to convey concepts rather than details, although detail is not completely absent. We have emphasized concepts because in government, as in medicine, the perfect textbook or classic case is a rarity. The practitioner usually confronts a new strain that exhibits many of the characteristics of previously studied cases, but has symptoms of various other problems. If the problem solver, in this case the public manager, has been trained to pigeonhole problems, he or she may be paralyzed by hybrid occurrences. Unless problems are viewed generically and with an understanding that they are more often admixtures rather than purebred, this paralysis may not easily be overcome. It is for this reason that we will focus on concepts to a greater extent than on details.

A second concern of ours is that the future public administrator be problem oriented. Good administrators do not concentrate on the taut parts of their ships. They devote most of their attention to torn sails, rebellious crews, and threatening seas. Yet, many books on public administration place considerable emphasis on instructing students in the routine, the nonessential, and the history of the great administrative successes. If that were all there is to public administration, most public executives could be replaced by computers that could remember the histories and process the uneventful and routinized business of the public administrator.

Unfortunately, such a computer would not make it to 9:05 AM behind the average government manager's desk. Public administration has problems. They are numerous and they are major. These problems stem from the organizational form and its effects on human beings; from the political process and the demands that it makes on limited public resources; from the almost total lack of planning anywhere in the United States.

This book highlights problems. Why? Because the people who read this book may someday have to solve these problems. We designed this book to train problem solvers. It is better, we feel, to have a first exposure to the problems in public administration in the classroom rather than in the free-fire zone of government employment.

There is also a pedagogical reason for including in the study of public administration the dramatic, the outrageous, the humorous, and the pathetic. It gets students out of their seats. We do not know the teaching predilections of others; but we prefer an emotional audience. Enthusiastic students provide the teacher with a tremendous source of energy to draw upon to guide and augment the learning experience. The teacher too can gain valuable insights, especially when two students take opposing sides.

In addition to the emphasis on concepts and problems, we have devoted a significant portion of this book to urban administration and the urban environment. Eighty percent of the government workers in the United States are employed by state and local governments. More than half that number work for local jurisdictions. Although the mass media may concentrate on the federal level, public management in this country takes place, in large part, in counties, cities, and special districts. Considering the present demographic patterns in the United States, it is in the urban areas, therefore, that the bulk of the public policy questions reside: How to achieve integration? How to prevent the deterioration of the housing stock? How to prevent the flight of middle-class taxpayers? How to avoid bankruptcy? Thus, approximately one-third of this book is devoted to the problems of urban areas. The systems analysis and evaluation sections focus almost exclusively on localities.

A SEND-OFF

There is a lot of material in the 13 chapters ahead of you. We have tried to make it readable and provocative. There are things to learn here and things to think about. We fully expect that you will know more when you finish this book. We hope, fervently, that you will also have a firmer commitment to figure out what is wrong and what is right with public administration. If this commitment stays with you through school and your public service career, government will be the beneficiary.

NOTES

1. Dwight Waldo, "The Search for the Substance and Boundaries of Public Administration," in Richard J. Stillman II, ed., *Public Administration: Concepts and Cases* (Boston: Houghton Mifflin, 1976), pp. 5–17; C. L. Sharma, "Administration as a Field of Study," *International Review of Administrative Science* 32, no. 4 (1966): 287–300.
2. John M. Pfifner and Robert V. Presthus, *Public Administration* (New York: Ronald Press, 1967); Philip Selznick, *T.V.A. and the Grass Roots* (New York: Harper & Row, 1949); Anthony Downs, *An Economic Theory of Democracy* (New York: Harper & Row, 1957); Herbert A. Simon, *Administrative Behavior: A Study of Decision-Making Processes in Administrative Organizations* (New York: Free Press, 1947); Daniel Katz and Robert L. Kahn, *The Social Psychology of Organizations* (New York: Wiley, 1966).
3. Aaron Wildavsky, *The Politics of the Budgetary Process* (Boston: Little, Brown, 1964). Glenn O. Stahl, *Public Personnel Management* (New York: Harper & Row, 1977).

4. Robert C. Fried, *Performance in American Bureaucracy* (Boston: Little, Brown, 1976); Anthony Downs, *Inside Bureaucracy* (Boston: Little, Brown, 1967).
5. Felix A. Nigro and Lloyd G. Nigro, *Modern Public Administration* (New York: Harper & Row, 1976).
6. Harold Seidman, *Politics, Position and Power* (New York: Oxford University Press, 1976).
7. Wassily W. Leontief, *The Structure of the American Economy* (Cambridge: Oxford University Press, 1951); Leontief, "The Structure of the U.S. Economy," *The Scientific American* 212, no. 4 (April 1965): 25-35; William H. Miernyk, *The Elements of Input-Output Analysis* (New York: Random House, 1965).
8. Guy Routh, "The Mist in Economics," *New York Times,* November 8, 1977, p. 33.
9. Reinhard Bendix, et al., *State and Society* (Boston: Little, Brown, 1968).

In addition to the sources cited in notes, the following *Public Administration Review (PAR)* articles are a convenient starting point for a more detailed exploration of the material in this chapter.

Bok, Derek C.   "The Role of the University in Educating Students for Careers in Public Service," *PAR* 35, no. 4 (July/Aug. 1975): 399-403.
Grode, George and Marc Holzer.   "The Perceived Utility of MPA Degrees," *PAR* 35, no. 4 (July/Aug. 1975): 403-412.
Henry, Nicholas.   "Bureaucracy, Technology and Knowledge Management," *PAR* 35, no. 6 (Nov./Dec. 1975): 572-578.
Henry, Nicholas.   "Paradigms of Public Administration." *PAR* 35, no. 4 (July/Aug. 1975): 378-386.
Siu, R. G. H.   "Chinese Baseball and Public Administration." *PAR* 34, no. 6 (Nov./Dec. 1975): 636-640.
Thayer, Frederick.   "The NASPAA Threat," *PAR* 36, no. 1 (Jan./Feb. 1976): 85-90.

PART TWO

ORGANIZATIONS

CHAPTER 2

PERSPECTIVES ON ORGANIZATIONS

INTRODUCTION

We are a society of organizations. Organizations come in all sizes and the large ones are huge indeed. The largest private industrial organization in the United States, General Motors, employs 800,000 workers. Our largest government organization, the Department of Defense, coordinates the activities of 3,000,000 employees. Although these organizations are the creations of society, one wonders if such behemoths become the creatures of society. Modern organizations, extremely large and complex, defy easy comprehension. As a result, most of us do not even try to figure out how, why, or for whom organizations operate. The purpose of this chapter is to answer these questions.

In seeking answers, we will explore the genesis of organizations, considering the factors that led to the formation of simple organizations and the forces that helped shape the development of intricate organizations that serve modern society. The relationship between organization and society will be our continuing focus, and we will consider how individuals relate to the organizations serving them.

A GENERIC PROFILE OF ORGANIZATIONS

Every day, each of us comes in contact with numerous organizations, such as schools, supermarkets, bus or railway companies, or the American Telephone and Telegraph Company. These organizations differ in size and complexity, and many research hours have been devoted to explaining these differences. More fundamental inquiries, however, are directed at the relationship between organizations and society. Why did society grant charters, whether formal or informal, authorizing the performance of tasks by certain groups? How did these groups evolve into what we now call organizations? What are the key factors that make the organizational form adaptable to a wide variety of tasks? In order to explore these questions, we shall consider our ancestors and speculate how the small-scale forerunners of organizations may have developed. Underlying our exploration shall be the proposition advanced by Simon, Smithburg, and Thompson: "All formal organizations in the community arise because some people feel that a new organization is needed to attain some desired goal."[1]

Evolution of Organizations

Organization as Resources   In many species the strongest gets to do what it wants. In a typical scene, a ponderous bull seal slushes onto the sand, chasing weaker and more youthful seals from his favorite spot in the sun or from his numerous mates. He rules the community through intimidation.

The origins of society may have been quite similar, with a territory of unaffiliated individuals under the control of the strongest person. When individuals grouped together to form a society, however, the intimidator operated under a new set of conditions: Community members could unite against bullies and punish them. Nonetheless, retribution may have given way to other considerations. The intimidator's superior skills in hunting or fighting off enemies may have compensated for local rowdiness. The bully, on the other hand, may have become convinced that forming a tribe was a pretty good idea and, as a result, resorted less often to acts of aggression against individuals in the community. In fact, intimidators who acquiesced to the society's values may have been selected to enforce the rules since they had the ability to make communal judgments stick.

As the society's police force, the bully again controlled the environment, but did so according to rules that society members agreed upon and with the understanding that the society would not tolerate indiscriminate bullying in disregard of those rules.

Thus, there was a change from a condition in which the "fittest" unilaterally ordered others about, to a condition in which nascent organizational characteristics emerged. Community members channeled the intimidator's energies to achieve group goals and compliance with the rules. Although a single individual, the bully served in a capacity that, today, is filled by police and judicial organizations. The intimidator, therefore, was a tool for carrying out a function deemed necessary by society: The first step in a series of developments that has led to the accomplishment of societal goals by modern organizations that, in essence, are merely bigger and better tools. As Victor Thompson has written, "it becomes possible to think of fashioning or designing organizations for achieving specific purposes just as we design physical tools or instruments for achieving certain purposes."[2]

Organization as Knowledge   The desires of members of ancient society were not always as "sensible" as effective rule enforcement. Protection from the unknown often ranked high on the society's list of values. Those who stood between the society and the unknown were high priests, shamans, and witch doctors. Elevation to these mystical positions may have been much more dramatic than the appointment of a physically strong individual as rule enforcer. "Predicting" a single celestial event or "driving out the demons" of an illness could catapult a person into the buffer position between the society and the elemental forces of nature such as death, the wrath of fire and comets, and the angry hand of a righteous God. For instance, if one reads the Bible as history, it seems as if the prophets, by virtue of their foresight and an occasional "miracle" or two, were constantly employed as kingly advisers.

Of course, much of this mystic knowledge was not mystic at all. The Priests of Egypt amazed the populace with predictions of eclipses and floods. What the people did not know was that the priests had become accomplished in mathematics, astronomy, and recordkeeping. Thus, they recognized the cyclical nature of the tides, the weather, and sun-moon overlaps. The Priests would not share this information with the masses, however, since it was the source of their "powers."

Organization as a Distribution Mechanism   In the above examples, a monopoly of resources such as strength and knowledge enabled certain members of society to carry out tasks that society wanted done. However, these resources were applied in a static fashion: The priest stood between god and the populace; the soldier/cop stood between society members and internal and external threats. Goliath and Samson made it on muscle; Daniel and Moses made it on miracles. They acted as buffers and were chosen accordingly.

In addition to these personal resources of knowledge and strength, there were also valuable physical, transferable resources such as crops, domesticated animals, and tools, whose distribution became a prime concern of society. As society developed, distribution mechanisms were set up.

In primitive society, one of subsistence farming, there was no need for transfer points of physical resources: Farmers produced only enough to feed themselves and their families. However, at some point, a surplus was produced and the individual farmer became a potential transfer point. Thus, physical resources stood ready to flow to other members of the society. The farmer's excess grain could be exchanged for the hunter's venison, or another farmer's surplus of a different crop. Farming families could also exchange their surplus for goods that were produced by their children who may have become artisans, since improved growing techniques reduced the need for their labor.

When individual exchanges became too cumbersome, mechanisms were set up to effect the necessary transfer of resources. Silos may have been set up to store the surplus and run by a person designated to dispense grain to community members based on need or necessary payment. A soldier also may have been assigned to the silo to prevent theft. Thus, the silo arrangement was a fledgling organization that distributed resources among community members according to rules and protected those resources against improper requisitions, whether by society members or foreigners.

In each of our examples, a person came to occupy a central position in the society through possession of a resource that was of value to the community. The value of the resource lay in its ability to fulfill community needs whether they be law enforcement, protection from evil spirits, or the effective distribution of goods. In all of the examples, the distinction between individual and organizational efforts is merely one of scale. If the intimidator deputizes several community members to suppress a dissident minority, we have a police organization. Issuing a general call to arms to fight off a foreign invader, the intimidator becomes commander in chief of the armed forces. The priest who decides that he is unable to minister to all those who seek him out may anoint several followers, conferring his powers upon them and, in the process, becoming the high priest of the ensuing religious organization.

Why Organizations Become More Complex

To this point, we have been looking at simple organizations. When simple organizations grow they do not necessarily become more complex. The high priest may have several hundred subordinates, but they may all be carbon copies of himself. A grainbroker may have several granaries staffed by many dispensers and guards, but their operation is not very different from that of the small granary that preceded them. The organization is a little bigger and a few employees have been hired to do tasks that the owner used to do. Modern organizations, however, are not merely big; they are complicated. The nature of these complications and their origin is the question at hand.

As organizations specialize their internal operations they become more complex. When our primeval granary owner expanded operations, it may have been necessary to choose among staffing arrangements. At its simplest, the choice may have been between employing one person to count the grain and one person to dispense it, or having two dispenser-counters. The decision to specialize the two functions could have come from any or all of the following.

Availability of Labor To dispense grain, someone strong is needed. To count, someone smart. By combining dispensing and counting in one job, two people who are both strong and smart are needed. However, the supply of multitalented people in the community may be limited. Smart children are all sent to school and never have to lift a finger, let alone a bag of grain; strong children are typecast by the community at an early age and are never taught to count. Thus, the type of labor available can force the specialization of function.

Price of Labor (Economy) A second consideration for separating the two jobs is that the services of multitalented people often cost more than individuals with a single talent. Physical labor may be compensated at a dollar an hour. The same price may be paid for accounting labor. However, the rate of pay for brains plus brawn labor may be $1.50 an hour. Thus, two multitalented individuals will cost three dollars an hour to accomplish the same tasks that two individuals, each with a single talent, could perform for two dollars an hour.

Reliability of Labor (Efficiency) A third consideration is that people who do two things at once might get a little confused and not do either task very well. A counter-dispenser, just up from the books to fill your order, may give you five pounds of grain, as you requested, but only charge you for four pounds, the number stuck in the employee's head from the entry being made in the books when you arrived. In theory, at least, the simpler the job the less likelihood there is of error.

Why Organizations Need Administrators

For economy and efficiency, organizations break up the jobs that they do. The assembly line is an illustration of how organizations grow wider to accomplish tasks better. However, organizations also grow taller. A *hierarchy* of command rises over workers performing specialized functions.

In part, the need for efficiency generates vertical growth in administration. Breaking up a task may mean faster and cheaper production; but it can also mean lower quality production. Imagine again our dispenser-counter operation. One worker doing a job may be 90 percent reliable. The organizational error rate is 10 percent. However, if one person dispenses and another counts, and both are 90 percent reliable, the organizational error rate for the dispensing/counting operation will almost double, since, in most instances, both workers will not make an error on the same transaction. Whether the dispenser errs while the counter performs correctly or vice versa, the dispensing-counting operation will be improperly performed. Thus, to reduce the number of errors, workers must be supervised. In addition, a quality control position may be created to check against error. Since efficiency is a major organizational goal, uncovering errors and eliminating their cause is the rationale for many administrative positions.

Technology is another prime factor contributing to organizational complexity. Technology requires horizontal specialization for efficient production and vertical administration for efficient coordination. Early military endeavors were rather simple affairs: Your group against my group, hand-to-hand. There is little specialization of function among the combatants. The leader of such a group needs to say little more than "charge" or "retreat." Under such circumstances, a king, who for forty years has ruled over a peaceful land, can, if the occasion arises, lead his troops against hostile forces. Until fairly recently this is exactly what happened; a course of action that contributed significantly to the high combat-mortality rate among kings. At some point, however, the military became more than a unitary mass that merely advanced and retreated in response to orders or the battle situation. Modern armed forces have become complex organizations that have significantly more administrative and coordinative personnel than combat personnel.

From king to West Point graduate is a leadership transformation that mirrors technological growth. It is one thing to use swords; it is another to use rifles. A sword needs no ammunition, a gun does. Rifle brigades need gunmakers and bulletmakers and someone to bring replacement ammunition. When a rifle becomes a cannon, two people are needed: One to fire and one to load. When the cannon goes to sea, sailors are needed; when it becomes airborne, a pilot. When the gun is used three thousand miles from homebase, transport is required to get it there, to fire it, to resupply it. When combat must be coordinated on land, sea, and in the air, and spreads over a thousand-mile front, the task seems beyond even Attila the Hun, no matter how inspirational he may have been in close combat. What is needed is someone with extensive training and experience who can coordinate all these activities. What has changed the nature of the military endeavor and its leadership requirements is technology. To organizations, developing technology brings:

1. An increased span of time separating the beginning from the end of any task.
2. A growing and increasingly inflexible investment in production technology.

3. Specialized manpower whose work has to be organized and carefully planned in order to maximize the technological investment.[3]

ORGANIZATIONS: A VIEW FROM BELOW

To this point, we have sketched a generic profile of organizations: Organizations are repositories of resources—people, material, and knowledge—that are arranged to carry out efficiently a task assigned by society. However, in everyday life, we do not see organizations in full perspective. The popular media zero in on scandalous blemishes or highlight handsome accomplishments. In our dealings with organizations, we look from underneath; often we are confused. Indeed, the mismatch between man and organization is a recurrent theme in twentieth-century literature. In Franz Kafka's novel *The Trial,* the central character, Josef K., runs up against an organization that is perverse, sinister, and inscrutable.

> Who could these men be? What were they talking about? What authority could they represent? K. lived in a country with a legal constitution, there was universal peace, all the laws were in force; who dared seize him in his own dwelling?[4]

Josef K.'s predicament is nightmarish. He has been arrested by faceless functionaries of a nameless organization on unspecified charges. Josef K.'s job is in jeopardy; he is treated like a leper by the rest of the community. The procedures of Josef K.'s case are endless; officials are too busy and important to see him. Lower-ranking clerks, whom he does see, give little information. Be patient, they say; the organization knows what it is doing. Officials whom he meets informally paint a picture of an organization that is based on favoritism, manipulation, and random judgments that have little to do with facts. His attorney spends half his time defending the organization and the other half telling Josef K. that he does not have the training or experience to understand the technicalities of K.'s defense. Josef K. teeters on the edge of sanity. The ordeal ends when K. is taken from his home by two more functionaries without voices or names and executed in a quarry. Even as he is about to die, Josef K. does not understand what went on; nor does anyone take the trouble to enlighten him. "Where was the Judge whom he had never seen?" Kafka asks. "Where was the High Court, to which he had never penetrated?"[5]

Josef K.'s nightmares did not spring full blown from Kafka's imagination. The scenery and actors in dramas are often familiar because the staging and casting have been drawn from real-life experiences. Kafka's *The Trial* draws upon his experiences as a government employee. Real life "authorities" can, also, give us nightmares that are all too real. The tragedy of Brian Russell is such an instance.

FATAL ERROR

Bureaucratic bungling by the Army sent Sgt. Brian P. Russell to his
death in Vietnam in 1971. More bungling today threatens to deny the
sergeant's mother the relief she deserves for the loss of her son.

Over Russell's protests and in violation of its own regulations, the
Army reassigned him to combat only nine months after his recovery
from battle wounds. The reason was that the Army had neglected to insert in his personnel file any record of his hospitalization.

Russell was killed by a booby trap in Vietnam, even though he was
ineligible for Vietnam duty. His grieving mother, Mrs. Loretta Sloan,
called the travesty to the attention of Sen. Strom Thurmond (R-S.C.)
and Rep. John Jenrette (D-S.C.). They introduced bills to award Mrs.
Sloan $500,000 for the loss of her son. Thurmond has done little to
push the bill, except to issue a press release. It has become lost, meanwhile, in the bureaucratic maze.

We tried to track it down. We learned that the Army is opposed to
paying Mrs. Sloan. Its report was submitted to the White House budget
office, which relayed it to the Justice Department for its recommendation. The Justice Department, according to our sources, will send it back
to the Army for revisions.[6]

Kafka wrote in the early part of the twentieth century. He was, his
biographers assert, an extremely neurotic individual. The anonymous
forces that assault Josef K. mirror the torments of Kafka. Yet, Josef K.'s
fictional fate, that of a rat in an exitless maze killed by the same unseen
hand that originally trapped him, pales before the real-life fate of
Sergeant Russell. Kafka may have been neurotic; but the death of
Sergeant Russell *is* a horrible instance of organizational bungling. When
we read Kafka's novels and consider Sergeant Russell's tragedy, we get
an eerie feeling. We have felt like Josef K. and we have confronted
situations that exhibit the same logic that sent Sergeant Russell into
combat. What tortured Josef K. and doomed Sergeant Russell was an
organization; in one case, surrealistic and bizarre and, in the other, grave
and depressingly realistic.

Josef K.'s perspective was that of the client, or more precisely, the
victim, of organizations. In a somewhat more intense way, his view is
much like ours. We look at organizations from the outside and from the
ground floor. We see retail clerks or leaders making announcements,
but we do not see the organization as a whole. The actual workings of the
higher levels or organizational authority lie somewhere in the mists
above the daily routine of clerks and beneath the oratory of leaders.

Yet these mists are not easily penetrated. Modern organizations can
be as secretive as Egyptian High Priests and for similar reasons: to make
the routine look spectacular or to make mistakes vanish. Moreover, today's organizations are so complex that even an individual with carte
blanche and unlimited time would face a formidable task. Specialization
in modern organizations has reached a state that can perplex those
within organizations as well as those on the outside.

Josef K. brings his "Case" to the Organization. To K., his protagonist is at once ephemeral and real. SOURCE: Franz Kafka, *The Trial* (New York: Alfred A. Knopf, Inc., 1968) p. 61; illustration by George Salter.

This confusion is not intentional and is certainly something that the manager would seek to remedy. However, specialization can be a problem even in organizations that send rockets to Mars or develop polio vaccines. Specialization is the face of modern organizations whether they serve us well or poorly. Our discussion dramatizes the latter; however, poor service is not the rule but the exception that illuminates the nature of specialization and gives future managers a glance at the problems they might face.

Specialization in Modern Organizations

When we come face to face with organizations, we are likely to feel a bit uncomfortable. While they do not grind up and spit out people, we are often left with the impression that they could do so rather easily. We feel that there is something impersonal about organizations, something missing. What is absent is a sense of wholeness. The organization is not a complete being like ourselves. In fact, it is not a being at all. It is a fragment of the machinery set up to perform the tasks that society wants done. Similar to the troupe that accompanied Dorothy to Oz, it has no heart, no brain, and no courage. It lacks all the things that we look for when we seek out human relationships. The organization also considers us a collection of fragments. It speaks only to a part of us; the totality of our being is not relevant. We are licensed drivers, tenants, or students. Thus, we are treated as a fragment by an organization that is itself a fragment. It is no wonder that many of us feel unfulfilled. It is also not surprising that we sense that organizations, designed to accomplish tasks we *could not* accomplish as individuals, are capable of doing what we *would not* do.

The fragmentation that we see in organizations, and the fragmentation that organizations see in us, is a reflection of the complexity of society. There simply is too much to know for any one person to know it all and too much to do for any one person to do it all. The attitude of Josef K.'s attorney is indicative of society's response to complexity and the personal consequences of that response. Society's response to complexity is specialization. The more complicated things become, the more specialization society demands. Yet as we, as individuals, specialize we lose our grasp of the totality of what is going on. The usual consequence is that the more we know about one thing, the less we know about everything.

If this is all upsetting, it may be even more upsetting to know that society denies certain rewards to those who refuse to specialize. In today's job market, for instance, the jack-of-all-trades and the renaissance man—versatile workers and people with Bachelor of Arts degrees—collide with a work environment that is increasingly disdainful of their generalized skills. Theodore Roszak's speculations on where this is all leading is also somewhat less than reassuring.

> Where everything - everything - has been staked out as somebody's specialized field of knowledge, what is the thinking of ordinary people worth? Precisely zero. For what do they know about anything that some expert does not know better? There are even experts in *their* sex life, *their* dreams, *their* relations with their children, *their* voting habits, *their* morals and manners, *their* tastes and needs.[7]

Specialization is not exclusively organizational. To attorneys we entrust our freedom or our resources. Yet, we are unlikely to get a detailed explanation of how the attorney is going about protecting them. To doctors we entrust our bodies. Yet few of us fully understand why we are swallowing the pills that we swallow. We do not have the specialized knowledge of the lawyer or the physician. Nor is their primary function to teach knowledge. Rather, doctors and lawyers apply their knowledge on behalf of individuals. The air of confidence and competence cultivated by lawyers and doctors is an attempt to reassure patients or clients they are in good hands, even if they do not know what is going on. The importance of professional bearing in compensating for our ignorance becomes apparent when we consider the individual to whom we entrust our automobile. The litany that the automobile repairman recites over your sputtering coupe—"Don't look good. Can see that it needs a fuel pump right now. Can't tell what else it needs until I get it apart. Call back at three"—is enough to bring on an attack of paranoia to the most trusting of souls.

In all of the above we are one with Josef K. Something is happening that will affect us and not only can we not control it, we cannot understand it. At the organizational level, multipaged insurance contracts written by lawyers for lawyers and credit card agreements with enough interest rate permutations to overload an electronic calculator are probably read by only a small number of consumers and understood by even fewer. In the day-to-day business of modern society, we are continually parceling out portions of our destiny and giving the "power of attorney" to those whom we have to trust because we have not the foggiest notion of what they are doing.

When these specialists are organizations, there is not even "professional bearing" to give us strength. Organizations cannot be touched or spoken to in the sense that a doctor or lawyer can. Not only a specialized entity, the organization is itself composed of a number of specialized parts. Each part is only concerned with a piece of us and the pieces seem to get smaller and smaller. The college office that used to deal with you as a student trying to finance your education may no longer be interested in such a large slice of your life. It may now be the Office of Student Loans as distinct from the Office of Awards and Scholarships, neither of which gets involved in helping students get part-time employment. This latter function remains the domain of the Employment Office. Bouncing around from one to the other trying to finance one's education could easily sow the seeds of a Kafkaesque nightmare. Figure 2.1 resembles an organization chart. It represents what *we* see as we take our first tentative step toward the "right office."

Customers often stop at several organizational doors before getting to the right one. Such experiences are commonly referred to as "bureaucratic runarounds." However, there is an implication of conspiracy in the term "bureaucratic runaround" that is basically not correct. To conspire, it is necessary to coordinate. Most of the difficulties that one experiences in "finding the right office" comes from the opposite direction. Ever narrowing functional specialization blinds individual employees to the overall organizational picture. Further, an inquiring client with a problem that is irrelevant to the job of a particular office interferes with what the employees consider their important business. The quickest way to remove the impediment is by referral. However, if the organization has failed to give a clear picture of itself to employees, the referral is likely to be to yet another wrong office. Rather than conspiracies, "bureaucratic runarounds" are usually defects in managerial control and coordination; that is, a failure to coordinate the flow of

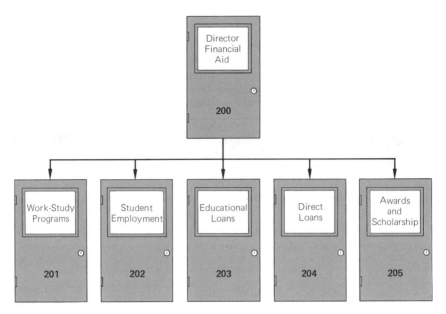

Figure 2.1 An Organization Chart: The Beginning of the Search for the Right Office. (Behind the Doors there are More Doors.)

information among "functionally specialized" units that carry on the day-to-day business of the organization.

Understanding the specialization among administrative levels in modern organizations is not any easier. Like Josef K., we too can be frustrated in reaching the administrative level which can resolve our problems. "Tell it to the Judge"; "I am not authorized to divulge that information"; and "We don't make the laws, we just enforce them" have a similar ring. All are rather stereotyped comments associated with lower-level employees in organizations. People do not speak like this because they read a lot of Kafka. Each of these statements defines the limits of the speaker's job, limits that have been set by the organization. In each instance—rulemaking, rule interpretation, and information release—there is someone above the speaker, either an organizational superior or owner, who performs these tasks and usually is hard to reach and slow to decide.

In modern organizations this layering often gets so thick that employees are unable to determine where the decision-making authority lies. The result is a statement such as, "I know the Issuance Office approved one of these yesterday, maybe it's worth a try but I wouldn't guarantee anything." The locus of decision-making authority on many matters in public agencies can be determined only after the fact. An informative case study that underscores this observation unfolds with the following passage:

In late May, an official from the *Rural Health Office* of the *Community Health Services* of the *Health Services and Mental Health Administration* of

TABLE 2.1   ASCENDING THE HIERARCHY

PERSON	APPROVAL
Receiving Clerk	Information complete, check enclosed and properly endorsed.
Accountant	Check cleared bank. Application fee in hand.
Investigator	Applicant has prior experience in business.
Police Clerk	No record of arrests.
City Planner	Business permitted at planned location.
Deputy Commissioner	Recommend Commissioner's approval.
Commissioner	Final Approval.

> the *Public Health Service* of the *regional office* of the *Department of Health, Education and Welfare* flew to Bakersfield to help KCLM prepare a formal application.[8]

The emphases are ours. We will not provide a chart. The passage portrays hierarchy as clearly as it can be done.

As hierarchy ascends and decision-making authority is dispersed among the numerous levels, the spectre of "red tape" abounds. Although high-level officials at the top of the hierarchy grant "final approval" on a given matter, various lower-level employees are responsible for approving certain components of the matter. Thus, your application for a license to operate a business may require a yes vote from numerous people within the bureaucracy, as Table 2.1 indicates.

This is not an atypical license issuance procedure and, if anything, might be somewhat oversimplified. A "tangle of red tape" can occur at numerous points. A person whose partial approval is necessary before the application document can move up to the next stage may be on vacation or backlogged with work. In moving from any one stage to another, the document may be misplaced. Background investigation procedures may be time consuming. Finally, a recent scandal in the licensing office might shift all decisions upward in the hierarchy. Rather than rely on the recommendations of lower level employees, executives with decision-making authority will dissect the procedure at each stage to determine that these recommendations are correct. These developments delay further the already lengthy seven-step procedure, which often is camouflaged by the government clerk's offhand comment that "these things take time."

THE RELATIONSHIP BETWEEN SOCIETY AND ORGANIZATIONS

To people like Kafka, it was clear that individuals were at a disadvantage when dealing with organizations. Others, however, addressed the relationship between organizations and society. Karl Marx and Adam Smith, for example, offered contradictory explanations concerning the degree to which organizations are responsive to the dictates of society. To Smith the organization was a competitive entity whose existence depended upon a favorable rating from the overall community. To Marx the organization was "an instrument by which the dominant class exercises its domination over other social classes."[9]

Socialists and capitalists—indeed, anyone who studied society—had to come to grips with the burgeoning organization of the nineteenth and twentieth centuries. With the coming of the industrial revolution and the nation-state, organizations suddenly came to the forefront. Factories replaced artisans and tradesmen; professional military organizations replaced the mercenaries of feudal times. The concentration of resources in these organizations made them powerful elements in national governance. As had the High Priests of Egypt and the militarists of Greece and Rome, Napoleon, Bismarck, as leaders of powerful organizations, dominated their nations.

It was indisputable that organizations had power; less clear was the source of organizational power. Did the organization appoint itself to a position of dominance? Or did society charter the organization and, if so, how? Max Weber addressed these questions in order to explain the emergence of modern organizations.

How Authority Is Achieved: Three Ideal Types

Max Weber may not have been a success in modern organizations. He was almost the exact opposite of the specialist. Perceptive and analytical, his fields of study included history, religion, the bases of government authority, and bureaucracy. In fact, Weber's inquiry into the bases for conferring authority in a society provided the starting point for his analysis of bureaucracy.

According to Weber, leaders who could impose their will on other people had power. Domination, therefore, was power legitimized. Domination existed when the "ruler believed that he had the right to the exercise of power and the ruled considered it their duty to obey his order."[10] Thus, for Weber, the question became: How does a person come to occupy a dominant position in society?

Weber identified three sources of power. First, one simply "had it": An elusive and almost mystic inner quality that convinces people that this person is the one to lead them. Second, one is born with power: The son of the king will someday be King. Third, one earned power: A person had to meet certain requirements in order to get the leadership job. Since everyone agreed upon the requirements, the leader was considered legitimate. Weber called the three leadership modes *charismatic, traditional,* and *legal-rational.*

Charismatic Authority Charismatic leadership is the stuff of epics. Indeed, many epical figures seem to have had special qualities that galvanized their followers. The charismatic leader does not rely on laws, traditions, or, in some cases, rational arguments. Jesus Christ is often cited as an example of the personal, nontraditional, nonlegal qualities of charismatic leadership. Moses and Mohammed, among religious leaders, and Hitler and Mao, among political leaders, certainly possessed charismatic qualities. The charismatic leader is often at the head of a fundamental change in society. The question whether the times made the man or the man made the times may be raised; but even in times ripe for change, it is the charismatic leader who organizes followers into a social movement that fundamentally changes the course of history.

Charisma cannot be transferred. Although the new rulers may glorify the charismatic leader's name, they cannot reproduce their predecessor's intensely personal leadership qualities. Moreover, in the wake of charismatic rule, stability is often desperately needed. The charismatic leader directs followers away from old paths and plunges them headlong into uncharted terrain. When the charismatic leader dies, devotees are likely to realize that they have not the slightest idea where they are. Thus, the successors set out to consolidate their power. To do this, according to Weber, they establish a system of "rational, impersonal rules or a traditional type of organization." In the process, the rulers become hostile to new forms of charisma.[11]

In the People's Republic of China, this was clearly the case. The charismatic Mao Tse-tung transformed a postfeudal society into a communist one in a decade. He launched an industrialization drive and, when he perceived an elite corps of specialists forming, threw it into reverse. Teachers and managers were sent to work the fields. Ideologically intense workers were promoted to management positions. *The Thoughts of Chairman Mao* guided the nation. Dramatic gestures—a vigorous swim in the Yangtze River in the wake of rumors that the Chairman was on his deathbed—galvanized mass support for Mao's new policy directions. Chairman Mao was China.

When Mao died, his wife, Chiang Ch'ing, lost the battle for his aura. Chiang Ch'ing wished to continue Mao's drive for ideological purity, but was defeated by more pragmatic leaders. The new leaders vilified Chiang Ch'ing but managed to associate Mao's name with their more conservative approach. The Chinese people, no longer energized by Mao's presence, accepted this anomaly. Stability was more attractive than continued adventure.

Traditional Authority Weber's second type of authority is traditional authority. As Stillman notes, "Time, precedent and the authority of tradition gave rulers their legitimacy in the eyes of the ruled."[12]

Here we are talking of kings, tsars, emperors, and hereditary rulers. Right to rule was hereditary, generally inherited by the oldest son of the monarch. Occasionally, another family, which felt it had better breeding, would overthrow the ruling clan and assume the right to rule.

Weber felt that traditional authority could be divided into "patrimonial" and "feudal."[13] Patrimonial authority was essentially an absolute monarchy; administrative officials were all appointed by the ruler upon whom they depended for their continued livelihood. Feudal authority was dispersed; retainers ruled domains of their own and were somewhat independent. They pledged their loyalty to the monarch more as allies than as subjects. The Magna Carta was a product of a feudal-traditional setting where the retainers were sufficiently independent to engineer a formal recognition of their rights by the monarch.

The traditional mode of authority produced some very bad leaders and widespread corruption. Nero, for instance, was undoubtedly crazy; Caligula was crazier still. Henry VIII made a shambles of the laws relating to marriage and murder; Richard III swam to the top through a sea of blood. Statements of the last French monarchs—"I am the state" and "Let them eat cake"—were ill-timed and inadvisable, given the developments that were under way. Court corruption and intrigue flourished as ministers vied for the monarch's favors.

Weber saw traditional rule weakening as society grew more sophisticated. "Divine right" became a questionable qualification for societal leadership. Hangers-on and dilettantes were suspect as first-line assistants. Moreover, as the mercantile class gained power and wealth through the efficient management of small-scale enterprises, the administrative machinery of the nation-state under traditional rule proved inadequate to meet its needs.

Legal-Rational Authority Legal-rational authority, the successor to charismatic and traditional authority, is appropriate to and can fully develop only in "the modern state" where "people obey laws because they have been enacted through legitimate channels, channels considered by the ruler and the ruled as correct. The ruler ruled by legal procedures."[14]

One major difference between legal-rational and other forms of authority is the presence of rules that set guidelines for leadership conduct. Charismatic leaders make up rules as they go along; traditional leaders dispense with rules by exercising regal prerogatives. Legal-rational authority operates under rules, set by the society, that provide orderly procedures for the removal of leaders who violate them. Moreover, under legal-rational authority, rules determine the structure of all the organizations serving society. Administration becomes bureaucratic.

WEBERIAN BUREAUCRACY: THE IDEAL TYPE

Weber's concept of *bureaucracy* was the organization form perfected. According to Weber, bureaucracy optimized "precision, speed, unambiguity, . . . continuity, unity, strict subordination, reduction of friction and of material and personnel costs"[15] in the performance of tasks. To achieve this level of performance, the bureaucratic organization was structured as follows:

1. Positions had fixed duties, legally prescribed. Similarly, organizational procedures were codified in written rules.
2. Clear lines of authority connected superior and subordinate positions.
3. Employment in a bureaucratic post required proven skill in the tasks involved. In return for compensation, the individual functionary devoted full working time to the organization and did not permit outside considerations to influence task performance.[16]

Structured in this manner, bureaucracy was a manageable and predictable tool. It was manageable because jobs were clearly defined; work was performed by experts; and lines of authority were clearly drawn. Bureaucracy was predictable because its rules were not formulated on a case-by-case basis. The rules, abstract and general, applied equally to everyone. Furthermore, by examining written records, authorities could determine if individuals dealing with the organization had been treated in accordance with uniform and impersonal rules. Bureaucracy thus avoided the arbitrary rule of the charismatic leader and the inbred, often incompetent, arbitrary rule of the traditional monarch. In bureaucracy, "whether public or private, the basic 'good' is efficiency. The fundamental objective . . . is the accomplishment of the work at hand with the least expenditure of manpower and materials."[17] Thus, to Weber and the theorists of "classical" bureaucracy, bureaucracy was an instrument of society. It was the best tool for the impersonal and efficient accomplishment of tasks assigned by society.

BUREAUCRACY: DEVIATIONS FROM THE IDEAL

Bureaucracy was far from a flawless mechanism. Even Weber was not completely at ease with the what he saw as the inevitable ascendancy of bureaucracy. His gloom is evident in the following Kafkaesque passage.

> It is horrible to think that the world could one day be filled with nothing but those little cogs, little men clinging to little jobs and striving towards bigger ones, a state of affairs which is playing an ever increasing

part in the spirit of our present administrative system . . . .This passion for bureaucracy . . . is enough to drive one to despair.[18]

Although Weber's occasional lack of enthusiasm was evident, it never blossomed into an antibureaucratic stance. Unlike the nineteenth-century Luddites, who destroyed industrial machines to prevent them from displacing and dehumanizing workers, Weber believed the benefits provided to society by bureaucracy outweighed the costs to organizational functionaries. According to Weber's calculus, society was growing more and more complex and at an accelerating rate. Thus, society had to depend on bureaucratic organizations to meet its needs. Furthermore, bureaucracy would evolve toward its pure form in order to achieve the efficiency demanded by numerous and complex problems. When, in his despairing moments, Weber tried to develop an alternative analysis, he came up empty. "What have we to set against this machinery in order to preserve a remnant of humanity?" was a question Weber could not answer.[19]

Weber also saw in bureaucracy a tool that could grow too big for society to handle. Bureaucratic resistance to change could spring from the same mechanisms that assured its reliability. Experts could disdain and resist policy changes proposed by amateurs; namely, elected or appointed "political" executives. Adherence to bureaucratic rules could become the organization's sole reason for existing. Reliability would give way to inflexibility as rules eclipsed task on the scale of bureaucratic values. Weber also understood that knowledge was power and that organizations, through secrecy, could hoard information necessary for societal control. Weber's foresight is borne out in the American context where legislation was needed to curb the indiscriminate use of the "secret" stamp by government organizations; and a president fell from power when his tape-recorded "files" were revealed.

In light of his awareness of the potential of bureaucratic abuse, one senses that Weber had his fingers crossed when he defined democracy as "a political system in which people elect a leader whom they can trust, whereupon, this accomplished, the elected one obtains the right to impose on peoples and parties the most absolute silence."[20] According to Weber, the leader's removal could follow upon "grave errors"; providing, of course, such errors were visible.

Weber's prebureaucratic administrative forms, the charismatic and the traditional, also exhibit a remarkable staying power. Robert Michels, a contemporary of Weber, viewed the traditional mode of authority as a mirror of human nature. "The instinct that impels men to retain the powers of government in the hands of their families, transmitting them wherever possible only to their own descendants," Michels wrote, "is so strong that every elective ruler tends to transform himself into a hereditary monarch."[21] Developments in India, Sri Lanka, and North Korea in the 1970s partially corroborate Michels's observations. In each country, the rulers maneuvered sons into heir apparent positions within the government. The result? In two of the three instances mother-son combinations fell from power.

While these outcomes are indicative of societies that are moving along the Weberian continuum and now prefer administration by bureaucracy rather than birthright, nonrational forces remain strong in organizations. As Stephen K. Bailey, a preeminent educator in the field of public administration and a shrewd observer of government organizations, points out:

> In all governmental policy, there have been overwhelming elements of personal favoritism and private gain ... this is owing to the fact that all governments are managed by human beings even if they are called kings, diplomats, ministers, secretaries or judges and hold seats in august legislative bodies. No process has been discovered by which promotion to a position of public responsibility will do away with a man's interest in his own welfare, his partialities ... and prejudices.[22]

So it is that Weber's bureaucracy stands as an "ideal" type. Although pure bureaucracy does not exist in the real world, it helps us understand organizations that do exist. It is a bench mark against which organizations can be classified. Clear patterns of authority, the efficient specialization of tasks, the impersonal and professional ethics of the bureaucrat, comprehensive recordkeeping to insure reliability and accountability: all serve as standards against which administrative practices can be measured. This is not to say that the standards are always superior. On the contrary, many unorthodox organizational practices enhance task performance more effectively than their ideal counterparts. (Beyond a certain point, increased specialization and more precise hierarchy leads to inefficiency.) Nonetheless, for relating the organizational form to developing societies and delineating the characteristics of bureaucracy, Weber is recognized as one of the giants of sociology.

THE LEGAL FRAMEWORK OF ORGANIZATIONS

Weber's field of inquiry was dominated primarily by government organizations. Even the Roman Catholic Church, which Weber considered one of the classical bureaucracies of the Middle Ages, was more of a government than a religious organization. Throughout the nineteenth and twentieth centuries the law that governed the operation of public bureaucracies came increasingly to reflect the Weberian design. Private organizations also operated according to such principles but were less often set forth in formal charters. Reproduced below is a typical legislative design for a government bureaucracy in the United States. It could have been written by Weber. Preeminence of rules, hierarchy, and expertise all figure prominently.

ARTICLE 2
DEPARTMENT OF AGRICULTURE AND MARKETS
JURISDICTION:
GENERAL POWERS AND DUTIES

§ 4. **Department of Agriculture and Markets**
There shall continue to be in the state government a department of agriculture and markets.

§ 5. **Commissioner of Agriculture and Markets**
The head of the department of agriculture and markets shall be the commissioner of agriculture and markets, who shall be appointed by the governor, by and with the advice and consent of the senate.... He shall be a person qualified by training and experience for the duties of his office.... In addition to the powers and duties specifically prescribed by this chapter, the commissioner shall have supervision over and direction of all officers and employees and of the affairs of the department. He shall be responsible for the enforcement and carrying into effect of the laws, rules and orders pertaining to matters as to which the department has functions, powers and duties.

§ 6. **Assistant Commissioners**
The commissioner shall appoint and may at pleasure remove two assistant commissioners of agriculture and markets and assign to such assistant commissioners the work which shall be under their respective supervision. Each of such assistant commissioners shall be a person qualified by training and experience for the performance of the duties so assigned to him.

§ 9. **Bureaus**
The commissioner may establish such bureaus as may be necessary for the administration and operation of the department and the proper exercise of its powers and the performance of its duties... under this chapter.

§ 1 h. **Other Officers and Employees**
There shall be such agents, inspectors, chemists, experts, statisticians, accountants and other assistants and employees, as the commissioner shall deem necessary for the exercise of the powers and the performance of the duties of the department under this chapter.

§ 12. **Oaths of Office**
The commissioner, the assistant commissioners, the counsel and the secretary shall, before entering upon the duties of their offices, take and subscribe the constitutional oath of office.

§ 13. **Salaries of Officers; Expenses**
The annual salaries and compensation of the assistant commissioners, the counsel, secretary and all other officers and employees of the department shall be fixed by the commissioner within the limits of appropriations made therefore.

§ 14. **Offices of Department**
The principal office of the department shall be in the city of Albany in rooms to be designated by the trustees of public buildings as provided by law.... The offices shall be supplied with all necessary books, stationery, office equipment and furniture, to be furnished and paid for in the manner provided by law.

§ 16. General Powers and Duties of Department

The department through the commissioner shall have power to: Execute and carry into effect the laws of the state and the rules of the department.

§ 19. Publication of Rules

Every rule or regulation enacted by the commissioner pursuant to the provisions of this chapter and intended to have the force of law shall be promptly published.[23]

Legally, the private organization remained much more obscure. The law described neither the organization nor its reason for being. Seeking a way to give standing to this mass of people performing a task for individual or collective owners, the law viewed the private organization as a big person. The corporation could sue and be sued, was subject to the laws of the land, and had personal possessions limited to the money that the owners put into it and the assets and liabilities generated by the original investment and any subsequent ones. Corporate managers had an obligation to follow the directives of the owners and, lacking such directives, to act in accordance with what was thought in the best interests of the owners.

As it has developed, the law concerns corporations rather than private organizations. Many nonorganizations incorporate to exploit the limited-liability provisions of the law. Fleet taxicabs often are incorporated vehicle by vehicle in order to insulate the owner's investment from legal claims by injured passengers, drivers, or pedestrians. People with large incomes at times incorporate to gain the tax benefits associated with the corporate state. While the law devises ways to deal with private organizations, it does not explain why they exist. Nor does the law explain why some tasks are performed by private organizations and other tasks are performed by public ones.

PUBLIC VERSUS PRIVATE ORGANIZATIONS

Economists saw organizational survival as dependent on acceptance by the consumer marketplace. In order to survive, the organization had to fulfill a need that society valued. Otherwise, the organization would be "voted out": the demand for its product would fall below the level necessary for continued existence.

Government organizations presented economists with a paradox: Payment for government goods was obtained by force not choice. Roads, for instance, are a highly valued government commodity. Yet, payment is not given freely but must be extracted from consumers in the form of taxes. One significant answer to this seeming paradox was advanced by political economists, who offered the "Theory of Public and Private Goods."[24] The traditional economic marketplace, according to the theory, provided individual consumers with the choice of supporting or not supporting a particular organization. In this beginning state, every organization would prosper or fail depending on the demand of individual consumers for its product. However, some organizations may provide benefits deemed necessary by society as a whole but not on an individual basis; many people would not want to pay their share of the costs. Some would refuse in order to improve their own economic position. Others might pay or not pay depending on their evaluation of the specific situation. Thus, a dilemma arises in this organizational free market: What to do with goods and services that have a favorable consensus from society but cannot survive in a marketplace of individual buyers? The answer, according to the Theory of Public and Private Goods, is to remove such goods and services from the "free market" of individual buyers.

The goods and services removed from the market of individual consumer choice become *public goods,* since they are intended to benefit all members of society. Payment for these goods is, therefore, extracted from all members of the society in the form of taxes. The decision whether the service is good or bad is made in the realm of public policy—the legislature. There is no subsequent test in the marketplace of individual consumers; individuals must pay for public goods. Dissatisfied individuals have only one recourse: Reverse the societal consensus that legitimized a particular service as a public good. This can only be done in the policy-making arenas.

According to proponents of the public goods theory, governments arise in order to make the societal consensus stick. Thus, government is a coercive institution designed to insure that everyone pays their share of the costs of public goods. The government accumulates the resources necessary to provide public goods through taxation. However, these resources are not necessarily tranformed into public goods by government organizations. When the United States government gives Lockheed several billion dollars to produce a military aircraft, it is a private organization that transforms the cash into resources and the resources into a jet fighter. Further, in the United States, full government funding is not a prerequisite for public goods. Some enterprises not quite making it in the marketplace of individual consumers may be deemed a public good. Government's response in such situations is to supply resources sufficient to keep the enterprise viable. Government subsidies to private mass transit and low interest loans to builders of middle-income housing in metropolitan areas help bridge the gap between what society believes to be the value of such enterprises and what individual consumers are willing or able to pay.

Increased government subsidies to U.S. railroads over the years, culminating with the Amtrak and Conrail takeovers of bankrupt lines, sought to offset financial losses caused by individual consumers' distaste for railway travel. Railway transport was considered a public good and each consumer's decision not to take a train trip generated a shift of some of one's tax monies to the railway industry. All of these situations, from Lockheed to Conrail, blur the distinction between public and private organizations.

Government, of course, also directly transforms resources into services. National defense, police and fire services, a whole range of social welfare services, and other tasks too numerous to mention are the province of the government organizations. It must be remembered, however, all public goods require forced payments—taxes—from a marketplace of individuals who, though they may benefit from the public good, are presumed to be reluctant to pay for them.

CATEGORIES OF PUBLIC ORGANIZATIONS

The Theory of Public and Private Goods offers a broad distinction between government organizations and their private counterparts. That is, private organizations are sustained by a free market of individual buyers; government organizations, with products that cannot succeed in the market, are sustained by taxes levied on the citizenry. In general terms, the Theory of Public and Private Goods defines what government's products are. For instance, government performs functions that cannot be entrusted to private concerns (e.g., military defense) or makes services available to all regardless of ability and wealth (e.g., education). However, the tasks performed by government organizations can be characterized more explicitly. We find the following categories useful: (1) service organizations; (2) regulatory organizations; (3) transfer-payment organizations; (4) maintenance organizations.

Service Organizations These are organizations whose primary purpose is to produce tangible goods and services. For example, schools, the military, police, fire, and sanitation departments provide services perceived as essential by society. Park and recreation and health care are also services directly provided by government jurisdictions.

Transfer-Payment Organizations These are agencies whose primary purpose is to provide resources to individuals, groups, or organizations that are, in society's estimation, resource deficient. Social security, welfare, and veterans' benefits are all transfer-payment programs managed by large government organizations.

Regulatory/Representative Organizations These are organizations whose primary purpose is to intervene in the marketplace in order to maintain, enhance, or diminish the economic leverage of particular industries or groups. Regulatory is here used in its broadest sense and includes representative organizations that advance the cause of a sector of the economy (e.g., Departments of Agriculture or Commerce) and those that serve as a watchdog (e.g., The Federal Trade Commission, The Securities and Exchange Commission).

Maintenance Organizations   These are organizations that provide support services to other government organizations. Civil service commissions, budget bureaus, and comptrollers offices provide services that are consumed within the government. The Internal Revenue Service and other tax collecting agencies gather resources necessary for government to operate.

These categories are not mutually exclusive. Transfer-payment organizations also provide services directly. Case workers counsel welfare recipients and the Veterans Administration runs an extensive network of hospitals. Regulatory/representative agencies also make transfer payments to farmers and businesses. Agencies of all types fund outside research. Finally, some agencies, particularly regulatory agencies, are accused of abandoning their primary prupose in favor of nearly opposite goals (see Chapter 4).

Nonetheless, these four classifications are useful. They delineate tasks that government undertakes and are sufficiently distinct and important to have been the focus of theories and conventional wisdom concerning the role of public administration in society. Political economists focused primarily on services to explain government's fundamental purpose. To Woodrow Wilson, who wrote that government "must make itself master of masterful corporations,"[25] regulation was a crucial government function. To Marxists, token transfer payments mollify the downtrodden workers without fundamentally changing the root causes of their plight and representational agencies preoccupy citizens with identities - worker, farmer, consumer, minority, elderly, female - that block the formation of coalitions based on economic class. For the average citizen, government's maintenance functions loom large as a bloated bureaucracy devouring their tax dollars. Regardless of their perspective, few people would disagree with Nicos Mouzelis's assertion that "whatever the political regime and whatever the political and social changes in the modern state, bureaucracy is here to stay."[26]

There is also general agreement on the type of person who will, increasingly, run society's institutions. James Burnham spoke for many when he said, "we are moving from a bourgeois, capitalist society to a managerial society. Not capitalists, not politicians or Congress, but managers in government and business will control society."[27] According to H. H. Gerth and C. Wright Mills, this is due to the fact that bureaucracy "is a power instrument of the first order for the one who controls the apparatus."[28] As we will see in the next chapter, however, controlling the apparatus is not an easy task.

SUMMARY

In this chapter, we explored the foundations of organizations in modern society: Our starting point was that organizations are all around us—schools, supermarkets, government agencies, the telephone company. We traced the evolution of organizations from simple social mechanisms accomplishing a single task to complicated social mechanisms specializing in various tasks. In this process increased technology was shown to be a prime contributor to increased organizational complexity and the consequent need for able administrators. The efficient arrangement of people, material, and knowledge was shown to be at the heart of effective administration.

Given these positive characteristics, our attention turned to the potential mismatch between organizations and individuals. Here the darker sides of organization emerge, particularly the dehumanizing aspects of specialization and the frustrating confrontations with red tape.

We then addressed bureaucracy as an ideal type in the classical constructs of Max Weber. We also discussed the theory that government organizations come into being in order to satisfy consumer preferences that could not be met by the marketplace. Finally, four types of organizations were distinguished—service, transfer-payment, regulatory/representative, and maintainence.

In summary, this chapter has been an introduction to some of the broad characteristics of organizations. In the next chapter, we will survey several approaches to the administration and control of the organization.

KEY TERMS AND CONCEPTS

Bureaucracy
Charismatic authority
Hierarchy
Legal-rational authority
Maintenance organizations
Regulatory organizations

Service organizations
Specialization
"Theory of Public and Private Goods"
Traditional authority
Transfer-payment organizations

NOTES

1. Herbert A. Simon, Donald W. Smithburg, Victor A. Thompson, *Public Administration* (New York: Knopf, 1950), p. 25.

2. Victor A. Thompson, *Without Sympathy or Enthusiasm: The Problem of Administrative Compassion* (University, Ala.: University of Alabama Press, 1975), p. 9.
3. John Kenneth Galbraith, *The New Industrial State* (New York: New American Library (Signet), 1967), pp. 25–28.
4. Franz Kafka, *The Trial* (New York: Knopf, 1968), p. 7.
5. Ibid., p. 286.
6. Jack Anderson, Syndicated Column, September 1976.
7. Theodore Roszak, *Where the Wasteland Ends: Politics and Transcendence in Post Industrial Society* (New York: Doubleday (Anchor) Books, 1973), p. 237; see also David Schuman, *Bureaucracies, Organizations and Administration: A Political Primer* (New York: Macmillan, 1976), Chapter 1, for an excellent analysis of the problems that arise when people confront modern organizations.
8. Michael Aron, "Dumping $2.6 Million on Bakersfield (Or How Not to Build a Migratory Farm Workers' Health Clinic)," in Richard J. Stillman II, ed. *Public Administration: Concepts and Cases* (Boston: Houghton Mifflin, 1976), p. 69. (emphasis added)
9. Quoted in Nicos P. Mouzelis, *Organization and Bureaucracy: An Analysis of Modern Theories* (Chicago: Aldine, 1967), p. 9.
10. Quoted in Ibid., pp. 15–16.
11. Quoted in Ibid., p. 20. For a fascinating theoretical discussion of charismatic authority see Ann Ruth Willner, *Charismatic Political Leadership: A Theory* (Princeton, N.J.: Princeton University, Woodrow Wilson School of Public and International Affairs, Center of International Studies Research Monograph No. 32, May 1968).
12. Stillman, *Public Administration,* p. 38.
13. Mouzelis, *Organization and Bureaucracy,* p. 16.
14. Ibid., p. 17.
15. Max Weber, "Bureaucracy," in Fred A. Kramer, ed. *Perspectives on Public Bureaucracy: A Reader on Organizations* (Cambridge: Winthrop Publishers Inc., 1973), pp. 6–9.
16. Ibid., p. 13.
17. Luther Gulick, "Science, Values, and Public Administration," in *The Administrative Process and Democratic Theory,* ed. Lewis Gawthrop (Boston: Houghton Mifflin, 1970), p. 100.
18. Quoted in Reinhold Bendix, *Max Weber: An Intellectual Portrait* (New York: Doubleday, 1960), p. 464.
19. Quoted in Arthur Mitzman, *The Iron Cage* (New York: Grosset & Dunlap, 1969), p. 178.
20. Quoted in *Robert Michels, First Lectures in Political Sociology,* ed. Alfred DeGrazia (Minneapolis: University of Minnesota Press, 1949), p. 90.
21. Ibid., p. 103.
22. Stephen K. Bailey, "Ethics and the Public Service," in Stillman, *Public Administration,* p. 315.
23. Article 2, Agriculture and Markets Law, State of New York (St. Paul: West Publishing, 1978), pp. 7–26.
24. This discussion is based primarily on L. L. Wade and R. L. Curry, Jr., *A Logic of Public Policy: Aspects of Political Economy* (Belmont, Calif.: Wadsworth, 1970). For a further discussion of public goods see Chapter 10.
25. Woodrow Wilson, "The Study of Administration," in Stillman, *Public Administration,* p. 271.
26. Mouzelis, *Organization and Bureaucracy,* p. 25.

27. James Burnham, *The Managerial Revolution* (New York: John Day, 1942).
28. H. H. Gerth and C. Wright Mills, eds., *From Max Weber: Essays in Sociology* (New York: Oxford University Press, 1946), p. 228.

BIBLIOGRAPHY

Burnham, James. *The Managerial Revolution.* New York: John Day, 1942.

DeGrazia, Alfred, ed. *Robert Michels, First Lectures in Political Sociology.* Minneapolis: University of Minnesota Press, 1949.

Galbraith, John Kenneth. *The New Industrial State.* New York: New American Library (Signet), 1967.

Gerth, H. H. and Mills, C. Wright, eds. *From Max Weber: Essays in Sociology.* New York: Oxford University Press, 1946.

Kafka, Franz. *The Trial.* New York: Knopf, 1968.

Mitzman, Arthur. *The Iron Cage.* New York: Grosset & Dunlap, 1969.

Mouzelis, Nicos P. *Organization and Bureaucracy: An Analysis of Modern Theories.* Chicago: Aldine, 1967.

Roszak, Theodore. *Where the Wasteland Ends: Politics and the Transcendence in Post Industrial Society.* New York: Doubleday (Anchor Books), 1973.

Simon, Herbert A., Smithburg, Donald W. and Thompson, Victor A. *Public Administration.* New York: Knopf, 1950.

Stillman, Richard J., II., ed. *Public Administration: Concepts and Cases.* Boston: Houghton Mifflin, 1970.

Thompson, Victor A. *Without Sympathy or Enthusiasm: The Problem of Administrative Compassion.* University, Ala.: University of Alabama Press, 1975.

Wade, L. L. and Curry, R. L. Jr. *A Logic of Public Policy: Aspects of Political Economy.* Belmont, Calif.: Wadsworth, 1970.

Weber, Max. *The Protestant Ethic and the Spirit of Capitalism.* New York: Scribner, 1958.

Weber, Max. *The Theory of Social and Economic Organization.* New York: Oxford University Press, 1947.

Willner, Ann Ruth. *Charismatic Political Leadership: A Theory.* Princeton, N.J.: Princeton University, Woodrow Wilson School of Public and International Affairs, Center of International Studies, Research Monograph No. 32, May 1968.

In addition to the sources cited in the notes and bibliography, the following *Public Administration Review (PAR)* articles are a convenient starting point for a more detailed exploration of the material in this chapter.

Carroll, James D. "Noetic Authority," *PAR* 29, no. 5 (Sept./Oct. 1969): 492–500.

Gross, Bertram M. "An Organized Society?" *PAR* 33, no. 4 (July/Aug. 1973): 323–327.

Landau, Martin. "Redundancy, Rationality, and the Problem of Duplication and Overlap," *PAR* 29, no. 4 (July/Aug. 1969): 346–358.

LaPorte, Todd R. "The Context of Technology Assessment: A Changing Perspective for Public Organization," *PAR* 31, no. 1 (Jan./Feb. 1971): 63–73.

McCurdy, Howard E. "Fiction, Phenomenology and Public Administration," *PAR* 33, no. 1 (Jan./Feb. 1973). 52–60.

McGill, Michael E. and Leland M. Wooten. "Management in the Third Sector," *PAR* 34, no. 5 (Sept./Oct. 1975): 444–455.

Murray, Michael A. "Comparing Public and Private Management: An Exploratory Essay," *PAR* 35, no. 4 (July/Aug. 1975): 364–371.

Rainey, Hal G., Robert W. Backoff, Charles H. Levine. "Comparing Public and Private Organizations," *PAR* 36, no. 2 (March/April 1976): 233–244.

White, Orion F., Jr. "The Dialectical Organization: An Alternative to Bureaucracy," *PAR* 29, no. 1 (Jan./Feb. 1969): 32–42.

RELEVANT PERIODICALS

Administration and Society
The Bureaucrat
Journal of Social Issues
Quarterly Journal of Administration
Social Science Quarterly
Theory and Society

CHAPTER 3

WHO RULES IN ORGANIZATIONS?

INTRODUCTION

In the previous chapter, we discussed some of the reasons why organizations have come to occupy a central position in the management of modern industrial society. This central position is not about to be relinquished by the organizational form. Nor should it be. Society's wants are filled by organizations. While anarchists and communards can imagine a society devoid of organizations that perform large-scale allocation, distribution, and maintenance functions, most of us find such an existence unthinkable. Making bread is good exercise and the end product is usually superior to the packaged supermarket variety, but how many of us have the time to bake a daily loaf? And who among us can make a television set or an automobile? It is clear that of necessity our relationships with organizations will be enduring. Thus, the question "Should we have organizations?" seems irrelevant. Rather, insights into the functioning of organizations can best be gained by asking such questions as "Whom shall organizations serve?"; "How can they function most effectively?"; "How do we make sure that organizations behave as society expects them to?" This chapter will address one such question. It is "Who rules in organizations?"

The question "Who rules in organizations?" has a simple answer. Organizational leaders are readily identifiable. They have titles such as president, chairman of the board, and commissioner. Pointing to the individuals in possession of these titles is the easy way to reply to the

"Who rules" question. As with most easy answers, this tells us very little. For instance, it tells us nothing about why certain persons come to be known as "the power behind the throne" or "the person to see if you want to get something done." It does little to explain why agencies can be "wracked by dissension." The simple answer also does not tell us how "lame duck" can be used to describe the person who occupies the office of president of the United States—one of the most powerful positions in the world. Nor does it explain why newly elected presidents invariably find that "mobilizing the bureaucracy" tends to be a frustrating, humbling experience.

None of these situations are unknown in the American context. Yet each complicates the search for a definitive answer to the question of how organizations are ruled. If authority is exercised reflexively by the chief executive in response to someone else, how do we know? If, as is more common, the chief executive delegates extensive authority to a subordinate who then becomes the "person to see" is it not the subordinate who actually rules? What kind of authority does a governor have over an elected attorney general who can quietly defy the governor without fear of formal sanction? How absolute is the authority of a bureaucratic leader who realizes that a mutiny among workers can have disasterous personal consequences? Finally, how can the president of American Telephone and Telegraph "lead" the physicists at Bell Labs, when it is likely that the president could not get by the first line of one of their reports?

A ROAD MAP

In pursuit of a better understanding of organizational governance, we will survey several major theoretical approaches to organizational rule. Weber's theories will be our starting point. Weber's executives ruled because they were able to combine authority and knowledge. Bureaucratic authority flowed from the leader to subordinates whose duty it was to obey lawful commands. This obligation was reinforced because the bureaucratic leader's knowledge, or competence, was recognized. Thus, to Weber and other "classical" theorists, organizational rule was exercised from the top down.

Next, we will turn to those theorists who enlarged upon the Weberian notion that unified command, a decent salary, and job security would be enough to ensure the obedience of organization members to leadership directives. Herbert Simon saw leadership as effective only when it partially relinquished, rather than hoarded, its decision-making authority. To Chester Barnard, authority was a dead-end device unless it was accepted by those it sought to direct. Their acceptance hinged on a for-

The Humbling of Bureaucratic Authority. SOURCE: "Shoe" by Jeff MacNelly, St. Louis *Post-Dispatch*, June 11, 1978. Reprinted by permission of the Chicago Tribune-New York News Syndicate, Inc.

mula of benefits and penalties far more complex than anticipated by Weber. Rule came from the bottom as well as from the top of the organization.

In the pages that follow, we begin by exploring these two approaches to rule in organizations: the *top-down* or formal and the *bottom-up* or informal. Subsequently, we will consider the political, societal, and ethical considerations that might favor a greater degree of subordinate authority.

BLUEPRINTS AND CALCULATIONS: TOP-DOWN RULE AND ORGANIZATIONAL DESIGN

Organizations begin as ideas. Someone sees a need and conceives of an arrangement of people and resources to meet it. A blueprint is designed. Whether the design creates a new bureaucracy or rearranges an existing one, the designer presumes it is the ideal mechanism for meeting the need.

Ideal blueprints are often used to form temporary, informal organizations. For example, a group of temporary neighbors at a vacation cottage community may want to have a party. However, no one wants to prepare singlehandedly a feast while on vacation. Moreover, sharing cooking duties among hosts on a rotating basis is impossible because people are moving in and out. One solution is to have each of the guests bring a portion of the party with him. To do this the group organizes itself. Each guest is assigned a specific responsibility to ensure that everyone does not show up with the same thing. The organization, although loosely structured, proceeds from an ideal blueprint. And participants consider it the best way to have a party without unfairly burdening any of the guests.

If blueprints could avoid the test of application, most would remain ideal solutions. However, most blueprints are carried out. Often they do not fare well. Even in the physical sciences, where the art of blueprint designing is most advanced, blueprints fail. In architecture, for example, the Tower of Pisa "leaned"; seaside structures dissolved because seawater had been used to mix the mortar; and modern buildings cracked because architects miscalculated the extent to which these buildings would settle into the ground.[1] In aeronautical engineering, ideal blueprints also failed in actual application. A number of early passenger jets crashed because designers failed to anticipate certain violent turbulences that the plane would create for itself as it approached the speed of sound.[2]

If physical scientists have been unable to design the perfect blueprint, what can we expect of social scientists? Organizational blueprints are actualized by people, not metal and plastic. People are highly complex, often unpredictable, and may rebel against, or be incapable of, performing the tasks required by the blueprint. Sports teams, for example, are organizations that have fixed blueprints that detail the number of players, the allocation of positions, and the sequence of operations. Each team stylizes its original blueprint design to make the organization more effective. Yet, when the game starts, the blueprint may be inconsequential. One team may dominate its league; another may lose most of its games.

One reason organizational blueprints may fail to produce desired results is a lack of talented workers. The New York Mets, in their infancy, were a laughingstock precisely because the team failed to perform up to the expectations of the organizational blueprint of a baseball team. The original Mets had excellent leadership personnel. Manager Casey Stengel had proven skills; loyal fans gave the team undying support. The blueprint seemed perfect. Stengel revealed the source of the Mets' problems when he queried, "Can anybody here play this game?"

Stengel accepted his lot graciously. However, most leaders of organizations that do not perform up to design specifications fail to see the humor in their predicament. Jobs and reputations are on the line and, besides, Max Weber, himself, said the bureaucracy is supposed to dance to the tune of the person in charge.

Weberian Bureaucracy: The Monocratic Blueprint

Weber conceived ideal bureaucracy as a smoothly functioning machine with a clearly defined hierarchical structure directed by a single leader who could elicit the willing compliance of functionaries. Indeed,

Weber clearly identified monocracy as the type of rule which would maximize organizational efficiency.[3]

In Weber's ideal *monocratic organization,* only the leader determined the organization's directions and goals. Workers merely followed orders.[4]

For Weber's monocratic organization to take hold, other forms of leadership and decision making had to loosen their grip. In describing the "collegial model," in which some organization members possess the formal right to vote on policy, Weber clearly sees collective decision making as dysfunctional:

> Work organized by collegiate bodies causes friction and delay and requires compromises between colliding interests and views. The administration, therefore, runs less precisely and is more independent of superiors; hence it is less unified and slower. All advances of the Prussian administrative organization have been and will in the future be advances of the bureaucratic and, especially, of the monocratic principle.[5]

Weber's structural blueprint for the institution of monocratic rule in organizations was hierarchy and its "levels of graded authority (with) a firmly ordered system of super and subordination in which there is a supervision of the lower offices by the higher ones."[6]

Although Weber was a giant in sociology and his insightful analyses ranged from religion to politics, his work was not translated into English until 1949. However, the principles of rigid hierarchy and strict subordination in organizational design advanced outside of Germany. Bureaucracy was coming to the forefront in all industrialized nations. In the United States in the 1930s, Luther Gulick and Lyndall Urwick gave the name *unity of command* to the monocratic form of organizational governance.[7] One of several administrative principles advanced by Gulick and Urwick, unity of command required each functionary to have one, and only one, boss. No one was to have more than one superior, since confusion could result if various superiors issued contradictory directives. Thus, subordinates would not be in a position to choose among alternative courses of action. If unnoticed and unchecked, the organization's direction would be partially determined by the decisions of subordinates who were not intended to have a policy-making voice.

The figures below demonstrate the unity of command principle and two deviations. In Figure 3.1(a), the organization is arranged and the messages flow according to the principle of unity of command. For example, when a conflict between two operating departments develops, the production chief appeals, through designated channels, to the organization head. Upon reaching a decision, the organization head issues

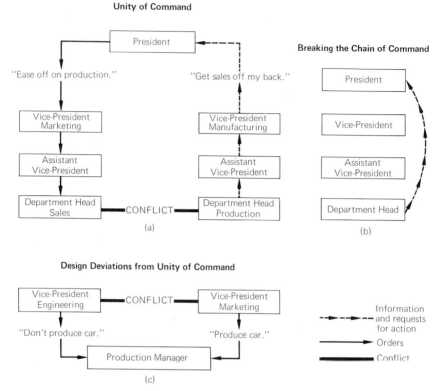

Figure 3.1   The Unity of Command Principle and Two Deviations

a directive, also through designated channels, to the sales supervisor. This decision is binding.

In Figure 3.1(b), the department head circumvents immediate superiors and appeals directly to the president of the organization. Unaware of the communication between their subordinate and their superior, the department head's immediate supervisors might embark on policies that deviate from the president's. There is also the possibility of offended egos even if contradicting actions do not take place.

Figure 3.1(c) demonstrates what might occur if a production manager was equally responsible to two superiors who disagreed on a particular policy. This could be the case, for instance, if the engineering department of an automobile company thought that a design feature precious to the marketing department was defective. In the ensuing conflict, the production manager might be unable to exercise decision-making authority, particularly if the production manager had to observe other tenets of unity of command and could not contact directly either the president of the organization or the immediate supervisors of the competing department heads.

HAVING TROUBLE MAKING PAYMENTS?

Sometimes we all need some help.

Call Us - We Can Help!
Call 1-877-891-STAR Today!

Credit Solutions Q & A:

Q. I'm already past due; what can I do?

A. Make a payment today online at www.milexch.com, at your local exchange or by mail with your remittance stub.

Q. What if I can't bring my account current?

A. Call us, we can help. We will work with you to set up a reduced payment plan which will get you back on track. Call us today!

Q. Can my past due status affect my credit report?

A. Any late payments can have a negative impact on your credit report, which may affect your ability to get additional credit, car loans, or a mortgage.

If payment is not received we can notify your unit commander, begin collection action and add additional fees. The Exchange Credit Program reports account status to all major credit bureaus.

**Don't let that happen!
We want to help!
Don't wait - Call us NOW!**

Exchange Credit Program customer service center telephone numbers.

CONUS (including Alaska and Hawaii) 1-877-891-7827

Overseas Toll Free Numbers

Germany 0800-812-4690
Italy 8008-72683
United Kingdom 0800-96-1843
Norway 800-14-199
Spain 900-971-394
Crete 00-800-1809200452

Netherlands 0800-022-9614
Belgium 0800-1-6374
Korea 00308-130663
Japan 00531-114239
Guam 1-800-546-7195

Collect Numbers: Turkey/Saudi Arabia 214-465-6030

For more information or to chat with a customer service representative, visit www.MyECP.com. Roll over the Credit Services tab at the top of the page and click on **MILITARY STAR® Card**

Unity of command or hierarchy does not presume that every act in the organization must be cleared through the chief executive. However, through established rules and delegation of authority to subordinates, the executive's stamp is on the design of all activities within the organization. Through *delegation,* the heads of the bureaucracy formally convey a portion of their decision-making authority to designated subordinates. Through bureaucratic regulations, the executive formalizes the standards of behavior that govern organization members. Therefore, when a lower-level official gives a command, the command has authority because it comes from the designated representative of the organization head. Similarly, behavior that accords with the general rules of the organization proceeds under the standing order of the executive. When questions concerning the delegation pattern of authority or the applicability of the rules arise, under unity of command, only the executive has the authority to provide the answers.

Gulick and Urwick also created the acronym *PODSCORB* (Planning, Organizing, Staffing, Directing, Coordinating, Reporting, and Budgeting) which subsumed other principles of management. Gulick and Urwick did not discover these characteristics or the concept of unity of command. For instance, in a book published in 1916, a Frenchman, Henri Fayol, formulated a similar list of managerial functions.[8] However, Gulick and Urwick were the first scholars to introduce to American managers a detailed conceptualization of what management was. Indeed, as a skeletal outline of the duties every organization must perform, PODSCORB remains important to the organizational designer.

Personnel Selection and the Organizational Blueprint

All forms of governance require two essential tasks: selecting an appropriate structure to realize the type of rule desired; and persuading people to operate under that structure. Of the two tasks, the second is the more difficult to accomplish. The structural blueprint merely designates one position as boss and other positions as subordinates. Persuading people to follow the blueprint's specifications, however, is not accomplished so easily. This is true in democratic settings (where apathy towards decision-making prerogatives can and does exist) and in more authoritarian settings (where outward obedience often masks varying levels of resistance.)[9]

When blueprints are to be filled by people, the designer must consider how to secure their compliance with blueprint requirements. To Weber the formula to secure compliance with the bureaucratic rules and respect for authority consisted of money, security, and esteem.[10] Adherence to authority would be further cemented by the congruence of superior expertise and superior position. Since promotions would be based on an individual's accumulation of expertise, subordinates, who through on-the-job training would become experts themselves, would readily accept this criterion.

Of course, fear of dismissal is one method of securing the compliance of functionaries. The person who cannot get along within the bureaucratic structure will most likely be told to find work elsewhere. Weber noted that "a greater dependence on the master is a greater guarantee" of the bureaucratic functionary's "conformity with status conventions."[11]

Thus, the blueprint for monocracy fell into place. Delegation of authority and rule adherence structured the monocratic rule. Money, security, and esteem secured the compliance of subordinates. The design was elegant but not even the draftsmen presumed it to be airtight. Weber, concerned about organizational rule motivated by power maintenance, warned of "guild-like closure" in high bureaucratic posts.[12] Gulick and Urwick, concerned about alien philosophies creeping into the bureaucracy, advised that professionals—lawyers, doctors, and the like—be kept "on tap, not on top."[13] Despite these cautions to blueprint implementers, the classical theorists thought highly of the bureaucratic design's potential for task performance. However, it was not long before the design's structural and compliance securing components were criticized. In fact, the ink was hardly dry on Gulick and Urwick's *Papers on the Science of Administration* when a telling assault was launched on the concept of unity of command.

CRITICIZING THE BLUEPRINT

The attack on the concept of unity of command was fierce. The leader of this assault, Herbert Simon, referred to it and Gulick and Urwick's other principles of administration as "proverbs."[14] The vehicle for Simon's broadsides at traditional organization theory and administrative principles was his book *Administration Behavior*. With this book, Simon, whose original training in political science had developed into a focus in public administration, broke ground in the field of management science. Management science, through careful organization design, analytic techniques, and computer applications, seeks to maximize the quantity and timeliness of relevant information available to the organizational decision maker. Simon, at the forefront in the development of management science, combined his efforts in management science with his investigations in political science and public administration. Simon's work with computers in the 1960s expanded further his range of academic expertise.

Simon considered unity of command an illusion with little hope for the future since its realization was a virtual impossibility. "It does not go too far to say that Unity of Command, in Gulick's sense," wrote Simon, "has never existed in any organization."[15] Simon felt that the unity of command concept was too simplistic as a guide for organizational governance and, in fact, was in conflict with another of the Gulick and Urwick principles—specialization.[16]

As administration specializes its functions, particularly in the public sector, support agencies, such as personnel departments and budget bureaus, come into being. Thus, the personnel or budget officer within an agency serves two masters. For instance, the agency head identifies employees who should be rewarded, reprimanded, or punished and the personnel officer acts accordingly. For guidance on withholding rates for health insurance plans, however, a separate personnel agency or civil service commission will supersede the agency head as the source of direction for the personnel officer. This is because negotiations for group insurance rates, collective bargaining, large-scale recruitment programs, and other activities that affect several agencies may be carried out more efficiently by specialized, independent agencies. In this way, agency administrators can concentrate on the substantive functions of their agencies, while jurisdiction-wide housekeeping functions are performed elsewhere. Thus, command is fragmented, not unitary. This fragmentation of command, observed Simon, was conducive to overall efficiency.[17]

It is not only the emergence of specialized agencies that fragments command. Major executive decisions are also often pro forma ratifications of subordinates' proposals. In large organizations, complex problems may be legal, financial, or scientific in nature. Thus, executives generally defer to the recommendations of their professional staff (e.g., accountants, lawyers, physicists) in matters outside their own areas of expertise. Although this action violates the principles of unity of command, no alternative seems possible. Specialization in modern organizations requires people with highly specialized expertise. Lawyers are valued for their knowledge of corporate law; nuclear physicists for atomic particles; and lathe operators for tooling metal.

The Gulick-Simon controversy was a battle of blueprint designers. Although some criticism of unity of command had heavy ideological overtones (i.e., it was undemocratic or stifled individual initiative), Simon saw monocracy as an ineffectual structure for decision making. People still were components, although somewhat more animated. However, the traditional way of arranging them was wrong. According to Simon, unity of command and other wooden concepts about organizations obscured the fact that "the task of deciding pervades the entire administrative structure quite as much as the task of doing."[18]

The Search for Hidden Authority

Simon's work kicked off a search for other decision makers who derived their authority from structural characteristics of the organization that were not accounted for by the classical bureaucratic design. This search revealed that a degree in physics or law was not a prerequisite for the "task of deciding." One could get the job by being in the right place at the right time.

When analyzing the organization as a communications system, one will discover that some positions are terminals and others, to a greater or lesser degree, are switching stations. At terminals, discretionary power is minimal. Commands are received and carried out. However, at switching stations, functionaries route commands and other information. Thus, persons who occupy positions at switching stations distribute the work of the organization rather than do it. The mailroom is an example of a low-level switching station. In his novel *Catch-22*, Joseph Heller describes an army mailroom. Heller's mailroom is fictional, of course, but it underscores the power implicit in positions at switching stations. Moreover, it would not be surprising if *Catch-22* routing techniques have been applied by real mail clerks.

> There then followed a hectic jurisdictional dispute [between General Dreedle and General Peckham] that was decided in General Dreedle's favor by ex-P.F.C. Wintergreen, mail clerk at Twenty-seventh Air Force Headquarters. Wintergreen determined the outcome by throwing all communications from General Peckham into the wastebasket. He found them too prolix. General Dreedle's views, expressed in less pretentious literary style, pleased ex-P.F.C. Wintergreen and were sped along by him in zealous observance of regulations. General Dreedle was victorious by default.[19]

There are Wintergreens in all organizations. However, they are not always in the mailroom. They often are at the higher levels of the organization in staff positions.

The staff member is a conduit of information to top management. Since only important information should flow to executives, the staff member is also a gatekeeper. Important information, however, is hard to define. In an organization, a matter that is important one week may be unimportant the next. Thus, the staff member, as conduit and gatekeeper, has considerable discretionary power. As the head of a major switching station, the high-level staff member becomes a key figure in organizational governance. By regulating the upward flow of information, gatekeepers shape the focus of top-management's attention. In addition, gatekeepers often reserve the right to make decisions that do not have to be endorsed by the top management. Thus, to those below, the executive staff member can be a boss, a bellwether of top-management thinking, an entree to the executive suite, or a buffer against management wrath. To superiors, the executive staffer is a major repository of organizational information and a filter against information overloads. (Secretaries also fit this description very well.)

Executive staff members are often perceived by organization members and outsiders as the "power behind the throne." It is easy to see why. Much of what the chief executive knows about the organization's operations has been learned from staff members. If the executive is unaware of a particular development, it is often because the staff has withheld this information. When attempts to communicate with the boss are blocked by gatekeepers, rebuffed individuals are likely to claim that the staff is all-powerful. The executive is seen as a figurehead imprisoned by gatekeepers and fed false optimism rather than the innovative ideas of those who were turned away. Even if the staff barrier is breached and the supplicant corners the executive at a party, likely as not, the executive will refer the supplicant to the staff.

Heavy reliance on the staff as a filtering device and decisional aid fits Simon's general notions of effective organizational structure. According to Simon, organizations not only wasted their time trying to achieve the proverbial unity of command, but would be in real trouble if, by some miracle, it was ever achieved. Paralysis would likely result, notes Simon, since the hierarchy of modern, complex organizations is incapable of channeling all of its decision activity to the top in a timely manner. Problems would either resolve themselves or become major crises while waiting on line to see the decision maker. Even when problems reach the top, their resolution by a harried, overworked chief executive would be as suspect as the battle strategy of a shell-shocked soldier.

Expanding on the Means of Compliance

Given the intensity of Simon's assault on the traditional notions of organizational leadership, one would expect that other basic principles would be found wanting, if only by association. This, indeed, was the case. Simon found Weber's compliance formula of money, security, and self-esteem too simplistic to insure good organization citizenship. Simon did not pioneer the study of the methods of securing employee compliance with organizational goals, but based his work upon a foundation laid by Chester Barnard in the 1930s. Barnard's major work, *The Functions of the Executive,* is a classic in organization theory and a practical management guide that retains much of its utility today.[20] Therefore, we will use Barnard's theories of *authority* to begin our exploration of why it is so difficult to keep organization members content, compliant, and productive.

Chester Barnard worked for the telephone company. He had a

good job. He was the president of New Jersey Telephone and Telegraph Company from 1927 until 1948. As a manager, he did things that were ahead of his time and maybe our time as well. For instance, he sent his middle-level executives, with families in tow, to the University of Pennsylvania at company expense and on company time. However, Barnard did not send them to study business administration. Barnard wanted them grounded in the liberal arts so that they could approach their jobs with broadened perspectives. In addition to managing the firm in an innovative manner, in his spare time, Barnard taught, lectured, consulted, and wrote about organizations.[21]

Barnard's focus was leadership and, as he saw it, leadership did not come from the top down as in classical bureaucratic design; it came from the bottom up. Leaders were ineffective, according to Barnard, unless they could make followers accept their leadership.[22]

Barnard identifies three postures that a subordinate can take towards an order: rejection, indecision, or acceptance. Rejection nullifies authority. The authority to command is meaningless if obedience cannot be obtained. Indecision, an intermediate stage that eventually leads to acceptance, rejection, or withdrawal of the order, puts authority on hold. Acceptance legitimizes authority. In all three cases, subordinates determine the effectiveness of executive authority.

Orders may not be authoritative if the subordinate has difficulty understanding them. In government, even the most intelligent subordinates often withhold obedience as they attempt to decipher a directive written in bureaucratese. Orders also may lack authority if they run against the personal principles of the subordinate. A first-grade teacher who is strongly opposed to "tracking"—assigning students to academic, artistic, or vocational programs based on an early evaluation of their aptitude—may resist an order to classify students in terms of their potential. The authority of an order also may be weak if it conflicts with the organization's perceived purpose. A forest ranger ordered to burn timberland is unlikely to act until a supervisor explains clearly how this action contributes to the preservation of forests. Orders issued by a questionable source may also meet resistance. If the vacationing boss's stand-in orders numerous changes, it is likely that subordinates will resist these changes until the vacation is over.

Even if leaders framed orders properly, there was no guarantee that subordinates would comply with organization regulations or fulfill production quotas. Thus, executives had to meet a whole range of subordinates' demands. Getting the right mix of inducements was one of the functions of the executive. Barnard called this the job of managing the *economy of incentives.*[23]

Barnard did not discard Weber's formula of compliance. Money, security, and esteem remained important factors in Barnard's formulation of the economy of incentives. However, depending on the situation, these factors might take second place to a comfortable work environment, advancement potential, or a crusading organizational mission. In Ralph Nader's original public interest groups in the 1960s, sense of mission was the primary method of attracting and keeping members. There is little else that can explain a Harvard Law School graduate turning down lucrative job offers to work a hundred-hour week for less than the minimum wage. Barnard notes, however, that sense of mission is a less compelling incentive in industrial organizations than in political and religious bodies. Nonetheless, asserts Barnard, this incentive is used anyway in most recruitment presentations. After all, sense of mission costs practically nothing, does little harm, and might convince a few prospective employees to accept a lower salary than they normally would.

In government service, where starting salaries are often low and have fixed increments, missionary approaches are frequently used in job interviews. The Peace Corps, which operates much like a religious mission, is the most obvious example, offering in its recruitment material "low wages, poor living conditions, and a chance to do some good." In some instances, a beneficial missionary aura can be thrust upon organizations from outside. Journalism, in the aftermath of Watergate, was annointed with a crusading image by many Americans. Idealistic students flocked to schools of journalism. The news media prospered: News executives and editors inherited highly qualified personnel at a lower price.

Offering prospective employees distinction, prestige, personal power, and the attainment of dominating position is another nonmonetary recruiting technique.[24] It is likely that many students of public administration will have firsthand experience with this approach early in the course of their careers. The job may be presented as being "where the action is." Therefore, the invaluable experience and proximity to breaking events offered by the job will more than compensate for the small salary. Furthermore, recruiters are not shy about identifying the position as a stepping-stone to bigger and better things. This is sometimes true; often it is not. In hierarchy, there are always more positions at the bottom than at the top. Some have to stay behind. Recruiters know this. However, they do not know which of the newly hired staff assistants will perform best on the job. Thus, recruiters emphasize the good news that the job is a springboard, rather than the not-so-good news that not everybody gets sprung. Those not chosen for promotion can always be dealt with later.

Money, prestige, advancement, good working conditions, an outlet for altruism, security, an action setting, comradeship, and a home away from home are all inducements that an organization can offer to individuals in return for their services. Barnard's list is even more extensive but this list adequately demonstrates our essential point: People work for organizations for a variety of reasons. The reasons change from person to person and from moment to moment. So do the inducements. Employees who are not promoted will reassess their commitment to the organization. Recruiters' promises no longer apply; a redefinition of commitment is necessary. If the organization wants to keep their services, it must restructure the inducement formula to compensate for opportunities lost.

Barnard's economy of incentives had another side. Inducements apply only to rewards. According to Barnard, one had to persuade as well. Termination of employment was one of Barnard's effective methods of persuasion. However, termination must not be an isolated, private act. Barnard envisioned a more public termination ceremony designed to quiet potential rebels.

> Coercion is employed both to exclude and to secure the contribution of individuals. Exclusion is often intended to be exclusion permanently and nothing more. . . . Exclusion of undesirables is a necessary method of maintaining organizational efficiency. . . . Forced exclusion is also employed as a means of persuasion by example, to create fear among those not directly affected, so that they will be disposed to render the organization certain contributions.[25]

Despite this cold treatise on termination, Barnard did not see exclusion as the most potent weapon for assuring organizational loyalty. Rather, society as a whole would be the most effective force. If the inducements that organizations offered were valued highly by the society at large, individuals would be predisposed to contribute their efforts. Similarly, if the things that organizations required of individuals, such as obedience, were universally inculcated, functionaries would arrive substantially premolded. No more than gentle persuasion would be needed to fit them exactly into the organizational design. "A fair day's pay for a fair day's work" is an American cliche that serves well the organization's blueprint. Societies that put stock in sayings such as "Don't kill yourself, you'll die soon enough, anyway," produce workers that drive executives to despair.[26]

Weber, Gulick and Urwick, Simon, and Barnard differed not only on technique but also in their interpretation of the problems faced. All agreed, however, that it was the executive who was to apply the techniques to the problem. Executives should delegate authority to subordinates, but with extreme care. Thus, the executive, and not subordinates, must determine the direction and destination of the organization.

PERSPECTIVES ON INFORMAL ORGANIZATION*

Barnard realized that a manager's authority was, to a great extent, vested in workers. However, one senses in Barnard's writing confidence that the veto power of subordinates could be manipulated by top management for organizational purposes. But Barnard may have underestimated the independence of the lower levels of organizations, suggests Melville Dalton, a sociologist who spent several years in managerial positions in organizations. In his study, *Men Who Manage,* Dalton contrasts the attitudes of employees who had risen to positions of leadership in the firm with the beliefs of individuals who had made little or no advance through the hierarchy.[27] The passage below is excerpted from an interview Dalton conducted with one of the unsuccessful employees, a foreman named Evans. Passed over three times for promotion, Evans is not at all circumspect in explaining why:

> There's no promotion system whatever. Seniority, knowledge, or ability don't count. You've got to be a suck-ass and a joiner. You've got to polish the old apple and have a lot of personality. I was once asked to join the Masons, and it was hinted that there'd be a good job in it for me. I told them it was against my religion. They said, "Why Jim! You're not a Catholic . What do you mean, it's against your religion?" "I mean that if I can't have a job on my own ability I don't want it!" Well, I cut off my legs by talking like that. . . . [28]

Can this be true? Is it possible that an organization might substitute Masonic membership for expertise or personality for seniority? Dalton's answer, based upon analyses of employee records, is yes. Being a Mason did count. So did Germanic or Anglo-Saxon origins. Although the company's top managers assured Dalton that skill, competence, and other more or less measurable criteria were used to promote people, 85 percent of the firm's "advisory or directive forces" were Germanic or Anglo-Saxon and 69 percent were Masons.[29] This system of higher management based on ethnicity and Masonic membership developed in this firm because formal standards for measuring promotion potential had not been established. In addition, jobs were often filled by subordinates who had no experience in equivalent positions.

Things are different for lower-level jobs where skills can be matched to position. Baseball players, for instance, must be able to hit, run, throw, and field. Those who throw best tend to become pitchers. Other players are assigned on the basis of a similar match between skills and position. Quantitative data about the players—batting averages,

*For a detailed treatment of the group influence in organizations, see Chapter 5.

pitching victories—are available and can be used to set a tentative starting lineup even before spring training begins. Usually, the team drawn
on paper during the winter layoff is substantially the same as the one
that takes the field on opening day.

A different set of criteria is needed to determine who would make a
good baseball manager. If a retiring star is being considered for the job,
there is no quantitative data on his leadership potential. He may relate
well to his teammates as "one of the boys" but how will he do as the boss?
Looking to other managers to find an ideal "managerial type" does not
help. Some successful managers are maniacs who punch their players;
other winning managers are low key, at times falling asleep on the
bench. Some have been great players; others have never played in the
major leagues. To confuse matters, for every successful manager there
are a dozen managers with the same mix of characteristics who have
failed miserably. The net result of the absence of reliable leadership
criteria is that one cannot make a selection based on a calculation of the
fit between position and individual.

In promoting individuals, the firm Dalton studied was faced with
the same dilemma. For promotion to the higher-level positions, hard
criteria were absent. Since the formal organization offered department
managers little guidance, they fell back on the informal organization.
Managers simply promoted friends who looked a lot like themselves.
Thus, the Masons and the Germanic and Anglo-Saxon types per-
petuated their rule at the plant.

Dalton's study highlights two aspects of informal organization.
First, the informal organization incorporates outside values in the organizational context. Masonic membership was an informal, external
value that affected formal staffing decisions. Second, the informal organization fills in gaps left by the formal organization's structure and
design. In the absence of promotional criteria based on job performance, informal criteria were used in the evaluative process. Thus, we
offer the following working definition of informal organization:

> *Informal organization is composed of individuals and groups who bring to
> the organization, or develop while in the organization, attitudes and values that
> are operationalized in the absence of, or in opposition to, formal organizational
> rules.*[30] *It is the mix of informal and formal rules that governs the organization.*

Informal Organization: Conflicts
with the Organization's Formal Goals

The cohesive Masons in Dalton's study were an informal group.
However, the group had many points in common with the formal organization. Its unorthodox methods of filling the higher ranks of the
hierarchy did not violate important organizational rules. Rather, the informal group filled a substantial void created by the absence of stan-

dardized promotional criteria. Lastly, as a high-echelon informal group, the stamp of official legitimacy was often available for the norms they developed informally.

Other cases show that informal policies can prevail in the organization even at the expense of formal goals. *The Demotion of Deputy Chief Inspector Goldberg* is a tale about a New York City Police Department division head who tried to enforce the law against bingo, even though unofficially the law was a dead letter. Goldberg held a high rank; his only superiors were the police commissioner, the top-ranking uniformed officer, and the borough commander. They tried desperately to convince him to lay off bingo. However, Goldberg's persistence forced his superiors to assume their formal roles. When they would hint to Goldberg that he was obsessed, overreacting, and that bingo entrepreneurs and players were nice folks, he would reply: "Are you telling me not to enforce the law?" Receiving the mandatory negative reply, Goldberg continued his campaign. However, within days Goldberg was charged with insubordination, demoted to captain, given a cut in pay, and assigned to a civil defense detail. Seeing the writing on the wall, Goldberg retired. A casualty of an indiscreet assault on an informal norm, Goldberg was relieved of his duties by the highest-ranking members of the formal organization.[31]

Group norms of lower level employees can also clash with formal organizational goals. Production schedules could be effectively reduced by a group that considered these quotas excessive. Important rules and regulations could be disregarded. In one such instance, reported by Peter Blau, inspectors in a law enforcement agency developed norms that included handling violations and bribe offers independently of the organization.[32]

There were several reasons why the inspectors decided that bribe offers should not be referred for prosecution. First, a bribe offer could imply provocation and criminal culpability on the part of the inspector. Second, the inspectors sympathized with the business owners and managers who had to wrestle with complex rules and regulations.[33] Third, a bribe offer was not viewed as a sinister act; it was seen as a natural cost cutting move on the part of business persons seeking to avoid lengthy and expensive administrative proceedings. All in all, it was felt that informal pressure would get the job done at less cost in time, money, and paperwork to all concerned. Thus, when bribe offers were made, inspectors would use the threat of exposure to secure voluntary compliance from violators.[34] In the process, some violations and almost all bribe offers went unreported to superiors.

This informal control over behavior, Blau observed, was possible because members valued what the group had to offer. Friendship, common interests, and mutual protection welded the group. Deviant behavior—in this case adhering to organizational values that conflicted with informal norms—was punished by a full or partial withdrawal of membership benefits. During Blau's study, two inspectors did report bribe offers. Although they complied with the law and the organization's rules, the inspectors were ostracized by the group. One inspector, a loner, was not overly concerned. The other outcast, however, felt miserable. Deprived of friendship and a sense of belonging, he could no longer count on the comfort and support of the group in the face of demands from the formal organization. The inspector became an enemy cast adrift in a hostile world—an example for those contemplating the exposure of bribers.

Group cohesion is also facilitated in another way. Groups tend to have a favorable self-image and a less than favorable image of other groups. It is an attitude of "us and them." If the stakes are high, as when two groups struggle for control of the organization, the attitude changes to "us *or* them." The "us or them" attitude goes a long way towards explaining what we read about organizations: "Enemies List Revealed"; "New Commissioner Gives Old Staff 24 Hours to Clear Out"; "Kissinger Wiretapped White House Aides." A memo that a new employee is likely to read upon entering government service may include the "us-them" statement: "Only authorized personnel may respond to inquiries from the press, legislature, or other agencies of the government." A boss who speaks of organization members who "are not *our* friends," or "are out after *their* own self-interest," or "get all the glory while *we* do all the work," is drawing a line between "us and them."

Informal Organization: A Societal Perspective

Informality is widespread in organizations. In the classical view of bureaucracy, where efficiency was the prime consideration in design, informality was dysfunctional. However, in the European and American contexts political ideals embraced the concept of a governing role for the majority of society's members. This concept often is carried over into the governance of public organizations.

We see the carry-over when work rules are subject to employee vote; when a community school board is given administrative or policy-making power; when a cooperative apartment house is directly managed by the residents. Each of these examples, particularly in the United States, is likely to be labeled *participatory democracy*. In the most general sense participatory democracy results when bureaucratic and political values intermingle in organizational governance. Proposals for participatory democracy generally indict organizational monocracy for being inequitable or for squelching, rather than reinforcing, attitudes or values important to society. The prescription for remedying this defect was bottom-up rule.

Bottom-Up Rule: The European Context The nineteenth century communist and socialist critiques of organization rule concentrated on the situation of the worker. To Marx, the organization was the workers. Yet workers were exploited in organizations controlled by capitalists. Owning the physical things—land, buildings, and machinery—necessary for a worker to be productive in modern society, capitalists forced workers to forgo, in return for employment reimbursed at a fraction of its value, their proprietary rights to what they produced. The owners made the decisions and reaped the profits. Workers were treated as mere cogs in the organizational machinery instead of the primary producers that they in fact were. Thus, workers were alienated from the means of production. Marx's remedy was organizations owned by, and run for the benefit of, the workers of the society.[35]

Other workers' movements of the early twentieth century had similar but less sweeping views than Marx. Guild socialists and syndicalists believed that each industry should be run for the benefit of the workers in that industry rather than all workers in the society. As a result, their organizational design was an eclectic mixture of communism, unionism, and the theories of Adam Smith. Workers in a particular industry would decide what to produce, determine production levels, and set salaries. Thus, if workers wanted to triple salaries and halve production, they had the authority to do so. Presumably, however, either the economics of the situation or the sensibility of the workers in their rightful position of responsibility would preclude such destructive actions.[36]

By the middle of the twentieth century, few influential political ideologies denied that the worker was entitled to a voice in the workplace. What differed were the relative values attributed to labor and capital. If labor input was seen as primary, the workers' voice was to be predominant. If capital was judged as the vital input, workers were to have less of a say. In the United States, legislation affirms the rights of workers to organize and to bargain with management. While our heavy reliance on arbitration indicates a straddling of the ideological fence (or perhaps an absence of ideology), we are beyond the point where public policy adheres to the bureaucratic ideal of the hegemony of overhead direction by corporate owners. Workers have rights, too, should they choose to exercise them.

Bottom-Up Rule: The American Context In the American experience, a distrust of powerful rulers and an abiding belief in democracy influenced the development of political thought. The American Revolutionary War was, in essence, a violent reaction against distant and unresponsive rule. The colonists' complaints against bearing what they felt was an unjust portion of the costs of the British Empire went unanswered. Feeling exploited and powerless, the colonists ended this arrangement and vowed never again to have a king or any ruler who could govern arbitrarily and arrogantly. Future American rulers would have to answer periodically to the citizens and their limited powers would be subject to countervailing influences of other government actors. If there were bureaucracies in those days, the U.S. Constitution could have been viewed as an antibureaucratic document.

The U.S. Constitution was based on democratic principles, even though democracy emerged in a somewhat diluted form. Only landowners could vote; specially designated electors decided electoral contests; and legislators and executives often decided what was good for their constituents rather than what was desired by constituents.

In the constitutional debates, those who placed full faith in the citizenry were not successful. However, their views continued to play a part in the debates over what form the United States government should take. Thomas Jefferson, who advocated a high degree of citizen involvement with government, is often cited as an authority by modern day proponents of participatory democracy. Jefferson saw the New England town meeting, with citizens exercising close control over their local institutions, as the epitome of democracy. Although he realized that New York, Philadelphia, and Boston had already become too populous for town meetings to be effective, this only heightened his concern. Jefferson feared that the urban citizen, whose exposure to democracy was limited to periodic and often ritualistic voting, would place a very low value on democracy. For democracy to thrive, according to Jefferson, a rural, dispersed population was necessary and should be encouraged.[37]

Alexis de Tocqueville, a French philosopher whose insights are those of an outside observer studying the United States in its initial years, supported Jefferson's views. De Tocqueville attributed the vitality of the democratic spirit in America to the high degree of citizen involvement with the institutions that governed them. The relative absence of class distinctions contributed to the citizens' willingness to exert influence. In Europe, according to de Tocqueville, this was not so. Bureaucratization had started earlier and progressed farther there than in America. The European bureaucracy had set itself apart from society as a bastion of expertise. Thus, it constituted a new superior class in a class-conscious society. Bureaucrats went by the book; rules and regulations were immutable. Citizen input was not invited since citizens were viewed as having little to offer the bureaucratic apparatus. Thus, de Tocqueville saw in European citizens a cynical attitude that undermined democratic principles. Reinforcing this cynicism, bureaucratic administration went its own way regardless of electoral changes.[38]

De Tocqueville and Jefferson feared that the citizen would feel incapable of ruling government institutions. However, there are two ways the citizen relates to public organizations. One is as boss—the voter. The other is as client. The client role was not as pervasive in the early days of the United States as it is now. Welfare and educational functions were carried on privately and taxes were paid only by landowners.[39] Municipal fire and sanitation services were private concerns. Volunteers fought the fires and animals ate the garbage.[40] Government was small and directly served only a few citizens. Thus, Jefferson and de Tocqueville could see participatory administration as citizens, in their democratically prescribed role of boss, closely overseeing the operation of government.

Jefferson's dream of a rural America and citizen supervision, however, never materialized. Today, even cities have billion-dollar budgets and it appears that the day has passed that the average citizen could ascertain the overall mix of government activity that would best serve the general welfare. Recognizing this, contemporary democratic theorists gradually have been taking the "boss" out of citizen. In the 1940s Joseph Schumpeter saw voting as merely a decision on candidates and parties rather than on policies.[41] In the 1950s Robert Dahl asserted that citizens rule primarily through their selective membership in interest groups: A process which moved citizens yet another step away from the government decision-making apparatus and narrowed their focus to a handful of issues.[42]

Modern proponents of participatory democracy also see the citizen as almost powerless to effect policy change through traditional electoral mechanisms. Yet they reassert the Jeffersonian notion of democracy devalued by the inability of citizens to influence their government institutions. Proponents of participatory democracy also adhere to de Tocqueville's vision of a bureaucratic monolith that must be checked by citizen involvement. Otherwise, it is slow to move, deaf to client suggestions, and resistant to the authority of elected superiors. Moreover, in jurisdictions that have grown large, government bureaucracy, no matter how pristine its motives may be, is likely to grow unresponsive in spite of itself. It will homogenize treatment of clients because the bureaucratic ethic says that standardization is efficient. As a result, everyday needs will become institutionalized and the specialized needs of particular geographic areas or specific social groups will be ignored.

Thus, the call for citizen participation heard today is a response to the defects in both big democracy and big bureaucracy. It is a bottom-up response. Clients—students, parents, neighborhood residents, the aged, and other service recipients—are to be the participants. In modern society, the argument goes, democratic spirit can be best reinforced by direct and meaningful client interaction with the government institutions that serve them. Furthermore, programs will only become responsive to local needs if community residents are afforded a policy-making voice. This last rationale is also advanced in support of greater decision-making authority for local program personnel. Being closest to the problem, employees based in the community can best tailor services to maximize impact.

Problems with Bottom-Up Rule   In organization, pure bottom-up rule works about as well as pure top-down rule. That is to say, it does not. One of the first to note this was Robert Michels. Michels was a student of democratic institutions who found precious little democracy. What he found was rule by the few. His findings led him to formulate the *Iron Law of Oligarchy*.

Michels's Iron Law of Oligarchy posits a dreary rule for organizations. It is governance by suppression and propaganda. It is rulers whose paranoia complements their aggression. It is an organizational citizenry that is either plotting or pliant, but always keeping a low profile. Most depressing is Michels's contention that this is likely to happen in all organizations regardless of type.[43]

Michels's Iron Law of Oligarchy is built upon several factors. First, he attributes considerably more weight to the xenophobia of informal groups than to their cooperation. Second, he sees elite groups, those who vie for the top positions in the organization, as more likely to have combative, aggressive members. Third, like Jefferson, Michels sees the rank and file becoming increasingly passive as the administrative machinery grows more complex.

One of Michels's prime focuses was the trade union movement. Michels's Iron Law of Oligarchy seems to explain, in part, the saga of Jimmy Hoffa and the Teamsters Union. When Hoffa's predecessor, Dave Beck, went to prison, Hoffa became the "caretaker" president of the Teamsters Union. When Hoffa fell victim to the occupational hazards of the post and was jailed, Frank Fitzsimmons became the "interim" union head. When Hoffa emerged from prison, the conditions of his parole barred him from holding union office for the duration of the sentence. (According to Hoffa adherents, Fitzsimmons traded Teamster support for President Nixon's reelection in return for Hoffa's neutralization.) Even in an informal role, there was no place for Hoffa in the high union councils dominated by his former assistant, Fitzsimmons. Prior to his mysterious disappearance, Hoffa was challenging the conditions of his parole in court and preparing another run for the union presidency. Even though Hoffa's fate is unknown, Michels's Iron Law of Oligarchy sheds light on the leadership transition in the Teamsters Union.

The problems with bottom-up rule are not limited to aggressive elites. With worker governance, experience seems to indicate that the "managers" often fail to live up to their billing. In Yugoslavia, where workers' councils were given a substantial organizational voice, some councils chose to sky rocket their salaries despite the societywide economic repercussions that ensued. Rather than confront complex administrative decisions, however, many workers' councils deferred to the factory manager.[44] Mixed reports emerged from the German experience. The German airline, Lufthansa, has reported success with worker democracy. On the other hand, studies on different firms have found that employee participants in organizational decision making were hardly enthusiastic. Unless meetings were held during working hours, turnout was meager.[45] These studies of workers' councils indicate that many workers view their jobs as instrumental, rather than central, to their way of life.

Client control exhibits similar problems. Where community elections have been held to choose governing boards for certain services, turnout has been low, often pitifully so.[46] In operation, community control has proceeded in a manner that often has exacerbated neighborhood tensions. Factions developed. Residents who had power excluded neighbors who did not.[47] The excluded neighbors often attempted to regain power through sit-ins, shout-ins, and service disruptions.

The relationship between newly elected governing boards and the existing administrative machinery was at times even more precarious. Service staffs were purged in disregard of civil service regulations and union contractual arrangements. In New York City, such personnel activity by community school boards led to a series of bitter and lengthy strikes and administrative closures both by local boards and the central board of education.[48]

Such results, of course, intensified the counterattack from bureaucratic purists. From the standpoint of the classical theory of bureaucracy, participatory rule subverts the instrumental nature of organization. The people, through their duly elected representatives, set the organization's general course and pay the freight. For instance, a welfare office is a coordinated group of experts addressing a problem—insufficient resources of certain individuals—at the behest of the society at large. It is not a device for instilling a democratic spirit, either in social workers or in welfare recipients. Nor is it meant to lay aside its professional standards and acquiesce to the self-diagnoses of its clients. The bureaucracy's core value should always be efficiency and effectiveness in the accomplishment of assigned tasks. The organization that sidetracks onto such issues as participatory democracy is insubordinate and squanders, on matters unrelated to its mission, the resources that society has provided to meet a certain need.[49]

Despite these objections and participatory democracy's poor showing, governing boards, advisory councils, and other input arrangements are common in public administration. These worker and citizen/client voices usually do not pack the punch that socialists or Jeffersonians would desire. Nonetheless they are a reality that the public administrator must deal with.

THE POTENTIAL OF
AUTHORITY: MILGRAM'S EXPERIMENTS

Clearly, there is tension between the informal and formal organization and between the bureaucratic and the democratic ideal. This tension is not unhealthy. If everything was subject to the citizens' vote or informality was the watchword for task performance, things could grind to a halt. On the other hand, there is much to fear in the perfection of authority. Even partially achieved, authority can be among the most compelling forces in modern society. Millions of people have died in the name of authority, even though authoritarians may have had a difficult time achieving their dominant positions. Authority can be either malevolent or benevolent; the agents of authority can do harm or do good. The laboratory experiments of psychologist Stanley Milgram make this abundantly clear.[50]

Milgram's experimental setting was simple. There was an "electric chair" in one room. In an adjoining room a control panel indicated voltages from 0 to 450. For emphasis, voltage ranges on the panel were designated as "Slight Shock," "Moderate Shock," "Strong Shock," "Very Strong Shock," "Intense Shock," "Extreme Intensity Shock," "Danger: Severe Shock," and, for the 450 volt range, "XXX."

There were three basic roles. Two were filled by actors and one by an unsuspecting citizen who answered an advertisement offering $4.50 for participating one hour in a learning experiment. One actor played the "experimenter"; the other played the "learner." The unsuspecting participant always played the "teacher."

In Milgram's experiments, the "experimenter" instructed the "teacher" to read word pairs to the "learner" and then test for retention. For example, if "blue sky" had been in a sequence of paired words and the "teacher" said "blue," the "learner" was expected to say "sky." If the "learner" gave a wrong answer, the "teacher" was to give the "learner" a shock and increase it in intensity for each successive mistake. The actor playing the "learner" always gave enough wrong answers so that the march up the shock scale to maximum voltage could only be halted if the unsuspecting "teacher" disobeyed the "experimenter" and refused to go on. If the "teacher" was hesitant, the "experimenter" ordered him to go on and asserted that the damage to the "learner," if any, was only temporary. The "experimenter" also said that the success of the experiment depended on proceeding to 450 volts.

The object of the experiment was to determine if one's aversion to inflicting pain on humans would be strong enough to overcome obedience to authority. Although the electric shocks were not real, the "learner's" protests were convincing. If obedience to authority—the "experimenter" was the figure of authority both as boss and as knowledgeable scientist—was a stronger force, the shocks would continue to be given despite the "teacher's" perception of the pain being inflicted. If concern for the welfare of the "learner" was paramount, the "teacher" would refuse to continue.

In Milgram's experiments, authority emerged victorious. Through experimental variations, which will be described below, factors that strengthen or weaken authority were highlighted. Although Milgram's findings are revealing, the implications of his experiment may be unsettling. Professor Milgram himself was dismayed by the results of the authority experiments.

When authority was successfully applied in the experiment, it neutralized core values held by the subjects. Academics and others surveyed before the experiment scoffed at the idea that subjects would deliver the maximum voltage. Yet, in the authority context, some obedient subjects tried to show the "experimenter" that they were good workers by administering the word test in a precise voice and methodically proceeding up the voltage scale. Others achieved self-absolution by defining themselves as merely an extension of the "experimenter." "OK," they said, "I'll do it, but it is your responsibility." A few assumed an air of righteousness. They saw their actions as justifiable because such a stupid "learner" deserved punishment.

In the initial experiments, at 300 volts the "learner" began to pound on the walls separating the two rooms. At 315 volts the pounding stopped. The "teacher" was free to draw his own conclusions about the cause of the commotion and its abrupt cessation. Whatever the conclusions, 65 percent of the "teachers" continued to administer shocks up to the 450 volt level.

Since the pounding had been limited to a single level and its meaning ambiguous, subsequent experiments provided clearer and more frequent clues. A preexisting minor heart condition was casually noted by the "learner" before the experiment started. The "learner" began grunting at lower shock levels and, at higher voltages, made increasingly insistent and pained demands to be released from the experiment. The "learner" also asserted that his heart bothered him as a result of the shocks. After 330 volts, dead silence set in. So what happened? 65 percent of the "teachers" continued to push the lever to 450 volts.

Next, the "experimenters" tried women "teachers." No difference was revealed. 65 percent of the women applied the maximum 450 volts, although they felt a little worse about doing it than the men.

In microcosm, these experiments show how effective authority can be if the formula is put together properly. The authority formula in the above experiments was: an overarching and respectable ideal—science; a knowledgeable and high-status superior—the "experimenter" scientist;

close supervision—the "experimenter" never left the room; continual reinforcement—the hesitant "teacher" was urged on by the authority figure; a contractual obligation on the part of the "teacher"—"teachers" had agreed to do the task in return for $4.50; a lifetime of socialization—those in authority are to be obeyed; and finally, uncertainty and fear as to the penalties for noncompliance—the authority might disapprove, or worse.

The centrality of authority as a motivating factor was underscored by further experiments. In one case, the "experimenter" ordered that the experiment be stopped because the "learner" was having severe reactions. Even though the "learner" assumed a macho stance and insisted that the experiment continue, every "teacher" stopped upon the "experimenter's" order. In another variant, the "experimenter," in the face of a reluctant "learner," agreed to assume the learning role. At 150 volts, the "experimenter" demanded to be let out; every "teacher" obeyed.

When the source of authority was absent, unclear, or vested in the "teacher," "teachers" treated "learners" in a much more humane way. With the "experimenter" out of the room, only 20 percent of the "teachers" gave the maximum shock. When there were two "experimenters" in violent disagreement whether the experiment should continue, every "teacher" grabbed the opportunity to break off the experiment. (Score one for humanity, but remember also Gulick and Urwick's dictums against split command.) When the intensity of the shock to be administered for a wrong answer was left to the discretion of the "teacher," only two "teachers" ventured out of the lower voltage ranges.

The "trappings" of authority were also tested in some of the experiments. When the locale was moved from the imposing environs of the testing laboratory to more nondescript locations, more "teachers" refused to administer the highest shocks. Compliance also waned when the imposing "experimenter" was replaced by a less authoritative-looking type. Finally, when a "common person" was given the authority position by the "experimenter," who was called away, only 20 percent of the "teachers" obeyed all the commands of the nonscientific type.

Another modification of the experiment assessed the relative strength of "fair play" and authority. Involved was the breach of a promise made by the "experimenter" to the "learner." Reluctant because of his "heart condition," the "learner" agreed to consent to the experiment only if he could call a halt should the pain become too severe. The "teacher" witnessed the "experimenter's" nodding agreement with this condition. At 150 volts, the "learner" asked to be let out. The "experimenter," reneging on the promise, ordered the "teacher" to continue. 40 percent obeyed the order to continue and proceeded to deliver the maximum shocks.

Milgram also introduced a peer group element into the basic exper-

The "Touch-Proximity" Variant of the Milgram Experiments. As a penalty for a wrong answer, obedient "teachers" must force the "learner's" hand onto a shock plate. SOURCE: Stanley Milgram, *Obedience to Authority* (New York: Harper & Row, 1974), p. 37. Copyright © 1974 by Stanley Milgram. Reprinted by permission of Harper & Row, Publishers, Inc.

iment. The results show that authority is weakened in the face of group solidarity among subordinates. The "teacher" role was broken into three parts. One actor asked the questions; another determined the correctness of the response. As usual, the unsuspecting participant delivered the shocks. Authority, in the form of the "experimenter," still hovered nearby and the "learner" delivered the standard rising crescendo of protests. In this instance, however, the co-workers of the "teacher-shocker" refused to go on at a certain point. Their example provided the "teacher-shocker" with support should he, too, choose to defy authority. With peers as a counterweight to the "experimenter's" authority, 90 percent of the naive participants refused to complete the experiment.

The results of another variation of the "specialized teacher" role are more disturbing for those concerned with the destructive potential of bureaucratic authority. The unsuspecting participant, rather than delivering the shocks, merely performed the subsidiary act of asking the questions. Although the participant was a link in the chain that led to the pain being inflicted on the "learner," the subject did not have to do the dirty work. This particular variation produced the fewest rebellions against the authority of the "experimenter." Only 3 out of 40 participants refused to continue to the end. Other experiments conducted by Milgram underscored the relationship between proximity to the victim and rebellion against the "experimenter's" commands. When the "teacher" had to sit next to the "learner," or make physical contact with the victim to effectuate the shocks, compliance was significantly reduced.

We have gone on at length concerning the Milgram experiments for two reasons: First, they help explain the exercise of authority, a central element in the effective functioning of organizations. Secondly, the experiments convey a warning that should be kept in mind. It is that bureaucratic authority is a potent force that can be applied to evil ends as well as to good ones. Where injury or destruction is desired by the bureaucracy, it can come about through the organized efforts of persons who, individually, would not think of hurting anyone. As Milgram writes:

> Consider the individual who, in everyday life, is gentle and kind. Even in moments of anger he does not strike out at those who have frustrated him.... Yet, when taken into military service he is ordered to drop bombs on people and he does so. The act does not originate in his own motive system and thus is not checked by the inhibitory forces of his internal psychological system. In growing up, the normal individual has learned to check the expression of aggressive impulses. But the culture has failed almost entirely in inculcating internal controls on actions that have their origin in authority. For this reason, (authority) constitutes a far greater danger to human survival.[51]

As a civilization that has had Crusades and Inquisitions, Hitler and Stalin, we cannot afford to ignore Milgram's warning. Sensitivity to the potential of authority is not a bad trait to nurture.

SUMMARY

We have looked at the question of who rules in organizations through several lenses. They are:

1. The classical bureaucratic perspective with its emphasis on formal rules.
2. The contractual-bureaucratic approach that emphasizes reciprocal benefits and penalties or a sharing of authority between the organization and workers.
3. The informal focus which attributes a high degree of policy control to lower-level organization members.
4. The political and social views that assign a normative value to policy control by worker and clients.
5. Michels's fatalistic vision of the inevitability of oligarchy.

The survey concluded with the experimental work of Milgram which covers much of the foregoing and raises important questions for future public administrators. Now that we have completed our study of authority within organizations we will turn our attention to the relationship between the organization and its environment.

KEY TERMS AND CONCEPTS

Authority	Monocratic organization
Delegation	Participatory democracy
Economy of incentives	PODSCORB
Iron Law of Oligarchy	Unity of command

NOTES

1. P. O'Hara, "Housing and Sub-Regional Population Movements: Studies in Shifting Demographic Patterns in the Bronx" (Master's thesis, Baruch College of City University of New York, 1976) p. 8.
2. Paul Eddy, E. Potter, and B. Page, *Destination Disaster* (New York: Quadrangle, 1976), pp. 94–95.
3. Max Weber, "Bureaucracy" in Richard J. Stillman II, ed., *Public Administration: Concepts and Cases* (Boston: Houghton Mifflin, 1976), p. 45.
4. Psychohistory has its pitfalls, but some contend that the Prussian gestalt is inseparable from Weber's analysis. Things are precise and people are obedient. For a thumbnail sketch of Weber's parental influence and a speculation that it turned him into a workaholic who prescribed his malady to the world, see David Schuman, *Bureaucracies, Organizations, and Administration: A Political Primer* (New York: Macmillan, 1976), pp. 54–59. For a complete psychohistorical treatment, see Arthur Mitzman, *The Iron Cage* (New York: Grosset & Dunlap, 1969).
5. Weber quoted in Stillman, p. 45.
6. Ibid., p. 41.
7. Luther Gulick and L. Urwick, eds., *Papers on the Science of Administration* (New York: Columbia University Press, 1937).
8. Henri Fayol, *General and Industrial Management* (London: Pitman and Sons, 1949), translated from the 1916 French edition.
9. Chester Barnard was pleased to note that this behavior, supportive of his theories on the legitimization of authority, was evident in his travels in both democratic and authoritarian countries. See his *The Functions of the Executive* (Cambridge: Harvard University Press, 1938) p. 83.
10. H. H. Gerth and C. Wright Mills, eds., *From Max Weber: Essays in Sociology* (Oxford: Oxford University Press, 1946), p. 204.
11. Weber quoted in Ibid., p. 203.
12. Ibid., p. 700.
13. Gulick and Urwick in Fred A. Kramer, ed., *Perspectives on Public Bureaucracy* (Cambridge: Winthrop Publishers, Inc., 1973), p. 29.
14. Herbert A. Simon, *Administration Behavior: A Study of Decision-Making Processes in Administrative Organizations,* 3rd ed. (New York: Free Press, 1976), p. 20.
15. Ibid., p. 25.
16. Ibid., pp. 22–25.
17. Ibid., p. 24.
18. Ibid., p. 1.

19. Joseph Heller, *Catch-22* (New York: Dell, 1961), p. 27.
20. Barnard, *The Functions of the Executive.*
21. William B. Wolf, *Conversations with Chester I. Barnard* (Ithaca: School of Industrial and Labor Relations, 1973).
22. Barnard, *The Functions of the Executive,* chapter 13.
23. Ibid., chapter 12.
24. Chester Barnard, "The Economy of Incentives" in Stillman, *Public Administration,* p. 295.
25. Ibid., p. 297. Barnard seems to get uncharacteristically forceful when he talks about firing people. In writing on authority, he mentions "incarceration or execution" as a not unthinkable penalty for organizational traitors in times of crisis. See Barnard, *The Functions of the Executive,* p. 171.
26. See Bernard C. Rosen, "Achievement and Economic Growth in Brazil" in Walter M. Gerson, ed. *Social Problems in a Changing World* (New York: Crowell, 1969), pp. 300–321. Rosen doesn't see a rosy economic future ahead for Brazilians unless they can shed their fatalistic attitudes, dissociate to a greater degree from family and geographic roots and get some of that good-old, in-control, Protestant Ethic.
27. Melville Dalton, *Men Who Manage* (New York: Wiley, 1959).
28. Melville Dalton, "Men Who Manage" in Derek Phillips, ed., *Studies in American Society, II* (New York: Harper & Row, 1967), p. 52.
29. Ibid., pp. 84–87.
30. This definition is based, in part, on Leonard Broom and Philip Selznick, *Principles of Sociology,* 4th ed. (New York: Harper & Row, 1970), pp. 201–203.
31. Edwin A. Bock and Philip Logue, *The Demotion of Deputy Chief Inspector Goldberg* (Syracuse: Inter-University Case Program, 1963).
32. Peter M. Blau, "The Taboo on Reporting Offers of Bribes" in R. Golembiewski, F. Gibson and G. Cornog, eds., *Public Administration: Readings in Institutions, Processes, Behavior* (Chicago: Rand McNally, 1972), pp. 27–35.
33. Ibid., p. 47.
34. Ibid., p. 48.
35. Henri Lefebre, *The Sociology of Marx* (New York: Random House (Vintage Books), 1969).
36. Daniel C. Kramer, *Participatory Democracy: Developing Ideal of the Political Left* (Cambridge: Schenkman, 1972). Kramer gives an interesting account of the various syndicalist movements as part of his rather evenhanded treatment of participatory democracy experiments. Less evenhanded is the work of C. George Benello and Dimitrios Roussopoulos, *The Case for Participatory Democracy* (New York: Grossman, 1971). They view participatory democracy as the end result of a revolutionary process rather than an addendum to the present state of affairs.
37. Kramer, *Participatory Democracy,* pp. 32–33.
38. Alexis de Tocqueville, *Democracy in America* (London: Oxford University Press, 1961), pp. 126–133; on associational ties, see pp. 376–391; on class distinctions, see pp. 445–484.
39. Participatory democrats argue that if the founding fathers could have foreseen the government assuming most of the welfare functions then performed by families, greater citizen participation would have been provided for in the constitution.
40. Bayard Still, *Mirror for Gotham* (New York: New York University Press, 1956), pp. 125–175, presents a vivid description of nineteenth-century city services or, more precisely, the lack thereof.

41. J. A. Schumpeter, *Capitalism, Socialism and Democracy* (London: Allen & Unwin, 1943).
42. Robert A. Dahl, *Pluralist Democracy in the United States* (Chicago: Rand McNally, 1967) is a good summary of Dahl's thoughts on interest group politics.
43. Robert Michels, *Political Parties: A Sociological Study of the Oligarchical Tendencies of Modern Democracy* (New York: Free Press, 1949). For transcription of lectures in which Michels ranges far, wide, and provocative, see also Robert Michels, *First Lectures in Political Sociology*, Alfred DeGrazia, ed. (Minneapolis: University of Minnesota Press, 1949).
44. Daniel C. Kramer, pp. 158–162.
45. Ibid., pp. 82–83.
46. Ibid., pp. 105–107.
47. State Charter Revision Commission for New York City, *School Decentralization in New York City* (New York, 1974), pp. 65–66.
48. Kramer, pp. 147–148.
49. See Victor A. Thompson, *Without Sympathy or Enthusiasm* (University, Ala.: University of Alabama Press, 1975) for a presentation of this view.
50. Stanley Milgram, *Obedience* (New York: Harper & Row, 1972).
51. Ibid., p. 146–147.

BIBLIOGRAPHY

Barnard, Chester. *The Functions of the Executive.* Cambridge: Harvard University Press, 1938.

Bendix, Reinhard. *Work and Authority in Industry.* New York: Chapman and Hall, 1956.

Benello, George C. and Roussopoulos, Dimitrios. *The Case for Participatory Democracy.* New York: Grossman, 1971.

Blau, Peter M. *The Dynamics of Bureaucracy.* Chicago: University of Chicago Press, 1955.

Broom, Leonard and Selznick, Philip. *Principles of Sociology,* 4th edition. New York: Harper & Row, 1970.

Crozier, Michael. *The Bureaucratic Phenomenon.* Chicago: University of Chicago Press, 1964.

Dalton, Melville. *Men Who Manage.* New York: Wiley, 1959.

de Tocqueville, Alexis. *Democracy in America.* London: Oxford University Press, 1961.

Gouldner, Alvin. *Patterns of Industrial Bureaucracy.* New York: The Free Press, 1954.

Heller, Joseph. *Catch-22.* New York: Dell, 1961.

Kaufman, Herbert. *The Forest Ranger: A Study in Administrative Behavior.* Baltimore, Md: Johns Hopkins Press, 1960.

Kramer, Daniel C. *Participatory Democracy: Developing Ideal of the Political Left.* Cambridge: Schenkman, 1972.

Lefebre, Henri. *The Sociology of Marx.* New York: Random House (Vintage Books), 1969.

Michels, Robert. *Political Parties: A Sociological Study of the Oligarchical Tendencies of Modern Democracy.* New York: Free Press, 1949.

Milgram, Stanley. *Obedience.* New York: Harper & Row, 1972.

Moynihan, Daniel P. *Maximum Feasible Misunderstanding: Community Action in the War on Poverty.* New York: Free Press, 1969.

Simon, Herbert A. *Administration Behavior: A Study of Decision-Making Processes in Administrative Organization,* 3rd ed. New York: Free Press, 1976.

In addition to the sources cited in the notes and bibliography, the following *Public Administration Review* (*PAR*) articles are a convenient starting point for a more detailed exploration of the material in this chapter.

Denhardt, Robert B. "Organizational Citizenship and Personal Freedom," *PAR* 28, no. 1 (Jan./Feb. 1968): 47–54.

Onibokun, Adepoju G. and Martha Curry. "An Ideology of Citizen Participation: The Metropolitan Seattle Transit Case Study," *PAR* 36, no. 3 (May/June 1976): 269–277.

Reidel, James A. "Citizen Participation: Myths and Realities," *PAR* 32, no. 3 (May/June 1972): 211–220.

Scott, William G. "The Theory of Significant People," *PAR* 33, no. 4 (July/Aug. 1973): 308–313.

Smith, Michael P. "Alienation and Bureaucracy: The Role of Participatory Administration," *PAR* 31, No. 6 (Nov./Dec. 1971): 658–664.

Starling, Jay D. "Organization and the Decision to Participate," *PAR* 28, no. 5 (Sept./Oct. 1968): 453–460.

Sternberg, Carl W. "Citizen and the Administrative State: From Participation to Power," *PAR* 32, no. 3 (May/June 1972): 191–198.

Strange, John H. (ed.). "Citizens Action in Model Cities and CAP Programs: Case Studies and Evaluation," *PAR* 32, Special Issue (Sept. 1972): 377–470. See especially John H. Strange, "The Impact of Citizen Participation on Public Administration," 457–470.

Vogel, Donald B. "Analysis of Informal Organization Patterns: A Training Technique," *PAR* 28, no. 5 (Sept./Oct. 1968): 431–436.

Walker, Donald E. "When the Tough Get Going, The Going Gets Tough: The Myth of the Muscle Administration," *PAR* 36, no. 4 (July/Aug. 1976): 439–445.

Zimmerman, Joseph F. "Neighborhoods and Citizen Involvement," *PAR* 32, no. 3 (May/June 1972): 201–210.

RELEVANT PERIODICALS
Academy of Management Journal
Academy of Management Review
California Management Review
Harvard Business Review
Organizational Dynamics
Sloan Management Review
Social Forces
Supervisory Management

RELEVANT CASE STUDIES
(Cases marked ICCH are available from the Intercollegiate Case Clearing House, Soldier Field, Boston, Mass. 02163; cases marked ICP are available from the Inter-University Case Program, Box 229, Syracuse, N.Y. 13210.)

Diver, C.S.   *Park Plaza* (A)(B)(C),* [ICCH]
Kaufman, H.   *The New York City Health Centers,* [ICP]

*Letters indicate that the case is presented in several installments.

Keeley, J. B.   *Moses on the Green,* [ICP]

Logue, J. and E. A. Bock.   *The Demotion of Deputy Chief Inspector Goldberg,* [ICP]

Rosenbaum, W. A.   *The Burning of the Farm Population Estimates,* [ICP]

Russell, J. R., W. D. Campbell.   *Department of Correction,* (A)(B)(C),* [ICCH]

Sheldon, A. P., A. Burst.   *Children's Hospital Medical Center,* [ICP]

Wolf, C., Jr.   *Indonesian Assignment* [ICP]

CHAPTER 4

ORGANIZATION AND ENVIRONMENT

INTRODUCTION

The classical notion of bureaucracy held that organizations, for the most part, did what they were told. Weber, however, also noted the potential for bureaucracy to be hostile towards political superiors.[1] Thus, discovering organization's major goals vis-à-vis society presents the student with a dilemma. Namely, "whether bureaucracy (is) still an administrative apparatus for the implementation of social goals or whether it has lost its instrumental character: whether from a tool in the hands of the legitimate policy-making body, it has become itself the master dictating the general goals to be pursued."[2]

In answering this question, we confront the same obstacles facing an investigative reporter or prosecutor trying to uncover organizational wrongdoing. The organization is, more often than not, inscrutable. Thus, according to Simon, Smithberg, and Thompson, "the day-to-day adjustment of the organization to its environment—the steps it takes to anticipate possible attacks from enemies, its efforts to win quietly important friends—are more often carried out in conversations and conferences that are hard to piece together, even when known, into a complete picture."[3] Indeed, with respect to the Watergate case, it is entirely possible that, without the revelation of the presidential tapes, Richard Nixon would have served out his term of office.

Despite the difficulties confronting them, researchers remained undeterred. And for good reason. Finding out what motivated the organization as an entity was, and is, crucial to understanding the role of organization in society. Rather quickly, researchers noted the tendency for organizations to be deflected from officially prescribed goals. Employees at all levels of the organization became committed to established routines. Institutionalization set in. Acting as an organism rather than as a tool, the organization factored its own survival and tranquillity into decisions relating to compliance with authoritative directives from legislators, stockholders, and other policy makers.

As it developed, institutionalization was something more than neurotic reclusiveness. The organization looks to the outside for direction but formal mandates are not the only sources consulted. The whole of the environment is surveyed. To guard against a misstep, the organization asks questions. What do the policy makers really want? Is that best accomplished through obedience to, or deviance from, specific directives? Are clients, constituents, or the news media more important than formal policy makers? With such questions, the organization becomes an information processor, scanning the environment for information that would help determine the most effective course of action.

Organizational interaction with the environment will be the theme of this chapter. Two modes of interaction, obedience and adaptation, will be our focus. As in the discussion of organizational authority in Chapter 3, the obedience to adaptation progression takes us from the Weberian period and the mechanistic view of organization to the organic approaches that dominate present day studies. In discussing the latter approach various modes of environmental interaction—*competition, coalition, cooperation,* and *bargaining*—will be discussed. We will also discuss the border-spanning agents of organizations who have primary responsibility for managing environmental relationships. Finally, we will take a look at information theory's utility as a framework for studying organizational adaptation.

CLASSICAL THEORY AND ORGANIZATIONAL OBEDIENCE

While Weber foresaw bureaucratic resistance to goals formally prescribed by legislators or chief executives, neither he nor the other "classicists" envisioned organizational autonomy becoming as significant a force as organizational obedience in modern society. In part, this myopia was a function of time and place. The time was the turn of the century when things were simpler and had a basis in tradition. The place was Europe—the homeland of the first systematic studies of organization.[4] As a result, the organizations studied by the classicists:

Responded to substantial and relatively stable demands. The organizational foundation consisted of the production of clothing, the exportation and importation of resources, the provision of military and police protection, and the collection of taxes.

Routinized operations because the demand for the product was predictable and the manufacturing or service delivery processes were relatively simple.

Operated under a higher degree of national control than was the case in the United States. Thus, there was less competition between organizations and more bureaucratization within organizations to comply with the requirements of the national governments.[5]

The European bureaucrat in the 1900s reinforced the notion that organizations were precise mechanisms where everyone knew their job and performed it in accordance with clear and unambiguous rules. Operating in class-conscious societies, continental bureaucrats adopted a distinctive style—formal, crisp, and somewhat aloof—reflecting their middle-class background.[6] Thus, it is no wonder that the classical theorists saw the organization as a tractable tool in the hands of legitimate leaders who, whether government officials or private entrepreneurs, pursued quite explicit goals.

If the classicists had studied American organizations, different formulations may have emerged. Whereas in Europe, government owned the rails, U.S. railroads were private concerns. Similarly, the electronic communications industry was a private enterprise in the United States but a public one in Europe. Thus, when the governments of Europe quietly built new rail lines or took over the emerging telephone network, it was business as usual—unruffled, methodical, bureaucratic. In America, however, the organizational tools were somewhat more manic. Competing railroads used cutthroat methods against each other, sought monopoly control, and extorted high rates from shippers when they succeeded. When Alexander Graham Bell invented the telephone, Western Union, which monopolized the telegraph lines but not Bell's invention, made a patentless plunge into the telephone business. Western Union's power play failed when Bell's patent was upheld upon judicial review. Nonetheless, in succeeding years, several other organizations made similar attempts, one of which featured the apparent bribing of the attorney general of the United States.[7]

In the late nineteenth century, public organizations were also something less than paragons of bureaucratic obedience. Elected political executives, ostensibly in charge, were often no more than figureheads. The "boss" usually ran the show from a seemingly inconsequential post and often had no formal connection with government. Nonetheless, such individuals diverted public funds for their own enrichment and the maintenance of their political organization's private welfare operations: an employment program highlighted by picnics in the summer, turkeys at Thanksgiving, and gifts at Christmas.[8]

A REDEFINITION OF
ORGANIZATIONAL FUNCTIONS IN SOCIETY

Viewing American bureaucracy in European terms—as society's well-mannered child—could only lead to one conclusion. The American children were uncontrollable ruffians and the parent was a schizoid who prohibited a certain type of behavior and then ignored it when it occurred. Many of its activities violated the law, yet the "machine" thrived. Another organization, the "mob," prospered despite the thoroughgoing illegality of its operations. Police chiefs and prosecutors campaigned against the mob's gambling czars and loan sharks and jailed many for income tax evasion. This, however, did not put the racketeers out of business. As with any good organization composed of positions rather than people, the mob handled its 1940s to 1970s leadership succession with aplomb. As chairman of the board, Carlo Gambino replaced Vito Genovese, who had retired to the federal penitentiary. Genovese, in turn, had assumed the position of "Lucky" Luciano, who had taken a permanent leave of absence via deportation. Through all of this, the organization hardly missed a beat. Bets were taken and loans were made; little attention was paid to the background din of crusading prosecutors.

Although the machine and the mob stood out, they were merely the biggest stars in a constellation of organizations discovered pursuing goals unarticulated or prohibited by superior authorities. Under scrutiny, such organizations were found to be controlled by more than a legal framework or a hierarchy of authority. Support could come from below in the form of influential constituencies as diverse as befriended immigrants, workers, and government contractors. Moreover, even nonconstituents, in their tolerance towards illicit activity, belied the law's stern prohibitions. When the patrolman ignored gambling violations, bribery was one factor; the belief that no real crimes were being committed was another.[9]

Confronted with a number of criminal organizations, theorists could not help but redefine the organizational environment. Thus, the organization, initially considered a component of the legal system, came to be viewed as a part of a social system. Social systems did not formalize all of their rules. Subparts of the system, organizations and individuals, responded to implicit as well as explicit expectations. Talcott Parsons offered the first and most abstract formulation of what society, as a social system, expected of its institutions. Parsons believed that no organization existed unless it served some societal purpose. Function, not law or profit, legitimized structure. Structural-functionalism, the study of institutions by examining the functions that they perform, was thus fathered by Parsons. According to Parsons, society assigned one or more generic functions to its institutions. They were: *goal achievement, adaptation, value maintenance,* and *integration.*[10]

Goal Achievement Putting a man on the moon or providing a minimum income to impoverished citizens are goals set by society. Organizations, government ones more often than not, are the institutions to which society explicitly entrusts such tasks.

Adaptation The ability to respond to changing circumstances is crucial in a dynamic society. Parsons identified the marketplace as an institution performing an adaptive function in capitalist society. Business organizations, with survival tied to marketplace success, are also adaptive institutions, as are state planning agencies in socialist countries. In the "mixed economy" United States of the 1970s, skyrocketing oil prices set off market mechanisms (higher petroleum prices at retail) and government policies (rationing, tax breaks for small-car purchasers, and toll reductions for car poolers). Both had the effect of adapting the society to the need for lower energy consumption.

Value Maintenance To function effectively, a social system requires a set of unifying principles. For society, laws and mores fulfill this requirement. Organizations can also symbolize values. For example, police departments and prosecutors stand for law and order, a powerful, mainstream value that partially insulates those organizations from outside criticism.[11]

Integration For smooth functioning, social systems strive to assimilate deviant individuals, cultural groups, and organizations. (Except, of course, those irredeemably opposed to salient points of the society's value system. Thus, criminal anarchists and psychopathic killers are incarcerated, not integrated.) Families are institutions for the integration of children. Schools are also. In areas where immigrant populations predominate, integration may have a higher priority than education. To further integration, social systems also take measures to guard against the emergence of deviant forces.

Parsons's functional breakdown provides the beginning of understanding how organizations can be "disobedient" or "illegal." As an illustration, let us consider the response of law enforcement agencies to gambling and marijuana smoking. The law prohibits both activities. Their elimination is, therefore, an explicit goal assigned to law enforcement agencies. Nonetheless, when adaptive, integrative, and value-maintenance criteria are applied, formally prescribed goals may be substantially deemphasized. With marijuana and gambling, it goes something like this.

Adaptive Criteria   The law enforcement system faces an overload of formal goals. Crimes range from murder to spitting on the sidewalk. They cannot all be covered and treating them equally is inconceivable. Priorities must be set and violent crimes against persons and property will rank high. This need to adapt to the goal environment often downplays enforcement efforts against gambling and marijuana.[12]

Integrative Criteria   Integration consists of assimilating deviant groups and avoiding the creation of new ones. The latter motive does much to explain the relaxation of law enforcement efforts against marijuana in the 1960s and 1970s. Marijuana smokers and anti-Vietnam War activists were disproportionately evident among the middle-class youth, including college and graduate students. Vigorous prosecution of the antimarijuana laws, therefore, would have further alienated anti-Vietnam War activists since many smoked marijuana and viewed enforcement campaigns as political persecution. Quiescent marijuana users could also act aggressively towards close surveillance and police harassment. Since most leaders of embattled government institutions had no desire to help unify antiwar protestors and pot-smoking concertgoers into an energetic, angry, and disaffected mass, marijuana enforcement became more lenient.[13] Also, given ghetto unrest, few wanted to alienate these predominantly middle-class groups.

Value Maintenance Criteria   In most parts of the United States, gambling and marijuana smoking are, at worst, minor sins, when measured against general societal values (laws and customs). For some, viewed as a risky venture to enhance one's capital, gambling is difficult to distinguish from stock market speculation whereby the near-patriotic act of powering the nation's economy is performed. Similarly, marijuana produced sociable intoxication: an effect familiar to most Americans and negatively valued probably by no more than a few. The means, inhalation rather than ingestion, and the milieu, unwashed hippiedom, did deviate from societal values; the ends sought by marijuana users, however, never strayed far from the value center.

Value maintenance and integrative and adaptive criteria can strengthen as well as weaken goal pursuit. For instance, prostitution, pornography, and homosexual sodomy generally make the list of victimless crimes. In 1972 a congressionally chartered study commission gave pornography a relatively clean bill of health.[14] Also, generally there is wider acceptance of gay life-styles. In areas with large gay constituencies, politicians have catered to the gay vote; openly gay politicians have been elected to office; gay political caucuses have actively lobbied for their constituencies; and gay-rights bills have been enacted. These efforts by gays to become part of the mainstream have given rise to a backlash in some areas; referenda so far have been passed rescinding gay rights laws in St. Paul, Minnesota; Dade County, Florida; and Wichita, Kansas. In general, the sex-related crimes, especially homosexual sodomy and pornography, are seldom prosecuted. However, in adapting to or activating strongly held sentiments in opposition to sex-related crimes, the voter-dependent organization can gain public support. Therefore, occasionally sex-related victimless crimes are prosecuted with great vigor and considerable public spectacle by the same district attorney who calls for liberal marijuana laws and off-track betting.[15]

THE ORGANIZATION AS A LIVING SYSTEM

Parsons made an additional observation that set the stage for further theoretical and empirical inquiry into the nature of the organizational/environmental interface. To Parsons, society was composed of systems within systems. The society was a system but so, too, in microcosm, were the organizations that served society. From the moment the first person steps into a position, the organizational mechanism becomes a social system needing a goal orientation, an adaptive capacity, a set of values, and an integrative structure. Thus, a prosecutor's office, assigned goal achievement and value maintenance functions on behalf of society, will adopt internal goals (the district attorney's reelection), internal values (the law is soft on offenders), integrative procedures (an apprenticeship for new attorneys), and adaptive responses (will the pursuit of certain offenses increase the budget?).

Parsons's elegant concepts "opened up" organization theory. Previous researchers had viewed the organization as a *closed system*—a value-neutral mechanism responding reflexively to explicit and authoritative mandates. With Parsons's *open systems* approach, the organization/environment perspective facilitated the search for previously ignored factors underlying organizational behavior. Unwritten laws, secondary objectives, and unconscious reflexes* rivaled formal goals in determining organization direction. Formal goals also competed with the self-interest of the organization and its members.

---

*One integrative institution that labors mostly in obscurity is courtesy. Courtesy permits strangers or casual acquaintances to interact cooperatively. Cooperative interaction benefits commerce and social stability and avoids the policing costs associated with antagonistic encounters. In organizations, courtesy often goes under the rubric of protocol. In the UN, for instance, protocol is ritualistic and ceremonial with many higher-ranking bureaucrats addressed as "excellency." The purpose, of course, is to make an extremely polyglot organization function more smoothly.

Social-systems theory promised to explain organizational phenomena that had been categorized as inexplicable or improper. Parsons's approach, however, was not without problems. In effect, it broadened research perspectives without sharpening the focus. Eight generic standards (four internal and four external) could govern organizational behavior. All could operate simultaneously. Therefore, matching two variables to explain organization behavior, a common characteristic of closed-system studies, would not suffice. To achieve full explanatory power under a social-systems paradigm, the functions served by organizational activity would have to be identified and ranked. Take, for instance, a community development office that is relocated from a middle-class neighborhood to a low-income area and, in the bargain, has its white, female director replaced by a Hispanic male. What goals have been served? Community development? Yes, by definition. The integration of minority groups? Yes, but less explicitly. Adaptation to the demands of the black/Hispanic coalition? Probably, but few might be willing to say so. An assertion of mayoral values against the previous director's deviant opinion that the ghetto was lost and, therefore, development funds should be lavished on middle-class areas? Perhaps. A little of everything? Most likely. Does anyone have the definitive, comprehensive answer? Insiders come close, particularly after they piece together their fragmentary knowledge. However, even they may be unable to sort out triggering factors, underlying causes, and smokescreen rationales. For the researcher, who is most often denied the insiders' entree, the task is even more formidable.

Societal Mandates
and Organizational Goals

While social-systems theory was not the key to all the mysteries of organization, it opened up several avenues of inquiry. One was the relationship between the formal overhead policy and organizational goals. Robert K. Merton, drawing partly on Parsons's work, categorized organizational goals in terms of their conscious legitimation from society. By analyzing societal intent and societal recognition, Merton asserted, goals could be viewed in four ways:[16]

> *GOAL DESCRIPTION*
> Intended and Recognized (Manifest)
> Intended and Unrecognized
> Unintended and Recognized
> Unintended and Unrecognized (Latent)

As arrayed, the categories are a continuum. Intended and recognized (manifest) goals are formally assigned by policy makers and are visible to the community. At the other extreme, unintended and unrecognized (latent) goals do not have the approval of policy makers and remain hidden from the general community. Such goals are latent in that they may or may not emerge as legitimate. Legislative or judicial condemnation may doom a latent goal. Such can be the fate of state special prosecutors who informally expand their prosecutorial mandate at the expense of local district attorneys. Local district attorneys, with the support of judges, legislators, and politicians, can frustrate the activities of the special prosecutor through adverse rulings, a barrage of legal actions, budget cuts, and pressure on the executive. However, when latent goals move towards manifest legitimation, they can pass through either or both of the intermediate stages. That is, they may be tolerated and then secretly endorsed by policy makers before formal approval is given.

Unintended and recognized goals are unilaterally assumed by the organization. Such policies win a measure of retrospective legitimation from policy makers by being recognized without being endorsed. Due mainly to disinterest, public awareness of unintended but recognized goals can be partial. The acquisition of additional resources is a common and vigorously pursued goal among government agencies. Legislators do not encourage this type of behavior but afford it tacit recognition by making automatic downward adjustments in budget requests. Another common organizational goal is a favorable public image. The means—press releases, brochures, guided tours—often annoy the owners. Indeed, the organization's stockholders frequently protest the expense of slick, high-quality, picture-laden, and self-congratulatory annual reports. In government, legislators are known to leap at the chance to deflate exaggerated claims of an agency. Nonetheless, even critics hold out little hope for the elimination of self-aggrandizing behavior by organizations. Thus, even as it is excoriated, it is tolerated.

Intended and unrecognized goals are approved, in advance, by policy makers. However, the mandate is implicit and unpublicized. For instance, the CIA's formal mandate does not include the overthrow of foreign governments. However, high-ranking officials in past administrations have authorized the CIA to encourage the overthrow of foreign leaders. Neither the general public nor the majority of governmental policy makers were aware of these maneuvers. Similarly, a municipal zoning board may quietly represent homeowners within government councils. Although the board's legal mandate dictates a dispassionate assessment of land use alternatives, legislators and public officials value the board's advocacy of the homeowners' tax plight. Business landowners, superiors feel, are more than adequately represented by the chamber of commerce and the municipality's economic development office. Nonetheless, holding down homeowners' taxes is unlikely to become an explicit goal of the zoning board. If it did, the planning ethic might be contradicted; the enabling legislation in question might undergo controversial amendment; and the final result might be a stern reaffirmation of the board's neutrality rather than approval of its advocacy. Thus, policy makers are content to keep the board's role informal and low key.

Merton's typology set the stage for numerous case studies that concentrated on what Merton termed "goal displacement." As designed, organizations fall into Merton's first two categories. They are fashioned tools "intended" to achieve the policy makers' intentions; that is, mechanisms dedicated to a goal. However, to adopt "unintended" behavior, the organization diverts resources from its original goals. It acts as an organism. Thus, the intended goals, to a greater or lesser extent, are displaced by the bureaucracy. In analyzing goal displacement, researchers have sought to discover organizations that break free of their creators.

Institutionalization and Goal Displacement

Philip Selznick conducted one of the first case studies documenting the phenomenon of *goal displacement*. Selznick's subject was the Tennessee Valley Authority (TVA).[17] The TVA had been envisioned as a means of providing electrical power and water resource control for the rural poor and marginal farmers of the Tennessee Valley. This goal was embodied in the enabling legislation and in the commitment of the New Dealers who formed the leadership core at the agency's inception. However, TVA executives quickly discovered that unless wealthy farmers could be won over political support for proposed policies would not be forthcoming. Thus, the wealthy farmers were brought into the agency's decision-making process. The results were predictable. Policies consonant with the TVA's original mandate were scrapped and programs beneficial to the prosperous farmers were substituted.

According to Selznick, the original goal—the betterment of the rural poor—was the victim of *institutionalization*. Formal goals had to compete with developing "precedents, alliances, effective symbols and personal loyalties which transform the organization . . . into something having sacred status to those within."[18] As a result, the organization began to see its continued existence as the overarching goal and, therefore, was willing to pursue the goals of whoever seemed the best guarantor of survival.

In large part, institutionalization, as a cause of unintended organizational behavior, was attributed to internal dynamics. Employees, at all levels, sought stability. Having become comfortably ensconced in established routines, no one wanted to rock the boat. In most organizations, steady sailing required an adjustment to external forces capable of making waves. However, as was the case with the TVA, it was often the formal goals of the organization that were thrown overboard in order to maintain a steady course.

In the public context, shifting goals to accommodate institutional concerns often draws accusations of treason. In most cases, enabling legislation extensively defines the duties and goals of a new agency. The definitions may be somewhat vague but are usually clarified through speeches by legislators and administrators. While such pronouncements do not have the force of law, they do strengthen, in the public eye, the agency's commitment to certain values and goals. Thus, when the organization partially abandons its original aims without a corresponding modification of its legal mandate, critics find ample documentation to support charges of a sellout.

In contrast to the government agency that deviates from its legislatively prescribed goals, few howls greet the business firm that adjusts its goals to meet changing market conditions. "Third sector" organizations—nongovernmental, not-for-profit concerns—also enjoy a latitude in goal setting that is denied to the government organization. Case studies of private philanthropic organizations, which uncovered the most extreme forms of goal displacement, only caused a stir in academe. One titillating study was of the National Foundation for Infantile Paralysis,"The March of Dimes."[19] The foundation's stated goal was the elimination of polio. In the 1950s, thanks to the Salk vaccine, that goal was achieved. Thus, in terms of its stated purpose, the March of Dimes had little to do. However, instead of dismantling the organization, the foundation turned its attention to the elimination of birth defects and continued to thrive.

Another example of goal displacement was reported by Charles Perrow.[20] Perrow studied a hospital founded by Jewish philanthropists. During their tenure on the board of trustees, the hospital adhered to the stated goal of treating indigent Jews. As the influence of the board of trustees waned with the death of the founders, doctors assumed policy control. When this happened, ability to pay became a more important criterion for treatment than Jewishness. Eventually, professional hospital administrators replaced doctors as the primary policy force and steered the hospital toward major medical center status. In the process, the original goal of the hospital receded from memory.

Perrow's studies led him to a conclusion rather distinct from Selznick's. Perhaps, he suggested, the leaders of the organization acted without giving a damn for traditional outside forces.

France's preparation for World War II may support Perrow's contention in a different way. French military leaders failed to adapt to the country's defense needs. In preparing for anticipated German aggression, the French relied heavily on the Maginot Line: entrenchments and artillery placements constructed according to World War I concepts of combat.[21] When tanks and planes, rather than infantry, attacked in 1940, the Maginot Line crumbled and the French army was rapidly defeated and demobilized. Of course, organizations that resist change do not always suffer such rapid denouements. As is the case with Western Union, vestiges of once mighty organizations may linger on to serve specialized or novelty needs, i.e., mailgrams or hand-delivered legal notices.

For many government organizations, the penalties for adamancy in the face of changing situations and policies can be postponed, often indefinitely. By the 1960s, FBI Director J. Edgar Hoover's preoccupation with internal communist subversion was somewhat of an anachronism. Most observers, including presidents and attorneys general for whom Hoover worked, scoffed at the notion. However, in books, speeches, and through "The FBI" television series, an image of the communist menace within was maintained before the public. Thus, the FBI continued to devote considerable resources to the surveillance of suspected communists. (To make the task commensurate with the organization's effort, Hoover included most civil rights organizations in the conspiracy.) Policy makers, aware of Hoover's damaging files on Washington influentials, were inclined to be tolerant of the director's obsession. In essence, although the tasks changed, Hoover and the FBI, with the rest of the environment well in hand, continued as if nothing had happened.[22]

Finally, if we may make the case that liberal policies are just as prone to institutionalization as conservative ones, there is the story of the Department of Health, Education, and Welfare (HEW) in the first years of the Nixon presidency. HEW had been in the forefront of President Johnson's Great Society programs. Robert Finch, with a go slow mandate from the new president, was the first HEW secretary in the Nixon administration. However, stemming HEW's momentum towards community action and other liberal policies was almost an impossible task.[23] Programs Finch ordered disbanded were not. Many community action legal offices, subsidiaries of HEW, prepared the briefs that stalled directives from the mother agency. Other offices marshalled community support to delay their termination. A sincere and conscientious man, Finch bent his entire being to the task and after two frustrating and exhausting years, resigned.

In such stories lies the explanation of why many chief executives, party affiliation notwithstanding, take office with plans for reorganizations and new agencies. It is a rare president, governor, county executive or mayor who assumes office without being forewarned of the intransigence of the existing bureaucracy. If they are not and happen to hear

"We can't do what you want because . . ." enough times, the same conclusion is arrived at independently. Nonetheless, for the executive, the cures are little better than the disease.[24] A thoroughgoing government-wide reorganization? HEW comes to mind. Massive resistance. Angry interest groups throughout the jurisdiction demanding to know what is being done to their agency. A new organization? Unless there is a near unanimous call for one, conceiving a new agency, shepherding it through the legislative process, and training it in the formative years promises to occupy much of the executive's precious time. Despite a pressing energy crisis in the 1970s, the creation of a department of energy, as a cabinet level department, took five years.

Moreover, since institutionalization can take hold quite rapidly, the agency may be an ingrate before it is out of diapers. Thus, in an increasingly common maneuver to move or outflank institutionalized bureaucracy, executives expand their personal staffs. Loyal staffers serve as supra-commissioners for line agencies and small staff organizations are created to handle issues important to the executive.

FORMS OF ADAPTATION

Studies such as those on the TVA, the March of Dimes, and the Jewish hospital point to an inescapable conclusion. All organizations interact independently with an extended environment in determining organizational objectives and policies. This holds true for the government agency, where many policies are legislatively mandated, as well as for the private organization. Both scan the environment for allies, enemies, and neutrals. The object of their search is to determine the relative balance of support and opposition to the organization and its policies. Activities, ongoing and proposed, are test marketed in the environment. "Trial balloons" are precisely of this order. Pilot programs often serve the same purpose for activities required by legislation. The information from such probes is fed back to organizational decision makers. The feedback is used to decide whether to pursue certain goals vigorously, lackadaisically, or not at all. Alternatively, the organization may respond actively to feedback by attempting to modify the environment. The following is a decidedly active organizational response to an external situation perceived as threatening.

> An ad agency representing a large retail chain in the snowy Northeast was disturbed by the impact of the weather on its clients. The weather, of course, can neither be scolded nor easily changed. However, people's perceptions of the weather, as gathered from news reports, can be modified. So, shortly before Christmas . . . (the) agency sent out a memo to "remind" radio and television stations of "the problems that arise in a retail establishment when you "editorialize" the weather. . . .

The most common error made by most air personalities is that they tell people to stay home prior to the arrival of bad weather. In most cases the storm never does arrive. This type of weather "editorializing" does terrible damage to retail store sales. . . . the type of damage that cannot be made up.

Occasionally, of course, a radio or TV report of bad weather does coincide with weather that is bad. Still, according to the memo, "It is a proven fact that people enjoy shopping in cold and inclement weather. Why not encourage their shopping rather than discouraging it. It's hard enough to create retail sales . . . we certainly don't need air personalities to discourage them."

The memo goes on to reassure the stations: "We are not trying to suppress the official weather forecast." The memo's advice on how to report the weather concludes . . . "If it becomes necessary that your station discourage driving we insist that all of our spots scheduled during that period be cancelled."[25]

The ad agency made a clear attempt to control the environment. The attempt was beaten back. To Watergate-hardened observers, the reason why is apparent. Coercive control techniques must be able to self-destruct so that they can be denied. A memo floating in the environment does not have this capability. Thus, when the memo surfaced, the ad agency was in trouble. The retailer-client, understandably wary of being associated with an attempt to control free speech, said that the agency had acted on its own.[26] The memo's author claimed, rather unconvincingly, that it did not mean what it appeared to mean. "I wouldn't really cancel any ads," he said.[27]

In the above case, with the spotlight on, control-oriented behavior changed into submissive, apologetic behavior. In one leap, the agency had covered the range of organizational responses to the environment, from tyranny to abject submission. Classifying the organizational environmental interface was the particular contribution of James D. Thompson and William McEwen to organization theory. "The organization can survive," they wrote in 1957, "so long as it adjusts to its situation, whether the process of adjustment is awkward or nimble becomes important in determining the organization's degree of prosperity."[28] According to Thompson and McEwen, adjustment to the environment was characterized by (1) competition or three cooperative strategies: (2) bargaining, (3) cooptation, or (4) coalition.

1. Competition Competition is interorganizational rivalry mediated by a third party. The marketplace is both the arena and the judge for organizational competition. Thompson and McEwen were careful to point out that marketplaces were more than economic. The electorate, budget-approving legislators, and research-supporting foundations, as well as clients and customers, could comprise the marketplace.

Through competition, the organization conformed to environmental demands in order to insure well-being. The organization that failed to respond would face a diminution of essential resources as demand for its product or services fell.

Competition is both muted and amplified as a factor influencing the government organization's response to the environment. It is muted because many government agencies enjoy a monopoly. Nonetheless, sensitivity must remain high because the government organization is confronted with several marketplaces—legislators, public opinion, clients, and constituents. Any one of these marketplaces may become crucial to the organization: legislators during budget hearings; public opinion during times of crisis; clients and constituents during changes in procedures. Thus, depending on time and situation, a different marketplace evaluates agency performance.

2. *Bargaining* "Bargaining involves direct interaction with other organizations in the environment."[29] Bargaining is a trade-off; for it to occur, each party must have something of value to the other. Thompson cites stool pigeon/police relationship. The stoolie has information; the cops have freedom. They trade. The ad agency cited above was bargaining, although from a position of considerable strength. It wanted the stations to trade their editorial latitude for continued advertising revenues. Bargaining is a fact of life among public organizations and between public and private organizations. Logrolling can occur between government agencies just as it occurs between legislators. Studies of the Joint Chiefs of Staff of the American military reveal air force commanders supporting aircraft carriers in return for navy support for bomber wings.[30]

Government agencies and private industry often negotiate regulatory policies. The agency avoids expensive, extended, and, perhaps embarrassing (if the regulation is questionable) legal battles and the private industry wins less stringent regulation.

3. *Cooptation* "The process of absorbing new elements into the leadership of the policy-determining structure of an organization as a means of averting threats to its stability or existence."[31] Thompson and McEwen saw cooptation as a means of bringing greater information to bear on organizational decision making. The result is a leavening of the organization's tendency towards a unilateral or arbitrary choice of goals. Financiers, for instance, are often added to the board of directors when corporations face money problems. Similarly, in financially strapped

New York City, the emergency financial control board, led by veto wielding businessmen, passed on the viability of fiscal policies.

An alternative interpretation of cooptation emerged in the 1960s. The new interpretation, consistent with, but not emphasized by, Thompson and McEwen, asserted that cooptation could be used to continue as well as modify existing organizational policies.[32] To defuse protests, opposition leaders were brought on board the organization and given important-sounding but impotent positions. With a hefty salary and intensive exposure to the organizational ideology, many coopted individuals emerged as apologists. Antiwar and civil rights activists of the 1960s were particularly sensitive to this form of cooptation as many sympathizers, not the least of whom were college professors, went in to change the bureaucracy only to be transformed themselves.

The advisory commission is another mechanism that can serve the status quo. From conception to final report, a commission's lifespan is measured in years. During this time, those who chartered the commission can plead for patience. When the report is complete, the furor that gave rise to the commission has often subsided. Therefore, its recommendations may be ignored with some impunity.

Stacking the membership is another organizational tactic for coopting advisory commissions. The voting members are chosen so that a majority favor the point of view desired by the organization. For good measure, commissions may be staffed with individuals sympathetic to organizational concerns. In effect then, the minority members are coopted. They lend their names to the venture without being able to influence the resulting policy recommendations.

It would seem that universities and professors are becoming the handmaidens of cooptation in all of its forms. Consultancies are lucrative and prestigious, even in schools of business and public administration. Analyses conducted by institutions of higher learning often buttress the contentions of private industry concerning the impact of proposed public policies. For a professor, a prominent appointment to an advisory committee can mean a high degree of recognition for very little work. As a result, many lend their names to foreordained conclusions that took two years to put into writing. Donald Schon sums up the fate of the coopted advisory mechanism rather neatly: "I have participated in about six and have inquired of other participants whether any had been a member of such a committee which was effective in carrying out the functions assigned to it. I have never received an affirmative answer. The principal force at work appears to be those of individual agency baronies and the demands of territoriality."[33]

4. *Coalition*   Thompson and McEwen also noted that the organization could join forces with other organizations in the environment.

Organizations entered into coalitions when a common goal could not be achieved by unilateral efforts. Trade associations greatly enhance the political clout of the member organizations. Similarly, for defense and space work, consortiums of contractors undertake major projects.

BORDER-SPANNING AGENTS

With the work of Thompson, McEwen, and others, the organization/environment perspective came to the forefront in organization theory. Researchers, notably Harold Wilensky, began studying the organizational mechanisms that monitored and shaped the outside world.[34] In evaluating the organization's contact points with the environment, it became apparent that there was a distinction between quantity contacts and quality contacts. High-quantity contacts—retail clerks, telephone operators, cashiers—have highly routinized tasks. In some organizations, telephones are answered according to a script. Such standardization is possible, in most cases, because the day-to-day business of the organization is highly predictable. In quantity contacts, then, there is high stability between the organization and the environment.

High-quality contacts, on the other hand, may be few in number. They are, however, quite important. They occur in very unpredictable circumstances. As compared with clerical personnel, who serve as static border guards for the organization, legal counsels, public relations officers, comptrollers, and marketing managers are *border-spanning agents*. They enter the environment to determine whether it is threatening, friendly, or neutral. From their analyses flow recommendations: should the organization act aggressively or submissively to threats; actively or passively toward favorable or neutral situations. The resultant decision may be implemented by the border-spanning agent as well. Thus, as illustrated below, the border spanners provide the organization with intelligence gathering, strategic planning, defense, offense, and diplomacy.

Legal Staff The organization must remain alert to a legal environment consisting of statutes, administrative regulations, pending legal actions, and legislative bills. Keeping the organization's knowledge of the legal environment up-to-date is the task of the legal staff. The task includes gauging the impact of anticipated legislation, indicating what is required of the organization by new legislation, and defending the organization against legal claims. For legislation that interferes with the organization's style of operation, the legal staff may compare the law's penalties with the cost of compliance. For example, the probability of offenders being detected, apprehended, tried, and convicted and the nature of the ensuing penalty can be compared with the cost of machinery modifications required by new safety regulations. While it is unethical for an attorney to advise that the law be broken, it is apparent that such an evaluation could underlie an organization's decision to evade statutory requirements.

The legal job is not limited to analysis. Indeed, when the organization manages to modify the legal environment, in-house attorneys are often responsible. Their briefs strike down threatening statutes; their lobbying campaigns can block or repeal unwanted legislation. By shifting into reverse, legal staffs can pursue the protective legislation and sympathetic regulation desired by the organization. When the organization buttonholes a congressman or breaks bread with a regulatory administrator, the emissary is often an attorney.

Public Relations The purpose of public relations is to keep the environment friendly. This usually entails the selective release of information: the favorable is disseminated, the damaging is withheld.

Public relations also seeks to change threatening attitudes in the environment. During the energy crises of the 1970s, oil companies proclaimed their innocence in the news media. Their ads pointed out the oil industry's high fixed costs and the need for intensive and expensive exploration to discover new energy sources to meet future demands. Subtle emphasis was given to uncontrollable leaps in the wellhead price of oil. (Subtle emphasis was necessary because the oil companies did not want to antagonize the oil-producing nations in the process of placating retail customers.) With their campaign, the oil companies sought to duck out of an angered public's line of fire without changing existing operations.

Public relations is more than imagery and defensive stonewalling. An assessment of the environment precedes both responses and can lead to a third—namely, a substantive change in the organization's policy. In the 1970s, the public realized, with some anger, that the fixed-income aged were more susceptible to the ravages of inflation and had specialized needs often ignored by the marketplace. Many organizations did not wait for public displeasure to crest in the form of legislation or regulation. Supermarkets packaged meat and produce in smaller quantities. Utilities, in addition to base-rate payment schemes featuring a minimum charge regardless of usage, offered payment/usage plans to accommodate the lower consumption patterns of the elderly.

Financial Relations Most organizations are dependent, to some extent, on outside investment. For the private firm, investment comes from the credit market; for the public agency, funding comes from a marketplace of legislators and executives. In either case, the financiers must be persuaded of the organization's future viability. For the business organization, a healthy growth rate and profit margin gain the confidence of the financial marketplace. In public budgeting, the indicators are more ephemeral but must still win the approval of legislative funders. If investors lose confidence, the corporation may find bankers calling the shots and public agencies may be forced to bow to legislative wishes in return for funding.[35] If the loss of confidence is complete, the organization may cease to exist.

Comptrollers and budget officers are the invisible border spanners. Public relations specialists, marketing managers, and attorneys occasionally enjoy resounding triumphs in the face of adversity. "Lost" legal battles are won; ridiculed new products take off; and vociferous public opinions are calmed by public relations coups. With mercurial adversaries—the public, juries, and the marketplace—such upsets are possible. The financial border spanner faces more stolid examiners in a low-key contest where the outcome may be decades away. The game pieces are statistics and reports, and victory may be viewed as "just another loan" or "a few more bucks in the budget." Nonetheless, with the ability to obtain hundreds of millions of dollars for the organization, financial departments are key links to the environment.

Marketplace Relations No organization wants a white elephant. Offensive or despised products embarrass the staff, frustrate employees, and upset the organization's environmental relationships; i.e., customer distrust can transform quickly into banker distrust. Therefore, in monitoring its environment, the organization pays particular attention to customers and clients. Market research is the firm's method of spotting trends in consumer preferences so that products or services can be adjusted to meet emerging demand. Government agencies are also sensitive to customer demand. A satisfied clientele (e.g., veterans, the business community, farmers) can be a bulwark of support for the organization in legislative and executive environments.

Occasionally, catering to its clientele can get the government agency in trouble. In situations requiring regulatory activity, agencies are often accused of neglecting the public interest in their eagerness to be responsive to the concerns of industry. The charge has validity but neglects the immediate environment of the agency in question. Here, the industry is a towering presence. It possesses a concentrated and powerful lobbying capability and the regulatory agency can be its beneficiary or target. When the public organization evaluates such a situation, accommodating the regulated industry can be perceived as more important to institutional survival than energetic and meticulous law enforcement. Indeed, the organization may seek to modify the more militant provisions of its enabling legislation to avoid being pushed into a confrontation.

Freelance Professionals and Others The above list of border-spanning situations is not exhaustive. Personnel officers perform a similar function when they recruit or encourage universities to develop a curriculum more in line with the organization's needs. Certified Public Accountants (CPAs) are border spanners with one foot in the legal environment and one foot in the financial environment. The resulting synthesis is oftentimes termed "creative accounting": the search for loopholes in the law and accounting practice that permit an organization to improve its financial status. The spirit, if not the practice, of creative accounting is often evident in the money-saving claims and productivity statistics of public agencies.

Border-spanning units are not always a part of the organization. For every activity listed above, there are firms that will attach to the organization to perform a border-spanning role. To augment in-house resources, the organization can hire law firms, accountants, advertising agencies, marketing consultants, executive search firms, and financial analysts. Moreover, many independent border spanners represent specialized and highly talented resources that the organization would find difficult to duplicate and costly to maintain: a well-connected lobbyist in Washington, the state house, or a foreign capital; a legal firm skilled in administrative law or product liability; a top-notch public relations firm or advertising agency. Each can help the organization meet a unique environmental challenge. Furthermore, outside border spanners are not embedded in the institutionalized framework of the organization. Thus, their perceptions may be more acute and, should fossilization set in, the relationship can be broken off without encountering the stubborn resistance that can confront internal reorganizations. (On the other side of the coin, however, organization members may be subtly uncooperative toward outsiders.)

Integrating the Border Spanners

Each border-spanning agent probes a particular sector of the environment. Lawyers recommend a certain organizational course with respect to existing statutes and pending legislation. Public relations specialists gauge public opinion. Comptrollers keep an eye on the financial environment and marketing specialists analyze consumer receptivity to the organization's products. However, if these piecemeal activities are not coordinated effectively, they can produce contradictory activities; e.g., public relations specialists launching a massive advertising campaign when financiers are withholding investment pending signs of conservative management. One way of integrating the findings and recommendations of the border-spanning agents is to have them meet in committee and arrive at a consensus. Final determination by the chief executive is the second, and more common, method of choosing among the recommendations of the border spanners.

John Kenneth Galbraith is one scholar who believes that, for major organizational decisions, the committee system is on the ascendancy. According to Galbraith, the chief executive in the mammoth organization is incapable of consolidating and understanding all of the information gathered by border spanners. The volume of information is too high; the complexity too great. It exceeds the integrative capacity of a single individual. Thus, Galbraith sees the border spanners ("technocrats"), with the help of integrative specialists such as systems analysts, charting the organization's course.[36] Subsequent approval by presidents and boards of directors becomes no more than a rubber stamp on the collective decisions of the technocrats. In the mammoth multinational corporations, Galbraith found evidence to support his contentions. However, in many smaller organizations and some large ones, it is still the executive who attempts to integrate the data provided by the border spanners and decides among the proposed policies.

The integration, of course, is not always carried out effectively. As executives delay, a fluid environment can petrify. Several policy options can be mooted and the organizational response can be dictated by circumstances that may have been avoided with timely action. To most observers, however, such results are attributable to the executive's misuse of time rather than a limited capacity for assimilating and synthesizing information. The most common advice is to quit meddling with routine internal operations and concentrate on the organizational/environmental relationship. Robert Townsend, an incisive critic of organizations and a former successful chief executive, puts the situation in perspective: "Marketing is the name of the game. So it had better be handled by the boss . . . not by staff hecklers."[37] His advice is similar with respect to planning, advertising, and public relations. Of course, Townsend is not recommending that the executive do everything. However, since the success of the enterprise depends on adaptation to the environment, executives are well advised to pay considerable attention to border spanning activities.

Environmental Destabilization
and Border Spanning: A Case Study[38]

The Bell System—the American Telephone and Telegraph Company (AT&T) and its subsidiaries—is vast. By the 1970s, its stockholders numbered three million; its employees nearly one million. The Bell System rested on $80 billion in assets, generating about $35 billion in annual revenues and $3 billion in profit. AT&T was the largest borrower of commercial credit in the United States. With 25 components—Western

Electric, Bell Labs, and the regional operating companies—the Bell System served, in whole or in part, every state in the continental United States.

Not surprisingly, the Bell System had been able to neutralize many environmental threats. Until 1969, Bell had convinced regulators and the courts that telephony was a "natural" monopoly—a product that would get higher in price and lower in quality with competition. Competitors thus were barred from duplicating the communication services provided by the existing telephone network. This prohibition applied to any device that intervened between the lips of the caller and the ear of the receiver. As a result, AT&T's marketplace environment was secure.

The Bell System's legal environment was also fairly stable. The Bell operating companies maintained a good relationship with state regulatory authorities. Legislators—federal, state, and local—were receptive to the concerns of a business that was often the jurisdiction's largest employer. The Justice Department was a little impetuous, but its occasional antitrust suits were successfully parried. The Federal Communications Commission (FCC) also was annoying but posed little threat to the system.

With both a monopoly of long-distance telephone communications and an exclusive franchise in regional operations sanctioned by government authorities, the Bell System operated in a receptive financial environment. AT&T's blue chip status was further reinforced by a regulatory rate-making philosophy that gave great weight to investor's rate of return.

In the 1960s, Bell's environment began to destabilize. First, bootleggers began to sell stylized phones that attracted consumers bored with the stolid black Bell units. Then, independent companies began to invade Bell's periphery with such services as a two-way outreach via CB radio. Furthermore, the FCC eventually sanctioned these incursions and the courts turned back Bell's appeals. In the 1970s, competitors became more active and began equipping office inner communications systems top to bottom with non-Bell hardware. Moreover, technological advances threatened to outflank the long lines, the heart of the Bell System's natural monopoly. Using microwave relays, competitors began to connect the geographically dispersed offices of business customers.

The Bell System counterattacked on all environmental fronts. Residential consumers were offered phones of varying colors and designs. Bell mounted an aggressive marketing campaign aimed at business customers contemplating competitors' equipment. Often, when rival equipment was installed, Bell, claiming that competitors damaged its wire network, refused to interconnect. In 1975 Bell launched a legal assault with the Consumer Communications Reform Act.

The Consumer Communications Reform Act was known as the

"Bell Bill" in recognition of the authorship role played by Bell's legal border spanners. The bill affirmed that an integrated, noncompetitive communications industry best served the public interest by providing quality service at low rates. Under the provisions of the bill, competitors, in seeking licenses or the renewal thereof, had to show proof that their services did not duplicate those offered by existing telephone companies; could not be matched by existing companies; and would not force existing companies to raise rates to compensate for lost business. State regulatory bodies, and not the FCC, were vested with the authority to approve the terminal and station equipment used for telephone exchange service. Finally, the bill permitted telephone competition to determine the cost of services and barred the FCC from setting minimum rates.

Through intensive lobbying, Bell managed to get over 100 senators and representatives to sponsor the Consumer Communications Reform Act. This support was noted by a financial environment that was already aware that the bill, if passed, was sudden death for competitors. Certain parts of the bill, if made law, were potentially fatal. With competition at cost, Bell could disregard many of the antitrust rules governing corporate combat. Competitors were no better served by state review of equipment. This promised 50 proceedings and the unlikely but nightmarish possibility of as many standards. According to one bankrupt competitor, Datran, the bill made investors cautious and rumors of the bill's likely passage, floated by AT&T financial border spanners, frightened them away altogether.

The bill also appears to have been a warning shot to the FCC. Attempting to stabilize the regulatory/legal environment, Bell wanted the FCC to be aware of its congressional clout. At the same time, public support was courted by an advertising campaign that emphasized the importance of a unified communications system to low-cost telephone services. Even though the Bell Bill did not pass, it helped AT&T beat back an impinging environment.

This is an archetypical story of the relationship between organization and environment. There is competition. There is coalition—the non-Bell operating companies, also exclusive franchises, were firmly in the AT&T camp. There is bargaining—the Bell Bill was partly an opening bid. There is cooptation—the National Association of State Regulatory Utility Commissioners was supportive of AT&T. Outside AT&T border spanners included law firms, research institutes, lobbyists, and college professors. Within Bell, the campaign staff included marketing, public relations, legal, and financial departments. AT&T's chairman of the board, John de Butts, took an intense leadership role. Like many open-systems theorists, practitioner de Butts saw the fate of his organization firmly tied to environmental relationships.

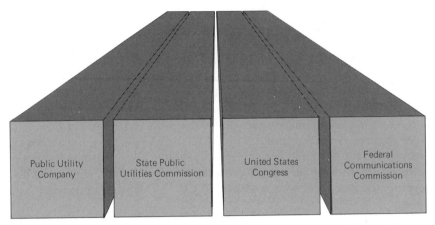

| Public Utility Company | State Public Utilities Commission | United States Congress | Federal Communications Commission |

A Public Utility Company's Perception of its Environment. This graphic appeared in a company's recent annual report, which devoted considerable space to governmental relations.

INFORMATION THEORY: A FRAMEWORK FOR ANALYSIS

Although a distinction is often made between closed-systems and open-systems theories, the distinction was, in many cases, quite blurred by the 1960s.[39] This is because both camps turned their attention to the role that information played in organizations. From the inside view, it became increasingly apparent that the way in which the organization processed information was the key to effective decision making. The attention paid to processing naturally led to the study of information gathering: a study that led closed-systems theorists into the organization's own environment. Open-systems proponents, however, made the opposite trek. When the organization triumphed over, succumbed to, or remained in equilibrium with the environment, the big picture was easy enough to see. The organization either had not kept pace with environmental demands or anticipated well enough to remain viable. However, this knowledge was slightly empty without some understanding of the internal processes that led to the adaptive or nonadaptive response. So organization/environment types delved within. Thus, one important bridge between the open- and closed-systems theorists was information theory.[40]

Information theory seeks to explain how any complex organism collects, processes, stores, and utilizes information. There has been some debate whether the bureaucratic organization, an artificial creation, can be subsumed under a theory originally concerned with living organisms.[41] However, we believe it can. The organization is created to solve problems. If it fails to solve enough problems, the organization, like any living species, becomes extinct. If it is an efficient problem solver

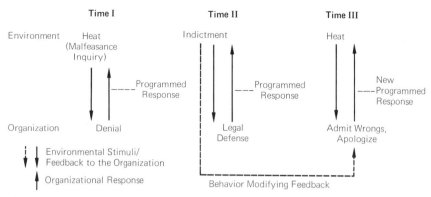

Figure 4.1   Organizational Response to Feedback

it survives. Insofar as information theory concerns an exchange between an entity and its environment, an organization in its goal achievement and adaptive functions is as fitting a subject as any.

Three Concepts: Homeostasis, Feedback, and the Law of Requisite Variety

Homeostasis is the adjustment of an organism to its environment. If it is hot, the body sweats to cool itself. If the heat is on, an organization is likely to say "no comment." Each response is programmed. In the case of the body, the program is genetic—built in from birth. In the case of the organization, the response is learned. Successfully applied in the past, "no comment" is assumed adequate for the present. However, if the warm organization found that "no comment" resulted in trial by fire, its repertoire of responses might change to include forthrightness as an alternative in future tight spots. Figure 4.1 illustrates how this might happen.

In the diagram above, the solid downward arrows represent *feedback* from the environment. The solid upward arrows represent programmed organizational responses. The broken line arrow represents response-changing feedback. At Time I, in responding to a reporter's inquiry, the organization's public relations office produces the standard time-tested response. At Time II, unsettling feedback kicks off two organizational activities. First, the indictment elicits a programmed response from the legal department. Second, public relations policy is reviewed. At Time III, that policy has been revised: Honesty has replaced evasion as the programmed response to embarrassing inquiries. Thus, feedback is of two types: response-inducing and response-changing.

The above model could be applied to most of the case studies cited thus far. Essentially, border spanners are feedback mechanisms. At organizational policy points, the feedback is used to plan future actions. It should also be noted that the environment consists of other organizations and individuals. Thus, the organization's response to feedback is, itself, feedback. Reporters and prosecutors might change their behavior and dig deeper as a result of the honesty policy. For their part, citizens might become more cynical or more trusting.

One more concept from information theory, the *Law of Requisite Variety*, is helpful in conceptualizing organizational growth and differentiation. As W. Ross Ashby, the creator of the law of requisite variety, summarizes it, "Only variety can destroy variety."[42] The implication for organizations is that for every pattern of information in the environment, a corresponding unit is required. Reporters produce spokespeople. Legislatures produce lobbyists. Customers produce assembly lines and so on. As the environmental groups get larger and more visible, the organizational resources devoted to them increase accordingly. In the 1970s a rise in consumer awareness led to an increase in both the government's allocation to local consumer protection agencies and business firms' devotion of resources to pacify consumer demands.

Information Utilization

One determinant of the value of information is the degree to which it reduces uncertainty. However, information-gathering activities are not subject to precise cost-benefit comparisons. As economist Kenneth Arrow points out, it is impossible to put an absolute value on the degree to which information reduces uncertainty.[43] In the first instance, no single bit of information has decision-making value; i.e., a single sale cannot guide a manufacturer's decision on how much of an item to produce. Thus, information must be patterned to be useful. For example, monthly sales figures showing peaks and valleys throughout the year and the figures from several years showing demand trends are good indicators upon which future expansions and contractions can be planned. As it develops, the information pattern is an additive mosaic. Although the mosaic may be transformed into a clear decision-making signpost by the final bit of information, the value of the last bit is contingent on all the information that has gone before.

Of course, the final bit of information may shatter rather than complete the mosaic. For instance, a commodities trader who has discerned a pattern in the fluctuations of the price of gold and is about to enter the market will skid to a halt if a massive gold strike is announced. The new information almost completely devalues the old information. In fact, if the slate is wiped completely clean, the gold strike is the first tile in a new information mosaic.

To Herbert Simon, Robert Cyert and James March, and others, the process of patterning environmental information, reducing it to key elements, and remaining alert for data that change the value of existing information patterns is a crucial organizational task. However, the flow of information from the environment to the executive is a lengthy chain that requires efficient and effective communications channels.[44] Simon, in particular, took pains to identify the weak links in this chain.[45] Although many associate Simon with internal organizational design—the context in which he first discussed communications dysfunctions—his observations apply equally to border-spanning information activities.

Information Dysfunctions

When information goes awry, there are three suspects: the sender, the receiver, and the channel through which it passes.

The sender can short-circuit a message by:

Retaining it
Misdirecting it
Making it ambiguous

The information channel can short-circuit a communication if it is:

Overloaded
Inoperative

The receiver can short-circuit a message by:

Misunderstanding it
Rejecting it
Being unable to act on it.

Chester Barnard was the first to offer a breakdown similar to the above.[46] However, Barnard's context was authority. His concern was for the waylaying of top-down messages from executives to employees. Simon, on the other hand, emphasized that the dysfunctions were multidirectional. Information flowing to the executive could get similarly misplaced, distorted, or misinterpreted. If border spanning was involved, an opportunity to determine further the nature of the organizational environment was lost. The fate of Presidents Johnson and Nixon hinged, to a significant degree, on such failures.

For Lyndon Johnson, it was a cornucopia of inflated body counts, imminent victories, and a host of other distorted messages from army commanders in Vietnam. Moreover, the rising tide of antiwar protests broke against Johnsonian stubbornness; staffers inclined towards more responsiveness were silenced by LBJ's legendary temper. The result was an ignominious showing in the 1968 New Hampshire primary and a sorrowful withdrawal from the presidential race.

Nixon, too, had his communications troubles. His reading of the

1972 political environment produced a campaign mentality that led to Watergate. The failure of his political lieutenants to read clearly the message of oddball staffers such as Gordon Liddy paved the way for spy novel tactics. Stonewalling, as it turned out, was another ill-conceived response to an environment determined to uncover the truth.

Information Costs

Some information comes easy. An indictment is a good example. The jurisdiction takes pains to convey the news to the organization. However, most information does not arrive prepackaged. Information is like any other crop. Money, time, and effort are required to harvest it.

Harvesting information is costly. The services of lawyers, market researchers, and other border spanners are not cheap. Their information sources are also expensive. Tens of thousands of dollars can be spent on law libraries, subscriptions to Poor's Register, and other periodicals that are indispensable to professional border spanners. Trips to professional conventions and conferences are necessary and costly. Moreover, border spanners often entertain clients in restaurants and other social arenas where the expense account reigns supreme. Finally, bribery is not an unknown means of acquiring information.

Harvested information has to be packaged and stored. This process adds to the costs of information. In most border-spanning situations, packaging requires memo dictation, secretarial transcription, tape recorders, and typewriters. Clerks are also needed to copy the memo, distribute it, file it, and perhaps lose it in a high-rental storage room. Information retrieval requires reversing most of the process above, which is why the process often sensitizes executives to the lure of the computer.

There are also premiums for insuring against theft or unwanted disclosure of information. Patents and copyrights are obvious premiums. However, the organization treats much of its information in a surreptitious manner. Few government agencies, for instance, want it publicly known that they are casting about for advice on whether to abandon a formal goal. Yet, slips of the tongue or egotistic cocktail party chatter can put such information in wide circulation. By making an extra Xerox copy of sensitive information, disaffected employees can directly supply reporters and others with hard evidence of organizational activity. To keep information from the indiscreet or rebellious employee, the organization incurs a variety of costs not the least of which is executive time spent trying to locate the source of the leak.[47] During the Vietnam War, when the press acquired an accurate but critical account of the U.S./ South Vietnamese war effort, the U.S. military command left no stone unturned in trying to expose and punish the leaker.[48]

Balancing Information and Action

One senses from the discussion above that there is a point where information is more trouble than it is worth. At some point, the organization becomes immobilized as collecting, packaging, storing, and securing information squeeze out other activities. Civil War General George McClellan demonstrated this rather well. As Commander of the Army of the Potomac, McClellan was an avid collector of organizational intelligence. He wanted to be absolutely certain of the battle readiness of his troops and preferred to know the whereabouts of every confederate soldier. According to McClellan, with each bit of new information this picture became clearer. Thus, the decision to engage the enemy was a function of the picture's completion. President Lincoln, impatient with his general's inactivity, pushed McClellan into battle. Not surprisingly, the result was indecisive. After regrouping, McClellan again tried to establish the exact order of the military universe; he was relieved of command by an exasperated Lincoln.

Even those who approach the study of decision making from different directions could agree that McClellan's management approach had one irredeemable defect: the need for certainty. The world of social systems—the organizational environments and internal dynamics—is not completely knowable. The future is probabilistic. The present goes by too fast; the past provides an uncertain guidepost for action. Even the combination of history, intuition, observations, and a resultant theory cannot account with certainty for a social system's future. Thus, the manager who strives for complete information is pursuing a mirage, one that disappears as time and circumstances force the organization to act. On the other side of the ledger, it would not pay for the organization to ignore processing information altogether. Students of decision making, therefore, advise that the organization strive for balance in information collection.

Amatai Etzioni's approach is a *mixed scanning* of the informational environment.[49] Under mixed scanning the informational horizon is frequently but superficially checked. The search is for anomalies; that is, information that does not fit the patterns of previous scans. When such deviations are uncovered, decision makers zero in. The deviation is analyzed to determine if a change is required in the existing organizational posture. Etzioni's approach is similar to "management by exception," which applies to the internal workings of the organization. With this approach, managers concentrate on the exceptional occurrence—highly inefficient units, habitually tardy employees, or unusually high performances which may indicate reporting errors. Again, the object is to zero in on problems.

Medical monitoring machines are mixed scanners. They are silent unless the vital signs being monitored deviate from a norm determined by the medical team. When the machines beep, human scanners—doctors or nurses—take a closer look.

Other analysts, including Simon, developed sophisticated models for assessing the likelihood of future events. These models included decision trees, probability distributions, linear regressions, and other mathematic formulations. The common purpose was to bring more information to bear on the organization's planning for the future.

MONITORING THE ENVIRONMENT: SOME IMPLICATIONS FOR ORGANIZATIONAL DESIGN

There are several prescriptions for avoiding dysfunctions and exceptional collection costs in environmental monitoring. One, already attributed to Simon and Townsend, is for the executive to get closer to the environment. The information is gathered firsthand and transmission distortion is avoided. Two alternative prescriptions are improving the communications linkages to the decision-making executive and adding highly skilled border spanners to the staff.

These two alternatives are, essentially, centralization versus decentralization. As with most alternatives, there is something to be said against both. If the executive becomes an inveterate eyewitness scanner of the environment, decision making becomes centralized to the point of overload. With overload conditions, decisions are delayed and often incorrect. Decentralization, i.e., more border scanners, usually harvests higher-quality information from the environment. However, this information does not always reach the executive intact. The collecting unit may distort or suppress the data to gain advantage.[50]

A third alternative, popularized by Franklin Roosevelt, was to set up redundant information channels. Roosevelt told departmental secretaries, staff assistants, and outside cronies, unbeknownst to each other, to monitor the same situation. If the reports were contradictory, Roosevelt often brought the intelligence gatherers together and let them battle it out. In looking for a winner, Roosevelt, the referee, sought an accurate environmental reading as well.[51]

To a certain extent, the traditional notions of organizational efficiency were compromised by decentralization and redundant channel approaches. The goal of the task-oriented organization was to eliminate mistakes. Indeed, avoiding errors is a prime objective in today's organizations. In adapting to the environment, however, fear of making errors can be dysfunctional. If the options are possible failure or inaction, border spanners who are afraid to make errors will choose the latter. If the executive's mindset includes a fixed picture of the environment, border spanners, fearing punishment, may withhold incongruent information. By failing to adapt to small changes in the environment, the organization could find itself so out of step that catching up would be impossible. Thus, some theorists propose that the organization should be consciously run as a learning system rather than an efficiency mechanism in order to respond more innovatively to environmental conditions.[52]

SUMMARY

Chapter 4 concludes the "organizations" part of this book. We began, in Chapter 2, by discussing the essential characteristics of organizations. Taking the client's perspective, we viewed the profile of organizations in modern society and considered the origins and contemporary roles of public organizations. In Chapter 3, we considered two patterns of organizational rule: the top-down and the bottom-up. The ideological overtones to bottom-up rule were explored and the potential of monocratic authority was considered.

In the chapter just concluded we turned from the internal characteristics of organization to the organization as a unit relating to its environment. In this latter role, the organization is no longer molded and directed exclusively by owners, boards of directors, or legislators. To some extent, the organization defines its own coordinates and sets a course. Formal superiors represent only a portion of the rocky shoals, safe harbors, and stormy weather that must be negotiated. For clear sailing, the organization relies heavily on border spanning activity to monitor and maintain the organization's environmental contacts. At the end of Chapter 4, we considered some of the more formal approaches to the basic elements of organizational adaptation: information management and processing. Information handling schemes were shown to have implications for the centralization and decentralization of organization functions.

In Part II, our emphasis has shifted from the structural characteristics of organization to the organization's behavior as an actor in a dynamic environment. Although people appeared in supporting roles, the organization was our primary unit of analysis. In Part III, however, the role of people in organizations and in public administration will be the center of attention.

KEY TERMS AND CONCEPTS

Adaptation	Coalition
Bargaining	Competition
Border-spanning agents	Cooptation
Closed and open systems	Feedback

Goal displacement   Law of requisite variety
Institutionalization   Mixed scanning
Integration   Value maintenance

NOTES

1. Max Weber, "Bureaucracy" in Fred A. Kramer, ed., *Perspectives on Public Bureaucracy: A Reader On Organizations,* (Cambridge: Winthrop Publishers, 1973), p. 19.
2. Nicos P. Mouzelis, *Organization and Bureaucracy: An Analysis of Modern Theories* (Chicago: Aldine, 1968), p. 7.
3. Herbert Simon, Donald Smithberg, and Victor Thompson, *Public Administration* (New York: Knopf, 1950), p. 25.
4. William G. Scott and Terence R. Mitchell, *Organization Theory: A Structural and Behavioral Analysis* (Homewood, Ill.: Dorsey Press, 1972), pp. 9–10.
5. Ibid.
6. V. Subramaniam, "Representative Bureaucracy: A Reassessment," in Robert T. Golembiewski, Frank Gibson, Geoffrey Y. Cornog, eds., *Public Administration: Readings in Institutions, Processes, Behavior* (Chicago: Rand McNally, 1972), pp. 535–552.
7. John Brooks, *Telephone: The First Hundred Years* (New York: Harper & Row, 1976), pp. 47–48.
8. William L. Riordan, *Plunkitt of Tammany Hall* (New York: Knopf, 1948).
9. See *Task Force Report: Organized Crime* (Washington: The President's Commission on Law Enforcement and Criminal Justice, 1967).
10. Talcott Parsons, "Suggestions for a Sociological Approach to the Theory of Organizations," in Amatai Etzioni, ed., *Modern Organizations: A Sociological Reader* (Englewood Cliffs, N.J.: Prentice-Hall, 1964), pp. 32–47. A liberty has been taken with Parsons's notion of "latency." "Value maintenance" has been substituted to avoid confusion with Merton's "latent functions." Although the term has been changed, the meaning has not.
11. See Burton R. Clark, "Organizational Adaptation and Precarious Values" in Etzioni, *Modern Organization,* pp. 159–167.
12. In New York City, on occasion, police have been formally directed, by the commissioner, to ignore certain minor offenses unless a citizen complaint has been received. See *The Knapp Commission Report On Police Corruption* (New York: Braziller, 1973), p. 278.
13. For a roughly parallel story concerning imbibers in a "dry" Kansas town, see Charles K. Warriner, "The Nature and Functions of Official Morality," in Walter M. Gerson, ed., *Social Problems in a Changing World* (New York: Crowell, 1969), pp. 91–96. Also, in the same volume, see Herbert A. Bloch, "The Gambling Business: An American Paradox," pp. 97–108.
14. *The Report of the Commission on Obscenity and Pornography* (Washington: U.S. Government Printing Office, 1970), pp. 52–53.
15. For a good profile of a crusading antipornography prosecutor, see Ted Morgan, "The United States Versus The Princes of Porn," *New York Times Magazine,* 6 March 1977, p. 16.
16. Robert K. Merton, *Social Theory and Social Structure* (New York: Free Press, 1957), pp. 50–53.
17. Philip Selznick, *The TVA and the Grass Roots: A Study in the Sociology of Formal Organizations* (Berkeley: University of California Press, 1966).
18. Ibid., pp. 258–259.

19. David L. Sills, "The Succession of Goals," in Etzioni, *Modern Organizations,* pp. 146–159.
20. Charles Perrow, "Goals and Power Structures: A Historical Case Study," in *The Hospital in Modern Society,* ed. Eliot Freidson (New York: The Free Press, 1973), pp. 112–146.
21. Omar N. Bradley, *A Soldier's Story* (New York: Holt, Rinehart and Winston, 1952), p. 243.
22. A stark example of corporate environmental control is offered by Benno Schmidt, *Freedom of the Press vs. Public Access* (New York: Praeger, 1976), p. 44. It seems as if DuPont owns both of Wilmington's daily newspapers and, through a holding company, controls all but one of the remaining dailies in Delaware.
23. Gary L. Walmsley and Mayer N. Zald, *The Political Economy of Public Organizations* (Bloomington: Indiana University Press, 1973), p. 69.
24. Harold Seidman, *Politics, Position and Power: The Dynamics of Federal Organization* (New York: Oxford University Press, 1970).
25. *Consumer Reports* 41, no. 3: March, 1976, 124.
26. Ibid.
27. Ibid.
28. James D. Thompson and William McEwen, "Organizational Goals and Environment," in Etzioni, *Modern Organizations,* pp. 177–186.
29. Ibid., p. 184.
30. Samuel P. Huntington, "Strategic Programs and the Political Process," in Lewis Gawthrop, ed., *The Administrative Process and Democratic Theory* (Boston: Houghton Mifflin, 1970), pp. 231–241.
31. Thompson and McEwen, "Organizational Goals," p. 184.
32. Norman I. Fainstein and Susan S. Fainstein, *Urban Political Movements* (Englewood Cliffs, N.J.: Prentice-Hall Inc., 1974), pp. 46, 121.
33. Donald A. Schon, *Beyond The Stable State* (New York: Random House, 1971), p. 5.
34. Harold L. Wilensky, *Organizational Intelligence* (New York: Basic Books, 1967). Wilensky's identification of "contact men" and "facts and figures men" underpins much of the discussion on "border spanners."
35. Technically, nonstockholding creditors are barred from charting the course of the debtor organization. In reality, however, the bankrupt firm has little choice but to modify policies if that is the only way to get a new loan or the relaxation of an existing repayment schedule.
36. John Kenneth Galbraith, *The New Industrial State* (Boston: Houghton Mifflin, 1967), p. 71.
37. Robert Townsend, *Up the Organization: How to Stop the Corporation From Stifling People and Strangling Profits* (New York: Fawcett, 1970), p. 87.
38. The materials are drawn from a case study being prepared by one of the authors.
39. One of the early calls for an open-closed synthesis came from Alvin W. Gouldner, "Organizational Analysis" in Robert K. Merton, ed., *Sociology Today* (New York: Basic Books, 1959).
40. Looking at objects as information processors is now widespread in science and may have been given significant impetus by the discovery that the DNA molecule was a collector, storer, and transmitter of information. Although in somewhat distinct fields, works that are considered seminal to the information approach include: Ludwig von Bertalanffy, *Problems of Life* (London: Watts and Company, 1952); Claude E. Shannon and Warren Weaver, *The Mathematical Theory of Communication* (Urbana: The University of Illinois

Press, 1949); Stafford Beer, *Cybernetics and Management* (New York: Wiley, 1959).
41. Tom Burns and G. M. Stalker, *The Management of Innovation* (London: Tavistock, 1961), detail nicely the distinctions between the mechanistic and organic theorists and come down on the side of the latter.
42. W. Ross Ashby, *An Introduction to Cybernetics* (New York: Barnes & Noble, 1956), pp. 206–218.
43. Kenneth J. Arrow, *The Limits of Organization* (New York: Norton, 1974), p. 38.
44. Robert Cyert and James March, *A Behavioral Theory of the Firm* (Englewood Cliffs, N.J.: Prentice-Hall, 1963).
45. Herbert A. Simon, *Administrative Behavior: A Study of Decision-Making Processes In Administrative Organizations* (New York: Free Press, 1976), pp. 154–171.
46. Chester Barnard, *The Functions of the Executive* (Cambridge: Harvard University Press, 1938), pp. 165–181.
47. Schon, again, opines that the "leaking" employee may very well be trying to wrench the organization into line with an already alienated environment. Therefore, uncovering and suppressing such employees is not only costly but foolhardy.
48. David Halberstam, *The Best and the Brightest* (New York: Fawcett, 1973).
49. Amatai Etzioni, *The Active Society* (New York: Free Press, 1968).
50. Wilensky, *Organizational Intelligence*, p. 58.
51. Ibid., pp. 50–51.
52. G. Zaltman, R. Duncan and J. Holbeck, *Innovations and Organizations* (New York: Wiley, 1973); Schon, *Beyond the Stable State*, pp. 116–179, comments extensively on just how poor a learning system he believes government to be.

BIBLIOGRAPHY

Arrow, Kenneth J. *The Limits of Organization.* New York: Norton, 1974.
Beer, Stafford. *Cybernetics and Management.* New York: Wiley, 1959.
Bertalanffy, Ludwig von. *Problems of Life.* London: Watts and Co., 1952.
Burns, T. and Stalker, G. M. *The Management of Innovation.* London: Tavistock, 1961.
Cyert, Robert and March, James. *A Behavioral Theory of the Firm.* Englewood Cliffs, N.J.: Prentice-Hall Inc., 1963.
Etzioni, Amatai, ed. *Modern Organization: A Sociological Reader.* Englewood Cliffs, N.J.: Prentice-Hall Inc., 1964.
Fainstein, Norman I. and Fainstein, Susan S. *Urban Political Movements.* Englewood Cliffs, N.J.: Prentice-Hall Inc., 1974.
Katz, Daniel and Kahn, Robert. *The Social Psychology of Organization.* New York: Wiley, 1966.
Lawrence, Paul R. and Lorsch, Jay W. *Organization and Environment.* Homewood, Ill.: Irwin, 1969.
Merton, Robert K. *Social Theory and Social Structure.* New York: The Free Press, 1957.
Perrow, Charles. *Organizational Analysis.* Belmont, Calif.: Wadsworth, 1970.
The Report of the Commission on Obscenity and Pornography. Washington: U.S. Government Printing Office, 1970.
Riordan, William L. *Plunkitt of Tammany Hall.* New York: Knopf, 1948.
Schon, Donald. *Beyond the Stable State.* New York: Random House, 1971.
Seidman, Harold. *Politics, Position and Power: The Dynamics of Federal Organization.* New York: Oxford University Press, 1970.

Selznick, Philip. *The TVA and the Grass Roots: A Study in the Sociology of Formal Organizations.* Berkeley: University of California Press, 1966.
Shannon, Claude E. and Weaver, Warren. *The Mathematical Theory of Communication.* Urbana: University of Illinois Press, 1949.
Task Force Report: Organized Crime. Washington: The President's Commission on Law Enforcement and Criminal Justice, 1967.
Townsend, Robert. *Up the Organization: How to Stop the Corporation from Stifling People and Strangling Profits.* New York: Fawcett, 1970.
Walmsley, Gary L. and Zald, Mayer N. *The Political Economy of Public Organizations.* Bloomington: Indiana University Press, 1973.
Wilensky, Harold L. *Organizational Intelligence.* New York: Basic Books, 1967.
Zaltman, G., Duncan, R., and Holbeck, J. *Innovations and Organizations.* New York: Wiley, 1973.

In addition to the sources cited in the notes and bibliography, the following *Public Administration Review (PAR)* articles are a convenient starting point for a more detailed exploration of the material in this chapter.

Brown, David S. "The Management of Advisory Committees: An Assignment for the '70's," *PAR* 32, no. 4 (July/Aug. 1972): 334–342.
Caiden, Gerald E. and Naomi J. Caiden. "Administrative Corruption," *PAR* 37, no. 3 (May/June 1977): 301–309.
Etzioni, Amatai. "Mixed Scanning: A Third Approach to Decision-Making," *PAR* 27, no. 4 (Dec. 1967): 385–392.
Kotler, Philip and Michael Murray. "Third Sector Management—The Role of Marketing," *PAR* 35, no. 5 (Sept./Oct. 1975): 467–472.
McGuire, John M. "Institutions and the World They Helped to Make," *PAR* 31, no. 6 (Nov./Dec. 1971): 653–657.
Porter, David O. and Eugene A. Olson. "Some Critical Issues in Government Centralization and Decentralization," *PAR* 36, no. 1 (Jan./Feb. 1976): 72–84.
Shipman, George A. "Complexities of Goal Attainment," *PAR* 29, no. 2 (March/April 1969): 210–213.
Sigal, Leon V. "Bureaucratic Objectives and Tactical Uses of the Press," *PAR* 33, no. 4 (July/Aug. 1973): 336–345.
Stallings, C. Wayne. "Local Information Policy: Confidentiality and Public Access," *PAR* 34, no. 3 (May/June 1974): 197–204.
Thompson, James D. "Society's Frontiers for Organizing Activities," *PAR* 33, no. 4 (July/Aug. 1973): 327–335.
Waldo, Dwight. "The University in Relation to the Governmental-Political," *PAR* 30, no. 2 (March/April 1970): 106–113.
Wamsley, Gary L. and Mayer N. Zald. "The Political Economy of Public Organizations," *PAR* 33, no. 1 (Jan./Feb. 1973): 62–73.

RELEVANT PERIODICALS
Academy of Marketing Science Journal
Administrative Science Quarterly
American Journal of Sociology
American Sociological Review
American Sociologist
Current Sociology

Journal of Marketing
Pacific Sociological Review
Public Relations Quarterly
Sociological Quarterly

RELEVANT CASE STUDIES

(Cases marked ICCH are available from the Intercollegiate Case Clearing House, Soldier Field, Boston, Mass. 02163; cases marked ICP are available from the Inter-University Case Program, Box 229, Syracuse, N.Y. 13210.)

Bower, J. L. *William D. Ruckelshaus and the Environmental Protection Agency.* [ICCH]

Eliot, T. *The Van Waters Case,* [ICP]

Henry L. *The NASA-University Memoranda of Understanding,* [ICP]

Lambright, W. H. *Launching NASA's Sustaining University Program,* [ICP]

Lovelock, C. H. *Stanford University: The Annual Fund,* [ICCH]

Maass. A. *Kings River Project,* [ICP]

Maloney, J. F. *"The Lonesome Train" in Levittown,* [ICP]

Robertson, T. S., L. S. Ward, S. L. Diamond. *Multiple Sclerosis Society: Fund Raising Strategy,* [ICCH]

Russell, J. R. *HSA Meets the Press,* (A)(B),* [ICCH]

Stratton, O. and P. Sirotkin. *The Echo Park Controversy,* [ICP]

Verma, D. T and F. Wiseman. *Massachusetts State Lottery,* (A),* [ICCH]

*Letters indicate that the case is presented in several installments.

PART THREE

PEOPLE

CHAPTER 5

HUMAN BEHAVIOR IN ORGANIZATIONS

INTRODUCTION

Organizations are mechanisms for getting people to work together toward the achievement of goals. In Part II, we concentrated on the organization as a structure and as an entity. We found that organizations are mandated by society, are designed as mechanisms, and behave like organisms. However, organizations are more than mandates of society, machines, or organisms; they are collections of people. The bureaucracy may be a machine but the people who populate it are certainly not machine parts. The bureaucracy may be an organism but the human beings who give it life are not simple cells. This proved a painful lesson for those who assumed that the fit between people and bureaucratic structure was an easy one.

In the United States, Frederick Taylor was one designer of bureaucracy who saw people as simple, rather than complex, beings who, if properly oiled by money, would serve as efficient components in the organization. This was the touchstone of managerial thinking in the United States at the beginning of this century. However, when it was discovered that personnel in "scientifically designed" jobs could be sad instead of glad, could produce less instead of more, and could leave the assembly line for the picket line, this thinking was questioned. Those who did so marched under the banner of the Human Relations Movement and, as the name implies, their concern was people.

The *Human Relations Movement* occupies a central position in the development of organization theory. Chronologically, it stands midway between Weber's development of the classic bureaucratic model and the "whole systems" approach that prevails today. Theoretically, Human Relations represented the first major break away from the mechanistic concepts of organization advanced by Weber and Taylor. The movement added immensely to the inventory of knowledge about organizations and the people in them. By applying the investigatory tools of sociology and psychology, the Human Relationists addressed the informal work group, the importance of emotional factors in organizational functioning, and the question of what moved people to act. The movement towards better working conditions, pension plans, and the "family" organization owed much of its impetus to the Human Relationists' influence. Long before Maharishi and self-awareness movements dotted the landscape, "self-actualization" was a major rallying cry of those who wished to inject humanism into the organizational structure. Human Relations is a rich area; we hope the following survey succeeds in highlighting its valuable insights.

TAYLORISM

Taylorism, named after the theories of Frederick Taylor, sought to maximize efficiency in the organizational machine by precision tooling people components to perform as reliably as the machine components of organization. Thus, when Taylorism was dominant in the study of organizations, scholars studied people as though they were machines.[1]

Taylorite methods of analysis included using stopwatches to time job performance, movies to break down a task into its smallest identifiable parts, treadmills to test the workers' threshold of fatigue, and meters to measure productivity effects of various levels of light and sound. The goal was to discover the optimum match between job requirements and the physical and mental capacities of individuals. Thus, staffing a 100 position organization required 100 matches between positions and people. Heavyweights would do the lifting, the agile would do the pole climbing, the mathematically inclined would do the books, and those with business administration degrees would do the managing.

To solve the person/position equation, Taylor proposed management science. However, finding the best worker for a particular job does not guarantee that the worker will perform up to expectations. The worker must want to do it. The organization's job is to instill this desire. Taylor did not see this as a very complex problem because he did not see people as very complex animals. Taylor saw people as rational and self-serving. Given sufficient facts upon which to base a decision, people would do that which best served their interests. To Taylor, best was what money could buy. Therefore, if payment was tied to production, organization members would produce at their maximum capacity. (Presumably, rational workers in scientifically designed jobs would be incapable of working themselves to death.)

One of the few problems that Taylor foresaw was educating the uninitiated to the economic facts of life. Thus, to the workers on the assembly line, Taylor patiently explained that more production meant more money and more money meant greater purchasing power to buy the good things in life. With this revelation in hand, employees were expected to work like beavers and not malinger on the job. Outside the organization, workers were expected to lead sensible, staid life-styles. Thus, they were expected to open and maintain bank accounts, live within their means, and avoid socially undesirable behavior. They would be fresh and industrious on the job and consider the organization's best interests, i.e., increased production, as their own.[2]

Although Taylorism dominated organization theory in the early part of the twentieth century, its reign was somewhat uneasy. There was no consensus on its theoretical foundations; alternative theories competed with Taylorism and eventually consolidated into the Human Relations Movement that dethroned Taylorism.

Historical Bases for the Attack on Taylorism

Taylorism annointed itself a "science," which by the turn of the century, was a surname much in vogue. Science, with its repeated observations, control of contaminating factors, and precise measurement made great breakthroughs towards a fuller explanation of the physical world. Newton's experiments with falling objects provided a universal law that helped to explain gravity and motion. Newton's formulations inspired others to seek universal laws of science and nature. Those in the hard sciences, physics and chemistry, often found them. The consequent impact on society often was staggering, although somewhat double-edged. For example, the laws of aerodynamics made possible applications that moved people as easily as they moved nuclear bombs (another gift of the diligent physicists).[3]

Science was as attractive to those who studied human behavior as it was to students of physical phenomena. Thus, eighteenth- and nineteenth-century economics offered a "scientific" explanation of human behavior in which motivating factors could be expressed in objective and measurable terms: money. Individuals, similar to the firms studied by the early economists, sought to maximize their monetary benefits while minimizing costs. Although this embodied a somewhat dismal view that people were motivated exclusively by self-interest, economics became the first "science" of human behavior.

Despite its dominant position in the study of human behavior, economics was never without its Doubting Thomases. The physiocrats, as economists were known in those days, were excoriated for both their theory and methodology. Studying people as objects from afar and totaling up the monetary pluses and minuses associated with the observed action struck critics as an inappropriate way of finding out how people behave. One such critic put it nicely:

> I cannot ask the clouds to tell me when and where they want to rain. I have to accumulate several thousands of observations. . . . But man, when interrogated, answers.[4]

The criticisms of the methodology were mild in comparison to the criticisms of economic theory. At worst, improper methodology could only impede the discovery of alternative explanations of human behavior. Economic theory, on the other hand, held that there was nothing else to discover, a proposition that set some opponents roaring. Economics, cried one, is "a sterile aberration to renounce the psychological."[5]

However, it was not the psychological perspective that presented the first strong challenge to the economic explanation of human behavior. A sociological perspective was evident in those analysts who studied the way people behaved as members of groups that endured for more than a short length of time. In 1789, as economics blossomed, Adam Ferguson, a noted scholar, observed that different trades "inspired certain sentiments."[6] Even Adam Smith, whose *Wealth of Nations* is the most well-known early treatise on economics, feared that the sullen listlessness of the early industrial worker could lead to a citizenry that exhibited a similar detachment towards the fate of their nation. Thus, as early as the eighteenth century, two themes that would later become central to the Human Relations Movement had been articulated. One was that the job affects the way workers think and behave. The other was that job-induced behavior could have negative consequences for society.

By the end of the nineteenth century, sociologists were beginning to analyze the role groups played in conditioning the behavior of members. Georg Simmel, a German sociologist, noted that people in modern society held membership in various social circles and asserted that each person's mental habits were conditioned by the combinations of these groups.[7] Wilfredo Pareto, an Italian economist, cited the proliferation of groups in a major criticism of Marx's two-dimensional, bourgeois-proletarian view of society. To prove that he was fair, Pareto then lambasted the classical economists for assuming that rationality was the mainspring of human action. To Pareto, faith, rather than calculation, was much more effective in motivating people to action. The belief that "man could do away with religion and substitute for it simple scientific notions," wrote Pareto, "is an infantile error."[8] This was to be a theme of the Human Relationists: Morale and esprit de corps would produce a workforce dedicated to the goals of the organization.

The final theoretical underpinnings of the anti-Taylorites were set in place by French sociologist Emile Durkheim. Writing at the turn of the twentieth century, Durkheim crystallized the vague fears expressed by Adam Smith more than a century before. He asserted that modern society tended to depopulate church, ethnic group, and family. It provided both the means—better transportation—and the compulsion—distant workplace—for a geographic dispersal of group members. Modern society also provided higher levels of education for the young and, in the process, weakened the hold of traditional rules and values. This is quite evident in the United States. Over 20 percent of its citizens change residences every year. People are more highly educated than ever before. Thus, it is not unusual to find the grandson of an immigrant laborer from the Lower East Side of New York City living the life of a corporate executive in California.

In France at the turn of the century, and on a smaller scale of course, Durkheim observed this same breaking away from traditional values. However, his studies showed something else: Those who had broken away were more likely to commit suicide.[9] To Durkheim, this was an indication that modern society had failed to develop the explicit rules of behavior and clearly defined roles that traditional groups provided for their members.

Instead, the newly liberated were offered a Protestant ethic that tied salvation to personal success and the closely allied theory of economic man that pitted individuals against the world. The message was clear: Individuals in modern society had to keep striving. Neglected, however, was guidance concerning what they were striving for. Thus, the entire weight of goal formulation was thrust upon individuals and many were unequal to the task. They became, in Durkheim's word, *anomic* or without rules.[10] Durkheim found that suicide was more likely among anomic individuals than among members of traditional, rule-laden groups. In addition, anomic individuals committed suicide for different reasons than those affiliated with groups whose rules more clearly defined acceptable behavior. A Judas Iscariot, for example, might kill himself because he knew that he had committed a heinous act by informing against his group and its leader. Individuals in modern society, according to Durkheim, often killed themselves out of frustration. Thus, anomic suicide was a response to a futile attempt to define right and wrong, good and bad; a definition that was once provided by the abandoned traditional group.

Even as Taylorism flourished, therefore, the philosophical groundwork had been laid for an assault on its domination of organization theory. Telling doubts had been expressed about its propositions and methodology. Thus, the task at hand for those dissenters who studied organizations was to coalesce and empirically verify these doubts. Beginning in the 1920s, such a mission was undertaken by Elton Mayo and his Harvard Industrial Research Group.

The Human Relations
Assault on Scientific Management

Elton Mayo was the seminal force in the Human Relations Movement. It was Mayo who launched the philosophical broadsides against scientific management. Mayo's first salvo was aimed at Taylor's assumption that individuals were concerned exclusively with their own welfare. Mayo attacked this as the *rabble hypothesis*.[11] Individuals were not merely acquisitive, according to Mayo, they were also cooperative. In taking this position, Mayo trained his guns on more than Taylorism. Classical economics was also in the line of fire. According to Mayo, the classical economists, particularly David Ricardo, advanced theories that were improperly constructed. Ricardo, Mayo tells us somewhat acidly, worked from the age of 14 to 21 in his father's brokerage house, at which point he retired to construct his economic philosophy based on the experience. It is no wonder then, according to Mayo, that Ricardo viewed humans as animals who always sought to buy low and sell high.[12]

Warming to the task, Mayo points out that it did not matter what businesses the classical economists had studied. Twentieth-century economic philosophy could not rest on generalizations drawn from eighteenth-century firms composed of, at most, a few hundred individuals. Although Mayo is unable to repress his skepticism, he allows that on such a small scale, economic considerations may have been primary in sealing and maintaining the work contract between individuals and organization.[13] In the twentieth-century corporate state, however, economic considerations cannot monopolize that relationship. Organizations grown large and complex are beyond the point of making precise economic calculations about employees. More and more people must contribute their time and energy to the completion of a single task and administrative positions must proliferate. Thus, the calculus of individual contributions relative to the overall effort of the organization becomes impossible in strictly economic terms.

Mayo also intoned a eulogy for "economic man" on mechanical grounds. Even if individuals wanted to use a rational selection process to decide which of several courses of action would be most beneficial to them, they had neither the time nor the brain power to collect and analyze all the information necessary for a truly rational decision.[14]

Mayo did not merely denigrate economics; he demoted it. He contended that economic rationality was no more than a secondary component in a multidimensional calculus. Individuals, said Mayo, were intrinsically social beings with a need for stable relationships with other social beings.[15] This relationship was achieved through membership in groups and associations. Such groups afforded the individual a sense of belonging and a familiar social situation in which behavior could proceed without calculation. Compared to the outside world, where the correct steps were unfamiliar and a misstep could cause disastrous consequences, the social group was a safe harbor from the maelstrom of uncertainty.

Mayo's observation that groups performed a useful function for their members did not break new ground. However, he was on more virgin soil when he suggested that the group, which in classical bureaucratic terms was little more than a malignant growth, must be factored into the organizational design. Thus, Mayo took pains to point out the consequences if groups were not factored in. With some passion, Mayo predicted disaster if group formation was discouraged by organizations. A dissolved group would likely produce anomic, uncommitted individuals. If carried out on a wide scale, this could produce an atomized society. If the attempt to dissolve the group was unsuccessful, the group would be justifiably antagonistic to whatever the organization might propose. Neither result would be beneficial.[16]

Mayo's warning also applied to organizations that remained oblivious to group behavior. Organizations, said Mayo, could not assume that a weakening of traditional ties among individuals meant the end of groups. They would continue to form because individuals needed them. Groups would develop wherever individuals spent significant amounts of their time. Thus, groups would form in organizations and influence the behavior of organization members. Executives who did not recognize this force did so at their own peril. At best, executives would see the subtle modification of their directives and know not why. At worst, they would show up at the plant someday and find that the employees had taken over and locked them out. Unless executives recognized that there were social needs within the organization that demanded their attention, befuddlement or banishment remained real possibilities.[17]

Mayo's broadsides at Taylor's economics indicated an ideological disagreement of such magnitude that economists who were dead for 200 years were battered around in the exchange. Equally intense was Mayo's fear that society could court disaster if it failed to tap the cooperative resources present in groups. Mayo was somewhat less violent in his criticisms of Taylor's scientific approach to job design and its consequent matching of personnel. This may be because Mayo's methodology in his initial experiments was not much different from that Taylor would have used. Indeed, it was the failure of his own scientific approach that crystallized Mayo's Human Relations philosophy.

THE HAWTHORNE EXPERIMENTS:
THE GROUP INFLUENCE IN ORGANIZATION

The first experiments that Mayo conducted in the United States were in a Philadelphia textile plant. It was well run and the labor turnover in the plant was 5 percent, except for one operation where the average worker left after 18 weeks or so. The sudden 250 percent turnover in a plant that averaged only 5 percent drew the attention of management. Elton Mayo and his Harvard associates were called in to see what was wrong. As it turned out, nothing was right.

Mayo found that workers left the job because it required constant attention at levels too high to permit talking among employees but not high enough to permit complete absorption in the work. Also, the job was never ending; the yarn spun and spun. There was no feeling of a job well done; no opportunity to close out a job quickly; and no reward of a well-earned break. In fact, there were no rest periods at all; employees worked for five consecutive hours before lunch and five consecutive hours after. Mayo's response to this situation was to institute rest periods. As a result, productivity went up, turnover went down, and Taylorism was reaffirmed.[18]

Mayo's next experiment was conducted at the Hawthorne works of the Western Electric Company. The Hawthorne experiment was significant because it produced the findings that eventually freed organization theory from the dominance of Taylorism. Yet, in the aftermath of the textile mill experiments, Mayo and his associates were intent on manipulating the physical elements of the job to improve performance. However, in the Hawthorne works, the application of the methods of management science explained virtually nothing.[19]

The first experiments at Hawthorne were designed to test the effects of illumination, working time, amount of sleep, and other physical variables on productivity. The researchers increased the illumination and lowered it. Work hours were shortened and then lengthened. Breaks were added, eliminated, and moved around. What were the results? Productivity almost always increased even though the changes did not represent a continuum. "Good" job designs followed "bad" and vice versa. Nonetheless, production went steadily up and, in the process, the theories of Taylor went steadily down.

At first, however, the only thing that was clear to the researchers was that they were disproving Taylorism. As for alternative explanations, they had none. One of the reasons for this void was that the experimenters were too close to one of the explanations to see it. Namely, the research team was one of the major reasons for the increase in productivity. The attention being lavished upon the workers in the experiment made them feel important. Thus, despite the changes in working conditions, output remained high. The workers produced be-

"Modern Times": 1936. In Chaplin's classic cinematic commentary on the scientifically designed job, an unsyncopated Charlie is about to be mangled by the tireless and unvarying machinery. (The Museum of Modern Art/Film Stills Archive, 11 W. 53rd Street, New York City)

cause the experimenters seemed to care. This discovery—that experimenters can unintentionally influence the results of an experiment—became immortalized as the *Hawthorne effect*. However, the Hawthorne effect only explained the impact of the experimenters' presence on the workers' behavior. The Harvard Industrial Research Group gained no real insights about what caused job behavior when there were no experimenters scurrying about.

The discovery of the Hawthorne effect did prompt the researchers to pursue a new direction of inquiry. Obviously, the workers' feelings had something to do with the way they behaved. Therefore, it was decided to find out how the workers felt about their jobs. Free-form interviews were held with thousands of Hawthorne employees. The strength or weakness of a worker's commitment to the job, it was discovered, was rooted in emotional as well as financial causes. For example, workers who disliked their supervisors generally produced less than workers who liked their supervisors. Chronically disgruntled employees often attributed their poor attitude to a single offense that occurred years before. Moreover, pouring out the tale often had a cathartic effect on the worker, reversing the individual's negative attitude towards the company.[20]

As the Hawthorne studies progressed, it became clear that social surroundings affected employee behavior. The discovery that the group was one of the strongest forces in the individual's social field came via a study in the Hawthorne Works bank wiring room. Here, the researchers found that the work group set production standards for members, despite a piecework payment scheme that rewarded individuals with high productivity. The group had basic work rules to which, with one exception, all members adhered. Three of the rules were:

1. You should not turn out too much work; if you do, you are a "rate-buster!"
2. You should not turn out too little work; if you do, you are a "chiseler."
3. You should not say anything to a supervisor which would react to the detriment of one of your associates; if you do you are a "squealer."[21]

The bank wiring room was the breakthrough that the researchers needed. Here was evidence that social being could exert a more powerful influence than economic being. Group dynamics in organizations became a major concern of the Harvard Industrial Research Group. Mayo retired to his study to turn out the Human Relations philosophy described above. Psychologists and sociologists became organization theorists overnight. The microscope was trained on the innards of organization and was to remain so for several decades.

Groups in the Laboratory

The discovery of the *informal group* prompted a number of laboratory experiments designed to find out how it functioned. In studies with student subjects, Bales and Borgatta explored the impact of group size on group cohesion and performance and found more consensus and tension in smaller groups than in larger ones.[22] The researchers also found that groups with even numbers of members have a harder time reaching agreement than those with an odd number of members. Other laboratory experiments have found that groups with five members seem to maximize member satisfaction; smaller groups tend to produce more tension among members and larger groups do not provide an adequate opportunity for everyone to participate.[23] However, the experimentally derived ideal group of five members does not necessarily mesh with or maximize satisfaction in real work situations.

In other studies, notably by Bavelas, group structure was analyzed.[24] Bavelas arranged the ideal groups of five members into four basic designs as shown in Figure 5.1.

Bavelas found that the central person tended to become the leader in each structure. Also, the patterns had differential applications to task performance. For simple tasks, the wheel was most effective. The leader could communicate with all members directly. The circle was the best design for difficult problems because it maximized interaction. Problem solutions and critical feedback came from all five members as the group

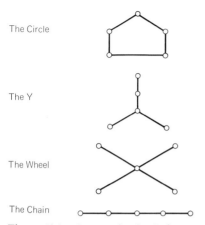

The Circle

The Y

The Wheel

The Chain

Figure 5.1   Groups in the Laboratory

worked toward a decision about what to do. More important from a Human Relations standpoint, the circle arrangement resulted in the highest level of satisfaction among group members.[25] This last finding helped explain the effectiveness with which informal groups retain the loyalty of members. Even if the workplace design precluded circular interaction, the egalitarianism usually present in informal groups provided a compensating circularity. For lunchroom chats and after-work get-togethers, workmates usually will arrange themselves in the round. This pattern, circular and satisfying, reinforces the group's solidarity in the workplace.

Bavelas's findings also lent support to the Human Relationists' prescriptions for organizational design. Worker satisfaction was a primary goal of the Human Relationists. Obviously, the organization is usually shaped like the "Y" or the "Wheel," with lower-level positions such as on assembly lines often arrayed in the "Chain." The circle is a much rarer occurrence. However, in proposing organizational redesign, the Human Relationists' emphasis on satisfaction led them to propose more circular arrangements. *Job enlargement* was an attempt to circularize the assembly line chain and participatory management sought to modify the "wheels" and the "Y's" of the organizational hierarchy.

FROM SOCIOLOGICAL
TO PSYCHOLOGICAL HUMANISM

Mayo had broken ground for a new line of inquiry into organizational behavior. He had developed a Human Relations philosophy that emphasized the cooperative potential of people in group and organizational settings. The research he instigated had brought into sharp perspective the interplay between group and organization. Still, something was lacking.

Mayo had viewed people chiefly as creatures of their surroundings. He set out to prove that humanity was not a disorganized rabble and the Hawthorne studies bore out his theses. Although Mayo felt the individual was instinctively cooperative, he had not ventured very far into the psychology of the individual. However, Mayo's criticisms of psychoanalytic theory indicate that he felt that the unsocialized individual was essentially benevolent. In discounting the Freudian notion of the Id—the primitive, infant mentality present in the psyche that seeks gratification regardless of the expense to others—Mayo wrote:

> The concealed assumption of the doctrine of original sin invalidates the psychoanalytic findings. The theory that life is a strenuous fight to subdue perversion, that the human mind is by nature pathological, is not a possible starting point for biological observation.[26]

Mayo followed up with a criticism of Freud's identification of sexual-familial factors as the primary determinants of psychological well-being. However, with the next breath, Mayo left individual psychology behind. "The unit of social explanation," he wrote, "is not the human individual, nor is it the family; it is a group of families living within an ordered relation with each other."[27]

Thus, in answer to the question of what made the individual tick, Mayo had not come up with much of an answer. He could refute the rabble hypothesis but was on shaky ground in his assertion that humans' affinity to form groups proved that people were not essentially bestial. After all, Hobbes had said that social arrangements were set up by humans to protect themselves against their own savage instincts.

Even though Mayo rejected Hobbes's concept and the Freudian notion of the Id, he offered no alternative theories concerning the intrinsic motivation of individuals. Mayo focused on environmental explanations. As a result, Mayo's approach did not offer a forceful argument that would discourage a management move to reassert "scientific management" by altering the environment in a manner designed to separate each individual from the group. After all, why not divide and conquer rather than expend resources to mollify groups that do not belong there in the first place and might very well rebel no matter how nicely you treat them.

In order to strengthen the position of the Human Relations Movement in the face of such arguments, it was important to show that the individual also was responsive to humanistic treatment. Mayo and his associates were too preoccupied with the study of groups to venture into this area. However, there was a string of psychologists, the first of whom was Kurt Lewin, that extended the Human Relations approach to include the intrinsic motivation of the individual.

Kurt Lewin, a German psychologist, provided much of the theoretical underpinning for the study of individual motivation. In a 1936 article entitled "The Psychology of Success and Failure," Lewin reported on research that showed that people tended to set levels of aspiration which, if achieved, led to the setting of even higher goals.[28] The successfully completed activity was not repeated. It had lost its motivating character. What did serve as a motivator, however, was the possibility of doing the task even better. For instance, the person who finally managed to bowl a 200 game did not go bowling again to repeat the performance. Rather, the next game was motivated by the possibility of bowling 205.

Lewin saw the level of aspiration as being determined by two factors. One was the person's actual achievements. That was the base from which the next level of aspiration was set. The second influence on the level of aspiration was the individual's social field.[29] If reaching a 205 bowling average means that the person must leave the team that he has been a member of for three years and go to a higher league that is populated, in the team's opinion, by "hustlers," the bowler may reduce these aspirations to remain with the familiar group. Like Mayo, Lewin took note of the group influence; however, Lewin's notion of achievement oriented people who value the self-esteem that success brings added significant impetus to humanistic organization theory.

Chris Argyris is a former student of Lewin's. The recipient of the first doctorate in organizational behavior, Argyris bridges two fields—psychology and sociology. His notion of psychological energy derives from Lewin's theories. A brief look at Argyris's concept demonstrates how individual motivation can be stifled by traditional organizational structure.

Psychological energy, says Argyris, is a concept designed to "explain observable human behavior that is not adequately explained by physiological energy."[30] Argyris notes that people find themselves either drained of energy or suddenly recharged when circumstances would seem to call for the opposite physical response. People can sleep all through the night and wake up tired, particularly if some distasteful task is scheduled. On the other hand, an unexpected evening invitation to something enjoyable can reenergize a person even after a grueling day at work.

Argyris states that psychological energy is the force that is activated when there is something that the individual wants and that something is attainable. Thus, psychological energy is the driving force towards psychological success. Both are internal to the individual.

Argyris did not see such opportunity for psychological success in the traditional organization. Rather, he saw the highly structured, formal work environment as a source of frustration to individuals in search of psychological success. Work procedures were fixed by management; rewards and punishments came from above. The employee was in a dependent position. Since psychological energy and psychological success were intrinsic properties, they were unlikely to be activated solely in response to external stimuli by the organization.[31]

In the failure of organizations to tap the psychological energy of individuals by providing opportunities for psychological success, Argyris saw, at best, a squandered resource and, at worst, a force that would work to undermine the organization. Individuals, frustrated in their need for psychological success, might decide to pursue it outside the organization. Thus, they would deny the organization their psychological energy, supplying only their bodies and reserving their creative efforts for other locales. Alternatively, employees may turn their psychological energy against the organization. According to Argyris, there is enough money embezzled, enough assembly line sabotage, and enough instances of diffident workers becoming enthusiastic union organizers to indicate that untapped psychological needs often come back to haunt the organization.[32]

Support from the Real World

The Mayo school and the Lewin school came at the question of employee motivation from different directions. However, there was mutual agreement that, whether the focus was the group or the individual, failure to fulfill their needs could have disastrous consequences for the organization. What the Human Relationists of both schools meant was that much of the organization's fate lay in the hands of the lower-level employees.

From his vantage point as president of New Jersey Bell, Chester Barnard seconded the motion of the Human Relationists. Barnard was a unique figure in organization theory. Whereas most theorists built upon the theories of others, Barnard's theories more or less materialized. In his works, Barnard cited almost no one. Yet, he was at the starting point of at least two distinct streams of thought about organizations: the humanist and the Simonesque. His impact was due, in large part, to the fact that his theories drew upon his personal experiences. In addition, his frank discussions of corporate life mesmerized students of organizations who were accustomed to hearing executives mouth chamber of commerce platitudes and great American success story fables. Thus, whether one was a follower of Mayo or of Lewin, Barnard was a man to be cited when he wrote,

> Authority fails because individuals, in sufficient numbers, regard the burden involved in accepting necessary orders as changing the balance

> of advantages against their interests. . . . Authority is the character of an
> order in a formal organization by virtue of which it is accepted by a
> member of the organization as governing the action he contributes.[33]

Here was an experienced administrator saying that the Human Relationists were right. The organization rested upon the consent of its members. Authority came from the bottom up. The formal structure was a nullity without the support of the people in it.

Barnard's theories added impetus to the Human Relations Movement. Moreover, Barnard's observations provided the Mayo and the Lewin schools with a vehicle for further research.

For the Mayo school, Barnard stressed the importance of compatible affiliations in the workplace. He advised the manager to avoid mixing antagonistic temperaments, nationalities, and races in forming work groups. Esprit de corps, according to Barnard, could elicit a greater degree of member commitment to the organization than money or other material rewards.[34]

For the Human Relationists of the psychological school, there was Barnard's identification of status, esteem, prestige, and opportunities for advancement and achievement as factors in an individual's decision to join and to remain in an organization.[35] Furthermore, at New Jersey Bell, managers had been sent to the University of Pennsylvania for intensive liberal arts training. Barnard's avowed purpose was to broaden their perspectives.[36] Psychological humanists were to embark on a similar course in training programs designed to modify the traditional, authoritarian outlook of management personnel.

With Barnard's authentication, the theories of Mayo and Lewin, already verified in serveral studies on organization, were ready for the transformation from explanation to remedy. It was the dawn of the age of organizational medicine and the Human Relations dispensary was to be amply stocked over the next few decades. We will not try to give a complete inventory. However, it is safe to say that the generic prescription was to make the organization better by making it nicer.

The Organization Man
Mayo and his associates emphasized that organizations were cooperative entities. Conflict was something to be avoided. With less of an emphasis on intrinsic motivation than the psychological humanists, the Mayo line prescribed amity and security rather than challenge. The organization was to be a family. It was to initiate the young, provide a comfortable and friendly environment for its adult citizens, and take care of them in their old age.

William H. Whyte's *The Organization Man* was perhaps the best illustration of the organization cast in the Mayo mold.[37] Compatibility was the key word. Conformity and security were not far behind. The organizations studied by Whyte administered psychological tests to incoming employees to ascertain their ability to get along. Spouses and other family factors of prospective employees also were considered. No uniform was prescribed, but the "button-down shirt" look prevailed. Pensions, profit sharing, and stock options sweetened the pot for employees who were expected to be on board when each matured. It was the era of the company person and the paternal organization. IBM and AT&T are excellent examples of this development. Even today, many employees of these two firms consider themselves IBM people or Bell people and give little thought to alternative career paths. This sense of family is, of course, what Mayo was aiming at.

INTERPERSONAL COMPETENCE

The psychological humanists were following a course somewhat more radical than the one that led to organization man. To them, organization man was merely the product of the traditional organization with an overlay of paternalism. Benevolence did not motivate organization members by providing an opportunity for psychological success. It merely made the employees more comfortable in their dependence.

Argyris was in the forefront of the theoretical drive to go beyond benevolence in organizational redesign. Organizations, said Argyris, needed to develop "interpersonal competence" among its members. However, Argyris's interpersonal competence was not the country club variety. Rather than a social facade allowing for routine trivialities to be exchanged as orders from above were carried out, Argyris's notion of interpersonal competence called for the facades to be abolished. Organizational decisions would take place in an environment where individuals related to each other and not to their roles.[38]

In continuing his emphasis on the intrinsic value of the individual, Argyris adds a few more concepts to psychological success and psychological energy. Each of us, says Argyris, has a self-image; that is, personal characteristics we are conscious of. The problem with self-image, for most of us, is that it is neither what we would like to be (ideal-self) nor what we are (self). However, to attain ideal-self we first have to understand self, and to understand self we need the help of others.

Argyris sees this problem as central to organizations. Formal position and authority often distort the awareness of occupants and silence others who see what the occupant does not but are afraid to speak. This combination of self-deception and fear can lead to grave problems. Part of Argyris's remedy is to play down the formal aspect of organization and convince people that they have a lot to learn from each other. Even if it is painful, knowing one's self is a requisite step to a better self.

According to Argyris, if individual self-esteem is present, the first step towards greater self-awareness sets off a chain reaction. If the person has self-esteem, critical appraisals from others will be accepted without hostility. Thus, the person with self-esteem can say, "nobody's perfect," and *mean it*. Defensiveness in others is reduced and they feel more esteemed. In addition, people will add this new information to their self-awareness inventory. It will make them better able to deal with the world, thereby further adding to their self-esteem.

The actual outgrowth of Argyris's constructs was *sensitivity train ing* for organization members. Training groups ("T-Groups") of managers were sent to a site outside the organization and, through role playing and discussion, sought to increase their interpersonal competence. In 1947, the National Training Laboratories were set up in Bethel, Maine. Brought into being by Kurt Lewin, Ronald Lippitt, Leland Bradford, and John R. K. French, among others, this first sensitivity training facility for organization members was the Mecca of the psychological Human Relationists. At Bethel traditional defensive organizational attitudes were "unfrozen," subjected to analysis, modified as self-awareness increased, and refrozen into a more open and aware attitude on the part of managers, who then returned to seed the organization.[39]

From a perspective similar to Argyris's, but somewhat less optimistic, Rensis Likert developed the concept of the *linking pin*.[40] The linking pin is an individual whose function is to act as a cohesive force between various parts of the organization. Part of the linking pin's job is to serve as a liaison between the formal organization and informal groups. In addition, a linking pin can bridge gaps in the formal structure. For example, operations personnel tend to keep their distance from research personnel. Also, newly promoted individuals are often advised by associates to tone down friendships with those who used to be peers but are now subordinates. The linking pin, however, has membership in both formal and informal organizational factions as well as the ability to feel as comfortable in a blue collar bar as at a suburban cocktail party. Linking pins are carriers of messages that are not entrusted to normal organizational channels. They will ensure that the message is not intercepted by enemies of the sender. If requested, they will withhold the name of their source. Although somewhat furtively, they link the organization together. The organization that must rely heavily on linking pins obviously has not scaled the heights of interpersonal competence. However, Likert considers the linking pin as a step in the right direction and that the participatory organization would legitimize the role.

THE HIERARCHY OF NEEDS

The psychological humanists advanced numerous concepts to explain motivation. However, they lacked an Elton Mayo—a unifying philosopher who could serve as a touchstone for those in the field. In 1954, in the person of Abraham Maslow, a psychologist who had never studied an organization in his life, they found their man.

In his book, *Motivation and Personality,* Maslow sought to "enlarge (the) conception of the human personality by reaching to the 'higher' levels of human nature."[41] In doing so, Maslow excoriated those who attributed individual behavior to base motivations. Mayo's target had been the economists; Maslow's aimed at those in the fields of psychology and psychiatry who, in their search for the underlying forces that motivate people to act, arrived at self-interest, survival, and the satisfaction of basic physiological drives such as hunger and sex. Maslow accepted these forces as partial motivators of human behavior; however, he did not see them as primary forces in the modern world. Food was only a motivator for hungry people. The well-fed person would seek out other things that would then replace hunger as the impetus to action.

Maslow also criticized psychologists who searched for the smallest part of the human psyche. This course, asserted Maslow, blinded the searcher to the fact that no individual part stands alone. Furthermore, since the fulfillment of elemental needs was readily observable, there tended to be a preoccupation with their study. To get food, rats ran mazes. Subjected to sensory deprivation, subjects, human and animal, became mentally lifeless. The search for the smallest part of behavior via the easiest route, according to Maslow, had led to simplistic and partial explanations of human behavior.[42]

Reductionism and expedience were not Maslow's only charges. If that were so, the debate would have been one of competing scientific methodologies. However, Maslow also charged opponents with a failure to act as scientists. They were predisposed to view humans as beasts. It was not merely that they saw the whole as being built upon easily understandable parts; or that they tended to pursue the experimental technology that promised clear findings without a measure of their importance. According to Maslow, they were basically unscientific in the first place. Going so far as to call them paranoid, Maslow asserted that their research was based on a pessimistic view of human nature that tainted both theory and methodology. To be sure, if one viewed humans as beasts, Maslow cautioned, there was no reason that experiments with rats could not be used to explain why human beings act as they do.

To Maslow, it was no more valid to say that humans were exclusively social animals than it was to assert that humans were merely biological animals. Biological needs explained some behavior as did environment. However, neither explained it all. In fact, those who set up society as the major behavioral determinant were attacked by Maslow for accepting the Hobbesian view of humans. Maslow did not reject socialization as a determinant of behavior. However, he did reject the premise that socialization was a device to mute human instincts that were savage, selfish, and destructive.[43]

For instance, Maslow questioned whether love was exclusively a gift of society. He noted the anthropological studies of Margaret Mead in Bali. There, adults were unloving toward the children, as ethnic norms required. However, the children were horribly put out by the lack of affection. They demanded love—an emotion they had not seen in their environment. This, concluded Maslow, was evidence that the need for affection was an intrinsic need, not a socialized one.[44] It was the same as the need to eat and the need to feel safe. Yet, said Maslow, those who studied society's effect on instinctual human behavior often started from the assumption that society existed to teach love.

Maslow questioned even the metaphors that had been used to portray the natural instincts of humans, charging that these metaphors were based on a Darwinian interpretation of human nature. Why, he asked, choose vultures, tigers, snakes, and wolves to characterize the "animal within us" when extremely intelligent species such as dolphins and apes exhibit a greater degree of cooperation than competition?[45]

After this skillfully argued attack, Maslow felt obligated to come up with an alternative or a synthesis and he did. Humans, according to Maslow, are motivated by a *Hierarchy of Needs*. By needs, Maslow means things intrinsic to humans that must be fulfilled in order to bring about a state of satisfaction. By hierarchy, Maslow means that certain basic needs had to be fulfilled first as a precondition to satisfying higher needs. In Maslow's scheme humans are motivated initially by physiological needs. Once satisfied, physiological needs give way to safety needs; as safety needs are satisfied, the needs for love and belonging are activated. When the needs for love and belonging are satisfied, self-esteem becomes the primary motivator of human behavior. Finally, when esteem needs are gratified, the person can turn to self-actualization. *Self-actualization* is the full realization of the individual's creative potential.[46]

The thrust of Maslow's thesis may be more evident if we try to imagine the Hierarchy of Needs operating in more concrete circumstances. If a small band of soldiers are starving to death in hostile territory, they will attempt to steal food from the enemy even though they may lose their lives in the process. Their immediate physiological needs demand that they seek food. However, if the theft is successful, the soldiers will quickly seek a safe hiding place. Starvation is no longer the primary threat; death at the hands of hostile individuals is. Hiding is a response to safety needs.

Assume now that both the hostile forces and the soldiers' own army vacate the territory. With no promise of rescue, the soldiers will seek out compatriots who also have been left behind. The need for belonging is at work here. Well fed and safe, the soldiers' need for companionship becomes the primary motivator. If a group of stragglers does form, the soldiers, satisfied in their need for companionship, become motivated by their desire for self-esteem. Each soldier wants to be a valued and respected member of the group. One soldier may take the lead by demonstrating a keen knowledge of survival in the jungle and putting it to work for the benefit of the group. Should this bring respect, the soldier may then turn to self-actualization, the need to realize one's full potential. In the case of the soldier, it may be the application of mechanical skills to construct a radio out of material left behind by the enemy. Even if only a receiving unit can be built, precluding the possibility of summoning help, the soldier builds the radio because it becomes a personal challenge. Thus, the soldier strives to fulfill a self-actualization need. The soldier is no longer motivated by physiological needs or survival needs. Neither does the need for belonging or acclaim serve as motivation. Rather, it is a personal desire to excel, to test the limits of one's capabilities.

SCORECARDS FOR MANAGEMENT

Soon self-actualization was the rage of many Human Relations types. However, the most wholesale espousal of Maslow's needs hierarchy was offered by Douglas McGregor. McGregor classified management styles into two categories, *Theory X* and *Theory Y*. Theory X was the traditional management approach. McGregor saw Theory X management was proceeding from several propositions. First, management as responsible for directing the enterprise. Second, employee behavior must be modified to fit the needs of the organization. Third, keeping the employees on the right track required constant management vigilance.[47] McGregor felt that underlying these propositions was an essentially dismal view of human beings. According to McGregor, the Theory X manager saw the average worker as,

> (naturally) indolent - he works as little as possible. He lacks ambition, dislikes responsibility, prefers to be led. He is inherently self-centered, indifferent to organizational needs. He is by nature resistant to change. He is gullible (and) not very bright. . . .[48]

McGregor did not dispute that managers may have had experience that would tend to support this ungratifying view of workers. However, he claimed that structuring organizations in the classical manner was the very cause of the observed behavior. Traditional management tended to put people in strong behavior-restricting cages. When, naturally enough, individuals tried to escape, executives would nod knowingly and write up another rule to strengthen the cage.

McGregor's alternative to Theory X was Theory Y. Based largely on Maslow's work, Theory Y encouraged organizations to eliminate obstacles to individual development. After providing the means to fulfill their members' physiological and safety needs, organizations should seek to make opportunities available for the fulfillment of social, esteem, and self-fulfillment needs. Only in this way could organizations get the most out of employees. In essence, Theory Y was the underlying philosophy that managers would have to adopt in order to commit themselves to a more loosely structured organization. McGregor sets forth Theory Y in the following manner:

> People are not by nature passive or resistant to organizational needs. They have become so as a result of experience in organizations.
>
> The motivation, the potential for development, the capacity for assuming responsibility, the readiness to direct behavior towards organizational goals are all present in people. Management does not put them there. It is a responsibility of management to make it possible for people to recognize and develop these human characteristics for themselves.
>
> The essential task of management is to arrange organizational conditions and methods of operations so that people can achieve their own goals best by directing their own efforts toward organizational objectives.[49]

To operationalize Theory Y, McGregor proposed that organizations decentralize their operations and delegate authority and responsibility downward. He also proposed that organizations enlarge lower-level jobs, encourage employee participation in decision making, and allow a self-evaluation of performance by organization members. McGregor's reformulation of Maslow's theories into a blueprint for organizational design set the stage for a period of experimentation in which many organizations embraced the Theory Y approach with varying degrees of success.

Theory X and Theory Y were joined by several other devices that sought to measure the management style of organizations. Rensis Likert designed one of the most thoroughgoing measures. Likert strung together a series of questions to be put to organizational employees. They covered the following six management characteristics; the range of possible answers is indicated in parentheses:

1. Character of motivational forces (Threats through achievement)

2. Character of communication processes (Top-down through all-around)
3. Character of interaction-influence processes (Paranoia through trust)
4. Character of decision-making processes (Hierarchical-unilateral through participative)
5. Character of goal setting or ordering (Fiat through group determination)
6. Character of control processes (Police state through self-policing)[50]

Depending on the answers, the organization management style fell into one of four categories: (1) exploitative-authoritative; (2) benevolent-authoritative; (3) consultative; and (4) participative. In a prototypical exploitative-authoritarian organizational setting the fear of dismissal is always present, orders come from above, reflexive and unquestioning obedience is expected, suggestions are frowned upon, and employee behavior is closely watched. At the other extreme, the participative organization uses individual achievement as a motivator, does not allow hierarchy to dictate who speaks to whom, builds trustworthy relations, opens decision-making processes, and delegates control responsibility to individuals. Likert used his questionnaire to diagnose the organization and then prescribe therapies to bring the organization to a more participative management style. Although an organization could rank as participative in one area and as benevolent-authoritative in another, Likert strongly felt that consistency was important for organizational coordination and that participative consistency was best.

Likert's book, *New Patterns of Management,* is one of the seminal works on organizational development.[51] Organizational development, or "OD," seeks to change the essential character and philosophy of organizations through sensitivity training for executives, increased participation for employees, and decentralization of the organizational structure. The ideal goal is a pure participative organization in which all members are satisfied, highly motivated, and individualistic. The group and the organization are also bound together by common purpose.

In more limited applications, organizational development is serially applied to problems. Of course, eliminating one serious problem area is no guarantee that another problem will not arise elsewhere in the organization. However, organizations may not want to pay the price of everlasting peace. It is expensive and may be disruptive—leaders may not like the idea of being led by workers. Moreover, it is still not clear whether an organization at peace is more effective than one that is anx-

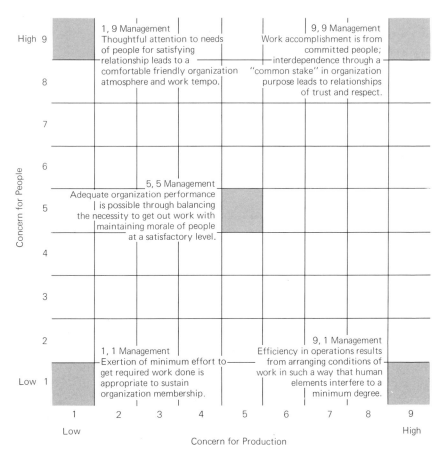

Figure 5.2 The Managerial Grid. SOURCE: Robert R. Blake and Jane S. Mouton, "Organization Excellence through Effective Management Behavior," *Manage*, Vol. 20, No. 2, 1967, pp. 42–47. Used with permission.

iety ridden. Lean and hungry is, by no means, a discarded concept in organizations.

Another diagnostic tool applied to organizations was the Blake and Mouton "managerial grid."[52] Blake and Mouton analyzed organizations in terms of "concern for production" and "concern for people." A score of 1 was the lowest for each category and 9 was the highest. Thus, a production score of 9 and a people score of 1 meant that the organization was obsessed with efficiency and expected people to fit into the organizational design with no questions asked. With a production score of 1 and a people score of 9, an organization's first priority was a comfortable, low-pressure work environment. For instance, an international organization might tend toward this approach to reduce the possibility of cross-cultural antagonisms surfacing as a result of organizationally induced stress. The experience of one of the authors at the United Nations Secretariat, where sociability is encouraged, seems to bear this out. As with Likert, however, Blake and Mouton offer not only a diagnosis but also a prescription. Their goal is an organization that scores a 9 on the production scale *and* a 9 on the people scale. In an organization that scores a 9 in each category there is mutual trust among organization members, the organization goals become the members' goals, and efficiency and satisfaction unite to enhance effectiveness (see Figure 5.2).

EXPERIMENTS IN ORGANIZATIONAL CHANGE

The prescriptions of the Human Relations movement have been applied in many organizational settings. However, nowhere have they been tried so comprehensively or over as long a period of time as in the Harwood Companies. Alfred Marrow, the head of the company, earned his doctorate in psychology under the aegis of Kurt Lewin. Thus, as early as 1938, experiments were being conducted at Harwood under the direction of leading human relations experts and with the full, knowledgeable, and enthusiastic support of the chief executive. The experiments continued, on and off, for over 30 years. Each new wave of humanist theory was put to the test at Harwood. The results were uniformly successful.

Since Harwood is a textile manufacturing company, the type of production oriented business that has been considered by some as inappropriate for participative approaches, the findings are significant. At the least, they raise the possibility that the full commitment of top management may lead to the successful implementation of the participative design in most cases.

Through the 1930s and 1940s, the Harwood experiments first analyzed job design from the standpoint of the psychological impact on employees. Researchers also initiated worker participation in the structuring of the work process and delegated to supervisors the responsibility for research into the company's personnel policies. Each innovation was successful. The first was designed to reduce the high turnover rate among new employees. It was found that new employees experienced deep frustration in trying to advance from the beginning workers' production rate to the expected rate of experienced employees, which was set at 60 units per hour. Early on in the training period, employee production increased rapidly; however, progress slowed around the 50 units mark and employees started to feel that they could never attain the 60 units figure. To escape these feelings of frustration and failure, employees left the firm. To reduce this turnover, Harwood scrapped the 60 units goal and substituted incremental goals. Successful training progress then consisted of producing two or three units more than the previous level. In this manner, most employees eventually reached the 60 units mark without experiencing the kind of frustration that caused their predecessors to depart.[53]

Harwood's experiments with worker participation in job design were equally successful. At Harwood, the need to accommodate changes in fashion and seasonal apparel caused frequent job redesign. The frequent relearning annoyed employees. Harwood, therefore, allowed a group of workers to participate in planning the transition to a new job design. Another group of workers underwent the identical job transformation without participating in the planning. The result was that the participation group made the transition smoothly and quickly reached a high production level on the new job. The second group did not adjust well and, in fact, deliberately restricted production to protest the change that had been imposed on them. On the basis of this experience, Harwood institutionalized worker participation in job redesign.[54]

Harwood was also an arly locale for sensitivity training. Harwood managers were brought together to discuss their problems and get a different perspective on their roles. One way this was done was to have managers act out the worker-manager interplay. This gave the managers a better understanding of how they looked to others and what it felt like to be on the receiving end of orders. This program also resulted in greater productivity by the employees of the managers who received the training program.[55]

Harwood also used an approach to change employee attitudes that is somewhat unique in organizations. Rather than laying down the official company line, Harwood let the employees find out for themselves. The personnel staff at Harwood felt strongly that older employees were slower learners and inferior workers. Top management thought differently but suspected that the attitude would be immune to executive fiat. Thus, the company assigned the personnel staff to the job of ascertaining just how inefficient the elderly workers were. The staff had full responsibility for the design of the study. When the results showed that the older workers outperformed the younger ones, the staff members, having no one to believe but themselves, reversed their attitude about the hiring of middle-aged workers.[56]

By the 1960s, Harwood was ready for a considerable experiment. It had purchased a large competitor, the Weldon Manufacturing Company. Physically, Harwood and Weldon were alike. Managerially, however, Weldon was chaos. Weldon's chief executive was extremely authoritative. He ruled with an iron hand; played off his subordinates against each other; and set a tone of management that had most of the managers twitching with paranoia. 40 percent indicated a desire to get out. Absenteeism and turnover among line personnel was high. The company was in bad financial shape. It was time to work a change in Weldon and fast; Marrow called in Rensis Likert to spearhead an army of behavioral scientists.[57]

Likert's first task was to rate Weldon on his organizational scale. Weldon straddled the borderline between exploitative-authoritative and benevolent-authoritative. Harwood, of course, was firmly in the participative category. Likert's next step was to organize an intensive program of sensitivity training to melt the authoritarian and distrustful attitudes of Weldon's management. Only Weldon's chief executive held out. He was finally dragged to a session where key subordinates, including his son and son-in-law, accused him of manipulation. The chief executive accused his former subordinates of being conspiring, traitorous ingrates; vowed never to change his style; and stalked out. With that outburst, his career ended. With the former owner out of the way, participation was extended from management down through line employees. Subsequent reports show that Weldon placed in the consultative category (as rated by the employees) and was continuing to make progress.

HUMAN RELATIONS
MOVEMENT: CRITIQUES FROM WITHIN

The Weldon experiments mark the zenith of the Human Relations Movement. The last major psychological humanist, Frederick Herzberg, reminds one of a Roman during the decline of the empire, still a citizen but critical of almost everything.[58]

To Herzberg, most efforts, Human Relations included, to motivate employees were variants of the Kick-In-The-Ass (KITA) approach. According to Herzberg, "KITA does not lead to motivation, it leads to movement." Threats, enticements, pleasant surroundings, a clublike relationship among employees, sensitivity training, job participation, and employee counseling all made Herzberg's KITA list. Each, according to Herzberg, did no more than boost the employees battery. Employees did not become self-charging. Rather, they put forth effort in spurts in response to inducements offered by management. However, when the inducement lost its appeal, employees once again were discontented and poorly motivated. Thus, the pay raise or the fringe benefit soon lost its motivating force. Employees started looking for the next round of inducements. Job enlargement or challenging assignments made Herzberg's list of KITA techniques because the employee had little control. The kick still was coming from outside. According to Herzberg, the only way successfully to motivate employees was to make them self-generating. Thus, according to Herzberg, "it is only when (the employee) has his own generator that we can talk about motivation. He then needs no outside stimulation. He wants to do it."[59]

The problem Herzberg saw with most motivation schemes was that they were directed at the individual's animal needs. Motivators directed at biological needs did not have an enduring impact, according to Herzberg, because they stimulated an equilibrating response in individuals. KITA involved either a threat or a temptation present in the work environment; that is, a potential change in the "hygiene" factors—salary, status, security, or task. Initially, individuals responded. However, once safe or satiated, individuals relaxed; they adjusted rather than achieved. According to Herzberg, real motivation could only occur if the job was designed to elicit self-motivation. The way to do this, noted Herzberg, was to build into the job achievement, recognition for achievement, responsibility, and the opportunity for growth or advancement.

Herzberg criticized most job enlargement schemes as being "horizontal." Horizontal enlargement was often no more than a physical manipulation of the work situation. Quotas were raised to "challenge" the employee. Employees were rotated through different jobs, each one as stultifying as the next. "Responsibilities" added to existing jobs turned out to be yet another mundane chore. Such activity, wrote Herzberg, "merely enlarges the meaninglessness of the job."[60]

Herzberg's alternative to job enlargement was "job enrichment." Job enrichment added a "vertical" load to the job. A vertically loaded job would have fewer controls but more individual accountability, give more "start to finish" tasks to the employee, and permit greater employee control over the pace, hours, location, and process of the work. In an experiment involving stockholder correspondents in a large corporation, Herzberg successfully applied vertical enlargement techniques.

Can Workers Manage?

To Herzberg, an underlying humanist assumption was that the dissatisfied worker was somehow sick, a charge not without foundation. When they discovered that work groups vetoed the production dictates of management, the Human Relationists considered this show of autonomy as a symptom of organizational illness rather than well-being. Therefore, those managers responsible for causing or correcting this aberrant behavior were instructed in the arts of humanism.

However, in disagreeing with the humanist view that group production decisions were pathological, critics such as Herzberg asserted that control over the work environment was a legitimate need of groups and individuals. Considering group recalcitrance as dysfunctional, it was also

charged, indicated a bureaucratic bias on the part of humanist researchers.

Erich Fromm pointed out that Mayo revealed his personal biases
when he chose to title his seminal work "The Human Problems of an
Industrial Civilization" rather than the "Industrial Problems of Man."[61]
Thus, the essential question was: "Who gets integrated into whom?"
From the Human Relations standpoint, it was the group that was to be
integrated into the organization. The process was to proceed with gentil-
ity and sensitivity. Nonetheless, one aim of the process was to ensure that
work groups did not negate organizational goals. Defining what was in
the overall interests of everyone was a function of the organization, not
of the group.

The notion that the group may have a better understanding than
management of what constitutes good job design received impetus from
the studies of the Tavistock Institute in London. Tavistock was extremely
concerned with the impact of technology (machines *and* work processes)
on organization. One of the key studies at Tavistock concerned the English coal mining industry where the introduction of new technology
made an assembly line operation out of tasks previously performed by
two-worker teams.[62] Under the new system, workers were assigned to
five task categories with five different rates of pay. Responsibility for
coordination and task definition shifted from the workers to management. The results were disastrous. Production was poor; absenteeism
was high. Workers often quarreled. Unhappy workers left the mines in
search of other employment.

The Tavistock researchers concluded that the new work arrangement was at the root of the problem. The introduction of five different
pay scales, where one had existed previously, caused the work force to
split into factions. The assembly line eliminated the cohesive and coordinative functions performed by the traditional work groups. As a result,
the operation flew apart.

In an attempt to correct the situation, the Tavistock researchers
reintroduced work teams to the mines. Wages for the team members
were equalized. The team was given the responsibility of task distribution. The full mining cycle was again assigned to the group. Output
increased and personnel problems decreased.

The Tavistock experiments demonstrated that there were alternatives to a strict organizational or technological approach to problem
solving. In the mines, technology was not ignored. However, machines
were modified to fit workers rather than workers being modified to fit
machines. This was a new turn of events. The early Human Relationists
proceeded from the question, "How can we help the workers adjust to
the organization?" Tavistock and similar studies, on the other hand,
seemed to ask, "How can the organization adjust to the worker?"

Refocusing on Executives

By the 1960s, the attention of the organizational psychologists was concentrated on the achievement urge. However, as studies zeroed in on achievement, they tended to cast doubts on the proposition that it was an intrinsic human need.

In one experiment, David McClelland asked managers and professionals in different countries to view a drawing of a worker tinkering at a workbench next to a family portrait and to write a story about what they saw.[63] The achievement-oriented persons saw the worker inventing something or thinking through an engineering problem. Less achievement-oriented types tended to see the worker doing some relatively unimportant task while daydreaming about a weekend trip with the family. Predictably, the achievers tended to be the higher-level managerial types. The respondents whose stories centered on family activities tended to be professionals and lower-level managers.

McClelland's findings were consistent from country to country. Although the respondents in some countries showed a lower achievement response, overall the gap between top managers and professionals held. Furthermore, political ideology seemed to be insignificant. In Communist Poland, high-level managers saw as much "achievement imagery" in the drawing as their counterparts in the United States. For those in public service, there was an additional piece of good news. High-level public administrators were as achievement oriented as top executives in the private sector.

McClelland's findings indicated that task was related to an individual's achievement urge. Although McClelland argued to the contrary, his findings could also be construed to mean that achievement was inherent in certain jobs rather than intrinsic to all individuals. Several studies by Lyman Porter added to this uncertainty. Individual feelings of esteem, autonomy, and self-actualization, according to Porter, were less prevalent on the lower rungs of organizations than at the higher levels.[64]

Porter asked managers at various organizational levels to indicate the amount of security, comradeship, esteem, autonomy, and self-actualization associated with their position. The managers were also asked how much of each *should* be associated with their position. The difference between what was received and what was expected was taken as a measure of satisfaction with the job.

Variants of Porter's studies controlled for age, company size, individual attitudes toward achievement, and cultural factors. No significant changes were recorded.[65] Although the Human Relationists cited Porter's findings as proof that organizations needed to strive for interpersonal competence at the lower levels, the Porter studies were a double-edged sword. Opponents of the humanistic approach used the studies to question whether self-actualization was possible in jobs that were structured and routine. If the obstacle to psychological success was the task itself, increased interpersonal competence was unlikely to lead to more satisfaction. Further, critics argued, perhaps some people did not have esteem and achievement needs; or perhaps these needs were minimal for others. And some people, the critics warned, were surely content to seek their fulfillment outside the organization. Thus, they seek out the routine, mechanical task. One might better satisfy such individuals by concentrating on material inducements, rather than attempting, through Human Relations approaches, to fulfill needs that do not exist in the workplace.

In the 1970s, the variety of personality types continue to be emphasized. Michael Maccoby, with his sights trained on the higher echelons of organization, finds "company men," "jungle fighters," and "gamesmen."[66] Company men are loyal, hard-working, and security minded in the mold of Whyte's organization man. Jungle fighters—Maccoby assigned Presidents Johnson and Nixon to this category—are snarling entrepreneurs who see the world as a kill or be killed proposition. According to Maccoby, both the company man and the jungle fighter are losing ground to the gamesman in the race for organizational leadership. Because he is innovative and adventurous the gamesman is more attractive to organization owners than corporate man. Lacking the unpredictable vindictiveness and obsessive suspicion of the jungle fighter, the gamesman gets more out of personnel; workers do not have to fear that every step might be their last. Although Maccoby sees more gamesmen assuming leadership roles, he stresses that the organization could utilize all types. The jungle fighter, for instance, handles dirty work, such as firing people, very well. The company man is a valuable check on the gamesman's propensity to go for broke.

The message of Maccoby and others is that the employee market is filled with a varied array of merchandise. Rather than adjusting operations to accommodate a single commodity market of self-achievers, Maccoby advises organizations to shop for the human resources that will fit in with its own operating style.

Maccoby's advice is consonant with that of critics of human relations who had been warning against an overemphasis on the psychological health of organization members. The internal tranquility of the organization is important, according to these critics, but so too is the environment.[67] If the customers of constituents are not satisfied, the organization might very well wither. A company that manufactures soap according to a rigid production schedule in a highly competitive industry may find that its production technology demands reflexive laborers. A drive towards the self-actualization of such labor may bring about production inefficiencies that devastate the firm's competitive position.

The response from the Human Relationists was more of a holding action than an assault. Abraham Maslow conceded that satisfaction may not always have a positive effect on the organization's bottom line.[68] However, he also argued that society was a net beneficiary of humanistic management. A self-actualizing worker would be a healthier citizen. The Theory Y employees were not likely to beat their spouses to release repressed aggression built up on the job. More Theory Y management meant fewer societal resources squandered on correcting the ills caused by Theory X management. If benefits external to the organization were factored in, argued Maslow, humanistic management would show a profit. Whatever the merits of Maslow's arguments, however, they were less than compelling to organizations.

Things were not much brighter for the Human Relationists on the motivation front. The theories of V. H. Vroom concerning worker motivation were gaining currency among organization theorists.[69] Vroom reinjected calculation and rationality into motivation. Humans ranked their desired outcomes and plotted and evaluated the paths leading to them. The possibility that the individual would fail to perceive the connection between a given path and a desired goal was the basic element in Vroom's formula. Vroom also allowed that the individual may not be goal oriented. Thus, Vroom's analysis reintroduced to the study of motivation a more hard-nosed appraisal of human motives. Some individuals would respond rationally to various stimuli; others irrationally. And some would not respond at all.

CONTINGENCY THEORY

One upshot of the critiques was *contingency theory*. Several studies suggested that organization design should be a function of the task to be performed. Depending on the circumstances, Theory X or Theory Y may be appropriate.

A study by John Morse and Jay Lorsch found that where the management style fit the nature of the work the organization was more efficient *and* the employees were more satisfied.[70] The subjects of the study were two manufacturing plants and two research firms. One manufacturing plant and one research firm had a rigid, rulebound, Theory X mode of operation. The other plant and research firm utilized a more participative, Theory Y approach. The Theory X manufacturing plant was more efficient than its Theory Y counterpart. In the research firms, however, the participative approach of Theory Y was more effective than the rigidity of the Theory X approach.

In both the efficient Theory X manufacturing plant and the efficient Theory Y research facility, the employees reported a higher feeling of competence than in the less effective firms. According to Morse and

Lorsch, this indicated that the effective firms had arrived at a better fit among task, management style, and employee attitudes. In the research firm, environmental demands were uncertain and the firm's researchers were inclined toward imaginative and inventive work. By cultivating this attitude via noninterference, the successful research organization remained ready to respond flexibly and creatively to sudden and unique demands from the environment. The successful manufacturing firm, on the other hand, knew what the environmental demands were, had the technology in hand to meet these demands, and needed a work force that would do the job put before it. Thus, its management was production oriented and sought to get the most efficient use out of its employees. The employees at the manufacturing plant had less need for independence than their counterparts in the research firm. They fit well into the rigid scheme and achieved a sense of competence through their work.

The above example suggests another question that might be asked about the applicability of the Human Relations approach to organizations. If it is not appropriate for all organizations, is it not possible that humanistic management may not be appropriate for all parts of a single organization? At the upper reaches of most organizations there are management cadres who are in positions similar to the employees of the research facility. They must stand ready to redirect the organization in response to demands from the environment. Furthermore, their work is likely to be varied and primarily involve problem solving. Their solutions, whether good or bad, are likely to have an immediate and visible impact. If problems are successfully handled, feedback is likely to be in the form of monetary rewards or additional responsibilities. Clearly, conditions conducive to self-actualization often exist at the upper levels of organizations. In many organizations, however, the soil is not so fertile at the lower levels. Somebody has to produce the widgets and process the papers; such tasks often are uninspiring or unrewarding.

In the vein of Morse and Lorsch, Warren Bennis predicts that organizations of the future will be staffed at the lower levels by persons who place a low priority on self-actualization.[71] At the higher levels, however, Bennis predicts increasing opportunities for self-actualization. Interpersonal competence will increase because organizations will be too complex for one individual to know everything. Management will be, of necessity, interactive. Bennis also sees organizations becoming more dependent on quick responses to environmental conditions. Indeed, he sees organizations forming to tackle problems in the environment and dissolving upon their solution.

This impermanence will eliminate the debilitating maintenance and political functions incumbent upon executives of organizations striving for immortality. The managers of such organizations, their esteem needs gratified by recognition from professional colleagues, will be placed in almost a pure self-actualizing situation.

What this bodes for the nonexpert, nonprofessional types of the future is another matter. The probability that most will have to seek self-awareness and achievement outside of the work environment has been advanced by several of the "post-industrial prophets." The organization will merely be the place to go to earn money to buy things of value to the individual.

SUMMARY

In this chapter, we have reviewed a number of approaches to employee motivation. We began with the straightforward notions of the efficiency-minded Taylorites and moved through the complex and sophisticated approaches of the behavioral scientists. We have seen the research microscope trained on the smallest elements of human interaction in organization and the findings extrapolated into a profile of the organization's management style. To this day, these studies represent the most extensive attempts to analyze the interplay between workers and organizations.

The Human Relations Movement remains a watershed, even though recent research has focused more on efficiency, and less on satisfaction, in the work environment. In the next chapter, which addresses public personnel policies, the efficiency criteria for job design will be much in evidence. This focus is not due primarily to the inapplicability of motivational research, but to the fact that precise task definitions and highly formalized employment practices are the signal design characteristics of the public organization.

KEY TERMS AND CONCEPTS

Anomic
Hawthorne effect
Hierarchy of Needs
Human Relations Movement
Informal group
Interpersonal competence
Job enlargement

Linking pin
Rabble hypothesis
Self-actualization
Sensitivity training
Taylorism
Theory X and Theory Y

NOTES

1. Frederick W. Taylor, *Scientific Management* (New York: Harper & Row, 1947).
2. See David Schuman, *Bureaucracies, Organizations, and Administration: A Political Primer* (New York: Macmillan, 1976) for a transcript of one of Taylor's economic enlightenment lectures and Schuman's comments.
3. See Theodore Roszak, *Where the Wasteland Ends: Politics & Transcendence in*

Post-Industrial Society (Garden City, New York: Doubleday (Anchor Books) 1973), for a ringing denunciation of where science has brought us and our ways of thinking.

4. Alfred DeGrazia, ed., *Robert Michels, First Lectures in Political Sociology* (Minneapolis: University of Minnesota Press, 1949), p. 27. The book is a transcription of lectures given by Robert Michels. Here Michels is quoting Maffeo Pantaleoni.

5. Ibid.

6. Ibid., p. 12, Adam Ferguson, "An Essay on the History of Civil Society" is Michels's source.

7. Ibid., p. 25.

8. Pareto quoted in ibid., p. 35.

9. Emile Durkheim, *Suicide* (New York: Free Press, 1951).

10. Ibid., p. 284.

11. Elton Mayo, *The Social Problems of An Industrial Civilization* (Andover: Andover Press, 1945), chapter II.

12. Ibid., p. 39.

13. Ibid., pp. 35–36.

14. Ibid., p. 42.

15. Elton Mayo, *The Human Problems of An Industrial Civilization* (Cambridge: Murray Printing Company, 1946), pp. 136–137.

16. Ibid., chapter VI. Several times Mayo mentions that a society composed of antagonistic, nonintegrated groups is ripe for a Hitler.

17. Ibid.

18. Mayo, *Social Problems*, pp. 40–52.

19. Fritz J. Roethlisberger, "The Road Back to Sanity," in Richard J. Stillman II, ed., *Public Administration: Concepts and Cases* (Boston: Houghton Mifflin, 1976), pp. 103–111. The description of the Hawthorne experiments is drawn mainly from this source. However, almost every book written by the members of the Harvard Industrial Research Group contains an account.

20. Mayo, *Social Problems*, pp. 77–78.

21. Roethlisberger, "Road Back to Sanity," p. 109.

22. R. F. Bales and E. F. Borgatta, "Size of Group as a Factor in the Interaction Profile," in A. P. Hare, Borgatta, and Bales, eds., *Small Group* (New York: Knopf, 1961), pp. 396–413.

23. P. E. Slater, "Contrasting Correlates of Group Size," *Sociometry* 21 (1958): 129–139.

24. Alex Bavelas, "Communication Patterns in Task Oriented Groups," *Journal of the Acoustical Society of America* 22 (1951): 725–730.

25. M. Shaw, "Communication Networks," in L. Berkowitz ed., *Advances in Experimental Social Psychology*, vol. I (New York: Academic Press, 1964).

26. Mayo, *Human Problems*, p. 152.

27. Ibid.

28. Kurt Lewin, "The Psychology of Success and Failure," in Timothy W. Costello and Sheldon S. Zalkind, eds., *Psychology in Administration: A Research Orientation* (Englewood Cliffs, N.J.: Prentice-Hall, Inc., 1963), pp. 67–72.

29. Ibid., p. 71.

30. Chris Argyris, *Integrating the Individual and the Organization* (New York: Wiley, 1964), p. 21.

31. Ibid., p. 38.

32. Chris Argyris, "A Few Words in Advance," in Alfred Marrow, ed., *The Failure of Success* (New York: Amacom, 1972), pp. 3–7.

33. Chester A. Barnard, *The Functions of the Executive* (Cambridge: Winthrop Publishers, Inc., 1938), chapter XIII.
34. Chester A. Barnard, "The Economy of Incentives," in Stillman, *Public Administration,* p. 296.
35. Ibid., p. 295.
36. John Brooks, *Telephone: The First Hundred Years* (New York: Harper & Row, 1976).
37. William H. Whyte, *The Organization Man* (New York: Simon & Schuster, 1956).
38. Argyris, *Integrating the Individual,* pp. 24–25.
39. See Argyris, "T-Groups for Organizational Effectiveness," in H. J. Leavitt and L. R. Pondy, eds., *Readings in Managerial Psychology* (Chicago: University of Chicago Press, 1973), pp. 501–527; also, Leland Bradford, "How Sensitivity Training Works," in Marrow, *Failure,* pp. 241–258.
40. Rensis Likert, *The Human Organization* (New York: McGraw-Hill, 1967), pp. 179–180.
41. Abraham Maslow, *Motivation and Personality,* 2nd ed. (New York: Harper & Row, 1970), p. ix.
42. Ibid., p. 44.
43. Ibid., pp. 86–87.
44. Ibid., p. 84.
45. Ibid., p. 83.
46. Ibid., Chapter 4.
47. Douglas McGregor, "The Human Side of Enterprise," in Leavitt and Pondy, *Readings,* p. 748.
48. Ibid., p. 749.
49. Ibid., p. 759.
50. Likert, *Human Organization,* pp. 14–24.
51. Rensis Likert, *New Patterns of Management* (New York: McGraw-Hill, 1961).
52. Robert R. Blake and Jane Mouton, *The Managerial Grid* (Houston, Texas: Gulf, 1964); also, "Organization Excellence Through Effective Management Behaviour," *Manage,* Vol. 20, No. 2, 1967, pp. 42–47.
53. Alfred J. Marrow, "The Effect of Participation on Performance," in Marrow, *Failure,* pp. 90–102.
54. Ibid.
55. Ibid.
56. Ibid.
57. Alfred J. Marrow, Stanley Seashore, and David Bowers, "Managing Major Change," in Marrow, *Failure,* pp. 103–119.
58. See Frederick Herzberg, "One More Time: How Do You Motivate Employees," *Harvard Business Review* (January-February 1968): 53–52.
59. Ibid., p. 53.
60. Ibid., p. 59.
61. Erich Fromm, "Thoughts on Bureaucracy," in Leavitt and Pondy, *Readings,* pp. 166–174.
62. Maxine Buchlow, "A New Role for the Work Group," in Leavitt and Pondy, *Readings,* pp. 458–475.
63. David C. McClelland, "Business Drive and National Achievement," in Leavitt and Pondy, *Readings,* pp. 178–202.
64. Lyman W. Porter, "Job Attitudes in Management: Perceived Deficiencies in Need Fulfillment as a Function of Job Level," *Journal of Applied Psychology* 46, no. 6 (December 1962): 375–384.

65. Lyman W. Porter and Edward E. Lawler, *Managerial Attitudes and Performance* (Homewood, Ill.: Irwin, 1968). Summarizes the various studies.
66. Michael Maccoby, *The Gamesman* (New York: Simon & Schuster, 1976).
67. See C. R. Walker, "The Problems of the Repetitive Job," *Harvard Business Review* 28 (1959): 54–58; R. H. Guest, "Job Enlargement: A Revolution in Job Design," *Personnel Administration* 20 (1957): 9–16; L. E. Davis and E. S. Valfer, "Intervening Responses to Changes in Supervisor Job Designs," *Occupational Psychology* 34 (1960): 109–132.
68. Abraham A. Maslow, *Eupsychian Management* (Homewood, Ill.: Dorsey Press, 1965), pp. 205–217.
69. V. H. Vroom, *Work and Motivation* (New York: Wiley, 1964).
70. John J. Morse and Jay N. Lorsch, "Beyond Theory Y," in Leavitt and Pondy, *Failure*, pp. 399–412.
71. Warren G. Bennis, *Changing Organization* (New York: McGraw-Hill, 1966), pp. 12–13.

BIBLIOGRAPHY

Argyris, Chris. *Integrating the Individual and the Organization.* New York: Wiley, 1964.

Bavelas, Alex. "Communication Patterns in Task Oriented Groups," *Journal of the Acoustical Society of America* 22 (1951): 725–730.

Bennis, Warren G. *Changing Organization.* New York: McGraw-Hill, 1966.

Blake, Robert R. and Mouton, Jane. *The Managerial Grid.* Houston: Gulf, 1964.

Costello, Timothy W. and Zalkind, Sheldon S., eds. *Psychology in Administration: A Research Orientation.* Englewood Cliffs, N.J.: Prentice-Hall Inc., 1963.

Durkheim, Emile. *Suicide.* New York: The Free Press, 1951.

Leavitt, H. J. and Pondy, L. R. *Readings in Managerial Psychology.* Chicago: University of Chicago Press, 1973.

Likert, Rensis. *The Human Organization.* New York: McGraw-Hill, 1967.

———. *New Patterns of Management.* New York: McGraw-Hill, 1961.

Maccoby, Michael. *The Gamesman.* New York: Simon & Schuster, 1976.

Marrow, Alfred J. *The Failure of Success.* New York: Amacom, 1972.

Maslow, Abraham A. *Eupsychian Management.* Homewood, Ill.: Dorsey Press, 1965.

———. *Motivation and Personality.* 2nd. ed. New York: Harper & Row, 1970.

Mayo, Elton. *The Social Problems of an Industrial Civilization.* Andover: Andover Press, 1945.

McClelland, David C. *The Achieving Society.* Princeton, N.J.: Van Nostrand, 1961.

Roethlisberger, Fritz J. *Management and Morale.* Cambridge: Harvard University Press, 1941.

Taylor, Frederick W. *Scientific Management.* New York: Harper & Row, 1947.

Vroom, V. H. *Work and Motivation.* New York: Wiley, 1964.

Whyte, William H. *The Organization Man.* New York: Simon & Schuster, 1956.

In addition to the sources cited in the notes and bibliography, the following *Public Administration Review (PAR)* articles are a convenient starting point for a more detailed exploration of the material in this chapter.

Argyris, Chris. "Organizational Man: Rational *and* Self-Actualizing," *PAR* 33, no. 4 (July/Aug. 1973): 354–358.

Argyris, Chris. "Some Limits of Rational Man Organizational Theory," *PAR* 33, no. 3 (May/June 1973): 253–267.

Eddy, William B. and Robert J. Saunders. "Applied Behavioral Science in Urban Administrative/Political Systems," *PAR* 32, no. 1 (Jan./Feb. 1972): 11–16.

Fox, Elliot M. "Mary Parker Follet: The Enduring Contribution," *PAR* 28, no. 6 (Nov./Dec. 1968): 520–529.

Gardner, Neely. "The Non-Hierarchical Organization of the Future: Theory vs. Reality," *PAR* 36, no. 5 (Sept./Oct. 1976): 591–598.

Gibson, Frank K. and Clyde E. Teasley. "The Humanistic Model of Organizational Motivation: A Review of Research Support," *PAR* 33, no. 1 (Jan./Feb. 1973): 89–96.

Golembiewski, Robert T. and Alan Kiepper. "MARTA: Toward an Effective Open Giant," *PAR* 36, no. 1 (Jan./Feb. 1976): 46–60.

Kaplan, H. Roy and Curt Tausky. "Humanism in Organizations: A Critical Appraisal," *PAR* 37, no. 2 (March/April 1977): 171–180.

Kirkhart, Larry and Orion F. White. "The Future of Organization Development," *PAR* 34, no. 1 (Jan./Feb. 1974): 129–140.

Lyden, Fremont J. (ed.). "Developments in Public Administration," *PAR* 36, no. 6 (Nov./Dec. 1976): 688–694.

McGill, Michael E. "The Evolution of Organization Development: 1947–1960," *PAR* 34, no. 1 (Jan./Feb. 1974): 98–105.

O'Leary, Vincent and David Duffie. "Managerial Behavior and Correctional Policy," *PAR* 31, no. 6 (Nov./Dec. 1971): 603–616.

Palumbo, Dennis J. "Power and Role Specificity in Organization Theory," *PAR* 29, no. 3 (May/June 1969): 237–248.

Ramos, Alberto. "Models of Man and Administrative Theory," *PAR* 32, no. 3 (May/June 1972): 241–246.

Scott, William G. "Organization Government: The Prospects for a Truly Participative System," *PAR* 29, no. 1 (Jan./Feb. 1969): 45–53.

Scott, William G. and David K. Hart. "Administrative Crisis: The Neglect of Metaphysical Speculation," *PAR* 33, no. 5 (Sept./Oct. 1973): 415–422.

Segal, Morley. "Organization and Environment: A Typology of Adaptability and Structure," *PAR* 33, no. 3 (May/June 1974): 212–220.

Simon, Herbert A. "Organization Man: Rational or Self-Actualizing?" *PAR* 33, no. 4 (July/Aug. 1973): 346–354.

Smith, Michael P. "Self-Fulfillment in a Bureaucratic Society: A Commentary on the Thought of Gabriel Marcel," *PAR* 29, no. 1 (Jan./Feb. 1969): 25–32.

Wilcox, Herbert C. "Hierarchy, Human Nature and the Participative Panacea," *PAR* 29, no. 1 (Jan./Feb. 1969): 53–64.

RELEVANT PERIODICALS
American Behavioral Scientist
American Journal of Psychology
Behavioral Science
Human Relations
Journal of Applied Behavioral Science
Journal of Applied Psychology
Journal of Applied Social Psychology
Journal of Experimental Social Psychology
Journal of Personality and Social Psychology
Journal of Social Psychology
Personnel

Personnel Psychology
Small Group Behavior

RELEVANT CASE STUDIES
(Cases marked ICCH are available from the Intercollegiate Case Clearing House, Soldier Field, Boston, Mass. 02163.)

Gabarro, J. J.   *Robert F. Kennedy High School,* [ICCH]
Lee, H. C.   *Lordstown Plant of General Motors,* [ICCH]
Healy, J. J. and A. D. Lundy.   *AB Volvo: Lundby Truck Production Plant: Redesigning the Work Environment,* [ICCH]

CHAPTER 6

PUBLIC PERSONNEL POLICIES, PROCESSES, AND PROBLEMS

INTRODUCTION

During the ascendancy of Taylorism at the turn of the century, government enthusiastically sought to keep administration free from political influence. When government's attention turned from moralistic management to scientific management, it stayed there throughout the period when Human Relations researches went forward in private industry and the university laboratory. Indeed, harmony and satisfaction in the workplace has never been more than a secondary criterion in government employment. Honesty and accountability have been two enduring guideposts for public personnel policy; the quest for a broadly representative government workforce has been a third.

In contrast to the emphasis on theory in Chapter 5, this chapter will concentrate on institutions and processes. First, we will trace the historical development of public personnel policies. Next, we will look at some of the mechanics of government employment—hiring, retiring, and points between. We also will discuss some of the innovative public personnel processes that began to appear in the 1970s. Equal employment opportunity policy, a new requirement rooted in a time-honored philosophy, will be reviewed. The dilemma of the personnel department, which often finds itself caught between top management and the rank and file, will also be considered. Finally, we will take note of the role conflicts and ambiguities that can confront the public employee and that may lead to "whistle-blowing."

GOVERNMENT BY ARISTOCRATS

The earliest answer to the question, "Who will work in the government?" was "The people who created it." The United States Constitution represented a synthesis of the philosophical perspectives of Madison, Hamilton, and Jefferson. The synthesis took place at the Constitutional Convention of 1787 chaired by George Washington. During the 30 years following the Constitutional Convention, one or all of these four gentlemen assumed leadership roles in the administration of the federal government. In supporting roles were John Quincy Adams, Samuel Adams, Charles Pinckney, John Jay, and others who had been present at the convention. "They were men of affairs, merchants, lawyers, planter-businessmen, speculators, investors."[1]

These men of affairs and their protégés performed honestly and efficiently, although the presidential transition from John Adams to Thomas Jefferson raised the specter of politics in administration. To ensure an active role in government for the members of his Federalist party, Adams made numerous fixed-term appointments to government posts on the eve of Jefferson's inauguration. Subsequently, Jefferson dismissed Federalist appointees without fixed-term protection and replaced them with loyalists from his own party.[2] As it turned out, the executive branch did not break into warring camps and, in Jefferson's wake, a succession of compatible regimes guided the United States government. In this "Era of Good Feeling," the federal service could be perceived as a politically neutral instrument.

There were, of course, differences in personalities, if not policies, and, as a result, each president filled top administrative posts with trusted associates. Still, from 1800 to 1828, the bulk of the federal government workforce remained intact from administration to administration. Also remaining intact was a personnel philosophy that viewed government service as an apolitical, professional, mildly aristocratic, lifelong career. This picture changed in 1829 when Andrew Jackson, a frontiersman and an anti-eastern establishment type, was elected president. Jackson brought with him new philosophies and a new breed of political actor—a combination that affected public employment in a major way.

ANDREW JACKSON: THE DEMOCRATIZATION OF THE CIVIL SERVICE

Jackson, with a few duels to his credit, was considered a crude ruffian, particularly by those who had not met him. However, condescension based on hearsay could turn to admiration when one met Jackson face to face. One New Englander, who had been in the forefront of that region's opposition to Jackson, was surprised to find that the president was "a knightly personage."[3] Still, the Jacksonian democrats did have their rough-hewn personages. Congressman Davy Crockett, according to a thumbnail autobiography, was "fresh from the backwoods, half horse, half alligator, a little touched with snapping turtle."[4] With the introductions out of the way, Crockett was eager to add that he could "wade the Mississippi, leap the Ohio, ride a streak of lightning, whip my weight in wildcats, hug a bear too close for comfort and eat any man opposed to Jackson."[5]

Crockett no doubt exaggerated his diet. However, the mercantile and agricultural men of affairs could not misinterpret the message behind the bluster. The pioneers of the frontier—meaning in those days such outposts as Ohio, Kentucky, and Alabama—had come into their own politically. Under Jackson, they joined forces with the emergent working class of the large eastern cities and opposed policies that had been dominant for the first 40 years of the republic.[6] One target was long tenure in office.

In comparison to Jackson's bare-knuckle clash with the eastern establishment that sunk the Bank of the United States, the battle over the make-up of the civil service was a largely rhetorical skirmish. During his presidency, Jackson removed no more than 20 percent of those serving in administrative posts.[7] Based on the federal workforce figures of 1831, this would mean that approximately 60 bureaucrats were removed during each year of the Jacksonian presidency.[8] This differed little from the replacement policies of Jackson's predecessors.[9] Still, on a philosophical plane, Jackson was the most eloquent voice for the democratization of the public service. With words directed at those who traditionally held public office, as well as those to whom he would open public employment, Jackson asserted:

> The duties of all public offices are . . . so plain and simple that men of intelligence may readily qualify themselves for their performance and I cannot but believe that more is lost by the long continuance of men in office than is generally to be gained by their experience. . . . In a country where offices are created solely for the benefit of the people no man has any more intrinsic right to official station than another.[10]

"The Spoils System"

Jackson did not want government run by an antiquated, eighteenth-century bureaucracy. He feared, not without reason, that the bureaucracy would become committed to the established way of doing things. Although it was an exceedingly mild version of the disease by present standards, Jackson was troubled by institutionalization. Both democracy *and* management would be served, thought Jackson, by opening up the federal service.

Indeed, Jackson's statements on the composition of the public service reflected these broad goals. It was a senator from New York, William Marcy, who articulated the political partisanship popularly associated with Jackson's quest for increased accessibility to public office and shortened tenure. "To the victor," Marcy pronounced, "belong the spoils," as he sought to get fellow New Yorker Martin Van Buren confirmed to an ambassadorial post.[11] Strangely enough, Van Buren's rejection set the stage for his ascension to the presidency in 1836 and it was he, not Jackson, who accelerated the politicization of the public service.[12] For the next four decades, the *spoils system* reigned triumphant.

It is not surprising that Marcy and Van Buren were in the vanguard of the push for more patronage on the federal level. Both had been key figures in New York's Democratic party machine, which had skillfully refined the practice of cementing party loyalty with public jobs.[13] Indeed, in scope and audacity, the federal version of the spoils system never matched the state/local variety, particularly in the 1840s when the urban political machine began to accommodate the waves of European immigrants.

A common image of the spoils system features inadequate government services delivered by illiterates, incompetents, and political hacks. There is truth to this but we must be careful when we look at nineteenth-century phenomena from a twentieth-century perspective. The immigrants did not come to America for government services. The "old country" governments did not provide social or welfare services and were usually more skilled at dishing out arrogance, oppression, and poverty. Thus, European peasants and artisans came to America to seek freedom and, above all, employment. The machine, therefore, fulfilled a primary need of the immigrants—a job in government or with firms doing business with the government. In appreciation, the jobholders activated a web of friends, neighbors, and fellow ethnics who sanctioned, by overwhelming majority vote, the performance of the machine.[14]

CIVIL SERVICE REFORM

The "spoilsmen," as the political leaders of the heyday of patronage have been called, were a colorful lot. They were outspoken, outgoing, and not the least bit shy about the way they ran things. Some politicians flaunted their extravagant life-styles (obviously supported by more than their government salaries or other visible income) as the products of an industrious, almost moral, exploitation of their elected posts.[15] Others felt just as righteous but emphasized the service nature of their posts.[16]

Whether they were moved by their own interests or the needs of their constituents—and it was probably a mixture of both—the spoilsmen had overextended and overexposed themselves by the 1880s. Mayors, governors, and even presidents had to knuckle under to party bosses and the demands of patronage from time to time. In 1889, six years *after* the first major civil service reforms, President-elect Benjamin Harrison found that he could not name his own cabinet. "Party managers," Harrison later lamented, "had sold out every place to pay election expenses."[17]

In the large northeastern cities, most mayors and local legislators would have had considerably more freedom if the dominance of local bosses extended only to appointments. Unfortunately, elected executives were often no more than costume jewelry—prominent but hardly necessary. Political clubhouses and local bosses mediated directly between the citizenry and administration for both services and jobs. Mayors of big cities, therefore, could usually count on a great many appointees being corrupt *and* incompetent. It was the era in which municipal engineers could neither read nor write. Some of the more talented employees were not required to show up for work at all. Rather, they ran neighborhood job referral services and expedited the resident's dealings with the bureaucracy from behind the desk of a local political clubhouse.[18]

The spoilsmen, who did little for their public image by flaunting their corruption, tarnished it further when they failed to pay lip service to constitutional government and the authority of elected officials. Citizens who believed in constitutional government, or who opposed corruption and inefficiency, began to coalesce. In 1871, they were rewarded with a fledgling *merit system* in the federal government. A commission established by President Grant was charged with setting up a system for filling government posts based on the job skills of applicants. As it turned out, the reform was premature. By 1875, Congress, by pressuring the president and refusing to fund the commission, rendered the merit system law a dead letter without ever repealing it.[19]

For the civil service reformers the setback was only temporary; their movement was gaining momentum. It needed but one big push and received it from a madman in 1881. Charles Guiteau had campaigned for President Garfield in 1880 and, as a result, felt entitled to a job. Spurned, Guiteau devised a plan to reverse his fortunes: He would assassinate Garfield; Chester A. Arthur, a notorious spoilsman from New York, would become president; and Arthur would reward Guiteau for his campaign efforts.[20] The first two parts of the plan worked out. The third did not. Guiteau succeeded only in resurrecting, once and for all, a civil service commission and injecting a strong dose of moral fervor into public personnel policies.

The Pendleton Act

The history of public personnel administration is one of overlays. No change sweeps out all that existed before it. Although a civil service system was established within two years of Garfield's death, it took nearly half a century to extend civil service coverage to 70 percent of all federal employees.[21] Patronage, with less fanfare and under a variety of aliases, continues to this day. Elitist recruiting practices have endured also. For example, in the State Department, which does its own recruiting, an Ivy League bias was still in evidence in the second half of this century.[22] Although steeped in professionalism and nonpartisanship, this self-perpetuating elite stood oblivious to cycles of reform and spoils.

Despite the coexistence of elitism, patronage, and reform in government personnel practices, it is reform that has been dominant. One major reason is that the formal structure of the personnel system employed by government is the product of reform architects. The rules are reform rules. The civil service concept is itself a reform concept. The dominant philosophy in public personnel management is a reform philosophy.

In the wake of Garfield's assassination the civil service reformers pushed through the *Pendleton Act* of 1883. Embodied in the Pendleton Act were requirements for competitive examinations, political neutrality for the civil service, and probationary periods for new employees. The Pendleton Act also created the United States Civil Service Commission—an agency headed by a bipartisan board of three members appointed by the president and subject to Senate confirmation. The commission conducted the examinations, made the rules, and certified the "eligibles" for any job covered by civil service. Although the commission was subordinate to the President, "in practice it assumed a much more independent posture."[23] Moreover, as recently as 1975, one observer noted that the Pendleton Act was "still at the heart of the federal civil service system."[24]

The framers of the Pendleton Act, perhaps unwittingly, created a genetic code. Features of the government personnel system that took decades to emerge were rooted in the act. Examinations were required to be practical in character; i.e., related directly to the job to be filled. In time, the demands of practicality required rigid descriptions of positions to which tests could correspond.[25] However, these rigid descriptions, which meshed well with the Civil Service Commission's testing needs, became a straitjacket for the government manager who desired flexibility in personnel utilization.

The "independence" of the Civil Service Commission, a matter of law in many jurisdictions, also posed long-range management problems. The personnel function, never well integrated into overall government management, developed separately. Because they were created primarily to combat corruption, civil service commissions, and their rules and regulations, became symbols of righteousness; that is, sacrosanct entities that could turn away proposals for change by resurrecting the ghosts of Boss Tweed and other spoilsmen.

MERIT SYSTEM PERSONNEL MANAGEMENT

The Pendleton Act was the initial beachhead in the campaign for a more trustworthy government personnel system. As the twentieth century opened, the reform movement concentrated on accountability and efficiency in government. To improve accountability, reformers recommended that each jurisdiction have a single elected executive (the "short ballot"). For more efficient management, "executive budgets" were proposed that would make the jurisdiction's chief executive the central repository and checkpoint for operating funds previously entrusted to separate departments.[26]

To achieve efficiency and accountability, the reformers wanted a clear chain of command. Thus, the beachhead established by the Pendleton Act expanded as more and more positions came under the jurisdiction of civil service commissions. During the early 1900s, public personnel management also picked up a healthy dose of Taylorism. Tasks were analyzed and broken into simple components where possible. Jobs became more specialized; their definitions more precise. Training entered public personnel management, as did performance ratings. Fred Taylor even made an appearance, but it was inauspicious. His work at the Army's Watertown Arsenal, replete with stop watch analyses, won Taylor an appearance before Congress and resulted in a ban on time studies for government tasks.[27]

When Mayo managed to discredit Taylorism, private industry eagerly explored the potential of the Human Relations approach. In government, despite the ban on one or two of Taylor's techniques, things were different. Additional steps were taken to root out sentiment. *Hatch Acts* passed at the federal, state, and local levels beginning in the 1930s prohibited civil servants from participating in partisan political activity. More government positions received civil service classification. The Civil Service Commission became more routinized, as did the positions it administered. Thus, the recommendations of the Human Relationists were not much in evidence.

Human Relations approaches did not make much headway in government for several reasons. First, images, as well as realities, shape the decisions of public policy makers, and the images associated with the Human Relations approach—"country club" work environments and "worker control"—mitigated against its adoption. Second, the Civil Service Commission had become a powerful institutional actor by the 1930s and was not about to relinquish authority to supervisors and work groups. Third, from the 1930s through the 1950s, the environment of public administration was in turmoil. The Depression gave way to World War II; the Korean War followed. Through it all, the government expanded at an unprecedented rate. Managers found it difficult to keep up, let alone innovate.

In this charged atmosphere, it was not surprising that those who diagnosed the administrative ills of the federal government offered time-honored remedies. The Brownlow Commission of 1937 and the First (1949) and Second (1955) Hoover Commissions recommended a more coherent, less fragmented, low redundancy administrative structure under the command of the president.[28] Some personnel recommendations were made. Brownlow advised that the powers of the Civil Service Commission be split between two agencies. One, performing a personnel management function, would be a staff arm of the president. The second agency would be an independent body charged with insuring the integrity of the merit system. A major proposal of the Second Hoover Commission—the *Senior Civil Service*—would have created a top management cadre independent of departmental career lines.[29]

Few of the personnel proposals made much headway prior to the late 1960s. When they did, a flood was loosed and, through the 1970s, the fundamental structure and premises of the civil service system were questioned or modified. We will focus on these new directions further along. For now, however, we will review the broad outlines of the personnel function in public administration.

Recruitment

If you persevere in your public administration studies it is certain (almost) that you will be exposed to government recruitment material. The material may be no more than an announcement in the local newspaper or on the bulletin board of a government office of a forthcoming "test" for one or another government position. ("Test," as we will discuss in more detail, can mean a comparison of resumes or a comparison of exam scores.)

At one time, the "test announcement" was the sum and substance of government's pursuit of employees to fill the great bulk of its positions. Lately, a bit more creativity and energy have been applied to the task. Ads appear in newspapers and professional journals. Recruiters visit college campuses. For certain job openings, mailings go to classes of individuals—professionals, college seniors, or those who have applied for similar jobs. Graduates of public administration programs, particularly those with master's degrees, have become prime targets for government recruiters.

Testing

Having secured a number of applicants for a position, the civil service authority seeks to evaluate their qualifications. This evaluation may include any or all of the following: resume, performance on written examination, "trial runs" (e.g., typing tests), reference checks. Multiple-choice/true-false questions remain the most common evaluative tool in written tests. (This reflects the staying power of Taylorism in public personnel management. Such tests permit maximum standardization.) All applicants receive the "same" test, although "same" does not mean identical. Questions may differ but evaluate the same trait. Asking Applicant A to determine the square root of 64 is assumed to be the same, in terms of evaluating mathematical skills, as asking Applicant B to determine the square root of 81. Through standardization, multiple-choice testing also eliminates such contaminating factors as skill of expression, evaluator bias, overblown resumes, and untrustworthy character references.

On the assumption that the tests measured one's ability to perform the job being filled, multiple-choice testing was long considered the purest method of evaluation. Nonetheless, attacks on its virtue increased through the 1960s and 1970s. In *Griggs* v. *Duke Power Company* [401 U.S. 424 (1971)], the Supreme Court found that aptitude tests and educational criteria were used improperly to disqualify blacks from positions calling for manual labor. Shortly thereafter, a suit was filed, charging that the Federal Service Entrance Examination was discriminatory [*Douglas* v. *Hampton*, 338 F. Supp. 18 (1972)]. Although the suit was not successful, many jurisdictions began to reevaluate and reformulate their tests.

In 1976, the Supreme Court, in *Washington* v. *Davis* [426 U.S. 229 (1976)], ruled that a racially discriminatory purpose was necessary to invalidate government acts. Merely showing that a test placed a disproportionate burden on one race was insufficient. Intent had to be established. Although this eased the pressure on civil service examination procedures, a search for inadvertent biases remains the hallmark of the professional tester. Thus, it is unlikely that those who ascertain the validity of civil service examinations will remove racial discrimination from their checklist.

In addition to bias, several other actual or potential shortcomings of standardized tests should be noted. First, since only high scorers are hired, it is difficult to judge if the test really picks the best person for job. To do that, some low scorers would have to be hired to see how they peformed. Second, when a group of applicants has test results that differ by a percentage point or two, the rankings within the group usually are meaningless as a measure of relative ability.[30] Of course, from the civil service commission's point of view, a waiting list is better than a waiting mob. Ranking prospective employees based on scores such as 99.8%, 99.7%, 99.6% gives the appearance of an objective ranking. Also, the precise rankings enable personnel departments to justify their selection of one applicant over another, even though both applicants may be equally qualified for the job.

Part of the reason for reliance on hairbreadth distinctions between test scores is the *rule of three*—a practice that has traditionally governed Civil Service Commission certification of candidates for vacancies occurring within the government bureaucracy. The rule of three requires that the hiring agency choose from among the three top-ranked individuals. In some jurisdictions, the rule of three is relaxed and all applicants within a specified range of scores (e.g., 95–100 percent) are certified as eligible. This practice, of course, expands the hiring options available to departmental managers.[31]

The *veterans' preference* also complicates civil service testing procedures. In most jurisdictions, veterans get five extra points and disabled veterans get 10 extra points. Thus, veterans can score 101–110 percent on tests. Where jobs are few and applicants are numerous, veterans may be the only candidates to achieve scores that provide a realistic opportunity for the position. Veterans see the preference as a well-deserved acknowledgment for serving their country. Veterans' organizations push this claim vigorously and many legislators also deem it meritorious. Still, there are moves to eliminate or modify veterans' preferences; we will consider them below.

Promotions and Transfers
In order to get promoted civil servants can:

pass a qualifications or "resume" test.
pass a written test.
impress superiors with their talents.
be durable.

In many jurisdictions, there are "resume tests" for supervisory level positions that permit "lateral entry" by those outside government service. Using resume information, for instance, the Federal Civil Service Commission ranks applicants for "mid-level career positions." The list is, to a degree, segregated according to occupations and is used in a flexible manner. For instance, when the Public Health Service has a mid-level opening, it does not necessarily choose from among the top three candidates on the overall list. Rather, the candidates who the Civil Service Commission deems best qualified in the area of health administration may be referred for interviews.

Promotions also can be judged by written test results. In many cities, written tests determine who becomes a police sergeant, a fire lieutenant, a senior clerk, or a sanitation department supervisor. The discretion of agency management is limited by the written promotion test. The candidate pool is restricted to those within the agency or those within a specific career line such as clerk. An outside authority, the civil service commission, determines who will be elevated to a higher rank.

Agency management is not always so restricted. For in-house promotions, discretion may be substantial although not entirely free of guidelines; for example, a person must have five years' experience as a clerk to be eligible for a senior clerk position. Nonetheless, management selects from the pool of eligibles. Performance on the job and job-related achievements can be factored into promotion decisions.

Seniority can also receive heavy emphasis in government's promotion decisions. The phrase that one may read at most civil service bulletin boards—"Applicants must have ten years of progressively responsible experience"—can reflect rules and regulations that require one year as a trainee in order to advance to junior engineer; one year as a junior engineer to qualify for an engineer's post; three years as an engineer to become a senior engineer; and five years as a senior engineer before ascending to a supervisory post. Even where there are no rules, an agency may have an informal "old boy" tradition that rewards endurance and longevity. Regardless of how such policies come about, they represent, in the opinion of at least one observer, "the dead hand of disincentive" and "stagnation."[32] There is considerable merit to this point of view.

Separation

One way or another, sooner or later, the individual's employment with government is terminated. Death, resignation, disability, retirement, and discharge are the exit ramps. Some are more pleasant than others for the departing employee and the involved administrators.

Death, disability, and retirement usually activate compensatory mechanisms such as life insurance, pensions, or disability benefits. Although none of these modes of separation evoke high drama on the public personnel front, one potential point of confrontation is the mandatory retirement age. The elderly resent being forced out of their jobs while they still have the ability and desire to make significant contributions to the organization. Legislators have been sympathetic toward this point of view and may force public and private organizations to rethink their retirement policies.

While older employees worry about the maximum mandatory retirement age, many observers of government personnel practices worry about the minimum voluntary retirement age. Partly as a result of union activity, minimum retirement ages have plummeted in many jurisdictions while pensions have skyrocketed. In the next chapter, which treats unionization, we will have more to say about this subject.

The most dramatic and controversial terminations of public employment are those instigated by the employer. Layoffs and dismissals tend to make page one in the news media, but *forced resignations* and other behind-the-scenes separations may be more numerous. A brief review of these employer-instigated terminations follows.

Layoffs   Layoffs, which were exceedingly rare in government until the 1970s, became a prominent feature in municipal management as fiscal crises struck many American cities. The civil service conducted the layoffs with much of the formality that marked the placement process. "Last in - First out" was the broad philosophy that guided workforce reductions. Employees in entry-level positions who had the least seniority lost their jobs first. When jobs were reduced at the supervisory level, excess supervisors were entitled to a lower-level post. Thus, in police force reductions, the sergeant whose job was eliminated dropped back to the rank of patrol officer. This set off a chain reaction that "bumped" the most recently hired off the force.[33]

Workers who were laid off, in order of seniority, were first in line when hiring resumed. However, many declined offers of reemployment. The inducement that had attracted some—government employment as secure employment—no longer appeared tenable. Others, having begun new careers while waiting months and even years to be recalled, were content to continue where they were.

Dismissals   Layoffs are like acts of God. They devastate without rhyme or reason, or spring from sources—inflation, recession, decades of mismanagement—that are remote and abstract. Dismissals, however, are face-to-face affairs. The dismissed employee, and not some abstraction, stands indicted. The boss who conveys the news is not a helpless agent but is investigator, accuser, prosecutor, judge, jury, and executioner. The employee may react hysterically or even violently to the dismissal. In short, firing someone is extremely unpleasant for all concerned.

Unpleasant things tend to be avoided and dismissals are no exception. One avoidance mechanism has been termed the *lateral arabesque* by the creator of the "Peter Principle," which states that everyone rises to his or her level of incompetence.[34] With the lateral arabesque the manager foists inept employees on some unsuspecting colleague in another office or agency.

Another way to avoid firing a person is the forced resignation. In many high-level posts it is understood that employees will tender their resignation upon the request of their superiors. Such arrangements are attractive from two standpoints. The superior avoids the red tape associated with firing, and the subordinate usually avoids the taint of dismissal and maintains an acceptable employment record and favorable references.

One type of forced resignation could be labeled *psychological termination*. This occurs when the employee will not accede to resignation demands and, for one reason or another, superiors wish to avoid the formal dismissal process. One example of psychological termination known to the authors proceeded in the following manner. The duties of the targeted official were transferred to others. Interdepartmental communications, even routine ones, were no longer routed to the official. The official's personal secretary was assigned elsewhere to perform top-priority duties—for eight hours a day. The government car assigned to the official was withdrawn. The official did not resign but began to search for another government post. His superiors eagerly helped him complete a lateral arabesque.

Forced resignations, lateral arabesques, *and* psychological terminations can be found in both private and public organizations. In public organizations, however, the strong procedural safeguards designed to protect employees from political dismissals force managers to rely on more indirect means of getting rid of deadwood. As Jay Shafritz points out, even the manager inclined towards dismissal must consider that:

> it will take months to build a case that will withstand appeals to the civil service commission and perhaps the courts.
>
> if the commission or the court reinstates the employee, other employees may decide to gear down to the appellant's level of performance, as abysmal as it may be, since it has been judged acceptable.
>
> if the employee secured union backing, the broader relationship between the organization and the union may destabilize.[35]

As a result, Shafritz writes, "managers find themselves in an almost untenable position. They can neither urge their charges on to greater productive heights nor effectively impose sanctions of sufficient weight to frighten workers into productive acts."[36]

Despite these obstacles, government managers do institute formal dismissal actions from time to time. What follows is an account of a formal dismissal proceeding.

CASE STUDY: Long Hair in the Merit System

In 1969, Salt Lake County, Utah came under the state's County Merit System Act. The circumstances that led up to the act's passage, notes William Timmons, were familiar: "Salt Lake County had had a long history of patronage, petty graft and corruption and had experienced a growth of the spoils system under recent county administrations by both major political parties during the 1950s and 1960s."[37]

The first controversial dismissal under the new merit system occurred in April, 1970. Bruce F. Williams, a laborer in the county's Facilities Maintenance Department, was fired for not having an acceptable haircut. Williams appealed to the Merit System Council—the county's civil service commission with a bipartisan membership of two Republicans and one Democrat. A hearing was held.

During the hearing, Williams's superiors detailed the dismissal process. First, a memorandum was issued reminding employees to be "clean shaven and have an acceptable haircut."[38] The memorandum was dated April 2. Almost immediately, Williams's immediate supervisor informed him of the unacceptable length of his hair. There ensued "two or three conversations" between Williams's supervisor and other superiors concerning the length of Williams's hair. On April 9, one week after the issuance of the "acceptable haircut" reminder, Williams's supervisor, in a letter to the department head, formally requested that Williams be suspended for five days. This was done and Williams was warned that the suspension would become a termination if he did not return with an acceptable haircut. Williams, standing by his "rights as a United States citizen,"[39] did not comply and on Monday, April 20, 1970, was fired for "misconduct."[40]

At the hearing, Williams's supervisors denied that the regulation on acceptable length of hair was directed at Williams. Previous problems with hair length involving other workers were cited. The supervisors, somewhat vaguely, intimated that long hair constituted a safety hazard and drew complaints from the citizenry. In zeroing in on the cause of the dismissal, Williams's attorney got the supervisors to admit that Williams "was one of the best workers that we had."[41] Further questioning by Williams's attorney highlighted the subjectivity of the supervisors' ruling and the imprecision with which the "acceptable haircut" standard was drawn. Lawyers for the county conceded these points but contended that the heart of the matter was not the letter of the rule but Williams's insubordination.

As the hearing progressed, Williams's supervisors began to echo the insubordination theme and stressed that it was a contagion that had to be eradicated. "As far as I was concerned, it was open rebellion," said the department head.[42] "He defied the administration," said another supervisor.[43] Thus, with management stressing insubordination, and Williams's attorney emphasizing the looseness of the haircut rule, the three Merit Council commissioners adjourned to make their decision.

While the Merit Council was deliberating, the head of Williams's department requested a private meeting. At the meeting, he suggested that Williams's reinstatement would cripple management. "These young kids in my department are just waiting to see what happens to Bruce. If you guys put him back on his job these kids are going to walk all over (my supervisors)." The department head asserted that Williams was "just testing us—pushing us to the wall. We have to show him who's the boss."[44]

Political pressure was also applied in order to prevent Williams's reinstatement. Apparently at the behest of management, the County Commissioner, an elected official, asked the Merit Council to "carefully consider the impact on my supervisors and departments heads of putting this kid back to work."[45] The Salt Lake City Commissioner of Streets and Public Improvements, also an elected official, chimed in with the assertion that "no long-haired kids are going to work in my department."[46] The head of the county's personnel department added that Williams was "tardy all the time and foments dissatisfaction with the other guys on the job."[47] Williams, called "one of the best workers" the week before, was identified as a "real ringleader of a little group of problem employees in (the) department."[48] Other calls and visits, most promanagement, were made.

Despite the pressure, the Merit Council, by a vote of 2 to 1, decided to reinstate Williams. Actually, Williams's hair was not very long and rivaled the hair style adorning one of the Merit Council commissioners. That commissioner voted in Williams's favor. A second commissioner voted for reinstatement on the grounds that there appeared to be no valid reason for the haircut regulation.[49]

Williams's victory was a costly one. His angered superiors perceived a spreading result and warned Williams's peers to keep their distance from him. Williams was reassigned to a detail that he did not like. Williams reacted with spotty attendance; as a result, he was fired two months after the reinstatement. This time his appeals were denied and the County Commissioner exulted that the Williams "example" had "taught employees a lesson—that no merit system could protect a troublemaker."[50] The lesson was effective as employees arrived well shorn in the wake of Williams's second dismissal. A year later, Williams was dead from an overdose of drugs.

FEDERAL PERSONNEL INNOVATIONS

In 1978, President Jimmy Carter launched another assault on the 95-year-old civil service arrangements. It appeared that the president meant business as his appointees lashed out at malingering in the civil service. One assistant secretary at HEW noted that "while there are many highly competent, dedicated civil servants, the percentage of civil servants who are not earning what the taxpayers are paying them is almost as high as any figure you ever heard. There is a very substantial number of people on the civil service rolls who are literally bilking the taxpayer."[51] The photo on page 180 portrays the OMB (Office of Management and Budget) director demonstrating the steps that must be followed in order to fire an employee. His chart's message is that "a manager can spend anywhere from 25 percent to 50 percent of his working hours for a period ranging from six to eighteen months at an estimated cost to the taxpayers of $100,000."[52]

The Carter plan resurrected a number of proposals that had been

The Chart of a Two-Year Dismissal Proceeding Against a Habitually Tardy Clerk. The clerk resigned before the dismissal proceeding could run its course. Her supervisor, who wrote many of the memos depicted on the chart, was reprimanded by his superiors for spending so much time on the case. (Photo © 1978 by Dennis Brack from Black Star.)

made previously. In keeping with the Brownlow proposals of 1937, the duties of the Civil Service Commission were to be divided between two separate agencies: Office of Personnel Management and Merit Protection Board. The Office of Personnel Management would handle placements, promotions, transfers, terminations, salary policy, and other managerial tasks. The Merit Protection Board would assume the appellate role with respect to the denial of salary increases or promotions that are deemed unjust by the employees affected.

From the recommendations of the Second Hoover Commission, the president revived the Senior Civil Service concept. Instead of regular salary increases, senior civil servants would receive performance bonuses that could equal 20 percent of their salaries. Incentives of a more negative character included no bonuses, no raises, and demotion to regular civil service status for senior civil servants who performed poorly. A shift from automatic to merit pay increases for 70,000 middle-management positions was also proposed. In addition, the Carter administration proposed a statute of limitations for the veterans' preference. After discharge, officers would have three years and enlisted men would have ten years in which to use their preference. Subsequently, they would have to compete on an equal basis with other applicants. Although the response to the Carter proposals was favorable, intense opposition from veterans' groups and government employees was expected.

STATE AND LOCAL PERSONNEL INNOVATIONS

In advancing the Civil Service Commission concept in the 1880s, the federal government took the lead. However, in the 1970s, state and

Variants of "The Bureaucracy Game" are a personnel management reality at all levels of government. With practice, managers can become skillful at shepherding recruits quickly through the maze. SOURCE: *National Journal*, October 29, 1977, p. 1677. © 1977 by *National Journal*.

local governments were in the forefront of attempts to modify personnel practices. As of 1975, 23 states reported that they had instituted "performance" or "output-oriented" pay increases or bonuses.[53] Fourteen percent of the localities and 20 percent of the states polled by the National Commission on Productivity reported attempts at job enlargement. Rotation schemes were most prominent and one of the more interesting was in Eugene, Oregon. In Eugene, departmental employees were assigned for six months to community relations posts in the mayor's or city manager's office. In addition to giving the employee a variety of responsibilities, the program exposed them to the jurisdiction-wide perspective that might not otherwise have been obtained on the departmental level.[54]

The state governments were also active with respect to the veterans' preference. Wisconsin prohibited its use on promotional exams. Oregon made the veterans' preference a one-time proposition; if applied to one's test score on the entry examination, the preference could not subsequently be used in promotional situations or to strengthen one's "bumping" rights. Also, Oregon sought to prevent retired military careerists from combining their 20 or more years of experience with preference points in order to gain an inside track on civilian posts in government. The result—"double-dipping" employees receiving salaries in addition to pensions—often shut out talented individuals in search of their first source of income. To remedy this situation, Oregon limited the veterans' preference to enlistees or draftees having no more than one reenlistment.[55]

Major structural changes in the civil service system were carried out in Wisconsin. Statewide personnel responsibilities were divided between a personnel management office and an appeals board. A senior civil service was created. In many cases, the development of position classifications and experience requirements was delegated to the agency manager. This latter step gave the agency a greater voice in the staffing process than was possible under the traditional civil service commission arrangement.[56]

In the 1980s and 1990s, the movement of personnel authority from civil service commissions to chief executives and operating departments probably will continue. Public managers will face a rapidly changing lineup of problems and will continue to demand flexible staffing policies and greater authority over employees. In states and localities, lingering financial difficulties will sustain calls for the modification of civil service procedures that impede the dismissal of "deadwood" and the chastening of idlers. However, as we shall see below, goals other than efficiency and managerial effectiveness also should continue to play a role in public employment policy.

THE SEARCH FOR REPRESENTATIVE BUREAUCRACY

We have looked at the development of public personnel policy as a succession of remedies. Democratization cured elitism; anticorruption measures curbed the excesses of democratization; efficiency therapy followed, and the management approach focused attention on overall administration. This progression represents a useful framework for viewing the history of public employment. From a slightly different perspective, however, public employment can be seen to cycle between two different philosophies.[57] One seeks a well-run government composed of an educated elite or one that is ruled by the principles of efficiency and management. A second philosophy seeks to insure widespread opportunity for entry into the public service. This latter goal can be achieved by "spoils," by merit system approaches that rely on practical tests and experience rather than educational achievement, and by equal employment opportunity requirements.

Neither position ever achieves absolute domination. The focus on well-run government never excludes concern over the composition of the workforce; nor does an emphasis on staffing demography shut out management concerns. At times, however, one or the other is predominant. From 1883 through the 1960s, management was dominant. Beginning in the 1940s, and gaining momentum through the next four decades, was a resurgent emphasis on the make-up of the public service.

Concern for the demography of public employment reemerged in the context of society's growth in size and complexity. In this century, elected officials have confronted an increasingly difficult management task. As government bureaucracy grew large, it grew unwieldy; as complexity increased, so did the inability of elected officials to comprehend fully the bureaucracies that they directed. Staffs, which augmented the elected officials' management capability, also grew cumbersome and complex. Thus, as management control techniques failed to keep pace with bureaucratic growth and specialization, policy prerogatives accrued to an eager bureaucracy, and the permanent civil service was perceived as a more potent influence than the electorate on the decisions of government.[58] Therefore, observers hoped that the government workforce would be "permeated with the democratic spirit and ideology—with respect for the dignity of man, (since) the real protection for the citizen lies in the development of a high degree of democratic consciousness among the administrative hierarchy."[59]

The first intensive search for *representative bureaucracy* was conducted in Britain by Donald Kingsley in 1944.[60] Kingsley found that the British civil service was representative of the middle class in that country both in make-up and outlook. A 1949 study of the United States civil service found considerably more demographic diversity.[61] Although the proponents of democracy in administration were heartened, Mosher pointed out that the findings demonstrated only *passive representativeness*— that is, people within the bureaucracy reflected the socioeconomic make-up of the citizenry. The question was whether passive representation gave way to *active representation* from bureaucrats who would go to bat on behalf of the people they represented.[62]

A bureaucrat's activism on behalf of his or her socioeconomic group is likely to be toned down or turned off by a number of factors. First, much of our administrative structure addresses specific problems—poverty, unemployment, ill health—rather than overall socioeconomic groups. Second, the bureaucratic functionary is required, in the ideal sense, to separate personal considerations from organizational deliberations. Third, when the organization's charter does permit activism, it is usually on behalf of economic rather than socioeconomic groups; that is, businesses rather than blacks; farmers rather than poor Hispanics. When activism is informally sanctioned the beneficiary is also likely to be a powerful institutional force in the organization's environment.

In short, activism in the bureaucracy is channeled towards assigned tasks. The nature of those tasks and the strength of the bureaucracy as a socializer favors passive socioeconomic representation. Nonetheless, activist socioeconomic representation can flourish in the gap between the bureaucratic ideal and the organizational reality. In some institutions, socioeconomic constituencies explicitly expect their points of view to be advanced in that gap. In the United Nations, for instance, member nations receive a proporitionate share of administrative posts, and many UN bureaucrats are expected by their governments to act with their national constituencies in mind.[63]

In the United States in the 1960s and 1970s, both active and passive representation were predominant features in public administration. Better known as *community control* and *equal employment opportunity,* these two approaches to representative bureaucracy are worth a closer look.

COMMUNITY CONTROL AND EQUAL EMPLOYMENT OPPORTUNITY

With the urban riots of the 1960s, there emerged new claimants to a share of the policy-making action in public organizations—the blacks and Hispanics of our depressed cities. The demand was for active representation—local services run by and for the members of the community. Community control was successful in some areas but often experienced setbacks when it collided with the administrative structure and unionized workforce of the larger jurisdiction. Moreover, black and Hispanic community "bosses," true to the traditions of the ethnic machine, occasionally channeled public resources to the community without benefit of an intervening public service. "Phantom" employees drew pay and some projects were illusions into which considerable funds disappeared. Since accounting procedures were generally atrocious, even money properly spent could not escape suspicion. Not unexpectedly, middle-class disapproval, symbolized by the election of Richard

Nixon in 1968, resulted in a sharp movement away from activist representation in the form of community control.[64]

The movement towards passive representation in the public service did not suffer such sharp reversals. The Civil Rights Act of 1964—passed overwhelmingly by Congress and enthusiastically implemented by President Johnson—carried forward, with renewed momentum, the battle against unequal opportunities that besmirched the democratic ideals of the United States. The Civil Rights Act overturned barriers that had kept blacks from the voting booth and from public accommodations. Civil rights in the workplace also became a concern of public policy as a result of the 1964 Act's creation of the Equal Employment Opportunity Commission.[65] Although its powers were not sweeping and its jurisdiction was limited to private firms, the commission represented a firm commitment to passive representation in the workforce.

In 1972, the Equal Employment Opportunity Act brought state and local employment practices under the jurisdiction of the Equal Employment Opportunity Commission. Employers were required to keep records regarding the sex, race, religion, age, and ethnicity of applicants. The "jawboning" powers (i.e., the power to seek voluntary compliance through persuasion) conferred upon the commission by the 1964 Civil Rights Act were augmented by enforcement powers that included the ability to bring civil action suits against employers engaged in discriminatory practices before the United States District Court. If the court concurs with the commission's allegations, immediate affirmative remedies can be ordered. For the individual who has been discriminated against, this can mean a job offer or the granting of a denied promotion or transfer. Back-pay awards may be made. Groups may be offered training or bonuses to compensate for past discrimination and their employer may be compelled to adhere to a plan for achieving racial, ethnic, and sexual balance throughout the organization.

In response to the major drive towards the equalization of employment opportunities in the 1970s, most organizations had to rethink their hiring and promotional practices. Achieving passive representation has become a major goal of personnel departments in business and at all levels of government. As enunciated in federal policy guidelines, "goals and time tables are appropriate as a device to help measure progress in remedying discrimination."[66] It is clear that anyone entering government service in the coming decades will come to grips with equal employment questions from time to time.

GOVERNMENT EMPLOYMENT AS PUBLIC POLICY

In addition to making equality of opportunity a reality, a responsibility it shares with other employers, the government also provides jobs designed to reduce unemployment. These jobs are provided under the *Comprehensive Employment and Training Act (CETA)* of 1973. Under CETA, federal funds are used to create state and local jobs for the unemployed. Ideally, CETA was designed to provide short-term remedies—public service jobs—and long-term solutions—enhanced skills for the hard-core unemployed. The manpower training component was not always activated, however, as jurisdictions placed CETA workers in menial jobs rather than in apprenticeship or paraprofessional positions. Nonetheless, CETA was providing 200,000 jobs throughout the nation in 1976.[67] In addition to the unemployed, many financially strapped jurisdictions benefited as imminent workforce reductions were avoided through CETA hirings.

CETA was one in a series of government employment programs. The Civilian Conservation Corps (CCC) of the 1930s was the prototype and spearheaded a number of Depression programs that employed everyone from bricklayers to Shakespearean actors. In a 1970 revival of the CCC, the Youth Conservation Corps provided summer employment for teenagers. An expanded version of this program, the Young Adult Conservation Corps, would have provided year round employment for persons 16–24 years of age. This 1976 proposal died in Congress, however, as did the Humphrey-Hawkins bill, which would have provided federally funded jobs for all unemployed individuals. In the same year, however, CETA was expanded in scope.[68] One suspects that, in times of economic distress such as the 1930s and the 1970s, public jobs will usually be created to employ the unemployed.

ROLE CONFLICTS IN THE PUBLIC SERVICE

"Being caught on the horns of a dilemma" is not an unusual posture in the public service. Sometimes, the dilemma has roots in the structure of the organization, and an entire function or office is caught betwixt and between. Unfortunately, this is often the fate of the personnel staff. Other public service dilemmas have more personal roots. Values that are deemed important by the employee and were acquired in some external setting conflict with the demands made by the organization. The predicament facing the personnel office and the painful choices that occasionally confront the public servant will occupy the remainder of the chapter.

The Personnel Officer: Dilemmas and Goals

The personnel office stands uneasily between management and the workers.[69] It is management's agent in achieving workforce efficiency. On the other hand, the personnel office has a responsibility for the morale of the rank and file. In this situation it is not difficult to generate animosity. Management may consider the personnel office as a spendthrift enunciator of the employee position. The workforce may view the personnel office as the oppressive enforcer of management's rules and regulations. When there is not hostility, there may be disdain. Management may see the personnel office as a paperwork processor rather than a policy maker. Similarly, to employees, the personnel office may be no more than the publisher of marginally interesting work rules and meaningless newsletters.

For their part, personnel managers are not entirely satisfied with their constituents. They are resentful when top management or union representatives veto proposed personnel actions. Similarly, personnel officers take a negative view toward line managers who obstruct personnel office inquiries and policies. As for civil service regulations, even the personnel office may become exasperated at times. This exasperation can place the personnel officer in the stressful position of paying lip service to regulations while violating the spirit and, on occasion, the letter of those regulations. In addition to their complaints about superiors, subordinates, and the rules, personnel officers complain of poor pay, limited authority, and low status.

The ideal professional environment of the personnel manager includes several items. Among them are the freedom to deploy workers and more latitude in the hiring, firing, and disciplining of workers. In order to achieve discretion in these areas, many personnel managers believe that it is important to win the confidence of top management through improved communications. The usual output of information—periodic statistical reports—is more likely to inspire drowsiness than a recognition that the personnel office has something to contribute. To remedy this impression, personnel managers recommend that more face to face meetings be held with superiors. At these meetings, positive recommendations supported by data analyses should be made. The personnel office has the raw material and imaginative statistical studies comparing work performance by sex, education level, test scores, previous position, or other readily available data to shed light on how well the organization utilizes its human resources.

Of course, the downward communications of the personnel office are important to its image and effectiveness. Newsletters, according to personnel officers, should not be cloying. The same goes for posters. Neither medium should puff up minor accomplishments. Deception should also be avoided. Cuteness, exaggeration, or lying may severely damage the credibility of the personnel office. Ideally, personnel office communications to employees should be truthful, unpretentious, and tactful.

The Many Roles of the Public Servant

The personnel office, because of its position in the organizational structure, divides its loyalties between two claimants. The individual public servant may contend with many more claimants. Through upbringing and education, the public servant may have acquired allegiances to family, religion, ethnic group, schoolmates, or a variety of ideologies such as socialism, democracy, or individualism. With exposure to the organizational form, productivity, efficiency, obedience to superiors, and value-neutral administration may compete as guideposts for the employee's decisions. Participation in informal work settings exposes the employee to additional influences such as the work group or professional colleagues. In government, other sets of concepts and entities may vie for the employee's loyalties. Included are political parties, clients, the law, and the "public interest." Finally public employees may view their tasks from the citizenship perspective.

Packages of loyalties and allegiances, some complementary and some contradictory, are a feature of modern life. This is due to the fact that all of us, to a greater or lesser extent, are called upon to fulfill a number of roles. *Roles* may be defined as "patterns of behavior associated with a distinctive social position."[70] Son, daughter, brother, sister, mother, father, Protestant, Jew, Catholic, Norwegian, Italian, student, teacher, Democrat, Republican, citizen, superior, subordinate, and technician are but a few roles, or patterns of behavior, that we might assume in our society.

Many of the patterns of behavior that we learn as children are partially abandoned as we grow older. The dependence that marks the son or daughter role is gradually reduced. By adulthood, religious and ethnic roles usually are deemphasized. However, most roles are not fully discarded and, indeed, may remain powerful background forces. For instance, weddings bring to the fore familial, ethnic, and religious roles that the guests may not have assumed for years. Still, the guests dance the traditional dances, participate easily in the religious ceremony, and reassume childhood roles—son, daughter, nephew, niece—with a certain enthusiasm.

At weddings, individuals consciously activate dormant roles. However, the norms associated with dormant roles may subconsciously influence behavior. For instance, youthful executives may not chew out an elderly subordinate for tardiness, even though they have reprimanded younger workers for the same offense. The executive might justify this special treatment (a probable violation of the norms of the bureaucratic role) in several ways; that is, "You can't teach an old dog new tricks"; "Retirement soon will solve the problem"; or "Nobody else is complaining." However, the real reason for the gentle treatment may be rooted in a norm internalized from childhood: A disrespect toward one's elders is improper.[71]

Whether it is conscious or unconscious, the typical legacy of an abandoned role is one or two norms that may conflict with the requirements of succeeding roles. Thus, it is not surprising that dismissals are reluctantly undertaken (or avoided) by bureaucrats who, as children, were told in no uncertain terms that harming others was wrong. Nor is it shocking that employees disapprove (or "leak" to the press), since their superiors "lie" by inflating accomplishments or making promises that cannot be kept.

It should be recognized that government employment, or service in any organized endeavor, is likely to involve conflicting roles and values. For instance, as a citizen one might be required to expose and condemn certain practices that as an employee demanded a vow of silence. There are several ways to resolve such conflicts. One method is to calculate the personal costs and benefits of each role. In the clash between the citizenship role and the workplace role, one might begin by noting that the former pays not a penny while the latter sustains the employee and his or her family. Another approach to resolving role conflicts is to make a fundamental commitment to one role or the other; that is, either uphold the citizenship "contract" or the employment "contract." The employee also may attempt to resolve role conflicts through means-ends analysis. For instance, an employee might question if a wiretap ordered by a superior in the name of "national security" actually benefits national security, and thus outweighs the wiretap's damage to constitutional principles.

In addition to conflicts arising out of roles and values external to the organization, contradictions and ambiguities may exist within organizational roles.[72] This is not uncommon on the supervisory or middle-management rungs that most public administration students will occupy. The supervisor, for instance, is both teacher and examiner to subordinates. However, the line between instructional supervision and production-oriented supervision is not easily drawn. It cannot be assumed that everyone masters a new job at the same rate. Shifting completely to a production-oriented supervision during the second week of a new work process might frustrate and alienate the slow learners. On the other hand, differential treatment and expectations may be perceived as unfair by the fast learners. Obviously, the decisions that face a supervisor in such situations are not easy ones.

The difficulty for the individual is heightened when the conflict or ambiguity involves superiors. As we saw with respect to the personnel office, employees who must accommodate the demands of superiors and subordinates walk a narrow line. The dilemma can become downright painful when contradictory orders come from above. In the public organization, role requirements may be defined differently by executive, legislative, and judicial superiors. Moreover, conflicting or ambiguous signals can emanate from different superiors within the organization.[73]

Whether external roles clash with organizational roles or the conflict involves two in-house roles, choosing one role over the other can exact a psychological or physiological toll from the individuals caught in the middle.[74] There are several ways to reduce the stress and tension associated with role conflict and role ambiguity. One is simply to acknowledge their existence. Another is to look at the positive, rather than the negative, aspects of role conflict and role ambiguity. Namely, role dilemmas are often a constructive, if somewhat painful, eventuality in individuals and organizations during times of change and uncertainty. The avoidance of role dilemmas might also be considered. Certain positions in the organization feature a high degree of conflict and ambiguity for which certain personality types exhibit a low degree of tolerance. Introverts who tend to internalize the tensions arising out of role conflict might seek detours around executive posts.[75] A detour may also be in order for highly empathetic individuals, since they may agonize over the impact of conflict on subordinates.[76] Instead of detouring, of course, individuals might seek to recast their work personalities in a more extroverted and less empathetic mold.

One also can prepare for possible role conflicts by periodically reviewing the values that guide one's behavior. Are there conflicts between values? Has it become more difficult to make decisions based upon a certain set of value premises? Are there dormant value conflicts which may soon be activated by the demands of the organizational role? To answer these questions one might keep track of *whistle-blowing* episodes—the revelation, by an employee, of organizational actions alleged to be illegal, improper, or immoral. In the 1960s and 1970s, such episodes featured:

> The Defense Department weapons cost analyst who exposed a $2 billion cost overrun in the development of the C-5A cargo plane to Congress and had his job abolished by superiors shortly thereafter.[77]
>
> The Food and Drug Administration virologist who warned loudly that the "swine flu" vaccine was dangerous to some people and that no evidence existed showing that the disease was severe enough to warrant a wholesale vaccination program. By the time vaccinated individuals had contracted paralysis and died, the virologist had been fired for "insubordination and inefficiency" and for directly challenging the "integrity of the scientific process."[78]

By assuming the whistle blower's position, individuals can decide how they would have acted in similar situations. Such self-analysis may come in handy in decision-making situations where two or more of the individual's roles or values are diametrically opposed.

Whistle blowing, generally, will continue to be a vexing problem for government. President Carter, in 1978, proposed that an independent Office of Special Council be created "to protect, through the courts if necessary, those who point out violations of ethics."[79] The president's personnel proposals, however, provided additional means by which management could terminate or transfer dissident employees. To confound things further, the line between "good" whistle blowing and "bad" whistle blowing is indistinct and can change over time. In the 1950s, it was respectable, even patriotic, to leak information about the "communist sympathies" of foreign-service officers, even though the evidence often consisted of adolescent political affiliations or other casual associations. In the 1960s, however, an employee who carried on about "subversives" in the State Department was penalized and hounded by superiors.[80] While hidden expenditures of $2 billion will likely continue as a respectable object of whistle blowing, one never knows. Ultimately, the decision to blow the whistle rests with the individual employees and their conception of right and wrong. Once the deed is done, vindication in the courts of law or public opinion may or may not be forthcoming.

SUMMARY

As we have seen, today's public personnel systems, which are developing in the direction of more managerial discretion, retain major features from earlier periods. The objective evaluation of merit through testing remains a prominent feature, as does vigilance against political "hacks," although in some cities this vigilance may be more symbolic than real. The passive (and sometimes active) representation of the country's socioeconomic groups, a policy for which Andrew Jackson carved out the first niche in 1829, is now required by law.

We saw that the public service is rich in history, but we also saw that it is well stocked with conflict. As with the personnel department, some conflict is structured into the organization. Other conflicts arise when external values confront organizational requirements. When this happens, the individual employee often bears the brunt of the battle. In the next chapter, we will again view conflicts centered in the world of public personnel—the battle fought among organized groups of political executives, civil service managers and professionals, and the unionized rank and file.

KEY TERMS AND CONCEPTS

Comprehensive Employment and Training Act (CETA)
Equal employment opportunity
Forced resignation
Hatch Acts

Psychological termination
Representative bureaucracy (active/passive)
Roles
Rule of three

Lateral arabesque
Merit system
Pendleton Act
Senior Civil Service

Spoils system
Veterans' preference
Whistle blowing

NOTES

1. Richard Hofstadter, *The American Political Tradition and the Men Who Made It* (New York: Random House (Vintage Books), 1974), p. 3. See also Sidney H. Aronson, *Status and Kinship in the Higher Civil Service* (Cambridge: Harvard University Press, 1964).
2. Robert A. Dahl, *Democracy in the United States: Promise and Performance* (Chicago: Rand McNally, 1973), p. 130.
3. Arthur Schlesinger, *The Age of Jackson* (Boston: Little, Brown, 1945), p. 99.
4. Crockett quoted in ibid., p. 278.
5. Crockett quoted in ibid.
6. See Leonard D. White, *The Jacksonians* (New York: Macmillan, 1954).
7. Jay M. Shafritz, *Public Personnel Management: The Heritage of Civil Service Reform* (New York: Praeger, 1975), p. 11.
8. Federal workforce figures are from Dahl, *Democracy in the United States*, p. 89.
9. Frederick C. Mosher, *Democracy and the Public Service* (New York: Oxford University Press, 1968), p. 62.
10. Hofstadter, *American Political Tradition*, p. 64.
11. Shafritz, *Public Personnel Management,* p. 12.
12. Schlesinger, *Age of Jackson,* pp. 55–56.
13. Ibid., pp. 50–52.
14. See Robert K. Merton, *Social Theory and Social Structure* (New York: Free Press, 1957), pp. 71–81; also, Edward C. Banfield and James Q. Wilson, *City Politics* (New York: Random House (Vintage Books), 1963), pp. 115–127.
15. Hofstadter, *American Political Tradition*, pp. 211–239.
16. William L. Riordan, *Plunkitt of Tammany Hall* (New York: Dutton, 1963).
17. Harrison quoted in Hofstadter, *American Political Tradition*, p. 222.
18. Banfield and Wilson, *City Politics*, p. 119.
19. Paul Van Riper, *History of the United States Civil Service Commission* (New York: Harper & Row, 1958), pp. 68–70.
20. Hofstadter, *American Political Tradition*, p. 222; Shafritz, *Public Personnel Management*, p. 21.
21. Shafritz, *Public Personnel Management*, p. 24.
22. Mosher, *Democracy and Public Service*, p. 156.
23. Mosher, *Democracy and Public Service*, p. 70.
24. Shafritz, *Public Personnel Management*, p. 23.
25. Mosher, *Democracy and Public Service*, p. 66.
26. See Richard Hofstadter, *The Age of Reform* (New York: Knopf, 1955).
27. John Rehfuss, *Public Administration as Political Process* (New York: Scribner, 1973).
28. See Harold Seidman, *Politics, Position and Power: The Dynamics of Federal Organization*, 2nd ed. (New York: Oxford University Press, 1975).
29. O. Glenn Stahl, *Public Personnel Administration*, 7th ed. (New York: Harper & Row, 1976), p. 70.
30. David Rosenbloom, "Public Personnel Administration and Politics: Toward

a New Public Personnel Administration," *Midwest Review of Public Administration* 7, no. 2 (April 1973): 98–110.

31. Stahl, "Public Personnel Administration," pp. 149–153.
32. Ibid., p. 164.
33. David T. Stanley, "Trying to Avoid Layoffs," *Public Administration Review* 37, no. 5 (September/October 1977): 515–517.
34. Laurence J. Peter and Raymond Hull, *The Peter Principle* (New York: Bantam Books, 1970), pp. 21–22.
35. Shafritz, *Public Personnel Management* pp. 51–56.
36. Ibid., p. 56.
37. William Timmons, *Long Hair in the Merit System* (Syracuse: Inter-University Case Program, 1972), p. 1.
38. Ibid., p. 5.
39. Ibid., p. 12.
40. Ibid., p. 3.
41. Ibid., p. 9.
42. Ibid., p. 10.
43. Ibid., p. 11.
44. Ibid., p. 19.
45. Ibid., p. 20.
46. Ibid.
47. Ibid.
48. Ibid.
49. Ibid., p. 21.
50. Ibid., p. 22.
51. *Time,* 6 March 1978, p. 13.
52. Ibid.
53. National Commission on Productivity and Work Quality, *Employee Incentives to Improve State and Local Government Productivity* (Washington: U.S. Government Printing Office, 1975), chapter 3 and appendix 4.
54. Ibid., p. 34.
55. *Public Administration Times* 1, no. 2 (February 1, 1978): 7.
56. *Public Administration Times,* p. 6. See also Governor Patrick Lucey, "Productivity: An Essential Strategy for Survival," *Public Productivity Review* 1, no. 1 (September 1975): 30–35.
57. See Herbert Kaufman, "Administrative Decentralization and Political Power," in Lewis Gawthrop, ed., *The Administrative Process and Democratic Theory* (Boston: Houghton Mifflin, 1970), pp. 404–406. Kaufman sees executive leadership as a third element in the cycle.
58. J. A. Schumpeter, *Capitalism, Socialism and Democracy* (London: Allen and Unwin, 1943).
59. David M. Levitan, "Political Ends and Administrative Means," in Ganthrop, *The Administrative Process,* p. 433.
60. J. Donald Kingsley, *Representative Bureaucracy* (Yellow Springs, Ohio: Antioch Press, 1944).
61. Reinhard Bendix, *Higher Civil Servants in American Society* (Boulder: University of Colorado Press, 1949).
62. Mosher, *Democracy and Public Service,* pp. 10–17; 91–95.
63. John P. Renninger, "Staffing International Organizations: The Role of the International Civil Service Commission," in *Public Administration Review* 37, N. 4, (July-August 1977): 391–396.
64. See Daniel P. Moynihan, *Maximum Feasible Misunderstanding: Community Action in the War Against Poverty* (New York: Free Press, 1969).

65. Harry Grossman, "The Equal Employment Opportunity Act of 1972: Its Implications for the State and Local Government Manager," in Jay M. Shafritz, ed., *A New World: Readings on Modern Public Personnel Management* (Chicago: International Personnel Management Association, 1975), pp. 100–109; see also Lloyd G. Nigro, ed., "A Mini-Symposium: Affirmative Action in Public Employment," *Public Administration Review* (May–June, 1974), pp. 234–246.
66. Grossman, "Equal Opportunity Act," p. 107.
67. *Congressional Quarterly Guide to Current American Government* (Washington: Congressional Quarterly, 1977), pp. 65–66.
68. Ibid.
69. This discussion is drawn from *Productivity—The Personnel Challenge* (Englewood Cliffs, N.J.: Prentice-Hall, 1973), which surveys the attitude of personnel managers toward their jobs.
70. Leonard Broom and Philip Selznick, *Principles of Sociology* (New York: Harper & Row, 1970), p. 18.
71. See John Finley Scott, *Internalization of Norms: A Sociological Theory of Moral Commitment* (Englewood Cliffs, N.J.: Prentice-Hall, 1971), chap. I.
72. Robert Kahn, et al., *Organizational Stress: Studies in Role Conflict and Ambiguity* (New York: Wiley, 1964).
73. Charles Wolf, Jr., *Indonesian Assignment* (Syracuse: Inter-University Case Program, 1963).
74. John R. P. French and Robert D. Caplan, "Organizational Stress and Individual Strain," in Alfred J. Marrow ed., *The Failure of Success* (New York: AMACOM, 1972), pp. 30–66.
75. Ibid., p. 38.
76. Ibid.
77. Helen Dudar, "The Price of Whistle Blowing," *New York Times Magazine,* 30 October 1977, pp. 41–54; see also *The Bureaucrat* 6, no. 4 (Winter 1977), which is devoted to "whistle blowing."
78. Ibid., p. 49.
79. Presidential Press Conference of Thursday, 2 March 1978, *New York Times,* 3 March 1978.
80. Dudar, "Price of Whistle Blowing," p. 52.

BIBLIOGRAPHY

Aronson, Sidney H. *Status and Kinship in the Higher Civil Service.* Cambridge: Harvard University Press, 1964.
Banfield, Edward C. and Wilson, James Q. *City Politics.* New York: Random House (Vintage Books), 1963.
Bendix, Reinhard. *Higher Civil Servants in American Society.* Boulder: University of Colorado Press, 1949.
Ermer, Virginia B. and Strange, John H., eds. *Blacks and Bureaucracies: Readings in the Problems and Politics of Change* New York: Crowell, 1972.
Golembiewski, Robert T. and Cohen, Michael, eds. *People in Public Service: A Reader in Public Personnel Administration.* Itasca: F. E. Peacock, 1970.
Harvey, Donald R. *The Civil Service Commission.* New York: Praeger, 1970.
Hofstadter, Richard. *The Age of Reform.* New York: Knopf, 1955.
———. *The American Political Tradition and the Men Who Made It.* New York: Random House (Vintage Books), 1974.
Kahn, Robert, et al. *Organizational Stress: Studies in Role Conflict and Ambiguity.* New York: Wiley, 1964.

Mosher, Frederick C. *Democracy and the Public Service.* New York: Oxford University Press, 1968.

National Commission on Productivity and Work Quality. *Employee Incentives to Improve State and Local Government Productivity.* Washington: U. S. Government Printing Office, 1975.

Nigro, Felix A. and Nigro, Lloyd G. *The New Public Personnel Administration.* Itasca: F. E. Peacock, 1976.

Peter, Laurence J. and Hull, Raymond. *The Peter Principle.* New York: Bantam Books, 1970.

Peters, Charles and Branch, Taylor, eds. *Whistle Blowing: Dissent in the Public Interest.* New York: Praeger, 1972.

Productivity—The Personnel Challenge. Englewood Cliffs, N.J.: Prentice-Hall, 1973.

Schlesinger, Arthur. *The Age of Jackson.* Boston: Little, Brown, 1945.

Scott, John Finley. *Internalization of Norms: A Sociology Theory of Moral Commitment.* Englewood Cliffs, N.J.: Prentice-Hall, 1971.

Shafritz, Jay M., ed. *A New World: Readings on Modern Personnel Management.* Chicago: International Personnel Management Association, 1975.

———. *Public Personnel Management: The Heritage of Civil Service Reform.* New York: Praeger, 1975.

Stahl, O. Glenn. *Public Personnel Administration,* 7th ed. New York: Harper & Row, 1976.

Timmons, William. *Long Hair in the Merit System.* Syracuse: Inter-University Case Program, 1972.

Tolchin, Martin and Tolchin, Susan. *To the Victor: Political Patronage from the Clubhouse to the White House.* New York: Random House (Vintage Books), 1971.

VanRiper, Paul P. *History of the United States Civil Service Commission.* New York: Harper & Row, 1958.

Vaughn, Robert. *The Spoiled System.* Washington: Public Interest Research Group, 1972.

White, Leonard D. *The Jacksonians.* New York: Macmillan, 1954.

Wright, Grace H. *Public Sector Employment Selection.* Chicago: International Personnel Management Association, 1974.

In addition to the sources cited in the notes and bibliography, the following *Public Administration Review (PAR)* articles are a convenient starting point for a more detailed exploration of the material in this chapter.

Beaumont, Enid F. "A Pivotal Point for the Merit Concept," *PAR* 34, no. 5 (Sept./Oct. 1974): 426–430.

Garnham, David. "Foreign Service Elitism and U.S. Foreign Affairs," *PAR* 35, no. 1 (Jan./Feb. 1975): 44–51.

Hellriegel, Don and Larry Short. "Equal Employment Opportunity in the Federal Government: A Comparative Analysis," *PAR* 32, no. 6 (Nov./Dec. 1972): 851–858.

Kranz, Harry. "Are Merit and Equity Compatible," *PAR* 34, no. 5 (Sept./Oct. 1974): 431–434.

Levitan, Sar A. and Joyce K. Zichler. "Block Grants for Manpower Programs," *PAR* 35, no. 2 (March/April 1975): 191–195.

McGregor, Eugene B. "Social Equity and the Public Service," *PAR* 34, no. 1 (Jan./Feb. 1974): 18–29.

Meier, Kenneth John and Lloyd G. Nigro. "Representative Bureaucracy and Policy Preferences: A Study in the Attitudes of Federal Executives," *PAR* 36, no. 4 (July/Aug. 1976): 458–469.

Morrison, David E. "Stress and the Public Administrator," *PAR* 37, no. 4 (July/Aug. 1977): 407–414.

Nachmias, David and David H. Rosenbloom. "Measuring Bureaucratic Representation and Integration," *PAR* 33, no. 6 (Nov./Dec. 1973): 590–597.

Newland, Chester A. "Public Personnel Administration: Legalistic Reforms vs. Effectiveness, Efficiency and Economy," *PAR* 36, no. 5 (Sept./Oct. 1976): 529–537.

Nigro, Lloyd G., ed. "Affirmative Action in Public Employment," *PAR* 34, no. 3 (May/June 1974): 234–245.

Reeves, Earl J. "Making Equality of Employment Opportunity a Reality in the Federal Service," *PAR* 30, no. 1 (Jan./Feb. 1970): 43–49.

Rosenbloom, David H. "Public Personnel Administration and The Constitution: An Emergent Approach," *PAR* 35, no. 1 (Jan./Feb. 1975): 52–59.

Rosenbloom, David H. "Some Political Implications of the Drift Toward A Liberation of Federal Employees," *PAR* 31, no. 4 (July/Aug. 1971): 420–426.

Rosenbloom, David H. and Carole Cassler Obuchowski. "Public Personnel Examinations and the Constitution: Emergent Trends," *PAR* 37, no. 1 (Jan./Feb. 1977): 9–18.

Schweitzer, Glenn E. "The Rights of Federal Employees Named as Alleged Discriminatory Officials," *PAR* 37, no. 1 (Jan./Feb. 1977): 58–63.

RELEVANT PERIODICALS
Compensation Review
The Journal of Human Resources
Personnel Journal
Public Personnel Management
Public Personnel Review
Training and Development Journal
Work Life

RELEVANT CASE STUDIES
(Cases marked ICCH are available from the Intercollegiate Case Clearing House, Soldier Field, Boston, Mass. 02163; cases marked ICP are available from the Inter-University Case Program, Box 229, Syracuse, N.Y. 13210.)

Godfrey, E. D., Jr. *Transfer of the Children's Bureau,* [ICP]
Lynn, L. E., Jr. *The C-5A,* (A)(B),* [ICCH]
Riker, W. *NLRB Field Examiner,* [ICP]
Timmons, W. *Long Hair in the Merit System* [ICP]

*Letters indicate that the case is presented in several installments.

CHAPTER 7

COLLECTIVE CONFLICT IN THE PUBLIC ORGANIZATION

INTRODUCTION

We closed Chapter 6 with a discussion of the dilemma of the individual confronted with contradictory role expectations. Supervisors did not know whether to assume the teacher or disciplinarian component of their role; whistle blowers had to decide between the roles of "John Q. Citizen" and "Bill Bureaucrat." Although in conflict, all of these role expectations were previously defined and formally approved by legitimate authorities, namely, the government or the organization. Friction, when it occurred, involved two authoritatively sanctioned roles. Thus, the whistle blower invariably sought to alert a higher authority—the chief executive, the legislature, the courts. Despite the harsh treatment afforded some whistle blowers by immediate superiors, higher-ups generally sought to resolve the contradictions underlying the original dilemma.

In this chapter, we will look at the more protracted struggles that mark the public organization. These struggles are collective, not individual. Coercion often is explicit. Management threatens unions with million-dollar fines should walkouts occur, and unions counter that a paralyzing transport strike could eat up as much in business taxes in a day. Of course, few labor disputes reach this stage; however, the possibility of a knockdown, dragout battle is always present. With less dramatic potential, but equal intensity, political appointees and career executives square off in the halls of administration. So, too, do administrative generalists and technical experts. At issue in all of these confrontations is the allocation of management authority in the public organization.

Thus, *conflict* will be the central focus of this chapter. Conflict theorists, those who reject the harmony themes of the Scientific Management and Human Relations schools, will be our first subject of attention. Public sector labor relations and the collective bargaining milieu will illustrate conflict in an organizational setting. Next we will consider the conflicting frames of reference of the political appointee and the career executive. The interprofessional rivalries that exist in the public service will also be reviewed. Finally, the growing professional status of the public administrator will be examined.

"THE HARMONY BIAS" IN ORGANIZATION STUDIES

In Chapter 5 we considered people in organizations from two broad perspectives. One was Scientific Management; the other was Human Relations. Both schools promised productivity. To Human Relationists, productivity was a function of an egalitarian (relative to the bureaucratic model) work environment; stimulating, self-satisfying tasks; and interpersonal competence. Taylorites and neo-Taylorites thought that most employees would produce in return for adequate material payoffs such as salaries and anticipated raises or promotions.

If both schools sought productivity, so, too, did they seek harmony in the workplace and in society. Conflict deeply disturbed the men and women who shaped organization theory in the United States. Taylor's career was contemporaneous with the bloodiest management-labor battles in U.S. history. Mayo wrote during Depression era factory seizures by workers and mass marches on Washington by the unemployed. To both Taylor and Mayo, societywide conflict was substantially rooted in the industrial setting. Thus, a generation apart, but with equal preeminence, Taylor and Mayo suggested that societal cohesion was dependent on the avoidance of intraorganizational conflict.[1]

Taylor saw piecework as the key that would calm industrial strife by forging a partnership between management and the individual worker. Mayo saw management's recognition and fulfillment of the work group's needs as the giant step towards industrial peace. And the search for harmony did not stop with Mayo. Through the sociological and psychological variants of Human Relations and through decision-making theories, there was one persistent theme—"the utility and functionality of consensus and the disutility and dysfunctionality of conflict in organizations."[2]

In their on-the-site experiments, Human Relationists successfully diminished conflict. In its place was group cooperation and/or worker satisfaction—and increased productivity, sometimes. Neo-Taylorites could point to rising salaries and increased overall output as proof that material remuneration was the crucial motivator. In support of both sides, neither bloodshed nor worker coup d'etats marked the industrial scene and, through the mid-1960s, the country was tranquil.

It seemed as if the researchers had covered all the bases. The individual employee was reasonably well paid, the work group was happy, and the country appeared productive and prosperous. Few organizational theorists, however, were looking very hard at the large groups within the organization. Those who did, found it difficult to reconcile strikes, work slowdowns, tension between organizational units, and equipment sabotage by industrial workers with the widespread harmony purported to exist in organizations. Where Mayo had seen a "cooperative system" as the natural order of things, Ralf Dahrendorf and Michel Crozier saw conflct, rather than cooperation and demands, rather than appeals.[3]

The conflict theorized by Dahrendorf and studied by Crozier was between aggregates of individuals within the organization. Dahrendorf theorized that there existed a single power boundary in organizations with positions of domination on the one side and positions of subjection on the other. Conflict would erupt as each side "sought to retain a share in the determination of future relations as well as for the retention of other benefits which may be the immediate reasons for the conflict."[4] To Dahrendorf, the struggle was not, in the final analysis, for higher wages, or better working conditions, or more respect. The struggle was for control, for the power to make the rules; the object was to get a piece (or a bigger piece) of the action.

Although Dahrendorf had proposed a single power boundary between dominant and subservient positions in organizations, he reserved spaces for the admission of expert positions and staff positions.[5] The studies of Michel Crozier filled in those reserve spaces. Crozier studied a French clerical agency and a manufacturing concern. In the former, there was conflict primarily between hierarchal levels.[6] In the manufacturing concern there was a vertical breach with management and the production workers set against the technical engineers and the machine repairpersons.[7]

The repairpersons were the key to the power alliances in the manufacturing firms studied by Crozier. They carved out their independence by declaring the production machinery off-limits to anyone else in the factory. The production workers were not to fiddle with their machines and, above all, supervisors were to keep their distance. Nosy production workers could find themselves laid off if a repairperson declared the machine "down" for major repairs. When one dogged supervisor found that a "major" repair was a missing screw, the strike-wary plant director chose to ignore the incident. Ultimately, it was the supervisor, not the guilty repairperson, who was forced to leave the plant.[8]

The plant's technical engineers allied themselves with the repairpersons and against management. Management, for its part, was outsmarted by the engineers and outmuscled by the repairpersons. The production workers were subordinate, but their tasks were bound by rules and required little management intervention. Moreover, as co-victims of the repair force's bullying, there was a certain affinity between the managers and the production workers.[9]

In its intensity, the conflict Crozier found was culture bound. Most French workers spent a working lifetime at a single task, therefore loyalty to their trade and hostility to trespassers could be fierce. Moreover, with the extreme bureaucratization that marked the French organization, such uncertainties as did arise found fresh, aggressive, and expansion-minded adversaries ready to do battle with hammer and tongs.[10] Although the commitments of the American workers are more muted than their French counterparts, due to occupational mobility and other factors, organizational combat in the United States is not, as we shall see, marked by timidity.

PUBLIC SECTOR UNIONIZATION

A *union* consolidates the voice of a group of workers in the persona of one or more employees or an external labor organization such as the American Federation of State, County, and Municipal Workers. The union assumes its representative position by virtue of a majority vote of the workers in a single department (police, fire), or a single occupational category (clerical, maintenance) that cuts across several departments. This collective voice may speak out on wider issues—for example, several public employee unions opposed the war in Vietnam—but in the main it advances the workplace-related interests of the employees. When those interests are contrary to what management perceives as its interests, the battle is joined and it is called *collective bargaining*. In collective bargaining, representatives of management and representatives of labor set forth their positions, negotiate the differences—with a strike as implicit or explicit leverage—and arrive at a written agreement that represents the work contract between the employees and the organization.

The average citizen has come to accept the above scenario as routine, even timeless. Our history books tell us that unionism in the United States began in earnest about a century ago with Samuel Gompers. The right of employees to organize, to bargain with management, and to strike has been recognized by the federal law for nearly half a century. This, however, is a chronicle of the rise of unionism in the private sector.

The history of public employee unionism is quite different. To this day, some jurisdictions refuse to recognize employee unions. Where there is recognition, strikes often are prohibited. In addition, few laws that grant public employees the right to organize, bargain collectively, and strike predate the 1960s. The reasons for this retarded development are worthy of examination.

The Right to Associate and to Bargain

Many scholars have commented that President Calvin Coolidge said little that was noteworthy. In 1919, however, as governor of Massachusetts, Coolidge made one of his more famous comments concerning public employee unionism. In response to the Boston police strike of 1919, Coolidge announced that "there is no right to strike against the public safety by anybody, anywhere, anytime."[11]

Coolidge's statement echoed the prevailing mood of the day. Government employment was seen as a privilege carrying more duties and obligations than were associated with private employment. The "people"—a powerful but somewhat hazy concept—were both the taxpaying stockholders and the consumers of public services. Strikes seemed to deprive the people of both their management rights and their rights to services. Moreover, the stability of government employment and the merit system that featured tenure protections, appeals processes, and politically neutral evaluation seemed a sufficient enough advance over the prevailing private sector practices to foreclose labor's major grievances. Thus, the tenor of the times supported harsh action, and, to perform the work of the striking police officers, Coolidge called out the National Guard. This response, used to this day, illustrates that management, at least, continues to believe that public services are essential and must not be interrupted.[12]

Coolidge broke the Boston police strike but did not prevent public employees from organizing to advance their interests. The model established by the postal workers in the 1880s—that of a workers' interest group lobbying with the legislature—had spread by the 1920s to fire fighters, the police, and teachers. Indeed, for 11 years (1938–1949), Michael Quill, the head of the Transport Workers Union, was a member of New York's City Council. His union constituents, meanwhile, ran the city's subways.[13] With the ability to marshal such strength, public employee organizations were influential even as their formal role was restricted by law.

By lobbying in the legislature or pressuring elected executives at the polls, public employee unions were indirectly and informally negotiating work terms for their members. This lobbying power also was used to achieve formal recognition of unions as the bargaining agent for public employees. Through the 1960s and 1970s, public employee unions charged that civil service commissions and personnel departments, despite their statutory "neutrality," were management tools. The unions wanted to be recognized as the true employee representatives, and, in 1962, an executive order issued by President Kennedy sanctioned "orderly and constructive relationships . . . between employee organizations and management" in the federal government.[14] During the 1960s and 1970s, numerous states, counties, and cities followed suit and legitimized collective bargaining between public management and government employees.[15]

Most people associate collective bargaining with its most prominent manifestation; namely, the contract negotiation. However, collective bargaining is an ongoing process and includes the formal resolution of disputes arising out of differing union-management interpretations of existing contracts. Because it breeds familiarity between union and management officials, collective bargaining creates informal channels of complaint resolution that feature verbal agreements between union shop stewards and middle-level managers that may or may not be institutionalized in succeeding contracts.

Despite this mid-term activity, drawing up the contract remains at the core of the collective bargaining process. The contract legitimizes the union, delineates its future role in the management of the enterprise, and, by conveying material rewards, strengthens the workers' support for their union. For management, the contract can mean a reduction or a reaffirmation of its discretion and authority. In short, the contract rearranges the power boundary that exists in the public organization between labor and management.

Who Bargains for Management in Government?

Although the contract has a major effect on management policy, collective bargaining rarely features the direct involvement of chief executives. While chief executives retain an authoritative voice, they remain in the background for several reasons. First, they do not have the time for a full commitment to the negotiation process, which is, usually, quite lengthy. Second, with the mayor, the county executive, or the governor present at the negotiating table, other management negotiators are likely to be ignored as union representatives zero in on the person who can finalize points of contention. Third, the union can, justifiably or unjustifiably, accuse elected officials of "grandstanding for votes." Such across-the-table name calling can cripple negotiations. Finally, the nuts and bolts of collective bargaining, such as the language of contract construction, may lie beyond the grasp of the political executive.

Management representatives at the bargaining table are more often the jurisdiction's chief legal officer, and/or the budget or personnel director, or the heads of the operating departments. In some jurisdictions, there are full-time offices of collective bargaining headed by professional negotiators who lead the management team at contract time. The political executive, by staying a respectable distance from contract negotiations, considers union proposals in a calmer setting. For similar reasons, arm's length participation may be advisable for legislators, who, like the political executive, define the parameters of management's position and retain partial authority to finalize the negotiators' commitments.

THE COLLECTIVE BARGAINING GAME: MOVES AND MOTIVES

Collective bargaining is wide ranging. Under the issue of "wages and hours," for example, overtime pay, holiday pay, uniform and meal allowances, vacation time, sick leaves, and personal days may be included. Benefits include life, health, dental, and disability insurance, and pension fund arrangements. Although management traditionally retains the "right" to set "on the job" rules, this too increasingly becomes a subject of bargaining. In short, current trends seem to indicate that less and less of the employment relationship will remain exempt from bargaining.

Most students are probably familiar with the fireworks that accompany collective bargaining. Threatening a strike if its demands go unmet, a union demands a hefty wage hike. "Impossible!" is the usual management response. Inevitably, it seems, when negotiations begin, agreement is hopelessly remote. However, this remoteness can be more apparent than real since most initial demands are bargaining ploys. On the union side, such ploys can serve several purposes. First, some demands are designed to test management's response to contract issues important to the union. Second, demands may set the stage for crucial battles in future years' negotiations. Third, demands may be a gesture of recognition or conciliation towards militant union elements. With demands of the second and third type, the union leadership may not desire to advance beyond a public presentation in this year's negotiations. Public managers also are skilled in the bluffs and countermoves of the collective bargaining game and may make demands with an eye toward future negotiations. Thus, as the collective bargaining game begins, one hand may be played for the benefit of onlookers. The drama may unfold as follows:

Union demand: Triple pay for holiday work.
Management Demand: All employees be subject to lie detector
    tests.

These are two constituent-satisfying moves. Workers' complaints that double pay for holidays does not compensate for the social benefits foregone have been recognized. So has the public's indignation over a recent embezzlement scandal in the jurisdiction. Each side permits the other to accommodate these sentiments. After these demands have been "considered" for a decent period, they are withdrawn by mutual consent. Witnessing this "trade-off," constituents are reassured that their representatives are doggedly slogging through the issues.

When negotiators get around to issues of immediate importance to the two sides, the lead-off bargaining moves change little. Exaggerated wage demands may be countered by management's assertion that bankruptcy is imminent. There is ritual to this since everyone involved knows that eventually the union will "come down" in its demands and management will "come up" in its offer. Indeed, most parties in the negotiations may have a good notion of where the eventual compromise point will be. Still, the parties hem and haw and cling to extreme demands until late in the grueling game. To the casual observer, much of this is a hypocritical waste of time. However, this attitude overlooks the situation of the actors in the collective bargaining process.[16]

Collective bargaining is structured as an adversarial proceeding. The key players act in a fiduciary capacity. That is, the union leader is supposed to advance the members' interests, not balance management needs and taxpayers' wallets against the workers' demands. Similarly, management must seek the best deal for their taxpaying clients. In short, the parties are charged with playing the game, not predicting the outcome. Moreover, even though the parties may know in advance the approximate outcome—say within 2 percent—they are committed to getting the better portion of that outcome for their clients. Since where one ends up in negotiations is sometimes a function of where one starts, an opening bid on an issue that will become a part of the work contract will look like this:

Union demand: 20 percent wage increase
Management offer: 2 percent wage increase

Although these bids may appear outlandish, the parties are sensitive to extreme positions that could poison the negotiating process. (This is why there may often be a tacit understanding about extreme *constituency bids*.) For instance, management, by taking a status quo position, might provide a dual impetus for worker unrest. Management could anger the workers; and their humiliated representatives could seek to channel that anger towards a strike.

Overall, the true bargaining moves of the participants may be constrained if the following outcomes are clearly associated with differing wage increases:

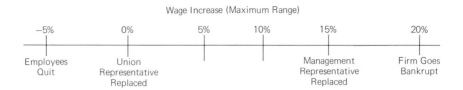

It is in the interests of the bargainers to stay within the 1 to 14 percent range. Indeed, since both the management negotiator and the union negotiator do not know the exact point at which they might be let go by their constituents, a margin of safety might be added. Thus, the union negotiator will not accept less than a 2 percent wage increase; nor will the management negotiator grant more than a 13 percent increase. Therefore, the real negotiating range becomes:

Within the negotiating range, each side will establish targets. Unions arrive at targets by estimating the needs of members, the capacity of management to meet those needs, and the political limits on the settlement range. Management arrives at targets by estimating its revenue capacity, the minimum needs of workers, and the political environment. For instance, a union's target will combine a high estimate of what members need, an optimistic estimate of what management can provide, and a favorable assumption about the political limits.

There are several reasons why the union negotiator tends not to aim to soak management for every possible cent. First, since the process is a continuing one marked by mutual accommodation, shoving for unconditional surrender invites retaliation and a breakdown in the union-management relationship. Second, excessive short-term gains may actually jeopardize the negotiator's job by raising the members' long-term expectations beyond what the negotiator can hope to achieve in the future.

During negotiations, the union's *target point* may change considerably. Management may demonstrate that its financial condition is much worse than the union thought. Additionally, management's negotiators may demonstrate extreme toughness by aggressively raising a variety of working condition issues as trade-offs against the wage package. In light of this, feedback from union members may indicate that certain working conditions are more valuable than the highest possible wage increases. Management also reassesses its negotiating position in response to the union's bargaining.

In this way each side modifies its target points in response to information from the other side during negotiations. However, the extent to which the union will lower its demands and to which management will raise its offer is bounded by a *resistance point*. For the union, for instance, this point is bounded by the lowest estimate of constituent needs, the most pessimistic estimate of what management can provide, and the least favorable assumptions about the union's political environment.

Much of the flavor and fireworks of the collective bargaining process is rooted in the fact that the primary determinant of one party's target is its perception of the other party's resistance point. That is, the union aims to get most of what management is willing to give. Management aims to give the minimum that the union is willing to accept. However, neither side can ever be sure if its perception is correct amid the bluff and bluster of the bargaining table. Thus, the process becomes very much like a game. For instance, we might look at one step in the process as a management bid—which may or may not be truthful—followed by a union play. The success of the union's play is dependent upon the accuracy with which management's veracity is estimated.[17]

> Management Bid: "We will accept a strike before agreeing to
> more than a 10 percent wage increase."
> Union Play: Accept or reject management's assertion

Thus, if the union accepts management's assertion as truthful, the union's wage increase target will be readjusted to 10 percent (Figure 7.1, Boxes A & B). If management has indeed been truthful, the union maximizes its gain (Box B). If management was lying, however, the union does not maximize its gain by accepting management's poverty plea (Box A). However, a rejection strategy by the union has the potential for greater gains *or* greater risks (Boxes C & D). If management has been lying, and its bluff is called, the union will probably win a wage increase higher than 10 percent (Box C). However, if management has been truthful, but labor is unbelieving, a strike may ensue that punishes everyone (Box D).

This maneuvering is prominent in newspaper accounts of labor-management disputes involving public and private organizations. There can be hundreds and even thousands of moves in a single contract negotiation as each side adjusts to the other. Demands are scaled down

CHARACTER OF MANAGEMENT'S ASSERTION

		Untruthful	Truthful
UNION RESPONSE TOWARD MANAGEMENT'S ASSERTION	Accept	(A) 10% wage increase	(B) 10% wage increase
	Reject	(C) 10%+ wage increase	(D) STRIKE

Figure 7.1 Management's "Final" Offer

where the opposition appears genuinely incapable of, or utterly opposed to, meeting them. Where less substantiation or resolve is evident, demands remain firm. Overall, both sides work toward a middle solution since, in most cases, neither wants to play its strike card. The strike starts a new ballgame and both sides may raise the ante. The union ups its wage demand to reimburse striking workers. Management may lower its offer to compensate for lost income. Often, a strike must drag on for several weeks before the proposals of opposing sides are again as close as they were on the eve of the walkout.[18]

PUBLIC SECTOR LABOR RELATIONS

Collective bargaining always takes place in the context of a larger system. That system constrains the parties to the negotiation. If management must draw upon a highly competitive labor market, such as electronic technicians, paying less than the market wage would attract marginally competent individuals who could detract from organizational efficiency. Similarly, labor must be careful when negotiating with employers who produce goods or provide services in a highly competitive market. Too large a wage package, relative to other firms in the industry, can place the firm at a competitive disadvantage and lead to bankruptcy or relocation. Thus, in private industry, where labor, product, or service markets are highly competitive and workers and firms are mobile, there are some built-in safeguards against extortionate behavior.[19] Of course, industrywide unions may enjoy an advantage in dealing with many small firms, and giant firms may bully small unions. Also, in oligopoly and monopoly industries, union and management may play a high stakes game—a game of collusion—with the knowledge that consumers will foot the bill. Nonetheless, in contrast to public sector bargaining, most people perceive private sector collective bargaining as a fair contest.

When public managers and public employees bargain collectively, many observers see a contest rigged in favor of unions that make and collect on extortionate demands. Robert Fowler nicely sums up this view:

"a government cannot change locations—it cannot go South; it cannot simply go out of business. . . . It is also likely to be under heavy citizen pressure to end any strike."[20] In the words of another observer, the public pressure for a settlement is likely to spring from "visions of rampaging criminals and unchecked holocausts, of empty classrooms and hospitals, of mountains of garbage and chaos in transportation."[21]

As for the elected public officials who engineer management's defense, many authors see them as ambitious jellyfish willing quietly to buy off unions with tomorrow's tax payments. Witness this query by two observers: "Was it simply a matter of indifference to New York's Mayor Lindsay in September 1969 whether another teachers strike occurred on the eve of a municipal election? Did the size and speed of the settlement with the United Federation of Teachers suggest nothing about one first rate politician's estimate of his vulnerability? And are the chickens now coming home to roost because of extravagant concessions on pensions for employees the result only of mistaken actuarial calculations? Or do they reflect the irrelevance of long run considerations to politicians vulnerable to the strike and compelled to think in terms of short run political impact?"[22]

Other fusillades charge that public management's conduct of collective bargaining is fragmented among personnel directors, chief executives, and legislators. Inexperience is also a liability as the jurisdiction's chief executive and management's top negotiators, who often change from contract to contract, confront veteran union negotiators with years of experience.[23]

There is another side to this rather dismal evaluation. One study found that city managers take an aggressive stance toward unions. Excessive demands are rejected, intrusions on managerial prerogatives are resisted, and strikes are approached with an eye towards outlasting the union.[24] It has been suggested that big city mayors adopt such an aggressive negotiating stance.[25] Indeed, this posture has been forced on many mayors as their cities flounder in seas of red ink. Bondholders, governors, and even the federal government are urging that a hard line be taken against union demands. Unions rampaging to huge settlements, a feature of the 1960s and early 1970s, appears to be a phenomenon of the past, outdated by the worsening financial conditions of cities. Unions are toning down their economic demands. As with negotiations in private industry, a "market" of sorts constrains the behavior of union and management in the public sector.

Productivity Bargaining

In the 1970s, there were additional indications that the resolve of public management was stiffening. Many jurisdictions, feeling a financial pinch or a taxpayer push, turned to productivity bargaining. *Pro-*

ductivity bargaining is "an attempt through the process of collective negotiations to obtain changes in work rules or practice that will permit the employer to reduce the cost and/or improve the quality or quantity of the service it provides."[26] Productivity bargaining can proceed in two ways. One is the *buy-out.* Management comes to the negotiations armed with work modification proposals to be traded off for benefits sought by the union. If the union consents to the work modifications, the productivity outcomes do not affect union benefits won at the bargaining table. However, *gain-sharing* clauses in work contracts do tie benefits to productivity increases. Union and management agree to "share the gains" from higher levels of service. If there are no gains, there are no benefits.

An offshoot of productivity bargaining is the *labor-management productivity committee.* These committees represent "formal negotiated arrangements by which labor and management cooperate in improving the quantity and quality of production."[27] In New York City, labor-management committees are set up at the departmental level and confer on productivity issues.[28] Generally, such committees are advisory in nature. Their proposals must be approved by management or, as the case may be, agreed to by labor and management as a part of a subsequent work contract.

Breaking Impasses

The relationship between union and management can seriously break down in two ways. First, an impasse can be reached at the bargaining table. Second, during the term of the contract, labor and management may be unable to dispose of a grievance—an allegation by one party that the other has violated the contract terms. These situations give rise to several *impasse procedures* designed to facilitate a resolution of the dispute through the formal intervention of a third party. Impasse procedures include: *conciliation, mediation, fact finding,* and *arbitration.*

> *Conciliation* Conciliation involves informal "efforts by a third party toward the accommodation of opposing viewpoints in a labor dispute, so as to effect a voluntary settlement."[29] A conciliator takes the stated positions of the parties and seeks to demonstrate that they are more compatible than the parties perceive them to be.

> *Mediation* Mediation is similar to conciliation in that it calls on a neutral third party to bring the two sides together. Mediators, however, may make proposals for settlement of the dispute that have not been made by either party.[30] Moreover, mediation generally occurs in a formal setting. Almost all states, along with the

federal government, provide formal mediation services for settling private as well as public labor-management disputes.

Fact Finding   The work of mediators and conciliators takes place, for the most part, behind closed doors. The task is to facilitate labor-management interchanges without formally judging the merits of the competing claims. Fact finding, on the other hand, features evidentiary hearings and formal opinions. Fact finders issue nonbinding recommendations to the parties on what the settlement ought to be. Often these recommendations are made public.[31]

Arbitration   In arbitration, as in fact finding, a neutral third party conducts formal proceedings to consider evidence and arguments submitted by labor and management in support of their respective positions. In arbitration, however, the decision of the arbitrator is final and binding and becomes a part of the contract.[32]

Impasse resolution procedures have their good points and bad points. On the positive side, since the disputants are too closely and passionately involved with the issues, a third party can see relatively painless solutions that have been overlooked. Also, when fact finders and arbitrators expose the bargaining process to public scrutiny, outlandish negotiating stances tend to wither away. In some states *all-or-nothing arbitration* procedures have been promulgated by law. Under such clauses compromises are barred and only one disputant will be upheld. Such procedures tend to pressure labor and management toward good faith negotiations.[33] In all cases, impasse resolution mechanisms put derailed contract negotiations back on track at least temporarily.

There are negative views of impasse mechanisms in the public sector. First, conciliators, mediators, fact finders, and arbitrators may "split the difference." Thus it can pay for one side to adhere to extreme demands, particularly if the opposition pursues a more moderate course.[34] In such a case, the stubborn side comes out ahead. Second, impasse procedures can be bypassed. The union may appeal to the legislature, or the personnel director may appeal to the mayor; thus, either quarter can force a decision prior to, or despite the recommendations of, the mediators, fact finders, or arbitrators. This clearly undermines the authority of third-party interveners and may render their participation little more than cosmetic.[35]

There are suggestions on how impasse procedures can better be utilized. To remedy the "bypass" problem, a clear legislative delegation of authority to management to conclude an agreement is advised. Also, for a more flexible response to differing contract disputes, jurisdictions are urged to relax their requirements for specific impasse procedures.[36]

The Putrefying Outgrowth of a Garbarge Strike. Such scenes fueled the arguments of those who sought to limit the activities of public employee unions. (United Press International Photo)

Whether these remedies are adopted, impasse resolution mechanisms will remain a major feature in conflict between union and management over the direction of public personnel policy.

Public Employee Strikes

Strikes by employees of the federal government are prohibited. Most states have followed suit, and the prohibition applies, as well, to county and municipal employees in those states. Nonetheless, when the "minute before midnite" negotiation session breaks up in acrimony, or when the entreaties of the mediator are rejected, the public may well "sniff through a garbage strike, walk through a transit strike or suffer through the blue flu" ("sick-out" by police officers).[37] These, and other employee work disruptions, amply demonstrate that antistrike laws are not always effective. This is because strikes have secured rewards for the employee participants that far outstrip the statutory penalties. Moreover, even though the coffers of many jurisdictions have been empty of late, union walkouts need not be tied to economic issues. New York City teachers have struck to thwart the decentralization of both policy-making power and management authority to community school boards.

It can be expected that law and practice will continue to diverge with respect to public employee strikes. So, too, will pressure be exerted, from opposite directions, in an effort to modify existing laws relating to public employee strikes. The union view is that the workforce is nearly impotent without the strike weapon; that is, collective bargaining becomes "collective begging." Additionally, public unionists claim that it is unfair to deny them the "right to strike" enjoyed by their counterparts in the private sector. Opponents point out that employee unions fared well during the period when legislative lobbying was the biggest gun in the public union's arsenal. Moreover, they contend, protection of the "public health and safety" justifies a denial of strike privileges.

Unionists retort that a general ban on public employee strikes disenfranchises many more clerical workers with menial tasks and low salaries than police officers with high salaries won by ransoming the public safety. Antistrike laws remain on the books in many states and, where strikes are permitted, there is often a distinction made between essential and nonessential services.

PUBLIC EMPLOYEE
UNIONISM: TRENDS AND PROSPECTS

Union membership among public employees grew rapidly during the 1960s and 1970s. This frightened some, as indicated by many of the measures proposed to curb unionized employee power in the public sector. Wellington and Winter proposed that the government contract out services such as refuse collection to private firms. They offered several arguments in favor of such a move. First, it lessens, in highly unionized cities, the impact of a general strike of government employees. Second, with competition among contractors, employees could not seek wage increases that would price their employer out of the market. Third, if there is a strike against a contractor, the atmosphere is depoliticized to a considerable degree. The mayor is not fingered by the union as the big bad boss and by the public as the managerial incompetent who has the streets awash in garbage.[38]

It is an extreme position, however, that the union grip on the public purse and on management discretion is a malignancy that must be combatted by casting off some of the host services. Actually, by the late 1970s, new union contracts were biting off much smaller chunks of the governmental budget than they had at the beginning of the decade. Of course, there were lower revenues on which to feast. Moreover, thousands upon thousands of union members were laid off across the country. This development tends to weaken arguments that unions have near insurmountable leverage vis-à-vis other groups in determining public policy with respect to government employment. Job losses are a bitter pill for labor leaders and that they were swallowed indicates that public employee unions are not invincible in the political arena.

If unions do not have a growing portion of public expenditures they do have a substantial piece of the management action.[39] This may be a legacy from the halcyon days of public employee unionism but, despite pay increases foregone and members laid-off, the union's voice in many management decisions is undiminished. The head of the sanitation workers' union in New York City is considered the de facto commissioner of the sanitation department by some. One former leader of the union is alleged to have shortened the tenure of several official commissioners whose managerial moves incurred his disfavor. Teachers' unions help shape major policy decisions in school systems throughout the country. Public employees, through their unions, sit in on the decision-making councils of the public organization. This is a crucial fact with which present and future public administrators must grapple.

On a jurisdiction-wide basis, the major potential casualty in the union's assumption of traditional managerial prerogatives is the civil service commission. As one observer has written, "because of the ever expanding scope of negotiations unions are gradually whittling away at some of the most sacrosanct practices of traditional merit systems."[40] Another adds that this "should rationalize and define the distribution of power" in the public organization.[41]

We end this discussion on public employee unionism by returning to an earlier theme. The unionized workers in public organizations have breached management's traditional power boundaries. They now make many of the rules to which they submit. This raises several questions for the future. Did public labor-management conflict peak in the 1970s much as private sector labor strife did in the 1930s after trade unions achieved a greater voice in industry? Are labor-management committees an indication that labor will use its new found strength to introduce participative approaches that were largely precluded under civil service regulations? Will worker (and manager) satisfaction, at taxpayer expense, be the only goal of participative management in the public organization or will a problem-solving, productivity-oriented approach prevail? It may be many years before there are clear answers to these questions. However, the emerging answers will have much to say about the shape of public administration in the last decades of the twentieth century.

CONFLICT IN THE EXECUTIVE RANKS

Union-management conflict is not the only struggle for control in the public organization. Within management, factions also struggle over the authority to make the rules. The battle is fought on two broad fronts which often overlap. Along one front are the appointed executives and the career bureaucrats. On the other, administrators confront technically skilled professionals. Schematically, one might view the overall battle lines as in Figure 7.2.

Depending on which battle is most intense at a given moment,

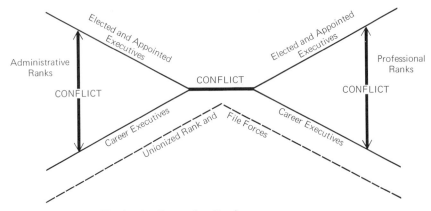

Figure 7.2 Conflict in the Executive Ranks

other conflicts tend to become muted. When unions attack at contract time, management is likely to put aside its differences and present a united front to meet the challenge. When elected officials aggressively seek to displace career bureaucrats with appointed loyalists, administrative generalists and scientific professionals of the career civil service are likely to join in concerted underground resistance. Finally, when the issue of management by administrative generalists versus management by professional specialists come to the fore, the experts, both appointed and civil service, will square off against a similar alliance of administrators. For the remainder of this chapter we will look at the four factions vying for control at the managerial levels of public organizations.

Politics and Administration

It was once fashionable to believe in the *politics-administration dichotomy*. This dichotomy dictated that elected officials and their appointees formulated policies, and a permanent, value-neutral administrative apparatus obediently implemented these policies. Chief executives were expected to exercise control over the bureaucracy through a small number of appointive posts located at the top of the administrative hierarchy. Thus, through this small cadre, public policy could be effectuated.

This approach was inadequate and drew a wholly artificial line between politics and administration. Worst of all, perhaps, it embodied concepts guaranteed to frustrate and polarize government executives. That the chief executive makes policy was one such concept. Thus, incoming chief executives were indignant when they discovered, deep within the administrative hierarchy, entrenched policy commitments under the guardianship of career bureaucrats who could not be dislodged. For their part, career bureaucrats resented being considered as quasi-robots or treated as saboteurs by frustrated political executives. Indeed, the artless political appointees could bring the permanent bureaucracy to a standstill.[42] Not knowing or not caring that the career executives represented the organizational memory, political executives, keeping their own counsel, "reinvented the wheel" or advanced policies that bore short-term fruit for the chief executive but promised long-term fallout for the careerists. After approximately two years, on the average, the political "leaders" departed, leaving behind a bitter bureaucracy.[43]

The politics-administration dichotomy, in addition to falsely attributing absolute policy dominance to the executive, erred in attributing absolute neutrality to the career civil servant. "Politics" was not expunged from administration. One reason is "sweat equity." After several years of intense effort accompanied by strong commitment, career bureaucrats become supporters of public policies as well as implementers. A second reason why reformers underestimated the careerist's influence is that they misunderstood the locus of power in the bureaucracy. Early civil service reformers believed that important policy-making authority is, or could be, located at the very top of the bureaucratic hierarchy. In reality, authority is distributed throughout the public organization. Third, early reformers underestimated the extent to which interest groups pervaded administration through direct contacts or through legislative channels. Civil service bureaucrats are very sensitive to these contacts and the role of interest groups in promulgating policies.

It might be noted in passing that executive posts are not the only ones filled by political appointees. The "policy makers" need secretaries and chauffeurs and these are often "confidential" posts filled by appointees. In jurisdictions where patronage remains a strong force, the lower echelons of certain agencies may be a fertile pasture in which political loyalists may graze. Recreation departments, for instance, tend to discover that the sons and daughters of politically involved citizens are highly desirable candidates for the annual crop of summer jobs. Occasionally, this practice results in a miniscandal featuring such actors as the lifeguard who does not know how to swim. Such actions are irresponsible but not incendiary since, at the lower organizational levels, the intense animosity that can arise between political and career executives is rarely reproduced.

Working Relationships

Whatever animosity they may have toward each other, political executives and career bureaucrats are locked in a relationship. This relationship may be stormy or placid, productive or unproductive; in any case, however, it is usually dependent on the political executive. The political executive must recognize that bureaucratic support is crucial.[44]

Bureaucrats know the ropes, and if they feel misused or abused they can, by withholding compliance, advice, and information, frustrate the political executive's efforts in the agency. To avoid this, Hugh Heclo recommends that the political executive be reconciled to sharing power in the government agency. This means drawing career officials into policy councils rather than issuing policy edicts to operating officers with 40 years of experience. And it means lobbying for the careerists' pet programs before the jurisdiction's executive as well as trying to sell the executive's program to the bureaucracy.

Of course, some chief executives and their staff assistants consider it somewhat traitorous when their delegates to the bureaucracy begin merchandising bureaucratic policies. "Going native" is the rather indelicate phrase used to describe such behavior. To diminish the careerists' influence, elected executives may seek alternative means of control. Expanding the number of positions subject to their appointment and dismissal authority is one. This was done in typical brass knuckles style by the Nixon administration. Nixon's personnel assistant authored the *Malek Manual* (Federal Political Personnel Manual): a compendium of dodges designed to evade the civil service regulations that protected career bureaucrats. "Dissidents" were to be the target. They were to be dismissed (or demoted to lower ranks) by changing job classifications from civil service status to political status, by filing unfavorable performance reports, and by a host of other maneuvers.[45] It may or may not have been bureaucratic retaliation, since Nixon was quite preoccupied at that time, but in 1973 and 1974, with the exception of defense and foreign policy, the administrative apparatus of government was operating with little regard for the White House.[46]

Prospects for the Future

As befitted the temperament of the Nixon White House, the Malek Manual was a strong-arm tactic. However, in a more legitimate way, President Carter's 1978 legislative proposals for a reformation of the civil service system also sought to bring the top civil servants under greater White House control. Under the proposals, top-level careerists could be reassigned from agency to agency and would be subject to presidentially controlled rewards (hefty bonuses) and penalties (demotions to permanent civil service rank).

Although the senior civil service would give the elected executive more control over careerists, it also may pave their way to the highest echelons of administration. Because the government bureaucracy chewed up a number of appointees there has been a move away from political selection criteria. Previous government experience is increasing in importance as a qualification for top posts. In part, this bill is filled by the *in-and-outers* who return to government whenever "their" party or an administration supportive of "their" policies is in power. However, with the senior civil service, chief executives may open up the very highest positions to careerists who are in emotional or intellectual accord with the personalities or policies of the party in power. Thus, elected public officials today may count among their "appointees":

the civil service party sympathizer.
the civil service program sympathizer.
the civil service expert.[47]

The last category reflects our next focus of attention—the increasing reliance on expertise in the administration of government.

PROFESSIONALIZATION

Mosher and Stillman have described a *profession* as "a more or less specialized and purposive field of human activity which requires some specialized education or training (though this may be acquired on the job) which offers a career of life work, and which enjoys a relatively high status in society. It normally aspires to a social, not selfish purpose. Usually but not always, it requires a degree or certificate or credential of some kind. Often its members join in a professional organization, local, state or national, which enunciates standards and ethics of professional performance, sometimes with powers of enforcement."[48] Those professions associated almost exclusively with government include the military, teaching, city management, urban planning, and the foreign service. We are, of course, familiar with those professionals who are found in and out of government: lawyers, doctors, engineers, economists, and scientists.

When a profession is primarily a government one, there can be a merger of identity between the sheltering agency and the profession. The Department of Defense is the military; the city planning board embodies the outlook of its planners; the local school system is a "teaching" place. In these organizations, the professionals substantially shape policy. Even where the professional contingent is in the minority, it is well equipped to engage in a struggle for control. Lawyers, scientists, and others can have a "degree of exclusiveness which underlines their unity."[49] They are the "cosmopolitans"—slightly alien, uncomfortably cohesive, and, in the eyes of the "locals" with careers in the agency, a definite threat.[50] This threat is especially clear to locals who agree with Mosher's contention that "a basic drive of every profession, established or emergent, is *self-government* in deciding policies, criteria and standards for employment and advancement, and in deciding individual personnel matters."[51]

In numbers, at least, the power of these cosmopolitans—the professionals—is growing. "Between 1960 and 1976, the number of persons who worked directly for governments and whom the census classified as 'professional, technical . . . ' doubled to 5.4 million."[52] Much of this growth takes place in the managerial ranks and is concentrated in staff positions. Although staff positions do not stand at the pinnacle of the organizational hierarchy, the subordination of professions can be a tenuous proposition. They are often "considered superior in educational and social terms."[53] If status alone is not enough, their expertise provides an exemption from scrutiny because "their tasks cannot be prescribed and regulated in a detailed way."[54]

Thus armed, professionals made the earliest and, to date, the most successful assaults on the domain of the civil service commissions. In the federal government, lawyers are exempted, by law, from civil service scrutiny. Agencies such as the State Department have fully autonomous in-house job classifications, salary scales, and promotion ladders. Often, when a profession seizes the personnel machinery in a entire agency, it gains a measure of control "over employees not in the elite profession."[55]

Professionals: A Threat to Whom?

Obviously, the professions are somewhat of a threat to the civil service commission concept (as is most everything else these days). In addition, according to Frederick Mosher, an elite profession in control of a public activity may resist supervision by democratically elected representatives. Mosher sees the professions as explicitly hostile to the players and the moves of the political process. Politicians are considered amateurs at best and corrupt at worst when they attempt to influence the professional group. "Professionalism rests upon specialized knowledge, science and rationality. There are *correct* ways of solving problems and doing things. Politics is seen as constituting negotiation, elections, votes, compromises. . . . Politics is to the professions as ambiguity to truth, expedience to rightness, heresy to true belief."[56] Others see professionals as something less than distrusters of politics but threatening nonetheless. Tunnel vision is the concern of Stephen K. Bailey when he identifies the "limited world" that professionals comprehend as a "constant threat to more general consideration of the public good."[57]

The increased professionalization of government agencies, however, is not an entirely negative development. First, the professional specialist is vital to government's functioning. None of the observers of public employment suggest more than keeping a watchful eye on professional hegemony. Second, professionals are not the first to be charged with myopia or a marked hostility toward the political process. In the heat of battle, this charge is often leveled at the career civil servants by the political executives. Indeed, in light of the personnel reforms of the

1970s, it may be that the battle for control in the managerial ranks between transients and careerists will become less important as the clash intensifies between transient professionals and transient administrative generalists. Third, in a public service that is remarkable in its inability to agree on general standards of ethical conduct, the ethos of a particular profession may come in handy. In part, the Watergate burglary cover-up was exposed because James McCord, one of the burglars and an ex-CIA employee, discovered that the White House planned to use the professional intelligence community as a scapegoat.[58] Nixon's last stonewall attempt was leveled when his attorneys, upon discovering that they had been deceived by their client, threatened to resign if the president did not release the incriminating tape recordings.[59]

Public Management: The New Profession

It is not implausible to suspect that there is an unconscious tinge of self-interest to the dire warnings concerning the consequences of the professional ascendancy. These harbingers (Gulick and Urwick, Mosher, Bailey), as professors of administration, belonged to the academic vanguard of the administrative profession and wrote at a time when the word "administrator" conjured up visions of some glorified, overpaid clerk. Mosher et al. quite rightly sought to counteract this false image and to nurture among administrators a sense of self-respect and a sense of professionalism.

In elevating administration to a profession, however, there were pointed comments about other professionals who had "not trained themselves for management."[60] Of course, it would be possible for a dean of a law school to advise against filling top posts with professional administrators who were not trained in the law. This aspect of the debate is normative. So also may be the assertions that administrative generalists are more likely than technicians to respect the American political system. Nonetheless, the efforts to make administration in the public sector a profession have been successful. Graduates of a public administration program have specialized training, may become members of the American Society for Public Administration, and should spend the bulk of their active careers in public management roles.

If the 1970s are any indication, the administrative profession is, at the least, holding its own against the more well-established professions. James R. Schlesinger and Elliot Richardson held a variety of high posts in the federal government during that decade. They were called upon by Republican and Democratic presidents. Richardson was Secretary of Defense; Secretary of Health, Education, and Welfare; Attorney General; and Ambassador to England. Schlesinger was head of the CIA, Secretary of Defense, and Energy Administrator. Obviously, these men were called upon for their managerial skills (and, in Schlesinger's case, general analytical skills as well). Simply, to be a specialist in areas as diverse as armaments, espionage, social welfare, and the law is nearly impossible and almost undesirable from the perspective of flexible management capability.

A Management Ethos?

Elliot Richardson was more than an administrative virtuoso. As Attorney General, he was also a pivotal figure when Watergate Special Prosecutor Archibald Cox was fired by the Nixon administration. In appointing Cox, Richardson had promised the Senate that Cox's investigations would be unfettered. When Cox's subpoenas and legal actions started closing in on the taped evidence that would expose President Richard Nixon, Richardson was ordered to fire the special prosecutor. Richardson declined. His resignation was demanded and received by the president. Deputy Attorney General William Ruckelshaus was ordered to fire Cox. He refused and was also fired.

Although we may be attributing the behavior of Richardson and Ruckelshaus to the wrong profession (both were lawyers), their actions may mark the beginning of a managerial ethos—an ethos that may solidify administration's claim to professional status. Obedience to superiors had always been a part of the administrator's formal bureaucratic charter. When a perceived responsibility to subordinates moved administrators to disregard or evade commands from above, the process was informal, surreptitious, and vaguely delinquent. Richardson and Ruckelshaus demonstrated that this need not always be the case. One could publicly declare allegiance to the integrity of the administrative structure and, in the process, hand down an indictment against those who would seek to compromise that integrity. While there is, as yet, no professional code of ethics for public administrators (although some exist for government employees generally), the rudiments may be present in the behavior of Richardson and Ruckelshaus.

SUMMARY

In this chapter we have looked at the government personnel picture from the perspective of collective conflict. We have seen forces arrayed along three broad fronts in the public organization: labor-management; political executive-careerist; and administrative generalist-specialized professional. Each of these forces seeks to retain or increase its autonomy. Total victory is unlikely in any of these three contests but, as the 1970s closed, the following state of affairs prevailed. Labor had gained substantial control over the terms of public employment. Careerists and political appointees intermingled in policy posts and their identities grew less distinct. Administrators were achieving professional recognition similar to that enjoyed by the more established technical professions.

Those entering public administration will doubtless have to deal with conflicts concerning the degree of influence to be exercised by various factions within the organization. However, as we shall see in the following sections, this is but a part of what awaits them. Program policy, as well as personnel policy, is shaped in the public agency, and external factions are not shy about marching in to advance their interests.

KEY TERMS AND CONCEPTS

All-or-nothing arbitration
Arbitration
Collective bargaining
Conciliation
Conflict
Constituency bids
Fact finding
Impasse procedures
Labor-management productivity
  committees

Malek Manual
Mediation
Politics-administration dichotomy
Productivity bargaining (gain
  sharing and buy-out)
Profession
Resistance point
Target point

NOTES

1. Elton Mayo, *The Social Problems of an Industrial Civilization* (Andover: Andover Press, 1945); Frederick W. Taylor, *Scientific Management* (New York: Harper & Row, 1947).
2. William C. Scott and Terence R. Mitchell, *Organization Theory: A Structural and Behavioral Analysis* (Homewood, Ill.: Irwin 1972), p. 190.
3. Michel Crozier, *The Bureaucratic Phenomenon* (Chicago: University of Chicago Press, 1964); Ralf Dahrendorf, *Class and Class Conflict in Industrial Society* (Stanford, Calif: Stanford University Press, 1959).
4. Dahrendorf, *Class and Class Conflict*, p. 252.
5. Ibid., p. 255.
6. Crozier, *Bureaucratic Phenomenon,* part I.
7. Ibid., part II.
8. Ibid., p. 127.
9. Ibid., pp. 89–139.
10. Ibid., pp. 213–227.
11. Coolidge quoted in Thomas R. Brooks, *Toil and Trouble: A History of American Labor* (New York: Dell (Delta Books), 1971), p. 321.
12. David T. Stanley, *Managing Local Government Under Union Pressure* (Washington: Brookings, 1972), p. 18.
13. Edward C. Banfield and James Q. Wilson, *City Politics* (New York: Random House (Vintage Books), 1963), p. 212.
14. Brooks, *Toil and Trouble*, p. 311.
15. Ibid., pp. 307–313.
16. The following discussion is based on Richard E. Walton and Robert B. McKersie, *A Behavioral Theory of Labor Negotiations* (New York: McGraw-Hill, 1965), chapters II and III. We find their analyses extremely informative and trust that our oversimplifications do justice to their work.
17. See R. D. Luce and H. Raiffa, *Games and Decisions* (New York: Wiley, 1957) for a thoroughgoing account of game behavior.

18. Walton and McKersie, *Labor Negotiations,* pp. 56–57.
19. See Harry H. Wellington and Ralph K. Winter, *The Unions and the Cities* (Washington: Brookings, 1971), p. 26.
20. Robert Booth Fowler, "Normative Aspects of Public Employee Strikes," in Joseph A. Uveges, Jr., ed., *The Dimensions of Public Administration,* 2nd ed. (Boston: Holbrook Press, 1975), p. 355.
21. Robert Miewald, "Conflict and Harmony in the Public Service" in Jay M. Shafritz, ed., *A New World: Readings on Modern Public Personnel Management* (Chicago: International Personnel Management Association, 1975).
22. Wellington and Winter, *Unions and Cities,* p. 31.
23. See Raymond D. Horton, *Municipal Labor Relations in New York City: Lessons of the Lindsay-Wagner Years* (New York: Praeger, 1973).
24. Alan L. Salzstein, "Can Urban Management Control the Organized Employee," in Shafritz, *A New World,* pp. 50–58.
25. Horton, *Municipal Labor Relations* p. 131.
26. Melvin H. Osterman, Jr., *An Occasional Paper: Productivity Bargaining in New York—What Went Wrong?* (Ithaca: Institute of Public Employment, 1975), p. 7.
27. H. M. Douty, *Labor-Management Productivity Committees in American Industry* (Washington: National Commission on Productivity and Work Quality, 1975).
28. Victor Gotbaum and Edward Handman, "A Conversation with Victor Gotbaum," *Public Administration Review* 38, no. 1 (January-February 1978): 21–23.
29. Labor Relations Reporter, *Primer of Labor Relations* (Washington: The Bureau of National Affairs, 1971), p. 87.
30. Ibid., p. 92.
31. See Mid-West Center for Public Sector Relations, *Questions and Answers on Collective Bargaining: A Practitioners Guide* (Bloomington: Indiana University Press, 1977), p. 29.
32. See American Arbitration Association, *Labor Arbitration Procedures and Techniques* (New York: n.d.), p. 1.
33. Wellington and Winter, *Unions and Cities,* p. 180.
34. Ibid., pp. 172, 179.
35. Ibid.
36. Ibid., p. 186.
37. Shafritz, *A New World: Readings on Modern Public Personnel Management* (Chicago: International Personnel Management Association, 1975), p. 33.
38. Wellington and Winter, *Unions and Cities,* chapter 4.
39. See David T. Stanley, *Managing Local Government,* appendix C.
40. Jay M. Shafritz, *Public Personnel Management: The Heritage of Civil Service Reform,* (New York: Praeger, 1975), p. 147.
41. Charles Feigenbaum, "Civil Service and Collective Bargaining: Conflict or Compatibility," in Shafritz, *A New World,* p. 48
42. Hugh Heclo, *A Government of Strangers* (Washington: Brookings, 1977), pp. 7–9.
43. See generally John Rehfuss, *Public Administration as Political Process* (New York: Scribner, 1973), chapter 6.
44. Heclo, *Government of Strangers,* chapters 5 and 6.
45. See *The Bureaucrat* 4, no. 4 (January 1976): especially pp. 429–509.
46. Theodore H. White, *Breach of Faith: The Fall of Richard Nixon* (New York: Atheneum, 1975), p. 243.
47. Heclo, *Government of Strangers,* chapter 4.

48. Frederick C. Mosher and Richard Stillman, Jr., "The Professions in Government," *Public Administration Review* (November-December 1977): 632.
49. Dahrendorf, *Class and Class Conflict,* p. 298.
50. Alvin Gouldner, "Cosmopolitans and Locals: Toward an Analysis of Latent Social Roles," *Administrative Science Quarterly* 2 (December 1957): 281–306.
51. Frederick C. Mosher, *Democracy and the Public Service* (New York: Oxford University Press, 1968), p. 124.
52. Mosher and Stillman, "Professions in Government," p. 631.
53. Mosher, *Democracy and the Public Service* p. 111.
54. Crozier, *Bureaucratic Phenomenon,* p. 192.
55. Mosher, *Democracy and the Public Service* p. 110.
56. Ibid., p. 109.
57. Stephen K. Bailey, "Ethics and the Public Service," in Richard J. Stillman, Jr., ed. *Public Administration: Concepts and Cases* (Boston: Houghton Mifflin, 1976), p. 321.
58. James Doyle, *Not Above the Law: The Battles of Watergate Prosecutors Cox and Jaworski* (New York: Morrow, 1977), p. 305.
59. Ibid., p. 345.
60. Mosher, p. 111.

BIBLIOGRAPHY

Brooks, Thomas R. *Toil and Trouble: A History of American Labor.* New York: Dell (Delta Books), 1971.

Crozier, Michel. *The Bureaucratic Phenomenon.* Chicago: University of Chicago Press, 1964.

————. *The World of the Office Worker.* Chicago: University of Chicago Press, 1971.

Dahrendorf, Ralf. *Class and Class Conflict in Industrial Society.* Stanford, Calif.: Stanford University Press, 1959.

————. *Conflict After Class: New Perspectives on the Theory of Political and Social Conflict.* London: McKay, 1967.

Douty, H. M. *Labor-Management Productivity Committees in American Industry.* Washington: National Commission on Productivity and Work Quality, 1975.

Doyle, James. *Not Above the Law: The Battles of Watergate Prosecutors Cox and Jaworski.* New York: Morrow, 1977.

Flynn, Ralph J. *Public Work, Public Workers.* Washington: The New Republic Book Company, Inc., 1975.

Heclo, Hugh. *A Government of Strangers.* Washington: Brookings, 1977.

Horton, Raymond D. *Municipal Labor Relations in New York City: Lessons of the Lindsay-Wagner Years.* New York: Praeger, 1973.

Loewenberg, J. Joseph, and Moskow, Michael H., eds. *Collective Bargaining in Government.* Englewood Cliffs, N.J.: Prentice-Hall, 1972.

Luce, R. D. and H. Raiffa. *Games and Decisions.* New York: Wiley, 1957.

Rubin, Jeffrey Z. and Brown, Bert R. *The Social Psychology of Bargaining and Negotiations.* New York: Academic Press, Inc., 1975.

Stanley, David T. *Managing Local Government Under Union Pressure.* Washington: Brookings, 1972.

Stieber, Jack. *Public Employee Unionism.* Washington: Brookings, 1973.

Walsh, Robert E. *Sorry—No Government Today: Unions vs. City Hall.* Boston: Beacon Press, 1969.

Walton, Richard E. and McKersie, Robert B. *A Behavioral Theory of Labor Negotiations.* New York: McGraw-Hill, 1965.

Wellington, Harry H. and Winter, Ralph K. *The Unions and the Cities.* Washington: Brookings, 1971.

White, Theodore H. *Breach of Faith: The Fall of Richard Nixon.* New York: Atheneum, 1975.

In addition to the sources cited in the notes and bibliography, the following *Public Administration Review (PAR)* articles are a convenient starting point for a more detailed exploration of the material in this chapter.

Balzer, Anthony J. "Quotas and the San Francisco Police: A Sergeant's Dilemma," *PAR* 37, no. 3 (May/June 1977): 276–285.

Derr, C. Brooklyn. "Conflict Resolution in Organizations: Views from the Field of Educational Administration," *PAR* 32, no. 5 (Sept./Oct. 1972): 495–501.

Donnelly, Bernard P. "Cheap Shots and Costly Pay-Offs: A Plea for Purpose in Public Programs," *PAR* 37, no. 2 (March/April 1977): 181–186.

Feuille, Peter and Gary Long. "The Public Administrator and Final Offer Arbitration," *PAR* 34, no. 5 (Sept./Oct. 1974): 431–434.

Goldoff, Anna C. and David C. Tatage. "Joint Productivity Committees: Lessons of Recent Initiatives," *PAR* 38, no. 2 (March/April 1978): 184–186.

Hershey, Clay S. "Limits of Federal Protest," *PAR* 34, no. 4 (July/Aug. 1974): 359–368.

Horton, Raymond D. "Productivity and Productivity Bargaining in Government: A Critical Analysis," *PAR* 36, no. 4 (July/Aug. 1976): 407–414.

Kliengartner, Archie. "Collective Bargaining Between Salaried Professionals and Public Sector Management," *PAR* 33, no. 2 (March/April 1973): 165–172.

McIntyre, Douglas. "Merit Principles and Collective Bargaining: A Marriage or Divorce," *PAR* 37, no. 2 (March/April 1977): 186–190.

Malek, Frederick C. "The Development of Public Executives—Neglect and Reform" *PAR* 34, no. 3 (May/June 1974): 230–233.

Mosher, Frederick C. "Professions in Public Service," *PAR* 38, no. 2 (March/April 1978): 144–150.

Mosher, Frederick C. "The Public Service in the Temporary Society," *PAR* 31, no. 1 (Jan./Feb. 1971): 47–62.

Newland, Chester A. "Personnel Concerns in Government Productivity Improvement," *PAR* 32, no. 6 (Nov./Dec. 1972): 807–815.

Nigro, Felix A. "Managers in Government and Labor Relations," *PAR* 38, no. 2 (March/April 1978): 180–184.

Nigro, Felix A. "The Implications for Public Administration," *PAR* 32, no. 2 (March/April 1972): 120–126.

Nigro, Lloyd G. and Kenneth J. Meier. "Executive Mobility in the Federal Service: A Career Perspective," *PAR* 35, no. 3 (May/June 1975): 291–295.

Rich, Wilbur C. (ed.). "A Mini Symposium: The Municipal Civil Service Under Pressure," *PAR* 37, no. 5 (Sept./Oct. 1977): 505–519.

Rinehart, Jeffrey C. and E. Lee Bernich. "Political Attitudes and Behavior Patterns of Federal Civil Servants," *PAR* 35, no. 6 (Nov./Dec. 1975): 603–611.

Schott, Richard L. "Public Administration as a Profession: Problems and Prospects," *PAR* 36, no. 3 (May/June 1976): 253–259.

Tyler, Gus. "Why They Organize," *PAR* 32, no. 2 (March/April 1972): 97–101.
Van Asselt, Karl A. "Impasse Resolution," *PAR* 32, no. 2 (March/April 1972): 114–119.
Wurf, Jerry. "Merit: A Union View," *PAR* 34, no. 5 (Sept./Oct. 1974): 431–434.

RELEVANT PERIODICALS
Industrial and Labor Relations Review
Journal of Conflict Resolution
Labor Law Journal
Public Productivity Review

RELEVANT CASE STUDIES
(Cases marked ICCH are available from the Intercollegiate Case Clearing House, Soldier Field, Boston, Mass. 02163; cases marked ICP are available from the Inter-University Case Program, Box 229, Syracuse, N.Y. 13210.)

Carper, E. T. *Reorganization of the U.S. Public Health Service,* [ICP]
Dickenson, C. and C. S. Diver. *Boston Police Negotiations,* (A)(B)(C)(D)(E),* [ICCH]
Diver, C. S. and H. Smith. *Bridgeport CETA,* (A)(B)(C)(D),* [ICCH]
Gordon, D. *Police Guidelines/Police Guidelines: Sequel,* [ICCH]
Kuechle, D. and R. Fearn. *New York City Sanitation Strike 1968,* (A)(B),* [ICCH]
Robinson, M. *The Coming of Age of the Langley Porter Clinic,* [ICP]
Timmins, W. *Arbitration: The Police Chief and the Four Day Week,* [ICP]

*Letters indicate that the case is presented in several installments.

A MID-BOOK CASE STUDY: INFORMATION FIELD DIFFERENTIALS BETWEEN ORGANIZATIONS AND INDIVIDUALS

INTRODUCTION

The following case study includes many of the concepts already covered. However, its aim is to provoke as well as review. We hope that when you have finished, these questions will be buzzing in your head. Are organizations often independent of societal control? If so, do organizations break free or are they let loose by society? If they break free, what penalties are imposed to prevent a recurrence? And, if weak penalties and strong inducements permit organizations wide latitude, can it be said that society charters the behavior that results? Finally, what confronts the individual when he or she decides that an organizational transgression should be revealed?

ONE AIRPLANE AND THREE INSTITUTIONAL ACTORS

Our focal point shall be the DC-10: a three-engine, wide-body flying machine capable of carrying over 300 passengers.[1] As this is being read, DC-10s ply the world's airways and, by all accounts, are reliable, easy-to-handle craft with an admirable safety record. This, however, was not always the case. In their first years of operation, DC-10s were time bombs. Three organizations possessed information that, if correctly patterned, pointed to a high probability of catastrophe. The descriptions of the three organizations below focus on the period from 1968 to 1972.

McDonnell Douglas Corporation McDonnell Douglas, it could be said, was an adaptive organization meeting marketplace demands for aircraft. The United States government and the commercial airlines were the customers. Competing with Douglas was the Boeing Corporation, which did well on all fronts, and the Lockheed Corporation, which primarily serviced Defense Department needs. As the 1960s drew to a close, the aircraft market appeared ready for a major reshuffling. With declining government purchases and an upward spiral in airline passengers, an upsurge in commercial purchases seemed likely. And, with the introduction of the Boeing 747, it was large planes that the commercial market wanted. The buyers' rough specifications, however, required an aircraft capable of landing where the 747 could not; namely, the smaller municipal airports. Boeing, which was selling 747s in vast quantities and buying back mortgaged assets with the income, was not ready to develop a more nimble jumbo jet. Thus, by default, the "air-bus" would have to be a Lockheed or a McDonnell Douglas product. The stakes, it appeared, were financial security for the winner and hard times, at best, for the loser. Lockheed was the first off the mark and unveiled the blueprint of the L-1011 TriStar: a 300-passenger, 3000-mile-range, three-engine craft. Shortly thereafter, McDonnell Douglas, which had suffered severe financial setbacks because of past tardiness in accommodating emerging tastes, entered the competition.

Convair Division of General Dynamics Convair was an adaptive organization satisfying environmental demands for aircraft parts. With respect to the DC-10, Convair's environment consisted of McDonnell Douglas. With a relationship forged by bargaining and formalized in contract, Convair built the fuselage and doors of the DC-10 according to Douglas's specifications. Convair's role was in all respects a subordinate one. It could only suggest design changes. Performance reports on DC-10 parts could be sent only to the Federal Aviation Administration (FAA) via Douglas with the latter retaining editorial discretion.

The Federal Aviation Administration The FAA is an organization created to work toward the goals of air safety. To this end, it oversees the manufacture and maintenance of airplanes, certifies pilots, and manages the nation's air traffic. In the FAA's immediate environment, airplane manufacturers, having the most at stake, loom large. Thus, regulation often blurs into coalition or cooptation. Coalition occurs because the agency lacks the manpower to make all required inspections. Thus, employees of the airplane manufacturers are deputized to run safety tests and grant FAA certification. Cooptation is a result of an intimate and long-standing relationship; the FAA understands the problems of the industry. When empathy is high, as it was during the unfolding of this story, even serious defects can elicit gentle jawboning rather than an administrative order requiring immediate compliance.

The Fatal Flaw

In the race between McDonnell Douglas and Lockheed, time and prospective customers were vital considerations. Indeed, to pave the way for TriStar purchases, Lockheed bribed officials in Japan and other countries. McDonnell Douglas eschewed payoffs, but took great pains to accommodate customer preferences. For instance, when American Airlines objected to a hydraulically latched cargo door, McDonnell Douglas switched to an electric latch system.[2]

Convair engineers did not appreciate the change. The electrical system, they felt, was more problematic. When, in 1969 and at McDonnell Douglas's request, Convair drafted a Failure Mode and Effects Analysis (a precertification document required by the FAA), several life-endangering cargo door failure sequences were identified. One failure involved the loss of the plane to an in-flight cargo door blow-out, the collapse of the passenger cabin floor, and resulting damage to the plane's control mechanisms and flying surfaces.[3] (The floor's inability to withstand rapid depressurization was crucial. Through the floor ran the hydraulic and electrical cables controlling the rear engine and rudder.)

The Convair analysis went to McDonnell Douglas and there it sat. On May 29, 1970, it was resurrected. On that day, during an air-conditioning test, with the cabin pressurized, the cargo door of the prototype DC-10 blew off and the passenger floor collapsed. McDonnell Douglas blamed a mechanic for improperly closing the door but set about modifying the design nonetheless. Convair again had reservations. "Less than desirable" was how one engineer viewed the modified system; other Convair personnel suggested a return to the hydraulic design.[4] McDonnell Douglas was unmoved. Indeed, through tough negotiating, it saddled Convair with the costs of modifying the door. Moreover, Convair was "prohibited from discussing any design feature with the FAA."[5] Douglas kept Convair's written objections in-house, and, eventually, a Douglas engineer, in his role as FAA inspector, approved the modified door as airworthy.

An Ineffective Alarm

Captain Bryce McCormick of American Airlines was an excellent pilot. He had to be. On June 12, 1972, 12,000 feet above Ontario, Canada, Captain McCormick's DC-10 blew out a cargo door, dropped a rear section of the cabin floor, and went into a dive. The tail engine and the rudder controls were inoperative. Fortunately, Captain McCormick had learned to steer the DC-10 by applying differential power to the engines in flight simulator training. With consummate skill, Captain

McCormick and copilot Paige Whitney landed the crippled plane and its 53 passengers at Detroit Metropolitan Airport.

The DC-10's flaw was about to become known to outsiders even though McDonnell Douglas again claimed human error and accused the baggage handler. National Transportation Safety Board inspectors swarmed over the plane. The FAA's Western Division office in Los Angeles acquired, from a reluctant McDonnell Douglas, previous reports of cargo door difficulties. There was a litany of complaints from several airlines. Doors had closed improperly despite positive readings from indicator devices. Touch was no better as a determinant of proper closure. Fully rotating the handle to the closed position could jam the locking mechanism in a half-opened state. Awkwardly located, the cargo door demanded much of the lowly baggage handlers. They had to crane and twist to read instructions, peer through a window into the locking mechanism, interpret the configuration, and use enough, but not too much, effort in closing a recalcitrant door. FAA field personnel were unmoved by Douglas's complaints about poorly designed baggage handlers and began drafting an Airworthiness Directive that would require specific modifications according to a fixed schedule.

For McDonnell Douglas, the Airworthiness Directive, a public document, would have been a staggering blow. The international marketing contest with Lockheed was at its height. To fulfill prospective and previously signed purchasing agreements, a number of planes were in production. A purchaser walkaway might have bankrupted McDonnell Douglas. Thus, the company went straight to the top. Incredibly, FAA Commissioner John Hixon Shaffer, who was told that the problem would be "fixed by Friday night," reached a gentlemen's agreement with a Douglas executive: no Airworthiness Directive.[6] Thus, it took two years for the new modifications to snake quietly through the DC-10 fleet. Frustrated FAA field personnel wrote a memo or two for the files in order to cover themselves, but otherwise remained mute. As the FAA indicated in a 1974 report, it had been generally "lax in taking appropriate Airworthiness Directive action where the need for AD's are clearly indicated."[7]

The Last Bureaucrat Signs Off

With the FAA neutralized, there were few sentinels left. However, one last impassioned warning was sounded by Convair's Director of Product Engineering, J. D. Applegate. On June 27, 1972, he wrote:

> Douglas appears to be applying more band-aids.... It seems to me inevitable that, in the twenty years ahead of us, DC-10 cargo doors will come open and I would expect this to usually result in the loss of the airplane. This fundamental failure mode has been discussed in the past and is being discussed again in the bowels of both the Douglas and Convair

The Exploded Rear Cargo Door of the DC-10 that Captain McCormack Brought Safely Back to Earth. (United Press International Photo)

organizations. . . . It is recommended that overtures be made at the highest management levels to persuade Douglas to immediately make a decision to incorporate changes in the DC-10 which will correct the fundamental cabin floor catastrophic mode.[8]

In response, Applegate's superior at Convair, J. B. Hurt, wrote, "we have in effect shared with Douglas the design philosophy. . . . This design philosophy . . . satisfied FAA requirements and therefore the airplane was theoretically safe and desirable."[9] Hurt went on to point out that past Convair protests had been imperiously ignored by Douglas. Hurt also established what was to become Convair's institutional position:

I am sure Douglas would immediately interpret such recommendations as a tacit admission on Convair's part that the original concurrency by Convair on the design philosophy was in error and therefore Convair was liable for all problems and corrections.[10]

Finally, Hurt raised the possibility of delicate, ongoing Convair/ Douglas negotiations being jeopardized. His memo concludes, "We have an interesting legal and moral problem, and I feel that any direct conversation on the subject with Douglas should be based on the assumption that as a result Convair may find itself in a position where it must assume all or a significant portion of the cost involved."[11]

The Applegate memo never emerged from Convair. The author went back to his desk. The voluntary "band-aid" revisions went forward, somehow missing one plane which, two years later, was Turkish Airlines flight 981 from Paris to London. Six of the 346 people on board fell through the floor and out of the plane when the cargo door blew out at 10,000 feet. With six times the load that had confronted Captain McCormick and a thousand more pounds of force behind the control-rupturing floor collapse, miraculous improvisations were beyond the ken of the Turkish pilots. Just over one minute after the door ruptured, the DC-10 hit the ground at 500 miles per hour.

A HYPOTHETICAL EXPLORATION

A plane is, in our opinion, fundamentally unsafe. It will, we are convinced, kill people. Nonetheless, our superiors tell us that the plane must fly and we must keep silent. What would we do? Shouting from the rooftops would seem apropos. We have been taught to place a high value on human life. What, then, can we say about the individuals in the DC-10 case? Consider something that might make our response a bit more explosive. Namely, the engineers of human habitations and conveyances may be, by academic training at least, more highly sensitized than we to the need for safeguarding human life. This sensitivity is embodied in "Murphy's Law" that Applegate alluded to in his memorandum—if anything can happen, it will.

When Murphy's Law is operational, a plane or a building design accounts for all known information and then some. Murphy's Law does not encompass the unknown since, even with wide margins of error built in, a system can fail when unanticipated or unknowable circumstances arise. However, if a probable system failure can be inferred from known information, Murphy's Law transforms the probability to a certainty. It is, in essence, a rough rule of thumb inducing engineers to err on the side of caution. Thus, we might assume that McDonnell Douglas's suspension of Murphy's Law severely compromised both the professional and humane principles of the quiescent engineers.

What now should we say about individuals who kept silent about a disaster that they perceived to be inevitable and deadly? Were these mutes cowards? Such judgments might best be reserved until a similar situation confronts us. However, we will examine the information envi-

The French Forest Where 346 DC-10 Passengers Met Their Death. (Photo by James Andanson-Sygma)

ronment that confronted these individuals and organizations to see if it favored, or even forced, their behavior.

The Employee's Information Environment

Disaffected employees, if they look before acting, will find two informational fields—organizational and extra-organizational—that emphasize the personal costs of pursuing one's ethical beliefs. Let us first look at the information available within the organization.

It takes little socialization in the organizational milieu to know that, for certain offenses, the organization is going to get you. One offense is flaunting the organization's dirty linen in public. The Defense Department analyst who exposed Lockheed's cost overruns on the C5A Air Transport contract during the 1960s—a time when official policy was that things were fine—ended up on the outside looking in. When such revelations can sink the organization, and McDonnell Douglas may have gone under if the DC-10's defects had been widely reported, the informer can be relentlessly pursued by an organization. Thus, the rebel can anticipate termination of employment; blackballing; ostracism by peers; a denial of charges; an attack on personal integrity, sanity, and character; and, finally, stubborn legal resistance should judicial vindication be sought. Stories of such developments are a part of the internal lore of most organizations. These tales can be a moving force at the highest levels and can affect an individual's behavior after the employee relationship has been severed. John DeLorean, a $600,000 per year Vice-Chairman of General Motors and heir apparent to the top spot, left GM in 1974 vowing to write an exposé. DeLorean received a hefty advance from a publisher and completed a widely publicized manuscript. Then, mysteriously, he refused to deliver his work to the publisher. "If they (GM) wanted to," he was reported as saying, "they could crush me like a grape."[12]

Assessing the information external to the organization can only reinforce the employee's perception of an unequal battle. If the organization fires the employee, it suffers no immediate penalty. In substantiating one's allegations, however, the ex-employee usually faces a long and costly process. The campaign for vindication is likely to be fueled, for the first year, by poverty level unemployment checks (assuming that the labor department rejects the employer's dismissal-for-cause claim) and savings. As cash reserves diminish, judicial redress remains distant and uncertain. Prior to a legal resolution, the objectionable practice may be quietly corrected, or run its natural course. The organization will continue to deny that it ever existed. If caught in this untruth, the organization will probably apologize, skillfully present the extenuating circumstances, pay the consequences, and be little the worse for the trouble. For the employee, even eventual victory can be bitter. Accepting reinstatement means reentry into a hostile environment, and back pay will be used, in part, to settle debts incurred during the course of battle.

The Organization's Information Environment

Before we paint the corporate organization as an ogre, we might assume the vantage point of a chief executive officer. The view is of stockholders and boards of directors who expect the organization to prosper, and employees who express similar wishes. As the executive scans the larger horizon there are competitors and customers, regulators and suppliers. Adaptation is the name of the game. Risk taking is the technique, but winning is the goal. Losing, after all, tends to put executives out of work.

So the game is played hard and with wide tactical latitude since there is little constraining information in the environment. For instance, not a single employee of Douglas, Convair, or the FAA was accused of any wrongdoing in the DC-10 affair. Fines for direct violation of the law do little to inhibit organizations, and penalties may never reach the individual violators (although the 1970s did see heftier corporate fines and more executives in the dock).

No personal liability was shouldered by Douglas and Convair executives as a result of negligence actions. Moreover, the corporate organization is a creature of limited liability. If it errs grievously, owners/

stockholders are responsible for damages only equal to their investment. Even cases of terminal litigation, however, are guarded against. Through insurance, losses arising from defective products, whether or not they occur, are paid for in advance.

Douglas, had little to lose and much to gain. Convair looked on. The FAA, lacking information because of Convair's closed contract with Douglas, pursued a time-honored policy of accommodation. In all three organizations, well-trained employees gritted their teeth. With the FAA, Convair, and all other knowledgeables silenced, it is not surprising that Douglas acted as it did in the high-stakes battle with Lockheed. Unfortunately, 346 unwitting people lost their lives.

SUMMARY

Who was responsible for killing those 346 people? No one? It is plausible. Everyone just seemed to be doing more or less what they had to do. Acting otherwise would have meant punishment: a loss of jobs, careers, and profits. However, we should consider the mechanisms that activate the rewards and punishments affecting organizations and employees: progress, growth, competition—organizational buzz words drawn from a list of society's favorites; unemployed, squealer, washed up—pejoratives in most circles. Judicial inequality between individual plaintiff and organizational defendant is not, apparently, a corporate conspiracy. Nor is the ponderous, indecisive state that often seizes regulatory agencies. Contracts that seal the lips of the parties involved are considered by law as private documents regardless of the public interest. And that is the point. Organizations adapt to an environment (values, customers, laws, regulatory mechanisms) structured by society. So do employees. If organizational risk taking is encouraged and employee exposés discouraged, public policy, in its broadest sense, is at work. But public policy is not immutable; we might just think about some modifications before *we* kill another 346 people.

NOTES

1. This case is drawn from Paul Eddy, Elaine Potter, Bruce Page, *Destination Disaster.* Copyright © 1976 by Paul Eddy, Elaine Potter, and Bruce Page. Reprinted by permission of Time Books.
2. Ibid., p. 72.
3. Ibid., p. 178.
4. Ibid., pp. 181–182.
5. Ibid., p. 182.
6. Ibid., p. 160.
7. Ibid., p. 161.
8. Ibid., pp. 184–185.
9. Ibid., p. 186.
10. Ibid., p. 187.
11. Ibid.
12. Quoted in *Newsweek,* August 15, 1977, p. 67.

PART FOUR

PUBLIC
POLICY
MAKING

CHAPTER 8

ADMINISTRATION AND THE PUBLIC POLICY ENVIRONMENT

INTRODUCTION

This chapter surveys the framework of public policy. Administration, in this survey, will be treated as more than an inanimate anchor for the public policy process. Although law or common wisdom may appoint legislators, chief executives, or the public as its superior, administration leads as often, perhaps, as it follows. This situation highlights administrative policy-making power that is real and is unlikely to diminish. Thus it is that administration is at the core of this treatment of the public policy environment.

Our survey will begin with a brief look at the constitutional foundations of the United States government. Next, we will take a historical view of the growth of executive power and the parallel growth of administration as a policy force. The codifications of administrative law, aimed at monitoring and controlling bureaucratic decision making, will be noted. What administrative law did not accomplish, and why, will also be the subject of some attention. Finally, two primary twentieth-century conceptions of the public policy process—elitism and pluralism—will be discussed.

PHILOSOPHIES FOR GOVERNANCE

It might be said that the founders who constructed our government represented three points of views: those who trusted administration; those who trusted the people; and those who trusted neither. These views were held, respectively, by Alexander Hamilton, Thomas Jefferson, and James Madison. All were shapers of the United States Constitution, although Jefferson, in France at the time, did not attend the Constitutional Convention.[1] Nonetheless, the Jeffersonian notions were well represented by those who took their philosophical cue from him.

Alexander Hamilton was the believer in administration. He wanted a strong central government and a strong chief administrator. Indeed, Hamilton proposed lifetime tenure for the president and preferred a more kingly title for the office.[2] Somewhat disdainfully, Hamilton looked upon the legislature as a contentious body with multiple voices that could not easily be held accountable for policy outcomes. For similar reasons, Hamilton was dubious about parceling out a significant portion of public policy responsibility to 13 states. Hamilton believed in an unimpeded leadership role for administrators once a task had been assigned by the legislature.[3] To accomplish this, Hamilton sought to have a strong and centralized administrative structure provided for in the constitution. In his opinion, the democratic dispersion of control over that structure was to be made with great care, lest voters, legislators, or state governments paralyze administration by their disagreements.[4]

Jefferson, on the other hand, thought that the constitution should subordinate administration to extensive and close democratic control. To Jefferson, democracy required administration that was close to the people; that is, decentralized to states and localities. Indeed, Jefferson even preferred that localities not become too big lest the spirit of democracy wither before the passive urban populations controlled by a few merchants and manufacturers. In stark contrast to Hamilton, who already was contemplating large industrial concentrations, Jefferson championed town meeting government.[5]

Given the ideological chasm between Hamilton and Jefferson and the divergence between their more moderate followers, the emergence of a centrist compromiser was to be expected. James Madison fulfilled such expectations, but it would be a mistake to see him merely as a broker. The philosophy advanced by Madison, who refused to put his unbounded faith in either an all-powerful executive or the wisdom of the people, dominated the Constitutional Convention. To Madison, the key question was whether an individual, as administrator or citizen, could set aside personal considerations in favor of broader societal concerns. Answering in the negative, Madison declared that "ambition must be made to counteract ambition."[6]

Madison had much in common with the architect. He was suspicious of the materials that were to comprise the government. Whether people, democracy, or unfettered executive management were advertised as ideal building blocks, Madison searched for defects and sought to account for them in the constitutional design. People sometimes acted selfishly; therefore, noted Madison, an adversary design would expose some self-interested assertions and counterbalance others. Also, in Madison's view, democracy could result in popular, but wrongheaded, movements, such as those championing religious, ethnic, or racial superiority, sweeping the country. In this case, Madison wanted plenty of checks on the majority and safeguards for the minority.[7] In a similar vein, the Madisonians did not deny that a powerful president would provide good management, but noted that the job might one day be filled by a mad and murderous individual. Thus, they thought it prudent to provide a way to turn the president out of office.

Unlike Jefferson, who wanted to guarantee the continued influence of small-town America, Madison wanted a generic constitution. Madison did not want to identify "good" and "bad" groups or prescribe a fixed distribution of influence. To be sure, this would favor the status quo at the time the constitution was adopted; namely, the small towners. However, if the status quo was the result of self-interested political struggle, it would be less than sporting to handicap groups for behavior that the constitution would approve. In Madison's view, the new government was to be an accessible arena for the clash between social and economic forces. Short of violence, the weaponry in this battle—rhetoric, facts and figures, emotions—was to be unrestricted. The primary and overarching restriction, which Madison strove mightily to build into our constitutional system, was that no one person or group would be allowed to win everything.

A Governmental Structure

In design, the constitutional structure sought to thwart unilateral control of the government in a number of ways. States were to be self-governing. Certain powers were assigned to the federal government. The states could not impinge on the federal mandate; nor could the federal government intrude on state functions. Within the federal government, power was to be divided among the executive, the judiciary, and the legislature. Each was provided with a counterweight to thwart domination by the others. The president could veto bills passed by the legislature. The legislature could reject proposed executive actions, override presidential vetoes, and pass laws requiring administrative action. The Supreme Court entertained suits against public officials and the government—an authority that was soon interpreted to mean that the constitutionality of legislative and executive acts was subject to judicial review [*Marbury* v. *Madison*, 1 Cranch 137 (1803)]. Presidents, vice presidents, and other administrative officials could be removed by the legislature if found guilty of "high crimes and misdemeanors," and judges could be impeached for violation of a concept loosely defined as "good behavior." (It might be noted that impeachments, and impeachment attempts, directed at judges have done little to make the definition more explicit.) All in all, this separation of powers between national and state governments and balancing of powers between the major institutions within the national government was an elegant reflection of the Madisonian philosophy which held that "all men having power ought to be distrusted."[8]

Even Congress, composed of representatives in pursuit of the narrow interests of diverse constituencies, did not escape Madison's suspicions. There was to be a bicameral legislature composed of a House of Representatives and a Senate. Both had to approve most legislation, and some authority was vested exclusively in one house or the other. In addition, it was intended that the House of Representatives and the Senate have differing philosophies. Under the pressure of biennial elections, members of congress were expected to represent the passions and ambitions of their small constituencies. Senators, on the other hand, were to be appointed, not elected, to a six-year term. Expiration dates were to be staggered; in the absence of physical or legal indisposition only one-third of the membership could change in a given year. The Senate, moreover, was to be stacked in favor of minority interests—namely, the less populous states. In total, the Senate was designed to check the excesses of the House by providing continuity of membership, a more contemplative view of the public interest, and a check against the oppression of the minority by the majority.[9]

In the constitutional scheme, the structural safeguards against tyranny were complemented by protections afforded the individual citizen. The *Bill of Rights,* appended to the Constitution in 1791, granted freedom of speech, a free press, and the right to assemble and petition the government. In addition, unjust search and seizure, self-incrimination, star chamber trials, and excessive bail were forbidden. These limitations were extended to the activities of state governments by the due process clause of the Fourteenth Amendment. Passed in 1868, the Fourteenth Amendment, with its declaration that every citizen is entitled to "equal protection of the laws," has been a touchstone for judicial rulings granting, to excluded groups, access to the councils and institutions of government.

The framers of the U.S. Constitution were less concerned about the electoral voice of the citizens than about citizens' rights. The determination of voting qualifications was left to the states and, for the most part, only white, male landowners were enfranchised. Voting for the president or vice-president was an indirect process buffered by electors who were not bound by the voters' choices. Direct citizen influence was limited to the House of Representatives. Each member of the House would represent 30,000 constituents (500,000 today), who, at the polls, could terminate or reelect the incumbent.

THE ASCENDANT PRESIDENCY

If we look at the Constitution of the United States and the debates that preceded its adoption, the subsequent rise of executive power is paradoxical. Although Hamilton's push for a strong national government was fairly successful, his push for a largely autonomous executive was not. In the Constitution, the structure of the administrative branch was mentioned only in passing; when it was noted, the purpose was usually to enumerate congressional prerogatives over the administrative process. Presidential appointees required congressional approval; Congress could grant the president unilateral appointment authority, but also could choose to deny the president any say in staffing a bureaucratic position. The president could negotiate a treaty, but two-thirds of the Senate would have to approve. Moreover, the legislature was to create post offices, provide for the printing of money, raise armies, declare war, make administrative rules, regulate interstate commerce, and guide international trade policy. Today, we see almost all of these activities as executive (or administrative) tasks. Presidents have waged undeclared war; struggles over trade policy can feature presidential subordinates such as the secretary of state and the secretary of the treasury; executive bureaucracies regulate interstate commerce, communications, and a host of other areas. Thus, through much of the United States' 200 years, in the absence of significant redefinitions of their relationship and powers, the presidency grew in power at the expense of the legislative branch.

Before the Constitution was 20 years old, a president moved boldly without congressional approval. Thomas Jefferson, in 1803, unilaterally purchased the Louisiana territories from the French, an act that contradicted his prior strong defense of legislative policy-making prerogatives. Indeed, Jefferson was moved to ask for congressional forgiveness for acting "beyond the Constitution."[10] Yet, with the same confession, Jefferson requested and received congressional authorization for the purchase. A quarter of a century later Andrew Jackson felt no need to apologize when he strayed beyond the Constitution. Unlike the parochial Congress, Jackson asserted, the president was responsible to a nationwide constituency.[11] Thus, Jackson felt that his policies, which included warfare against the Cherokee nation in violation of an existing treaty, were properly counterposed against legislative or judicial dictates.[12] Abraham Lincoln, in an exercise of emergency powers during the Civil War, suspended provisions of the Bill of Rights, thus permitting warrantless searches and seizures in defiance of a bristling Supreme Court.[13]

When Jefferson, Jackson, and Lincoln seized the policy-making reins, each was convinced of the necessity of doing so. Moreover, Jackson and Lincoln were "strong" presidents seeking to expand the authority of the executive branch. During other nineteenth-century administrations, however, chief executives such as Van Buren, Tyler, Fillmore, Pierce, and Buchanan stayed in the background as legislators such as Henry Clay and John C. Calhoun made Congress the fulcrum of public policy action. After Lincoln, Congress reasserted itself and sought to impeach President Andrew Johnson in a showdown that centered as much on the legislative-executive balance of power as on Johnson's alleged violations of the Tenure of Office Act.[14] The move failed by a single vote, but Congress had put on an impressive show of muscle.

Whether through the effectiveness of the Johnsonian example or the timidity of his successors, presidential aggrandizement at the expense of the legislature was not a prominent feature during the last quarter of the nineteenth century. The bureaucracy grew, but it was not until the twentieth century that presidents resumed flexing their muscles in earnest. Men like the Roosevelts, Wilson, Truman, Kennedy, and Johnson were dominant personalities committed to policies that would strengthen the executive. Each was in office during times of war, economic depression, or civil unrest; and three—Teddy Roosevelt, Harry Truman, and Lyndon Johnson—succeeded to office upon the sudden death or assassination of popular predecessors.

During such crises, there was a tendency to look toward the executive for leadership—an opportunity that few presidents failed to grasp. After McKinley's assassination, Teddy Roosevelt seized on muckraking exposés of monopolists and meatpackers to become a "trustbuster" and a pure foods advocate, thus paving the way for the Federal Trade Commission and the predecessor of the Food and Drug Administration. Woodrow Wilson, who had spent his professorial years championing administrative efficiency, used a boost from World War I to put theory into practice during his presidency. Franklin Roosevelt's massive administrative responses to the Great Depression and the Second World War resulted in a permanent expansion in the size and power of the executive branch. Similar growth occurred as a result of Truman's conduct of the Korean War, Kennedy's response to the Soviet Union's space supremacy, and Lyndon Johnson's Great Society programs aimed at curbing urban riots.

During the twentieth-century growth of presidential power, Congress was not always docile. However, its rebellions seemed more like holding actions than major offensives. When Wilson committed the United States to membership in the League of Nations, an isolationist Congress said no. Since President Wilson's one-man-show approach was most evident in foreign policy, there was also an element of congressional pique in the refusal. Twenty-five years later, however, Franklin Roosevelt's unilateral agreements at Yalta and Tehran—which, among other things, committed the United States as a core member of the

United Nations—were endorsed rather perfunctorily by the Senate. More recently, the bloody conflicts in Korea and Vietnam never became "wars" because presidents did not seek such a declaration from Congress, which, for its part, did not press for one. The electorate's support for "antiwar" candidates Eisenhower and McCarthy turned out to be a more potent check on presidents Truman and Johnson than the full weight of Congress. When Congress did not rely on the voters, it relied on the Supreme Court. It was the Court, not the Congress, that voided Harry Truman's nationalization of the steel industry in 1952.[15] When President Nixon refused to spend congressionally authorized funds, the Congress did not strike back with legislation until the Supreme Court ruled that an unconstitutional act had indeed occurred.

Legislative Deference

When one hears of the removal of property or power from the authorized holder, the search is usually for a perpetrator. Little attention is given to the victim or the circumstances. The power shift from the legislature to the executive, however, is marked by legislative deference and the firm push of circumstances as well as by executive acquisitiveness. The presidency's power rests partially on personnel and budgetary powers conferred by the Congress. In addition, the inexorable growth of the executive branch in response to society's increased size and complexity has chipped away at the legislature's supervisory role.

Congress augmented executive power early on. During Washington's administration, the legislature gave the president the power to remove bureaucratic officials.[16] With an executive bureaucracy of several dozen souls and a president of unquestioned integrity, this did not seem too momentous a grant of authority. With twentieth-century hindsight, however, we know that it was. Few recent presidents had awe-inspiring integrity, and several displayed an instinct for power politics. The federal bureaucracy now numbers 3 million. Tens of thousands of appointed policy makers are without a civil service buffer against presidential removal. Nor is removal the sole penalty. The offending official's program can be drained of funds by presidential budgetary powers conferred by Congress during the Reform Era.[17] Thus, presidential removal powers and budgetary powers, both granted by Congress in the name of administrative efficiency, have contributed to the diminution of legislative authority.

Another factor that weakened legislative policy-making authority was the increase in the government workload. Almost from the start, for instance, the Post Office Department grew like topsy. Constitutionally empowered to create post offices, the Congress, by 1901, had established 77,000. Congress supervised postal operations, but the oversight was more political than administrative. Getting a post office in one's congressional district meant a hard-working image and increased patronage for congresspersons. Similarly, holding down the first-class mail rates paid by most voters made sense politically if not managerially. In defense of Congress, it should be noted that effectively managing the mails was often beyond the ken of the administrators who devoted their full time to the task. Nonetheless, if size partially neutralized the efforts of a management cadre, it had an even greater effect on congressional oversight. Thus, by the 1970s, Congress substantially severed the postal service from legislative and executive control, mandated nonpartisan professional management, and established a Board of Governors to make policy and a Postal Commission to set rates.[18]

Complexity was also a factor confounding the legislature's attempts to make policy. The post office may have grown beyond the legislature's ability to supervise, but in a century of atomic energy and space travel, many government operations achieved a state of complexity that exceeded the legislature's capacity to think. As one observer of science and technology in government puts it, "Congress must act on behalf of the people as buyers. Unless a buyer is sophisticated and can challenge the agency or identify what it needs, the buyer can become the victim of the seller."[19] The usual response of Congress to sales pitches by high-technology agencies is to counterpose dissenting experts whose testimony is equally unfathomable. In this milieu, the pressure that the opposing sides can exert, rather than the relative weight of their technical arguments, usually carries the day. With the nongovernmental scientific community increasingly dependent on federal underwriting, the high-technology government organization can usually amass compelling support for its policies.

A FURTHER SEPARATION OF POWERS: THE EXECUTIVE AND ADMINISTRATION

In removing the postal service from the direct command of the president, Congress took a step that had been taken many times before. Since 1887, with the passage of the *Interstate Commerce Act,* Congress had been granting independent policy-making power to administrative agencies while closing off several avenues of presidential control. Congressional control was not necessarily enhanced as a result, but the bureaucracy, already growing in size and intelligence, was boosted towards a fourth branch of government role.

In granting independence to the Interstate Commerce Commission (ICC), Congress targeted not only the presidency but a specific president, Benjamin Harrison, who once had been a railroad lawyer. If the ICC was to regulate railroads properly, thundered a sponsoring senator, it had best be shielded from the presidential interference of a seasoned railroad advocate. Therefore, the ICC, which became the model for the regulatory agency, was separated from the hierarchy of command leading to the president. The president could not remove agency administrators unless malfeasance could be demonstrated. Policy-making power was assigned to several "commissioners" whose terms were staggered and exceeded the president's term of office. This arrangement prevented the president, who retained appointment authority with Senate approval, from loading the independent agency with loyalists. Congress's intent was that the "independent" agency be its own source of expertise and policy guidance, a fact that some agencies make a point of noting. Witness the Civil Aeronautics Board's formal assertion that its decisions "are not subject to review or approval by the President or by any department or agency of government."[20]

The Interstate Commerce Commission had an imposing array of powers, and its arsenal was duplicated by the independent agencies that Congress subsequently created. The ICC could legislate by formulating rules and regulations binding on the licensed railroads and, later, on licensed bus and trucking companies. It could enforce those rules and regulations through inspectors empowered to issue summonses to violators. It could judge the licensees' guilt or innocence of the charge at an administrative hearing.[21] Thus, the ICC became legislator, executive, prosecutor, and judge. The agency, moveover, was partially shielded from scrutiny. The Interstate Commerce Act provided protection from the president, and the complexity of ICC rate regulations offered insulation from Congress. The courts, which could overturn agency findings, were always at a distance due to the lengthy appeals process. With respect to the traditional branches of government, particularly the executive, the independent agency often lived up to its name.

The Informal Separation of
Executive and Administrative Powers

In discussing administrative autonomy, it would be a mistake to overemphasize formal independence from, or subordination to, presidential authority. Often, it is not what its statute says as much as what the agency does that demonstrates the degree of autonomy that it enjoys. The FBI under J. Edger Hoover (1924–1972) is the prime example. One way the agency cultivated a nationwide constituency was by exploiting the "public enemies list," a device that took care to include the objects of whatever hysteria might be widespread in the land: gangsters in the 1930s; communists in the 1940s and 1950s; and black nationalists and dirty, long-haired, antiwar radicals in the 1960s and 1970s. Such public relations made for overwhelming support, and by combining that support with a roomful of damaging files on Washington influentials, the FBI achieved autonomy from other government actors. Presidents left it alone; so did attorneys general; and the Congress treated the FBI with conspicuous generosity when budget time rolled around.

With difficult to understand missions, high-technology, scientific agencies may continue to retain substantial policy independence from the president as well as Congress. Agencies with less obtuse missions, however, may have a more difficult time achieving a Hooveresque sanctity from outside interference as long as legislators and presidents remember that an unfettered FBI and CIA routinely trampled on the Bill of Rights in the 1950s and 1960s. Instead, as has been the usual case in the past, securing autonomy from one of the traditional branches will require a partial surrender of the agency's independence to another branch.

Fending off presidential supervision with congressional muscle was a maneuver perfected by the U.S. Army Corps of Engineers. Engineer corps' projects are major undertakings featuring local employment in the short run and flood protection and recreation facilities in the long term. The corps, of which the president is also commander in chief, judicially distributes its projects so that a large percentage of Congress is grateful for past, present, or forthcoming largesse.[22] As a result, legislators look askance at presidential meddling with engineer corps' plans; they can display their disfavor by threatening to cut the budget of the president's pet programs. It is at such times that the president realizes that he is in charge of certain things so long as he does not try to run them.

It might also be noted that, to a large extent, independence is a function of the sheer incapacity of the president (governors and mayors, for that matter) to supervise all that goes on in administration. Richard Neustadt has identified the president as having five constituencies: subordinate bureaucratic officials, members of his or her political party, the Congress, the citizenry, and foreign governments.[23] The president, in serving these five constituencies, is responsible for domestic policy and foreign policy, the leadership of a political party, and the ceremonial obligations of the office. This does not leave much time for the administration of the country's largest bureaucratic organization.[24]

In the traditional scheme of things, the president's need to delegate control over the buraucracy has been realized in the person of the cabinet secretary—an appointee/loyalist placed at the helm of the federal superagencies such as Health, Education and Welfare; Housing and Urban Development; Defense, etc. Although the president's chosen legate, the cabinet secretary may "go native" when confronted with a substantial constituency of employees and clients with strongly held and well-documented views on policy.[25] If the cabinet secretary adheres doggedly to the presidential line, things can get rough. Assigned tasks may come back mangled from employees anguished and apologetic for having misunderstood what was desired. Citizen-critics, armed with copies of yesterday's confidential memo, may blast policies barely announced. With enough of this, administrators soon realize that although their jobs come from above, a significant part of their authority comes from below. As a result, obedience to presidential wishes becomes less absolute.

Even when bureaucratic pressure is absent, executive requests may wither before the personal values of the appointee. President Kennedy, for instance, wanted his Federal Communications Commission (FCC) chairperson, Newton Minow, to pressure the electronic news media for more favorable coverage. Minow refused.[26] Kennedy neither renewed the request nor punished Minow. Presidential soul searching may have caused the matter to be dropped, but a calculation of the damage attendant upon a Minow exposé of the attempt to suppress the news media may also have played a part in Kennedy's decision.

With bureaucratically proselytized or ethically inclined appointees, chief executives can feel alone, frustrated, and ineffectual. President Harry Truman described his job as "trying to persuade people to do things they ought to have sense enough to do without my persuading them."[27] Thus, in recent times, chief executives relied increasingly on their immediate staffs. As the names Haldeman, Ehrlichman, and Lance would indicate, some of the reliance was ill placed. Nonetheless, staffers keep at a distance from the ideology of the agencies that they supervise and are more likely to consider themselves soldiers of the president. Interestingly enough, when Nixon sought to intimidate the electronic news media, the assault was by the White House staff with Vice President Spiro Agnew on the point. FCC Chairman Dean Burch, who had long been moderately critical, intensified neither the quantity nor quality of his remarks to any great degree as Agnew leveled polysyllabic, inflammatory harangues.[28]

Although presidential staff assistance has increased enormously during the second half of the twentieth century, there are limits to what staff can do. A staff large enough to monitor the bureaucracy itself would be unwieldy. Thus, even without formal independence or protective legislative patrons, the government organization can evade executive supervision to a large extent.

Shared Powers and Administrative Brokerage

It is common to describe our government system as one of separated powers. That is, different duties are assigned to the executive, the legislature, and the judiciary; one branch can check or balance another branch but cannot take over another's duties (e.g., the president can veto a bill but cannot, at the same time, write and sign into law a preferred version). Increasingly, the characterization *separated powers* has given way to *shared powers*.[29] This is not altogether startling when we realize that courts, in effect, legislate. Segregation, as public policy, no longer exists in the United States because of *Brown* v. *the Board of Education* [347 U.S. 483 (1954)]; the "one man, one vote" concept on legislative districting is the product of several rulings culminating in *Reynolds* v. *Sims* [377 U.S. 533 (1964)], and not an output from the legislative process.[30] Presidents, as we have already noted, have acquired (by hook, crook, or legislative philanthropy) many of the powers vested in Congress by the Constitution. For its part, Congress has created administrative agencies "independent" of the executive hierarchy and, in the case of the General Accounting Office, set up a large-scale government organization to do the legislature's bidding.

Of a greater import, perhaps, than the blurred boundaries between executive, legislation, and judiciary is that administration is the repository of power and authority. Some is self-developed (the Hoover FBI; the Army Corps of Engineers); other powers are conferred through delegation or default by the traditional branches. Regardless of the initial source of authority, it assures a strong brokerage role for the bureaucracy. Managing and, to a large extent, controlling the bulk of government's resources, the bureaucracy becomes the quartermaster in the system of shared powers.

As quartermaster, the bureaucracy need act little different from the traditional branches of government. At times it defers to the traditional branches; on other occasions presidents, legislators, and the court justices are persuaded, maneuvered, or manipulated into supporting the programs of a bureaucratic agency. Presidents can punish agencies and remove officials but also require image-enhancing programs that are unlikely to emerge from an antagonistic bureaucracy. Legislators can, and do, cut budgets, but agency contracts for corporate constituents and bureaucratically ghost-written reports or bills are a potent countervailing currency.[31] The courts are a valuable check on administrative excesses, but if an agency is so inclined, the judicial system can be exploited. With overloaded dockets, the waiting time for a day in court is usually several months. To exhaust all appeals takes years.

Since bureaucracies have abundant endurance, they do not shy away from judicial wars of attrition. Even vindicated opponents may, after several years of costly legal wrangling, look more like losers than winners. This image, so intimidating for others who might want to challenge agency policy, may have been the agency goal from the minute the first brief was filed.

"Hot Oil, Sick Chickens," and
the Administrative Procedures Act

By 1934, the decision-making power of administration had grown in numerous ways. As one student of this development noted, administrative powers conferred on the early regulatory agencies had been concrete, specific, rulebound, and proscriptive.[32] That is, the agency enforced prohibitions against specified acts defined by law. Gradually, between the creation of the ICC in 1887 and the Franklin Roosevelt administration, there was a loosening of agency mandates. Regulation, in its initial ICC stage, was directed at specific acts such as rebates by railroads. Soon, generic business behavior, such as the formation of cartels, came under administrative scrutiny with the Sherman Anti-Trust Act in 1890. By 1906, with the passage of the Pure Foods Act, regulation began to encompass such abstract phenomena as impurity or rancidity.

Since such terminology was insufficient for administrative leeway, in 1914 Congress gave the Federal Trade Commission (FTC) as broad a berth as had yet been granted. The FTC could make its own rules, case by case, and in addition to determining what should not be done, could also determine what should be done. By 1934, the flood of New Deal legislation designed to combat the Great Depression had given administrative agencies the power to set prices and wages, regulate production, and control entry into certain businesses (radio and TV). Thus, over a half century, Congress had delegated increasingly broad authority to administration that, by 1934, was making laws, investigating violations, citing violators, judging their guilt or innocence, assessing penalties, and dictating future courses of conduct.

As administrative power grew, the courts made passing reference to the need for legislative standards and overruled a number of specific administrative decisions but never struck at the enabling legislation which undergirded administrative authority.[33] Finally, in two rulings arising out of the National Industrial Recovery Act of 1933, the Supreme Court called administrative policy making to task. Although both rulings struck down broad delegations, they also addressed, in critical terms, the haphazard way in which the policies of the National Recovery Administration (NRA) were carried out.

In the *"Hot Oil" case* [*Panama Refining Co.* v. *Ryan,* 293 U.S. 388 (1935)], the court noted that the NRA had "failed to observe minimum procedural decencies" in prohibiting certain shipments of oil in interstate commerce. As Gellhorn writes, "not only was the criminally enforceable petroleum code unpublished or unavailable to affected parties but . . . a careful examination disclosed that the code had in fact been amended out of existence."[34] In short, an industry kept in the dark was being managed by an administrative agency with a near limitless mandate.

"Hot Oil" did not sink the National Industrial Recovery Act, it merely left a hole where the administrative control of oil shipments used to be. Several months later, however, the *"Sick Chicken" case* [*Schecter Poultry Corp.* v. *United States,* 295 U.S. 495 (1935)], blew the National

Recovery Administration out of the water. Schecter Poultry was a small wholesaler supplying local butchers. Somehow, Schecter became the test case for the NRA's Live Poultry Code which, itself, was one of the more niggling industry codes. Even NRA supporters thought the choice ill-advised and they were soon borne out by the Supreme Court.[35]

The NRA had informed Schecter that its poultry business fell under the jurisdiction of interstate commerce. The Supreme Court ruled the opposite. In microcosm, Schecter exemplified the NRA's unacceptability to both the conservative and liberal factions of the Supreme Court. Conservative justices—annoyed that the NRA set uniform prices in many industries, limited overall production, and established quotas for individual firms—inveighed against NRA's attempt to fix Schecter's wages. When the Court's liberals found out that the NRA had permitted the large firms in many industries to formulate economic control policies that weighed heavily on smaller competitors, they too were dismayed. Justice Cardozo called the NRA "delegation run riot," the vote of the justices was 9–0 in favor of Schecter, and the National Industrial Recovery Act was ruled unconstitutional.

Despite this ringing denunciation, most legal scholars note that the "Hot Oil" and "Sick Chicken" cases were singular judicial stands and that subsequent legislative delegations of authority conferred NRA-type power with slight modifications. There was, however, a continuing recognition by the Court that some form of administrative due process was required to protect parties affected by administrative decisions. This was also the 1941 view of the attorney general's Committee on Administrative Reform. In 1946, Congress responded with the *Administrative Procedures Act (APA),* which provided that:

> (1) The functions of the prosecuting agency and the hearing officer are separated, and a separate corps of hearing officers has been created. (2) Agencies are required to inform the public of their structure, procedures and rules by publication in the Federal Register. (3) Notice must be given of proposed rules or changes therein. (4) Hearings are to be conducted in accordance with definite rules. (5) Courts are to review agency action . . . by the test of whether it is supported by substantial evidence on examination of the whole record.[36]

The Administrative Procedures Act, and the state and local statutes modeled after it, was one of the important bureaucracy-wide checks on administrative activity. Even so, it was only a compilation of rules of procedure with many exceptions and qualifications. In 1974, the Freedom of Information Act, an amendment to the APA, further strengthened the citizens' rights vis-à-vis administration; it also was duplicated by state and local versions. Equal opportunity and environmental protection standards provide additional checks on administration discretion.

ADMINISTRATIVE RULES

As a result of the Administrative Procedures Act and judicial rulings, the formal administrative process is characterized by rules. Gellhorn identifies three types: *procedural, interpretive,* and *legislative.*[37]

Procedural Rules Every agency has rules that detail the manner in which it makes decisions or conducts business. *Procedural rules* indicate who signs what document; what constitutes "evidence"; who is entitled to submit it and in what form; what records are kept and where. Procedural rules are not only numerous, they are often complex, leaving the average citizen befuddled and put off. Critics have charged that industry lawyers and regulatory agency personnel welcome this isolation. In recent years, however, administrative agencies have broken down many of the barriers to citizen input. The FCC solicits viewer comments on the performance of local TV outlets. Ad hoc groups concerned with televised violence have aired their views in FCC hearings. Even utility rate hearings have been opened to the public. Letters from the public—once ignored by some agencies if they did not follow the proper format—now become a part of the record for licensing determinations and policy decisions.

Interpretive Rules Firming up vague legislation is a common chore in administration, and one tool is the interpretive rule. Interpretive rules set forth the agency's understanding of its statutory authority. It notifies regulated parties of the agency's enforcement intentions. The notification medium may be a press release or an "authoritative ruling binding upon the agency and issued after interested and affected persons are given notice and an opportunity to be heard."[38] In the latter case, interpretive rules, by giving an explicit green light to certain behaviors, effectively bind the agency. For instance, if a municipal franchise board originally rules that sidewalk cafes may occupy half the sidewalk but subsequently shortens the maximum cafe width, it may not swoop down and demolish restaurant extensions built in good faith under the original rule. For their part, clients are not bound by interpretive rules. However, defiance will usually draw administrative action that can be stayed only by appeal to the courts. This can be risky since courts are inclined to defer to administrative expertise, and when this happens, interpretive rules acquire the force of law.

Legislative Rules An agency mandated to "promulgate such rules and regulations as are necessary to carry out the provision of this act" is authorized to decide what the law says. It does so through *legislative rules.* If proper notification and hearing procedures are followed, courts rarely overturn legislative rules. Judicial review is usually reserved for those rules that clearly exceed the legislative intent or are promulgated under statutes of dubious constitutionality.

Administrative Enforcement and Adjudication

With procedural, interpretive, and legislative rules, the administrative agency is ready for business. This is not to say that business is at a standstill while the framework of rules is being constructed. Quite the contrary, much of the framework is built upon the trial and error of early agency enforcement attempts. In time, however, the enforcement and adjudication activity of most administrative agencies rests on a formal and sturdy base.

Administrative enforcement starts simply enough. Agency inspectors or unaffiliated peace officers issue summonses of violation to persons or firms that are in apparent violation of agency rules and regulations or statutes administered by the agency. As a result, the alleged offender must appear before an administrative tribunal or a court of law. (The trend, it seems, may be toward more administrative adjudication. In many jurisdictions, for example, motor vehicle bureaus, parking violation bureaus, and housing code offices adjudicate complaints that were once handled by the courts. "Trial by mail"—where fines are fixed and offenders admit guilt—is also on the rise.)

The administrative hearing process for violations of law or administrative regulations differs from the judicial variety in several respects. First, informality often reigns. Complainants can confront licensees in administrative hearings held by consumer affairs agencies. Second, the rules of evidence are relaxed. The standard is not "beyond a reasonable doubt" or "a preponderance of evidence" but the kind of evidence on which responsible persons are accustomed to rely in serious affairs.[39] Third, the hearing officer is not the final decision maker in the administrative process; that authority rests with the heads of the agency. Fourth, the carrying out of the administrative decision is often stayed pending judicial review if it imposes severe penalties, such as a license revocation, and the defendant appeals.

A second type of administrative hearing does not seek to uncover and punish wrongdoing. Rather, it seeks to determine the "facts" so that a public policy decision can be made. Thus, when utilities apply for a rate hike, an administrative hearing is usually held. The object may be to determine whether the utility is making "a fair and reasonable rate of return" or whether pay phones are underpriced. Although such criteria sound economic, much more is involved. Pay phones may remain underpriced—and be subsidized by residential and business subscribers—because low-cost public phones are deemed necessary by the administrative agency in light of its mandate to see that phone service is provided in "the public interest."

Some fact-finding hearings can drag on for years when an agency seeks to establish crucial policy criteria. Such was the case when, through the 1960s and 1970s, the Federal Communications Commission sought to determine what constituted a "fair rate of return" for the American Telephone and Telegraph Company. The FCC went over AT&T's books—by the roomful. Economic and accounting analyses, prepared by FCC staff and AT&T representatives, bombarded the hearing examiners. After some years, FCC Docket 18128 *Private Line Ratemaking Principles* arrived at an acceptable rate of return and addressed some of the accounting practices of AT&T. For instance, the FCC thought that some promotional expenses were unbecoming a monopoly and prohibited their deduction from gross revenues in the calculation of rate of return. In no way was Docket 18128 the final say on the matter. Almost immediately, AT&T persuaded the FCC to permit a higher rate of return. Through the middle of the 1970s, the issue of profits, pricing, and accounting practices remained open as the FCC probed the reemergence of competition in the telephone industry. AT&T contended that the FCC cost assumptions, predicated on a monopoly situation, were no longer valid in a competitive milieu. On and on it went with no end in sight.

Judicial Review of
the Administrative Process

When an agency renders a decision or takes an action that adversely affects firms or individuals, the aggrieved parties may appeal to the courts. This appeal, however, is subject to some statutory exemptions and some procedural requirements. As soon as one is summoned before an administrative body, judicial relief can be sought by questioning the legitimacy of the administrative proceedings. (It need not be sought. Ignoring the subpoena will force the agency to start the judicial ball rolling.) When this occurs, newspaper accounts usually feature attorneys' charges that the agency has "exceeded its mandate," is engaged in a "fishing expedition," or is "harassing" their clients. The courtroom version of such tirades differs mainly in tone. To rebut, the agency must show that what it is doing is authorized by law; that those called in have been informed of the purposes of the investigation; and that the demands for evidence or testimony have not been unduly burdensome or in violation of constitutional privileges such as the protection against self-incrimination. These obstacles are not as formidable as they may sound. As Gellhorn notes, "If the agency is persistent and careful there is little beyond its reach."[40] Or, to put it in agency terms: "New subpoena? We have lawyers! More time? We have plenty!"

When challenges to their validity fail, administrative proceedings are free to run their course. That is, a hearing officer's opinion cannot be appealed until it has been approved by the department head. If two departments must review the matter, both must issue the decision before the courts will intervene. In short, the court reviews administrative activity at two points: when it starts and when it is finished.

Over one-third of the Supreme Court docket, and perhaps a greater share of the lower courts' time is devoted to appeals from the decisions of administrative agencies.[41] In nonemergency situations, courts will sometimes stay, pending a hearing, administrative decisions that deprive petitioners of property, licenses, or franchises. Recently the Supreme Court has taken the same position with respect to the denial of certain government benefits. Despite access to judicial review, it is unusual for a challenge to succeed in obtaining a reversal. First, agencies are not likely to go to court with "weak" cases. Second, agency judgment in its area of expertise is often unquestioned by the courts. The reasoning is that the legislature created the agency to make expert judgments and it is improper for the court to assume that role. Of course, the subject may well be beyond the ken of the judges, regardless of their philosophy toward the separation of powers. (There does, however, appear to be a trend toward specialization within the judiciary as some judges have become experts on communications law and aviation law.)

While courts will defer to administration on matters of fact and expert judgment, agency decisions are reviewed to see if the rules of procedure—both in agency regulation and in the body of the law—have been followed. Was the violator properly notified of the rules, of the actual violation, of the attendant penalties? Was the violator singled out or prosecuted for reasons other than the alleged violation? Was there a fair hearing? Was all the evidence heard? If any of these questions can be answered in the negative, the court may order a rehearing by the agency or overturn the administrative decision.

Exemptions to the APA

In a way, the APA was akin to throwing flour over a powerful, invisible presence. As a result, administration was more exposed to scrutiny although not necessarily weakened. Even the exposure, however, was less than complete. Some administrative agencies were exempted. Other agencies, those without quasi-legislative or quasi-judicial duties, were beyond the purview of the APA.

One of the agencies that awarded itself an APA exemption was the United States Immigration Service. Much like the U.S. Army Corps of Engineers, the Immigration Service did nice things for the members of Congress. If constituents wanted their relatives to come to the United States, a congressperson, with the help of the Immigration Service, could oblige. Since the émigrés were a diverse lot—members of Congress sponsored suspected gangsters as well as dissident intellectuals—the Immigration Service preferred loose, case-by-case decision making to the more restrictive APA-style standards. In addition, if the game of international intrigue required that foreign agents be deported rather than publicly exposed or if espionage was suspected but not provable, a malleable undesirable alien category came in handy. Thus, when the APA was passed, immigration authorities did nothing to comply with its provisions.

Congress ignored the Immigration Service's noncompliance until 1950. In that year, the Supreme Court ruled that the Immigration Service must comply with hearing provisions of the APA (*Wong Yang Sung* v. *McGrath,* 339 U.S. 33, modified, 339 U.S. 908). Congress, coming to the rescue of its ally, almost immediately reexempted the agency.[42] A number of years later, the Administrative Conference of the United States, an agency established to study ways of improving the administrative process, suffered a similar rebuff when it renewed the suggestion that the Immigration Service's case-by-case and highly discretionary mode of decision making be replaced by general rules.[43]

Many agencies are not considered for APA coverage. Technically, there is no need. The police, for instance, are not authorized to make decisions about what the law means or what constitutes a minor or major violation of a specific statute. Despite the lack of authority, however, the police exercise discretion that is extensive and profound; decisions to arrest or not arrest an individual are made regularly and can change the course of a suspect's life.[44]

That the police edit the law as well as enforce it was shown by James Q. Wilson. Wilson, in a multicity study, found three distinct enforcement patterns: the *legalistic* style, the *watchman* style, and the *service* style. *Legalistic* police operations observed the letter of the law. Enforcement did not vary from group to group or from infraction to infraction. In contrast, *watchman* enforcement ignored gambling and public intoxication in neighborhoods where such offenses were common. Indeed, many violations of law were permitted as long as they did not erupt into violence. With the *service* style, which was found in the suburbs surveyed by Wilson, police sought to keep the peace and enforce the law but much of the activity was informal. Teenage violators, for instance, were likely to be reported to their parents instead of being hauled into court.[45]

Besides exempting certain administrative agencies and excluding "nondiscretionary" agencies, the sweep of the APA was limited by another factor. Informality was often preferred by the agencies covered by the APA. Administrative hearings could be lengthy and expensive. They subjected the agency to the limelight and a potentially hostile audience. In addition, lower-level personnel could opt for informal settlements even if their superiors did not.[46] Where the trouble of an administrative hearing was considered a greater penalty than the offense warranted, violations could be ignored.

According to most observers, the net effect of these exemptions, exclusions, and evasions is that the bulk of administrative decision making is informal.[47] In this obscurity, facts and values can become indistinguishable as premises underlying administrative decisions that do much to shape public policy.

ADMINISTRATION AS A FOCUS OF VALUES

The organizational form embodies values: Efficiency is good; wastefulness is bad. The organization as a peopled entity becomes value conscious: Survival is good; threats to survival, and those who make them, are bad. The political arena often influences institutional values: Parties in power make better allies than parties who are not. Individual employees hold values: Fat people are lazy; thin people are energetic. These four value orientations—the bureaucratic, the institutional, the political, and the individual—permeate administrative policy. Although their presence is ubiquitous, their influences are overlapping and variable. Thus, it would be impossible to label the value component of an administrative decision as 25 percent bureaucratic, 15 percent institutional, 50 percent political, and 10 percent individual. However, a brief look at each value component, accompanied by illustrative examples, should make the categories clearer.

Bureaucratic Values and Administrative Decisions

The *bureaucratic values* of efficiency and "value neutral" expertise endow the government organization with much of its power and autonomy. Efficiency and expertise win deference from the traditional branches of government. This deference was dramatically illustrated when the Supreme Court upheld the Social Security Administration's denial of survivors' benefits to a woman widowed after several months of marriage [*Weinberger* v. *Salfi*, 422 U.S. 749 (1975)]. According to the Social Security Administration, when a death occurs within nine months of marriage the nuptial was arranged solely to secure lifetime social security benefits for the survivor. (Congress was persuaded by this view and incorporated it into the Social Security Act.) Understandably, the plaintiff in the above case wanted to be recognized as an innocent victim entitled to payments rather than a ghoulish conniver. She was unsuccessful as the Supreme Court endorsed the use of "irrebuttable presumptions" in determining eligibility. Such decisions legitimize administrative expertise as a basis of public policy and bless the bureaucracy's tendency towards standardization.

Despite the Supreme Court's sympathy toward irrebuttable presumptions in the Salfi case, it has required more procedural safeguards for citizens denied various forms of public assistance. Some welfare benefits for the destitute are treated as rights rather than privileges, and recipients must be notified of the reasons for an ineligible classification and afforded an opportunity to dispute the ruling. Still, the strength of bureaucratic values is not to be underestimated. An order from the Court requiring procedural niceties may be mooted by the Court's inclination to defer to administrative expertise. Efficiency may also be on the administrator's mind when formal proceedings are abandoned in favor of informal, and less public, policy making.

Institutional Values and Administrative Decisions

Organizations, as peopled structures, are social systems and have goals such as survival. Survival is an *institutional value* expressive of the investment that employees have sunk into the organization. One survival tactic is to maintain and augment supportive elements in the environment while intimidating or otherwise neutralizing detractors. The Selective Service Commission's prosecution of heavyweight boxing champion Muhammad Ali in the 1960s can be seen as an agency's quest for an environment less threatening to institutional survival.

Because of the unpopularity of the Vietnam War, things were not going well for the Selective Service Commission in the mid-1960s. Draft evasion was on the rise with border crossings to Canada, scrambles to enter exempt occupations, and the consumption of imaginative concoctions of drugs to mimic disqualifying physical symptoms at preinduction medical examinations. Many of the evasive tactics were legal; some were illegal but undetectable. Expatriate evaders were unreachable and some stay-at-homes merely hid in the cracks of an enforcement system unable to keep pace with the growing tide of violations. Embarrassingly for the commission, even traditional supporters, such as the American Legion, wondered aloud why more was not being done to bring "draft dodgers" to justice.

In view of the commission's rocky position, Muhammad Ali's application for conscientious objector status based on his Muslim faith was made to order. Commission supporters had little love for the brash Ali. Moreover, the average American was somewhat discomfited by the Black Muslims, who, at the time, were militant, separatist, and marred by an internal power struggle capped by the assassination of Malcolm X. In the decade of urban rioting, this imagery was certain to evoke suspicions. Thus, with many fearful of the Muslims and others incredulous at the notion of a boxer who was a conscientious objector, a prosecution of Ali promised widespread popular support.

The Ali case also could make the commission's conscription task easier. Youths would be dissuaded from swearing allegiance to the Muslims, or any pacifist religion without traditional Anglo-Saxon roots, in order to beat the draft. In addition, potential draft evaders—seeing that wealth and fame did not stay the wrath of the Selective Service Commission—would have second thoughts. This message was to be punctuated when Ali was denied state boxing commission approval to engage in his profession as he sought vindication in the courts. Thus, Ali's prosecution informed potential draftees that evasion could mean legal fees, loss of income, and several years of uncertainty topped off with a possible fine and prison term.

As it turned out, the Supreme Court unanimously reversed the commission's findings that Ali was not entitled to conscientious objector status. However, this judicial rebuff may have been outweighed by the institutional benefits derived from bringing the case. The world of administration is complex and, on occasion, losing is no more than winning in disguise. Witness the rewards that New York City reaped for willingly instigating, vigorously contesting, and graciously losing a law suit brought by municipal bondholders. The city, at the brink of bankruptcy, had refused to make bond interest payments. At the time, there was a near unanimous opinion—city lawyers dissenting, of course—that the withholding of interest violated the bondholders' agreement. The bondholders sued, and after a year of court activity, the city was ordered to make the interest payments. The city, which had acquired some financial breathing space, obliged.

Political Party Values
and Administrative Decisions

Bureaucratic values are part and parcel of the organizational form. Institutional values arise out of an ideological or pecuniary commitment to particular organizational goals. Political-party values, however, are rather unique to the government organization. When political party values are operative, administrators attribute extra weight to policy proposals solely on the basis of the political coloration of their source. Consider the following: A cafe, located at the base of a building inhabited by two powerful politicians, sought to expand and needed a license to do so. The politicians, one a reform leader and the other a machine power, were equally at odds over the quantity of night life that should take place under their bedroom windows. They launched separate telephone blitzes on the hierarchy of the licensing agency while an unsuspecting hearing officer sought to delve into the facts bearing on the application. The machine leader favored expansion—a conclusion the hearing officer was independently arriving at as the hearing progressed. The reformer, who favored the status quo, was lobbying with a reform administrator in a reform administration. Not surprisingly, the original hearing officer, on the brink of recommending expansion, was replaced with one who, the administrator was confident, would view the matter differently. The administrator's confidence was rewarded: The reform leader slept soundly, and the dispassionate record of the hearing and the referee's decision gave little hint of the background maneuvering that played such an important role.

Cases such as this usually highlight calls for the removal of politics from administration. The calls usually come from two sources: the radical surgeons and those who would keep political influentials within bounds. The radical surgeons would expunge all political influence except that embodied in the legislation under which the agency operates. Those who would control, rather than eradicate, political influence recognize that elected representatives will advance the interests of their constituents before administrative agencies. However, they caution administrators against an uncritical acceptance of a politician's point of view, particularly when it comes from a party official without an electoral base. As in the above case, the politician may be carrying the ball for a constituency of one.

While suspicion of politicians' overtures is not ill-advised, it may threaten long-standing relationships that, to those involved, are legitimate and rewarding. Appointed administrators are often associated with the dominant political party and may be acquainted with many of its officials. Those officials may have been crucial in securing the administrator's job. Thus, what the public sees as a "powerful politician's" request for "preferential treatment" may look different to the administrator. Instead of powerful politicians securing improper access to administrative councils, appointees see long-time friends and generous patrons whose sage advice need not negotiate cumbersome administrative channels. Moreover, for a party leader who obviously controls a substantial bloc of votes, the lack of an electoral mandate can be viewed as a mere technicality by the eager-to-please administrator. Indeed, this point of view may be accurate, as well as self-serving, in jurisdictions where party discipline is strong.

Individual Perceptions and Administrative Decisions

Individual perceptions are the media through which values are translated into administrative policy. Decision makers often are aware of their perceptions. Consequently, decisions are consciously filtered through one or more biases; that is, efficiency is good; the agency cannot show weakness; helping reform politicians fosters good government. Although some of the foregoing would not pass public muster, they are not ruled out as policy criteria in the inner councils of administration. Other perceptual filters, however, work subconsciously; thus, they distort facts but not the decision makers' feelings of objectivity.[48] In the following case, public safety was, ostensibly, the sole criterion for the administrative decision. As you will note, however, a welter of values and perceptions surrounded the decision.

The Word from the Tower: A Case Study

In the picture on page 263 is an administrator prepared to exercise discretion. He is in the tower (upper-left corner) wearing a white hat and sunglasses and, at the time, was the chief of the Bureau of Fire Prevention for the city of Syracuse.

The chief is suspended above a street on the grounds of Syracuse University, which had been the object of a month-long controversy. It started when university officials, primarily to facilitate snow-plowing, attempted to designate the street a "fire lane," with parking prohibited at all times. Vigorous resident protests—the nearest parking alternatives required a quarter-mile walk—led to willingness on the part of most university officials to accept a daily two-hour ban to permit effective snow-plowing. One official, however, withheld approval pending a dry run by fire trucks over the plowed road. This brought the Bureau of Fire Prevention into the picture.

The chief of the Bureau of Fire Prevention was not a stranger to the road in question. Prior to heading up the Bureau, the chief had moonlighted with the university department responsible for plowing. Those years had left a perceptual legacy. One week before the truck test, in the wake of a major snowstorm, the chief had toured the road and what he saw reaffirmed his enduring perceptions. Confronted with curbside snowbanks, cars were forced to park away from the curbs and narrowed the road considerably. Thus, when the residents met with the chief on the eve of the test, they found that a decision had already been made. The chief dismissed the tenants' argument that a daily no parking period to permit thoroughgoing plowing would result in a roadway wide enough for any fire vehicle. Indeed, he went so far as to "go on record as saying we can't get fire apparatus out there."[49] Perhaps to guarantee his prophecy, the chief assigned the department's largest vehicle—a tower truck designed primarily to combat blazes in high-rise buildings—to the test.

When, on Tuesday, January 24th, the tower truck arrived for the test, it confronted a road that clearly contradicted the chief's assertions. The road had been plowed clean, despite record-breaking accumulations of snow on the ground. Cars were parked close to the curb. The remaining width was clearly adequate for the tower truck's passage. Nonetheless, the chief, bound by past perceptions or the previous day's bravado, continued to term the road unsafe. To prove his point, the chief waved the truck onto the road, stopped it alongside a car and ordered the extension of the stabilizer mechanisms necessary for the raising of the tower ladder. All of this was accomplished and the chief went for an aerial ride. At about the point shown in the picture, he discovered why the truck was not fully operable in the road. "Had a van been parked there," the chief stated, "the ladder would not have gone much lower." Exasperated residents protested that

Administrative Discretion. As residents and university officials stand by, the fire chief is descending to announce that the tower truck is not fully operable on the road and that parking must be banned. SOURCE: Glen Ellman, *The Daily Orange* (Syracuse, New York), January 27, 1978.

the truck was never meant to scale eight-foot heights but the chief was unmoved.

The next day in an interview with a reporter, the chief downplayed the test but did not retreat from his decision. "They (university officials) called it a test," he said. "That isn't why I brought the apparatus out there. *I had already made up my mind.*"[50]

When a situation is certified as a clear and present danger to life, questions usually come after its correction, not before. The public safety prevails over the need to guard against procedural irregularities. Indeed, as the chief intimated, he need not have conducted the test at all in order to prohibit parking on the road. When public safety is involved, professionalism often substitutes for administrative law as a reassurance to the citizen that the power to make high-impact and often irreversible determinations is not being politically influenced. Immunity to politics—and most police and fire departments achieve this to a large extent—does not shut out other values, however. In the case above, the decision maker's previously acquired perceptions, largely inaccurate under the daily plowing scheme, helped determine the administrative decision. In addition, the chief had staked his reputation and, to a large extent, that of the department, on a negative outcome. Thus, the decision may have been influenced consciously or subconsciously by a desire to avoid personal and organizational embarrassment.

ADMINISTRATION AND PUBLIC POLICY

To this point we have sketched administration as a major actor sharing public policy power with the legislature, the judiciary, and the executive. The sketch has been generic. Administration grew powerful because it grew large; it purchased more autonomy with an increasing wealth of knowledge. Administration became a repository of shared government powers and exercised its residual authority in accordance with bureaucratic, institutional, and employee needs. Although size, complexity, and the organizational dynamic are significant factors, it would be a mistake to assume that administrative policy power is exclusively self-developed or naturally derived.

A glance at any government directory will show that administrative agencies embody explicit, legislatively conferred perspectives on public policy. Public organizations are dedicated to consumers, workers, farmers, and business persons; airlines, power companies, the radio and TV industry; the poor, the aged, and the unhealthy. The guardianship, moreover, can range from close regulatory supervision to an explicit support and advocacy role. However, varying degrees of policy-making latitude exist in most statutes. When laws are vague—and many simply require that X, Y, or Z be regulated or promoted in the public interest— the affected parties descend on administration to make sure that specific regulations embody their interests. Thus, the government agency becomes a focal point for public policy formation.

As regulated groups become successful in shaping agency policies, their role shifts.[51] They become clients or partners in administration. No role transformation is required for societal groups whose clientele relationship with the government has been legally sanctioned from the start. Labor, business, and agriculture all have agencies watching out for their interests. Some industries have press agents as well as guardians. Aviation and telecommunications have agencies that promote their expansion and see to it that damaging internal struggles do not arise.[52]

That much of public policy is made in administration is an unassailable proposition. Agencies and their major clients fill in the details of legislative policy, draft legislation that expands the administrative mandate, and lobby with the legislature or the executive in order to advance such policy initiatives. The questions that arise from this reality are several. What is the voters' role in public policy formulation? If their role is minimal, who are the major actors? If the real policy makers do not spring from the electoral process, what are the implications for democracy?

Whatever Happened to Voter Sovereignty?

In our popular conceptions, voters have always been somewhat larger than life. The majority of the voters spoke with the "voice of the

TABLE 8.1

Voter	First Choice (×3)	Second Choice (×2)	Third Choice (×1)
Joe	Movies	Ballgame	Dancing
Mary	Movies	Ballgame	Dancing
Harriet	Ballgame	Dancing	Movies
Mike	Ballgame	Dancing	Movies
Joann	Movies	Ballgame	Dancing

people." In an elegant and perceptive analysis, Kenneth Arrow showed that this voice could be false where there are more than two policy options and the order of preference is factored in.[53]

As an example, let us consider the following: Five people are deciding where to go on a Friday night. Three alternatives are put to a vote. The results are shown in Table 8.1.

If, as is arbitrarily assumed in the example, a first choice has three times the commitment and a second choice twice the commitment accompanying a third place vote, this group might feel a bit uneasy going to the movies. This feeling would not be unjustified. In actuality, as Table 8.2 illustrates, the group prefers to go to the ballgame.

What this shows is that the majority vote does not always favor the preferred option if varying degrees of intensity are present. Now one cannot, of course, arrive at measurements of relative intensity as precise

TABLE 8.2

Activity		Votes	(×)	Weight (Intensity)	=	Weighted Preference
Movie	1st Place	3	×	3	=	9
	2nd Place	0	×	2	=	0
	3rd Place	2	×	1	=	2
						11 = Total weighted vote for movie.
Ballgame	1st Place	2	×	3	=	6
	2nd Place	3	×	2	=	6
	3rd Place	0	×	1	=	0
						12 = Total weighted vote for game.
Dancing	1st Place	0	×	3	=	0
	2nd Place	2	×	2	=	4
	3rd Place	3	×	1	=	3
						7 = Total weighted vote for dancing.

as those used in the example. The point is that there is a qualitative, as well as a quantitive, aspect to citizens' preferences. Therefore, if the ballgame lobby in the above group swayed the rest toward the stadium, majority vote would have succumbed to intensity, but the group would have been more satisfied with the result.

Arrow's Theorem, as it was called, added impetus to an ongoing analysis of the voter's role in public policy formation. Over a decade before Arrow's 1951 analysis, Joseph Schumpeter had questioned the coherence and impact of the people's voice in two-party elections.[54] In a bigger and more haplessly tangled version of Arrow's paradox, candidates in the United States represented a raft of issue-positions. Moreover, Schumpeter observed, a plethora of political rhetoric obscured just what these issue-positions were. If, through sheer perseverance, voters managed to board the raft and sift through the rhetoric, they were likely to come across uncrackable nuts such as atomic energy or genetic research. As a result, said Schumpeter, most citizens fell back on sentiments and prejudices when voting. Political parties, aware of this, bombarded the electorate with imagery designed to please the majority of the voters. The pitch, as campaign managers in the 1960s and the 1970s were to make explicit, was to "Middle America."

From this perspective, the ballot box and the campaign trail did little to shape public policy. Vote totals, unless substantially one-sided or clearly tied to an issue, provided little policy guidance to elected officials. Campaign promises designed to please the ears of an electorate with short memories were flimsy policy commitments. Clearly, intensity of preference must be conveyed through means other than the ballot box. Upon taking a closer look, sociologists and political scientists found that an intense message was being sent to elected officials. Decoded so as to be clear to political parties and candidates, the message reads as follows: "We understand the costs and moves of the political game. If you will back our policies when in office (not necessarily during the campaign, of course), we will help fund and staff your candidacy. If you refuse, we will work for your defeat, using all the techniques of innuendo and vilification at our disposal." However, the two disciplines could not, at first, agree on who was sending the message. Most political scientists saw groups as the source; most sociologists saw a particular stratum of society.

The Power Elite

Beginning in the 1920s, sociological studies of American cities delved into community politics and found stratification. According to the researchers, decisions on a wide range of community affairs were heavily influenced by a few individuals. These community influentials, in the main, were wealthy members of "old-line" families.[55]

On the national level, C. Wright Mills, in the 1950s, singled out the "military-industrial complex" as the *"power elite."* Again, the members of the complex were from the "right" families, the "right" schools, the "right" clubs, and populated the highest policy levels of industry and government.[56] In 1960, President Eisenhower, with a farewell speech warning against the growing power of the military-industrial complex, gave a boost to the Millsian point of view.[57]

Despite a seeming presidential endorsement, the social stratification/power elite notions were a bit too rigid for later researchers. They noted that the Social Register did not represent a homogeneous point of view; there were "liberals" scattered about. Furthermore, after they moved on to bigger and better things, even Harvard classmates came at public policy from different institutional perspectives. Moreover, "Brahmin" families were not prolific enough to populate all of the key public policy positions in postindustrial society. Still, the criticisms of Mills did not mean an abandonment of elite theories. According to Gabriel Kolko, elitism was plain to see if one stopped concentrating on family trees and alma maters and looked at the larger institutional picture in society.[58] From this vantage point, the upward path to policy-making positions would be seen as a powerful socializer. For those who make it through, college instills a respect for book learning, a skill at writing reports, and a belief that rites of passage are proper and lead to bigger and better things. Graduate schools—particularly for law, business, and public administration—provide further reinforcement. By the time tomorrow's policy makers rise through the educational system and up the organizational ladder, they think alike and look alike. As the "institutional elitist" might point out, Henry Kissinger, the immigrant from the upper-Manhattan tenements, was not, philosophically, a radical departure from his blue-blood predecessors as secretary of state.

Pluralism: Rotating Elites

When political scientists looked at the public policy process, they also saw elitism. However, this elitism differed from the sociological version and was not deemed a significant factor in explaining public policy outcomes. To the pluralist school, groups were the heart of the matter.[59] Once mobilized around issues of interest to it, the group became a prime impetus in public policy formation. *Interest groups* were organized to a greater or lesser degree, and this produced the elitism that existed. As organizations, the interest groups usually had identifiable spokespersons. Thus, the intergroup policy competition was spearheaded by corporate chairpersons, union heads, trade association presidents, religious leaders, and others.

The term *rotating elites* was used by the pluralists to characterize the participants in the public policy process. First, the leadership within interest groups rotated. Union leaders lost elections. Corporate executives were kicked up or out. Although the *institutional elite* school would charge that such changes were largely illusory, pluralist political scientists felt that group members made significant changes when incompetent or intractable leaders failed to advance their interests. New leaders with new outlooks would be installed.

According to pluralist thought, individual groups, through their spokespersons, also rotated in and out of the policy arena because their interests were not embodied in all public policy questions. Thus, minimum wage policies brought labor and management to the halls of Congress and the corridors of administration. The Sierra Club and the Friends of the Parks were not likely to be in evidence. If the issue became saving the redwoods, however, these groups would come to the fore as the unions and corporations faded into the background.[60]

By the 1960s, the pluralist perspective was widely accepted. Descriptively, it seemed to correspond with what was going on in the real world. Although somewhat remote from the ballot box, *pluralism* was more palatable ideologically than the elite theories of aristocrats and mind control. If interest group leaders who played a public role were legitimized by some expression of member preference, was that not democratic? Interest group theorists, moreover, had little trouble linking back to Madison. Here were multiple and diverse factions struggling to influence public policy. Low-intensity feelings remained unaffiliated; moderate-intensity feelings coalesced into a group; a bit more intensity guaranteed a meaningful hearing from government decision makers; and continued high-intensity activity produced public policies desired by the group. Thus, when it was said that pluralism produced government policies shaped by a "majority of minorities," people felt reassured that the U.S. Constitution was in working order.[61]

Pluralism as Private Interests with Public Power

The interest group, in the pluralist view, exhibits organizational traits. The larger and more successful interest groups—the AFL/CIO or the National Association of Manufacturers—are full-fledged organizations. So, too, are the administrative agencies of government. Even in the legislature, committee staffs have been powerful in setting the agenda of elected representatives. This triumvirate of interest group bureaucrats, administrative bureaucrats, and legislative bureaucrats has been identified as a prime loci of public policy. Of the three, we are interested in the administrative agency and the interest group. Legislative policy making, evaluation, and oversight will be treated in subsequent chapters.

Armed with resources, a formal mandate to advance the interests of their clients, and an informal obligation to advance the interests of their employees, the administrative agency and the interest group are key policy initiators in the pluralist arena. Often, the administrative agency and the interest group concerned with the same policy area support similar policies.[62] As is the case with the Department of Agriculture and the nation's farmers, this policy partnership can be legislatively blessed. However, similar understandings often arise between agencies and interest groups which are in a regulatory relationship. Over time, through constant contacts and a process of mutual accommodation, regulatory policy reflects industry preferences; that is, public power comes to serve the private interests that it was designed to control.

That familiarity breeds tolerance is not the only explanation of how special interests become ingrained in government administration. Some claim that even the paternity of the regulatory agency can be traced to the regulated industry. In this view, the ICC was welcomed by the railroads. Although small firms were on the bottom of the pecking order, the railroads were also being bullied by industrial giants who sometimes made good on their threats to buy or build competitor lines and instigate price wars. Similarly, even before the Food and Drug Administration (FDA), meatpackers had supported federal inspection because some in the industry, fixated on profit and deaf to pleas of their more image-conscious brethren, were putting out such a squalid product that foreign nations refused to import U.S. meat.[63] In the 1930s, imagery was also important to the stock market, which, in the eyes of the public, had somehow made 33 percent of the nation's wealth disappear. The Securities and Exchange Commission was a desperately needed imprimatur.

Government also could be, for regulated businesses, a pleasant substitute for competition rather than a mere damper on competitive excesses. For the telephone and electric industries, now composed of companies with government-granted monopoly privileges in their areas, regulation replaced aggressive, free-wheeling, cost-cutting competitors. Instead, there was a relatively gentle adversary. The regulatory agency did not seek to seize a portion of the utility market. Indeed, "regulation in the public interest" served the private utilities well in fending off radical calls for their nationalization.

Regardless of how it came about, the embodiment of private interests in government agencies is criticized for assigning the responsibility for public policy to the objects of that policy.[64] One example often cited is the domination by practicing physicians of the state boards that certify new doctors. This arrangement, critics say, leads to the government's perceptions of society's medical needs being shaped by the members of the medical profession, and not by the public at large. Thus, the medical school curriculum may be shaped to produce specialists who must have access to major medical center facilities while the region may have a real need for general practicioners willing to work in rural areas.[65]

The situation in the legal profession is somewhat similar. State Bar

Associations, on behalf of the judiciary, test law school graduates and certify them as qualified to represent clients in legal proceedings. The bar exam—the final hurdle to the practice of law—helps shape law school curricula and the question is to what end: that is, filling future vacancies in existing law firms or creating advocates for previously neglected rights? There is a noticeable tilt towards the former in many of the law courses that comprise the bulk of the law school curriculum. Books on the real property law, for instance, offer an exhaustive preparation for a landlord's lawyer while substantially neglecting the residential tenant's rights and remedies. If, as it seems, existing lawyers, primarily serving an institutional clientele, shape the law school curriculum into a cloning mechanism, the question is whether a broader-based licensing authority would not prefer more public interest advocates, or even administrative law judges, as the conscious product of a legal education.

A further criticism of pluralist administration comes from some economists. Regulation often insures higher prices (minimum price requirements) and reduces competition (one license per township limitation). Many economists are critical of such rules and think that the overall costs of regulation may outstrip the benefits. Rate determination hearings by regulatory agencies often lend credence to the latter assertion. To protect itself, an agency may seek both economic justifications and political justifications for rates. Thus, hearings are usually lengthy and feature economists, politicians, citizens' groups, and industry representatives on both sides of the issue. As a result, rate hearings can run on for months and years. The expense, ultimately, is borne almost entirely by the public through taxes to pay for the agency's role; higher prices to pay for the industry's arguments; and contributions to pay for the objections of the private, consumer advocacy organization. Economists wonder whether the improper rate requests uncovered and denied by the regulatory agency compare with the total costs of the discovery. The queries are particularly pointed when an industry is easy to enter and able to sustain a high degree of competition (e.g., taxicabs), yet government regulation limits entry and sets rates.[66]

As he assumed office in 1977, President Carter, in a reaction to the intricate and thick webs binding regulated industries and regulatory agencies, promised to pursue a policy of "deregulation." Government's rate-making activities and its awarding of "market shares"—airline routes, interstate bus routes, and other franchises—was to be reduced and competition allowed to reemerge. As of 1978, the airline industry had been subject to some deregulation. However, it was difficult to discern any immediate reduction in government's role, particularly since the Civil Aeronautics Board was highly active in overseeing the deregulation.

THE PUBLIC INTEREST REASSERTED

In the pluralist view, special interests were the alloys of public policy. If backed by numbers and intensity, special interests mobilized group efforts powerful enough to impact on policy. Options that did not appear on the public policy agenda simply did not have the necessary support, according to the pluralist view.

One of the earliest broadsides hurled at the pluralist model was E. E. Schattschneider's *The Semi-Sovereign People;* it set the tone for subsequent criticisms.[67] Schattschneider attacked the pluralist presumption that groups had an equal opportunity to enter the public policy arena. Entry, Schattschneider pointed out, was costly. Money was needed to pay lawyers, lobbyists, and press agents. Printing leaflets and placing ads also required ready cash. Time could substitute for money but that too was a limited commodity for citizens who worked a 9 AM to 5 PM job trying to influence bureaucracy that kept the same hours of operation. Knowledge was also an important but limited currency in pluralist policy making. If a group is interested in preserving a condemned building, for instance, it helps to know that the landmarks commission can perpetuate what the building department is prepared to destroy. A certain bearing also is helpful in reaching administrative and legislative policy makers. Welfare clients, Indian-Americans on reservations, students, and others who lack this carriage, may find themselves disenfranchised in the political and administrative sectors of the pluralistic arena.

Interestingly enough, by the late 1970s, one of the seminal pluralist theorists, Charles Lindblom, was moving towards the Schattschneider point of view regarding differential access to the pluralist arena.[68] Business, Lindblom contended, was the most powerful pluralist force and was taking over permanent possession of large swaths of the government's policy-making apparatus. Seeing a growing mismatch, Lindblom advised that ways be sought to restore a balance among interests lest we find ourselves with a business elite at the helm of public policy.

Schattschneider, in addition to his critique of the accessibility of pluralist policy making, questioned whether public policy was due exclusively to the clash of special interests. Could not the laws against murder and mayhem, he asked, be attributed to a "public," as distinct from a "special," interest? Answering affirmatively, Schattschneider suggested that the interest group efforts were directed towards winning widespread public support for their policies. For this, a campaign of persuasion was required. While certain groups in society could afford such campaigns and others could not, resources and skills could not push through a special interest group's policy in the face of widespread public resistance.

Support for the notion that special interest proposals must satisfy a broader public interest may be found by contrasting the fate of the chemical sweeteners, cyclamate and saccharin, when they were found to cause cancer in test animals. Under the Delaney Amendment, the Food and Drug Administration must prohibit the use of any cancer-causing, chemical food additive. In the 1960s, cyclamate, the base of a multibillion-dollar diet-food industry, was prohibited when shown to be a carcinogen. This culminated a decade-long battle in the administrative arena, where the industry fought hard and successfully to discredit earlier reports implicating cyclamates. Faced with positive proof, the manufacturers shifted into the legislative arena but found their representatives reluctant to go on record in favor of cancer. Bemoaning the expense involved, the industry replaced cyclamates with saccharin, the last available artificial sweetener.

When saccharin was found to be a cancer-causing substance in the 1970s, the scenario differed radically. Tens of millions of Americans were reliant on diet products for weight control. This time, the ban was opposed by the industry *and* a significant portion of the public. As a result, Congress partially exempted saccharin from the requirements of the Delaney Amendment.

SUMMARY: DOES PUBLIC POLICY SERVE A PUBLIC INTEREST?

One approach to the role of administration that has been evident in this chapter is one of reliance. The need for expertise and for massive institutional structures to process the work of postindustrial society causes many to cede a central policy making role to administration. Glendon Schubert has termed this the *"idealistic" approach to achieving the public interest.*[69] There is an abiding faith in, or a fatal resignation toward, administration. As we have seen, this faith must be strong to contend with the institutional, political, and individual factors that distort bureaucratic decision making.

We also have seen, in this chapter, a more distrustful approach to administration. This approach is realized in many of the provisions of the Administrative Procedures Act. Still, the APA treats administration much like a machine that needs its bugs ironed out. The underlying presumption is that the administrative apparatus is perfectable, and when perfection is achieved, it will be an instrument for carrying out the policies set by legislators and executives. In Schubert's typology this is termed the *"rationalist" approach to achieving the public interest.* The problem, of course, is that superiors can hone the machine as much as they like, but it will still act erratically if it continues to receive conflicting orders and vague commands from numerous quarters.

A third approach is to accept that administration is a maelstrom of facts and values and a prime target for those who wish to influence public policy. Schubert terms this the *"realistic" view of the public policy process.* It is, of course, the pluralist view. Schubert, however, rightly notes that pluralism does not claim to arrive at the public interest. Rather, a balance between competing special interests is the end product of pluralist public policy.

In the following chapters we will return to these three themes. Our next focus of attention, the budget, is largely the product of a pluralistic policy process. However, recommendations for improved budgeting techniques presume that administration can be given explicit directions and workable controls so that policy can be rationally implemented. The tendency of the institutionalized government bureaucracy to appropriate public policy decisions unto itself also will be in evidence from time to time.

KEY TERMS AND CONCEPTS

Administrative Procedures Act (APA)

Administrative rules (procedural, interpretive, legislative)

Arrow's Theorem

Bill of Rights

Institutional elitism

Interest group

Interstate Commerce Act

Pluralism

Police styles (legalistic, service, watchman

Power elite

Public interest (idealistic, rationalist, realistic)

Separated and balanced powers

Shared powers and administrative brokerage

Values in administration (bureaucratic, institutional, political, individual)

NOTES

1. The primary source for exploring the Constitutional Convention of 1787 is Alexander Hamilton, James Madison, and John Jay, *The Federalist* (Cambridge: Harvard University Press, 1961). *The Federalist* consists of separately authored but unsigned position papers. Detective work by political historians has resulted in the attribution of the individual pieces to the appropriate author.
2. Robert Dahl, *Democracy in the United States: Promise and Performance* (Chicago: Rand McNally, 1973), pp. 68–69.
3. Alexander Hamilton, *The Federalist*, no. 70; see also John C. Miller, *Alexander Hamilton and the Growth of the New Nation* (New York: Harper & Row, 1959).
4. Hamilton, *Federalist*, no. 70.
5. Lynton K. Caldwell, *The Administrative Theories of Hamilton and Jefferson* (Chicago: University of Chicago Press, 1944).
6. James Madison, *The Federalist*, no. 51.
7. James Madison, *The Federalist*, no. 10.
8. Reinhold Niebuhr, *Moral Man and Immoral Society* (New York: Scribner, 1960), p. 164.

9. Dahl,*Democracy in the United States,* pp. 79–83; for a somewhat critical view of what the Senate does, see Rexford Tugwell, *The Emerging Constitution* (New York: Harper & Row, 1974), pp. 426–432.

10. Jefferson quoted in Tugwell, *Emerging Constitution,* p. 65.

11. Arthur M. Schlesinger,*The Age of Jackson* (Boston: Little, Brown, 1945), p. 43. Jackson, according to a contemporary, felt that "to labour for the good of the masses was a special mission assigned to him by his Creator . . ."

12. Tugwell, *Emerging Constitution,* p. 172.

13. Alpheus Thomas Mason and William M. Beaney, *The Supreme Court in a Free Society* (New York: Norton, 1968), p. 64.

14. Tugwell, *Emerging Constitution,* p. 234.

15. *Youngstown v. Sawyer,* 343 U.S. 579 (1952).

16. James Q. Wilson, "The Rise of the Bureaucratic State," *The Public Interest* no. 41 (Fall 1975): 78.

17. It was the Budgeting and Accounting Act of 1921 that dramatically increased the president's fiscal leverage over the federal bureaucracy.

18. *The Report of the Commission on Postal Service* (Washington: U.S. Government Printing Office, 1977) details some of the post-1970s' changes and is testimony to the enduring nature of postal administration problems.

19. W. Henry Lambright, *Governing Science and Technology* (New York: Oxford University Press, 1976), p. 203.

20. *United States Government Organization Manual, 1972-3* (Washington: U.S. Government Printing Office, 1972), p. 387.

21. Robert Fellmeth, *The Interstate Commerce Commission* (New York: Grossman, 1970), pp. 327–338.

22. Arthur Maass, *Muddy Waters: The Army Engineers and the Nation's Rivers* (Cambridge: Harvard University Press, 1951); Also, by the same author, *The Kings River Project* (Syracuse: The Inter-University Case Program, 1963).

23. Richard E. Neustadt, *Presidential Power: The Politics of Leadership,* as excerpted in Robert Golembiewski, Frank Gibson, and Geoffrey Cornog, *Public Administration* (Chicago: Rand McNally, 1972), pp. 401–407.

24. Thomas E. Cronin, "The Swelling of the Presidency," *Saturday Review,* 20 January 1973.

25. Hugh Heclo, *A Government of Strangers* (Washington: Brookings, 1977), chapter 3.

26. David Wise, *The Politics of Lying* (New York: Random House (Vintage Books), 1973), pp. 370–371.

27. Truman quoted in Neustadt, *Presidential Power,* p. 403.

28. Wise, *Politics of Lying,* pp. 336–338.

29. Neustadt, *Presidential Power,* p. 404.

30. *Brown v. Topeka* (347, U.S. 483 (1954).

31. See J. Lieper Freeman, *The Political Process: Executive Bureau–Legislative Committee Relations* (New York: Random House, 1965); Norman C. Thomas and Karl A. Lamb, *Congress: Politics and Practice* (New York: Random House, 1964); and Mark J. Green, James N. Fellows, and David R. Zwick, *Who Runs Congress?* (New York: Grossman, 1972) for views on the relationship between Congress, administration, and interest groups.

32. Theodore Lowi, *The End of Liberalism: Ideology, Policy and the Crisis of Public Authority* (New York: Norton, 1969), p. 134.

33. Ernest Gellhorn, *Administrative Law and Process* (St. Paul, Minn.: West Publishing, 1972), pp. 14–15.

34. Ibid., p. 17.
35. Tugwell, *Emerging Constitution,* p. 517.
36. Mason and Beany, *Supreme Court,* p. 43.
37. Gellhorn, *Administrative Law,* pp. 122–127.
38. Ibid., p. 122.
39. Ibid., p. 184.
40. Ibid., p. 70.
41. Mason and Beany, *Supreme Court,* p. 34.
42. Ibid., p. 44.
43. Abraham Sofaer, "Judicial Control of Informal Discretionary Adjudication and Enforcement," *Columbia Law Review* 72, 1293 (1972).
44. See Kenneth Culp Davis, *Discretionary Justice: A Preliminary Inquiry* (Baton Rouge: Louisiana State University Press, 1969), pp. 80–90.
45. James Q. Wilson, *Varieties of Police Behavior, The Management of Law and Order in Eight Communities* (Cambridge: Harvard University Press, 1968).
46. Peter M. Blau, *The Dynamics of Bureaucracy* (Chicago: University of Chicago Press, 1955), pp. 151–155.
47. Davis, *Discretionary Justice,* p. vi, estimates that 80–90 percent of administrative decisions are informal; Gellhorn, *Administrative Law,* p. 100, estimates that the "great bulk" of administrative decisions are informal; Peter Woll's book, *Administrative Law: The Informal Process* (Berkeley: University of California Press, 1963) is, as the title suggests, wholly devoted to the subject.
48. See Herbert Simon, *Administrative Behavior: A Study of Decision-Making Processes in Administrative Organization* (New York: Free Press, 1976). Chapters III, IV, and V are a seminal treatment of the intrusion of values into the administrative decision-making process.
49. *The Daily Orange,* 24 January 1978.
50. *The Daily Orange,* 24 January 1978.
51. Marver Bernstein, *Regulating Business By Independent Commission* (Princeton, N.J.: Princeton University Press, 1955), was one of the first to treat the metamorphosis of the government agency from public interest regulator to industry bedfellow.
52. James Q. Wilson, "The Rise of the Bureaucratic State," pp. 87–91.
53. Kenneth J. Arrow, *Social Choice and Individual Values* (New York: Wiley 1951).
54. J. A. Schumpeter, *Capitalism, Socialism and Democracy* (London: Allen & Unwin, 1943).
55. Floyd Hunter, *Community Power Structure* (Chapel Hill: University of North Carolina Press, 1953); William Lloyd Warner, *Democracy in Jonesville* (New York: Harper & Row, 1949).
56. C. Wright Mills, *The Power Elite* (New York: Oxford University Press, 1956).
57. Dwight D. Eisenhower, "The Military-Industrial Complex," in Samuel Heldel ed., *Basic Issues of American Democracy* (Englewood Cliffs, N.J.: Prentice-Hall, 1973).
58. Gabriel Kolko, *The Roots of American Foreign Policy* (New York: Beacon Press, 1969).
59. Robert A. Dahl, *Who Governs? Democracy and Power in an American City* (New Haven, Conn.: Yale University Press, 1961); Nelson W. Polsby, *Community Power and Political Theory* (New Haven, Conn.: Yale University Press, 1963).
60. Two books that set the stage for pluralist theories were Robert A. Dahl and Charles E. Lindblom, *Politics, Economics and Welfare* (New York: Harper & Row, 1953) and Anthony Downs, *An Economic Theory of Democracy* (New

York: Harper & Row, 1957). Dahl and Lindblom thought that things had become too big for anyone to formulate a grand plan. To Downs, grand plans might be possible but few would be willing to pay the costs of gathering the information. The common result: Everyone concentrated on his own corner of the universe.

61. Robert Dahl, *Polyarchy* (New Haven, Conn.: Yale University Press, 1971).
62. See John Kenneth Galbraith, *The New Industrial State* (Boston: Houghton Mifflin, 1967) for a general discourse on the mutuality of interest between government and private corporations.
63. Gabriel Kolko, "The Triumph of Conservatism," in Allen F. Davis and Harold Woodman, eds., *Conflict and Consensus in Modern American History* (Lexington, Mass.: Heath, 1972), pp. 247–265.
64. Lowi, *End of Liberalism.*
65. Robert R. Alford, *Health Care Politics: Ideological and Interest Group Barriers to Reform* (Chicago: University of Chicago Press, 1975) surveys the parceling out of public health care to factions of the medical community.
66. Alfred E. Kahn, *The Economics of Regulation* (New York: Wiley, 1970); William S. Moore, *Regulatory Reform* (Washington: American Enterprise Institute, 1975).
67. E. E. Schattschneider, *The Semi-Sovereign People* (New York: Holt, Rinehart and Winston, 1960).
68. Charles Lindblom, *Politics and Markets* (New York: Basic Books, 1978).
69. Glendon A. Schubert, *The Public Interest* (New York: Free Press, 1960).

BIBLIOGRAPHY

Alford, Robert R. *Health Care Politics: Ideological and Interest Group Barriers to Reform.* Chicago: University of Chicago Press, 1975.
Arrow, Kenneth J. *Social Choice and Individual Values.* New York: Wiley, 1951.
Caldwell, Lynton K. *The Administrative Theories of Hamilton and Jefferson.* Chicago: University of Chicago Press, 1944.
Dahl, Robert. *Polyarchy.* New Haven, Conn.: Yale University Press, 1971.
Dahl, Robert and Lindblom, Charles E. *Politics, Economics and Welfare.* New York: Harper & Row, 1953.
Davis, Kenneth Culp. *Discretionary Justice: A Preliminary Inquiry.* Baton Rouge: Louisiana State University Press, 1969.
Fellmeth, Robert. *The Interstate Commerce Commission.* New York: Grossman, 1970.
Freeman, J. Lieper. *The Political Process: Executive Bureau–Legislative Committee Relations.* New York: Random House, 1965.
Gawthrop, Lewis C. *The Administrative Process and Democratic Theory.* Boston: Houghton Mifflin, 1970.
Gellhorn, Ernest. *Administrative Law and Process.* St. Paul, Minn.: West Publishing, 1972.
Green, Mark J.; Fellows, James N. and Zwick, David R. *Who Runs Congress?* New York: Grossman, 1972.
Hamilton, Alexander; Madison, James, and Jay, John. *The Federalist.* Cambridge: Harvard University Press, 1961.
Lambright, W. Henry. *Governing Science and Technology.* New York: Oxford University Press, 1976.
Lindblom, Charles. *Politics and Markets.* New York: Basic Books, 1978.
Lowi, Theodore. *The End of Liberalism: Ideology, Policy and the Crisis of Public Authority.* New York: Norton, 1969.

Mason, Alpheus Thomas and Beaney, William M. *The Supreme Court in a Free Society.* New York: Norton, 1968.

Mills, C. Wright. *The Power Elite.* New York: Oxford University Press, 1956.

Moore, William S. *Regulatory Reform.* Washington: American Enterprise Institute, 1975.

Niebuhr, Reinhold. *Moral Man and Immoral Society.* New York: Scribner, 1960.

Neustadt, Richard E. *Presidential Power: The Politics of Leadership.* New York: Wiley, 1960.

Polsby, Nelson W. *Community Power and Political Theory.* New Haven, Conn.: Yale University Press, 1963.

Rourke, Francis E. *Bureaucracy, Politics and Public Policy.* Boston: Little, Brown, 1969.

Schattschneider, E. E. *The Semi-Sovereign People.* New York: Holt, Rinehart and Winston, 1960.

Schubert, Glendon A. *The Public Interest.* New York: Free Press, 1960.

Schumpeter, J. A. *Capitalism, Socialism and Democracy.* London: Allen and Unwin, 1943.

Thomas, Norman C. and Lamb, Karl A. *Congress: Politics and Practice.* New York: Random House, 1964.

Tugwell, Rexford. *The Emerging Constitution.* New York: Harper & Row, 1974.

Wilson, James Q. *Varieties of Police Behavior, The Management of Law and Order in Eight Communities.* Cambridge: Harvard University Press, 1968.

Woll, Peter. *Administrative Law: The Informal Process.* Berkeley: University of California Press, 1963.

Woll, Peter. *American Bureaucracy.* New York: Norton, 1963.

In addition to the sources cited in the notes and bibliography, the following *Public Administration Review (PAR)* articles are a convenient starting point for a more detailed exploration of the material in this chapter.

Browne, William P. "Organization Maintenance: The Internal Operation of Interest Groups," *PAR* 37, no. 1 (Jan./Feb. 1977): 48–57.

Galnoor, Itzhak. "Government Secrecy: Exchanges, Intermediaries and Middlemen," *PAR* 35, no. 1 (Jan./Feb. 1975): 32–42.

Hamilton, Randy H. and Judy Kelsey. "The Administrative Conference of the U.S.," *PAR* 29, no. 3 (May/June 1969): 286–290.

Harmon, Michael Mont. "Administrative Policy Formulation and The Public Interest," *PAR* 29, no. 5 (Sept./Oct. 1969): 483–491.

Heaphey, James J. "Legislatures: Political Organizations," *PAR* 35, no. 5 (Sept./Oct. 1975): 479–482.

Herman, William R. "Deregulation: Now or Never! (Or Maybe Someday?)," *PAR* 36, no. 2 (March/April 1976): 223–228.

Horowitz, Donald L. "The Courts as Guardians of the Public Interest," *PAR* 37, no. 2 (March/April 1977): 148–153.

Ink, Dwight A. "The President as Manager," *PAR* 36, no. 5 (Sept./Oct. 1976): 508–511.

Kaufman, Herbert. "Administrative Decentralization and Political Power," *PAR* 29, no. 1 (Jan./Feb. 1969): 3–15.

Long, Norton. "Reflections on Presidential Power," *PAR* 29, no. 5 (Sept./Oct. 1969): 442–450.

Lorch, Robert S. "Toward Administrative Judges," *PAR* 30, no. 1 (Jan./Feb. 1970): 50–55.

Lowi, Theodore. "Decision Making vs. Policy Making: Toward an Antidote for Technocracy," *PAR* 30, no. 3 (May/June 1970): 314–325.

Lowi, Theodore J. "Four Systems of Policy Politics and Choice," *PAR* 32, no. 4 (July/Aug. 1972): 298–310.

Moore, John E. "Recycling the Regulatory Agencies," *PAR* 32, no. 4 (July/Aug. 1972): 291–298.

Schick, Allen. "Congress and the 'Details' of Administration," *PAR* 36, no. 5 (Sept./Oct. 1976): 516–528.

Woll, Peter. "Administrative Law in the Seventies," *PAR* 32, no. 5 (Sept./Oct. 1972): 557–564.

Worthly, John A. "Public Administration and Legislatures: Past Neglect, Present Probes," *PAR* 35, no. 5 (Sept./Oct. 1975): 486–490.

RELEVANT PERIODICALS
American Journal of Political Science
American Political Science Review
Bell Journal of Economics
Congressional Digest
Congressional Quarterly
Law and Society Review
National Journal
Policy Studies Journal
Polity
Public Interest
Public Opinion Quarterly
Social Policy
Society
The Review of Politics
Western Political Quarterly

RELEVANT CASE STUDIES
(Cases marked ICCH are available from the Intercollegiate Case Clearing House, Soldier Field, Boston, Mass. 02163; cases marked ICP are available from the Inter-University Case Program, Box 229, Syracuse, N.Y. 13210.)

Bailey, S. K.   *The Office of Education and the Education Act of 1965*, [ICP]

Bauer, K. G., J. S. Schulman and R. Bernstein   *Prospective Rate Setting for Hospitals: Experience of a Regulatory Agency in Massachusetts*, [ICCH]

Lawrence, S. A.   *The Battery Additive Controversy*, [ICP]

Lynn, L. E., Jr.   *Reorganization of Florida's Human Services Agency*, (A)(B)(C)(D),* [ICCH]

Redford, E.   *Congress Passes the Federal Aviation Act of 1958*, [ICP]

Robinson, M. and C. Silverman.   *The Reorganization of Philadelphia General Hospital*, [ICP]

Sherwood, F. P.   *A City Manager Tries to Fire His Police Chief*, [ICP]

Westin, A. F.   *The Miracle Case: The Supreme Court and the Movies*, [ICP]

*Letters indicate that the case is presented in several installments.

CHAPTER 9

THE ROLES OF THE BUDGET: SETTING POLICES AND REVIEWING ORGANIZATIONAL PERFORMANCE

INTRODUCTION

In the previous chapter, we discussed the relevance of rules to administration. In doing so, we considered that, under a variety of circumstances, public agencies may evade, abuse, or bend the laws governing their activity. However, there is another device that the legislature and the executive have at their disposal to bring deviant agencies into line. It is money. Weber noted that the lifeblood of bureaucracy was a steady income flow. Most public agencies do not generate their own operating revenues.* For transfusions of the cash flow necessary for survival, public agencies must look to the executive and the legislature. The device by which public enterprise is funded is the budget. Since the budget struggle is one in which bureaucracies compete for "the bread of life," it assumes crucial importance for the administrator. While the following statements may overdramatize the case, they indicate the perspective from which many public executives view the budget. "The budget," said New York's former Mayor Abe Beame, "is everything." Mayor Henry

---

*Some bond issuing authorities do generate their own revenues, particularly those that are involved in highway, bridge, and tunnel operations. Further, the written obligations to the bond holders often preclude such revenues from being diverted to other government activities. Thus insulated from the financial retribution of other government actors, authorities have a wider behavioral latitude than most government agencies.

It was Robert Moses who raised the public authority to its pinnacle of independence. At the height of his power, Moses controlled several New York State authorities and operated with little reference to legislators, governors, mayors, and such. If they wanted to speak with him, they could always call.[1]

Maier of Milwaukee chimes in, "the budget is the World Series of Government."[2] And from the national perspective, Frederick J. Lawton notes that "the budget has emerged as the key document which controls the entire business of the Federal government."[3]

This is a remarkable series of statements about a governmental device that receives relatively little public attention. The president's annual budget message is hardly prime-time material. The legislative evaluation of executive budget proposals generally proceeds in obscurity. Even in the states where legislative-gubenatorial battles frequently erupt over the budget, the clash generally comes on the eve of the next budget year. Accumulated tension plus the knowledge that time is fast running down causes the participants to go all out in an attempt to embody their point of view in the budget. However, as the clock strikes twelve, the final budget renders a largely unappealable verdict on the success or failure of the combatants. The shape of the allocations are subject to only minor changes in the coming fiscal year, and the battle over the budget retreats from public view as quickly as it appeared. Yet, the brevity of the budget's annual appearance in the public limelight belies its importance. It may sparkle only briefly over a sea of issues and policies that evoke considerably more notice, but the magnitude of the budget's role is far greater than most suppose it to be.

THE BUDGET AS PUBLIC POLICY

The budget is vital because it is the device whereby plans and policies are put into action. It converts broad ideas into concrete activities and resources. In so doing, the budget serves as the final determinant of the degree to which legislatively enunciated policy will be translated into reality.

> Legislation, of necessity, confers responsibilities and grants authorizations to departments in quite general language. If an agency is directed to perform defined functions under law, it would still have wide discretion in determining how much or how little should be done in the performance of each individual function. Budgeting is like a mechanism for pumping fuel into the engines of government. It reserves for Congress the full opportunity for saying, on a year to year basis, in what scope and at what rates of progress departments should carry out their statutory assignments.[4]

In the federal government, congressional procedures bring the budget to center stage in the policy arena. When launched by *enabling, or "authorizing" legislation,* a program is little more than an unseaworthy hulk in dry dock. Funding may be "authorized," but another legislative enactment, an *appropriations bill,* is required to get the money to the program. For an agency, navigating the appropriations process can be like running the gauntlet. Legislators who championed the general aims of a program by sponsoring the enabling legislation are replaced by penny-counting, appropriations committee members familiar with agency finances. Sensitized to inflated budget requests and other ploys, committee members are predisposed to slash funds, and since the appropriation need not conform with the funding levels in the authorizing legislation, they often do.

If the program emerges unscathed, a government-wide lineup before the Congressional Budget Committees awaits. There, if compared to malnourished counterparts, the well-endowed program may fall victim to a spread the wealth drive. In short, a program's success in the budget process can determine whether it sets sail as a leaky, underfunded scow or a sleek, well-financed vessel. Thus, in the federal government, the budget finalizes legislative decisions and is the vehicle whereby policies are operationalized. The budget is a dollars and cents expression of the value society places on various public sector activities. If one looks to the clientele served by those activities, the budget tells us the relative standing of various segments of society in the claims line for the public dollar.

The budget is also a device for value adjustment. Not all substantive legislation receives financial support equal to the rhetorical support with which it was passed. As a powerful legislator in the budget process once remarked, "Appropriations Committees are the saucers that cool the legislative tea. Just because you have an authorization (enabling legislation) does not mean a thing to us. . . ."[5] In fact, the amount appropriated by Congress for a given program is almost always less than the amounts authorized in the legislation creating the program. The budget is, in effect, the legislature's second vote on any issue. The issue that receives strong rhetorical support from legislators, but little money, does not yet stand very high on society's list of priorities.

The budget is more than just a second legislative vote. For programs that have been in the budget in previous years, the budget is a third, fourth, and even fortieth vote on their value. It is an annual opportunity to adjust old values. Moreover, the budget's low profile allows these adjustments to proceed in relative privacy. It allows legislators quietly to modify those programs that it brought into the world with a blare of trumpets and a sea of dollars. Thus, last year's $50 million appropriation to wipe out black lung disease becomes this year's inefficient Bureau of Industrial Illness Control whose funds are reduced.

In sum, the budget is the nuts and bolts of public policy. Public pronouncements and sympathetic speeches may indicate that a problem is in the running for corrective resources. However, as currency in the domain of public policy, talk is cheap. It serves a purpose in indicating the government's concern, but it takes hard cash to back up concern with action. Most competitors for public goods are not in the race for verbiage. The battle is for tangible benefits. The battlefield is the budget. Its final form tells us who won or lost. In the words of one observer:

> If politics is regarded in part as conflict over whose preferences shall prevail in the determination of national policy, then the budget records the outcome of this struggle. If one asks: "Who gets what the government has to give?" then the answers for a moment in time are recorded in the budget. If one looks at politics as a process by which the government mobilizes resources to meet pressing problems, then the budget is a focus of these efforts.[6]

How different this view is from that commonly expressed about the budget. To most of the public, it is an unintelligible waste of paper. In the world of administration, the budget often comes to be viewed as a routine bookkeeping device. It keeps the accounts straight and provides some basic information that can be utilized in management analysis. However, the overarching characteristic of the budget is that it is a policy document. The average citizen may remain blissfully unaware of this. The public administrators who fail to comprehend the budget's policy implications, however, do so at their own peril. Agency members should be perturbed when their operating budget is decreased as "an economy measure." Unless there are many such cuts across the bureaucratic structure, "economy measure" is likely a euphemism for lack of support. The tides of public favor, as measured by executive and legislative protectiveness, are shifting away from the "economized" agency. As for the constituency served by the cut agency, their claim on the public goods provided by society has lost some of its strength.

The budget cut should signal the administrator to look toward strengthening or redirecting services and mobilizing constituent support. If this is not done, the budget's policy message has been missed. The likely result, no matter how fastidiously one uses the budget to account and manage, is that there will be less agency to account for every year. The administrator who looks at the budget and sees only "the books" is a throwback to earlier times. However, the budget's evolution, which we will address in the next section, challenges the public executive to keep pace or else join the list of endangered species.

Budgeting for Accountability

The *executive budget*, a jurisdiction-wide accounting of expenditures in a single document, is a twentieth-century phenomenon. The budget, as we know it today, was nonexistent in the nineteenth century. In those days, most jurisdictions paid for their activities out of a general account. Individual agencies went directly to the legislature for funding. Mayors, governors, and presidents had little control over the allocation of resources among departments under their command. Lump sums flew hither and yon. Bookkeeping was sloppily done. And, for the larcenous public executive, there was little reason to institute neatness. After all, building a $1 million courthouse for $13 million—a feat New York City's "Boss" Tweed managed in the 1870s—was a good way to line one's pockets.

In late nineteenth-century America, Tweed's style was widely imitated even though protegés rarely matched his grandiosity. The response to this chicanery was the Reform Movement, and one thing it wanted was executive responsibility for the jurisdiction-wide budget. The target of the executive budget was the misappropriation of the public dollar. Thus, the budget would list every position, every piece of equipment, and every maintenance function for the next fiscal year. Then, with a clear itemized expenditure prescription, negligent management would be more visible to both executive and legislative probes. Thus, writes Schick, "the executive budget was intended to strengthen honesty and efficiency by restricting the discretion of administrators. . . ."[7]

The reformers were not denied. Most states adopted the executive budget during the first quarter of the twentieth century. The Budget and Accounting Act of 1921 mandated an executive budget at the federal level. These developments ushered in a budgeting era, lasting into the 1940s, that was characterized by a "control orientation." Control was facilitated by several *budgetary principles* that, in either the original or slightly modified form, continue to influence budget formats. The principles are:

1. *Annuality*—Funds are authorized and appropriated for a single year. There is a yearly legislative review of bureaucratic activity.
2. *Comprehensiveness*—The budget contains all receipts and outlays for every government unit. Nothing is excluded. No spending authority exists without having undergone the annual budget review.
3. *Unity*—The budget is to contain both short-term expense items (annual operating funds) and long-term expenditures (capital expenditures).
4. *Exclusiveness*—The budget is concerned only with money, not issues.
5. *Specificity*—Money is allocated to identifiable objects—positions, programs, equipment.
6. *Accountability*—Money is to be spent as indicated in the budget. The budgetary allocation for any item is not to be exceeded. Spending more than the allocated amount or the transfer of funds between accounts requires executive or legis-

lative approval. Every transaction is identified in carrying out the budget.

7. *Publicity, clarity, and accuracy*—The budget is to be a public document clearly informing the citizenry of governmental expenditures.[8]

The last principle suffered somewhat at the hands of the first six. The budgetary principles produced mammoth, complex, and hard to understand budget documents. Almost every expenditure, no matter how small, had a "line." Hence, the "control" budget was more commonly known as the "line-item budget." Budgets today still bear a striking resemblance to their "control" ancestors. Federal and state budgets, and those of large municipalities, consist of numerous facts and figures that are incomprehensible to the average citizen. Even for those involved in budgeting, total comprehension is extremely difficult, and as a result, the budget is reviewed in fragments. Not until 1975 did Congress institute mechanisms to integrate the piecemeal reviews and evaluate the budget in its totality.

The control orientation also lingers on in contemporary legislative and administrative budget behavior. "Lack of adequate fiscal controls" is a phrase that drops with regularity from the lips of federal, state, and local auditing executives. Hints that an agency is spending money in an "unauthorized manner" is still one of the better ways to instigate a legislative investigation into the agency's affairs. In fact, much of the business of Congress is devoted to quizzing agency executives over budgets, whether the subject is future requests, the nature of past expenditures, or deviations from congressionally approved methods of spending.

Budgeting for Management

The control orientation gave way, in the 1940s, to a "management orientation." To administrators, and legislative and executive study commissions, the notion took hold that the budget was a device with applications beyond the realm of accounting. The budget's detailed listing of equipment and personnel could be rearrayed into a number of patterns useful to management. Jurisdiction-wide clerical, administrative, or maintenance expenditures could be determined. More important, the budget could indicate the amount of money being expended on a specific project. Combined with output measures, such as the number of forms processed or clients interviewed, specific project budgetary data could provide a measure of performance. Thus, while it still retained much of its "line-item" character and control utility, the budget became, also, a performance indicator with management utility.

As a device to determine the efficiency with which the bureaucracy is carrying out its job, the budget has several uses. Unit performance from year to year can be compared. Broad activities can be broken down into their constituent parts. For instance, the budget of a building department might lump all inspectors together, although some inspect commercial buildings and others inspect residential structures. By segregating the inspectors by function and distributing equipment, material, and support service expense, the budget can be used to compare residential inspection costs to commercial inspection costs.

The budget formats that have been adopted by many government jurisdictions reflect this management approach. The budget is broken down into things that are being done by the individual departments, rather than merely serving as a listing of the personnel positions and salaries. Thus, the budget can be used by the jurisdiction's management to monitor agency activities. It is little wonder, then, that the Federal Bureau of the Budget is now the Office of Management and Budget (OMB). In addition, state budget directors are assuming a greater managerial role. Indeed, at all levels of government, executive staffs now use the budget for the "programming of approved goals into specified projects and activities, the design of organizational units to carry out approved programs, and the staffing of these units and the procurement of necessary resources."[9]

Budgeting for Planning
In a study of controllership activities within organizations, Simon, Kozmetsky, Guetzkow, and Tyndall identified three questions that can be asked on the basis of accounting figures: "Am I doing well or badly?"; "What problems should I look into?"; "Of several ways of doing a job which is best?"[10] The first two questions apply to the accounting and management budget orientations that have been discussed. The third addresses the budget's potential as a device for planning and the evaluation of alternative courses of action.

While not utilized until recently, the planning application has always been latent in the budgetary process. The budget lists public activities. It is an aggregate of public sector expenditures in a given jurisdiction. Rearrayed in decreasing order of expenditures, it is a priority ranking of governmental functions and, by extention, an indicator of the importance that society attaches to various groups.

The budget bestows benefits and extracts costs from individuals outside the government structure. Yet, even though it tells much about external impacts, the budget fosters an extremely introspective view on the part of public servants. The control orientation fixates on detail. The management orientation on internal process. However, throughout the 1960s and 1970s, demands increased for budgetary applications that focus on the external impacts of government activity. Whereas previous orientations had as their goal accountability and efficiency for internal purposes, the planning orientation looks to external effectiveness. Will spending proposals and the programs they represent achieve the goals set by society? What works and what does not work is a segregation that the planning budget hopes to achieve. Once the segregation is accomplished, the ineffectual can be eliminated and its funds transferred to programs that better fulfill society's goals.

Planning-oriented budgeting is being emphasized by many jurisdictions, and in 1977 President Carter promised to institute *Zero-Base Budgeting (ZBB)*. ZBB is the most recent of the planning approaches to governmental budgeting. ZBB and similar techniques are largely a response to perceived deficiencies in the budget process. Therefore, we will take a closer look at planning approaches after the budgeting process has been explored.

The control, management, and planning stages discussed above are not separate and distinct. One does not arise out of the ashes of the other. Rather, earlier orientations continue to thrive as later ones enter the picture because none are without a life-sustaining constituency. Auditors and legislators still use budgets for control. Managers still play with budgetary figures to get a handle on operations. Executives are increasingly aware of the budget's applicability as a planning tool. Each new orientation has combined with, rather than displaced, existing orientations. While a new thrust may occupy the center of attention, it does not assume exclusive dominance over the budgetary process. In fact, many scholars believe that the budgetary "process" is the true dominant force and that "orientations" change the essential character of the "process" about as much as tablecloths change the essential character of tables.

THE INCREMENTAL CHARACTER OF BUDGETARY DECISION MAKING

Some researchers who have conducted empirical studies of government budgeting tend to look askance at characterizations such as control, management, and planning and are particularly leery of the last. Aaron Wildavsky and Ira Sharkansky, in separate studies, found a complex process little influenced by planning and analysis.[11] On a more theoretical plane, Charles Lindblom asserts that, in complex decision situations where the interests of policy makers conflict and time is of the essence, analysis will give way to rules of thumb, bargaining, and compromise.[12]

What Lindblom conceptualized, the budget process epitomized. The perspectives of budgeting participants differ drastically. To a budget official, evaluation is the name of the game. To the head of an agency, survival and growth are somewhat more compelling. To the legislator, the taxpayer's pocketbook looms large. Whenever and wherever they can enter the process, pressure groups forcefully interject their views about the budget.

On top of these differing perspectives comes an overwhelming multitude of decisions associated with the budget process. Programs are numerous; their activities specialized and complex. All have advocates and detractors. Few programs are free of mistakes, although administrators try to hide them. All can show accomplishments and do so without shame. There is a public dollar that every program is scrambling for, and executive and legislative decision makers have to figure out who gets what portion. In the federal government, the economic pie now approaches $.5 trillion; the employees to be fed 3 million plus; the programs to be fueled are in the thousands. Not surprisingly, the decisions that emerge from this budgetary milieu often are not based on rigorous analysis. Rather, the decision makers "muddle through." Indeed, to observers such as Lindblom and Wildavsky, it is the only solution possible where perspectives and priorities differ and the potential decisions are almost unlimited.

The budget that emerges from the "muddle" is rarely a dramatic document. From year to year, changes are made by inches and degrees. Thus, Wildavsky applies the term *incrementalism* to budgetary decision making.[13] Lindblom's characterization is "successive limited comparisons."[14] Both descriptions indicate that the budget process not only eschews analysis but tends to ignore proposals that depart significantly from the status quo. As a result, important possible outcomes are neglected and strongly held values are muted. However, for the individual participant in the budget process, introducing new programs that will evoke adamant opposition from other budgetary actors is likely a waste of time. Similarly, there is little point in opposing a policy that enjoys a consensus of approval. In Lindblom's words, "a 'good' policy" is one about which various actors agree, "without their agreeing that it is the most appropriate means for achieving some objective."[15]

In his book, *The Politics of the Budgetary Process*, Aaron Wildavsky cites several instances in which the participants make a choice between the ideal and the reality. "Another agency," he writes, "concluded that a new pet program simply would not be approved and decided to wait for a more propitious moment lest antipathy caused by inclusion of this item jeopardize the rest of its budget."[16] Where the other actors are extremely powerful and perceive of an agency head as "greedy" or "wasting their time," programs with a good chance of being funded may be shot down in the fusillade that is aimed at the program that did not stand a chance to begin with.

In looking for barometers that will help them assess the prevailing mood, decision makers turn first to previous budgets. A precedent-laden document, it contains last year's decisions built upon the decisions of the year before that and so on. Decisions legitimized by previous budgets represent the result of compromise between powerful institutional actors. Unless there are many new actors or the environment had changed radically, the previous year's budget lies very close to the zone of agreement for the next year's budget. Thus, in making decisions about the budget, the previous year's allocation to a department is viewed as already legitimized. It is the *base*. Differences from this base are what budgetary decision makers concentrate on. As Wildavsky writes:

> The largest determining factor of the size and content of this year's budget is last year's budget. Most of the budget is a product of previous decisions. . . . Budgeting is incremental, not comprehensive. The beginning of wisdom about an agency budget is that it is almost never actively reviewed as a whole every year in the sense of reconsidering the value of all existing programs as compared to all possible alternatives. Instead it is based on last year's budget with special attention given to a narrow range of increases or decreases. Thus the men who make the budget are concerned with relatively small increments to an existing base. Their attention is focused on a small number of items over which the budgetary battle is fought.[17]

Most research affirms Wildavsky's conception of the base. It is treated as a given. Little attention is paid to it by decision makers. On the state level, research by Sharkansky uncovers the same incremental approach identified by Wildavsky in the federal government.

> In order to cope with their difficult economic and institutional surroundings, budget makers have devised simplifying procedures. These resemble the incremental decision making that is used at the federal level, but the state and local procedures appear to be simplified even further. . . . We have found the weight of incremental budgeting to be a pervasive influence. . . . the total expenditures of state governments tend to remain within a limited range of previous expenditures.[18]

Further, the total budget is more or less an aggregate of many individual decisions using the base as a guidepost. Within the budgetary process, departmental, executive, and legislative actors keep the base firmly in mind. An agency requesting a substantial increase must decide if it looks too extravagant in relation to the base. Executives and legislators, in trimming agency budget requests, impose the most severe cuts on those that stray farthest from the base. (Despite this, brazenness appears to pay. An agency request for 130 percent of its base might be cut back to 106 percent of the base. The timid agency requesting 110 percent of its base might end up with 105 percent. The budget of the brazen agency is slashed much more than the timid agency, but it still comes out better.)[19]

Closely related to the concept of the base is the idea of "fair share."[20] *Fair share* is the proportion of the jurisdiction's budget that an agency has been receiving from year to year. It, too, serves as a guidepost for subsequent decisions about an agency's budget. An agency that ranks fifth in the budget allocations for 1978 is unlikely to find itself ranked fortieth in 1979. The participants in the budget process, particularly agency heads, are cognizant of how agency budgets stand in relation to each other. Thus, fair share combines with the base to narrow the range of budgetary decisions; each removes a substantial portion of the agency budget proposal from scrutiny. That portion of the budget so removed is "waved through." It passes on to approval unscathed, unseen, and unencumbered.

BACKDOOR SPENDING:
CONSTRAINTS ON BUDGETARY DECISION MAKING

Base and fair share are simple decision mechanisms that allow budget actors to come to quick conclusions. Although nearly automatic, such conclusions represent conscious decisions that are made about the budget. While it rarely occurs in practice, there is always the possibility that the executive or the legislature can take the ax to an agency's base or radically change its fair share standing in relation to other agencies. However, substantial portions of the budget are immune to change via the annual budget process. Often called "uncontrollable expenditures," such allocations are required by law. Only a change in the basic legislation can prevent the inclusion of these expenditures in the budget.

Congress has another term for uncontrollable expenditures. It is *backdoor spending*. This somewhat more pejorative term stems from congressional annoyance at being denied the opportunity to review uncontrollable expenditures. As noted earlier, appropriations legislation is the mechanism whereby Congress infuses cash into programs. Authorizing or enabling legislation deals with substance; appropriations bills deal with sums. With backdoor spending, the original bill includes sum and substance; Congress's financial review mechanism, the appropriations committees, never comes into play. Thus, the Congressional Joint Study Committee on Budget Control defined backdoor spending as "any budget authority which is provided other than through Appropriations Committees or (where), in substance, the decision is not made by the Appropriations Committees."[21] The Joint Study Committee estimated that nearly half of all federal expenditures were made without annual scrutiny. *Permanent appropriations, borrowing authority,* and *contract authority,* which were identified as three prime evaders of budgetary review in the 1974 report, are discussed below.

Permanent appropriations   These are items such as interest on the national debt and the Social Security Trust Fund. The bankers and policy holders must be paid, and while Congress might seek to reduce the national debt to lower interest payments in succeeding years, it can do little to prevent social security eligibles from "coming of age."

Borrowing authority   The ubiquitous "federally guaranteed loan" backs up everything from homes and schooling to small businesses and foundering aircraft manufacturers. While not every endeavor or applicant is eligible for such loans, neither is the amount borrowed amenable to the budget process. The total is tied to the number of qualified applicants, and if twice as many apply this year as did last, the expenditure will be correspondingly, and uncontrollably, higher.

Contract authority   Agencies are often permitted, by law, to enter into contractual obligations to purchase goods or services without the prior approval of Congress. While the debt so incurred requires a subsequent appropriation by Congress to liquidate it, the contract authority statute requires that the obligation be met. For instance, in 1973, contract authority commitments in the area of low-rent housing totaled $150 million. In the same year, the contract authority available for water pollution control efforts was a whopping $11 billion.[22]

Permanent appropriations, borrowing authority, and contract authority do not exhaust the list of items that bypass annual budget review. Furthermore, other government jurisdictions also have uncontrollable expenses, although the terminology used by the Congress to identify various types is not universal. Your state or locality might designate the uncontrollable portion of its budget as "fixed expenses," "bond obligations," or "general obligations." Whatever the terminology, a significant portion of most governmental budgets represents funds already committed for various purposes. The expenditures are keyed to the number of poor people, civil service pensioners, the elderly, the sick, or the student population. According to Murray Weidenbaum, HEW, the federal agency that counts most of the foregoing as its clientele, has a budget of which only 10 percent is amenable to change during the annual budget cycle.[23] The Office of Management and Budget reported that, in 1971, over 75 percent of the federal government's nondefense outlays were uncontrollable.[24]

When uncontrollability is added to fair share and base, it becomes evident that the bulk of the governmental budget is enacted with very little study. Only a portion of the budget is subject to change and, of that, an even smaller portion is subject to scrutiny. The result, according to Weidenbaum, is that the process of public resource allocation is hardly that deliberate and systematic choice among alternatives that economists try to envision. Rather, it is a fragmented and compartmentalized affair. Many of the key decisions are not made during the budget process or within the budgetary framework at all. . . . The President and the Congress do not face each year's budget preparation and review cycle with a clean slate: they must take account of a large accumulation of legal restraints within which they must operate.[25]

In 1974, the Congressional Joint Study Committee on Budget Control recommended that *Sunset Laws* be enacted to reduce the amount of uncontrollable expenditures. Under the proposal, enabling legislation that calls for formula payouts, earmarked revenues, and other reflexive expenditures must lapse after a number of years. As the "sun sets" on the bill, Congress would be forced to reevaluate the backdoor spending involved.

As of 1977, Sunset Laws still languished in Congress. Some states, however, have been quicker off the mark. Colorado, Florida, and Louisiana now "terminate" state agencies periodically. Prior to refunding, an audit determines whether, legislatively and organizationally, the agency should continue in its present form.[26]

Despite the forces gathering against them, backdoor spending remains a major factor in government budgeting, and the base and fair share persevere as benchmarks in the process. Thus, as we proceed to examine the budget cycle and the struggles that take place within it, keep in mind that many of the questions are irrevocably settled before the process starts. Remember, also, that as the process gets under way, many issues are quickly and perfunctorily resolved.

PUTTING TOGETHER THE BUDGET MANUSCRIPT

Viewpoints and Ground Rules

The budget that emerges from the Congress, state legislature, or city council is a prodigious document. It has hundreds and, sometimes, thousands of pages. It generally has been months in preparation, and as is the case with the federal budget, may have been percolating for a year and a half. It has numerous authors—including, but not limited to, legislators, chief executives, and agency heads. Moreover, most of the authors have distinctly different views on what the final manuscript should look like. These views are often advanced with no small amount of vigor, and the ensuing clashes are often characterized by such terms as "the annual budget battle." Indeed, the fight may continue after the final bell. When their bitter opposition to programs did not prevail in the budget process, presidents have "impounded" appropriated funds. In response, legislators howled, program supporters sued, and the courts told the executive that bankrupting legislatively funded programs was unconstitutional.[27] The impoundment episode highlights the intensity of the participants in the budget process. Legislatures jealously guard their role in the allocation of public funds. Executives, equally intense, may test even the limits of the law in frustrating budgetary requirements that they oppose.

Congress and the executive are not the only institutional combatants in the budget arena. The federal agency plays a part, and it is neither small nor casual. The institutional dynamic of organizations leads them toward growth and expansion. To accomplish this, additional resources are needed. The budget is the place to get resources, and agency executives spend considerable time in the preparation of arguments to justify increased agency expenditures.

Thus, within the government structure, the budget assumes a central position for all the major actors. To the members of the legislature, representing the people, it is "their money" and they had better have a say in how it is being spent. To executives it is their bureaucracy and certain prerogatives accrue to them as heads of it. To agency heads, socialized to equate expansion with survival, the budget represents a crucial annual struggle to do better than competing agencies and better than last year. Each of these authors—legislators, executives, and bureaucrats—spends considerable time and energy in pursuing those concerns that are perceived as vital.

Even though the authors struggle to assert their prerogatives, the competition is far from a no holds barred affair. Since many proposed expenditures are assured safe passage through the budgetary gauntlet, only a portion of the budget is contested. Moreover, institutional retaliatory capacity serves as a deterrent to unsporting behavior. Presidents who severely violate the fair share principle might find themselves astride a runaway bureaucracy. Agency heads who refuse to cooperate with the legislature might find their domains riddled with gaping holes as legislators sheath their red pencils and uncover the cannons. In the face of such reserve weaponry, budget authors fight hard but not recklessly. Thus, although the budget arises out of conflict, the struggle is muted by mutual respect or fear and an understanding that, under the incremental rules, few are faced with do or die choices.

In states and municipalities, budgeting is also an incremental process. However, unlike the triangular struggles surrounding the federal budget, the institutional interplay tends to be bilateral in states and localities. The bureaucracy is an ex-officio participant. It is the prime client of any government budget. The second participant varies. Since there is rarely a fine balance between governors and state legislatures or mayors and city councils, either the executive or the legislature is clearly the dominant force. Thus, if the governor is dominant, the legislature is largely ignored by agency fund seekers.[28] Agency heads' time is spent developing strategies that will maximize the agency's gain but fall short of incurring executive wrath. Where executives are weak and legislatures are strong, the same tactic is used on legislators.

Regardless of jurisdiction, most budget authors approach the process in the same general manner. Before trying to shape the budget manuscript, the authors seek to determine the bounds of permissible behavior. Then, without overstepping these boundaries, each author endeavors to make the budget "his book."

The Budget Outline

The executive prepares the preliminary outline for the budget document. In the federal government and in most states this job is performed by a budget office that is part of the executive staff. The *Office of Management and Budget (OMB)* carries out the president's budgetary policies. Generally, budget offices are specialized bodies that deal almost exclusively with budgetary matters. Where the office is highly respected for its professional expertise, as is the case with OMB, it is regarded as "the executive" in the executive budget. Agencies deal with the budget office and rarely make direct appeals to the executive.

Well in advance of the publication date, OMB, in consultation with other executive officials, determines the overall shape of the budget manuscript. This is done by estimating the revenues that will be available for the budget year in question. In the states, where a balanced budget is a legal requirement, revenue estimates serve as boundaries for the total expenditures that can be proposed. In addition, since budget deficits are not very attractive political propositions for state and local executives, revenue estimates tend to be conservative. Most incumbents, it seems, produce a year-end surplus.

In the federal government, budget surpluses and deficits have become institutionalized as economic governors. Thus, the original outline of a given year's federal budget aims at anticipated and planned expenditure totals that will produce a surplus or a deficit deemed desirable by presidential advisers. (See Chapter 10 for a detailed discussion.)

After the budget office has determined a government-wide expenditure total, each agency is sent preliminary guidelines for the preparation of its budget request. The guideline includes a ceiling figure that represents the agency's share of the expenditure limit and that, in theory, is not to be exceeded. Based on the budget office's analysis of the agency's programs, it may be suggested that some be expanded and others cut back. Recommendations might also be made for inclusion of

---

*A prominent exception to the pattern of cautious revenue estimates is, of course, the city of New York. Either through hallucination, or something more sinister, it managed to foresee property taxes coming in from burnt out buildings and, in fact, based its revenue estimates on the assumption that *no one* would fail to pay the property tax.

items that the executive favors but that are not yet a part of the agency's program. In memo form, this initial outline is transmitted to the bureaucracy as early as 16 months before the budget must be approved by the legislature.

The First Draft

The first draft of the budget is prepared with the bureaucracy. The agencies and organizations within the bureaucratic structure ascertain their needs for the coming budget year. Even in the preparation of an agency's spending requests many authors may be involved. "In most agencies," according to the federal Office of Management and Budget, "preparation of the budget begins at the field station level."[29] Through unit heads, bureau chiefs, and department heads, superiors make decisions as to the relative merits of the competing claims made by the organizational components under their command.

Not all budget decisions have purely programmatic motives. Budget choices might be aimed at what the administrators see as the maintenance of internal order. Unit heads who have incurred an administrator's disfavor might find it expressed in a partial denial of requested operating funds. The amount denied may then be shifted to another unit. As Wildavsky observes, budgets can "be put together primarily to discipline subordinate officials within a government agency by reducing amounts for their salaries and their pet projects."[30]

The intraagency conflict over the budget pie is perhaps the most subtle in the budgetary process. It proceeds by way of offhand comments and peripheral messages. "I hear," the unit head comments casually to the administrator, "that Joe's unit is caught up on its work. It sure must be nice to remain current. I wouldn't mind having the staff that he does so I could get out from under our backlog." Bureaucrats fight for a bigger share by intimating that they are overwhelmed with work—and thus deserve more money—while many of their peers are underwhelmed—and thus deserve less.

Of course, the administrators, particularly in smaller agencies, may forego participatory budget preparation. Sitting down with the last year's budget, administrators may unilaterally modify it for submission to the executive. Knowledge gained from their interactions with their unit chiefs may influence their decisions, but their formal access to agency budget preparation via memos or meetings is denied.

Regardless of the manner in which it is formulated within the agency, the agency budget request that emerges, in almost all instances, says "We need more!" Even the administrator who is intent on using the budget to discipline subordinates, according to Wildavsky, will not do so to the extent that overall agency income is reduced.[31] In studies of federal, state, and local governments, the overwhelming preponderance of agency budget requests asked for an increased budgetary allotment.[32]

There are several reasons for this. Some are related to institutional dynamics. Others to the agency's role as a representative of certain clientele groups. Still others are adaptations to the mechanics of the budgetary process.

Organizationally, the budget represents the agency's share of the territory it occupies along with the other organizational actors. Expansion or protection of that environmental space is a primary agency concern. However, expansion may be out of the question unless the agency asks for more money. The agency's environment is populated with actors who have their own institutional concerns. Agency passivity is unlikely to induce them to champion its cause. The jurisdiction's executive, for instance, is confronted with a mass of competing claims. The executive's attention naturally gravitates to those agencies that stand out. Unless the agency's prominence is of the "sore thumb" variety that sets the executive to thinking about amputation, meekness is unlikely to be rewarded. The budget process is not characterized by the financiers seeking out the deserving. Things are rather the other way around. It is the "squeaky wheel that gets greased," and it is a good bet that other agencies will be making dramatic noises about their need for more cash. Therefore, unless agency heads make their bid, the money that they fail to ask for may go to others by default.

The organization also represents its constituency in the scramble for scarce public funds. Most citizens, even the sophisticated, are befuddled by the budget process. They tend not to get involved. Even though the budget represents the share of public benefits available to an agency's constitutuents, few view it in this light. They are usually more concerned with substantive legislation that promises dramatic changes in their condition. Minimum wage laws, an increase in social security payments, or an income tax cut are clearly understandable issues that will visibly impact on the lives of significant segments of the population. The budget, however, has low visibility. It will be formulated largely behind the scene. The individual "items" around which budget decisions revolve—for example, principal supervising building inspector, vehicular maintenance services—are virtually incapable of capturing the public imagination. The impacts of adverse budgetary decisions—one less social worker or a $200 reduction in the money available for duplicating—are so diffuse that they may not even be noticed by clientele groups. Thus, it is left to the agency to represent the interests of its clients in the budget process. The agency's fight is to preserve the benefits that already accrue to constituents and advance the argument within the bureaucracy that they deserve more. In advancing its arguments, the agency speaks from a position of expertise concerning client problems and needs. This advocacy continues through the legislative stages of the budget cycle.

The agency also is motivated towards expansionism by the character of the budget process. Administrators know that those to whom they pass on the budget are likely to cut it. There is nothing punitive or malicious in this nearly inevitable reduction. It is part of the ground rules of the game. Over a half-century of putting together the budget document, a set of mutual expectations build up among the authors. Agencies advocate; they seek increases. Executives economize and balance; they cut and redistribute. Legislatures check administrative excesses; they cut out the fat. Authors are socialized to their roles to the extent of acting reflexively at times.[33]

Thus, when agency heads prepare the first draft, they make allowances for the inevitable cuts. Their budgets contain desired program increases and increases thrown in to account for shrinkage. Agency heads also know from experience that, with rare exceptions, the legislative and executive scythe mechanistically and methodically trims off the top. It does not matter whether the request is much more than last year's, the same, or less. Administrators who fail to account for this by requesting additional funds will probably end up with less than they now have. It might be added that, through the 1970s, inflationary pressures played an independent role in increasing expenditure requests by government agencies.

Editing the First Draft
After the agency has prepared its budget request, it is sent to the budget office for review. Quite often, what is received bears little resemblance to the outline that the budget bureau sent down to the agency several months before. The request might exceed the ceiling, and there may be a different program emphasis. Once again, consternation is unlikely to ensue unless the deviations go beyond the latitude permitted by the informal rules. The agency has merely fulfilled its budgetary role as the other authors anticipated it would.

Beyond acting out its appropriate part in the set of mutually anticipatory, budgetary relationships, the agency has other good reasons for making its push in the first draft. Chief executives usually demand that disputes within the bureaucracy be kept in-house. Agency heads who unilaterally announce to the world that the president has squelched their budgets likely will end up on the street. (Saying the same thing in a legislative hearing in response to a question is okay. The oath compels an honest answer—one that an aggrieved bureau chief is quick to give.) Therefore, unless they feel assured of a safe legislative forum, the administrators' final impassioned defense of their agencies' requests must come before the budget is submitted to Congress.

Then, too, there are valid divergencies in the perspectives of the president, as represented by the budget director and his appointed department heads, and the bureau chiefs within the departments. To complicate matters, there is also a symbiosis. As Freeman notes:

> It is [the job of the appointed executive] to attempt to assert the views of the Administration before the array of bureaus in their charge and to gain compliance with these views. At the same time . . . they must rely on the bureaus for expertise and special knowledge and they must often accede to what may appear to them to be "bureaucratic inertia" or "bureaucratic eccentricity." The bureaus, composed wholly or almost wholly of career personnel and possessed of the technology and the capacity to perform the tasks of the agency, are neither easily moved by the party in power nor overly embarrassed at urging their time-tested viewpoints upon non-career leaders in the Administration. The result is a not too delicate see-saw between the politics of the administration's party and the politics of bureaucratic expertise, specialization and self-preservation, with bureaucratic leaders frequently fulcrums in the balance.[34]

Furthermore, even the department head who owes his position to the president may succumb to the organizational imperative. According to Lawton, "department heads may be conscious of standing in a competitive position to the President. They may show little solidarity with him on issues affecting their own agencies."[35]

Thus, as noted above, the disparity between budget bureau guidelines and agency requests represents policy differences as well as budgetary strategies. The agency budget serves as a vehicle for discussing policy differences within the bureaucracy. In fact, the federal Office of Management and Budget has institutionalized the ironing out process between agency requests and executive policy guidelines by conducting hearings at which the agency presents its case to OMB.

As agency administrators see several reasons for a larger budget, they tend to be very active participants in this process. The budget office, acting on behalf of the executive, substantially determines the final shape of the budget to be submitted to the legislature. If the agency's program is going to be "sold," OMB is the place to do it. Yet there are many agency "salespersons" plying their wares. Halfhearted approaches are likely to be unsuccessful in this milieu. Thus, administrators devote considerable time and attention to substantiating and defending their budget requests. Indeed, maintaining good relations with the Office of Management and Budget is a year-round affair. The budget hearing is just one of many interactions. Agency heads seek to maintain a continuing dialogue. Even before inclusion in the budget request, new programs or expansions of existing ones may be informally proposed in order to get a reading on its likely reception. Both before and after the OMB hearing, agencies follow the fate of their budget by keeping in close touch with budget officials. It is here that the agency's reassertion of need is likely to be most effective. After the budget is a 500-page

President Jimmy Carter and OMB Director James McIntyre: Overseers of the Federal Budget as the 1970s Drew to a Close. (United Press International Photo)

document on the president's desk, agency appeals directed upward through the bureaucracy are likely to be ineffectual.

After the budget hearings are conducted by the Office of Management and Budget, OMB sits down to complete its editing of the budget documents submitted to it by the various agencies. Like the agency, OMB's editing rationales are numerous and range from the near involuntary response to analytical choice. The budget reviewers may blue-pencil the "padding" that is presumed to exist in the agency's first draft. The executive role set in the web of mutual anticipation is thereby fulfilled. Studies by Wildavsky and Fenno on the federal level and Sharkansky on the state level, indicate that the executive editor always cuts something.[36] A study by Davis, Dempster, and Wildavsky indicated that mayors also routinely pare agency requests.[37]

Executive editing also has a programmatic purpose. Presidential priorities deemphasized by agency budget drafts may be restored. Additionally, in the process of ballooning their requests, some agencies will expand more than others. Thus, the budget office tries to bring the various requests more in line with the existing fair share arrangement. Reference is made to the base as well. Wildavsky reported that the base is as central a concept in the budgeting offices as it is throughout the entire budgetary process. A later work by Davis, Dempster, and Wildavsky established all but a fixed mathematical relationship between the agencies' base and subsequent presidential recommendations to the Congress.[38] Finally, the budget office edits with the knowledge that there is yet another editor, the legislature, down the line. Therefore, while agency requests are reduced by the budget office, they remain above the previous year's base. The resulting document consists primarily of old programs retained and slightly expanded plus a smattering of new proposals.

Appealing to the Publisher

Before the budget emerges from the bureaucracy, the dissatisfied agency has one more chance to engineer a more favorable request. It is the direct appeal to the president for the restoration of cut funds and the somewhat more sensible application of indirect pressure to that end. Protesting to the president might have value to agency morale in demonstrating that the administrator is fighting down to the wire. However, given the standing of OMB, such appeals are likely to be rejected, and given the nature of bureaucracy, OMB may very well draft the letter for the president's signature. Finally, the plea to the president may tarnish the agency head's reputation as a "team player" within the administration.

Applying indirect pressure is a bit safer and may be more successful. If the agency can mount a campaign of support by its clientele that is capable of reching the Executive Office, a last-minute reprieve is possible. Wildavsky has identified the discreet arousal of clientele support as an agency strategy in the budget process. (Discreet because it would not do to have the administrator lead a horde of complainants against the president's policies up the White House steps.) If carried out with élan, this final agency maneuver to modify the budget within the bureaucracy may be successful. The president, as publisher, does hope to produce a manuscript that has some appeal. Thus, if confronted with a campaign that seems strong enough to convince Congress to restore the cut program, the president may decide to take credit for the inevitable. Nobody wants to appear as a loser in the budget process, so where funding is assured, one might well see former critics cheering "their" program on to approval.

It is also at this point that agency cultivation of influential congresspersons can pay off. If one or two legislators who can make or break an appropriations bill are sympathetic to a program, they may be the only clientele group that needs to be activated. Even in OMB, it has been rumored that the most highly regarded budget analysts are those whose budget recommendations are least changed by Congress.[39]

At the state and municipal level, it appears that clientele mobilization is somewhat less effective. According to John Crecine:

> The presence of external influence in the political sense was not detected in the budget formulation process. . . . influentials play a very minor role in the formation of municipal operating budgets. . . .budgets in municipal governments are reasonably abstracted documents bearing little direct relationship to specific community pressures.[40]

Generally, it appears that state and local governments lack the elegant dispersion of budgetary authority that moved Wildavsky to state: "Nowhere in the Federal Government does a single authority have the power to say what is going to be in the budget."[41] In states and municipalities, the budget staff often is an ad hoc committee of various aides. The executive tends toward direct involvement and may occupy a powerful position vis-à-vis the other authors. At all levels of government, however, when the executive gets the manuscript back from the printer, he sends it off to the legislature for review. This is a necessary step, even if the review is pro forma. In the federal government, the reviews are anything but perfunctory. They are caustic, hilarious, philosophical, homey, outraged, and outrageous. And, they mean something. The legislative critics revise the manuscript.

Congressional Critics and Cutters
The Congress is not the first to excise the budget manuscript. As we have seen, the Office of Management and Budget on behalf of the president has already trimmed down the requests emanating from the bureaucracy. However, whereas the OMB goes about its chores in a sober manner, Congress criticizes and cuts with the flare of a circus ringmaster. This is not to say that Congress acts irrationally. Far from it. Beneath the flamboyance of congressional budgetary action lies a serious attempt to create a document consonant with society's wishes as expressed through the legislature. The difference in presidential and congressional behavior as they both set out to do essentially the same thing is attributable to the roles that each has come to play in the budgetary process.

The president is the manager of the bureaucracy. In rendering decisions about its operations, the president is expected to be sober and analytical. After all, the president is in charge. If something is wrong, the chief executive is not expected to carry on about it, but to change it. The budget that the president sends to the Congress represents the administration's program and management plan for the coming year. Presidents, when they do deliver their budget messages to Congress in person (often they do not), speak with the air of a chairman of the board and chief operating officer at a stockholders meeting. With assurance, the president says, "This is how we plan to run the government this year."

Yet, the president's audience is not composed of timid stockholders. They are congresspersons. There are no proxy votes here. Moreover, legislators do not cast secret ballots in the budgetary process. Votes are shouted out. Extemporaneous speeches or written statements often embellish them. The congressperson speaks critically and loud for three reasons. First, he or she is a legislative watchdog, and watchdogs bark. Second, he or she is keyed to attack overspending. Third, "back home" constituents are presumed to be listening for evidence of activity on their behalf.

Legislators are "overseers" of administration, not managers. Unlike the president, it is not their job to run the bureaucracy. The legislature's role is to make recommendations that will make the bureaucracy run better. Implementation is left to others. In practice, the "oversight of administration" role boils down to finding fault. Either something is being done that should not, or something is not being done that should. Legislators zero in on what they perceive as defects, whereas the president is somewhat more required to maintain an overall perspective.

In the budget process, the legislative role is that of the "cutter." The search for budget defects invariably uncovers extravagance. Even without a search, the mutual expectations of the budget process demand a legislative reaction to the presumed prolificacy of the other authors.

The role of the congressperson is also that of fighting advocate. A constituency is keeping an eye on him. Sending quiet little memos into the bureaucracy suggesting changes is unlikely to score points with the people back home. The legislator is a "representative." There are few better ways to demonstrate this than by uncovering "wastes of the taxpayers' money." Of course, in the budget process, opportunities for such demonstrations abound.

> REPRESENTATIVE ROONEY: I find a gentleman here, an FSO-6. He got an A in Chinese and you assigned him to London.
> MR. X: Yes, sir. That officer will have opportunities in London—not as many as he would have in Hong Kong, for example—
> REPRESENTATIVE ROONEY: What will he do? Spend his time in Chinatown?
> MR. X: No, sir. There will be opportunities in dealing with officers in the British Foreign Office who are concerned with Far Eastern affairs. . . .
> REPRESENTATIVE ROONEY: So instead of speaking English to one another, they will sit in the London office and talk Chinese?
> MR. X: Yes, sir.
> REPRESENTATIVE ROONEY: Is that not fantastic?
> MR. X: No, sir. They are anxious to keep up their practice. . . .
> REPRESENTATIVE ROONEY: They go out to Chinese restaurants and have chop suey together?
> MR. X: Yes, sir.
> REPRESENTATIVE ROONEY: And that is all at the expense of the American taxpayer?[42]

The above jewel is from Aaron Wildavsky and, as he notes, there are many more where that came from.

Prior to 1975, fragmentation was the hallmark of congressional budget review, and Representative Rooney's grilling of Mr. X was an oft-repeated scenario in legislative-executive interaction. If there were skeletons in an agency's budget closet, a single legislator was responsible for uncovering them. As the above dialogue indicates, the search was often successful. However, even as congresspersons exposed minor transgressions, a rising flood of information from the bureaucracy taxed their ability to evaluate the overall impact of programs. Every year, more numbers, reports, expert testimonials, and economic projections added weight to already ponderous budget proposals. The budget approved by Congress increasingly resembled the presidential request because there was neither the time nor the analytic resources for a thoroughgoing review. In 1975, Congress sought to reassert its oversight role by setting up mechanisms for centralized budget review and staffing them with experts capable of dissecting the technical rationales advanced on behalf of the president's budget. However, even in Congress the executive request continues to traverse the numerous, albeit weakened, appropriations subcommittees; and in many state legislatures, fragmented review remains dominant. Thus, since legislative budget review is at present a mixture of fragmented and centralized approaches, both will be discussed below.

Contained Specialization

Since all revenue bills originate in the House of Representatives, it is there that the executive's budget received its initial and major congressional review under the old system. The budget was not considered as a whole; sections and even pages were assigned to individual House members who made it their business to be thoroughly familiar with the budget of a particular agency or bureau. The term *contained specialization* is often applied to this division of legislative review.

The evolution of contained specialization essentially mirrors the growth and differentiation of the bureaucracy. At one time a single House committee considered all financial matters: taxation, expenditures, and the budget allocations for individual agencies. In 1865, the burden having grown too large, separate committees were formed and expenditures became the domain of the Appropriations Committee. However, the budget workload eventually outstripped the capacity of the Appropriations Committee as a unitary body. As a result, the Appropriations Committee was divided into 12 Appropriations subcommittees. Since reevaluating the product of its twelve subparts was impossible, the full Appropriations Committee became the collator of subcommittee decisions. In time, even a twelve-way specialization proved incapable of dealing with the proliferating bureaucracy. Thus, individual subcommittee members were assigned to review the budgets of single agencies or functions. As the Appropriations Committee basically collated the subcommittee's product, so too did subcommittees collate the product of their contained specialists. Thus, since the specialist's judgment rose relatively unscathed through Congress, an agency's budget fate could hinge on the decisions of a single Congressperson. Quite naturally, many administrators sought to get on the friendliest possible terms with "their" specialist.

In the era of contained specialization, the Senate appropriations process was less audit oriented than its House counterpart. As a body with broader constituencies, longer terms, and no requirement to perform the initial groundwork on expenditures and taxation, the Senate tended to be more sympathetic to program concerns. Moreover, with only one-quarter as many members in the Senate as in the House, Senate Appropriations Committee members usually served on other committees where programs were considered in a context largely divorced from financial considerations. As a result, the Senate often served as a "court of appeals" for agencies hit by House cuts. However, the Senate docket could not accommodate all plaintiffs. Thus, under the old system, the audit-oriented contained specialists of the House Appropriations subcommittees were the key force in most legislative budget decisions.

Centralized Budget Analysis

Under contained specialization, the budget was analyzed by hundreds of people. However, the review proceeded in the absence of a single unifying vision. Taxing and spending were considered separately. Tax matters were the domain of the Ways and Means Committee in the House and the Finance Committee in the Senate. Each house of Congress had an Appropriations Committee to review expenditures. Agency budgets were dispersed to no less than a dozen subcommittees for scrutiny. As the fiscal year approached, and often after it had arrived, the fragmented reviews collided to produce the federal budget. Budgeting by collision rather than coordination had consequences that disturbed Congress. Among them were the increasing budgetary dominance of the president and budget deficits that, although the result of legislative budget decisions, deviated from congressional expectations with regularity. Thus, by 1974, Congress perceived "a need for identifying and agreeing on the kind and amount of information that is required to evaluate both the budget as a whole and its thousands of component parts. . . . There is a need for providing within the Congress itself the kind of arrangements to insure the best use of this information."[43]

As a cure for its ills, Congress passed the Budget and Impoundment Control Act of 1974. With respect to impoundment, the legislatively approved flow of money to programs was substantially immunized against presidential stoppage. Institutionally, the act added Budget Committees to both houses of Congress and established a *Congressional Budget Office (CBO)*. The new committees, which consider revenues and expenditures simultaneously, are composed of members of both the Finance Committees (Ways and Means in the House) and the Appropriations Committees. The House and Senate Budget Committees jointly determine the desired level of deficit or surplus and impose an expenditure ceiling to achieve it. Overall tax levels are fixed as well. For these tasks, a staff of 150 assists the Budget Committees with general analytical skills, knowledge of economics, and expertise in specific program areas. Through the 1970s, many state legislatures followed the lead of the Congress.

With an overall spending limit set in advance, the budget is parceled out to the Appropriations subcommittees for review. However, to a much greater degree than under the old system, subcommittee discretion is circumscribed. The contained specialist can still diagnose programs. However, if shortages are found, the subcommittees must work within existing appropriations since the subcommittees' largess may not exceed Budget Committee guidelines. In the defense budget, for instance, adding an aircraft carrier requires a corresponding reduction in other armed services expenditures.

The Budget Committees and their staffs were not the only way Congress beefed up its budgetary power. In the Congressional Budget Office, the legislative budget director oversees a staff of 200. The CBO helps Congress monitor the status of budget legislation. It serves as a financial housekeeper to prevent the disarray that, in the past, hampered the congressional budget role. Generously endowed with economists and management specialists, the CBO is capable of critically reviewing the administration's economic forecasts and program estimates. Thus, when the Carter administration predicted a daily savings of 4.5 million barrels of oil as a result of proposed energy programs, the CBO branded the projection as "overly optimistic" by 1 million barrels.[44]

Such pronouncements make for great debates and, to observers such as Lindblom, that is the problem.[45] One benefit of incrementalism is that it mutes conflict. Budgets take shape in the center of the pluralist arena where the traditional budget authors—legislators and administrators—are skilled in negotiation and compromise and where even the visible clashes may serve as a safety valve. If analysts come to the fore, it is claimed, so too will rigidity. A researcher whose analysis leads to certain conclusions is not likely to compromise them away. Indeed, academics representing different schools of thought often engage in venomous exchanges. Some fear a similar animosity and resultant polarization if analysis becomes the primary medium for public policy debates.

The incremental/analytical dichotomy surfaced in the dispute over the Carter energy proposals. Although the CBO was an arm of a Democratically controlled Congress and the energy program was the creation of a Democratic administration, the CBO, nonpartisan by statute, publicly announced that its analysis refuted the energy saving claims of the President's energy advisors. As a result, the chairman of the House Budget Committee, a distressed Democrat, proposed that the CBO be more circumspect.[46] The perceptual differences are clear. To the congressperson, the administrative and legislative environment favored an agreement on energy policies. It was not the time to complicate matters with charges of duplicity, even if true. Inflated claims were a standard part of, and secondary to, reaching a decision. To the CBO, on the other hand, the disagreement over facts had to be resolved for a decision to be reached. Whereas the analyst tends to say "Let's do it right," the incrementally socialized tends to say "Let's do it."

Regardless of which approach prevails, legislative budget review is important to administration. The appropriations process represents the bureaucracy's annual exposure to scrutiny. The legislative specialists and the professional staffs are a valuable resource for probing bureaucratic activity. These individuals take their functions seriously; their recommendations are neither frivolous nor lightly taken. The power of the purse is a potent weapon in persuading agency heads to change quickly behavior patterns that the legislature finds unacceptable. Given bureaucracy's natural tendency to go its own way, legislative budget review serves as one of the more valuable checks in the array of checks and balances that characterize our political system.

Pardons and Commutations

Once the budget, or budget bills for separate programs, is passed by the Congress, the president signs it. Although the president can veto, this is rarely done. The budget appropriations now stand ready to be disbursed to the bureaucracy. This final stage, called budget execution, sees revenues allocated periodically through the year to the departments and bureaus. In the federal government, agencies receive their allocations quarterly. The money is doled out a little at a time so that the agency cannot miscalculate and spend its annual allotment before the year's end.

Of course, it is possible that agencies can run out through no fault of their own. Inflation, extraordinary costs, or new developments might require a mid-year increase in the agency's budget. When this happens, there is a mechanism to handle such needs. It is the supplemental appropriation. It moves through the same process as does the whole budget. However, it moves more quickly and quietly in the absence of the budget season crush. In this sedate and less visible milieu, the really dogged agency may be able to sneak on the supplemental appropriations line to win a reprieve for funds and programs denied during the regular budgetary process. Budget actors occasionally conspire to allow a program to be struck down in the regular budget process with the understanding that it will be quietly resurrected via a supplemental appropriation.

When the last supplemental appropriation goes through and the end of the fiscal year nears, the curtain falls on a budget that, in the federal government, has been nearly a year in executive formulation; 9 months in legislative review; and 365 days in the bureaucracy. Thus, as the 1980 budget is in its last month, the 1981 budget is being scrutinized by the legislature and the 1982 budget is being outlined by the executive Office of Management and Budget. In its omnipresence, the budget serves as an anchor for government institutions. It forces continual interaction among lawmakers, executive policy makers, and bureaucrats. To the legislature and the executive, the budget is also a bellwether. Unlike one-time issues where winning may be attributable to a host of factors, the budget, by providing a standard battlefield year after year, can indicate if the institutional balance of power is shifting. It was in response to such a shift that Congress reformed its budgetary practices. Still, the budget's valence is strongest with respect to the administrator. The budget is organizational sustenance and administrators participate actively and creatively in the process to keep their operations well financed.

BUDGETARY GAMESMANSHIP
FOR THE PUBLIC ADMINISTRATOR

In many ways the budget process is a game. In it agencies try to increase their holdings. In absolute terms, they want more money than last year. In relative terms, improving the agency's position vis-à-vis competing agencies is also an indicator of successful gamesmanship. Yet the competition is fierce and the game board is strewn with pitfalls. Misjudging the reactions of the other players can be dangerous, as the administrator on the receiving end of the following casual but potent remark discovered. "I was wondering whether there was someplace in this appropriation where we could make a substantial cut for the purpose of impressing upon you the desirability of making this study." Thus spoke the congressperson in response to the administrator's reservations about implementing a program favored by the appropriations subcommittee.[47]

Thus, in the budget game, the stakes can be high, the penalties for a misstep severe. However, failing to play the game can result in the agency losing merely because the other participants expect at least a degree of gamesmanship on the part of the agency administrator. Even if the administrator does not play, cuts will be made. On the playing field of the budget process, every agency is presumed to have on protective equipment and padding. Once the game is on, no agency is immune to blocks and tackles.

While the agency cannot drop out of the game, it does have some discretion regarding the intensity with which it will play. The game can be played easy or hard. However, research indicates that the hard-playing agency comes out ahead of the game. According to Sharkansky, "assertiveness" is one factor that corresponds with higher budget increases. The assertive agency:

> requests the biggest increases
> takes the most pains to highlight programs
> shows a willingness to appeal cuts
> both answers and evades the inquiries of legislative and executive budget reviewers
> disregards specific legislative instruction about methods of expenditure
> pursues supplemental appropriations after the regular budget season is over.[48]

In the annals of administrative assertiveness, Robert Moses is a legend. A guiding force in the construction of New York public facilities for nearly half a century, Moses popularized the oft-imitated budgetary tactic of "laying stakes."[49] To stake out a claim on future budgets, the administrator requests a small first year allocation to begin a project, the overall cost of which has been grossly and deliberately underestimated. With the initial funds, the project is brought to an irreversable stage. Thus, a wedge has been driven into the budget. As it is hammered home in succeeding years, legislators are likely to be astounded at the costs. With each blow, the administrator, with a pained expression, humbles himself before legislative inquisitors. "How wrong we were. Nonetheless, I guess a half of a bridge won't do." Usually, it does not.

In *The Politics of the Budgetary Process,* Wildavsky's play-by-play description of the game captures the full flavor of the contest.[50] The aggressive administrators are almost shameless in marketing their programs. In appealing for more money, programs that conduct research into the causes of a particular disease open with a memorial list of its congressional victims. As the eulogy ends, a litany of the disease's gruesome symptoms begins. In another case, the U.S. Weather Service holds itself responsible for a substantial portion of the antifreeze purchases in the United States and the cracked engine blocks thereby prevented.

Aggressive merchandising is but one weapon in the arsenal of the assertive agency. Budgeting is also a positional game. When the blame for having cut a program falls, an agency skilled in budgetary gamesmanship will see to it that it falls on somebody else. If asked to reduce its budget, the agency cuts out its most popular program. The administrator washes his hands by saying, "The budget office made me do it." In the embarrassing furor that ensues, the program, of course, is restored. Now, in the aftermath of the controversy, the options of the executive with respect to the agency's budget have been reduced. First, the executive, already embarrassed, may well keep a low budget profile. Second, the agency has managed to get its best profile firmly imprinted on the public's mind. Further cuts, even if directed at ineffective programs, will be seen as unjustly directed at a "good" agency. Finally, executive cuts in other parts of the agency are likely to appear vindictive.

Of course, not all strategies pack the punch of the popular program cut. More subtle tactics are also a part of the agency's overall attack plan. For instance, state and municipal legislatures are inclined to cut budget requests for maintenance, equipment, and supplies rather than personnel allocations.[51] (People, after all, are votes.) The skillful administrator will be sure to include prominent, but needless, requests for such items so as to accommodate these legislative propensities. On the federal level, legislators are fond of cutting administrative and public relations staff. In the first place, such cuts are presumed to have no effect on programs. In the second, the common feeling that there are "too many bureaucrats" affects legislators as well. Lastly, public relations specialists are, not unjustifiably, considered inappropriate in a public setting. Thus, administrators might temporarily assign program personnel to such functions. Thus, in the budget, administrative and public relations staffs appear to have fewer employees than are actually assigned. If the ploy is successful, the administrator wins points for having a skeleton staff and secures gentle budgetary treatment.

The strategies listed above are but a sample of those available to help preserve and improve the position of the government organization in the annual budget process. All of these maneuvers can be characterized as attempts to control the organization's environment. Where possible, external decision makers are denied access to information that they require. Pains are taken to cultivate or otherwise neutralize actors who pass on the organization's fate. In the budget, as in all other interactions with its environment, the organization seeks to reduce uncertainty and to minimize threats to its existence.

BEYOND INCREMENTALISM: PPBS AND ZBB

As we discussed, the budget process, as complicated and convoluted as it may seem, is seen by many as the only feasible way to arrive at decisions on an issue as massive, complex, multifaceted, and controversial as the federal budget. Indeed, incrementalism does permit a broad range of programs to be viewed in a number of different ways. By the time it has wound its way through the budgetary process, the program proposal has been looked at as money, people, services, and an activity among various other activities. Bureaucratic, executive, and legislative actors all get to flex their muscles to see if the governmental center of gravity can be moved in one direction or another. What emerges is most certainly a consensual document. Some are more happy than others with the result, but no one is entirely displeased; nor is anybody ecstatically happy. Besides, in the budget process, there is always a next year.

Still, there are those who question the efficacy of the incremental approach, and some striking examples are emerging to back up the doubts. New York City's journey to the brink of bankruptcy in the 1970s proceeded along the incremental path. To continue programs at base and fair share levels, the city begged, borrowed, and, in the opinion of some, lied. (City officials foresaw a nationwide economic upsurge pouring tax money into their mortgaged coffers. To most sober observers, who saw no such thing, the estimates were either irrational or duplistic.) Before creditors forced the city's hand, attempts to cut programs were substantially neutralized by vigorous budgetary gamesmanship. Unions, when not on strike, seemed forever on the verge of walking out. Clientele groups would appear frequently and vociferously on the steps of City Hall or in front of the State Capitol Building to protest threatened budget cuts. Lunches for school children were one of the favorite cutbacks of school administrators. The "$24 million" renovation of Yankee Stadium ended up costing five times as much. Gaming pervaded even the highest executive levels. State governors and New York City mayors tried to outmaneuver one another to fix the blame for financial difficulties or to bequeath the consequences to their successors in office.

Incremental budgeting, to a large extent, institutionalizes the past and dismisses the future. Viewing the budget primarily through the base presents a vision formed in the past. Protecting the base, a key administrative mindset in the budget process, is neither innovative policy making nor rational management. The base can obscure bad policies. Moreover, budget scrutiny should be a primary device for the administrative review of operations. However, if the process designates the base as a given, the opportunity is often overlooked.

Cavalier treatment of the future is also a much criticized characteristic of incremental budgeting. In effect, when a government jurisdiction deliberately underestimates long-term project costs, it mortgages the future of its citizens without informing them of the true interest rates. (If a bank did this to a homeowner, it would be in violation of the law.) While the future is not fully knowable, incremental budgeting often proceeds as if it were completely indecipherable. In this milieu, any program projection becomes valid. Proponents base estimates on the assumption that nothing will go wrong; opponents estimate program results as if nothing will go right. Often, a stiff dose of optimism or pessimism is added to each projection to account for acts of God. With this type of information, the public policy vision of the future is arrived at through negotiation rather than calculation.

In place of the incremental model, "comprehensive" budgeting approaches have been advanced. Heavily emphasizing the management and planning utility of the budget, alternatives such as the Planning-Programming-Budgeting System (PPBS) and Zero-Base Budgeting (ZBB) have been applied in administrative settings. Regardless of the initials, the key techniques of comprehensive budgeting approaches are (1) subjecting the base to scrutiny; and (2) calculating the future in a rational manner. The aim of these techniques is to direct resources more accurately to the achievement of goals.

PPBS and ZBB came to the fore as administrative tools. Executives used these budget techniques to rank funding requests that came up through the bureaucracy. Legislatures, lacking the personnel resources of the executive and more reliant on incremental analysis, were slower to adopt comprehensive techniques. However, in the mid-1970s, congressional budget reform and the advent of state Sunset Laws signaled the emergence of comprehensive budget analysis on the legislative scene. Nonetheless, as of 1977, the major experiences with comprehensive budgeting have been administrative ones.

PPBS PPBS was the first of the comprehensive budget approaches. In the early 1960s, the *Planning-Programming-Budgeting System* was introduced in the Department of Defense. Implementation was facilitated by a large analytical staff backed up by ample computer resources; weapons programs amenable to quantification and comparison; and 20 years of experience with systematic weapons analysis. Robert MacNamara, Secretary of Defense at the time, gathered together analysts and resources, conferred high-level authority upon the new unit, and assigned it the task of reviewing the defense budget. Analysis had entered the budgetary arena, but incrementalism did not leave. Even in the Department of Defense incrementalism remained a strong force. Nonetheless, executives were now armed with information that had general management utility and the potential for thwarting feebly supported budget requests that, before analysis, may have blustered through. Impressed, President Johnson prescribed PPBS for the entire federal budget in 1965.

PPBS did not take the administrative world by storm. Analysis was new to many agencies and as many used it incorrectly as used it correctly. Besides, incremental thinking, deeply entrenched, was a formidable foe.

Agencies found ways to make standardized analytic forms sound like press releases when complete. End runs to Congress negated other unfavorable analyses. PPBS paléd somewhat as a budgetary cure-all but broadened the analytical base underlying budget requests and management decisions. As James R. Schlesinger noted, analysis illuminated the true costs of programs that basked previously in an ideological glow.[52] Moreover, asserted Schlesinger, analysis often uncovered a "dominant solution"; that is, a course of action that everyone could agree upon if only its existence were known.[53] A brief sketch of how PPBS is applied indicates how blemishes invisible under other budget formats might emerge.

The first step in PPBS is to specify objectives. This is "outside-in" budgeting. It asks, "What are the things out there that I am looking to effect?" Once objectives are specified they form the skeleton of the PPBS budget document. After the objectives are in place, all government programs relevant to an objective are arrayed about it regardless of their formal placement within the bureaucratic structure. Thus, if a municipality's goal was to insure safe buildings, inspection units from both the fire department and the building department would be considered a part of the program to insure that buildings were safe. With activities viewed in this light, it becomes easier to determine if they are competing or complementary. As alternative means toward a single end, a comparison of their relative effectiveness is facilitated.

This comparison of relative effectiveness is carried out in a rigorous manner. The alternative programs are analyzed to determine which has greater impact. Furthermore, the analyses extend several years into the future. Long-range program costs enter into the budget picture heretofore characterized by an annual time frame that could obscure the true cost of programs. The long-range vision of PPBS seeks to prevent unanticipated costs whether they arise from poor foresight or some bureaucrat's strategic ploy.

As noted, the bureaucracy resisted PPBS. Moreover, neither legislatures nor interest groups were enamored of the "Planning" in PPBS. To them, planning meant policy making. However, to those in the legislative setting, policies were not precise formulas developed by analysts with computers. Policies were fluid and shaped, for a moment in time, by the interaction of individuals with a stake in the outcome. In the face of this attitude, PPBS was unable to transform radically congressional decision-making patterns. Nonetheless, analysis was not banished from administration. Even with planning deemphasized, PPBS was a useful management tool. Lumping programs around goals, even vague ones, highlighted redundant, feeble, and misdirected efforts.

In weakening the incremental rules of thumb, PPBS did a better job on fair share than on the base. When considered as one among hundreds of diverse programs, an agency that lays claim to its traditional budget ranking is difficult to challenge. However, when viewed as one of two or three programs, a program may clearly present a woeful effectiveness profile. If so, even appeals to tradition may not forestall radical surgery. Thus, with PPBS, the key question—"How can we budget better?"—weakened fair share claims and could lead to a reduction in the base. Until the 1970s, however, the base was not the primary target of administrative budgetary analysis. When administrators did train their sights on this most ubiquitous of incremental givens, the weapon they used was Zero-Base Budgeting.

ZBB   For the United States, the 1970s were a time of economic turbulence. Oil prices skyrocketed, the Vietnam war ended, population growth slowed. In response to these and other factors, the rate of increase in the country's output of goods and services slowed. The public's demand for goods and services, however, remained high. As a result, there was an inflationary price spiral. Many government jurisdictions found operating expenses leaping ahead of revenues. For states and municipalities, this meant less services and/or more taxes. The latter course, by making prices higher, only threatened to worsen the economic outlook. Taxpayer revolts, moreover, were beginning to materialize. Budget cutbacks, on the other hand, brought fear and trembling to the hearts of the incrementally trained administrator and legislator. One reason incrementalism had worked was because it gave everybody a little more every year. Suddenly, the wherewithal to do this was unavailable. Thus, under duress, the PPBS question—"How do we budget better?"—was replaced by "How do we budget for less?" The budgeting technique that addressed this question was Zero-Base Budgeting.[54]

Zero-Base Budgeting's unique feature is its explicit evaluation of the base. It requires unit managers, program heads, and departmental executives to detail the effect of lower than present allocations on operations and service levels. Instead of "base-plus" budget requests kicking off the process, "base-minus" estimates form the core of ZBB. Furthermore, to give superiors a range of choices, unit budgets are prepared at several base-minus and base-plus levels. In New Jersey, for instance, program impacts must be estimated at 0 percent, 50 percent, 75 percent, 100 percent, 125 percent, and +125 percent of current funding levels. Other states, Georgia is one, eschew percentages but require graduated estimates beginning at the lowest level, beneath current funding, that maintains program viability. Thus, under ZBB, each manager prepares impact analyses for several funding levels. Each analysis is called a "decision package."

After unit decision packages are prepared, they must be ranked by the manager. The "highest priority" decision package is the one that uses the minimum amount of resources necessary to continue the program or unit as a viable entity. From the managerial level, as decision packages move upwards, ranking procedures continue through the hierarchy. At each level, the decision packages are prioritized. For example, a park commissioner would review decision packages for golf courses, beaches, swimming pools, and playgrounds. For each, 80 percent of current funding level analyses would detail the loss of revenue, drop in patronage, and physical deterioration that would accompany the 20 percent savings. After this review, the commissioner would be required to identify first, second, third, and fourth program preferences. Unlike incremental budgeting, where all existing programs could be loved equally, ZBB forces administrators each year to decide on the absolute and relative value of programs.

By the time the decision packages reach the executive, all of the jurisdiction's programs are ranked and, for each individual program, the consequences of funding alternatives are displayed. Thus, the executives are presented with an information base that assists them in deciding which programs to fund at what levels, and where, within existing resources, money can be found to finance important programs. In actual practice, many budget decisions make themselves in the course of the ZBB process. The last crucial units or programs, for example, those ranked 175–200 on a list of 200, are likely to be clear candidates for discontinuance. Conversely, funding is guaranteed to the highest ranked operations that are generally the providers of essential services such as police and sanitation. It would be an exaggeration to say that all of the funds from the program ranked number 200 would go to the program ranked number 1. However, that is the general idea. Since ZBB views programs at basic, minimal funding levels, in the final analysis high-priority programs are likely to be financed with funds expropriated from the budgets of last place finishers.

In between the quick and the dead, there are the middle-range programs: the ones ranked from 50 to 150 in our illustration for instance. Here choices are a little harder. (It should be noted that ZBB does not lay claim to precision ranking. Actual applications usually follow our example—that is, several priority categories are established and the programs in each are considered equivalent.) However, even with rough rankings, the executive has a valuable decision foundation. Programs closer to the 150 mark might be funded at minimum levels such as 75 percent of current budget. Programs hovering near the 50 mark would likely be supported at 90 percent of current levels.

As with all management applications of budgetary analysis in government, the results of ZBB are subject to legislative revision or statutory veto. A sheriff's office may duplicate everything in the police department except efficiency and effectiveness. However, if the office is legally mandated or a rich patronage source, it will survive and thrive even if it is the uncontested last place finisher in the ZBB race.

A CLOSING THOUGHT

We would not venture a guess as to whether incrementalism or analysis will prevail in the budgetary process. Indeed, we predict that, for the foreseeable future, both will help shape governmental funding decisions. However, one thing does seem certain: Analysis will play an increasing role in the administrative environment. Since the budget is a natural focal point for analysis, variants of PPBS and ZBB will be widely used. Thus, it is important that the future public administrator be familiar with them. Furthermore, even though the planning component of techniques such as PPBS seem to be overshadowed by management applications, administrators should not lose sight of the external picture painted by the budget. Goals *are* important. Budget analysis can help measure progress towards them. Public managers should not forgo this opportunity to measure their organization's impact on the outside world. The organization was, after all, created by that world to serve it.

In the next chapter we will look at government's overall financial picture. The budget will be viewed as a component that is adjusted to achieve broad societal goals.

KEY TERMS AND CONCEPTS

Appropriations bill
Backdoor spending
Base
Budgetary principles (Annuality; comprehensiveness; unity; exclusiveness; specificity; accountability; and publicity, clarity, and accuracy)
Congressional Budget Office (CBO)
Contained specialization
Contract authority

Enabling or authorizing legislation
Executive budget
Fair share
Incrementalism
Office of Management and Budget (OMB)
Permanent appropriations
Planning-Programming-Budgeting System (PPBS)
Sunset Laws
Supplemental budget
Zero-Base Budgeting (ZBB)

NOTES

1. Lewis Friedman and Gregory Morton, *Municipal Performance Report: City Budgeting* (New York: Council on Municipal Performance, 1974), p. 3.
2. See Robert Caro, *The Power Broker* (New York: Knopf, 1974).
3. Frederick J. Lawton, "Legislative-Executive Relationships in Budgeting as Viewed by the Executive," in Robert J. Golembiewski and Jack Rabin, eds. *Public Budgeting and Finance: Readings in Theory and Practice,* 2nd ed., (Itasca: F. E. Peacock, 1975), p. 56.

4. Ibid.
5. Quoted in Aaron Wildavsky, *The Politics of the Budgetary Process,* 2nd ed. (Boston: Little, Brown, 1974), p. 100.
6. Ibid., p. 4.
7. Allen Schick, "The Road to PPB: The Stages of Budget Reform," in Fremont J. Lyden and Ernest G. Miller, eds. *Planning Programming Budgeting: A Systems Approach to Management,* 2nd ed. (Chicago: Rand McNally, 1972), p. 20.
8. S. Kenneth Howard, *Changing State Budgeting* (Lexington: Council of State Governments, 1973), pp. 3-8.
9. Schick, "The Road to PPB," pp. 25-27.
10. Herbert Simon, George Kozmetsky, Harold Guetzkow and Gordon Tyndall, "Management Uses of Figures," in Golembiewski and Rabin, *Public Budgeting and Finance,* p. 15.
11. Wildavsky, *Budgetary Process;* Ira Sharkansky, *The Politics of Taxing and Spending* (Indianapolis: Bobbs-Merrill, 1969).
12. Charles E. Lindblom, "The Science of Muddling Through," in *Public Administration Review* 19 (Spring 1959): 79-88.
13. Wildavsky, *Budgetary Process,* p. 15.
14. Lindblom, "Muddling Through," p. 81.
15. Ibid., p. 81.
16. Wildavsky, *Budgetary Process,* p. 30.
17. Ibid., p. 15.
18. Sharkansky, *Politics of Taxing and Spending,* pp. 142-143.
19. Ibid., pp. 104-105.
20. Wildavsky, *Budgetary Process,* p. 16.
21. *The Report of the Congressional Joint Study Committee on Budgetary Control,* 18 April 1973.
22. Ibid.
23. Murray L. Weidenbaum, "Budget 'Uncontrollability' as an Obstacle to Improving the Allocation of Government Resources," in Golembiewski and Rabin, *Public Budgeting and Finance,* pp. 95-180.
24. Office of Management and Budget, "Preparation and Execution of the Federal Budget" in Golembiewski and Rabin, *Public Budgeting and Finance,* p. 50.
25. Weidenbaum, "Budget Uncontrollability," pp. 96-97.
26. Allen Schick, "Zero-Base Budgeting and Sunset: Redundancy or Symbiosis?," Vol. 6, No. 1, *The Bureaucrat* (Spring 1977), pp. 12-32.
27. See J. D. Williams, *The Impounding of Funds by the Bureau of the Budget* (New York: Inter-University Case Program, 1955); Louis Fisher, "The Politics of Impounded Funds," *Administrative Science Quarterly* 15, no. 3 (Sept. 1970): 361-377.
28. Mayoral dominance in municipal budgeting is noted by John Crecine, *Governmental Problem Solving: A Computer Simulation of Municipal Budgeting* (Chicago: Rand McNally, 1969); Howard, *Changing State Budget,* pp. 264-273, notes gubernatorial dominance over the legislature but sees the bureaucracy as a strong force; Lewis B. Friedman, *Budgeting Municipal Expenditures: A Study in Comparative Policy Making* (New York: Praeger, 1975), notes mayors and agencies joining forces against legislatures.
29. Office of Management and Budget, "Preparation and Execution," p. 48.
30. Wildavsky, *Budgetary Process,* p. 4.
31. Ibid., p. 20.
32. Ibid.; also Friedman, *Budgeting Municipal Expenditures;* Sharkansky, *Politics*

of Taxing and Spending; Thomas J. Anton, *The Politics of State Expenditure in Illinois* (Urbana: University of Illinois Press, 1966).

33. Wildavsky, *Budgetary Process.*
34. J. Leiper Freeman, "The Setting and the Participants in Bureau-Committee Relations," in Golembiewski and Rabin, *Public Budgeting and Finance,* p. 67.
35. Lawton, "Legislative-Executive Relationships," p. 57.
36. Richard Fenno, *The Power of the Purse: Appropriation Politics in Congress* (Boston: Little Brown, 1966); Wildavsky, *Budgetary Process; Sharkansky, Politics of Taxing and Spending;* Friedman, *Budgeting Municipal Expenditures.*
37. Otto Davis, M. A. H. Dempster, Aaron Wildavsky, "A Theory of the Budgetary Process," IX *American Political Science Review* (Sept. 1966): 529–547.
38. Ibid.
39. Wildavsky, *Budgetary Process,* pp. 39–40.
40. Crecine, *Governmental Problem Solving,* pp. 189, 191, 192.
41. Wildavsky, *Budgetary Process,* p. 131.
42. Ibid., p. 96.
43. Committee on Budgetary Control.
44. *Time,* 18 July 1977, p. 66.
45. Lindblom, "Muddling Through."
46. *Time,* 18 July 1977, p. 66.
47. Quoted in Wildavsky, *Budgetary Process,* p. 99.
48. Sharkansky, *Politics of Taxing and Spending,* p. 61.
49. "Laying Stakes" was coined to describe Robert Moses's budgetary faits accomplis in public works. Caro, *Power Broker,* p. 218. "Wedge" is Wildavsky's term, as is "Camel's nose," and describes the same maneuver. Wildavsky, *Budgetary Process,* pp. 111–112.
50. Wildavsky, *Budgetary Process.*
51. Sharkansky, *Politics of Taxing and Spending,* p. 95.
52. James R. Schlesinger, "Systems Analysis and the Political Process," in Louis C. Gawthrop, ed. *The Administrative Process and Democratic Theory* (Boston: Houghton Mifflin, 1970), p. 353.
53. Ibid.
54. The discussion of ZBB is based on Schick, "Zero-Base Budgeting and Sunset: Redundancy or Symbiosis"; Graeme M. Taylor, "Introduction to Zero-Base Budgeting," *The Bureaucrat* (Spring 1977): 33–55; Walter D. Broadnax, "Zero Base Budgeting: New Directions for the Bureaucracy?" *The Bureaucrat* (Spring 1977): 56–66; Donald F. Haider, "Zero Base: Federal Style," *Public Administration Review* 37, no. 4 (July-August 1977): 450–470.

BIBLIOGRAPHY

Barber, David. *Power in Committees: Experiments in the Governmental Process.* (Chicago: Rand McNally, 1966).

Braybrooke, David and Lindblom, Charles E. *A Strategy of Decision.* (New York: Free Press, 1963).

Burkhead, Jesse. *Governmental Budgeting.* (New York: Wiley, 1956).

Crecine, John P. *Governmental Problem Solving: A Computer Simulation of Municipal Budgeting.* (Chicago: Rand McNally, 1969).

Fenno, Richard, Jr. *The Power of the Purse: Appropriations in Congress.* (Boston: Little, Brown, 1966).

Friedman, Lewis. *Budgeting Municipal Expenditures: A Study in Comparative Policy Making.* (New York: Praeger, 1975).

Howard, S. Kenneth. *Changing State Budgeting.* (Lexington: Council of State Governments, 1973).

Meltsner, Arnold. *The Politics of City Revenue.* (Berkeley: University of California Press, 1971).

Minmier, George S. *An Evaluation of Zero-Base Budgeting System in Governmental Institutions.* (Atlanta: Georgia State University, 1975).

Novick, David, ed. *Program Budgeting: Program Analysis and the Federal Budget.* (Cambridge: Harvard University Press, 1965).

Pyhrr, Peter A. *Zero-Base Budgeting: A Practical Management Tool for Evaluating Expenses.* (New York: Wiley, 1973).

Schick, Allen. *Budget Innovation in the States.* (Washington, D.C.: Brookings, 1971).

Schick, Allen and Keith, Robert. *Zero Base Budgeting in the States.* (Washington, D.C.: Library of Congress, 1976).

Schultze, Charles L. *The Politics and Economics of Public Spending.* (Washington, D.C.: Brookings, 1968).

Smithies, Arthur. *The Budget Process in the United States.* (New York: McGraw-Hill, 1968).

Wildavsky, Aaron. *The Politics of the Budgetary Process,* 2nd ed. (Boston: Little, Brown, 1974).

In addition to the sources cited in the notes and bibliography, the following *Public Administration Review (PAR)* articles are a convenient starting point for a more detailed exploration of the material in this chapter.

Adams, Bruce and Betsy Sherman. "Sunset Implementation: A Positive Partnership to Make Government Work," *PAR* 38, no. 1 (Jan./Feb. 1978): 78–82.

Baily, John J. and Robert J. O'Connor. "Operationalizing Incrementalism: Measuring the Muddles," *PAR* 35, no. 1 (Jan./Feb. 1975): 60–66.

Beckman, Norman. "Policy Analyses for the Congress," *PAR* 37, no. 3 (May/June 1977): 237–244.

Finley, James J. "The 1974 Congressional Initiative in Budget Making," *PAR* 35, no. 3 (May/June 1975): 270–278.

Harder, Donald F. "Zero Base: Federal Style," *PAR* 37, no. 4 (July/Aug. 1977): 400–407.

Phyrr, Peter A. "The Zero Base Approach to Government Budgeting," *PAR* 37, no. 1 (Jan./Feb. 1977): 1–8.

Schick, Allen. "A Death in the Bureaucracy: The Demise of Federal PPB," *PAR* 33, no. 2 (March/April 1973): 146–156.

Schick, Allen. "Beyond Analysis," *PAR* 37, no. 3 (May/June 1977): 258–263.

Schick, Allen. "Systems Politics and Systems Budgeting," *PAR* 29, no. 2 (March/April 1969): 137–151.

Schick, Allen. "The Road From ZBB," *PAR* 38, no. 2 (March/April 1978): 177–180.

Wildavsky, Aaron. "Rescuing Policy Analysis From PPBS," *PAR* 29, no. 2 (March/April 1969): 189–202.

Worthy, Joseph. "PPB: Dead or Alive," *PAR* 34, no. 4 (July/Aug. 1974): 392–394.

RELEVANT PERIODICALS
GAO Review
Managerial Planning
Municipal Finance
National Civic Review

RELEVANT CASE STUDIES
(Cases marked ICCH are available from the Intercollegiate Case Clearing House, Soldier Field, Boston, Mass. 02163; cases marked ICP are available from the Inter-University Case Program, Box 229, Syracuse, N.Y. 13210.)

Christenson, C. J.   *The New York City Financial Crisis,* [ICCH]
Christenson, C. J.   *Budgeting in State Government,* [ICCH]
Silvers, J. B. and C. K. Prahalad.   *Cook County Hospital,* (A)(B),* [ICCH]
Vancil, R. F.   *Post Office Department,* [ICCH]
Vancil, R. F.   *Office of Economic Opportunity* (B),* [ICCH]
Weinberg, R. M. and F. G. Feeley.   *Illinois Budget Bureau,* (A)(B)(C),* [ICCH]
Williams, J. D.   *The Impounding of Funds by the Bureau of the Budget,* [ICP]

*Letters indicate that the case is presented in several installments.

CHAPTER 10

FINANCING GOVERNMENT

INTRODUCTION

This chapter concerns the financing of government. It is a three-level survey. First, we will review the nature of public goods and how they are financed. Federal government finance will be treated next. State and local considerations will occupy the remainder of the chapter. For both federal and subnational governments, there will be two prime foci. The first will be the financial environment of government. That is, what concepts in the world of theory and what forces in the world of reality shape ensuing financial decisions. Our second focus will be on the revenue-gathering methods of federal and state and local jurisdictions; namely, who pays what, when, where, and how.

THE EMERGENCE OF PUBLIC FINANCE

There is little doubt that government finance is in the public eye. Words such as unemployment, inflation, taxpayer revolt, revenue crunch, and layoffs pepper headlines in both national and local media. Courts have judged certain school financing schemes unconstitutional. Cities, counties, and special districts have flirted with bankruptcy. Citizens' rejection of proposed property tax increases have threatened to shut down schools in mid-term.

This torrent of crisis-related information is enough to make one yearn for the good old days when government finance was a once-a-year phenomenon. When April 15 passed, most citizens were happy to forget the ordeal as their financial dealings with government reverted to sub-liminal paycheck extractions, ubiquitous tax additions at the checkout counter, and irrelevant imposts at the liquor store, racetrack, or tobacco shop. Now, we worry about throwing kids out of school in November, laying off cops on January 15, and having no pool for the summer months. Indeed, to many people this onslaught is as anesthetizing as the yearly tax form and brings the same response. Namely, "Let this cup pass as quickly as possible and bother me not with the details."

Whether or not public finance is a hot issue for the general public, it is a crucial one for students of public administration. Increasingly, economic impacts are factored into policy proposals. Government re-sources devoted to financial management continue to expand. For ob-servers, participants, and practitioners in the public policy arena, an understanding of the financial environment of government is of prime importance. Therefore, the following survey of the goals, mechanisms, and theories that shape government's financial policies is not merely an academic exercise. Whether as citizen or civil servant, what you learn may well be put to use.

THEORETICAL APPROACHES
TO PUBLIC FINANCE

In sharp distinction to the incremental views highlighted in the previous chapter on the budget, societal goals are a central concern when government's revenue and expenditure activities are considered together. Thus, with broad strokes, analyses of public finance seek to explain what society seeks to accomplish through taxing and spending; why and how it does so.

The goals of public finance are identified as the maintenance of a stable economic environment, the efficient allocation of resources, and an equitable distribution of resources among the citizenry.[1] These goals, formulated by Richard Musgrave, arise out of the neoclassical approach to public finance.[2] This is because Adam Smith, the eighteenth-century progenitor of modern economics, called upon government to repel in-vaders, keep the peace, and provide a public works infrastructure to stabilize the operation of the marketplace.[3] The second goal, the effi-cient allocation of societal resources, is more or less the behavior of the economic person in the aggregate. If each individual seeks to maximize his benefits from the resources available, society by extension, is doing the same.

The third goal, the equitable distribution of resources, is not a classical economic concept, per se. Rather, it is a combination of norma-tive criteria and mass market necessity. Normatively, we have decided not to have a mass of severely impoverished people in this country for reasons that may be humanitarian (no one should starve) or self-interested (what happens if they get mad?). Also, the modern, postindustrial marketplace needs multitudes of consumers with money to spend. If a few were rich and most were poor, it would be difficult to sell several million cars and employ the thousands of workers now in the automobile industry.[4]

The neoclassical goals are important for U.S. national policy. Defense is a primary federal government product. Efficient resource distribution and full employment are given high priority at the federal level. Achieving these goals, most admit, requires a managed national economy. Indeed, what we have in Washington are financial officials who see themselves as economic managers.

At the state and local level, government's economic management role is much diminished. Economic competition is more evident as jurisdictions scramble for the jobs and taxes provided by business enterprises. Thus, in states and localities, government's financial decisions can be viewed through the prism of "public choice." According to public choice theorists, governments must respond to institutions and individuals who compare the benefits derived from a given mix of goods and services with the tax costs associated with the package.[5] A dissatisfied constituency can produce tax revolts, tax flight, or electoral defeat for the incumbent administration.[6] These scenarios have occurred. Therefore, public choice theories shall be prominent in our discussions of state and local finance.

Market Inadequacy and
Government Services: Public Goods

Both the neoclassical and public choice schools use, as a starting point, the *theory of public goods*. This approach assumes that the marketplace is the prime mechanism for meeting society's demands for goods and services. However, society will not always get what it wants because the market is an imperfect allocator. Private firms will not provide desired products if doing so is unprofitable. Thus, government is called upon to fulfill product demands rejected by private producers. In the argot of public finance, government's stock and trade is providing or regulating high externality goods and services. Since the concept of externalities is a crucial one for public finance, we shall look at it in more detail.[7]

Externalities are product benefits or costs that do not accrue to the producers or paying customers. They are "external" to the marketplace transaction. Benefits that escape the sellers or buyers are termed *positive externalities*. *Negative externalities* are costs evaded by the buyers or sellers.

Positive Externalities To a greater or lesser degree, many public goods defy marketplace pricing. National defense is the most extreme example. It is *indivisible*. It cannot be broken up into units and put on a shelf so that individual citizens can purchase the shares desired. Some public goods, such as a highway, can be priced, but payment cannot be exacted from all beneficiaries. Nearby homeowners and business persons profit from the road, but only drivers pay the toll. If an entrepreneur of a private highway tried to bill the nonpaying beneficiaries, they would likely assert that the highway was valueless to them, and they had not asked for it in the first place. Regardless of the "free riders" truthfulness, they would not be obliged to pay a cent under the rules governing marketplace transactions. Thus, the inability to exclude nonpaying beneficiaries is also a characteristic of public goods. Although businesses are not doctrinaire—fees are not charged to lunchtime loungers in the pleasant plaza of a corporate headquarters—they are understandably reluctant to manufacture a product or provide a service if the market could expropriate much of its value without paying the price. Thus, high externality projects such as dams and highways are usually built and maintained by the government.

Negative Externalities   These are costs shifted to individuals who are neither producers nor consumers of the product or service. For instance, every day we as citizens cover a negative externality by paying for the collection of nonreturnable cans—a cheaper proposition for manufacturers—littered about by individuals who prefer not to spend the time and energy necessary for proper disposal. Government's heavy involvement in the correction of negative externalities can be seen when garbage collectors sweep the street, when clean air regulations are issued, and when the residential neighbors of a polluting firm commence legal action. Thus, with respect to negative externalities, government either absorbs the cost, legislates against the offending activity, or assesses damages against parties who evade costs. As you might imagine, a considerable amount of government effort is expended on such activity.

Modern-Day Externalities   The development of technology has become, in many instances, a stupendously expensive, high-risk venture. Relatively short-term patent rights do not adequately guard against nonpaying firms expropriating the value of a business's invention. Moreover, even though the developing firm stands to reap substantial benefits from technological innovation, failure could be fatal. Thus, in the United States, government, not the utility companies, shouldered most of the research and development costs for nuclear power plants. Similarly, aerospace innovation is often a public good even though commercial aircraft builders may eventually benefit.

Before leaving the subject, it is worth noting that externalities have a value component as well as a factual component. Heavy industrial and automotive pollution had been a reality for decades, but it took a considerable amount of old-fashioned lobbying before congressional recognition was forthcoming in the 1960s. Indeed, as the energy shortage took hold in the late 1970s, pollution became a somewhat more respectable externality as coal, a much dirtier fuel, replaced higher priced gas and oil in the furnaces of America.

Societal Preferences and Government Services: Merit Goods

In some cases, society may decide to provide goods and services, available on the marketplace, to all citizens regardless of their ability to pay. Such goods and services are often termed *merit goods,* and education is a prime example.[8] Children cannot be excluded from primary education in most industrialized nations of the world. Although, in some countries, education is exclusively a state enterprise and, in others, a public/ private mixture, the market mechanisms that deny educational services to those lacking the wherewithal is neutralized in all instances.

Economic rationales can also be applied to merit goods. Education makes for a better work force, higher productivity, and future economic growth. Thus, the cost of universal education is a rational investment. With regard to low-cost government housing for the elderly, however, the economic rationality argument becomes strained. More likely, we feel a social responsibility to make decent housing available to the aged at prices that they can afford.

As has been pointed out, *efficiency* (economic criteria) and *equity* (social criteria) both play a part in our allocation of goods, services, and individual rights and prohibitions.[9] Minimum wages, in part, reflect social criteria concerning the value of labor, not economic criteria concerning efficient production. Antitrust laws evince a distrust of oligarchic concentrations of power and can stand in opposition to the economic efficiency often associated with size. Thus, although our concern in this chapter is primarily economic, it must be remembered that social goals and economic goals, not always compatible, can impact on government's financial policies.

CATEGORIES OF GOVERNMENT SERVICES

Different public goods can be provided in different ways. However, even the provision of a single service may not be consistent from place to place. Sanitation services are directly provided by some municipalities; contracted to private firms by others. Although the search for rhyme and reason in all of this has not been very successful, public goods can be categorized, and the following breakdown is worth remembering:

General Revenue Public Goods (Direct Provision) These are goods and services paid for out of general tax funds provided by government employees using publicly leased or owned facilities and equipment. Police, fire protection, and most highly visible government activities fall into this category.

General Revenue Public Goods (Indirect Provision)   These are goods and services paid for out of general tax funds provided by private firms and applied to specified public purposes. For instance, many "Medicare" facilities are privately owned and operated but are reimbursed, from general tax revenues, for treatment given to persons eligible under government health care regulations.

Segregated Revenue Public Goods   These are goods and services paid for by specific taxes. Interstate highways, for instance, are paid for out of the Highway Trust Fund: the repository for the federal excise tax levied at the gasoline pump.

Direct User Charge Public Goods   These are governmentally provided goods and services paid for by users at the time of consumption. Bridges, tunnels, toll highways, and mass transit are all direct user charge public goods. Of all public goods, the direct user charge variety most closely ties payment to the value of the product to the individual citizen. Due to this approximation of the market model, transit authorities and government-operated utilities are often referred to as "public enterprise."

Income Transfers   Some public monies are simply bestowed on members of the society to do with as they please. In this operation, government is merely a transfer mechanism.[10] It takes from some taxpayers and gives to other persons who may or may not be taxpayers. Social security and certain welfare payments are income transfers.

Income transfers operationalize the income distribution standards formulated by the legislature. Involved, among others, are the Social Security Administration, the Veterans Administration, and national welfare system—all huge bureaucracies. (It is important to note that each has a public goods component—medical services, etc.,—as distinct from a transfer component—direct payment to eligible recipients. "Welfare mess" charges are generally aimed at the transfer components.)

Proposals for a "negative income tax" center on income transfers and the costliness of their administration.[11] Simply put, those falling short of the income standard desired by public policy would fill out a return, pay no tax, and receive a check to cover the deficiency. The proposal seeks to cut through the miasma of rules and regulations of the taxation and transfer systems that can result in a person paying a tax to the IRS while receiving low-income subsidies through a separate bureaucracy.

PAYING FOR PUBLIC GOODS

One thing apparent from the discussion so far is that everyone, to a greater or lesser degree, benefits from public goods, services, and income transfers. Everyone is covered by the national defense umbrella; school is a mandatory passage in our lives; the community benefits from police protection. Other programs have a narrower impact. They supplement the income of the aged, homeowners, the unemployed, the impoverished, farmers, and a host of other groups. Some of these programs have ripple effects that are assumed to benefit society as a whole, but others merely transfer funds that would be spent by taxpayer A to citizen B. Other government services, offered on a pay-as-you-go basis, apparently benefit the voluntary customers without affecting nonpatrons. Even here, however, the picture is not so clear. Drivers may pay a higher toll than they would if the "Exit Ramp Diner" was taxed by the Thruway Authority for the value derived from the road. Moreover, mass transit riders may pay a lower fare because the bus or subway line is subsidized from general tax revenues paid, in part, by nonriders.

Although obviously a sticky one, the question of "Who benefits from a public good?" is crucial to tax theory. If the answer is "Identifiable direct and indirect beneficiaries," tax policy would seek them out and charge them for their use of public goods. If the answer is "Everyone!" or "Impossible to determine," the cost of public goods is spread among all citizens. In the former case, taxation would proceed under the *benefit principle*. In the latter case, it would proceed under a *cost distribution/ability to pay principle.*[12] Let us look briefly at each.

Benefit Principle Charging the cost of negative externalities, such as pollution, to the offending firm through taxation would be an application of the benefit principle. The firm pays because it has benefited—saved money—that will be spent by society on street sweepers or surgeons removing pollution-diseased lungs. Raising the tax assessment of homeowners whose property fronts on governmentally improved roads would cover the positive externalities generated by that particular public good. The benefit principle is of growing importance in studies to determine the impact of public goods, particularly those delivered locally. Localities also utilize benefit-based taxation to a greater extent than the federal government. When we discuss state and local finance later in the chapter, the benefit principle will be an important focus.

Cost Distribution/Ability to Pay Principle In one sense, the cost distribution principle is a backup position for the benefit principle. If you cannot determine the beneficiaries of a particular public good, you levy a tax as if everyone benefits. However, this would merely result in a head tax—everyone paying the same amount. To reach the ability to pay criteria, a distinction must be made among incomes. If a society decides, as ours has, that some people (the lower-income classes) have a more crucial need for their money than others (the rich), taxation is based on ability to pay.

The federal government relies heavily on the ability to pay criteria for several reasons. First, a large proportion of its expenditures are transfer payments. The beneficiaries cannot pay; thus the cost must be distributed among nonbeneficiaries. Second, more than one-quarter of the federal budget goes to national defense—the nearest thing to a pure, indivisible, nonexclusionary, externality-laden, universal public good. Since all benefit, all pay according to their means. Third, the federal government deals in macroprograms with millions of clients and has about 100 million taxpayers: numbers that defy the application of benefit-based taxation in most cases. Lastly, national economic policy has been heavily influenced by theorists inclined toward ability to pay taxation, and even the advocates of benefit taxation would concede that calculating benefits might not be worth the cost on the federal level.

THE FEDERAL FINANCIAL SETTING

The financial managers of government, particularly those at the federal level, tend to look at the big picture. Unlike budgeteers who, although also concerned with larger objectives, cannot help but get involved in pluralistic bargaining over program specifics, financial managers stay a bit more aloof. They are concerned, first and foremost, with macroeconomic effects. That is, the manner in which government's projected expenditure totals and anticipated gross revenues (1) contribute to the economic growth of the country; (2) achieve a given distribution of income among the citizenry; and (3) enhance the efficient utilization of human and physical resources. At this initial, holistic, and number-laden phase, pluralism is somewhat muted but ready to spring. The expenditure total, of course, is the budget writ large. The revenue total will be comprised of a myriad of taxes benefiting some and penalizing others. However, when the financial managers make their initial calculations, many expenditure and revenue particulars are unresolved. When they are later worked out in executive conclaves and the halls of Congress, pluralism reasserts itself. However, even at the initial, highly esoteric stages, a theoretical pluralism is operative. Quite simply, there is an earnest, heated, and indecisive debate between economic policy makers who label themselves *Keynesians* and those identified as *monetarists*. Since it is important to be aware of these two perspectives, a brief review is in order.

The Keynesian Approach

Economic growth and the efficient societywide allocation of resources are relatively new goals of conscious public policy. Prior to the 1930s, government saw itself as a parsimonious service provider collecting taxes to the extent of expenditures—no more and no less. It was the era of the balanced budget, and government noninterference with the marketplace was the reigning economic philosophy, if not always the practice. Then in 1936, John Maynard Keynes, a British economist, stood the governmental world on its ear with the publication of *The General Theory of Employment, Interest and Money*.[13] Keynes's radical proposition was that service provision was not the major purpose of national government activity. According to Keynes, the budget and all of the financial activities of government were devices for stimulating the demand for goods and services throughout society. Lack of demand, Keynes asserted, was the root cause of economic depression. Low demand meant idle workers and resources. Unemployment exacerbated the demand deficiency, and the sight of idle plants drove investors into hiding. Keynes, writing during the heart of the Great Depression and surrounded, as it were, by evidence, stated that the low demand-unemployment-noninvestment spiral could bring a nation to economic depths and keep it there. A lot of people in the United States were listening, and with the Employment Act of 1946, Keynesian economics, already influential among financial decision makers, was formally introduced. The act called for the reduction of unemployment, created the Council of Economic Advisors in the Office of the President, and transformed government from a passive observer of the economic scene to an active intervener.[14]

Keynes's prescription for national government—one that was not fully embraced in this country until the 1960s—was to discard the notion of a balanced budget. According to Keynes, a balanced budget during economic downturns could only deepen the slide. When tax receipts fall, as they do during recessions, effecting a balanced budget requires a reduction in expenditures or, in other words, an additional dose of economic depressant. Thus, Keynes recommended exactly the opposite course, deficit spending, to combat a depressed economy. Cutting taxes and increasing expenditures would give consumers and investors more spending power. Demand would rise; investor confidence would be restored; and more workers would be hired to handle the resultant economic activity. Just as the economy spiraled downward in depressions, the upward boost provided by demand stimulation was, to a certain degree, self-sustaining. A $10 tax reduction for Joe Smith meant a little extra disposable cash for the butcher, the tailor, and the grocer. Similarly, wholesalers supplying the local merchants would reap, and partly spend, a bit more income. This was the "multiplier effect" of economic stimulation, and in macroterms, a little more employment all along the line meant a sizable nationwide drop in the jobless rate.[15]

In Keynesian terms, there is a limit to economic recovery; a point at which the cure becomes the disease. If the demand generated by government economic policy exceeds the economy's capacity to provide goods and services, inflation results. Consumers, by demanding more than the country can conceivably produce, bid up prices. Workers demand and get higher salaries because their services are difficult to replace and necessary if the employer is to meet product demand. Producers, chugging away at capacity, scramble to purchase raw materials that, as a result, also increase in price. With lenders wary of price spirals that will erode the value of their money, the cost of borrowing increases as well.

Keynesians had an answer for inflation. It was demand management. When demand exceeds the productive capacity of the nation's economy, Keynesians recommended that the antidepression remedy be reversed. Taxes were to be increased. Alternatively, or concurrently, government expenditures were to be reduced. For firms and individuals, decreased budget flows and increased taxation meant a lower income. Thus, through the multiplier effect, demand would moderate to a level consonant with the productive capacity of the nation.

The Monetarist Approach

Upon succeeding the balanced budget approach in the 1950s, demand management became the touchstone of federal fiscal policy. Even non-Keynesian economists accepted government's role in regulating the economy. Nonetheless, not everyone worshipped the Keynesian gospel. In the 1960s, a small dissident band of "monetarist" economists was led by Milton Friedman.[16] At the crux of the monetarist-Keynesian schism was the money supply. Monetarists, like Keynesians, believed that, in response to fiscal stimulation, consumers would spend most of their additional dollars. However, the monetarists charged that Keynesians, by underestimating the number of transactions generated by new dollars, injected more purchasing power into the economy than its productive capacity could handle; in a word, inflation. Inflation, monetarists held, was more serious than unemployment. Moreover, monetarists warned, even with slack production capacity, firms could not always be relied on to produce more goods in response to additional demand. If they did not, of course, unemployment would not be reduced either.

To monetarists, demand stimulation was more than ineffectual; it was a culture that could nurture the disease of inflation. With a constant supply of goods and services, and eager consumers with extra cash, prices would be bid up. When this happened, according to the monetarists, the stage was set for a wage-price spiral; the most damaging and uncontrollable form of inflation. The collective American consumer would get the same amount of product but pay more; the same consumers, as workers, would demand more wages to maintain their standard of living; producers would close the circle by granting the wage requests and further raising prices. While on the surface this appears to balance out, inflation has winners and losers. The winners are the producers and workers who can raise prices or win higher wages (without producing more) in order to keep pace with inflation. On the losing side, the standard of living for those on fixed incomes, including the unemployed who were not helped by demand stimulation, goes steadily down.

For the most part, the monetarist indictment was summarily dismissed in the 1960s. By the 1970s, however, there was new evidence. Economic recession, high unemployment, and rapid inflation made a simultaneous appearance in defiance of Keynesian precepts. Defensively, Keynesians viewed the situation as an aberration, and true enough, the early 1970s showed plenty of mutational potential. There were Arab oil boycotts, Vietnam withdrawals, world food shortages, and a host of other happenings capable of derailing well-laid plans and sound theories. Unfortunately for the Keynesians, the mess defied analysis, and the results, if not the reasons, were consonant with monetarist predictions.

With Keynesian antidotes for economic distress apparently failing, attention turned to monetarist remedies that, Doctor Friedman admitted, were harsh but unavoidable after years of malpractice.[17] Monetarist proposals included tax increases, short- and long-term decreases in government expenditures, and an eventual return to the balanced budget. At that point, and increasingly during the transition, *fiscal policy*— budget deficits and surpluses—was to be replaced as an economic governor by *monetary policy*—direct control of the dollars in circulation. Other monetarist proposals to restore price stability included a lower minimum wage and a less dominant role for unions in the fixing of employment terms. As side effects, the monetarists predicted extended periods of high unemployment and low economic growth lasting until the effects of the government's diminished role and increased fiscal responsibility took hold.

During the mid-1970s, even Keynesians were edging away from the demand stimulation/full-employment approach.[18] Some called for renewed wage-price controls. Others admitted that even the maintenance of full employment levels appeared prone to inflationary levels of economic growth.[19] Therefore, going from high unemployment (8 percent) to full employment (4 percent) would require a multiyear regimen of delicate and gradual stimulation. Although the Keynesian-monetarist debate was not settled as he began his term, President Carter seemed inclined to experiment with monetarist approaches. For instance, he promised to balance the budget through expenditure reductions by 1980. On the other hand, the president also supported an increase in the minimum wage. One suspects that the two economic management approaches will be with us for some time with monetarism enjoying considerably more real world applications than in the past.

THE NATIONAL ECONOMIC POLICY PROCESS: EXECUTIVE STYLE

Anyone who sets out to study the making of economic policy would be well-advised to bring a scorecard. Congress versus the president is but the beginning. The Federal Reserve Board also can challenge the president on fiscal policy. Moreover, the headline "Presidential Advisors Bicker on Economy" likely refers to the chairman of the Council of Economic Advisors, the secretary of the treasury and the director of OMB. All three have to run the gauntlet of the president's Domestic Policy Staff where analysts can modify policy proposals. Even spectators can score points. The Brookings Institution, a private thinktank, has a formidable array of economists who have influenced economic policy during Republican administrations and have come on board to formulate it during Democratic regimes. The up-and-coming American Enterprise Institute, a bit more monetarist, serves as a bullpen for Republican administrations.

The formulators, if anything, are outnumbered by the implementers. To begin with, all federal agencies are employment-providing users of land and capital. Then, there are tax collecting agencies, of which the IRS is but one. Borrowing is the province of the Treasury Department and the Federal Finance Bank. Looking for a loan? Start with the Small Business Administration, the Veterans Administration or the Federal Home Loan Bank Board. The Treasury Department borrows and lends—in mind-boggling amounts. This list is not exhaustive, but you get the idea.

Of this array, four organizations stand out as a major force in setting and carrying out the nation's economic policy. They are the *Council of Economic Advisors,* the *Treasury Department,* the *Federal Reserve Board* and the *Office of Management and Budget.* OMB evaluates the economic impact of existing and proposed federal programs as a part of the budget process that was detailed in Chapter 9. The remaining three agencies are profiled below.

The Council of Economic Advisors   The *Council of Economic Advisors* (*CEA*) was established by the Employment Act of 1946. The act authorized government intervention in the economy and provided for an office of economic experts to help the president formulate policy. The council was charged with analyzing the economy, monitoring the effect of fiscal policy, and preparing the president's economic report to Congress. Through the years, CEA influence has varied. Dynamic CEA chairpersons, such as a Walter Heller during the Kennedy and Johnson years, have had a profound impact. After 20 years of halfhearted efforts, Heller moved national economic policy into unabashed Keynesianism. "Full-employment budgets" featured stimulative deficits and produced "fiscal dividends"—increased tax revenues from heightened economic activity—corresponding to Heller's predictions.[20] Although Heller's approach fared less well as the Vietnam war and inflation intensified, he had shown that the council could assume a major role in economic policy making.

The Treasury Department   From time to time, the secretary of the treasury, rather than the chairperson of the Council of Economic Advisors, looms as the chief economic adviser to the president. During the Nixon and Ford administrations, Treasury Secretary William Simon was highly influential. Actually, in light of the Treasury Department's day-to-day management of the government's economic affairs, it is not surprising that the secretary can supplant presidential advisers whose baliwick is analysis rather than action. The Treasury Department collects the preponderance of federal revenues. It is the central accounting office for all executive expenditures. The Treasury Department also manages the public debt and prints our money.

The Treasury Department's chores are not merely housekeeping ones. It can siphon money from the economy. The U.S. Savings Bond is a familiar mechanism, but the savings plan for banks, featuring million dollar treasury notes, is a more potent economic force. The Treasury Department's Comptroller of the Currency regulates banking practices and can have a long-term impact on the way money moves about in the economy. Being on top of the nation's tax system also gives the secretary of the treasury considerable leverage in U.S. tax policy.

The secretary of the treasury also has international stature. As a member of the International Monetary Fund and the International Bank for Reconstruction and Development, among others, the treasury secretary is viewed abroad as the chief spokesperson for U.S. economic policy. At home, the growing importance of international economic developments, such as rising oil prices and the standing of the U.S. currency in world trade, enhance the standing of the secretary as a presidential adviser.

The Federal Reserve System   "Ours is the responsibility to act in the monetary area, and we intend to exercise that responsibility in ways that promote the long run, as well as the immediate, interests of the nation."[21]

With this statement, Arthur Burns declined to commit the "Fed" to economic policies desired by President Carter. As chairperson of the Federal Reserve Board, Burns's wants were at least as good as the president's wishes. The "Fed," an independent body, is not subject to presidential directives. Although the chairperson is a presidential appointee, the two terms do not coincide, and Burns, a Republican holdover, was solid through 1977. Moreover, the president's choice requires Senate approval, and Burns was not without support in that body. Although Burns eventually was replaced by an appointee more in tune with Carter's fiscal philosophy, the "Fed" always has the potential to play an independent role in economic policy making.

The Federal Reserve System was originally created to back up the nation's banks. In the halcyon days of go-for-broke banking, all deposits were loaned out on occasion. When this occurred, a few large defaults or withdrawals could render the bank unable to pay depositors on demand. Naturally, this led to depositor panics, mattress banking, reduced investment, economic downturn, and a rapacious image for bankrupt financiers and their more solvent cousins. Thus, in 1913, the Federal Reserve System was created and was given three tools for regulating bank behavior. These tools, which have become far more important as economic governors than as banking backstops, are: (1) *Reserve requirement;* (2) *Federal funds rate;* and (3) *Open market activity.* Let us take a look at each.

> *Reserve Requirement*   Every member bank must keep a percentage of its deposits in a Federal Reserve Bank account. The initial purpose of the reserve requirement was to guard against banks overextending themselves. Over time the reserve requirement began to be used with an eye towards economic impacts. Simply, if the Federal Reserve System wished to reduce the amount of money available for lending, it raised the reserve requirement. To put more money into circulation, the reserve requirement was lowered.
>
> *Federal Funds Rate*   At the close of every business day, banks must have the required reserves on deposit with the Federal Reserve Bank. Banking, however, remains a hectic business; because of accounts closed out, investments gone sour, or an upsurge in demand for loans, the reserve requirement may not be met. When this happens, the deficiency must be covered by a di-

rect loan from the "Fed" or by borrowing from another bank with excess reserves. The rate for this borrowing is the *federal funds rate*. In effect, this rate is the minimum rate for all commercial borrowing in the country. If the federal funds rate rises, borrowing should drop and so should the money in circulation. If the rate drops, loans (investments) should increase, as should the money supply.

Open Market Activity   Besides being a repository and a lender, the Federal Reserve dabbles in the treasury bill market. It sells treasury bills to the banks; it buys them back. In each case, the terms usually are attractive enough to assure the desired transaction. Thus, by selling treasury bills, the Federal Reserve takes cash out of circulation. Conversely, the money supply is increased when the "Fed" buys.

Thus, the Federal Reserve Bank can expand or contract the supply of money by taking the following steps:

CONTRACT (TIGHT MONEY)	EXPAND (EASY MONEY)
Raise reserve requirement	Lower reserve requirement
Raise federal funds rate	Lower federal funds rate
Sell treasury bills and other securities	Buy treasury bills & other securities

This is the imposing arsenal of economic weapons that is at the disposal of the chairpersons of the Federal Reserve Board in their role as head of the bank's Open Market Committee. As we have seen, this committee is not at the disposal of the president. When and if a rift occurs, the presidential *fiscal policy*—revenues, expenditures, and the target deficit or surplus—may be neutralized by the Federal Reserve Board's *monetary policy*—the mixture of reserve requirement, the federal funds rate, and the open market posture. Thus, a presidential tax break to business to promote investment may be nullified by a discouragingly high rate of interest arising from Federal Reserve Board actions.

TAX LEGISLATION

The executive branch may be the home of Keynesian economics, and the Federal Reserve Bank may be a powerful bastion of monetarist restraint. However, the acid test for any economic policy still takes place in the Congress. Expenditure totals and specifics must be approved by Congress. Only the Congress has the power to levy taxes. In Congress, the technical arguments of presidential economists, Treasury Department tax experts, and Federal Reserve Board money supply wizards confront the crucible of interest group politics.

We have already discussed the congressional expenditure process, and in many respects, the taxation process is similar. However, to a degree, tax policy can elicit a bigger display of interest group muscle than expenditure policy. Most tax proposals do not affect one industry, specific workers, or the sale of certain items. Hiking the corporate income tax is likely to get the entire business and investment community up in arms. By virtue of their position, some 100 million drivers and the powerful transportation industry are members of the lobby against increases in the gasoline tax. Such numbers make for intense and powerful lobbying in the halls of Congress. Moreover, if broader arguments fail, equally intense but more concentrated pressure can be exerted to exempt specific groups from the new tax.

The congressional tax process begins when presidential tax initiatives are presented to Congress in January or February. The president, or a surrogate, may use several media: The State of the Union message; the following year's budget submission; the Economic Report of the President; or a special tax message. Whether one or more presentation modes are used, a tax bill must follow. And, since all revenue bills must originate in the House, that is where it goes. The first stop is the Ways and Means Committee. There, the traditional advocate for the administration's position and the first witness is the secretary of the treasury. What happens next is captured with remarkable conciseness by Joseph Pechman:

> the committee may hear witnesses from . . . the Office of Management and Budget . . . the Council of Economic Advisors and the Federal Reserve Board. Testimony is then heard from bankers, businessmen, lawyers, economists, and others representing the interests of private groups (and sometimes of individual clients). Except when the administration's witnesses testify, the broader "public interest" is not well represented. In recent years (1970s), representatives of public-interest organizations have begun to appear . . . but the preponderance of the testimony is from special interest groups. Meanwhile, the committee members are besieged in private by large numbers of people seeking changes in the bill. The length of the hearings depends on the importance of the bill, the controversy it has aroused, and the positions of the committee chairman and ranking members. If there is considerable opposition, the hearings may continue for months.[22]

The Ways and Means Committee is the primary House battleground. Contained specialization (see Chapter 9) is, more or less of necessity, at work. Tax bills can approach a thousand pages, and as anyone who has ever read IRS tax instructions might suspect, the material is complex and technical. The members and staff of the Ways and Means Committee, with the ability to decode the technicalities and wade through the complexities, become the House experts on tax matters. As

Pechman writes: "Only on rare occasions has a major tax bill reported by the Ways and Means Committee been rejected by the House."[23]

On the Senate side, the Finance Committee gets first crack at tax bills emerging from the House. The parade of witnesses before the Ways and Means Committee usually reassembles for the Senate Finance Committee. In the Senate, where contained specialization is less of a factor, Finance Committee recommendations are often amended from the floor. As in budgeting, appellants petition senators for last ditch commutations from forthcoming tax burdens. The supplicants are likely to include White House advisers seeking to salvage endangered presidential policies and prestige. When the Senate passes its tax legislation, a Senate-House conference committee is convened if there is a disparity between the two versions.[24] When the differences are ironed out, a tax law emerges from Congress for the president to sign. As with the budget, the signature is not often withheld.

Tax Guidelines

In this country, there are certain benchmarks against which proposed taxes are measured. For any tax, we ask the following questions. Is it equitable? Is it easy to administer? Does it distort marketplace decisions?

Before proceeding, it must be noted that these questions pertain to the United States. Other countries, for ideological or structural reasons, may approach taxation differently. For instance, noninterference with the marketplace would certainly not loom large as a criterion in a socialist country. Similarly, easy administration and equity may be luxuries that the less-developed country cannot afford.[25] Visible wealth—property, livestock, machinery—may be the only calculable tax base and must be used even though administratively cumbersome, prone to corruption and inequitable. Tax assessors who take inventory can be bribed, and those engaged in commerce "off-the-books"—workers, money lenders, bazaar merchants—can evade taxation. Nonetheless, the tax administrator in a less-developed country must take what is available or give up the chase. Lest we feel superior, "Who will offer the least resistance?" may serve as a tax policy question in this country more often than we think. Be that as it may, let us look now at our tax policy benchmarks: *administrative efficiency, equity,* and *marketplace neutrality.*

Administrative efficiency This is rather straightforward. Cutting administrative costs frees more taxes for the production of public goods and services. A companion goal is a tax system that is understandable to the average taxpayer. Clarity reduces taxpayer frustration and allays the suspicion that others, able to hire experts to navigate the process, fare better. Efficiency and clarity go together in that low-cost administration requires voluntary compliance arising out of a belief in the equity of the tax system.

Equity Equity is the touchstone criterion for United States tax policy. However, as one might expect, equity, a macrocultural concept embodying a world of meaning, poses definitional problems. No one, after all, proposes "inequitable" taxes. Equity, as it is used to measure tax policy, relies heavily on the *ability to pay principle*. That principle is presumed to be equitable. Thus, the twin measures of a good tax become *horizontal equity*—those similarly situated pay the same tax—and *vertical equity*—those who are well off pay a proportionately higher tax than those who are not. As a closer examination will show, these two concepts are extremely useful as measuring rods.

Horizontal equity addresses the evenhandedness of a tax. If two individuals are earning an identical amount but one pays a higher tax, horizontal equity is apparently compromised. However, further analysis may show that one taxpayer has seven children and the other is single. Therefore, since their income equality masks a real disparity in liabilities and overall financial condition, horizontal equity is not violated. Alternatively, analysis may show similar family situations. However, the taxpayer with a $300 a month mortgage (tax deductible, in part) pays a lower tax than the one who rents a $300 a month (nondeductible) apartment. In this case, with similar incomes and expenses, horizontal equity is violated when tax liabilities differ.

Vertical equity measures a tax against the ability to pay criteria. An ability to pay tax scale is pretty much an arbitrary formulation. Can a low-income person afford to pay a 15 percent tax? Should middle-income persons pay a 30 percent rate and 8 percent of the value of their property? Do we charge a Rockefeller 70 percent or 91 percent? There is no scientific answer to these questions. However, the broad outlines of vertical equity are not in dispute. Vertical equity is met when the tax system is *progressive;* that is, when the tax rates are higher for the rich than for the poor. Vertical equity is violated when the tax system is *proportional;* that is, when the tax rates are the same for everyone. Vertical equity is severely violated when the tax system is *regressive;* that is, when the poor pay a higher tax rate than the rich.

Marketplace neutrality This tax criterion has theoretical roots in the *benefit principle.* Under pure benefit taxation each individual would get, and pay for, exactly the amount of public goods desired. Since the cash remaining after the purchase of public goods would be exactly what the individual had intended to save or to spend on private goods, the marketplace would be unaffected. Despite this theoretical elegance, benefit-based taxation is administratively expensive; the pure form is likely unachievable; and the ability to pay principle is widely accepted. Nonetheless, with respect to business firms, our tax policies take possible marketplace distortions into account. For instance, federal taxation is proportional for all corporations making over $50,000. Thus, the tax does not upset marketplace results by rewarding incompetent firms and penalizing successful ones through a progressive system. In general, neutrality in the business marketplace is achieved if all firms and all industries are affected equally by a tax.

Tax Shifting: A Dilemma for Policy Makers

Tax guidelines are fine if you can determine who pays a given tax. However, this is not always easy. If you impose a tax on a landlord, rents may be raised a corresponding amount. The employer portion of social security and unemployment taxes may be borne by workers through lower salaries or by consumers through higher prices. GM's corporate tax may be paid by car purchasers rather than stockholders. In all of these cases, tax shifting is a possibility.

Tax shifting occurs when the nominal taxpayer does not bear the ultimate cost of a tax. When shifting is involved, measuring a tax against equity and marketplace neutrality guidelines requires a determination of *tax incidence*. That is, the ultimate payers of the tax must be identified. The questions of tax shifting and tax incidence are crucial ones for tax policy. The dilemma for the policy maker is that they are not easy ones to resolve. For some taxes, there is wide disagreement as to whether shifting occurs. Even when it is agreed that the tax has been shifted, there is often a dispute about who eventually pays. Therefore, the equity and marketplace impacts of a tax remain highly uncertain in many cases.[26]

Four Federal Taxes

We will look at specific federal taxes from several of the above perspectives. Taxes will be viewed as tools of economic management and measured against the administrative, equity, and marketplace criteria. We will note if questions of tax incidence fog the picture. The object is not so much to give you a detailed knowledge of the taxes mentioned as to acquaint you with the issues central to tax policy. With this in mind, let us take a look at the personal income tax, the corporate income tax, the payroll (social security) tax, and the excise tax.

Personal Income Tax   The personal income tax has been called the "nation's fairest and most productive source of revenue."[27] It accounts for one-third of all taxes collected in the United States and generates almost half of the federal government's revenues. Administrative costs, as a percentage of collections, hover around 1 percent; tax leakage is minimized through payroll withholding. Income is broadly defined; and interest, dividends, capital gains, and other income sources are subject to taxation. In overall structure, the personal income tax is designed to achieve vertical and horizontal equity. Tax rates are based on income, and the percentage ranges from 14 percent to 70 percent as one's income rises from the nether regions to the $100,000-plus class. Moreover, in determining income, allowances are made for extraordinary financial burdens that may have befallen the taxpayer in the course of a year. Medical expenses are deductible; uninsured property losses are also.

With wide coverage and weekly withholding, the income tax is useful as a stabilization tool. A tax cut can put large amounts of money into circulation and stoke up demand. A tax increase does the opposite. Moreover, since the tax is paid weekly through withholding, the impact of tax stabilization measures are felt quickly. In addition, the progressive structure of the personal income tax acts as an automatic stabilizer. As individual incomes drop during economic downturns, the tax bite goes down even farther. Thus, a person's ability to purchase goods and services does not drop as precipitously as personal income. Upsurges in demand due to income jumps are also muted by the progressive tax structure. Approximately 40 percent of salary increases that put individuals in higher brackets goes to taxes.

Automatic stabilizers, however, can break down during inflation. Let us consider, for instance, a typical student income, a common student diet, and for clarity, a hypothetical inflation rate and tax structure. Before inflation, a $50 income taxed at 10 percent could purchase 45 one-dollar hamburgers. However, if inflation doubled wages and prices, but progressive tax rates remained unchanged, a $100 income taxed at 20 percent could only buy 40 two-dollar hamburgers. Real purchasing power has dropped by 11 percent. Since legislators are understandably reluctant to reduce their constituents' standards of living, rebates or increased exemption and deduction allowances often are enacted to protect inflation-threatened purchasing power.

Tax shifting is not a major concern with respect to the personal income tax. However, the question of *tax erosion* is. Erosion occurs when income is excluded from the taxable base. Some of the income exclusions associated with the income tax are universal and fairly noncontroversial. For supporting a dependent through the year, $750 is removed from the tax base. Much of the money spent on health care is deducted from taxable income. There are, however, deductions and exemptions that apply only to certain classes of taxpayers—stockholders, homeowners, municipal bondholders. According to most observers, these deductions dilute the horizontal and vertical equity of the personal income tax.

Once called tax preferences, deductions and expenditures that erode the tax base are now known as *tax expenditures*. In part, the new name is reflective of the trend toward viewing expenditures and revenues together. Thus, exemptions and deductions began to be seen as allocations of funds—tax expenditures—that could be made through the budget process. As a result, the value of tax exemptions to the beneficiaries must now be included in the budget the president submits even though the tax system remains the distribution medium. Some illustrative tax expenditures for 1978 were:

$6 billion for the holders of state and municipal bonds;
$7 billion for those who contributed to charity;
$10 billion to homeowners.[28]

These are startling figures for items (interest deductions, property tax deductions, charitable contributions) that had long been considered idiosyncrasies of the tax structure.

Occasionally, tax expenditures have a pinpoint aim. Although the one-person tax amendment is rare today, it was common in the 1950s and 1960s, and the story of the "Louis B. Mayer amendment," drawn from that era, is a tax break classic. Mayer, about to retire as head of MGM Studios, had reservations about his severance pay—a percentage of the profits for the next five years. In the volatile movie industry, this was a highly uncertain nest egg. Therefore, Mayer requested, and the studio agreed to, a lump-sum cash payment. However, this would have subjected Mayer to the highest tax rate (91 percent) prevailing at the time. So, off went an emissary to Congress; the result was "Taxability to Employees of Termination Payments," an abstruse mouthful that amended the tax law so that lump-sum termination payments were treated as a capital gain and taxed at a rate of 25 percent. This amendment to the tax law bestowed on Louis B. Mayer, who was to be its sole beneficiary, a $2 million tax expenditure.[29]

Whether or not tax expenditures have an exclusive list of beneficiaries—and some in the corporate area still do—the cost to nonbeneficiaries is high. It has been estimated that the elimination of tax expenditures could lead to a 30 percent across-the-board reduction in tax rates.[30] Thus, tax expenditures can violate horizontal equity as is the case when homeowners and renters with identical salaries and family situations pay a different tax. Vertical equity is also violated since many deductions are more valuable and often only available to the wealthy. Erosion can also shake the citizens' confidence in the fairness of the entire tax system, particularly since tax expenditures also are made through the property tax and the sales tax.

Corporate Income Tax The corporate income tax is the third largest generator of federal revenues, ranking behind the personal income tax and the payroll tax. As a flat-rate impost on corporate profits (48 percent for $50,000+; 20–22 percent for less than $50,000),[31] it is easy to administer. The tax directly taps an income-producing source and, moreover, reaches income, "retained earnings," that might otherwise be sequestered. Marketplace equity and neutrality are achieved to some degree. Although the firm that bounces back from a bad year may carry over losses and, as a result, keep a larger share of future profits, the rate structure is not a progressive one that distorts the market and penalizes success and rewards failure. As might be expected, the corporate tax expenditure is not unknown, and defense contractors seem particularly adept at winning them.[32]

Although the corporate tax is one of our oldest and most established taxes, there are a few who advocate its elimination. Moreover, because of an unresolved question concerning tax shifting, the call comes from two quarters. One faction sees the tax as onerous to stockholders. First, the corporate tax chops the stockholders' return on investment by 48 percent. Then, when dividends are paid from the remaining 52 percent, personal income taxes are levied at the rate applicable to the individual stockholder. As a result, critics charge, corporations are rendered unattractive vis-à-vis other investment possibilities. On the other side of the argument are those who point out that corporate America is reasonably well nourished by investment and has maintained a steady diet through periods of higher and lower tax rates. From this point of view, the consumer pays because management treats the tax as a cost of doing business and incorporates it into the price of the product.[33]

Upon the "consumer-stockholder" debate rests a determination of the vertical equity of the corporate income tax. If stockholders bear the brunt of the tax, it is slightly progressive. If consumers pay the tax, it is regressive. Either way, the corporate income tax is likely to persist. It helps regulate business conduct; it exacts payment for corporate benefits derived from public goods; it is a potential medium for charging the costs of negative externalities to their corporate producers; and it is a well-established money maker.

Payroll Taxes   Payroll taxes are the second largest source of federal revenues. As the name indicates, salaries and wages provide the tax base for the payroll tax. Social security, the first program funded by payroll deductions, continues to be the primary recipient of such taxes.

As a fixed-rate paycheck deduction, the social security tax is easy to administer. However, for economic regulation, the flat-rate, single-bracketed deduction is unwieldy. On equity grounds, the tax is shaky indeed. Investment income, far more important to the higher economic classes than the lower, is exempt. Moreover, as of 1977, the social security tax (5.85 percent for employees; 5.85 percent for employers) was levied only against the first $16,500 of one's wages. Thus, as one's income exceeded that figure, the effective tax rate was reduced.

As with the corporate tax, there is a debate over who pays the payroll tax. However, whatever side one subscribes to, vertical equity is again a loser. At issue is whether employers shift their share of the tax to the workers or consumers.[34] (There is general agreement that the employer does not pay.) If employees pay their share of social security taxes through payroll deductions *and* their employer's share through lower wage rates, an already regressive situation is exacerbated. Vertical equity also is diluted if consumers indirectly pay the employer's social security tax. Taxes implicitly or explicitly tied to consumption extract a greater percentage from the poor—who spend a higher proportion of their income—than from the rich.

Social security taxes are earmarked; they go only to the aged, widows and widowers, and other specified beneficiaries. Although designated as Social Security Insurance, social security tax reserves are inadequate for the maintenance of a true insurance fund, and most of the taxes go rapidly back out as payments to beneficiaries. In the process, a good deal of the social security tax's regressivity is balanced. As a percentage of total income, social security payments benefit the low-income aged more than the affluent. In relation to social security taxes paid during one's working years, retirement benefits are proportionately higher for those with low, lifetime contributions than for those who paid the maximum tax throughout.

Excise Taxes Excises are taxes on goods and services. They account for 6 percent of federal revenues. Excise taxes are imposed at the manufacturing or wholesale level (e.g., whiskey) or at retail (e.g., gasoline taxes). Because of fewer collection points, excise taxes on manufacturers and wholesalers are easier to administer than the retail variety. Regardless of whether the manufacturer, wholesaler, or retailer pays initially, the consumer pays the tax in the end. Thus, excise taxes are regressive. As a percentage of income, the poor pay more.

Three points concerning federal excise taxes are worth remembering. First, international trade relations affect excise taxes. Imports from friendly countries may be taxed gently. Imports that threaten U.S. industries may be taxed heavily. In either case, "friendly" and "threatening" are likely to have been defined largely in the arena of interest group politics. Second, federal excise taxes are occasionally earmarked. Federal gasoline taxes, for instance, go to the multibillion dollar Highway Trust Fund.

Third, the excise tax is the mechanism for the "sumptuary" levy—that is, taxes designed to render vices that are immune from prohibition more expensive. Alcoholic beverages and cigarettes are chock-full of excise taxes. Indeed, in some states, taxes may be added at the manufacturing level (federal), the wholesale point (state), and the checkout counter (state, municipal, or county sales). Most users could not care less. The demand for alcohol, tobacco, and gasoline is not very responsive to price. It is no wonder then that taxing authorities may prefer sumptuary increases to tax hikes that are partially negated by reduced purchases or workers declining overtime to avoid a higher tax bracket.

THE FEDERAL
FINANCIAL PICTURE: AN OVERVIEW

As we have seen, the federal government manages its financial picture through numerous actors and multiple mechanisms to reach several goals. Presidential economic policy is formulated by several agencies—The Council of Economic Advisors, the Office of Management and Budget, and the Treasury Department. Also powerful on the executive level is the substantially autonomous Federal Reserve Board. Outside thinktanks, such as the Brookings Institution and the American Enterprise Institute, are also influential. The Congress, still heavily reliant on contained specialization for tax matters and jealously guarding its constitutional role as originator of revenue legislation and allocator of operating funds, is a powerful force in federal government finance. Interest groups often impact at executive and legislative levels but, for tax matters, concentrate on Congress.

The mechanisms at the disposal of the president, the Congress, and the Federal Reserve Board are powerful shapers of the economy. They include the provision of public goods, income transfers, interest rate controls and tax devices: any or all of which can slow the economy down or speed it up; bestow benefits or exact penalties; or pursue a wide range of specific public policy objectives.

The objectives of federal financial policy—the efficient allocation of goods and resources, an equitable distribution of income, and economic stabilization—are not always compatible. However, the right mix of efficiency and equity, and a tranquil economic environment is the goal of most financial policy makers even though their definition of right may differ. Thus, the incremental process—where agreement, rather than righteousness, is the measure of policy success—is well represented by this multiplicity of actors, mechanisms, and goals.

THE FEDERAL FINANCIAL PICTURE: A CRITIQUE

There are, of course, plenty of things to criticize in the financial policy-making process at the federal level. Depending on where one stands, one can rail at the special treatment given to Louis B. Mayer; complain over the astronomical rise in social security withholding tax; decry the "them that gots, gets" result arising from tax free bonds; blast the work disincentives of transfer payments; or wonder why bankers' interests should be embodied in the Federal Reserve Board. If you want to yell loud and long, there are books that will provide sufficient grist for any of the above.[35] Here, however, we would like to touch briefly on criticisms that see the current system as a deficient means of national economic planning.

With our "riotous pluralism" as operative in economic planning as in other spheres, certain problems arise.[36] Economic stabilizers, for instance, often are instituted too late. By the time that a tax decrease to stimulate spending emerges from Congress, a spending upsurge already may be underway. What results is not more employment, the original goal, but inflation, a disease to be treated with tax cuts, not increases. To achieve more timely applications of fiscal remedies, it has been proposed that the president be empowered to raise or lower taxes, on a temporary basis, without congressional approval. Congress, not surprisingly, demurred. Impoundment, often rationalized by presidents as necessary for cooling down the economy, has been struck down by the courts. Thus, on both taxes and expenditures, congressional prerogatives have prevailed over presidential attempts to centralize economic planning.

In 1974, following judicial and self-assertions of its independent role, Congress sought to bring more coherence to its own economic policy making by creating the Congressional Budget Office (CBO) and Budget Committees for the joint consideration of taxes and expenditures. Nonetheless, the overarching adversarial nature of the public policy-making process and the numerous agencies impacting on one or another area of economic activity remain problematic. National economic planning, notes one observer, will not come until we can achieve "horizontal integration" with government, business, and labor viewing themselves as partners, not adversaries, in the determination of economic policy.[37] While "co-determinism" has made strides in Western European countries with a longer history of central planning, the United States may be another matter.[38]

National planning in the United States is hampered by more than an adversarial, tripartite breakdown between business, labor, and government. Often, there is a jealous guarding of territory, industry by industry, that is reinforced by alliances formed with government agencies. General Motors does not talk with General Foods, for example, and the Department of Transportation keeps its distance from the Department of Agriculture. However, the alignments that can arise between General Motors and the Department of Transportation and General

Foods and the Department of Agriculture can be vertical bastions impervious to the information-seeking assaults of the national economic planner.

Of course, if Balkanized institutional arrangements cannot be analyzed, they can be outflanked. Macroeconomics does this and, despite some poor showings, continues to do so, in part, because it need not consider the specifics of an industry. However, aggregate demand, employment, and investment—although they reduce complexity and provide a useful handle—may mask important facts and, moreover, rest on assumptions that could stand reevaluation. We have become resource conscious and with good reason. National planning of the future may concern itself more with industry by industry utilization of natural resources, and how such usage fits in with an overall economic plan. The "market" may also be disaggregated with closer study given to monopoly, oligopoly, and institutionalized, nonprofit-seeking behavior as a major factor in corporate responses to national economic policy. In any event, government and the economy are not likely to move off of the front pages for very long at any time in the foreseeable future.

THE STATE AND
LOCAL FINANCIAL ENVIRONMENT

State and local finance is radically different from the federal variety, and the distinctions provide a good jumping off point for discussion. Thus, we shall briefly note the administrative, demographic, electoral, constitutional, and theoretical factors that set states and localities apart from the federal government. Next, we will note two opposing viewpoints on future directions for subnational administration. One approach favors administrative consolidation and service equalization, while the other supports continued, and even increased, diversity in localized government services. Revenue sharing, which partically accommodates both philosophies, will be discussed. In addition, we will review selected state and local taxing and borrowing tools.

Multiple Jurisdictions   As noted above, one critique of federal fiscal policy is aimed at the fragmentation of policy-making authority, the dispersal of the tools of economic governance, and the paucity of joint planning within government and between the public and private sector. For those who subscribe to this point of view, the federal government is a model of coherence when contrasted with state and local governments. They are multitudinous, numbering close to 80,000.[39] States contain counties, and counties contain towns and municipalities, although some of the largest cities contain, or overlap with, several counties. The real overlap champions, however, are school districts and special districts.

There are nearly 40,000 cutting hither and yon.[40] The small ones cover a few towns; the medium-sized ones span counties; the giants can cover an entire state, and a few transcend state borders. Almost all possess some degree of autonomy from municipal, county, and state governments.

The Service Mandate   In this country, most public goods and services are delivered by state and local governments. Indeed, a great deal of federal expenditures reach clients by way of state and local authorities. Federal funds account for much of a welfare recipient's allotment, but the locality handles most of the spadework through eligibility determinations, lost check verifications, and the like. Many state expenditures also are disbursed through local mechanisms. Of course, police, fire, and sanitation, the most visible government activities, are carried out almost exclusively by localities.

This heavy service delivery responsibility has important implications for local government. First, services are labor intensive. Employee salaries are the highest expense item. Second, for many services, the work force is irreducible after a certain point. Busses, for instance, cannot operate without drivers. Third, service salaries are high in most sectors of the economy. Thus, to be competitive, government must offer comparable wages. The alternative is to pay lower salaries for less talent.[41]

All of this presents a painful dilemma to financially troubled localities. With labor intensive services that are resistant to efficiency remedies, a work force reduction is often unavoidable when costs must be reduced. However, since the level of services is dependent, to a large degree, on the number of employees, cutting costs usually translates into diminished services. Even the financially secure jurisdiction confronts rising labor costs that will require additional tax burdens in order to maintain existing service levels.

The Open Economy   The national economy is a closed system in many respects. Taxpayers do not flee en masse, immigration does not double the welfare rolls, and few businesses relocate to foreign shores. However, for the states, and most crucially, for county and local governments, the economic boundaries are wide open. As the experiences of the central cities in the Northeast show, a significant percentage of taxpayers can leave in a decade and be replaced by service needy, low-income populations that fail to replenish the tax base. Another scenario, not uncommon, is the tax-induced departure or shutdown of a major business employer from a smaller city. What ensues is best described as a localized economic depression.

The other side of the coin is graced by winners. In the movement of taxpayers, employers, and workers, the regional winner has been the

Sunbelt. From Florida to Arizona and at points in between, business and worker émigrés swell both populations and local economies. Yet, from the rural south and the barren hills of Appalachia, the poor continue to follow the traditional path of hope to the north. Within regions, suburbia has reaped the fruits of dissatisfaction with central city conditions. Whether through better schools, tax breaks for businesses, enhanced public safety, or high-priced segregation, the suburban community has snared much of the tax base lost by the central city.[42]

Electoral Choice   Characterized by hugeness and complexity, federal government activity often presents an unmeetable challenge to individuals who wish to calculate the net benefits or costs they derive from a particular program. According to Anthony Downs, the federal taxpayer copes with this informational dilemma by drawing up a rough balance sheet. Thus, taxpayer A may view welfare programs as "bad" and defense and transportation programs as "good." The entire federal package is endorsed if "good" prevails on the bottom line. When presidential elections come around, taxpayer-voter A audits the platforms of both parties and chooses the one with the most personally rewarding bottom line.[43]

If this approach indeed describes taxpayer-voter behavior, the difficulty of calculation is markedly reduced on the local front. Special district taxes—those levied to finance school systems and water authorities—often require ballot box approval. Voters' opinions are voiced annually or, through special election, shortly after an issue has erupted. Moreover, the issue is not one of many embodied in difficult to distinguish candidates. The choices are specific, few in number, and have identifiable impacts. They involve school budgets or water bonds, and service benefits and tax costs that can be ascertained by individual citizens.

Constitutional Restrictions   State budgets, and those of counties, municipalities, and special districts, are required to be in balance. Thus, the budget deficit, a keystone of national economic management, is a proscribed tool for state and local officials. Of course, the tools of monetary management, the printing of money, and the manipulation of interest rates cannot be used either.

The balanced budget requirement does not forbid all borrowing. However, the purposes for which borrowed funds may be used are limited, and an overall debt ceiling is usually imposed. Moreover, debt repayments become a fixed expenditure in future budgets. If debt and operating expenses do not equal revenues, taxes must be raised or services must be cut.

THEORIES OF STATE AND LOCAL FINANCE

In government finance, it is always difficult to separate theories of economics from theories of government. However, on the federal level, economic policy is a distinct element although formulators and implementers represent diverse ideologies. The argot of economics is also familiar to legislators and, even as they factor in noneconomic concerns, overall fiscal policy remains a focus. Moreover, the bulk of the federal bureaucracy is, by design, a unitary structure answerable to the president. Of course, the federal bureaucracy can be unwieldy and, at times, defiant. Nonetheless, the defiance is largely situational rather than constitutional; the unwieldiness is due as much to bureaucratic dynamics as to legislative design. Few see the fundamental structure of our national political institutions threatened by monetarist or Keynesian ideology or by the difficulties in planning and implementing economic policy.

State and local finance is another matter. Theories of economics, government, and administrations are virtually inseparable. If one talks about centralizing the financial administration of locally delivered services in Washington or a state capital, one must also address the role of subnational jurisdictions in the governance of the country. Are they guarantors of diversity? Are they trustees of power that was never intended to be centralized? If one accepts these propositions, new questions arise. Can we afford atomized administration when centralization would free resources for the actual delivery of badly needed services? Does diversity translate into inequality for students in districts with low educational expenditures or for senior citizens in jurisdictions with minimal health care programs? Does fragmented planning produce disastrous results in a highly interdependent society? These are questions of intergovernmental relations, equity, diversity, and administrative efficiency and are all highly important in state and local finance. Indeed, economics often retreats from view even as opposing sides purport to be debating economic theories. Thus, in the discussion below, the pure flavor of the Keynesian-monetarist debate will, to the delight of some, be absent.

The Marketplace of Governments

At the simplest level, those who look at the current profile of state and local finance are of two persuasions. There are those who like it and those who do not. Those who like it favor *public choice*. Many jurisdictions are preferred; so is a high level of diversity in the jurisdiction by jurisdiction provision of services. With many jurisdictions providing a diversity of services, there is creted a marketplace of governments.[44] Interregional and intraregional population mobility permits citizens to locate in areas that provide the desired mix of goods and services both public and private. In the words of a seminal public choice theorist, people "vote with their feet" when jurisdictions are multiple and diverse.[45] The public choice school also embraces frequent, issue oriented elections because they give the local citizenry a continuing say in determining the quantity and quality of their public goods.[46]

Public choice theorists also subscribe, where possible, to benefit-based revenue collection. Thus, the property tax, insofar as property values represent the worth of the surrounding environment of public goods, is not found to be objectionable. Indeed, some call for increased government efforts to identify the beneficiaries of public goods so that charges can be levied in accordance with usage. The indivisibility of public goods, according to this view, is often assumed too readily.[47] The third lane of most metropolitan highways, for instance, is only needed for rush hour commuters. By apportioning the full cost of that lane to commuters through higher rush hour tolls, payments would be more in line with individual benefits.

Support of public choice rests on more than a marketplace model. There is also a belief in the tendency of large bureaucracies to move towards the institutionalized state where policies become immutable, the "uninformed" citizenry is disregarded, and the organization becomes the reason for its own existence.[48] According to public choice theorists, this substantially disenfranchises the citizenry of large and heterogeneous jurisdictions. They choose among candidates representing the sum of a nearly incalculable array of positions with respect to numerous public goods and services. Even if the successful candidate closely reflects public preferences for goods and services, implementation may be thwarted by the institutionalized bureaucracy.

According to public choice theorists, the diverse population of a large jurisdiction is no better served by the "most common denominator" service delivery mode favored by big organizations. Most clients are likely to have needs that differ markedly from the "average" and are ill-served by a standardized approach.[49] Only by decentralizing administration, it is maintained, can the responsiveness of government be increased.[50]

The public choice school is not doctrinaire in its rejection of centralized administration. Regional transportation or air quality authorities, for instance, would not be condemned. Indeed, when a public good has high positive externalities throughout a region (highways) or a locally produced public good generates high negative externalities (waste incineration), an organization that transcends jurisdictional boundaries is often the only practical administrative unit. Nonetheless, public choice theorists would urge a critical review of "super-agency" proposals. If it is found that the public good in question can be provided by units large or small, the latter course should be followed.

The Government Reform
and Equal Rights Influences

As a theory of state and local government, public choice is somewhat paradoxical. It more or less supports the status quo yet is relatively new and is considered somewhat radical. An explanation of this anomaly lies in the ideologies opposed to public choice and the inertia of state and local institutions. On the issue of public finance, public choice runs counter to government reform and equal rights: two movements whose broad goals have captured the American imagination in the twentieth century. Yet, states and localities often reject reformist and egalitarian principles in administrative councils and at the ballot box. Nonetheless, government reform and equal rights proponents, ofttimes allied, are a major influence on state and local financial policy.

As we have noted at several points in this book, the impact of the reform movement has been great. Government reorganization is a major reform focus and this has resulted in fewer administrative authorities within and among jurisdictions. Our 80,000 local governments represent a reduction, primarily through the merger of school districts, from almost 200,000 in the 1930s.[51] Most government reorganizations continue to strive for the consolidation of functions, the elimination of waste, and bureaucratic accountability via the elected executive. Nonetheless, reform proposals have not always carried the day. Decentralization has been the watchword of some reorganizations. Metropolitanization—the consolidation of the numerous jurisdictions in an urbanized area into a single government—was implemented in Dade County (Miami); Minneapolis-St. Paul; Toronto; and Phoenix, Arizona. In other locales, however, suburban opposition has thwarted central city/suburb unification attempts.

The push for citizen equality is manifest in employment practices, voting requirements, and a host of other areas. In state and local finance, equality has been sought in the funding of poor and wealthy areas. The call has not been for complete service uniformity but the elimination of financing levels based on area tax levels or other wealth criteria. Thus, in the early 1970s, a legal campaign succeeded in reducing, but not eliminating, the expenditure disparities between rich and poor school districts. Moreover, the gains were often extended by state legislative actions subsequent to the judicial decisions. There was, however, a setback. In 1973, the United States Supreme Court refused to declare unequal school financing unconstitutional. The ruling did not effect most of the states that had moved towards equalization but, at the same time, it did not compel a leveling of financing where large differentials existed.[52]

Even though the Supreme Court's decision could be labeled public choice, as could voter rejections of metropolitanization, it would not be wise to underestimate the forces of reform and equalization, particularly when they can make a common cause out of issues such as standardized service delivery. Public choice has made inroads in some areas, but we daresay that it is not about to win the day.

STATE AND LOCAL TAXES

State and local taxes are shaped by their surroundings. Balanced budget requirements force tax rates upward if services beset by rising costs are to be maintained at existing levels. Population mobility forces a reliance on levies against immovable bases (real property) or on presumably stable activities such as retail sales. Confronting an informed citizenry armed with tax and expenditure ballots, administrators are likely to feel that proposing small increases in existing taxes is safer than introducing a new tax. In addition, tax choices may effectively be preempted by the prior claims of other jurisdictions. A locality, for instance, may be reluctant to tax resident income even if it promises to be a productive source and no legal barriers exist. Even though the local tax would merely top off state and federal levies, the local executive stands to be identified as the sole villain if the public becomes angered.

With the foregoing in mind, we can draw a broad profile of state and local taxation in the 1970s. First, tradition and necessity combined to make the property tax the largest generator of state and local revenues. It accounted for one-third of nonfederal tax collections, but for localities, provided four out of every five tax dollars. Second, the sales tax nudged the property tax for first place by bringing in just under one-third of state and local tax revenues. Due to the relative stability of commercial activity over time and the more or less painless, protest-dampening collection mode, the sales tax was attractive to states and localities. In third place, and accounting for about 20 percent of subnational tax revenues, was the income tax.[53] It was primarily a state levy and, with an eye towards the federal presence, featured low rates and only mild progression.[54]

One generic factor that sharply distinguishes the state and local tax structure from the federal is tax elasticity. Federal taxes are very elastic. Economic doldrums can bring on a tax cut. Even without legislation, the progressive federal tax structure automatically responds to economic fluctuations: As income drops, a lower percentage goes to taxes. By comparison, the state and local tax structure is substantially inelastic in responding to economic conditions. Legislative tax relief is difficult to accomplish. During recession, services are already threatened by reduced tax collections at existing rates. Under balanced budget requirements, lowered rates would likely diminish services: a "bad" for "bad" substitution that does little to intrigue legislators. The "automatic" response of the state and local tax structure to income variations is also poor. Goods, services, and housing comprise two-thirds of the tax base. Since consumption levels (which include the "necessities" and the "joys" of life) do not respond immediately or fully to income drops, tax rates, in relation to income, go up, not down. Take, for instance, an 8 percent sales tax. If one's salary drops from $200 to $150 and purchases remain constant at $100, the tax jumps from 4 percent to 6 percent of income.

As you might have suspected, regression is the second factor that sharply distinguishes state and local taxes from federal taxes. The sales tax bite becomes less consequential as one's income rises; the same is true of the property tax. Both are fixed-rate taxes tied to consumption. Although state income taxes are mildly progressive, they do not fully counterbalance the regressivity of other taxes at the state and local level.

Critiques: Tax Inequality, Maladministration, Service Inequality

There is no dearth of tax critics at the state and local levels. Many of the critiques should be familiar, since we have already discussed them under federal taxation. Regressiveness, of course, is a violation of vertical equity. As a percentage of income, the rich pay less. Sales taxes, by randomly exempting this item or that, violate horizontal equity by discriminating among those with similar incomes but different tastes.[55] Similarly, property assessments, the basis for property taxes, can fluctuate widely within jurisdictions for houses that have similar market value.[56]

Administration, particularly for the property tax, is also criticized. Tax assessors may work part-time, lack professional training, and apply exotic, self-developed evaluation criteria.[57] Performance borders on impropriety when cronies receive favorable assessments or local property is grossly underevaluated in order to qualify the community as "needy" under certain state and federal aid formulas. The sales tax also exhibits administrative drawbacks. The recordkeeping for retail sales ranges from the precise to the nonexistent. While the degree is unknown, sales tax evasion is undoubtedly a reality.

Tax preferences are also a reality on the state and local levels. The primary manifestation is in the exemptions of nonprofit organizations from property and sales taxes. Thus, universities, churches, foundations, and philanthropic institutions often occupy, and thereby remove from the tax rolls, valuable parcels of municipal real estate. Government land and buildings are similarly exempt—an eminently logical proposition that begins to break down when public authorities locate such things as money-making convention centers on prime real estate. As with federal exemptions, the more open forum of substantive legislation, rather than the labyrinth of tax policy, may be the locale for future decisions concerning these subsidies.

Finally, there is concern over differing tax capacities and service responsibilities among jurisdictions. As we have seen, tax rich communities, whether blessed with a high income population or a lucrative commercial tax base, often far outspent less affluent jurisdictions for basic services. In addition to funding differentials, there were also wide disparities in clientele. The inner city student, for instance, was often the product of broken families, mean streets, and a low standard of living. The suburban student, while not free of problems, usually had a social background that facilitated the educational task. In short, the resource rich community had a low level of service problems and the resource poor community often had them by the bucketful.

In response to inefficiency in tax administration, the disparity in tax wealth and the differing service demands, there has been a growing reliance on the redistribution of federal, state, and local tax revenues. Since these *intergovernmental transfers* are a growing factor in state and local finance, they will be our next subject of attention.

INTERGOVERNMENTAL TRANSFERS

Grants are funds distributed to states and localities from above. States and localities are the recipients of federal grants; localities receive support from state grants. This process has been going on for a long time. In the 1800s, federal grants of land and money were made to finance the establishment of state universities. With the New Deal of President Franklin Roosevelt in the 1930s, the federal government began to defray the cost of state aid to the needy. A major, direct conduit between the federal government and localities was established by the Housing Act of 1949. Local redevelopment plans meeting federal guidelines could receive substantial federal funding. Finally, in the 1960s, federal largesse reached the community level. Under Model Cities and Community Development programs, neighborhoods received federal funds and were given a policy voice in their application. State grants to localities also date to the nineteenth century and, by the mid-1970s, accounted for 80 percent of local welfare funds and 50 percent of educational funds.[58]

There are three types of grants, flowing from either general or earmarked revenues, that can be identified. *Categorical grants* must be applied to specific activities approved by the funding authority; for example, the modernization of local feeder roads adjacent to an interstate highway. *Block grants* are more broadly directed federal and state outlays to smaller jurisdictions. Grants may go to education, for instance, but the local jurisdictions retain a measure of discretion in applying the funds. Finally, there is *general revenue sharing*. Through general revenue sharing, states and localities receive a portion of federal tax revenues to do with as they please. Taken together, these three devices comprise the intergovernmental grants economy.

The revenue base of the intergovernmental grants economy is rationalized on efficiency and equalization grounds. In the first instance, many taxes are more efficiently collected by larger administrative units. Local sales tax administration, for instance, would be a nightmare. State collection, with the locality's percentage subsequently remitted, is more efficient. Similarly, when a state and city both utilize the personal income tax, taxpayers often calculate state and local imposts on the same form and write out a single check to the state which then reimburses the locality. As a result, some state to local revenue flows, by simply returning the taxes collected in a specific jurisdiction to that jurisdiction, are based solely on efficiency.

In addition to its efficiency, the intergovernmental grants economy is applauded for the "vertical equity" of its revenue base. Grants draw on federal revenues, the most equitably collected, and on state tax revenues, which generally are deemed more equitable than the local variety. Thus, the intergovernmental "grant pie" contains a larger contribution—proportional to income—from the rich than from the poor.

For the distribution side of the intergovernmental grants economy, equity is the major rationale although the occasional denials of eligibility to jurisdictions below a certain size reflect consolidation-efficiency criteria.[59] More compelling, however, is the view that states, counties, and municipalities are merely the locale, not the cause, of poverty, poor housing, and other ills and, therefore, should not bear the full burden of problems that are the responsibility and concern of the nation as a whole. Thus, the federal grants system fosters interregional equity by funding poorer communities and states more heavily than well-to-do areas. Similarly, state grants, particularly for education, have increasingly been used as equalization tools among jurisdictions.[60]

Although some would discount the efficiency and equalization effects of the intergovernmental grants economy, almost no one would deny the political aspects. The name of the game is formula politics since, for most grants, a transfer formula determines a jurisdiction's entitlement. Thus, the declining central city would want low income weighed heavily. Suburbs would want population growth criteria. Giving added weight to population density would favor the Northeast; the rapidly expanding Southwest would benefit if high public works expenditures was a crucial factor. Given this situation, what emerges from the arena of pluralistic compromise is a multifactor formula worthy of a theoretical mathematician.[61]

Through the 1960s, abstruse formulas were compounded by grant proliferation and increasing specificity in the definitions of fundable programs. Some eligible jurisdictions, boggled by the complexity, missed lucrative opportunities or dropped out of the grant game completely. Not surprisingly, this brought categorical grant critics out of the woodwork. Accusations were made that grant programs preempted the policy prerogatives of local jurisdictions. By way of exhibit, critics pointed out localities with program profiles that matched the grants available from superior jurisdictions.

These critiques, partially in line with public choice philosophy, strengthened during the Nixon Administration. With presidential support, proposals to reduce the quantity and complexity of grants and to diminish the federal policy-making role moved forward. One result was block grants that combined and simplified a few categorical grants. The second and most important result for the structure of intergovernmental relations was general revenue sharing. Approved by Congress in 1972, general revenue sharing transferred funds to states and localities with minimal restrictions as to use. Moreover, the application procedures were so simple that jurisdictions needed to do little more than make a request.

While only a small portion of the intergovernmental grants economy was given over to revenue sharing by the initial legislation, public choice ideas had been translated into policy. Although the equalization-consolidation approach remained dominant—even revenue sharing formulas factored in low income—proponents were disturbed. They pointed to jurisdictions that had used revenue sharing funds to shift expenditures from the poor, the designated beneficiaries of discarded categorical grants, to middle- and upper-class citizens.[62] Thus, income redistribution, if that indeed was the aim of federal grant policy, was being thwarted by local initiatives permitted by revenue sharing. Despite such objections, revenue sharing has remained on the books and the long-term outcome of the public choice-equalization debate is unclear. However, whether dispersed or centralized policy making prevails, intergovernmental transfers are sure to continue. So is the larger debate over the appropriate federal, state, and local roles in this country's governance.

STATE AND LOCAL BORROWING

In addition to taxes and grants, states and localities have a third major source of revenue. It is borrowing. It may be that borrowing is the most public of all state and local revenue tools. In many instances, proposed government bond issues for major projects have been subject to referenda. As a result, multimillion dollar expenditures and a few decades of tax payments became the subject of widespread debate. Not infrequently, voters rejected the projects. In the 1970s, the spotlight on borrowing grew brighter. An inability to meet debt repayments brought cities to the brink of bankruptcy, closed down state construction projects for several years, and wiped out at least one public bond issuing authority. Moreover, overall state and local debts grew rapidly. This, combined with the possibility of long-term economic stagnation, portended a troublesome future. As a fixed, multiyear expenditure item, debt repayments cannot be reduced. If the tax base does not grow, or shrinks, services must be held at existing levels or cut back. Thus, state and local debts, once projected as an increasingly smaller portion of growing tax revenues, loomed as an albatross.

In one way the surge of borrowing in the late 1960s and early 1970s is understandable. Before the faith was substantially shattered by the economy's prolonged slowdown, "economic growth" qualified as a core belief among government planners. From another angle, however, the borrowing spree is a bit more difficult to comprehend. Counterposed against the "every day in every way things get better and better" philosophy of the planners were laws that, in the name of fiscal responsibility and intergenerational equity, restricted the nature and extent of state and local borrowing. By looking at three categories of borrowing, we might better see the rationales, restrictions, and circumventions that are operative in state and local debt financing.[63]

Tax Anticipation Notes For current operating expenditures— employee salaries, office rents, and state and local shares of transfer payments to eligible residents—borrowing usually is limited to *tax anticipation notes*. Funds are borrowed to pay current operating expenses pending the imminent receipt of tax revenues. For instance, a loan to meet a jurisdiction's March 20 payroll is secured by quarterly sales taxes due from retailers on April 1.

Using imminent taxes as collateral for loans to cover operating expenses illustrates a primary rationale behind state and local borrowing restrictions. Simply put, tomorrow's citizens should not pay for today's public services. The reasoning is sound, but financially or politically pressed jurisdictions have ignored it on occasion. To qualify current operations for longer term borrowing, jurisdictions have considered planning personnel and everyday supplies as capital expenses— enduring investments that can be mortgaged in the name of future taxpayers. Such rationales are flimsy, at best. A blunter ploy is consistently to underestimate tax revenues so that the legislature will grant permission to "stretch out" the ballooning short-term debt.[64]

Capital Borrowing Long-term borrowing is permitted for capital projects such as land acquisition, major equipment purchases, and building construction. The justification for *capital borrowing* is that these expenditures provide benefits over time and, therefore, it is legitimate to pay for them in kind. Multiyear payments spread project costs more equitably among present and future beneficiaries. Today's taxpayers do not pay the full cost of a project that might outlive them, and tomorrow's taxpayers share the cost from the time they locate in the jurisdiction.

Besides masquerading operating expenses as capital items, jurisdictions have misused capital borrowing by underestimating the true cost of proposed projects. As was discussed in the budgeting context, low-ball estimates usually come to light when the project is irreversible and the response is limited to increasing expenditure and borrowing obligations.

Circumventions such as low-balling often neutralize another tool—the *debt ceiling*—that is designed to control borrowing. Tax anticipation loans, by definition, are limited. In most states and localities, capital debt obligations also may not exceed a legislated limit. Often, there is an overall debt ceiling on short- and long-term loans. The purpose, of course, is to prevent onerous burdens from being passed on to tomorrow's citizens. However, with deliberate underestimates of project costs and anticipated revenues, the debt ceiling can be exceeded. Legislators, presented with a fait accompli, have little choice but to raise the maximum.

Revenue Bonds   Capital and tax anticipation loans generally are effected through the sale of "full faith and credit bonds" whose collateral is the short- and long-term tax revenues of the issuing jurisdiction. However, there is another type of bond—the *revenue bond*—which is not backed by tax collateral. Rather, the bonds finance specific, money-making public ventures—bridges, port facilities, hydroelectric projects—and are secured by anticipated revenues. The project is structured so as to be attractive to investors. In most cases, the project is set completely apart from the budgetary process. If any public funds are involved, ironclad legislation often guarantees the promised government investment. The repayment of principal and interest to bondholders has first claim on project revenues. Management "in the interests of the bondholders" is the usual legislative charge and top executives are, for the most part, highly respected as administrators or specialists in the project area. In most areas of the country, the administrative unit that displays these characteristics is known as the "public authority."[65]

Numerous *public authorities* were created during the 1940s, 1950s, and 1960s. Most were for single endeavors, but others were multiproject giants that became an important force in regional policy. Their large scale construction projects were big-ticket items for banks, investors, unions, and local legislators seeking facilities and employment for constituents. With self-funding, large reserves and statutory obligations to bondholders, public authorities often remained independent of political executives. In the 1960s and 1970s, however, political actors began to reassert themselves. Legislation whittled down the public authority's discretion over the profits from fully paid projects on the grounds that the

The Verrazano-Narrows Bridge in New York City. Built by the Triborough Bridge and Tunnel Authority, it is the world's longest suspension bridge. It is one of dozens of New York State bridges, dams, and highways built by various public authorities under the direction of Robert Moses. (Wide World Photos)

interests of the original bondholders had terminated. Profits produced by projects that already had been paid for were used to subsidize floundering services unconnected to the public authority. In some cases, the same result was accomplished by merging a thriving public authority with an unprofitable one. Nonetheless, the public authority remains an important element particularly in the management of the transportation networks of our large metropolitan areas.

Revenue bonds are not immune to criticism. On occasion, project viability has been sorely overestimated and, perhaps, misrepresented. As a result, tax revenues have come to the rescue of more than one "self-sustaining" enterprise. The revenue bond also draws fire when it is used for the purchase of real estate or the construction of industrial parks and office buildings. Such actions, it is charged, exploit the lower cost of state and local borrowing (because investors factor in federal tax savings) to compete unfairly with private realtors and landlords for capital. The competitive edge extends to operations if rents in the public facility undercut the market rate. In addition, below-market rents give business tenants a government subsidized advantage over their competitors. This, of course, is a travesty to those who believe that government activity should strive for marketplace neutrality. Regardless of the validity of this argument, it is not always compelling to the jurisdiction seeking more jobs and an expanded commercial tax base.

SUMMARY

We saw that government responds to marketplace imperfections when it provides goods and services. In the provision of public goods, government seeks to affect income redistribution, economic stability, and the efficient allocation of resources. Among theorists, Keynesians and monetarists share the goal of long-term growth but are locked in a fierce debate over how to achieve it. "No-growth" economists, alarmed at the rate at which we are using up resources, are substantially excluded from economic policy councils, perhaps mistakenly.

The formulation and implementation of national economic policy remains fragmented. Presidents, administrators, and Congress engage in a pluralistic tussle, and again, there are critics who decry the lack of centralized planning. Policy results often are marked by inequity and preferential treatment, but the federal tax structure, on the whole, is fair, efficiently administered, and a valuable economic governor.

On the state and local level, questions of autonomy, efficiency, and equality make for a lively dialogue, and since no one concept dominates, the profile of local governance is extremely heterogeneous. Administration is centralized or decentralized; professional or political; largely independent of voters or quite beholden to them. The state and local revenue structure is also diverse. The income tax is primarily a state tool. Localities are dependent on property taxes. The sales tax is attractive to both. Because of a growing belief that states and localities service national problems, tax revenues collected by larger jurisdictions are an increasing proportion of state and local revenues. State and local borrowing is also substantial and needed, but an overreliance on debt, often slyly achieved, may set the stage for a hard fall if the economy continues to falter.

All in all, public finance is a crucial growth industry in government. Financial managers, tax specialists, and economic planners should be in high demand. What they decide will have far-reaching implications for all members of this society.

KEY TERMS AND CONCEPTS

Ability to pay principle
Benefit principle
Block grants
Capital borrowing
Categorical grants
Cost distribution/ability to pay
   principle

The Council of Economic Advisors
  (CEA)
Debt ceiling
Equity (vertical and horizontal)
Externalities (positive, negative,
  and modern-day)
Fiscal policy

General revenue sharing
Income transfers
Intergovernmental transfers
Keynesians
Marketplace neutrality
Merit goods
Monetarists
Monetary policy
Progressive taxation
Public authorities

Public choice
Public goods
Regressive taxation
Revenue bonds
Tax anticipation notes
Tax erosion
Tax expenditures
Tax incidence
Tax shifting

NOTES

1. Richard A. Musgrave, *The Theory of Public Finance* (New York: McGraw-Hill, 1959), chapters 1 and 2.
2. Paul A. Samuelson, "The Pure Theory of Public Expenditures," *Review of Economics and Statistics* 36 (November 1954): 387–389.
3. Adam Smith, *The Wealth of Nations* (New York: Oxford, 1976), pp. 689–731.
4. See Kenneth E. Boulding, *The Economy of Love and Fear* (Belmont, Calif.: Wadsworth, 1973), chapter 1; and Thomas M. Kando, *Leisure and Popular Culture in Transition* (St. Louis: Mosby, 1975), chapter 1, for a potpourri of views on why relative income equality is better than great disparities in wealth.
5. Anthony Downs, *An Economic Theory of Democracy* (New York: Harper & Row, 1957).
6. Charles M. Tiebout, "A Pure Theory of Local Expenditures," *Journal of Political Economy* 54 (October 1956): 416–424.
7. Public goods-externality discussions often are as complex as they are legion. Ours, a stab at clarity, is a composite. For rigorous and highly regarded treatments see Robert W. Ayres and Allen V. Kneese, "Production, Consumption and Externalities," *American Economic Review* 59, no. 3 (June 1969): 282–297; James M. Buchanan and William Stubblebine, "Externality," *Economica* 29 (November 1963): 371–382; Richard A. Musgrave and Peggy B. Musgrave, *Public Finance in Theory and Practice* (New York: McGraw-Hill, 1976), pp. 56–61. Finally, Otto Eckstein, *Public Finance* (Englewood Cliffs, N.J.: Prentice-Hall, 1973), chapter 1, is an excellent source for those with an aversion to numbers and charts.
8. Musgrave and Musgrave, *Public Finance in Theory and Practice,* p. 65.
9. Arthur M. Okun, *Equality and Efficiency: The Big Trade-Off* (Washington, D.C.: Brookings, 1975).
10. See Kenneth E. Boulding and Martin Pfaff, *Redistribution to the Rich and the Poor* (Belmont, Calif.: Wadsworth, 1972), particularly section 2.
11. See Milton Friedman, *Capitalism and Freedom* (Chicago: University of Chicago Press, 1965).
12. Musgrave and Musgrave, *Public Finance in Theory and Practice,* pp. 212–223.
13. John Maynard Keynes, *The General Theory of Employment, Interest and Money* (London: Macmillan, 1936).
14. For a look at Keynes and his impact, see Robert Lekachman, *The Age of Keynes* (New York: Random House, 1966).

15. For a more detailed exposition on demand management and the multiplier effect, see Charles L. Schultze, *National Income Analysis*, 3rd ed. (Englewood Cliffs, N.J.: Prentice-Hall, 1971), chapter 3.
16. For an excellent review of the national economic policy debates of the 1970s see Peter D. McClelland, ed., *Focus Macroeconomics* (Guildord, Conn.: Dushkin Publishing, 1976).
17. Milton Friedman, "Letter on Economic Policy," in ibid., pp. 46–48.
18. Robert Lekachman, "The Inevitability of Controls," in ibid., pp. 54–56.
19. James P. Gannon, "Slow Recovery, A Debate Over Okun's Law," *Wall Street Journal*, 29 January 1975; reprinted in ibid., pp. 32–33.
20. Eckstein, *Public Finance*, pp. 102–105.
21. *The New York Times*, 8 November 1977, p. 49.
22. Joseph A. Pechman, *Federal Tax Policy*, 3rd ed. (Washington: Brookings, 1977), p. 39.
23. Ibid., p. 41.
24. For a Naderesque slant on tax legislation, see Richard Spohn and Charles McCollum, *The Revenue Committees* (New York: Grossman, 1975).
25. See Musgrave and Musgrave, *Public Finance in Theory and Practice*, chapter 34, for a discussion of the finances of less-developed countries.
26. See Joseph A. Pechman and Benjamin A. Okner, *Who Bears the Tax Burden* (Washington, D.C.: Brookings, 1974).
27. Pechman, *Federal Tax Policy*, p. 54.
28. *The United States Budget for Fiscal Year 1978* (Washington, D.C.: U.S. Government Printing Office, 1977).
29. Phillip M. Stern, *The Rape of the Taxpayer* (New York: Random House (Vintage Books), 1974), pp. 42–43.
30. Musgrave and Musgrave, *Public Finance in Theory and Practice*, p. 264.
31. All rates are for 1977, as per the Internal Revenue Code.
32. Michael Barone, Grant Ujifusa, and Douglas Matthews, *The Almanac of American Politics, 1974* (Boston: Gambit, 1974), pp. 1158–1159.
33. Pechman, *Federal Tax Policy*, pp. 129–135.
34. See John A. Brittian, *The Payroll Tax for Social Security* (Washington, D.C.: Brookings, 1972).
35. See, for instance, Friedman, *Capitalism and Freedom;* Spohn and McCollum, *The Revenue Committees;* Stern, *The Rape of the Taxpayer.*
36. See Andrew Shonfield, *Modern Capitalism* (New York: Oxford University Press, 1969), pp. 323–329.
37. Edward S. Mason, "Address to the American Economic Association," quoted in ibid., p. 333.
38. See Shonfield, *Modern Capitalism,* chapters V-VIII.
39. James A. Maxwell and J. Richard Aronson, *Financing State and Local Governments* (Washington, D.C.: Brookings, 1977), pp. 77–80.
40. Ibid.
41. William Baumol, "Macroeconomics of Unbalanced Growth: The Anatomy of Urban Crisis," *American Economic Review* 57, no. 3 (June 1967).
42. Richard Muth, "Migration: Chicken or Egg?" *Southern Economic Journal* 37, no. 3 (January 1971).
43. Downs, *Economic Theory of Democracy.*
44. Robert L. Bish and Vincent Ostrom, *Understanding Urban Government: Metropolitan Reform Revisited* (Washington, D.C.: American Enterprise Institute, 1973), chapters 2 and 3.
45. Tiebout, "Pure Theory of Local Expenditures."

46. Robert L. Bish, *The Public Economy of Metropolitan Areas* (Chicago: Markham Publishing, 1971), p. 70.

47. For the logic behind more benefit-based taxation see Wilbur Thompson, "The City as a Distorted Price System," in Harold M. Hochman, ed., *The Urban Economy* (New York: Norton, 1976), pp. 74–76. While Thompson is somewhat at odds with the "public choice" school in several areas, his imaginative approach to taxation is congruent and, indeed, explores areas that "public choicers" had, to a degree, neglected.

48. Robert L. Bish and Robert Warren, "Scale and Monopoly Problems in Urban Government Services," *Urban Affairs Quarterly* 8, no. 1 (September 1972): 97–122.

49. Vincent and Elinor Ostrom, "Public Choice: A Different Approach to the Study of Public Administration," *Public Administration Review* 31, no. 2 (March-April 1971): 210–211.

50. For a view that leads more towards consolidation, see The Advisory Commission on Intergovernmental Relations, *The Challenge of Local Government Reorganization* (Washington, D.C.: U.S. Government Printing Office, 1974).

51. Maxwell and Aronson, *Financing State and Local Governments*, p. 77.

52. Betsy Levin, ed. "Future Directions for School Finance Reform," *Law and Contemporary Problems* 38, no. 3 (Winter-Spring 1974).

53. Percentages are from Pechman, *Federal Tax Policy*, p. 2.

54. Musgrave and Musgrave, *Public Finance in Theory and Practice*, pp. 281–282.

55. Maxwell and Aronson, *Financing State and Local Governments*, pp. 106–110.

56. Ibid., pp. 146–148.

57. Ibid., pp. 150–152.

58. Ibid., p. 87.

59. Paul R. Dommel, *The Politics of Revenue Sharing* (Bloomington: Indiana University Press, 1974), pp. 75–76.

60. See "Reform Through State Legislatures," in Levin, "Future Directions," pp. 436–492.

61. Dommel, *Revenue Sharing*, pp. 155–162.

62. Ibid., chapter VII.

63. See, also, Maxwell and Aronson, *Financing State and Local Governments*, chapter 9.

64. For a primer on circumventions, see Fred Ferretti, *The Year the Big Apple Went Bust* (New York: Putnam, 1976).

65. The epic work on public authorities is Robert Caro, *The Power Broker: Robert Moses and the Fall of New York* (New York: Knopf, 1974), especially sections VI and VIII.

BIBLIOGRAPHY

Bish, Robert L. *The Public Economy of Metropolitan Areas.* Chicago: Markham Publishing, 1971.

Bish, Robert L., and Ostrom, Vincent. *Understanding Urban Government: Metropolitan Reform Revisited.* Washington, D.C.: American Enterprise Institute, 1973.

Blinder, Alan S., et al., eds. *The Economics of Public Finance.* Washington, D.C.: Brookings, 1974.

Boulding, Kenneth E. *The Economy of Love and Fear.* Belmont, Calif.: Wadsworth, 1973.

Boulding, Kenneth E., and Pfaff, Martin. *Redistribution to the Rich and the Poor.* Belmont, Calif.: Wadsworth, 1972.

Burkhead, Jesse, and Miner, Jerry. *Public Expenditure*. Chicago: Aldine, 1971.

Caro, Robert. *The Power Broker: Robert Moses and the Fall of New York*. New York: Knopf, 1974.

Dommel, Paul R. *The Politics of Revenue Sharing*. Bloomington: Indiana University Press, 1974.

Downs, Anthony. *An Economic Theory of Democracy*. New York: Harper & Row, 1957.

Ecker-Racz, L. L. *The Politics and Economics of State-Local Finance*. Englewood Cliffs, N.J.: Prentice-Hall, 1970.

Eckstein, Otto. *Public Finance*. Englewood Cliffs, N.J.: Prentice-Hall, 1973.

Ferretti, Fred. *The Year the Big Apple Went Bust*. New York: Putnam, 1976.

Friedman, Milton. *Capitalism and Freedom*. Chicago: University of Chicago Press, 1965.

Keynes, John Maynard. *The General Theory of Employment, Interest and Money*. London: Macmillan, 1936.

Lekachman, Robert. *The Age of Keynes*. New York: Random House, 1966.

Maxwell, James A., and Aronson, J. Richard. *Financing State and Local Governments*. Washington, D.C.: Brookings, 1977.

Musgrave, Richard A. *The Theory of Public Finance*. New York: McGraw-Hill, 1959.

Musgrave, Richard A., and Musgrave, Peggy B. *Public Finance in Theory and Practice*. New York: McGraw-Hill, 1976.

Okun, Arthur M. *Equality and Efficiency: The Big Trade-Off*. Washington, D.C.: Brookings, 1975.

Pechman, Joseph A. *Federal Tax Policy*. Washington, D.C.: Brookings, 1977.

Pechman, Joseph A., and Okner, Benjamin A. *Who Bears the Tax Burden*. Washington, D.C.: Brookings, 1974.

Pierce, Lawrence C. *The Politics of Fiscal Policy Formation*. Pacific Palisades, Calif.: Good Year, 1971.

Shonfield, Andrew. *Modern Capitalism*. New York: Oxford University Press, 1969.

Spohn, Richard, and McCollum, Charles. *The Revenue Committees*. New York: Grossman, 1975.

Stern, Philip. *The Rape of the Taxpayer*. New York: Random House (Vintage Books), 1974.

In addition to the sources cited in the notes and bibliography, the following *Public Administration Review (PAR)* articles are a convenient starting point for a more detailed exploration of the material in this chapter.

Almy, Timothy A. "City Managers, Public Avoidance and Revenue Sharing," *PAR* 37, no. 1 (Jan./Feb. 1977): 19–27.

Aron, Joan B. "Regional Governance for the New York Metropolitan Region: A Reappraisal," *PAR* 34, no. 3 (May/June 1974): 260–264.

Ayres, Douglas W. "Municipal Interfaces in the Third Sector: A Negative View," *PAR* 35, no. 5 (Sept./Oct. 1975): 459–463.

Bahl, Roy. "The Outlook for State and Local Government Finances," *PAR* 36, no. 6 (Nov./Dec. 1976): 683–687.

Burkhead, Jesse. "Fiscal Planning–Conservative Keynesianism," *PAR* 31, no. 3 (May/June 1971): 335–345.

Campbell, Alan K. "Approaches to Defining, Measuring and Achieving Equity in the Public Sector," *PAR* 36, no. 5 (Sept./Oct. 1976): 556–562.

Caputo, David A. and Richard L. Cole. "General Revenue Sharing Expenditure Decisions in Cities Over 50,000," *PAR* 35, no. 1 (Jan./Feb. 1975): 136–142.

Carroll, Michael A. "The Impact of General Revenue Sharing on the Urban Planning Process—An Initial Assessment," *PAR* 35, no. 2 (March/April 1975): 143–150.

Chitwood, Stephen R. "Social Equity and Social Service Productivity," *PAR* 34, no. 1 (Jan./Feb. 1974): 29–35.

Elazar, Daniel J. "Fiscal Questions and Political Answers in Inter-governmental Finance," *PAR* 32, no. 5 (Sept./Oct. 1972): 471–478.

Harman, B. Douglas. "The Bloc Grant: Readings from a First Experiment," *PAR* 30, no. 2 (March/April 1970): 141–153.

Hart, David K. "Social Equity, Justice and the Equitable Administrator," *PAR* 34, no. 1 (Jan./Feb. 1974): 3–11.

Lovell, Catherine H. "The Future of the Intergovernmental Process: Will Revenue Sharing Be Continued," *PAR* 36, no. 2 (March/April 1976): 211–216.

McCaffery, Jerry M. "Knowledge Management in Fiscal Policy Formation," *PAR* 35, no. 6 (Nov./Dec. 1975): 598–602.

Mikesell, John L. "Administration and the Public Revenue System: A View of Tax Administration," *PAR* 34, no. 6 (Nov./Dec. 1974): 615–624.

Ostrom, Elinor and Dennis Smith. "On the Fate of 'Lilliputs' in Metropolitan Policing," *PAR* 36, no. 2 (March/April 1976): 192–200.

Ostrom, Vincent and Elinor Ostrom. "Public Choice: A Different Approach to the Study of Administration," *PAR* 31, no. 2 (March/April 1971): 203–216.

Pachon, Harry P. and Nicholas P. Lovrich, Jr. "The Consolidation of Urban Public Services: A Focus on the Policy," *PAR* 37, no. 1 (Jan./Feb. 1977): 38–47.

Porter, David O. and Teddie Wood Porter. "Social Equity and Fiscal Federalism," *PAR* 34, no. 1 (Jan./Feb. 1974): 36–43.

Ross, John P. and Richard D. Gustely. "Changing the Intrastate General Revenue Sharing Formula: A Discussion of the Issues," *PAR* 36, no. 6 (Nov./Dec. 1976): 655–660.

Traylor, Orba F. "State Level Financial Management of the Revenue/Expenditure Gap," *PAR* 35, no. 5 (Sept./Oct. 1975): 523–537.

Zimmerman, Joseph. "Metropolitan Reform in the U.S.: An Overview," *PAR* 30, no. 5 (Sept./Oct. 1970): 531–543.

RELEVANT PERIODICALS
American Economic Review
American Journal of Economics and Sociology
Federal Reserve Bulletin
Journal of Economic Issues
Journal of Public Economics
Journal of Taxation
National Tax Journal
Public Finance
Public Finance Quarterly
Taxes

RELEVANT CASE STUDIES
(Cases marked ICCH are available from the Intercollegiate Case Clearing House, Soldier Field, Boston, Mass. 02163; cases marked ICP are available from the Inter-University Case Program, Box 229, Syracuse, N.Y. 13210.)

Langston, E. *Choosing an Inflation Projection for Army Tanks,* [ICP]
Russell, J. R. and S. N. Chakravarty. *New York City Tax Program - 1971–1972,* [ICCH]
Tillet, P. and M. Weiner. *The Closing of Newark Airport,* [ICP]

CHAPTER 11

INCREASING THE RESPONSIVENESS OF GOVERNMENT ORGANIZATIONS

INTRODUCTION

In this chapter we will focus on the crucial issue of the responsiveness of government organizations. The responsiveness question is twofold. Are government agencies responsive and respectful towards the public? Are all citizens afforded meaningful access to the administrative, legislative, and political arenas where public policy is formulated? This issue surfaced again and again in the preceding chapters.

This issue was prominent in our discussions of institutionalization. An organization seeking to control its environment could become less responsive to the individuals and groups which it was mandated to serve. Responsiveness also surfaced as an issue in our discussion of pluralism. The pluralist milieu of the United States political process favors the access of organized interests to the public policy arena and can shut out the policy preferences of the poorly organized and underfunded.

A variety of remedies have been proposed to moderate the less than desirable consequences generated by institutionalization and pluralism. To counteract institutionalization class actions, the ombudsman and other devices that carry the case of the aggrieved citizen to the offending organization and beyond have been proposed. To moderate the pluralist policy-making environment's bias towards the established and highly organized interest groups, reformers have called for new methods of financing political campaigns, an expanded role for public interest research groups, a more vigilant role for the press, and more ethical behavior on the part of public servants. In this chapter, we shall scrutinize some of these remedies for institutionalization and antidotes for pluralism.

REMEDIES FOR INSTITUTIONALIZATION

The institutionalized organization often is accused of callousness and inefficiency. The charge is not unjust although the magnitude of the offense is open to question. In most cases stockholder and taxpayer losses due to inefficiency and the costs accruing to mistreated clients and customers do not outweigh the overall benefits. Still, this has not, and should not, foreclose attempts to reduce the negative consequences of institutionalization.

The 1970s featured some techniques that promised to mitigate the inefficiencies of institutionalization. Zero-Base Budgeting, which we reviewed in Chapter 9, swept through government and business circles. One heard of Zero-Base Media Planning or Zero-Base Marketing programs as well as Zero-Base Budgeting. In government or industry, zero-base approaches were attractive as remedies for institutionalization because programs lost the immunity from scrutiny that they had achieved over time.

To temper their callousness, whether real or perceived, organizations took steps to improve the performance of personnel who deal directly with the public. In business, flight attendants, salespersons, and receptionists often receive varying degrees of training in handling the public. In many cities public transportation authorities award cash bonuses to courteous bus drivers or railway conductors. Although service styles may be tailored to fit the clientele, substantive organizational policies may continue to be self-serving. When client-organizational conflicts arise, the pleasant clerk (or assistant commissioner) does little more than take the heat with a smile as citizens blow off steam to no avail.[1] Nonetheless, a smile is better than a snarl, particularly in the noncontroversial agencies—motor vehicles, post office—where the client is a paying customer.

ZBB and personnel training are not the only treatments for institutionalization. When wronged citizens are the symptom, class action lawsuits, the ombudsman, and citizen review boards are advanced as remedies. For the inefficiencies associated with institutionalization, project management is prescribed by many as the number one cure. In the following pages we shall take a closer look at these recommendations for eliminating the ills—or the ill effects—of the institutionalized organization.

Class Actions, the Ombudsman, and Other Citizens' Safeguards

When the citizen is bruised in a collision with the bureaucracy, help is often sought from unaffiliated persons or institutions. The crop of bureaucratic accident victims is sufficient to sustain a number of such champions. Thus, private law firms have invaded what was in the 1960s the bailiwick of the public interest lawyer by bringing *class action lawsuits*—a single action on behalf of a number of similarly aggrieved clients. Although the targets have been private organizations primarily and the courts have made things more difficult for plaintiffs, the class action suit, when successful, is an expensive lesson for the offending organization and a lucrative proposition for the attorneys representing the injured individuals. Multimillion-dollar claims are not unheard of in these cases. With class actions the assumption that only a few will bother to recover trivial damages is potentially invalid. Administrators, as a result, may be more reluctant to cut corners at client expense.

When the offending organization is a government one, legislators and their staffs, newspaper "help-line" columnists, and TV "action reporters" complement the work of the lawyer. Interventions from these sources have a good chance of success. Legislators hold the purse strings; the media can enhance or besmirch the organizational image. Thus, the inquiries of legislators and reporters are afforded top priority by organizations. The complainant may receive the benefit of the doubt, as well as a rapid response, as the organization seeks to mollify powerful elements in the environment.

Since the early 1960s, there have been several analyses of the mechanisms for the resolution of citizen complaints against the government bureaucracy. Investigators studied methods, both in the United States and abroad, whereby government handled citizens' complaints against itself.[2] American methods did not fare well. One congressperson might be more skilled than another at making the bureaucracy see the error of its ways. Thus, a citizen from neighborhood A might have her problem straightened out while a citizen from neighborhood B, with an identical problem, might not. Media intervention, primarily a marketing tool, was limited to a few dramatic cases. If a class action lawsuit was impractical, judicial redress often involved an expense that exceeded the damages sustained by the wronged citizen and/or was prohibitive vis-à-vis the individual's resources. Looking to the Scandinavian countries, analysts thought they saw a more effective method of resolving citizens' complaints against the bureaucracy.[3] It was the ombudsman.

The *ombudsman* has nearly a two-hundred-year history in Sweden as a government office designed to put muscle behind the citizens' attempts to reverse bureaucratic wrongs. The ombudsman is an independent and nonpartisan officer of the legislature, provided for by law, who supervises administration; deals with specific complaints from the public against administrative injustice and maladministration; and has the power to investigate, criticize and publicize, but not to reverse, administrative action.[4]

The idea of a full-time office devoted to keeping the bureaucracy honest was attractive. The ombudsman could pick apart the agency's work and, if necessary, expose defects to the glare of publicity. The ombudsman promised more even and focused citizen advocacy than was available from individual legislators who had other duties and varying degrees of skill at storming the bureaucratic battlements. Thus, in the 1960s and 1970s, states such as Hawaii, Nebraska, and Iowa created ombudsman offices.[5]

Many jurisdictions have offices that do not meet the above criteria—they report to the executive rather than the legislature—but that nonetheless investigate citizen complaints against the bureaucracy.[6] These offices include departments of investigation, attorneys general, and consumer affairs offices. Of course, such offices, as members of the chief executive official family, may be ordered to keep all bureaucratic problems in-house. Thus, public exposure, an effective prod and deterrent, is deleted from the weaponry that can be brought to bear in order to resolve the citizens' complaints.

While all may not meet the ombudsman criteria and none may be equal to the quantity of citizen-bureaucracy disputes, complaint resolution offices represent an additional check on the harmful side effects of institutionalization.

Citizen Review Boards and Juridical Democracy

Another check on the institutionalized bureaucracy—one that has been the center of much controversy—is the *citizen review board*. The urban riots of the 1960s spurred a reevaluation of the delivery of government services.[7] Because of instances of brutality and racially motivated selective enforcement, the police received the lion's share of attention.[8] The charge often leveled was that higher-ups would rather back up patrol officers than uncover brutality. Thus, it was recommended that outside observers—a citizen review board—entertain and investigate allegations of police brutality.

Citizen review boards have had a stormy history with numerous incarnations.[9] One manifestation of the review board concept has been the "blue ribbon" panel. Formal boards usually were composed of recognized community leaders such as the head of the area's chamber of commerce or the local NAACP director. Even though such boards were hardly radical, the police fought aggressively for their elimination and, in many cities, succeeded.[10] In place of formal review boards, ad hoc surveillance groups sprang up in some cities. When instances of brutality were observed, the group would apply political pressure in an attempt to insure a thoroughgoing investigation.

The civilian review board concept seems to have waned through the 1970s. There is a legacy, however. Police departments have formulated guidelines governing the use of force, in-house review boards have become more probing, and their proceedings have become more public. (For a discussion of law enforcement data banks in the context of the Freedom of Information Act implications, see Chapter 14.)

A general external check on administrative discretion involves the legislature and courts.[11] To circumscribe administrative latitude legislators can write statutes more precisely. Judges can require that administrative decisions proceed with clear-cut rules rather than in arbitrary fashion. However, a different pattern of legislative and judicial oversight is often present. Legislation is vague. Often, the public agency is born in a turbulent environment and its legislation mirrors this uncertainty. The agency is charged with finding answers to questions that have stumped the legislators. In delegating this task, legislators are reluctant to hamper the administrative search with rules. This autonomy is often compelling when the public agency is sued. Courts rarely overturn legislative delegations to administrative agencies.

In the 1960s several critiques were leveled at legislative and judicial policies that permitted public agencies broad discretion. First, agencies could refuse to fill out their legislative mandate. Second, even when they were intent on rule making, bureaucrats could attempt to "see all around a subject" before issuing an authoritative statement. Thus, Kenneth Davis recommended that legislative charters and judicial directives require a continuing effort toward more precise and detailed rules.[12] In addition, Davis proposed that "these rules not be in the form of generalizations."[13] Rather, Davis said that administrators should formulate hypothetical cases and announce why the actions therein are considered improper. Thus, the public would not be on tenterhooks as the administrator, gropingly and unpredictably, brings a series of exploratory actions, with the sometimes futile hope of arriving at an all-encompassing rule. Davis was particularly concerned with the need for rules in police and prosecutorial agencies where, he believes, discretion is most often and most harmfully exercised. Building on Davis's proposals, Theodore Lowi reasserted the need for "overhead control" on administration with judges and lawmakers drawing stricter limits. With *juridical democracy,* as Lowi terms this state of affairs, citizens or corporate clients can be made more aware of what to expect in their dealings with public organizations.

Project Management

Class actions, the ombudsman, citizen review boards, and juridical democracy can constrain the institutionalized organization. They do not, however, touch, in any significant way, the technological and human investments that are at the core of organizational inertia. People still have a stake in the organization's survival; all that expensive equipment, physical plant, and land defy the administrator to close up shop. Thus, as we saw in Chapter 4, survival becomes an informal goal, displacing to a greater or lesser extent the formal organizational goals. To refocus the organization on assigned tasks, some recommend a move toward temporary organizations and temporary program units within administration. Indeed, there are those who believe that transient organizations are inevitable in postindustrial society.

Warren Bennis is the foremost spokesperson, among organization theorists, for "adaptive, rapidly changing *temporary systems*, organized around problems to be solved by groups of strangers with diverse professional skills."[14] Bennis sees this as the wave of the future because:

> the routine jobs which require bureaucratic administration will be computerized.
> individuals will possess highly specialized skills as a result of extensive education.
> the organization will become an umbrella enveloping distinct, highly specialized units which will have to interact to accomplish tasks.
> interdependence will increase (and competition will decrease) between organizations as partnerships become necessary for task accomplishment.[15]

In the view of Bennis and others, temporary projects will increasingly become the administrator's prime concern. The organization will be composed of employees on retainer, equipment on call, and money on account. When a task arises, a project team containing the appropriate mix of professional personnel will be assembled. Organizational resources—computer time, office equipment, floor space, secretarial and clerical personnel—will be made available. So, too, will a healthy budget, should the team need to purchase that which the organization cannot provide. For high-technology projects these outside purchases can include university faculty, research organizations, and millions of dollars in sophisticated equipment. This ad hoc approach to task performance—bringing together what you need, when you need it, and only for as long as you need it—is called *project management*.

The essence of project management is change and impermanence: the bane of the employee in the institutionalized bureaucracy. However, the retainer concept, by providing a security that is partially unrelated to task, reduces the employee's resistance to change. Since members of the project team have home bases elsewhere in the organization, the end of a project does not mean the end of a job. As one might suspect, it takes a big organization to provide a reservoir of "retainer" jobs or enough tasks to occupy project specialists over an extended period. Similarly, a substantial technological inventory and the ability to write blank checks is the mark of the large organization. Indeed, some predict that the ascendance of temporary organizations will occur within the framework of increasingly large organizational structures. However, they do not feel that these structures will become an irresistible force in the hands of a few. Willingly or unwillingly top management in the "mega-organization" will grant autonomy to its project teams. Superiors, at a distinct knowledge disadvantage when confronted with teams of highly specialized individuals, will be reduced to retrospective approval or disapproval.[16] For most of its operations, the "mega-organization" will be decentralized.

Already there is a high degree of intraorganizational and interorganizational job mobility among professional employees. Even in government, the tabernacle of tenure, mobility is on the rise. For instance, with numerous study commissions precipitating and dissolving through the 1960s and 1970s, many researchers had staccato employment patterns. Often, a researcher's professional ties, as a sociologist or an attorney, for example, provided a steadier anchor than his or her rapidly changing employment relationships. Characterized by an acceptance of uncertainty and impermanence and an ability to develop and discontinue close working relationships quickly, these researchers provide a taste of what some see as the freelance work project cadres of the future.

Project management also may dampen the hierarchical struggles that can occupy the time and dissipate the energies of the employee in the traditional bureaucratic organization. The project unit and its positions are fleeting. With the careful scheduling of tasks, the establishment of intermediate goals with completion dates, and the regular monitoring of progress, the overall goals of the project are kept in sharp focus. Moreover, the highly specialized skills of the project personnel encourage a collegial, rather than a hierarchical, approach to problem solving. Indeed, the project manager is viewed more as a provider of services than as an issuer of orders. As a professional administrator, the project manager removes roadblocks, within or outside the organization, encountered by the project specialists in their attempts to meet the project goals.

Project Management in Action   In private industry, the "product group" is an erstwhile example of the project management approach.[17] In government, the premier example of project management is the

Apollo space program. With teams of physicists, geologists, engineers, and other high-technology specialists, a nationwide network of interconnected computers, and a raft of private subcontractors, NASA met, with room to spare, President Kennedy's goal of a manned moon landing by 1970.[18] Since this is an often told tale, we will not recount the saga of project management and the flight to the moon. However, we would like to share with you a local version of project management with which we are familiar.

PROJECT WILDCAT[19]

Project management is a tool for grappling with problems that go beyond an organization's borders or cut across its traditional framework. One such problem faced by localities is the tendency of rehabilitated addicts and offenders to backslide because employment is not available. In the late 1960s a project management assault—one replicated since by 13 other jurisdictions across the country—was launched on the problem by the Vera Institute in New York City. It was called "Project Wildcat" and those spearheading it had to convince reluctant city agencies, skeptical public employee unions, and wary welfare officials to work together in establishing more than 1000 jobs for former drug addicts.

Project Wildcat faced a tougher challenge, perhaps, than did the Apollo program. No presidential or mayoral declaration had stirred up citizen support. Unlike the expansive funding levels of NASA in the 1960s, the budget check made out to Project Wildcat was severely limited. From old-line welfare agencies—institutionalized to a greater extent than relatively new techno-space structures faced by NASA project managers—the Project Wildcat managers had to pry, coax, or steal personnel, money, and new methods of operation. For starters, the project was separated into four distinct components: (1) developing a job inventory; (2) identifying and overcoming legal and financial constraints; (3) modifying welfare requirements; and (4) recruiting, training, and placing ex-addicts.

Developing a job inventory required that public employers—the building department, the parks department, etc.—be convinced that the output of the Project Wildcat workers would be worth the supervisory and equipment expenditures that would be required. Moreover, the municipal employee unions had to be reassured that no existing jobs would be replaced or modified as a result of Project Wildcat. Thus, the deputy project manager responsible for the job inventory had a task chart that read like a "Who's Who" of agency commissioners and labor leaders.

The deputy project manager responsible for identifying legal and financial constraints was immensely successful. He found 250 such constraints. Removing these constraints, however, was a more difficult task. Welfare recipients—a category that included most of the ex-addicts signed up with Wildcat—could not hold jobs and continue to receive payments. To get around the barrier it was necessary to change the processing procedures and create a new assistance category so that welfare could become "work-fare." The Human Resources Administration (HRA), in the midst of a budget squeeze, saw little reason for setting up a special category for a handful of recipients and even less reason for diverting personnel for the task. The welfare check distribution system, after all, was complex and expensive to modify. Using all their persuasive powers, project team members sought to convince HRA officials that Project Wildcat could not succeed without the change. To punctuate their message, the team members offered to rewrite the applicable procedures and make the necessary computer program modifications. As a result, HRA officials agreed to cooperate and the program went forward through the recruitment, training, and placement stages.

The efforts of the project team were well rewarded. Garbage was removed and pests were eradicated from the backyards of poverty area tenements; abandoned buildings were rehabilitated; road markings were repainted; and parks were cleaned up. The Wildcat workers performed, or freed regular city personnel to perform, jobs that would not otherwise have been done. The work not only benefited the city, but clearly made a dent in the recidivism rate of the ex-addicts and ex-offenders in the program. Over half of the initial participants were working a year later— 42 percent in Wildcat-supported jobs and 12 percent in open-market jobs. Of those who moved on to nonsupported work, nearly 80 percent held the job for 18 months or more. Vera Institute estimated that the taxpayer received $1.03 in public services, reduced welfare payments, and taxes paid by workers for every $1.00 invested in the project. The success of the Wildcat project prompted five federal agencies and the Ford Foundation to finance the extension of the supported-work concept to other areas of the nation through a special nonprofit agency called the Manpower Development Research Corporation.

A Short Assessment   In the succeeding chapters we will delve further into the techniques and tools associated with problem-oriented management. However, we might briefly note the factors that are important to project management's success. First, there should be adequate resources and sufficient time. Second, communications skills and persuasive power should accompany the administrative talents of the project managers and their deputies. Third, since the project manager operates across a broad swath of the pluralistic bureaucracy, public support is helpful. Finally, the support of high-ranking superiors (including the jurisdiction's chief executive, if possible) is essential. In short, to take personnel and other resources from entrenched units, the project manager needs all the support available and a high level of interpersonal skills.

Project management cannot always be used. It is inappropriate for routine and repetitive functions or specialized research functions carried on by experts working alone. It also may not be advisable to use project management when there is major conflict within or between agencies.

This may guarantee clashes between the project manager and department heads. Finally, project management should not be undertaken hastily. In deciding to proceed, the costs involved in establishing and operating a project organization should be measured against the expected savings or anticipated income.

In sum, project management provides a means for organizational flexibility. It enables a response to the needs of clients even as the needs shift with time. Although difficult to implement, project management can be an effective antidote to organizational calcification.

ANTIDOTES FOR PLURALISM

Most analyses of the public policy process admit to the influence of special interests. In Chapter 8 we reviewed these analyses in detail, closing with Schubert's tripartite analysis of the public interest.

As you recall, Schubert considered the concept of competitive special interest groups as the "realist" view of the public policy process. In the 1960s and 1970s, there were several assaults on the pluralist "reality" that sought to diminish the influence of the special interest and to reassert the public interest. They included the formation of *public interest research groups* and the reform of campaign-financing requirements. Long-standing safeguards against special interest influence on public policy—the press and codes of ethics—were also brought to bear with a renewed vigor.

Public Interest Research Groups

"Public interest" lobbyists of the 1960s analyzed the legislation of various regulatory agencies, and charged that "regulation in the public interest"—a phrase found in most enabling acts—had been abandoned and industry-agency symbiosis had been substituted. For instance, according to public interest lobbyists, the FDA was not as interested in pursuing the pure food called for in its legislation as it was in reaching an amicable agreement with the food industry over what constituted an acceptable level of dirt. Such charges were repeated again and again in a remarkable series of books published by associates of Ralph Nader.[20] Muckraking, high-minded, and gloriously revealing, *Nader's Raiders* tore apart agency after agency. When agency activity was measured against the statutorily prominent criteria of "public health" and "public safety," it fared poorly. Instead, the "Raiders" charged, agencies were moved by the industry's version of "industry economics" or inducements such as the *deferred bribe:* the acceptance of a high-salaried post in the regulated industry upon the regulatory official's termination of government service.[21]

As a result of these books the administrative policy-making process

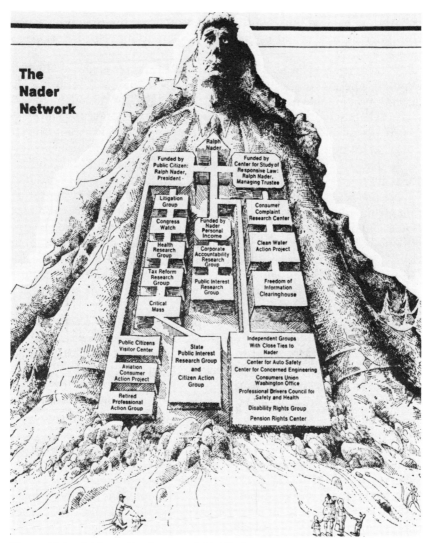

Figure 11.1 A Mount Rushmore of "Public Interest" Organizations with Ralph Nader at the Pinnacle. In comparison to the government activities that they monitor, these groups range from small to tiny. Nonetheless, their impact—on car safety, airline regulation, and government information policy—has been substantial. SOURCE: *The New York Times,* January 29, 1978, p. E-3. Copyright © 1978 by The New York Times Company. Reprinted by permission.

and the role that special interests played was exposed to public scrutiny. The nonrole of the "consumer" was also highlighted and there followed a period of "consumer" awareness. In a true special interest response many jurisdictions created consumer offices. As for the regulatory agencies, they expanded the opportunities and relaxed the requirements for consumer input, but did not end their relationship with the regulated industries.

In his early efforts, Nader had attacked the bureaucracy through exposés. These exposés precipitated a public outcry and served as the ammunition in lobbying for corrective legislation. As the 1970s opened, Nader abandoned neither exposés nor "ad hocracy" but put more emphasis on establishing a firm base for the continuous monitoring of government by general purpose "public interest" organizations.

In rapid succession, Nader created the Center for the Study of Responsive Law and Public Citizen, which, in turn, begat the Consumer Complaint Research Center, Congress Watch, the Public Citizens Litigation Group, and others (see Figure 11.1). Non-Nader groups also have flourished on the national scene. These organizations are funded by contributions from individuals and foundations. The bulk of the funding comes from relatively small contributions. Public Interest Research Groups in states and localities also receive citizen funding that includes a portion of the student activity fee at universities where the student body has elected to make a contribution.

These organizations have accomplished much. They were a major force behind "Freedom of Information" legislation that improved the citizen's access to files in both public and private organizations. (See Chapter 14 for a more detailed discussion.) Auto safety devices from the seat belts of the 1960s to the air bags of the 1980s received their major boost from the efforts of the Nader groups. The authorship role of the public interest research group is reflected in the safety regulations for mines, nuclear power plants, drugs, and chemicals.

It is possible to question whether the public interest group has wrongly assumed its name by asking, "Who chooses the issues?" The Nader groups, for instance, often go after their founder's pet peeves. Even though the targeted policies—for example, the overbooking of airline flights—potentially affect a large portion of the public, their modification does not necessarily reflect public wishes. Still, at the risk of heresy, one can justify the public interest group in pluralist terms. To wit: The organizations purport to represent an overriding public interest. Their charters are generic; their specific activities freelance, various, and unpredictable. They are funded. Therefore, somewhere out there is a "public interest" willing to pay money to perpetuate itself.

The Power of the Press
Characterized as early as the 1950s as the "fourth branch of government," the press demonstrated its power in the 1970s.[23] Although a writ of indictment or a bill of impeachment was never handed up, the dogged investigative reporting of the press helped try and convict Rich-

ard M. Nixon in the court of public opinion. Nixon's resignation closed out an administration that had tried, as had no other in modern times, to intimidate the press.

With its triumph, the news media (print and electronic) looked indomitable, and many felt assured that the "fourth branch" was keeping a close eye on the other three. It would be a mistake to assume, however, that the news media are omniscient, ever vigilant, or impervious. For various reasons the press may overlook as much as it uncovers. Part of the reason is that the press and the government have a symbiotic relationship.[24] To the press, administration provides news. From the press, administration gets publicity for ongoing and proposed programs. The government organization is one of the more prolific producers of press releases and the newspaper is the most gluttonous consumer. The newspaper, however, cannot afford to analyze all that it consumes. Every 24 hours, large volumes of information must be digested and printed. Thus, pressed reporters conduct sample analyses or, on the basis of past performance, take what is offered at face value. If the agency has a record of putting out accurate and interesting news, its press releases are likely to appear in the newspaper intact and unchecked. More problematically, the agency that can conduct its operations in secrecy can build a reputation for credibility upon a superstructure of lies. Although "credibility gaps" are uncovered, checking out every story is prohibitively expensive. Thus, the temptation is always present for the administrator to slip half-truths or even falsehoods into the news if the odds of getting caught are low.[25]

The media can also shut out points of view that lack resourceful, sophisticated proponents. Mimeograph machines, public relations officers, and envelope stuffers are helpful in making the front page or the six o'clock news.[26] Moreover, the "institutional elitists" discussed in Chapter 8 would note that newspaper publishers and editors hold a conception of the acceptable limits of public policy that does not differ radically from that held by government officials.

Nonetheless, the press, as a force to be contended with, looms large in the vision of most elected and appointed officials. A career can be shattered on the front page; a program can be exposed and discredited. The press is, and shall continue to be, one of the most potent safeguards against administrative excesses.

Campaign Financing Reform

Campaign financing is one of the major conduits for special interest entry into the public policy-making process. The movement for the reform of campaign financing has been led in the 1960s and 1970s by the non-Nader citizen lobby Common Cause. Reform proponents claimed that financing campaigns from private contributions opened the way for improprieties. The argument became more persuasive in the wake of the Watergate scandal.

Nixon's campaign staff wheedled, cajoled, extorted, and bargained for campaign funds. As implicit barter, the staff used the prospect of government benefits for the generous and government penalties for the tightfisted. The Nixon campaign committees "laundered" the money of shy contributors—so that it would appear to come from another source. It gave pointers to corporations—barred by law from contributing—on how to funnel funds through its executives in the form of private contributions. In one frantic period, trying to beat the effective date of a law requiring disclosure of the source of contributions, some Nixon fund raisers adopted the modus operandi of the "bagman"—the person who collects the daily take in a brown paper bag from scattered illegal betting parlors.

The Nixon campaign was a sorry spectacle, perhaps even the low point in our electoral history.[27] However, the abuses illuminated a fundamental and long-standing situation: Running for office requires a lot of money and those who provide it expect certain tokens of appreciation from the successful candidate. As David Adamany and George Agree write:

> The pattern of giving distorts American elections. Candidates win access to the electorate only if they can mobilize money from the upper classes, established interest groups, big givers and ideological zealots....The pattern of giving also threatens the governmental process. The contributions of big givers and interest groups award them access to office holders, so they can better plead their causes. In some cases, contributions directly corrupt by purchasing decisions....Campaign financing policy should allow all citizens a roughly equal opportunity to participate in financing as well as voting.[28]

Both before and after the Nixon campaign's sordid performance, presidential elections were the target of major campaign financing reforms. The first, the Federal Election Campaign Act of 1971, required extensive disclosures of the sources and amounts of contributions. In 1972, the Campaign Communication Reform Act limited the amount of money that could be spent on media advertising. After the 1972 campaign showed that the 1971 act's disclosure provisions were riddled with holes, Congress passed a stronger version. As a result of the *Federal Election Campaign Act of 1974,* contributions of over $100 had to be by check, so did campaign expenditures exceeding that amount. Campaign accounts were required to be kept in single banking institutions (one in each state was permitted for presidential races), and a principal campaign committee was to keep a master set of books that would include the income and expenditures of all committees working on behalf of the candidate.

The Election Campaign Act of 1974, by imposing limitations on contributions, significantly reduced the electoral leverage of special interests. The individual's maximum campaign contribution to any candidate for federal office was limited to $3000 ($1000 for the primary; $1000 for any run-off election; and $1000 for the general election. If only the general election was held, the limit would be $1000). Overall, no individual could contribute more than $25,000 to campaigns for federal offices. Loopholes remained but the 1974 act resembled Swiss cheese to a lesser extent than its 1971 predecessor.

In terms of long-range impact, the severest blow to special interest influence through campaign financing may have been the creation of the *Presidential Election Campaign Fund*. The fund is stocked by individual citizens who choose to divert a dollar of their tax liability to public campaign financing. The election fund was available to political parties and presidential candidates on the following basis: Candidates, upon raising $100,000 in the prenomination stage, were entitled to matching grants for all contributions of $250 or less. The two major political parties were entitled to $2 million in convention expenses from the fund. If public funding was rejected, $2 million was still the limit. Similarly the $20 million in public campaign funding available to each major party's presidential nominee was as much as could be legally raised from private sources. The limits could be revised upward to account for inflation.

With individual contributions curtailed, and the total of those contributions limited, the Republicans and the Democrats, enticed by the low overhead and prodded by the "post-Watergate" morality, opted for full federal funding in the presidential campaigns of 1976. Overall, some $72 million was distributed to parties and candidates in 1976: $24 million to various candidates during the primaries; $4 million for the conventions; and, in the general election, $21.8 million for Republican candidate Gerald Ford and a similar amount for Democratic candidate Jimmy Carter. Thus, for the major candidates, no private funds from either individuals or groups were directly available. (Of course, the campaigns for state and local candidates have spill-over effects that benefit national candidates. These campaigns remained privately funded since senators and representatives, as of 1978, would not mandate full public funding for their own campaigns.)

The election of Jimmy Carter was a direct outgrowth, perhaps, of the new funding scheme. Little known to the public and hardly a power within the Democratic party, Carter, with the value of small contributions enhanced by the federal funding laws, beat out such stalwarts as Henry Jackson, whose access to large contributors was substantially mooted by the limitations of the federal funding laws. Similarly, the equal funding of the Democratic and Republican candidates wiped out a financial edge traditionally enjoyed by the Republicans. It is not surprising, then, that one of President Carter's first acts was a call for election reforms including the public funding of congressional campaigns. Again Congress demurred, but the suggestion, often raised during the 1960s and 1970s and receiving a bit more support each time, is certain to be raised again. In the states, over 40 election reform measures were passed in the 1970s that limited the amount and source of expenditures and contributions.[29] If the trend toward public financing continues, we may see a major reduction in the impact of special interest groups.

Codes of Ethics

Public funding will not close off all of the express lanes that speed special interest views to key administrative decision points. As we noted in Chapter 8, the president's constituencies include those party members holding or aspiring to elective office. Those incumbents and aspirants—mayors, governors, and legislators—still mounted privately funded campaigns for office as the 1970s closed. Thus, the "party constituency" can urge upon the president policies that secretly reflect the preferential treatment of campaign contributors.

Of course, administrators may also have direct contact with elected officials who surreptitiously advance special interests. If administrators suspect, or are certain, that ulterior motives are behind requests or orders, they may resist. In Chapter 7 we took note of Richardson and Ruckelshaus, who drew the line and refused to obey an order that they deemed improper. As is the case with many dilemmas that pit personal ethics against organizational obedience, these two gentlemen acted without formal guidance. With the same absence of guidance but with less drama and a happier ending for the administrator, the ethics-obedience battle is frequently played out in administration. Politically referred clients are graciously received but the standards governing their requests are not relaxed. Unqualified candidates for patronage positions are turned away by snails-paced processing and verbal descriptions of a miserable and demeaning job.

For the administrator who wants formally to parry requests perceived as improper or to punish behavior deemed unethical, many jurisdictions have codes of conduct. These codes also help employees determine whether or not a planned action is proper.[30] Codes of conduct can be positive or negative. Positive codes are in the nature of oaths to uphold the law or to comport oneself in a manner becoming a public servant. Negative codes are the "shalt nots," and penalties for transgressions may include dismissal or criminal prosecution. In jurisdictions where *codes of ethics* exist some of the more commonly prohibited actions are:

> on-the-job political activity.
> the use of government property for private purposes.

the participation in regulatory or contractual decisions by government employees who hold a financial interest in the affected firms. (In the trade, this is known as *conflict of interest.*)

the administrator's employment by a firm within a year of his or her separation from the government agency regulating that firm.[31]

As the 1970s closed, "financial ethics" were heavily emphasized. Thanks to Watergate and the creative personal financing of President Carter's first OMB director, Bert Lance, "full financial disclosure" has become fairly well established as a rite of passage for those aspiring to higher administrative positions. Although the search is more for shady dealings than for financial or fiduciary relationships with special interests, the latter are revealed as well. Most nominees sever potential conflict of interest relationships, or put their holdings in a "blind trust," in order to clear the way for appointment.

It should be noted that codes of ethics are as much probureaucratic as they are antipluralist. As we discussed in Chapter 2 and Chapter 6, the bureaucratic functionary separates work from personal affairs. Codes of ethics seek further to insure value-neutral employees. However, in the process, they may expose special interest values in administration.

SUMMARY

In this chapter we looked at some specific remedies for institutionalization, such as the ombudsman and project management. We also touched upon several prescriptions for reinjecting the "public interest" into the pluralist policy-making process, such as the "citizen's lobby" and public financing of political campaigns. In the following final three chapters we will take an in-depth look at some analytical approaches to public policy making which attempt to skirt the shortcomings associated with institutionalized organizations living in an environment that tends to be dominated by special interests. These include systems analysis, program planning and evaluation, and computer-based management information systems.

KEY TERMS AND CONCEPTS

Citizen review boards
Class action lawsuits
Codes of ethics
Deferred bribe
Federal Election Campaign Act of 1974

Juridical democracy
Ombudsman
Presidential Election Campaign Fund
Project management
Public interest research groups

REVIEW KEY TERMS AND CONCEPTS

Elitism

Incrementalism

Institutionalization
Interest groups
Realistic, rationalist, and idealist
views of the public interest

Planning-Programming-
Budgeting Systems (PPBS)
Pluralism
Zero-Base Budgeting (ZBB)

NOTES

1. Victor Thompson, *Without Sympathy or Enthusiasm: The Problem of Administrative Compassion* (University, Alabama: University of Alabama Press, 1975), chapter 3; Tom Wolfe, *Mau-Mauing the Flak Catchers* (New York: Bantam Books, 1971).
2. Walter Gellhorn, *When Americans Complain* (Cambridge: Harvard University Press, 1966); Walter Gellhorn, *Ombudsmen and Others: Citizens' Protectors in Nine Countries* (Cambridge: Harvard University Press, 1966).
3. Bernard Frank, "The Ombudsman and Human Rights," *Administrative Law Review* 23, no. 3 (April 1970): 467–492.
4. Donald C. Rowat, *The Ombudsman Plan: Essays on the World-Wide Spread of an Idea* (Toronto: McClelland and Stewart, 1973).
5. Ibid., pp. 76–85.
6. David J. Olson, "Citizen Grievance Letters as a Gubernatorial Control Device in Wisconsin," *Journal of Politics* 31 (August 1969): 741–755.
7. *The Report of the National Advisory Commission on Civil Disorders* (New York: Bantam Books, 1968), pp. 283–293.
8. Ibid., chapters 11, 12, 13; Jerome H. Skolnick, *The Politics of Protest* (New York: Ballantine Books, 1967); David W. Abbot, Louis H. Gold, Edward T. Rogowsky, *Police, Politics and Race* (New York: American Jewish Committee, 1969).
9. Murray Stedman, Jr., *Urban Politics* (Cambridge: Winthrop Publishers, 1972), pp. 271–292.
10. Ibid.
11. Theodore Lowi, *The End of Liberalism: Ideology, Policy and the Crisis of Public Authority* (New York: Norton, 1969), pp. 297–299.
12. Kenneth Culp Davis, *Discretionary Justice: A Preliminary Inquiry* (Baton Rouge: Louisiana University Press, 1969), p. 219.
13. Ibid., p. 220.
14. Warren G. Bennis, *American Bureaucracy* (New Brunswick: Transaction, 1972), pp. 3–17, 165–187; see also Bennis, *Changing Organizations* (New York: McGraw-Hill, 1966); and Alvin Toffler, *Future Shock* (New York: Random House, 1970).
15. Bennis, *American Bureaucracy*, pp. 3–17.
16. John Kenneth Galbraith, *The New Industrial State* (New York: New American Library (Mentor), 1967), chapters VI and VII.
17. Victor A. Thompson, "Bureaucracy and New Product Innovation," *Academy of Management Journal* 16 (September 1972): 361–372.
18. James Webb, *Space Age Management* (New York: McGraw-Hill, 1969).
19. Arthur L. Levine, "Project Management in New York City Agencies," unpublished paper based on a study of project and task force management in five cities, under a grant from the City University Research Foundation, BHE-PSC Award Program.
20. Edward F. Cox, Robert C. Fellmeth, and John C. Schulz, *The Nader Report on the Federal Trade Commission* (New York: Barron Publishing, 1969); Robert

C. Fellmeth, *The Interstate Commerce Commission* (New York: Grossman, 1970); James S. Turner, *The Chemical Feast* (New York: Grossman, 1970).

21. Fellmeth, *Interstate Commerce Commission*, p. 312.
22. *The New York Times*, 29 January 1978, p. 3.
23. Douglas Cater, *The Fourth Branch of Government* (Boston: Houghton Mifflin, 1959).
24. V. Sigal, *Reporters and Officials* (Lexington, Mass.: Heath, 1973). One of the sharper thrusts at the government-press symbiosis comes from Tom Bethell, "The Myth of an Adversary Press," *Harper's*, January 1977, p. 33.
25. David Halberstam, *The Best and the Brightest* (New York: Random House, 1972).
26. For a thoroughgoing treatment of the issues surrounding media access, see Benno Schmidt, *Freedom of the Press vs. Public Access* (New York: Praeger, 1976), p. 60.
27. Frederick C. Mosher, et al., *Watergate: Implications for Responsible Government* (New York: Basic Books, 1974).
28. David Adamany and George E. Agree, *Political Money: A Strategy for Campaign Financing in America* (New York: Johns Hopkins Press, 1975).
29. Ibid., p. viii.
30. Joseph F. Zimmerman, *Ethics in Local Government* (Washington, D.C.: International City Management Association, 1976).
31. See also *A Suggested Code of Ethics for Municipal Officials and Employees* (Washington, D.C.: International City Management Association, 1962).

BIBLIOGRAPHY

Abbot, David W.; Gold, Louis H.; and Rogowsky, Edward T. *Police, Politics and Race.* New York: American Jewish Committee, 1969.

Adamany, David, and Agree, George E. *Political Money: A Strategy for Campaign Financing in America.* New York: Johns Hopkins Press, 1975.

Alexander, Herbert. *Campaign Money: Reform and Reality in the States.* New York: Free Press, 1976.

Bennis, Warren G. *American Bureaucracy.* New Brunswick, N.J.: Transaction, 1972.

Cox, Edward F.; Fellmeth, Robert C.; and Schulz, John C. *The Nader Report on the Federal Trade Commission.* New York: Barron Publishing, 1969.

Gellhorn, Walter. *Ombudsmen and Others: Citizens' Protectors in Nine Countries.* Cambridge: Harvard University Press, 1966.

———. *When Americans Complain.* Cambridge: Harvard University Press, 1966.

Halberstam, David. *The Best and the Brightest.* New York: Random House, 1972.

Kaufman, Herbert. *Are Government Agencies Immortal?* Washington, D.C.: Brookings, 1976.

Magruder, Jeb Stuart. *An American Life.* New York: Atheneum, 1974.

Mosher, Frederick C., et al. *Watergate: Implications for Responsible Government.* New York: Basic Books, 1974.

The Report of the National Advisory Commission on Civil Disorders. New York: Bantam Books, 1968.

Rowat, Donald C. *The Ombudsman Plan: Essays on the World-Wide Spread of an Idea.* Toronto: McClelland and Stewart, 1973.

Schmidt, Benno. *Freedom of the Press vs. Public Access.* New York: Praeger, 1976.

Sigal, V. *Reporters and Officials.* Lexington, Mass.: Heath, 1973.

Stedman, Murray, Jr. *Urban Politics.* Cambridge: Winthrop Publishers, 1972.

Toffler, Alvin. *Future Shock.* New York: Random House, 1970.

Turner, James S. *The Chemical Feast.* New York: Grossman, 1970.

Webb, James. *Space Age Management.* New York: McGraw-Hill, 1969.

Wolfe, Tom. *Mau-Mauing the Flak Catchers.* New York: Bantam Books, 1971.

Zimmerman, Joseph F. *Ethics in Local Government.* Washington, D.C.: International City Management Association, 1976.

In addition to the sources cited in the notes and bibliography, the following *Public Administration Review (PAR)* articles are a convenient starting point for a more detailed exploration of the material in this chapter.

Balloun, James S. and John F. Mahoney. "Beating the Cost Service Squeeze: The Project Team Approach to Cost Improvement," *PAR* 32, no. 5 (Sept./Oct. 1972): 531–538.

Cupps, D. Stephen. "Emerging Problems of Citizen Participation," *PAR* 37, no. 5 (Sept./Oct. 1977): 478–487.

Dunn, Delmer. "Transmitting Information to the Press: Differences Among Officials," *PAR* 28, no. 5 (Sept./Oct. 1968): 445–452.

Fredrickson, H. George. "Public Administration in the 1970's: Developments and Directions," *PAR* 36, no. 5 (Sept./Oct. 1976): 564–576.

Graham, George A. "Ethical Guidelines for Public Administrators: Observations on the Rules of the Game," *PAR* 34, no. 1 (Jan./Feb. 1974): 90–92.

Lewis, Jack. "The Gentle Art of Good Listening," *PAR* 32, no. 5 (Sept./Oct. 1972): 544–545.

Paglin, Max D. and Edgar Shor. "Regulatory Agency Responses to the Development of Public Participation," *PAR* 37, no. 2 (March/April 1977): 140–148.

Schuch, Peter H. "Public Interest Groups and the Policy Process," *PAR* 37, no. 2 (March/April 1977): 132–140.

Wakefield, Susan. "Ethics and the Public Service: A Case for Individual Responsibility," *PAR* 36, no. 6 (Nov./Dec. 1976): 661–666.

PART FIVE

ALTERNATIVE CONCEPTS AND APPLICATIONS FOR GOVERNMENTS' POLICY PROBLEMS

CHAPTER 12

THE SYSTEMS APPROACH TO POLICY ANALYSIS

INTRODUCTION

In public administration, there has been raging a debate between those who see incrementalism as the most practical adaptation to decision making in complex situations and those who feel that a comprehensive approach promises better solutions to society's problems. In the view of the latter, incremental decision making, "muddling through," is not sufficient for the management of modern society (see Chapter 9).

According to critics, incrementalism is a blinder, one that obscures the vision of administrators, legislators, and even analysts. The narrowest perspective belongs to the administrators. The organizational machinery demands their continued attention and the organizational mission demands their committed leadership. In charge of a fragment of government in a competitive milieu, administrators are rarely motivated to take a holistic view of government enterprise.

Critics also contend that incrementalism beclouds legislative and executive outlooks. In an incremental response to the complex panorama confronting them, legislatures and executive staffs do two things. First, they zero in on the most prominent features; squeaky wheels are greased without checking for bald tires or defective suspensions. Second, the oversight job is broken up. Individual legislators and analysts oversee an agency or functional area. Their fragmented perspectives produce topical remedies that are added together, rather than integrated, into a legislative or executive program. It is rarely determined if two or more remedies, in combination, have harmful effects.

In this chapter, we will explore an alternative to incrementalism. It is the systems approach to policy analysis. To set the stage, some of the policy failures of incrementalism will be considered. Throughout the chapter, the emphasis will be on urban areas. Cities highlight the deficiencies of incrementalism. Moreover, the highly complex and interrelated urban infrastructure serves to illustrate the usefulness of the systems perspective.

CIRCUMSTANCES
BEYOND INCREMENTAL CONTROL

Incrementalism attacks problems as they arise, where they arise, and to the extent that they arise. The approach is similar to cutting weeds without uprooting them, or patching sod on bare spots without turning the earth. The weeds keep growing; the grass keeps dying; and the garden remains a mess. The urban garden has been incrementally tended. Yet, despite massive government expenditures, our cities do not flower. Indeed, in many metropolises, it appears that the long-term fruits of incrementalism are bitter, expensive, and damaging to the quality of life. An observer describes the crop:

> It is virtually impossible to be original describing the status of the central cities of our major metropolitan areas. The problems abound: Congestion, pollution, slums, poverty, racial strife, crime, drug addiction, dirt, noise. People still argue about whether conditions are better or worse than they used to be and whether the people who now live in these cities are or are not better off than they used to be. This much is certain: not many are happy with conditions as they are.[1]

Yet, these conditions exist in the wake of decades of programs that were designed to improve city life. Urban renewal sought to remove the aged and decrepit structures that lay close by the downtown areas in most central cities. It did. In the process, it neglected to account for the poor people thus removed. Urban renewal made middle-income housing in what was formerly lower-income residential areas. It did not, however, make middle-income citizens out of the poor who were displaced by demolition and urban renewal construction. They had to move to other low-rent areas, the supply of which had been reduced by the renewal's emphasis on middle-class construction. So the poor became more concentrated, providing a richer culture in which despair and anomie could thrive. Thus, a nationwide program designed to improve the quality of city life had contrary effects, such as the further segregation of the poor. Indeed, Theodore Lowi, in his book *The End of Liberalism*, cites one town that consciously applied urban renewal in a way that increased the residential segregation of blacks.[2] However, the framers of urban renewal legislation had not accounted for either mistakes or misuse. Both occurred because policy makers had not anticipated them and made no provision to deal with them.

Perhaps because it hit so close to home, the environmental issue sharply underscored the boomerang effect of many government policies. The emphasis on economic growth could bring us not only prosperity but waters that we could not swim in and fish that we could not eat. The plastics that wrapped our foods so neatly could turn into gaseous acid when burned and eat away at the insides of our incinerators. At the other end of the four-pound Sunday *New York Times* was a considerable chunk of forest cut away. For many heavy smokers there lurked in the future what Kurt Vonnegut has called "a fairly sure, fairly honorable form of suicide."[3] However, it was the automobile and its highways, long considered an unqualified boon to society, that was the focus of the environmentalists' attack. Lead particles, carbon monoxide, and other hydrocarbons that spewed out as cars consumed gasoline on highways encircling cities combined under the right condition into clouds that could kill. Although the most dramatic, pollution was only one of the many dark results that tarnished the once bright hopes of supporters of highway programs. One before-and-after perspective proceeds thusly:

> The highway program was attractive, politically, largely because it made sense in the popular economic thinking of the time. It seemed to support a growing economy. It was a boost to employment. . . . Unforeseen or neglected side effects which have gained importance to the public since the 1960s include pollution, accident rates, energy consumption, segregation and the undermining of mass transit . . . the destruction of neighborhood communities and diminution of housing stock, historic sites and open space.[4]

All this and more. The great, looping bypass highways were designed to speed "through" traffic via less congested suburban routes; they did. In addition, the highways facilitated the middle-class exodus from the central city. On the heels of their clientele, central city retailers occupied the shopping malls springing up along the new highways. Suburban industrial parks also blossomed, enticing manufacturers with cheaper land, lower taxes, and better transportation. As a result, many manufacturers and retailers completely abandoned their operationally inefficient, multistory, traffic-paralyzed downtown structures.

Firms fleeing to the suburbs left behind workers as well as structures. Low-income workers, minority workers, and those dependent on mass transit often could not follow their employers to the suburbs. Many could not afford to leave low-rent, central city housing. Zoning policies, often racially motivated, held suburban housing costs beyond the reach of low-salaried employees. Mass transit from central city residential areas to new suburban work locations was either nonexistent or required a lengthy and expensive trip. The alternative for reaching relocated jobs was the automobile, which, if the unskilled employee had one, was usually too unreliable for the daily round trip from city to suburb. The result for many workers who were left behind was unemployment, depriving some poor city families of their only source of income. Meanwhile, some middle-class, suburban families added second and third incomes as housewives and teenagers filled the relocated jobs.[5]

Those who favor comprehensive planning over incremental policy making often point to the "unanticipated" consequences of major endeavors such as the highway program. However, critics of incrementalism do not confine themselves to major social policies that they feel have gone awry. Some see little evidence of systematic planning or coordination anywhere. "Priorities," writes one, "are horribly mixed up in single agencies, let alone across the federal structure."[6] From an observer of the state scene comes an echo:

> Few states have any capability to relate their social service delivery systems to each other. . . . (for instance) one problem is the extent to which persons whose primary mental health problems do not require institutionalization should be discharged. . . . many decisions are made on the basis that released mental patients, particularly geriatric patients, simply go on welfare and place other burdens on the state social service delivery systems. Fact or fiction? Who can tell unless patient discharge records can be related systematically to welfare records and records of community mental health and aging programs—a comparison that cannot be made in most states.[7]

It seems that even a descent to the municipal level fails to bring an escape. The following tale of local agencies bumping into each other appeared in *Fortune* magazine:

> For example, (in the South Bronx), piecemeal urban renewal efforts wasted millions of dollars of capital improvements, while the burden of high and rising taxation encouraged businessmen to move away and landlords to let their buildings rot. That hopeless tangle of mismanagement called the New York City government deserves a considerable share of the blame. On several occasions, rehabilitation teams and demolition crews working under separate city programs have appeared at the same building on the same day.[8]

Finally, intergovernmental collisions can be highly dramatic, particularly when law enforcement agencies are involved. There have been several reports of "Mexican standoffs" as federal and local narcotics officers descended on the same cache of drugs at the same time. Since each is reluctant to forgo the credit for "the bust," a joint and mutually antagonistic watch develops as a decision from superiors is awaited. The recent trend toward joint federal-state-local task forces for many law enforcement areas indicates that efforts are being made to define areas of responsibility and emphasize a team approach rather than a competitive one. It is too early to tell how successful these programs will be in modifying organizational dynamics. However, as a roadblock to systematic planning, an agency's preoccupation with securing and expanding its environmental space is a prime impediment.

Proponents of increased government planning and coordination also criticize fundamental and long-standing constitutional, legislative, and executive designs. The constitutionally prescribed terms for legislators and federal, state, county, and municipal elected executives—ranging from two to six years but closer to two on the average—are attacked for inducing a shortsightedness that is inadequate for dealing with the long-term consequences of programs. Governors, for instance, are identified as having interests that "tend to be short range, innovative and opportunistic, rather than long range."[9] Executive staff agencies, particularly those concerned with budgeting, are often somewhat less than visionary. "Department of Finance . . . review gives precisely the same attention to every appropriation item, which is to say that each item is treated as an entity completely within itself, related to nothing except its own record."[10] Within the legislature, the committee system is seen as further narrowing the focus of individual legislators.

Congressional budget reform and the increasing role of the Office of Management and Budget indicate a growing awareness of the need for a systematic evaluation of government activity. This is not to say, however, that failure or success in the legislative and administrative arena will no longer be dependent on the amount of support that can be marshaled. Nonetheless, the implications of a given policy or program will be, at the least, more fully evident. It is a step in the direction "of putting the facts in control of the situation."[11] Looking down the road, proponents of factually based public policy see an analytical approach that will better "interrelate taxation, government expenditures, fiscal and monetary policy, economic output, unemployment and inflation."[12]

What the above statements envision is a systems approach to the setting of public policy. Environmental pollution and central city decline are seen as an indictment of the incremental approach. Compartmentalized solutions have a habit of getting out of their compartments, and when they get into others they may be anything but solutions. In fact, the environment with which policy makers deal is not really composed of distinct compartments, although the functional nature of most agencies might cause executives to have such a perspective. The public policy maker's decision arena is a system. Not only is it uncompartmentalized, it is uncooperative and hard to figure out. Jay W. Forrester, one of the pioneers in the analysis of urban systems, describes some system characteristics below.

> Complex systems actively resist most policy changes.... They respond to policy changes in directions opposite to what most people expect.... the short term response is often opposite to the long term effect.... We develop experience and intuition almost entirely from contact with simple systems, where cause and effect are closely related in space and time. Complex systems behave very differently.[13]

No wonder policy makers make mistakes! The remainder of this chapter is about systems and the systems concept as applied to the analysis of government organizations and the decision environment in which government executives operate. Systems analysis is gaining currency as a tool managers can apply to discover and correct organizational problems and to chart an organizational course that avoids many of the pitfalls that remain hidden when viewed from the incremental perspective. Systems is a general concept and *systems analysis* is a general tool. Therefore, what follows may at times seem elemental and, at others, somewhat theoretical. However, the essence of what the chapter conveys is a way of thinking, one that has a wide variety of applications which you might find yourself applying sooner than you expect.

WHAT ARE SYSTEMS?

System is becoming one of the most widely used words in the English language. Every day, we are bombarded with one or another variation. "Educational system," "ecosystem," "information system," "solar system," "government system," "the System"; no matter what we read, it seems to be about a system.

The frequent use of the word leaves everyone vaguely sure of what it is even if they cannot quite define it. System is accepted without ever being dissected. Part of this is due to the fact that it serves as a "last name" to so many other words. People find it hard to describe system without relating it to a given "first name." Thus, people might define systems as planets, computers, roads, or government agencies. All are, in fact, systems. Knowing this, however, brings us no closer to a meaning of system. This is because system does not relate primarily to the physical characteristics of things or even to the effects things have on the world outside of them. System refers to the way that a thing is put together. Von Bertalanffy makes it short, neat, and to the point: "A system can be defined as a complex of elements standing in interaction."[14]

The definition is skeletal, but then, so is the concept. System speaks of structure and functioning. It is a description of how parts are put together and how those parts work. This is why systems have "bugs" and "bottlenecks," not to mention dysfunctions. Something is not meshing. Either the system is at a standstill or it begins producing the wrong thing. Government systems often exhibit such behavior. The highly computerized Bay Area Rapid Transit System in California was, on one occasion, completely shut down when safety devices picked up several phantom trains about to crash into real ones. Prison systems are often accused of being institutions for graduate study in crime techniques rather than mechanisms for the rehabilitation of criminals. Stories about systems "not working" often provide touches of humor among otherwise dismal news reports.

A PARKING BUREAU COMMITS FETAL ERROR

Chicago (AP)   Frank Gauss 4th tore up the legal notice that declared him a fugitive from justice, stuffed some of it in his mouth and burped.

The Springfield, Ill., Traffic Violation Dept. had just charged him with refusing to pay a parking fine.

Gauss had no comment when he got the notice this week. He's four months old, the violation was on Sept. 3, 1975, in Springfield, and that, said his parents, is an airtight alibi. "He wasn't born until May 21, 1976," said Mr. and Mrs. Frank Gauss 3rd, both 22.

The father said he himself wasn't near the Springfield area at the time.

Mrs. Eleanor Baker, Springfield city treasurer, said, "Let's just call it a combination of computer error and a human error. The baby will not go to jail."[15]

It is a good bet that a "systems analyst" was put on the trail of this particular error. After all, agencies do not like to be ridiculed. However, the systems analyst will not analyze the external impact of this child-chasing computer. What he will do is recheck the computer program, look at the keypunch entries, and examine the original ticket. The search of the systems analyst is for what went wrong with the system.

Often, the job of finding out what went wrong entails a detailed study of the system, its parts, and its interconnections. In this sense, automobile mechanics are a systems analysts when they take apart your automobile to discover "the problem." Psychoanalysts perform a similar search in trying to get to the root of psychological difficulties. Also, much of academic research is devoted to analyzing the essential components of phenomena. A sociologist, in trying to discover the root cause of the hostility between certain ethnic groups, might ask the following questions: Do the groups compete for the same housing? Employment? Are their religions different? Is animosity traditional between the two mother countries? With the answers, the researcher draws a picture of each group and intermeshes them to see where they fit squarely together and where incompatible edges cause intergroup friction.

In this case, the sociologist is analyzing a system. This system (the neighborhood) has two major subsystems (ethnic groups A and B). These subsystems are not working very well together, thereby bringing a certain amount of instability to the neighborhood system. The sociologist, by asking the above questions, is trying to discover exactly which linkages between the subsystems are "shorted out." If the linkage that is causing the sparks can be discovered and repaired, the larger system, the neighborhood, is likely to function better.

It is not only existing systems that can be analyzed. Proposed systems can be analyzed as well. Years before the first 747 jumbo jet and its 350 passengers left the ground, a midget version, about eight feet long, had "flown" millions of miles. Through artificially created weather extremes, with various loads, and under a range of emergency conditions, the 747 system was analyzed through a mock-up that was identical in detail but a fraction of the size. System malfunctions were discovered and corrected by an analytical process, a simulation, that allows for the exploration of the actual consequences of the proposed system design.

Analyzing systems, thus, can be useful in several ways. System components can be identified and their interrelationships established. Bad components or bad connections can be discovered. A full understanding of a malfunctioning system is also an understanding of how it could work better. A system that works well, if the dynamics of its successful functioning are clear, can be duplicted elsewhere. When a system can be abstractly reproduced so as to preserve its essential structure and function, the analyst can change the system on paper to explore the likely consequences of actual modifications.

As should be evident, systems need not be of a certain size in order to be worthy of the name. Nor need they be of a certain degree of complexity. The solar system is huge, yet the sun and the planets rotate and orbit in relation to each other according to laws that are few and elementary, as applicable to planets as to apples. The fertilized ovum cannot be seen with the naked eye, yet contains incredibly complex instructions for the development of a complete living organism. Both are systems. One large and not very complex, the other minuscule and marvelously complicated. In fact, from the perspective of systems analysis, a system springs to life the moment an analyst points to a given thing or area and says, "That is my system."

System Definition

The first job of the analyst is *not* to discover the system, but to define it. While our first sociologist was studying the neighborhood, a second may have studied only one of the ethnic groups. The question thus is whether this second study is of a system. The answer is yes because in any systems study there is an arbitrary inside and outside. It is the analyst who draws the boundaries in the study of social systems.

Thus, the second sociologist would study the ethnic group as a system and the neighborhood would be external to the system. Families, ethnically oriented stores, churches, and social organizations would be the subsystems of the ethnic system.

Chadwick suggests that system definition include environment, system, subsystems, and elements.[16] The *environment* consists of all systems other than the one being considered. *Subsystems* are distinct parts of the larger system (ethnic groups in a neighborhood). *Elements* are the lowest level of detail that your study is going to consider (family units in a sociological study; buildings in a planning study).

System definition is essentially a way of limiting the scope of study. The environment is part of the study but only to the extent that it provides inputs to the system and receives some outputs in return. The environmental processes that determined the shape of the inputs upon systems entry are not considered. The further utilization of the systems output by the environment is not studied either. For instance, street litter is the amount of packaging and other materials flowing into a neighborhood minus the amount flowing out or retained for other purposes by the residents. The manufacture of the packaging and the landfill impact of its disposal are not relevant to the study of the neighborhood as a solid waste flow-through system. Factors that are relevant include the number, frequency, and type of sanitation services in the neighborhood; the capacity of the neighborhood's garbage cans relative to the quantity of disposable materials; the attitude of neighborhood residents toward litter.

Of course, studying only the above factors does not mean that the modification of inputs would not significantly impact on a system. Returnable bottles, for instance, can significantly reduce the level of street trash. However, the analyst cannot study the universe. If certain things are not considered as givens, this is precisely what can occur. Thus, the environmental boundary serves to define the outer limits of the system for the purposes of study and analysis.

Just as environment represents the outer limits, elements define the inner limits of systems study. The composition of a soda can may be a factor in the municipalities disposal system, but it is not a factor in a given neighborhood's litter problem. In the neighborhood analysis, the can is important as a unit of litter on the street. Similarly, people's attitudes toward litter need be determined only to a certain point. For instance, while some new neighborhood arrivals may come from a country where farm animals make quick work of discarded trash, knowing that the residents do not perceive of littering as improper may be all that is necessary. Finding out whether it was pigs or goats who vacuumed up the garbage back home is not particularly pertinent to the analysis.

It should be evident that one could substitute problem definition for systems definition in the above without losing very much. In any analysis, some definition of "study area" is useful so that investigatory energies do not lose their effectiveness by being spread all over the lot. This does not mean that root causes will not be located outside of the study area. Indeed, analysis may clearly point to external factors. However, often such discoveries cannot be made without a thorough analysis of the originally defined problem area. Pluto, the most distant planet in our solar system, was discovered before it could be seen because astronomers, in analyzing the movement of the eight known planets, saw patterns that could be accounted for only by the existence of a ninth. Without a thoroughgoing analysis of the eight-planet system, Pluto would have remained unknown despite being an integral part of the system. Analysis, regardless of its scope, should always seek to have strong explanatory power. If this is accomplished, clues pointing you in the right direction should emerge even if the central problem is not within the study area.

What Systems Do

System is a dynamic concept. It is concerned with movement. The streets of an abandoned city are not transportation systems. For the streets to be activated as a transportation system, traffic—pedestrian or vehicular—is necessary. Similarly, buildings are brought to life as systems by people living and moving about within them. Factories are collections of brick and machinery without a flow of materials and resources that can be transformed into finished goods. Shut-down factories, bricked-up buildings, or closed highways are architectural corpses. To come alive, they need flows of activity.

Systems, then, are devices for getting things from here to there. One measure of their success is the efficiency with which they accomplish this movement. Often systems do more than move, they transform. The mix of metal, rubber, glass, and plastic that enters the assembly line in Detroit emerges as an automobile. The assembly system not only moves things, it changes them. Many government activities are directed at effecting a change in people. Prisons, job training programs, and mental health programs all seek to make the clients something that they were not before.

Beyond movement and transformation, every system does one more thing. It interacts with other systems. As mentioned before, anything that has been defined as a system has merely been given an artificial boundary to make studying and understanding it easier. If everything interrelates, the only real system is *all* systems combined. For instance, our ethnic group was part of a neighborhood, that was part of a city, that was part of a region, that was part of a country, and so on. Minnesota supplies iron, some of which gets turned into automobiles that become scrap metal which is then made into something else. When the supply of oil is reduced, everything from iron mining in Minnesota to an ethnic family living in a city apartment will feel the effects.

For any system, therefore, how it stands in relation to the environment is central to its existence. Its inputs are outputs from other systems in the environment. Similarly, its outputs flow to other systems as inputs. In fact, comprehensive systems models and policy analysis essentially serve as means for better determining the relationship between a given government activity and its environment. In business, this picture is neatly summed up in the "bottom line"; that is, profits indicate a good input-output relationship between the firm and its environment and losses indicate a bad one.

Government does not have an easily readable bottom line. Balancing the public program ledger is a formidable task. Indeed, a belief in the impossibility of a comprehensive audit underlies incrementalism. With the search for net policy effects abandoned, the incremental bottom line becomes the top line—the initial prospectus that launches a policy. Interested parties author the prospectus in an adversarial process. The major authors are those with the most to gain or lose as an immediate result of policy enactment. The emphasis is on concluding the decision-making process to the mutual satisfaction of the authors rather than reaching conclusions about the impacts of policy alternatives. However, from the systems perspective, government decisions affect an environment wider than that represented by interested parties. Governments output—who gets what, where, when, and how—and its input—who gives what, where, when, and how—reverberate through the economic, political, and social spheres and help mold the physical environment. Therefore, if casual analysis leads to the wrong who, at the wrong place and time, getting the wrong thing in the wrong way, what accrues to the intended beneficiaries often is very little, as "yesterday's solutions . . . become the cause of tomorrow's problems."[17]

Systems analysis, when used to gauge the impact of policy options, is one way of avoiding unanticipated and possibly irreversible consequences. Also, since lack of time, money, or political sophistication denies policy authorship to some, and others will not be affected until the policy gathers momentum, analysis factors in the incrementally disenfranchised. Thus, systematic analysis of policy, by accounting for excluded individuals and obscured outcomes, provides decision makers with a broader view of the impact of government on its environment.

What Systems Cannot Do

Things that limit the operation of systems are called constraints. When people say, "I would if I could, but I can't," they are talking about constraints. There are two basic types of systems constraints—internal and external. Most of us cannot fly a plane. We do not have the capacity to do so. This is an *internal constraint*. Unless we restructure our system of being to include a subsystem called "flying skills," piloting a plane will be impossible. Systems can also have *external constraints*. Some years ago, in New York, there was a man named Fitzpatrick who could fly a plane very well. He was also, as fate would have it, both a betting and a drinking man. Not once, but twice, he wagered with some barmates that he could land an airplane on the city streets. And so he did, winning some money and losing his freedom in the process, six months being the price for driving a stolen plane while intoxicated.[18] Now, Fitzpatrick was not internally constrained from flying a plane. He was obviously a crack pilot (who may have been somewhat cracked himself, not to mention lucky). It was the environment that kept Fitzpatrick out of the air and off the streets. The constraints of Fitzpatrick's derring-do were external.

Internal Constraints   In man-made systems, internal constraints usually evolve around physical capacity. A subway line can transport, for a given distance and in a certain time, only as many people as can fit on trains available. Once there are more people than the maximum, they will be delayed. Thus, internal constraints—systems incapacity—create waiting lines. The materials being processed are delayed. These delays occur either prior to systems processing or at points further along in the system.

If delays occur in people processing systems, the materials may seek out alternative paths. This is what often happens when people see a movie line that stretches around the block. They may very much have wanted to see the movie, but are not willing to pay the costs—time lost that could be *spent* somewhere else, frostbitten toes, or the psychic aggravation of standing around. So, they choose another system: perhaps the movie across the street that, although originally less attractive, now prevails because it offers immediate systems entry.

Systems overloads are also put "on hold" after the initial processing. When people are the materials being processed, this procedure can often be exasperating. For instance, looking at the line for an attraction in an amusement park, you decide that waiting on it to purchase a ticket is worthwhile. So you wait, purchase your ticket, and, lo and behold, once inside the door, you find yourself on another waiting line that is longer and slower moving than the one selling the tickets. Similarly, high-pressure salesmen seek to get customers past the initial processing point in a one-way, no-exit system. They sell systems entry—signing the contract—without regard to any processing incapacities that may exist beyond the entry point. Thus, a home improvement contractor may verbally promise to start work as soon as you sign the contract, all the while knowing that:

1. The contract does not require the contractor to start work immediately.
2. The contractor is incapable of starting and finishing the work within the promised time because of the many other jobs the firm has (system overloads).
3. The contract requires you to pay the contractor whenever the firm does get around to doing the work.

The frustration of the amusement park patron and the homeowner is due to the fact that no single-line, processing system is stronger than its weakest link. For instance, assume that you have a single transportation system that links the suburbs with a central city. It is a railroad that runs under the wide bay separating the city from the suburbs. It can carry 10,000 people an hour and looks like this:

| | MORNING RUSH HOUR | | | | |
INBOUND	The Heights	Plains	Bayshore	Bay City Port	Bay City Downtown
Capacity	10,000	10,000	10,000	10,000	000
Total Demand (On & Getting On)	2,000	5,000	10,000	10,000	000

From its last suburban stop, Bayshore, the system carries 10,000 people per hour to the Bay City Downtown stop 7:00–9:00 A.M. daily. The Bay City Port stop is hardly used at all, since the port is way past its glory days, and what little employment it has does not attract the white-collar suburbanites. Now, let us assume that one day ominous cracks are discovered in the railroad tunnel under the bay and the tunnel is shut down pending engineering studies. The authorities press into service the only alternative means of traversing the bay, two large, but antiquated and slow, ferry boats. The problem is that they can transport only 8,000 people per hour over the bay. The system looks as before—the trains still run through the suburbs and from Bay City Port to downtown and still have a capacity of 10,000 people per hour—except for one thing: The cross-bay link in the new transportation system can carry only 8,000 persons an hour. The result is that the capacity of the entire transportation system is only 8,000 passengers per hour even though individual parts of the system are capable of handling 10,000:

| INBOUND | MORNING RUSH HOUR | | | | |
	The Heights	Plains	Bayshore	Bay City Port	Bay City Downtown
Capacity	10,000	10,000	8,000	10,000	000
	Bayshore Waiting Line = 2,000 per hour (7:30–9:30 A.M.)				
Total Demand (On & Getting On)	2,000	5,000	10,000	8,000	000

It is on this basis, of course, that many proposals for subsystem improvement may actually be meaningless. If the courts can process only 1000 criminal cases a month and must release untried suspects after 90 days, beefing up the police force to produce 2000 arrests per month would soon result in one suspect being set free by the courts for every one arrested by the police.

External Constraints   External constraints are environmentally imposed. In government systems the external constraints can be behavioral, material, or financial. Behavioral constraints are those that forbid the system to act in a certain way even though it possesses the capacity to do so. The laws relating to privacy and to illegal search and seizure are formal constraints on institutions, public and private. Although these constraints are not always abided by—prosecutors have been known to lose evidence beneficial to defendants; corporate bribery appears to be somewhat routine—they exist.

Material constraints exist when the environment no longer supplies inputs to the system. Ending the draft changed the selective service system. It maintained its recordkeeping and initial registry components, but the machinery for processing draftees has been substantially dismantled. An environment that is unable or unwilling to consume the outputs of a system also materially constrains its operation. Until its recent revival, the coal industry had additional mining capacity but nobody to mine for.

Financial constraints are those that hold systems capacity at a level where it is unable to process all the inputs available. In government, where most systems are in this position, financial constraints loom large.

LOOKING AT A
GOVERNMENT SYSTEM: CRIMINAL JUSTICE

The term "criminal justice system" is beginning to be heard with increasing frequency. Unfortunately, it is generally heard as part of a statement such as "The criminal justice system is a mess." However, from

Figure 12.1 Criminal Justice System

a systems view, such a statement, even if disparaging, makes eminently more sense than "The police aren't doing their job"; "The courts are too lenient"; or "The prisons don't shape up the criminals." These latter statements identify bad results as stemming from poor performance by individual agencies and institutions. A systems critique allows that there might be something more. Poor interrelationships may be a major part of the problem, and beyond that, there is a recognition that, if interrelationship dysfunctions are serious enough, good individual performances by agencies can be negated. Poor systems coordination is somewhat like two people in a boat rowing furiously in opposite directions—everyone may be working as hard as he can, but little progress is made if the efforts are not mutually supportive. Viewing the agencies and institutions involved in criminal justice law enforcement as a system makes it easier to recognize that many of the problems arise in the gaps between the components rather than in the components themselves.

Figure 12.1 is an elementary model of the criminal justice system. The system processes those accused of crimes. It moves people from Point A, arrest or notice of violation, to Point B, reentry into the environment. As a result of the process, it is hoped that the outputs will be significantly different from the input. (Upstanding citizens should emerge whence lawbreakers entered.) Thus, the little box above is a model of a mechanism that processes and transforms—the criminal justice system.

The criminal justice system is not quite so simple of course. Within it are subsystems that process, hold, and transform the material that feeds into the system. Each has a limited capacity. To illustrate, let us imagine the three major components of the criminal justice system—the police, the courts, and the prisons—as a succession of subsystems with diminishing capacities. Thus, the input material in the environment, "the criminal element," exceeds the arrest capacity of the police. The arrest output of the police exceeds the processing capacity of the court. The holding needs and sentencing outputs of the courts exceed the detention capacity of the prison system. This hypothetical situation (although it is not hypothetical by very much) is illustrated in Figure 12.2.

Since the capacity diminishes at each step, something must be done with the overloads. There are several alternatives. Either suspects re-

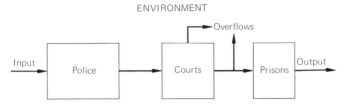

Figure 12.2   Criminal Justice System: Successive Subsystems with Diminishing Capacities

main in the environment—they are not apprehended—or they are returned to the environment as subsystem overflows—prisoners released for failure to be given a speedy trial. Another alternative is to reduce the processing time for each person. This tack, pursued by many jurisdictions, has resulted in arraignment procedures that last an average of 60 to 90 seconds, and trials that finalize frenetic plea bargaining between prosecutors and defense attorneys almost as quickly.[19]

Interrelating the Criminal Justice Subsystems

The criminal justice system's processing of persons suspected of crimes is not one continuous operation. There are numerous stops and starts between systems input and systems output and several paths that the person being processed might take. A person being processed might be at various times characterized as a suspected offender, indicted suspect, prisoner awaiting trial, suspect on bail, defendant, convicted offender, imprisoned felon, probationer, or parolee. It is conceivable that one person could be all of these things in the course of his movement through the system. The names refer not to who the individual is but to where the individual has stopped. In addition, the person being processed can be characterized in several other ways depending on the way the individual has left the system. The individual can be an acquitted defendant (either on the evidence or because systems overloads or dysfunctions compelled a dismissal of the case; e.g., no speedy trial), a bail jumper, a parole violator, in contempt of court (which is often one's status when the individual ignores a parking ticket), or rehabilitated. Rehabilitated, of course, embodies the systems function of transformation. It is hoped, of course, that when the person emerges from the criminal justice system by the normal channels the individual will choose to become a law-abiding citizen. The individual who is not so transformed and passes through the system yet another time, will have earned the additional title of recidivist.

Figure 12.3 is of the criminal justice system. It traces the paths that can be followed in systems processing, the interrelationships between the subsystems, and the interplay between the system and its environment. You will note that the prison subsystem occupies a central place in the

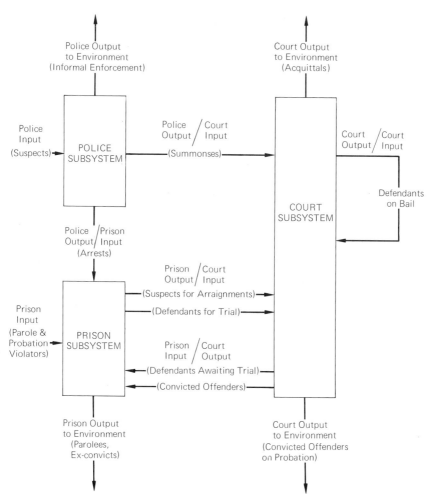

Figure 12.3 Criminal Justice System: Interrelationship of Subsystems

systems diagram. It interconnects with all of the other subsystems. It is the mechanism whereby the system puts the information being processed "on hold." The arrested suspect's first contact with the prison subsystem will probably occur in the "holding pen" as the individual awaits an appearance before the arraignment judge who will make a decision about bail.* The holding pen is one of several waiting lines that the prison subsystem manages for the criminal justice system. Considerable detention resources are expended on holding pens and proposals

---

*In some cities, this "holding pen" is part of the police department, either in station houses or at headquarters; in others, it is part of the courts. From a criminal justice *system* perspective, it does not much matter. Wherever located, it is a "holding" mechanism, not an intake unit, or a distribution unit, or a process unit.

have been made concerning the reduction of this particular waiting line. Since the prison subsystem responds primarily to inputs from other subsystems, these proposals call for changes in other parts of the criminal justice system. One is that minor crimes such as marijuana possession be charged via summons rather than arrest, thereby reducing inputs into the holding pen and to the arraignment parts of the court.

If holding pen and arraignment inputs could be significantly reduced, subsystem resources could be shifted to other activities, such as increasing the number of trial personnel or enlarging the prison systems capacity for housing convicted criminals. Indeed, the minor offense summons would even free police time since issuing a citation consumes considerably less time than an arrest. The procedure clearly would save a lot of systems time (as compared to saving subsystems time that might just cause time loss in another subsystem for a net system effect of zero). The question that remains is the effect the procedure would have on the incidence of the crimes so treated. Would they increase enough to negate the savings?

The activity of the arraignment part of the court subsystem also responds primarily to inputs from the police subsystem. In turn, the decisions that the arraignment part makes directly affect the operations of the prison subsystem. The primary arraignment decision is whether the person will be put on systems "hold" at the individual's own personal potential expense (bail) or at the systems expense (jail). If many suspects are denied bail, or bail is set at levels higher than most can afford, a large part of the prison subsystem capacity will be devoted to housing the waiting line for the trial part of the court subsystem. Police arrest activities and decisions of the arraignment court determine the length of this waiting line.

There have also been proposals aimed at reducing this particular waiting line. In one, bail would be set at the usual fine for the type of violation, rather than at some figure based on the likelihood of the person's showing up for trial. (Insuring the suspect's court appearance is the fundamental reason for bail. This is why congresspersons are usually released in their own recognizance—they are unlikely to disappear—while Patty Hearst, the wanderer, had to ante up $1,500,000 to get on the outside waiting line.) In the "bail as fine" proposal, the suspect's failure to appear at trial becomes a guilty plea; the bail becomes the fine and that is that. No court warrants to draw up, no police to search for the delinquent individual, and no prison capacity expended on guaranteeing the appearance of petty offenders.

Subsystem Behavior

Subsystems are not a unitary mass. They are made up of components that can undergo change. Our review of the criminal justice system

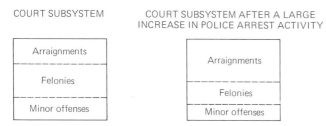

Figure 12.4   Involuntary Input Response

has shown that resources devoted to different prison and court activities shift in response to inputs from other subsystems. However, subsystems do not respond only to physical stimulation from other subsystems or the environment. The behavioral latitude of a subsystem is often dependent on its location within the system. For instance, the police stand on the environmental border of the criminal justice system. They gather the system's input materials from the environment. Since there are usually more criminals than can be arrested, picking and choosing occurs. Thus, police departments often make decisions to ignore certain offenses.

Subsequent subsystems do not enjoy quite the behavioral latitude of the police. Their behavior is more directly tied to the behavior of other subsystems. For instance, arraignment is directly tied to the number of arrests that are made. The courts, in allocating arraignment time, are responding to police activity rather than an internal court decision. The prisons, in setting aside space for suspects awaiting trial, are responding involuntarily to court decisions. Figure 12.4 shows an involuntary change in subsystem behavior.

The physical materials that a system processes tend to proceed through the system in a fixed direction. As the formal workload of the system, such materials, with stops and starts and an occasional doubling back, tend to proceed fairly predictably from input and processing units through to the output units of the system. However, there is a system's commodity, information, that moves about in any direction. Information not only flows freely within systems composed of people, it flows quickly. These information flows are often not a part of the system's design. They proceed through an informal network composed of the individuals within the system. Nonetheless, information exchange has implications for systems functioning.

Feedback is one systems' message that can modify both the relationship between, and the activity within, subsystems. Feedback responses occur when one subsystem evaluates the response to its behavior of another subsystem and changes its activity patterns as a result. For instance, if the police discover that their arrests of prostitutes result in routine court dismissal, they are likely to make fewer such arrests. In-

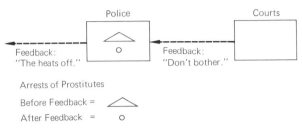

Figure 12.5 Voluntary Feedback Response

formation on the consequences of their activity has fed back from the courts and, in this case, the police response is "Why bother?" Thus police decisions to pursue a certain crime will be based, in part, on conviction and detention feedback from the courts. Figure 12.5 illustrates the feedback response, which, you will note, continues beyond the system's borders, a characteristic of many systems' messages.

The environment responds to the system's behavior as well. The broken lines back into the environment on Figures 12.3 and 12.5 are feedback flows. They indicate that other systems are keeping a close eye on what the criminal justice system does. Data on its performance continually feed back into the environment and its criminal subsystem causing these areas to modify their behavior. A study prepared for the Council on Municipal Performance notes that "those disposed to criminal behavior are apparently aware of differentials in the vigor of law enforcement and respond accordingly."[20] For their part, citizens are likely to howl when they read about a particularly nasty felon released on minimal bail or pleading to a lesser charge because of systems overloads. Since systems are continually interacting, some corresponding shifts are likely to occur in the criminal justice system in response to citizen complaints or an upsurge in certain types of criminal activity.

Often, behavior by individual subsystems proceeds in a manner that could be characterized as selfish or self-aggrandizing. For instance, although administrators may know that other subsystems cannot handle more than certain amounts of their output, this knowledge does not always deter them from overloading the subsystems. Individual agency concerns may be deemed more important. Thus, a police department that is under pressure due to a rising crime rate may sweep the streets of petty offenders even though such actions will clog the judicial mechanism and run up against a prison system filled to capacity. The result is an enhancement of the police image and a shifting of the public outcry to "revolving door justice." District attorneys may wage crusades—a holy war against pornography is always good press— without regard to the police, prosecutorial, and court time thereby diverted from other activities. The result, as with most systems overloads, is that some of the indictments being processed escape from the system due to speedy trial requirements, improvised prosecutions and plea bargaining, or the reduced capacity of the prison holding mechanism. "Ticket blitzes," a tactic sometimes employed by rank-and-file police officers to highlight a grievance, also clog succeeding system components; the "rules slowdown," another employee expression of unhappiness, not only slows down the system, it casts certain doubts on the system design as well. After all, if "going by the book" can bring the system to a grinding halt, management should give some thought to rewriting the book.

In any case, the burdens on subsystems are substantial enough without being added to by other members of the system's "team." The problems of the court subsystem, for instance, are legion, and as with most systemic problems, many are not of its own making. The burden of a tremendous workload; innumerable hearings; the scheduling difficulties of getting together prosecutors, defense lawyers, defendants, and witnesses at the same place and time is compounded by prosecutors and defense attorneys who use delay as a strategy or to hide the fact that they are unprepared. As a result, back and forth between court and the prison system go defendants who occupy spaces that might be better filled by convicted criminals.

For its part, the prison subsystem is plagued by problems and it is little wonder. It has to accept inputs from all points on its environmental horizon. There is almost no opportunity to reject inputs. Thus, it either must release some inmates from the other end of the prison pipeline or allow overcrowding. One governor conferring blanket pardons on a number of prisoners admitted that reducing the strain on the prison system's capacity was as important as the traditional goodwill motivations. Whatever the cause—and problems within the criminal justice system undeniably play a part—prisons are going through a period of great institutional stress with a more assertive prisoner population that is growing in size.

For both the courts and the prisons, analysis of existing operations may do much to suggest internal improvement that would alleviate some of their problems. However, as we hope the foregoing has made evident, without studying the relationship of the prisons and the courts to each other *and* to other subsystems within the criminal justice system, many problems will remain oblivious to "in-house" assaults.

URBAN SYSTEMS

We would never attempt to send a space ship to the moon without first testing the equipment through prototype models and computer simulations of the anticipated trajectories. No company would put a new kind of household appliance or electronic computer into production without first making laboratory tests. Such models and laboratory tests do not guarantee against failure, but they do identify many weaknesses that can be corrected before they cause full-scale disaster.

The social and economic phenomena with which public administrators deal, although far more complex and difficult to understand than technological systems, should be approached with the same goal in mind. Both in planning and evaluating programs, devices to facilitate the comparison of performance with expected or predicted results are needed. To do this, the reality of the program environment must be reproduced. The effective planning of policy demands an understanding of the system in which that policy is to be implemented.

Urban areas, in particular, have been the focus of studies from the systems perspective. This is partly because the physical planning function is most developed at the municipal level. City planning, in one form or another, has been with us for nearly two centuries. When Alexander Hamilton selected Paterson, New Jersey, to be the country's "industrial city," he set about encouraging manufacturers to locate there. The urban interplay among transportation, economics, and social dynamics was being recognized by government administrators as early as 1811, when the commission that drew up New York City's street plans considered "whether they should confine themselves to rectilinear and rectangular streets, or whether they should adopt some of those supposed improvements, by circles, ovals and stars, which certainly embellish a plan, whatever may be their efforts as to convenience and utility. In considering that subject, we could not but bear in mind that a city is to be composed principally of the habitations of men, and that strait sided, and right angled houses are the most cheap to build, and the most convenient to live in. The effect of these plain and simple reflections was decisive. . . . (Given) the price of land (it seems) proper to admit the principles of economy."[21]

Zoning—no matter how terribly it may have been done in certain instances or what ulterior motives, such as segregation, it may have hidden in others—is essentially the most comprehensive planning tool that existed in government until very recently. The relationships among residential, retail, and manufacturing locations and the interplay of transportation with each formed the decisional components of the zoning approach. The techniques may have been less than reliable, but the perspective was one that led to a wide appreciation of urban areas as

> complex, dynamic systems with many interrelationships existing between their various economic, social and physical attributes. . . . (Where) programs instituted in one functional segment of the city or metropolitan system (such as transportation) can have both direct and indirect effects,

both productive and counter-productive, in other functional segments, especially over time.[22]

Conceptualizing Urban Areas

Observers have been trying to dissect the "complex, dynamic" urban system for some time. Theories of residential and business locations trace their beginnings to the classic nineteenth-century economic treatise *The Isolated State*, by Johann von Thunen.[23] As a result, the first systematic observers of the urban environment conceptualized it as an "*economic landscape.*" Next, there were attempts to explain population behavior in terms of Newtonian physics. This approach viewed locational activity as dependent on the attractiveness of alternative sites as modified by the distance that the person would have to travel to reach them.[24] The interplay of gravitational forces was the key to urban development in these "*physical analogy*" *models.* Finally, the *economic-sociological models* of urban areas combine elements of the "economic landscape" and "gravity" approaches with sociological explanations of locational behavior. "Quality of life," as perceived by the individual or firm, was factored in as a force affecting the urban system.

These three types of models—economic landscape, physical analogy, and economic-sociological—are the building blocks of the intricate techniques used to analyze policy impacts on urban areas. In addition, the individual approaches can be utilized by the public manager to better allocate organizational resources. Thus, they are worth a closer look.

Economic Landscape Models The concentric-ring theory is perhaps the most familiar economic landscape model.[25] It says that as cities develop, and residence separates from workplace, the residences that are located nearest the working area at the center of the city will be the oldest and most crowded. The poor will locate near the center to minimize travel costs to work and reside in aged structures that have been broken up into small apartments that provide sufficient income to the owner while keeping down individual rentals. People with higher incomes will be able to afford the higher transportation costs from the outlying districts and, thus, avail themselves of the low-density living conditions that exist there. Not all affluent individuals reside on the city's periphery. Some, financially able to satisfy their preference for spacious living quarters close to their employment, populate the "silk stocking" districts that share the fringe of the business district with low-income neighborhoods. In explaining the "silk stocking" district and other variations from the original concentric-ring hypothesis, economic landscape models continue to analyze the interplay between employment and residential locations, the monetary costs and physical characteristics that make a given location more or less desirable, and the ability of the locatee to shoulder such costs. August Losch and Walter Isard are two more recent modelers of the economic landscape.[26]

Physical Analogy Models   Following upon the economic landscape models, gravity models added attractiveness to the locational formula:

> In the application of the gravity concept to the analysis of urban systems, the gravitational pull exerted by two bodies has been interpreted as the amount of interaction between two areas, and the mass of the bodies has been measured in terms of size or attractiveness of the areas. The earliest and simplest gravity models were based on the proposition that the amount of interaction between two areas is related directly to the size (or attraction) of the areas, and inversely to the distance separating the areas.[27]

Indeed, many of the gargantuan amusement parks, which often locate many miles from urban areas, operate on the principle that their attractiveness is sufficient to induce 60-mile car trips. One such park is located halfway between, and at least an hour's drive from, the centers of New York and Philadephia. Disneyworld, located in what was one of the more sparsely settled sections of Florida, apparently has a gravitational pull that covers the eastern portion of the United States.

The addition of time was an important modification to the distance component of gravity models. Distance has both a physical and temporal meaning. "How long did it take you to get here?" is as much a question about distance as "How many miles apart do we live?" Anyone who has ever struggled for half an hour to cover a mile during the central city rush hour, need only compare that to a 30-mile drive on the open highway to realize that time is part of distance. In terms of the gravity models, the suburbs became more attractive locales when they moved closer to the city in terms of time-distance. It was the highway that altered the city-suburb spatial separation. The time-distance implications of transportation channels can radically affect the urban system. As Benjamin Chinitz has written:

> The automobile and the truck and even the airplane ... alter the balance of advantages and disadvantages at different locations and therefore undermine the very motive for concentration at particular points.[28]

In addition to attractiveness and distance, expansions of the gravity model began to include the attractiveness of competing areas. The effect was to raise the gravity model from a two-dimensional to a multidimensional tool for analysis. In its earlier stage, the gravity model looked at the world in such terms as city-suburb. The addition of relative attractiveness was a recognition that suburb was more than a unitary mass; that is, it was a collection of little suburbs, each of which had its own attractiveness score. Essentially, the extent to which a given area could grow was constrained by competition from other areas. To refer again to amusement parks, those in the industry have estimated that the present number of parks is sufficient for the customer population throughout the country. Furthermore, their locational distribution is such that all major population areas are covered. Additional parks, industry representatives warn, would be more than the market could handle. The "catchment areas" of the parks would then overlap. As a result, some of the parks, either the new or the old, would go under. While one senses a possibility of overprotection of the organization's environmental space in this statement (they were probably saying the same thing when there were half as many parks), what the industry is wary about is the addition of relative attractiveness to the attractiveness-distance formula that customers now use in making attendance decisions.

Similarly, the location of public facilities such as health centers often hinges on the concept of "catchment areas." A catchment area is the space surrounding a public facility from which it will draw its patronage. A bus stop may have a catchment area of five blocks. A health center may pull residents from as far as 10 blocks away. A park may have an even longer reach. In the planning for the location of public facilities, the consideration of catchment areas is important. From the standpoint of getting the maximum use out of limited resources, it makes little sense to locate similar public facilities so that their catchment areas overlap.

The location of prospective patrons is also an important consideration in the placement of service centers. A senior citizens' center, even if it is placed equidistant from existing locations, does little good if the location is an area largely populated by swinging singles and young marrieds. Trends in the future location of the target population should be considered as well. If the poor happen to live in an area where buildings are being burned or abandoned daily, a welfare center that will take two years to build might find itself with no customers when it is complete. It might be better placed in an area where the burnt-out target population is relocating. Unfortunately, many public facilities do seem to be placed on the basis of pin-and-map techniques. A colored pin representing a new facility is placed on a street map so that it is neatly spaced and, if possible, geometrically in tune with the pins representing existing facilities. The location of the potential patrons is given nary a thought.

Economic-Sociological Models   As gravity models built upon the economic landscape models, economic-sociological models begin with a foundation that consists of the economic and physical models. On top of this foundation is laid the sociological component of the model.

Quality of life is a key concept in sociological modeling. Pollution levels, incidence of crime and fire, health of the population, and quality of education all have impact on the citizens' perception of their neighborhood's, and their city's viability. Amenities are also important to an area's quality of life. The availability and accessibility of parks, playgrounds, libraries, stores, and movies help determine an area's attractiveness.

As should be evident, the quality-of-life picture is a composite. Many factors, deemed intangible by early economic landscape and physical analogy models, combine to measure the social attractiveness of an area. Modeling the social subsystem of the urban environment depends to a great degree on attitudinal and behavioral measurements. This contrasts with the economic and physical spheres where census information, Bureau of Labor Statistics data, engineering specifications, building permits, and property tax rolls are but a few of the sources that make the job of subsystem description easier. In the social sphere, however, citizen surveys to determine the community impact of crime rates, sanitation performance, education levels, and other services can play an important part in giving form and substance to the subsystem. Despite the difficulty in formulation—it is often necessary to start from scratch with a questionnaire that itself has to be tested for adequacy before use—attitude measures provide something that many collections of raw statistical data do not. Whereas aggregate statistics paint a picture based on circumstantial evidence, attitude surveys directly examine the people who make urban areas living systems.

Attitude surveys also get a lot closer to things in terms of time. Most aggregate statistics used in economic modeling indicate what the system looked like one or two years ago. In the meantime, the system may have changed radically. However, this will not be apparent until the information—for example, a precipitous drop in tax revenues—travels through time and space to reach us. In contrast, asking, "What do you think of the police protection and does that play a part in your deciding to live here?" gets the information from the source and gets it now. Client and citizen surveys such as those pioneered by the University of Michigan Institute of Social Research should play an increasing role in the analysis of social systems in future years.

The completed profile of the social subsystem must be interrelated with those of the other urban subsystems—the governmental, economic, and physical. The economic and physical may be profiled using landscaping and gravity approaches. The governmental subsystem can be factored in via budget analysis, a process that also helps measure the economic, social, and physical subsystems by way of tax and service levels and capital construction expenditures. The budget/governmental component should not be constrained by political boundaries. In keeping with the systems perspective, city and suburban budgets and state and federal outlays affecting the region should be included.

Models that incorporate governmental, social, physical, and economic indices are known as whole systems models. There are whole systems models in use by urban governments in the United States and Canada. Pittsburgh's whole-systems model and Toronto's PROMUS (Provincial-Municipal Simulator) tie in the city and the suburbs and interrelate the physical, social, economic, and government subsystems. Ira Lowry, whose work undergirds the Pittsburgh model, conceives of each firm and household as having an equation in which the value of its present location is a function of individual preferences (the social component) and the attributes of the site (the physical and economic components).[29] During a decision period, each establishment considers all possible sites, prices them, and bids on them with the highest bidder receiving the location. More complex and abstract formulations of the urban dynamic are offered by J. W. Forrester, who believes that systems modeling has the potential for accurately determining the major implications of proposed policies.[30]

Urban Subsystems

As the preceding discussion indicates, locational theorists gradually worked toward a conceptualization of the city as composed of four major subsystems: *physical, economic, social,* and *governmental.* However, the subsystems are important not only as factors in a locational equation; public managers in planning, economic development, or social services focus on individual subsystems. Moreover, the physical, economic, and social components of urban areas will reflect increasing government involvement in years to come. Thus, we will look briefly at how these subsystems can be conceptualized.

Physical From the physical perspective, the city processes and stores information. The information is people. They are processed, moved by the transportation network, and are stored for varying lengths of time in physical structures such as houses, offices, movie theaters, and museums. This physical subsystem, according to Robert Dorfman, is:

> a large and complicated machine for housing, maintaining and transporting its population and for storing and transporting the materials they use and disposing of their wastes.... In contrast with most other machines, a city comes into being by growth rather than design. As a result, the parts are not well designed to fit to each other; they are in varied states of disrepair and obsolescence, and they are replaced and modernized seriatim.[31]

Much public debate is addressed to physical subsystems. This is so for several reasons. First, government plays an extremely important role in shaping the physical subsystem. Planning boards and other such agencies generally have to approve all new structures and modifications of existing ones. Publicly supported housing, whether partially funded by subsidy or fully funded by tax funds, is a growing factor in urban areas. Roads within and around urban areas are planned, built, and maintained under government auspices. Railway networks, when built today, are generally government operations, and the older commuter lines look more governmental every day as subsidies and outright takeovers increase. Bus systems, too, are turning into public goods in many cities.

Modifications of the physical subsystem also engender controversy because they are fraught with major implications for the other subsystems in the urban environment. Many of these implications are far-reaching and irreversible. When the first bridge from a central city to the rural area on the other side of a wide river begins to be built, the farmers might as well pack their bags. The urbanization of their domain is inevitable. A new highway that offers better access in and out of a region is likely to be lined by manufacturers dependent on raw materials transported by truck. Low-income housing locations that threaten the existing social patterns in an area are likely to elicit howls of protest from long-term residents and may set off a flight response that fundamentally changes the social makeup of the neighborhood.

Economic   As an economic entity, the city "serves as a communications center or market for some industries."[32] The urban area has to produce goods or services that other urban areas want. This is the basic, or export, component of the economic subsystem. If this economic component is healthy, then locally dependent industries will arise to serve it and its employees. At present, some basic industries are physically welded to certain locations. Mining, timber cutting, and other resource extractions must be carried on at the source. Such industries will depart only if the source is exhausted or if there is no longer a demand for the product. Other industries have greater degrees of mobility as the competition among various regions and states to lure industry their way indicates. For these industries, availability and cost of labor, the advantages and disadvantages of the physical facilities such as highways, and the governmentally imposed costs such as taxes play an important part in the decision about where to locate.

Social   The social subsystem of the urban environment has been receiving increasing attention recently. Such concepts as the "quality of life" indicate a realization that the social needs of the population affect their activities within the urban system. Crime, poor sanitation, and substandard schools can destabilize the population of an urban area even in the face of physical and economic subsystems that are well designed and have capacity to spare. The 30–60 mile leap out to the suburbs that some central city industries make often encounters little resistance from employees who either already live there or are happy to relocate because they see the urban area as failing to meet their social needs.

There is ample evidence that the social subsystem in urban areas is undergoing substantial change. The white, middle-class migration away from most central cities is an accelerating reality, as is the corresponding growth in minority populations and increase in the number of low-income and unemployed workers. People do withdraw from the urban system because "the schools are no good." Statistical analyses have shown extremely strong correlations between white middle-class outflows and crime increases. In a study of 29 cities, a large number that substantially cancels out possible physical and economic explanations, the Council on Municipal Performance found that "very roughly, for every robbery reported in . . . 1960's, two white people moved out."[33] Of course, racial and ethnic prejudice may, in fact, be the ultimate reason for middle-class departures. Indeed, observers of the urban system have acknowledged ethnic and racial tension as a characteristic of the social subsystem.

Anthony Downs has ventured that there is a "Law of Cultural Dominance."[34] Downs asserts that an established group will feel dominant, and remain in an area, if it comprises over 60 percent of the population. However, the established group will disperse quickly if an incoming group appears to be achieving dominance; a perception that occurs, according to Downs, when the new arrivals exceed 40 percent of the neighborhood population. Robert Dorfman sees this phenomenon rooted in a deep-set human need to be a "loyal member of a well defined and somewhat exclusive social group."[35] Part of the glue that holds the group together, according to Dorfman, is hostility toward other groups. Moreover, says Dorfman, "certain occupations and industries become segregated just as neighborhoods are. It would be surprising if it were otherwise. People like to work, as to live, among people with whom they feel most at ease."[36]

Of course, it is illegal, many would say immoral, to deny individuals employment or housing because of group membership. Further, what is rightful superiority, pride, and solidarity to the group is xenophobia to the outside world. Xenophobia can also lead to physical conflict between groups if the flight response is economically foreclosed. Understandably, public policy seeks to change group mindsets supportive of such behavior. None of this is news to Downs and Dorfman. However, they view social systems as slow to change and urge that both the law and group dynamics be accommodated where possible. Downs, for instance, advises administrators to keep his "law" in mind when integrating housing to avoid almost immediate resegregation via "white flight."[37]

In a development that might ease intergroup friction in the central city, suburban zoning patterns designed to perpetuate segregation in housing and education have been struck down by the courts. Taking what could be called a systems view, judges have ruled that the central city has borne the brunt of integration, and is leaning toward resegregation because of suburban barriers to minority entry. Pending appeals, however, this is still a very fluid area and administrators, in dealing with the social subsystem, continue to face a difficult and crucial task; for when social breakdowns occur, the physical, economic, and governmental subsystems feel punishing effects.

Governmental Government, "a fantastically complicated and unwieldy institution,"[38] is a major subsystem in the urban system. Dorfman notes that there are 1300 separate governmental jurisdictions in Cook County, Illinois; a circumstance that can certainly lead to interrelationship difficulties and governmental impacts that arise out of the gaps between the decision makers rather than from the decision makers themselves.[39]

It should be clear that government does not make the list of urban subsystems because it is powerful or because legislation gives it a controlling position in city affairs. Both may be true but both are irrelevant to the attainment of subsystem status. In fact, the government employee who sees only power ("When the Mayor speaks, everybody listens") or a benevolent but detached control ("We just sort of keep the lid on things") is likely to miss the systematic nature of the urban environment altogether. Government is an urban subsystem because it provides outputs to the other subsystems and receives inputs in return. Things that happen outside of government impact on its operation; downward trends in the municipal bond market are likely to immerse mayoral staffers in a review of "contingency budget reduction plan no. 1"; high wages for managerial personnel in the private sector may prevent the city from getting the quality of manpower it needs; outflows of middle-class residents may have negative impacts on the tax base, the educational system, and the mayor's reelection.

Conversely, government policy sends ripples through the physical, economic, and social spheres. Tax rates can hold or drive away businesses and residents. Transportation placement can cause one area to develop while another deteriorates; poor fire protection can cause insurance rates to skyrocket, and thus drive out homeowners. The situation in even a single urban area can have national repercussions. During New York City's flirtation with bankruptcy, interest rates for municipal borrowing increased across the nation.

In the playing out of the systematic relationships that exist in the urban environment, the government is neither off stage nor above it. It is both actor and acted upon. It is part of the system and a complex part at that. This is why exposure to a number of disciplines, state Blanning, Lewin, and Uretsky, "is especially important in training urban managers, who must have some understanding not only of management principles and methods, but also of subdisciplines such as urban sociology, urban economics and urban politics."[40]

THE BASICS OF MODEL BUILDING

System theorists and analysts are eager to learn how things look and how things work. When they find out, a *model* is likely to result. The model represents reality. It can be highly abstract, a blueprint or an organization chart for instance, or a virtual replica of the system studied. A model that reproduces reality with great precision is the flight simulator. A detailed, full-scale reproduction of the pilot's cabin, it is mounted on movable platforms and suspended by cables so that it pitches forward and backward, and tilts left and right in response to the pilot's ascent, descent, and banking maneuvers. To highlight the reality, a screen outside the pilot's window runs film of airport runways photographed during actual landings. The whole setup is a grander version of the driving games often found in amusement parks, which are also simulations. While the purpose of the one is enjoyment and the other is rigorous training, both imitate reality. One of the very few actual ingredients that is missing is the consequences of making a mistake, which is pretty much the whole idea.

Even a food recipe, according to our definition, is a model. It describes the ingredients that go into a dish and the order in which they are added. Many good cooks and gourmets can actually reverse this process and build the model out of the dish. They taste, smell, and look. One by one they identify the ingredients and make educated guesses as to the proportions of the various ingredients and how and when they were combined. The resulting recipe is a model of reality. Thus, the gourmets have built this model to explain the dish before them. It is a verbal representation of actuality. To test just how good their model is, the gourmets could follow the recipe to see if their version tastes like the first. If it does not taste *quite* like the first dish, the gourmets would reanalyze their model, adding a little bit of this and taking away a little bit of that, tasting all the while, until they arrived at a version that tasted identical to the first. Correcting their recipe to account for their additions and subtractions, the gourmets would then have a precise written model of the orginal dish.

The urban models that are built to explain the dynamics of city life and the interplay between its various subsystems are really no different. Model builders postulate a set of relationships based on their observations or intuition such as:

1. Low median income = High unemployment
2. Poor educational system = Middle-class outflows
3. High sales taxes = Loss of retail trade
4. One lane of highway = 10,000 new suburban homes

In building an actual model, many more relationships would be postulated. Some of the largest models, those that describe the nation's economy for example, have thousands of such relationships as a starting point. Obviously, such a task would be unthinkable without a computer. Making a series of guesses about the relationships of things in a complicated system would not be much fun if the likelihood were that they would not be proved right or wrong for the 40 years that it would take to compile the necessary data. Fortunately, the computer can swallow, store, digest, reformulate, and spit out mountains of data. If the data are available, the analyst need only tell the computer, "Here are my theories about these two-part relationships, run the data on each against each other and tell me if I'm right or wrong." After model builders have verified the accuracy of their initial guesses, they begin to mix them with still other factors, including the individual part of their guesses that were wrong. Thus, they start intermingling like this:

1. Low median income = High unemployment except where low salary, light manufacturing is a primary industry
2. Poor educational system = Middle-class outflows except where the middle-class population is primarily middle-aged and older
3. High sales taxes = Loss of retail trade to the extent that transportation networks allow access to alternative retail locations with lower sales taxes
4. One lane of highway = 10,000 suburban homes if the median income of the closest city is above $7500

If the researchers have enough time, money, and computer, they keep running these ideas together. Instead of one or two factors combining to equal the extent of middle-class outflows, there can be dozens, and each of these factors, in turn, rests upon others. For instance, middle-class population becomes a function of:

1. Educational levels that are a function of expenditures, teacher-student ratios, teaching methods, community attitudes toward learning.
2. Median age that is a function of employment opportunities, property tax rates, land values, and low-income population.
3. Quality of life that is a function of crime rates, incidence of fires, street cleanliness, availability of recreation.

What begins to emerge is the systematic nature of these relationships. Like the police, the prisons, and the courts in the criminal justice system, for example, each factor begins to connect to others. What also begins to happen is that some factors are eliminated because full analysis shows some relationship to be spurious.

For example, the "high sales taxes = loss of retail trade" association may have been established by a comparison of the city sales tax to the average sales tax in all adjacent suburbs. However, further analysis shows equal numbers of city residents being drawn off by a shopping center in a northern suburb where the sales tax is identical to the city's, and a shopping center to the south where the sales tax is 2 percent lower. With sales tax weakened as an explanatory force, causes for the decline of central city retail trade must be found elsewhere. The physical and social subsystems are a good place to look. Usually, in downtown shopping areas, parking is scarce, physical facilities are old, and high crime is either a real or perceived problem. The suburban malls suffer none of these physical or social drawbacks. Thus, the orginal association:

High sales taxes = Loss of retail trade to the extent that transportation networks allow access to alternative retail locations with lower sales taxes

becomes:

Poor physical and social conditions = Loss of retail trade to the extent that more attractive shopping locations are accessible.

In this manner, much like the gourmets adjusting and readjusting their recipe, model builders are continually testing and retesting their model. Called *iteration,* this process of feeding back later stage findings to question the design and underlying assumptions of earlier stages is a continuing and vital part of model construction.

A report on city crime prepared by the Council on Municipal Performance illustrates the actual application of this approach. A summary of its findings indicates the mixing and matching procedures that led to its conclusions:

Robbery rates are significantly associated with several factors: police per capita, income inequality, two measures of the percentage of high income families, net emigration of whites in the 1960's, racial composition and density. . . . We tested ten other factors and found them not significant.[41]

This report was built on data from 30 of the largest cities in the United States. The cross comparisons among cities were used to build a model of robbery rate causes. The passage below, although only a sketch of what was a sophisticated statistical study, conveys the overall investigative approach by describing how poverty was eliminated from the original list of postulated causes of robbery.

> There is no relationship in our study between a high incidence of poverty and a high incidence of reported property crimes. Compared to the other cities, Los Angeles and Boston experience a relatively high incidence of such crimes, though a relatively small proportion of families there live in poverty. On the other hand, Baltimore and Philadelphia have relatively little property crime although a relatively high proportion of families there live in poverty.[42]

What emerges from the report is a model of robbery. In combination with other models, such as those relating to the location of economic activity, the relationship between robbery and white, middle-class migration away from cities might be significantly modified. However, as we mentioned before, systems studies have boundaries. These boundaries are drawn by the time and money available to the analysts and their own investigative focus. Thus contained, analysts seek to explain what goes on within the system with the proviso that the addition of unstudied environmental factors might modify the findings.

CONCLUSION: THE GOALS OF SYSTEMS ANALYSIS

Systematic modeling is not like taking a snapshot. It is expensive; the pictures are often fuzzy; and the subjects usually have not the slightest idea of what is going on. Thus, the question might be asked, "Why analyze and model systems?" Well, there is always the joy of finding out. Indeed, many of the original econometric and sociometric models were the brainchildren of academics whose purpose was to prove the existence of certain relationships. However, from the perspective of public policy, a model is more than a likeness, it is a tool for finding ways to improve the reality. It is a means to an end, rather than some marvelous device to stand around and admire. Treating the model as an object of art or as a toy exhibits a penchant of the modern analyst rather chillingly described by R. W. Churchman. "Probably the most startling feature of twentieth century culture is the fact that we have developed such elaborate ways of doing things and at the same time have developed no way of justifying any of the things we do."[43]

The goal of urban models is to help develop policies by examining the short- and long-term impacts of program proposals within the various subsystems and throughout the urban system. The goals of systems analysis thus differ markedly from the narrower incremental goals with which we are familiar. Getting a hospital for neighborhood A or putting a new road through are, at the most, only subparts of system goals.

From the systems perspective, the hospital is seen in terms of the overall need for hospital beds in the urban area; the degree to which the catchment areas of existing facilities cover the urban area including neighborhood A; the trends in employment and location that will affect the target population in future years; the benefits that would occur if the investment for the new hospital were applied to another subsystem. The focus is not on the neighborhood, but on the way the entire urban system will change as a result of constructing the new hospital.

Similarly, a new road from the central city to the suburbs is not just something that makes getting around easier. It is migrating retail businesses. It is low-income clerks left behind because they have no car. It is the wives, sons, daughters, and husbands of middle-income suburban families taking their place. It is workers in the central city who have been laid off becoming a drain on governmental resources through unemployment and welfare. It is a shift of tax revenues from one sector of the urban system to another. All this and more is what the systems perspective sees when it looks to the implications of a given policy.

The goals of the model, then, are to enhance the decision makers' appreciation of the scope of their decisions, to provide them with a means of ascertaining whether alternatives would have a more favorable overall impact and, generally, to maximize the information underlying public policy decisions to protect against today's solutions becoming tomorrow's problems.

This is not to say that the incremental method of making public policy decisions will wither away. The sheer weight of government activity, the complexity of society, the fragmentation and compartmentalization of interests: all contribute to the endurance of incremental decision making. Still, the systems approach can overcome some of incrementalism's negative consequences: the occasional gross pluralist maladjustments that create more problems than they solve. Overcoming problems is the generic mandate of the administrator, and systems thinking helps carry out that mandate. To advance the analytic approach, administrators may have to convert skeptical pluralist policy makers in state houses, city halls, and legislative bodies.

To the administrator who is committed to systematic analysis and who understands the public policy environment, converting skeptics will be treated as a part of the job. In the next chapter, on program evaluation, we will see that those who bring small-scale versions of systematic analysis to government may need as thick a skin as the analytically inclined administrator. However, the people lining the evaluator's gauntlet often are not legislators but the vested interest personnel of the institutionalized bureaucracy.

KEY TERMS AND CONCEPTS

Economic landscape model	Environment
Economic-sociological model	External constraints
Elements	Input-Output Analysis

Internal constraints   Subsystem
Iteration   System
Model   Systems analysis
Physical analogy model

NOTES

1. Benjamin Chinitz, "The Economy of the Central City: An Appraisal," in *The Urban Economy,* ed. Harold Hochman (New York: Norton, 1967), p. 94.
2. Theodore J. Lowi, *The End of Liberalism: Ideology, Policy and the Crisis of Public Authority* (New York: Norton, 1969), pp. 250–283.
3. Kurt Vonnegut, Jr., *Welcome to the Monkey House* (New York: Dell, 1970), p. xi.
4. Kenneth J. Dueker and Richard Talcott, "State Land Use Planning Process Issues: Geographic Information System Implications," in *Computer Systems and Public Administrators,* eds. Richard A. Bassler and Norman L. Enger (Alexandria, Va.: College Readings, Inc., 1976), pp. 292–293.
5. John F. Kain and John R. Meyer, "Transportation and Poverty," in Hochman, *The Urban Economy,* pp. 180–194.
6. Daniel B. Magraw, "Societal Change and Information Systems," in Bassler and Enger, *Computer Systems,* p. 4.
7. Harold Hovey, "Some Perspectives on Data Processing," in Ibid., p. 10.
8. Herbert E. Meyer, "How Government Ruined the South Bronx," *Fortune,* November 1975, p. 140.
9. S. Kenneth Howard, *Changing State Budgeting* (Lexington, Ky.: Council of State Governments, 1973), p. 214.
10. Thomas J. Anton, *The Politics of State Expenditure in Illinois* (Urbana: University of Illinois Press, 1966), p. 74.
11. Magraw, "Societal Change," p. 4.
12. Jay W. Forrester, "Overlooked Reasons for Our Social Troubles," in Hochman, *The Urban Economy,* p. 259.
13. Ibid., p. 161.
14. Ludwig Von Bertalanffy, quoted in George Chadwick, *A Systems View of Planning* (Elmsford, N.Y.: Pergamon Press, 1971), p. 37.
15. *New York Post,* 29 September 1976, p. 37.
16. Chadwick, *A Systems View of Planning,* pp. 42–43.
17. Jay W. Forrester, "Comments on National Growth" in Hochman, *The Urban Economy,* p. 138.
18. *The New York Times,* 27 January 1959, p. 35.
19. Edward H. Blum, *The Community Information Utility and Municipal Services* (Santa Monica, Calif.: Rand Corporation, 1972), p. 26.
20. Arthur Carol, *City Crime* (New York: Council on Municipal Performance, 1973), p. 16.
21. Susan Elizabeth Lyman, *The Story of New York* (New York: Crown, 1975), p. 5.
22. Donald F. Blumberg and Dilip R. Li Maye, "Promus: An Urban Planning and Management System," in *Computers in Public Administration,* ed. Samuel J. Bernstein (Elmsford, N.Y.: Pergamon Press, 1976), p. 167.
23. Johann von Thunen, *The Isolated State* (Hamburg, Germany: 1826).
24. An early gravity construct was put forth by Charles C. Colry, "Centrifugal and Centripetal Forces in Urban Geography," *Annals of the Association of American Geographers* 23 (1 March 1933): 1–21.

25. See R. E. Park and E. W. Burgess, *The City* (Chicago: University of Chicago Press, 1925).

26. August Losch, *The Economics of Location* (New Haven: Yale University Press, 1954); Walter Isard, *Methods of Regional Analysis: An Introduction to Regional Science* (Cambridge: MIT Press, 1960).

27. Colin Lee, *Models in Planning* (Elmsford, N.Y.: Pergamon Press, 1973), p. 58.

28. Chinitz, "Economy of the Central City," p. 122.

29. Ira S. Lowry, *A Model of Metropolis,* Rand Corporation Memorandum RM-4035-RC (Santa Monica, Calif.: Rand Corporation, 1964).

30. Jay W. Forrester, *Urban Dynamics* (Cambridge: MIT Press, 1969).

31. Robert Dorfman, "The Function of the City," in Hochman, *The Urban Economy,* p. 32.

32. Ibid., p. 34.

33. Carol, *City Crime,* p. 10.

34. Anthony Downs, "The Future of American Ghettoes," in Hochman, *The Urban Economy,* pp. 185–210.

35. Dorfman, "Function of the City," p. 34.

36. Ibid., pp. 35–37.

37. Downs, "Future of American Ghettoes," p. 201.

38. Dorfman, "Function of the City," p. 32.

39. Ibid., p. 32.

40. Robert W. Blanning, Arie Y. Lewin, and Myron Uretsky, "Issues in the Design of an Urban Game," in Bernstein, *Computers in Public Administration,* p. 409.

41. Carol, *City Crime,* p. 3.

42. Ibid., p. 12.

43. C. W. Churchman quoted in Chadwick, *A Systems View of Planning,* p. 115.

BIBLIOGRAPHY

Altschuler, Alan. *The City Planning Process.* Ithaca, N.Y.: Cornell Press, 1966.

Bourne, Larry S. *Internal Structure of the City: Readings on Space and Environment.* New York: Oxford University Press, 1971.

———, ed. *City and Suburb: The Economics of Metropolitan Growth.* Englewood Cliffs, N.J.: Prentice-Hall, 1964.

Churchman, C. W.; Ackoff, R. L.; and Arnoff, E. L. *Introduction to Operations Research.* New York: Wiley, 1957.

Downs, Anthony. *Urban Problems and Prospects.* Chicago: Markham, 1970.

Emery, F. E. *Systems Thinking.* Baltimore, Md.: Penguin Books, 1969.

Forrester, Jay W. *Urban Dynamics.* Cambridge: MIT Press, 1969.

Gorham, William, ed. *Urban Processes.* Washington, D.C.: Urban Institute, 1972.

Habert, Richard. *Highways to Nowhere.* Indianapolis: Bobbs-Merrill, 1972.

Isard, Walter. *Methods of Regional Analysis: An Introduction to Regional Science.* Cambridge: MIT Press, 1960.

Jacobs, Jane. *The Rise and Decline of the Great American Cities.* New York: Doubleday, 1969.

Lithwood, Martha B., ed. *Public and Business Planning in the United States.* Detroit: Gale, 1972.

Losch, August. *The Economics of Location.* New Haven: Yale University Press, 1954.

Lowry, Ira S. *A Model of Metropolis.* Rand Corporation Memorandum RM - 4035 - RC. Santa Monica, Calif.: Rand Corporation, 1964.

Lupo, Alan; Colcord, Frank; and Fowler, Edmund P. *Rites of Way: The Politics of Transportation in Boston and the U.S. City.* Boston: Little, Brown, 1971.

Manoni, Mary. *Bedford Stuyvesant: The Anatomy of a Central City Community.* New York: Quadrangle, 1973.

Owen, Wilfred. *The Metropolitan Transportation Problem.* Washington, D.C.: Brookings, 1966.

Pascal, Anthony H., ed. *Thinking About Cities: New Perspective on Urban Problems.* Belmont, Cal.: Dickenson Publishing, 1970.

Pikarsky, Milton, and Christensen, Daphne. *Urban Transportation Policy and Management.* Lexington, Mass.: Lexington Books, 1976.

Rivlin, Alice M. *Systematic Thinking for Social Action.* Washington, D.C.: Brookings, 1971.

Taeuber, Karl E., and Taeuber, Alma F. *Negroes in Cities: Residential Segregation and Neighborhood Change.* Chicago: Aldine, 1965.

VanGigch, John P. *Applied General Systems Theory.* New York: Harper & Row, 1974.

Zadek, L. A., and Polak, E. *Systems Theory.* New York: McGraw-Hill, 1969.

In addition to the sources cited in the notes and bibliography, the following *Public Administration Review (PAR)* articles are a convenient starting point for a more detailed exploration of the material in this chapter.

Bloomberg, Warner. "Governing Megacentropolis: The Goals," *PAR* 30, no. 5 (Sept./Oct. 1970): 513–520.

Caldwell, Lynton K. "Managing the Transition to Post Modern Society," *PAR* 35, no. 6 (Nov./Dec. 1975): 567–572.

Chamberlain, Neil W. "Private and Public Planning," *PAR* 31, no. 3 (May/June 1971): 382–388.

Cleveland, Harlan. "Systems, Purposes and the Watergate," *PAR* 34, no. 3 (May/June 1974): 260–264.

Coates, Joseph F. "Why Think About the Future: Some Administrative-Political Perspectives," *PAR* 36, no. 5 (Sept./Oct. 1976): 580–585.

Cohen, Henry. "Governing Megacentropolis: The Constraints," *PAR* 30, no. 5 (Sept./Oct. 1970): 488–497.

Crecine, John P. "Computer Simulation in Urban Research," *PAR* 28, no. 1 (Jan./Feb. 1968): 66–71.

Dyckman, John W. "New Normative Styles in Urban Studies," *PAR* 31, no. 3 (May/June 1971): 327–333.

Fitch, Lyle C. "Governing Megacentropolis: The People," *PAR* 30, no. 5 (Sept./Oct. 1970): 481–488.

Friedmann, John. "The Future of Comprehensive Urban Planning: A Critique," *PAR* 31, no. 3 (May/June 1971): 315–326.

Friesen, Ernest C. "Constraints and Conflict in Court Administration," *PAR* 31, no. 2 (March/April 1971): 120–124.

Henderson, Hazel. "Philosophical Conflict: Reexamining the Goals of Knowledge," *PAR* 35, no. 1 (Jan./Feb. 1975): 77–80.

Hoos, Ida R. "Systems Techniques for Managing Society: A Critique," *PAR* 35, no. 2 (March/April 1975): 157–164.

Keating, William Thomas. "On Managing Ignorance," *PAR* 35, no. 6 (Nov./Dec. 1975): 593–597.

Kennedy, David J. "The Law of Appropriateness: An Approach to a General Theory of Intergovernmental Relations," *PAR* 32, no. 2 (March/April 1972): 135–143.

Kramer, Fred A. "Policy Analysis as Ideology," *PAR* 35, no. 5 (Sept./Oct. 1975): 509–517.

Long, Norton. "Have Cities a Future?" *PAR* 33, no. 6 (Nov./Dec. 1973): 543–552.

Long, Norton. "The City as Underdeveloped Country," *PAR* 32, no. 1 (Jan./Feb. 1972): 57–62.

Munro, Jim L. "Intersystem Action Planning: Criminal and Non-Criminal Justice Agencies," *PAR* 36, no. 4 (July/Aug. 1976): 390–397.

Munro, Jim L. "Towards a Theory of Criminal Justice Administration: A General Systems Perspective," *PAR* 31, no. 6 (Nov./Dec. 1971): 621–632.

Mushkin, Selma J. "Policy Analysis in State and Community," *PAR* 37, no. 3 (May/June 1977): 245–253.

Rehfuss, John. "Suburban Development and Governance," *PAR* 37, no. 1 (Jan./Feb. 1977): 111–120.

Stillman, Richard J., II. "The Bureaucracy Problem at DOJ," *PAR* 36, no. 4 (July/Aug. 1976): 429–439.

Ukeles, Jacob B. "Policy Analysis: Myth or Reality," *PAR* 37, no. 3 (May/June 1977): 233–238.

RELEVANT PERIODICALS

AIP Journal
Annals of Regional Science
Environment and Behavior
General Systems
Interfaces
Journal of Regional Science
Journal of Social Policy
Management Science
Nation's Cities
National Civic Review
Policy Analysis
Social Problems
Urban Affairs Quarterly
Urban Life

RELEVANT CASE STUDIES

(Cases marked ICCH are available from the Intercollegiate Case Clearing House, Soldier Field, Boston, Mass. 02163; cases marked ICP are available from the Inter-University Case Program, Box 229, Syracuse, N.Y. 13210.)

Altshuler, A. *The Ancker Hospital Site Controversy,* [ICP]
Altshuler, A. *A Land-Use Plan for St. Paul,* [ICP]
Altchuler, A. *Locating the Inner City Freeway,* [ICP]
Bower, J. L. *Transportation Policy in Massachusetts,* (A)(B)(C),*[ICCH]
Campbell, W. *Campus Expansion and the City of Berkeley,* [ICP]
Elynn, L. *Land Use(A): The Dimensions of the Problem/Land Use (B): National Land Use Legislation,* [ICCH]
Johnson, G. G. *MBTA,* [ICCH]

*Letters indicate that the case is presented in several installments.

CHAPTER 13

EVALUATING PROGRAMS

INTRODUCTION: TOWARD DETAILED ANALYSIS

Program evaluation has, in one sense, always been with us. The traditional budget deliberations of legislators and executives detailed in Chapter 9 were evaluations of government programs. In most cases, however, only the new parts of programs were analyzed. Often overlooked was the underlying program structure upon which the additions were built. In the 1970s, things began to change. A new commitment to the comprehensive analysis of public programs was evident in congressional budgetary deliberations, Government Accounting Office (GAO) audits, Office of Management and Budget reviews, and agency self-evaluations required by statute. Thus, evaluation came to mean an intensive examination of how programs functioned, what they achieved, and the costs associated with the accomplishments. In this chapter, we will review the development of evaluation, the problems that confront evaluators, and some of the techniques that aid in the comprehensive analysis of public programs.

DEFINING PROGRAMS

People in government often talk about the "program level." The implication is that there are boundaries in the bureaucracy that can be discovered that will distinguish "program" functions from other functions. By alluding to "level," the impression is conveyed that this boundary cuts horizontally across the bureaucratic hierarchy; that is, above a certain point is not "program level," while below it is. What does this tell us? Absolutely nothing.

Carol Weiss is considerably more helpful in providing us with several *program* characteristics, the range and mix of which make clear that program level is not a very helpful term. Programs, she writes, can differ in size, scope, duration, clarity of inputs, the complexity and time span of goals, and the methods of operation. Let us look at some of these characteristics.[1]

Scope. "The program being evaluated may cover the nation, a region, state, city, neighborhood or be limited to one specific site."[2] Swine flu vaccine to prevent disease nationwide is a program as is a local effort to curb illness by preventing the consumption of fish from polluted local waterways.

Size. "Programs can serve a few people or reach thousands or even millions."[3] Social security reaches most Americans, either as contributors or as beneficiaries. The federally guaranteed loan to the Lockheed Corporation was a program with a pinpoint aim.

Clarity of program input. It may be very clear who is involved in administering and staffing a specific program, but it often is not. If the local meter maids are given exclusive responsibility for issuing parking tickets and the police prohibited from doing so, the government factor in the rise and fall of illegal parking is the meter maid contingent. However, if both issue parking summonses, one faces the problem of determining the relative impact each has had on the parking situation. When a problem is the focus of attention of several agencies, figuring out who did what becomes exceedingly difficult. A disreputable mail order firm, bilking customers both within and without of its home state, could be the subject of investigation and prosecution by several agencies including local district attorneys and consumer protection offices, the consumer frauds bureau of the state attorney general's office, the Federal Trade Commission, or the U.S. attorney having jurisdiction. Additional government offices, while not having enforcement power, may receive and use the complaints as a basis for drafting legislation to curb mail order abuse. The president's Office of Consumer Affairs is one such agency. Of course, any legislator can also submit a bill in response to constituents' complaints about mail fraud. If mail order fraud is reduced, who gets the credit? One suspects that calculating the relative impacts in this case is either impossible or not worth the costs.

Complexity and time span of goals Eliminating double parking is a goal that is easy enough to measure. However, "'improving the quality of urban life' contains within it not only a large number of subgoals (which must be made explicit) but also ambiguous subgoals (improving the esthetics of the urban scene) that pose awesome problems of conceptualization and measurement."[4]

Innovativeness Some programs depart radically from the accepted ways of doing things. Some community improvement functions may be assigned to youth gangs, for instance. Other programs may operate under traditional routines. A municipal health department's campaign against venereal disease may be identical to the one it waged against measles.

It should be clear that there is no single ruler by which one measures programs. They operate in a variety of ways and under various guises and begin to look similar only when treated generically rather than specifically. In its most generic sense, a *program* consists of the resources that are to be used, the method in which they are to be applied, and the result that they are designed to obtain.

Programs, as government activities, are directed at a specific problem external to the unit assigned to deal with it. Units can be large or small; the problems can be general or specific. All meter maids can be charged with enforcing all the traffic laws, or a portion can be assigned to clear double parkers from Main Street. The measure of program success is whether the efforts of the unit accomplish the task that it has been assigned. If the largest department store on Main Street burns down, thus eliminating the double parking problem, the unit's efforts cannot be said to have been responsible. Further, intermediate steps that are taken by the unit to attack the problem cannot be calculated as program success. For instance, the unit assigned to issue tickets for double parking may increase its ticket issuance twofold. However, most of the violators are from across the state line. Coming to the city to take advantage of lower sales taxes, they feel beyond the reach of the local authorities. Though the increase in summonses may look impressive and represent a lot of work, the activity has not contributed to the resolution of the problem. *Evaluation,* then, is determining whether your activities are effective in resolving the problem and determining the extent to which other factors have contributed to the resolution. If your program is ineffective or if the problem would have gone away in any event, the evaluation of your program's worth cannot be very high.

THE EVOLUTION OF PROGRAM EVALUATION

While there have always been government programs, there has not always been evaluation in the sense of a systematic undertaking to determine if the objectives are being met. Traditionally, operations, not results, have been the object of evaluation. Allen Schick refers to the period from 1920 to 1935 as one in which government executives emphasized "expenditure control."[5] This accounting orientation led just where one would expect it to lead. The reporting integrity of the government machine became the criterion by which it was judged as effective. Schick identifies the post–1935 period as one of "management orientation."[6] Many of the concepts of the early management scientists such as Taylor were applied to the government. Thus, writes Schick, there developed "management improvement and work measurement programs, and the focusing of budget preparation on the work and activities of the agencies."[7] Those with a management orientation were still evaluating the bureaucratic machinery to a much greater extent than they were evaluating what that machinery was accomplishing.

This bureaucratic, and even congressional, preoccupation with the internal workings of government did not mean that legislation calling for evaluation was nonexistent. On the contrary, over 50 years ago the comptroller general of the United States was delegated the responsibility for reviewing the results and effectiveness of programs in the federal government. The Budget and Accounting Act of 1921 called for the general evaluation and analysis of federal programs and activities, and as Schick has noted, its passage was preceded by considerable debate over how to determine the effectiveness of public programs.[8] The Accounting and Auditing Act of 1950 again called for evaluation and analysis. Throughout the middle third of this century, however, this "call" generally fell upon deaf ears in the bureaucracy. Indeed, one of the more receptive administrators, Secretary of Defense MacNamara in the Kennedy administration, was more likely moved by his experience as head of the Ford Motor Company than by legislation. Beyond the Department of Defense, evaluation appeared to have made few inroads, even as of 1970, when a report prepared for the government stated, "the most impressive finding about the evaluation of social programs in the federal government is that substantial work in this field has been almost non-existent."[9]

While evaluation may have been nonexistent, congressional calls for it were becoming louder and more explicit. Under the Kennedy and Johnson administrations, the response to social problems and the social disruptions such as riots came in the form of rapidly increasing government activity. Williams and Evans cite as an example "the explosive expansion of Head Start from what was originally conceived as a limited experimental program to a large national program almost overnight."[10] Social programs proliferated. Many seemed to accomplish very little. Others accomplished things that appeared to have little connection with social welfare. Some local poverty programs started acting like political machines. Employment was reserved for loyalists. Program executives started running for city councils. Money occasionally disappeared only to be found in administrators' wallets. In the face of such unanticipated and, most often, undesirable consequences—politicized antipoverty groups could, and did, cut into the power of some inner city congresspersons—Congress reacted. In broad legislation relating to its own structure and in specific bills establishing programs, the legislature inserted the word "evaluation" prominently and often. With respect to the Office of Economic Opportunity, 1967 amendments to its enabling legislation called "explicitly and at several points for evaluation studies" both by agency staff and outside consultants.[11] Section 204 of the Legislative Reorganization Act of 1970 supplemented the authority of the comptroller general to perform evaluations and clearly demonstrated Congress's interest in program analysis. By the time Congress passed the Congressional Budget Act of 1974, it was demanding that "the Comptroller General . . . develop and recommend to the Congress methods for review and evaluation of government programs carried on under existing law."[12] The following year the General Accounting Office published a document, *Evaluation and Analysis to Support Decision Making*, that, as its title suggests, presented evaluation as an integral component of governmental decision making.

The push for evaluation was evident on several other fronts as well. In the executive branch, President Nixon's Reorganization Plan No. 2 of 1970 assigned the Office of Management and Budget the task of placing "much greater emphasis on the evaluation of program performance: on assessing the extent to which programs are actually achieving their intended results, and delivering the intended services to the intended recipients. This is needed on a continuing basis, not as a one time effort. . . ."[13]

In the private sector, various evaluative techniques and tools had been tested, refined, and applied. In business, as well as in the fields of academic endeavor, the computer had been utilized to mimic actual events, to analyze mountains of data that would take years to process manually, and to estimate the probability of future events as an aid to decision making. The application of the techniques of scientific experimentation in the social sciences, particularly the measurement of traits and attitudes pioneered by psychology, made it possible to show if a given treatment had caused a change in an individual. Businesses, such as the Rand Corporation and A. C. Neilson, had sprung up with evaluation as their primary product. Policy analysis was becoming increasingly important as a field of study in schools of public administration. The bureaucracy, confronted with calls for evaluation from all sectors of its environment, was compelled to respond by moving toward a result orientation. "Evaluation," according to Wholey, et al., "is becoming increasingly important in the development of federal social policies and in the management of federal social programs. To make certain that these policies and programs meet the needs of society, it is necessary to analyze programs to determine their consequences—that is, to measure their successes and failures in meeting the nation's goals."[14]

It is too early to see clearly the results of this initial embrace between government organization and evaluation. However, the remainder of this chapter is based, in part, on the reports of maiden evaluators confronting an equally inexperienced administrative apparatus. Often, therefore, as the evaluators tell us how to do it, they tell us, also, how to do it when the subject is resisting.

EVALUATING ORGANIZATIONAL ACHIEVEMENT

When the evaluator comes face to face with the government agency, there exists the potential for hate at first sight. From the evaluator's viewpoint, "the staff running the program tend toward optimism and, in any case, have a stake in reporting success. Many programs provide a variety of services and deal with a large number of participants. A handful of 'consumer testimonials' or a quick tour of inspection can hardly gauge their effectiveness."[15]

For its part the agency is not likely to be cheered by someone, particularly if that someone is an outsider, who wants to compare "both outcomes—what happened that would not have happened in the absence of the programs—and relative effectiveness—what strategies or projects within the program work best?"[16] To an organization trying to maintain a precarious internal and external equilibrium, the exploratory operation of evaluation that could lead to the removal or rearrangement of organizational parts may not be a very exciting prospect. According to Carol Weiss, practitioners "as they see it, are on trial. If the results of the evaluation are negative, then the program—and possibly their jobs—are in jeopardy."[17]

However, Weiss also feels that there are times when the agency welcomes the evaluator with open arms that hide ulterior motives. If the heat is on a program, a full-scale evaluation can buy time during which the outcry may die down. A decision maker confronted with a clear, but potentially dangerous, decision about a program may order a needless evaluation in order to shift the responsibility to the evaluators. On the other hand, evaluations may be ordered for programs that are obviously effective in order to gain favorable exposure or to obscure other programs that would disintegrate under scrutiny. As an antidote to this type of behavior, Weiss suggests that evaluation not be undertaken when:

> there are no questions about the program's accomplishments.
> there is insufficient money or staff.
> there is a free-form program improvising its activities day-to-day.
> there is no agreement on goals among policy makers.[18]

This last criterion should be leavened by the knowledge that, in public policy, a general consensus is more likely than an explicit agreement on goals. The evaluator who cannot discover even vague consensual backing for a program might well heed Weiss's advice.

Searching for Goals

Assuming that the organization and the evaluator overcome the initial hurdles that stand in the way of their getting together, the evaluator now stands ready to "assess the effectiveness of an ongoing program in achieving its objectives (by relying) on the principles of research design to distinguish a program's effects from those of other forces working on a situation (and aiming) at program improvement through a modification of current operations."[19]

In order to measure the effectiveness of a program, the evaluator needs something to measure it against. The definition above gives us *objectives* as a yardstick, although "goals," "aims," "purposes," or "targets" are just as likely to spring from the lips of program administrators. Often, however, no matter what you call them, the things that a program is trying to accomplish are not very clear at all. This lack of clarity can be a premeditated administrative ploy to frustrate evaluation or insure that success is easily achieved. However, the fogginess of goals is often rooted in equally misty legislation. "Providing a decent home for every American" or "high quality comprehensive medical care" sound fine, particularly in speeches by legislators or administrators. For many public executives, the agency task definition is composed almost exclusively of such phrases. Below is a portion of the enabling legislation of the New York State Department of Environmental Conservation. It is a good example of what the administrator (and evaluator) runs up against in the attempt to define objectives on an operational level. According to law, the agency should:

> encourage industrial, commercial, residential and community development which provides the best usage of land areas, maximizes environmental benefits and minimizes the effects of less desirable environmental conditions.
> assure the preservation and enhancement of natural beauty and man-made scenic qualities.
> provide for prevention and abatement of all water, land, and air pollution including but not limited to that related to particulates, gases, dust vapors, noise, radiation, odor, nutrients and heated liquids.
> promote control of pests and regulate the use, storage and disposal of pesticides and other chemicals which may be harmful to man, animals, plant life, or natural resources.
> promote control of weeds and aquatic growth, develop methods of prevention and eradication, and regulate herbicides.

provide and recommend methods for disposal of solid wastes, including domestic and industrial refuse, junk cars, litter and debris, consistent
with sound health, scenic, environmental quality, and land use practices.[20]

There are a lot of things to be done and none of them are very
clear. The commissioner has to do a lot of providing, promoting, and
encouraging. So what? Does the commissioner provide a little or a lot?
Does the commissioner promote with money, moral suasion, or education campaigns? Or does the commissioner encourage with a smile or
with a club? Does the agency "abate . . . water, land, and air pollution" to
99 percent of current levels? 75 percent? 50 percent? Does the commissioner recommend one "method for the disposal of solid waste" or several dozen? It appears that it is up to the commisioner to decide on so
many issues. Since this is the type of legislation that passes on value-laden
judgments to administrators, the agency is likely to become the arena for
the clash of values advanced by interested parties. Thus, giving hard
numbers to the vague legislative directives may take considerable time.
Indeed, avoiding a commitment to the specific may be the best way to
maintain a truce between the agency and the interest groups in its environment.

Operating under the legislation's lack of specificity has other advantages. If the administrator chooses not to elaborate on the legislation,
the zone of positive accomplishment is very easy to reach. A single vacant
lot transformed into a playground "promotes the restoration and recla-
mation of degraded or despoiled areas." Similarly, for most of the other
legislative requirements "more than nothing" can be pointed to as success regardless of how much more than nothing has been accomplished.
If vague legislation represents assigned duties that are easy to fulfill,
while specific program goals represent administrative promises that may
be difficult to keep, the administrator will always be somewhat tempted
to avoid goal definition.

The law, thus, can be a roadblock and a temptation to administrators. We hope that it is a minority of administrators who throw up
their hands and say, "What can we do?" or rub their hands gleefully
together and think, "We needn't do much of anything!" Evaluators,
however, should never succumb to amorphous goals. If muddy water is
accepted as the evaluation milieu, evaluators should not be surprised if
they end up in the swamp. For the evaluation that emerges from the
mire of unenunciated goals—probably a report on how confusing it all
is—"much of the blame . . . must be placed with program managers for
failure to be explicit about their objectives and with evaluators for failure
to insist on the guidance they need to define evaluation criteria."[21]

For evaluators, lack of goal definition can be such a major stumbling block that, if it cannot be remedied, there may be little point in proceeding. "Unless goals are precisely stated," notes Wholey et al., "there is no standard against which to measure whether the direction of a program or its rate of progress is satisfactory."[22] Thus, before evaluation can proceed, it often becomes necessary to thrash out goals. There can be no precise measurement of program effectiveness without a clear standard to measure against. Since these goals and standards are, as often as not, nonexistent, the methods of formulating objectives and establishing criteria to measure their attainment become of prime importance to a successful program evaluation.

Giving Form to Goals

To discover program objectives, or even to create them, if necessary, one needs to know the thinking of the policy makers. Even vague statutes are backed by legislative reports, hearing transcripts, and speeches by individual legislators. Presidents may express certain views as they sign bills into law. Their executive staff, or staff agencies such as the Office of Management and Budget, may recommend certain directions for the programs. The agency head and various staff may prepare memoranda concerning program objectives. Minutes of staff meetings may contain summaries of discussion or debate over program aims. All of these sources can be used by the evaluator in constructing a clear and precise program objective in conjunction with agency personnel. Program executive and staff inclusion in the goal formulation process is important for several reasons. One, they are close to the problem. Two, they are familiar with the program machinery. Three, without staff support or cooperation, the evaluator is unlikely to make much headway.

At the end of this study and consultation process, explicit statements of objectives should emerge. These statements of objectives should capture a complete understanding of the intended benefits of the program. The beneficiaries should be clearly identified. The level of attainment expected—the degree to which the problem will be eliminated—is a vital part of the objective. One may think beyond the immediate program and include spin-off benefits that will accrue to society when program goals are achieved. Reducing alcoholism by 20 percent may have positive effects on unemployment, employee absenteeism, and productivity. In any event, once program objectives have been clearly defined, the question becomes: How will we know when the objective has been reached?

Giving Substance to Goals

The ideal measure of program achievement would do two things. It would indicate when the objective has been met and, at any point prior to that, give a clear indication of what has been accomplished and how much remains to be done. While program evaluation measures are by no means ideal, there has been increased attention paid to replacing rhetoric with facts in the measurement of social programs. These facts are the subparts of a well-defined objective. The facts of the objective of reducing alcoholism could be: the number of arrests for public intoxication and drunken driving; the number of alcohol-related hospitalizations and deaths; the Monday absenteeism rate among workers; the amount of participation in private and public treatment programs; or the demand for alternative intoxicants such as marijuana. These facts that give measurable substance to program objectives are called criteria. As the measuring devices for program accomplishment, *criteria:*

> should be relevant and important to the specific problem for which they are used.
> should cover all major effects of a program.
> should be capable of meaningful quantification.[23]

The sample criteria reproduced below, which were formulated by Harry Hatry, show clearly that they are tools for measurement. Hatry's "program objective," under which the criteria have been formulated, is "to provide opportunities for satisfactory homes for the citizenry, including provision of a choice, at prices they can afford, of decent, safe and sanitary dwellings in pleasant surroundings."[24] (It is interesting to note that Hatry includes "at prices they can afford" in his definition. Occasionally, "middle-class" housing programs, by the time they reach the occupancy stage, rent at levels that are higher than the middle class can afford.) Some of Hatry's criteria for the housing objective are:

1. the percentage and number of substandard dwelling units. (Hatry suggests the use of several categories, not just "standard" and "substandard," each fully defined in terms of crowding, physical deterioration, insanitary conditions, etc.)
2. acres of blighted areas eliminated and other areas prevented from becoming blighted.
3. total number and percentage of persons and families living in substandard dwelling units.
4. number and percentage of persons and families upgraded from one level of housing to a higher level or prevented from degrading to a lower level.
5. measure of neighborhood physical and psychological attractiveness.
6. average and distribution of property values adjusted for price level changes and compared against the expected change from year to year.
7. number of fires, accidents, deaths, and injuries resulting from housing deficiencies.[25]

There is a noticeable difference between these measures of success and such statements as "Last year the Department did more for the people of the state than ever before," or "The agency built 3500 new dwelling units in 1976." Hatry's criteria give more dimension to the objective. The program is no longer a one- or two-dimensional entity that can claim success on the basis of equally shallow rhetoric, press releases, or single statistics. Good housing becomes a mix of several factors. For housing to improve, all or most of the factors must improve. Hatry's basic approach to criteria formulation can be used to develop evaluative measures for a wide variety of programs and includes three essential questions that one should find in any evaluation: (1) What do the clients think? (2) What's going wrong? and (3) Are things curing themselves?

Clients and Goals

Hatry's criterion of "psychological and physical attractiveness" takes evaluation beyond structures, investments, and acreage; it seeks to determine what the client thinks. To be heard, however, the client's voice must overcome several barriers. Administrators may resist being evaluated by the "ill-informed and the nonprofessional." Easily gathered "hard statistics" may be pushed as a low-cost alternative to expensive and administratively cumbersome client surveys. Nonetheless, the evaluator should resist jettisoning attitudinal measurements. If attitudes are ignored, a program may look good when, in actuality, it is a time bomb.

Public housing, scarred by unexpected explosions both large and small, illustrates the importance of attitudes to the evaluative formula. In the 1960s, Lewis Mumford unilaterally evaluated the psychological attractiveness of public housing. "There is nothing wrong with these buildings," he wrote, "except that, humanly speaking, they stink."[26] At the time, Mumford's was a minority opinion. The figures showed that public housing provided modern spacious accommodations at low rents to individuals previously housed in decrepit structures. Maintenance expenditures were adequate and the overall public-housing population was racially and ethnically mixed. All in all, the "hard statistics" indicated a pleasant environment. Time, however, has vindicated Mumford. Projects have become high-crime areas. The scars of vandalism disfigure even newly constructed public housing. Long-term residents, perceiving an increasingly hostile environment, have left. In some developments, the vacated apartments, no longer physically or psychologically attractive enough to lure renters, remained empty and were the first malignancies in an often fatal disease. The Pruitt-Igoe Houses in St. Louis, desolate and abandoned within two decades of construction, could easily bear the words of Lewis Mumford as an epitaph. "Sanitary, steam-heated apartments," he wrote, "are not a substitute for warm-hearted neighbors."[27] Mumford's words have general applicability in the evaluative milieu. When resources are available, evaluation should always explore the attitudes of the people who are the object of the program.

Pruitt-Igoe Going Down. A youthful physical plant succumbing to the ravages of untreated social ills. (Wide World Photos)

What's Going Wrong?

Hatry's criteria not only measure upgrading but backsliding as well. Overall increases or decreases in substandard housing and the population of substandard housing will be evident as measures are compared over successive periods. This is important because, more often than not, administrators fail to view accomplishment as the net result of positive and negative program effects. Rather, a preoccupation with the positive—"getting the job done"—often causes policy makers to lose sight of what is getting undone in the process. In the 1950s, urban development, by relocating thousands of people during site clearance, often forced tenants at these sites into housing that was inferior to the structures that had been demolished.[28] In addition, the noise of construction and the forced departure of many of their friends often induced residents in surrounding areas to move. Finally, when the development was completed, "first-choice" tenants in buildings surrounding the site transferred en masse. The result was neighborhood dislocation, severe strain on the surrounding structures, and a project population that differed radically from the long-time neighborhood residents.[29]

Other programs administered by the federal government also created unnoticed negative impacts almost as fast as they created positive ones. For instance, federally guaranteed, low-interest loans to home purchasers were intended to make home ownership available to most Americans, thus upgrading housing overall. The ensuing rush to the suburbs, however, has other consequences. As an observer notes: "The effects of the FHA insurance policies and practices on segregation, urban sprawl and the decline of the central cities, for example, went virtually unnoticed for years."[30]

The job of evaluation is to ferret out "unnoticeable" program impacts that, quite likely, are negative. Program assets, assiduously compiled by administrators, usually include the obvious and the obscure. The "program liabilities" column, on the other hand, is likely to have few entries. Often, the major job of evaluation is to complete the ledger by asking, "What's going wrong?"

Are Things Curing Themselves?

Hatry's criterion relating to property values—"Average and distribution of property values adjusted for price level changes and compared against the expected change from year to year"—embodies the essence of program evaluation. What is important is the change that the program causes *in addition* to what was going to happen anyway. If property values go up at 6 percent a year, the rate of inflation, that increase is *not* a program accomplishment. If, in addition to inflation, property values had been trending upward in the project area for several years prior to the program's initiation, a continuation of that trend is not the miraculous result of the program. While the numbers may be higher, they were growing just as healthily with no program in sight. Inflation and the continuation of historical trends are *not* program achievements.

QUANTIFYING CRITERIA

After compiling the data called for by a criterion, one is confronted with the problem of combining the data in a way that is meaningful. Structural quality, crowdedness, and the surrounding environmental conditions play a part in determining whether urban housing is good or bad. The critical questions are: What is the relative importance of each? How do we add them together to arrive at a single indicator? To answer the first question, we have to find a way to rank each of the characteristics. To answer the second question, we have to find a way to add apples and oranges.

Weighting is probably the most familiar way of attributing rank to numbers. Let us imagine that, in a certain neighborhood, the incidence of crime is 52 occurrences per 1000 residents per year. Let us suppose that the incidence of fire is also 52 occurrences per 1000 residents per

TABLE 13.1   ADDING APPLES AND ORANGES

Item	Expected Crop (in Bushels)		Expected Market Price Per Bushel		Hurricane Loss		Loss in Dollars
Oranges	100,000	×	$1.00	×	.4	=	$40,000
Apples	100,000	×	$1.00	×	.6	=	$60,000
Totals:	Expected Revenues $200,000	−	Hurricane Losses $100,000	=	Actual Crop at Market $100,000 or a 50% loss		

year. However, it has been determined that the residents of this area are twice as concerned about crime as about fires. An accurate index would have to show that, although the incidence of fire and crime were identical, crime was twice as important in determining the community's perception about its level of public safety. This could be accomplished by multiplying the crime incidence figure by two while leaving the fire figure unchanged. (e.g., crime indicator = 104; fire indicator = 52)

Ranking can be a value-laden exercise, particularly if survey instruments cannot be used. When an independent reading of attitudes is not available, administrators may contend that what the citizens want most is what the program does best. In such instances, the evaluator should use common sense and a dash of skepticism. Painted park benches outside of public housing obviously are less important than painted apartments within.

Whereas ranking presents valuation problems, combining the ranked *indicators* presents technical and conceptual problems of varying magnitude. Combining similar measures with different constructions can be easy. If the county sheriff's office calculates its arrest figures on a per 10,000 basis while the municipal police use a per 1,000 scheme. converting the figures to a common base is simple. However, combining income and age indicators seems to present somewhat more difficulty.

The solution is really no more difficult than adding apples and oranges. Let us say that a farm devotes one-half of its acreage to apple orchards and the other half to orange groves. A hurricane destroys 60,000 bushels of the farm's 100,000 bushels of apples and 40,000 bushels of its 100,000 bushels of oranges. Apples and oranges may not add up as raw numbers, but they certainly can combine as percentages of an expected market price. Having lost 60 percent of the apple crop and 40 percent of the orange crop, the farmer can state with assurance that the crop is just about 50 percent as well off as expected. Once in percentage form and viewed as a part of a larger entity, the crop, adding apples and oranges is not only easy, it is meaningful. (See Table 13.1.)

Income and age combine for much the same reasons. Used in an evaluation criteria, they are a part of a larger crop: the overall population picture of a given area. In a conversion that is proportional, each can be stated in terms of a relationship to all the ages and all the incomes throughout an area.

Thus if $7000 is the median income of a city, a neighborhood showing the median could be indexed at .5 on a scale of 0 to 1. The age of the population of a neighborhood could be similarly indexed vis-à-vis its relation to the median age citywide. For each indicator, then, one determines the norm for a larger area and the relation of the collected data of the area under study to that norm. Since all of the indicators are now expressed in terms of a deviation from a standardized point, their combination becomes possible.

Where indicators are combined into a quality index, it is important that they all proceed in the same direction, either from good to bad or from bad to good. If you mix up the directions of the individual indicators that add up to the housing sketch, you are more likely to end up with modern art than a likeness of housing conditions. For instance, a high initial investment in building materials indicates a well-built structure. A high number of violations issued to the building indicates that it is not being taken care of at the present. If you look across the indices for high scores, this building will look great when, in fact, the current lack of maintenance is eating away at the housing quality provided by the high initial investment. In this particular case, a .6 on the initial investment index would be better than average (.5), whereas a .6 on the violations index would be worse than average. With investments, the measure of goodness is the index score. With violations, the measure of goodness is one minus the index score. Therefore, in order to transform the violations index into a "goodness score," the actual rating, the "badness score," is subtracted from one. Thus, even though the raw index score is .6 for both indicators, the violations score has to be transformed to .4 in order to give a true "index" picture of the building conditions.

There are additional techniques for making sure that the numbers paint real pictures. Where you have *time series data*—that is, readings from several previous years—the higher the number of previous years for which you have data, the more accurate the prediction for future years is likely to be. By collecting data from several previous years, the evaluator hopes to cancel out "flash in the pan" occurrences. For instance, a normally quiet neighborhood, located by a college, may have a low crime rate. However, the traditional rivalry football game last year ended in a full-scale riot. The 200 arrests that resulted doubled the neighborhood's normal yearly total. Unless arrest information was collected for several years, so that last year's undergraduate binge appeared as unusual as it really was, the impression of a soaring crime rate would be conveyed.

Deciding How Much Program to Evaluate

When program objectives and criteria for the measurement of their attainment are set, evaluation falls back into the more mundane task of making the most of the resources available.

The availability of resources plays a large part in determining just how comprehensive the evaluation is going to be. Ideally, the environment at which the program is directed should be defined as accurately as possible. If a city is fortunate enough to have a computerized "whole systems model" such as Toronto's PROMUS, many of the program alternatives can be fed into the existing model. These complex and costly analytical tools will project program impacts on the target population or environment and across a wide spectrum of urban indicators. Unfortunately, most program evaluations will be undertaken with considerably fewer resources. Time constraints also may preclude a full analysis. Even a sketch, however, can provide more information than intuition or "conventional wisdom."

For years it had been alleged that the high level of welfare payments in northeastern states was responsible for the migration of poor people from states with lower payment levels. However, the preliminary results of a recent study indicate that this is not so. It seems that rather than being pulled by welfare rates, migrants come in search of job opportunities. Higher welfare rates do, however, discourage migration out of the state by people who have been laid off and are unable to get another job. Thus, a program encouraging people to move on in search of relocated employment may be as effective in reducing the "welfare population" as a program discouraging people from moving into the area. This is particularly true if, as the study suggests, new residents arrive with an attitude that could lead to their becoming productive community members. When such inferences can be made, even preliminary analyses enhance decision making. Long held assumptions can be challenged. Broad patterns of interrelationships can be established. The effects of various program options become clearer. It need only be remembered that the analytical sketch, as a predictive tool, provides a greater or lesser degree of accuracy depending on the rigor with which it has been constructed, a rigor that often bears a direct relationship to the resources available.

If one's resources are limited, some determination has to be made as to the scope of the evaluation. Obviously, an evaluation that is incomplete when the money runs out is worse than no evaluation at all.* If the evaluation cannot be comprehensive, an in-depth study of a program

---

*Somehow, we do not feel that evaluators should engage in the tactic of deliberately running short to secure further funding on the grounds that, without it, the entire original investment will go down the drain. Doing so would be contrary to the principles underlying evaluation.

component might be more useful than a fleeting glance at the overall program. The question then becomes one of seeing the program as parts and selecting for study those parts that the evaluator believes are central.

Some of the major divisions into which programs can be broken down are apparent—clients, program staff, individual facilities, and functional areas, such as the educational and treatment components of a venereal disease program. From such a perspective, however, there is always the danger of confusing the routine and the trivial with the substantive. Client processing, while it may be remarkably efficient and comprehensive, may do nothing to change the lives of the clients. "Problem magnitude" functions, the number of complaints received by an agency for instance, show the program as an adjunct to the problem rather than as a force working to change the underlying causes. Agencies do not exist to point to all their complaints. The legislature was aware of citizens' distress when it created the organizational remedy. The agency's purpose is to eliminate complaints rather than swallow whatever comes its way while boasting about its wonderful appetite.

A SYSTEMATIC APPROACH

Edward Suchman has conceptualized five ways of viewing the agency for evaluation purposes. One or several of the perspectives in combination might be used by the evaluator who is precluded from a comprehensive study due to lack of time or money. Suchman's focus is on effect rather than structure. Except for the first category, effort, the criteria are a mix of program and results.

1. *Effort*—the quantity and quality of activity that takes place . . . it is an assessment of input (workload) without regard to output.
2. *Effectiveness*—the result of the effort rather than the effort itself.
3. *Impact*—the degree to which effective performance is adequate to the total amount of need.
4. *Cost effectiveness*—the evaluation of alternative methods in terms of costs . . . a ratio between effort and impact.
5. *Process*—an analysis of the process whereby a program produces the results it does; it is descriptive and diagnostic and looks for unanticipated negative and positive side effects.[31]

The first two categories, effort and effectiveness, address input and output. Studying them, we can learn about what an agency is doing in terms of the quantity of its activity. For measures of program quality to emerge, however, effort and effectiveness must be mixed with other factors. Suchman's last three categories encompass this mixing process and flesh out a program portrait that begins with an analysis of effort.

Effort   A man shoveling sand with a teaspoon accomplishes little but expends great effort. If we evaluate him on his effort, he is doing a good job. If we evaluate him on his accomplishments, he could be doing better. When we speak of improving *effort* alone, all we are asking the man to do is shovel harder with his spoon. To improve the man's effectiveness in any substantial way, we had best give him a shovel.

Looking at effort alone tends to narrow one's focus to what exists, rather than what could be. The evaluation concerns itself with production processes rather than with the overall external effects of the program. The study of effort is essentially an internal audit.

This is not to say that internal audits are improper. Rather, from a perspective of program evaluation, such audits are secondary to the primary purpose of appraising results. *Productivity evaluation* certainly has a place in the spectrum of activities that seek to maximize the public's investment in government. Cumbersome, archaic, wasteful, and just plain stupid bureaucratic procedures need to be identified, studied, and eliminated. Agency efficiency should be a goal of every public manager. Yet, it must be recognized that *efficiency* is a measure of how well inputs are processed. It is a means-oriented criterion; thus, it can generate a preoccupation with the internal workings of the organization. The manager thus preoccupied can easily neglect to analyze the external impacts of the program. If we concern ourselves exclusively with evaluating efficiency, all we are doing is fine tuning the program vehicle. We are not asking if it is the right vehicle or if it is being driven in the proper direction.

Effectiveness   *Effectiveness* is the output of the program. It tells us what is being accomplished. As with effort, it tells us little by itself. Our poor soul with the spoon may shovel ten tons of sand a day, which sounds pretty impressive. If we look at the effort that he is putting into it and realize that he is probably killing himself, the effect begins to look less desirable. If we compare this effect with a bulldozer program that removes ten tons of sand per scoop, the effectiveness looks poor indeed. Output, then, is an almost meaningless figure without comparison either to the input, the magnitude of the problem, or outputs from alternative programs. The next three categories concern themselves with such comparisons.

Impact   *Impact* asks whether a given program is merely a drop in the bucket. "A little success can be a bad thing" may be more than just an old saying. A highly touted program that accomplishes very little may actually have negative overall effects. The expectations that the program raises and then leaves unfulfilled lead to frustrations that may be internalized or let out against society. "The Revolution of Rising Expectations" identified by the National Advisory Commission on Civil Disorders is, no doubt, fueled by programs that promise and then advertise magical results that are largely nonexistent. Evaluating impact is one way of identifying such programs and is the first step in a rational decision as to whether alternative means would better attack the problem.

Impact relates program accomplishment to the magnitude of the problem. It is more concerned with strategies than with volume or costs. Some early studies on impact were conducted during World War II. In one, the Allies were concerned over their failure to make a large dent in the German submarine fleet even though they were carpeting the oceans with depth charges dropped from ships and planes. After detailed study, it was determined that the charges had been set to explode at too great a depth and that maximum damage could be inflicted with detonations 25 feet below the surface. The modified antisubmarine program subsequently had a much greater impact in preventing submarine attacks on Allied vessels. By studying impact, rather than cost or quantity of effort, decisions about program direction were made on the basis of information that may not have been uncovered through other analytical perspectives.

Cost Effectiveness   When there are several programs attacking the same problem, *cost effectiveness* tells us how much each has to spend to achieve a certain level of impact. For example, a residential neighborhood near a school becomes concerned with traffic safety as a result of several children being struck by cars. With the objective of "reducing the number of pedestrians struck by motor vehicles in neighborhood A," several programs could arise. A police officer could be placed on a key corner. The speed limit could be reduced. Stop signs and traffic lights could be installed. Signs warning motorists of "children at play" could be erected at numerous spots. The school could institute a safety education course. Bumps could be constructed on the streets to compel motorists to drive slowly.

Each of these programs has different costs and impacts. A full-time police officer may cost $20,000 per year. The police officer will have an impact on the safety habits of the children and motorists, although the impact is likely to be less the farther one gets from the officer's post. Reducing the speed limit and installing warning signs are programs that cost less than full-time patrol, but their impact on drivers also is likely to be less. Traffic controls, also cheaper than a police officer, may have no effect on speeding between intersections, an area where many children are likely to play. Safety education programs at school will have some effect on children but none on drivers. Bumps in the road would be fairly inexpensive to construct and would modify driving habits while having little impact on play habits.

It would be ideal to have all of these and more. A police officer on every corner, speed limits, warning signs, traffic controls, safety educa-

TABLE 13.2   ALTERNATIVE PROGRAMS FOR
REDUCING THE NUMBER OF PEDESTRIANS HIT BY CARS

Program	(Effort) Cost Per Year	(Effectiveness) Accidents Prevented	(Impact) % of Problem Resolved	(Cost Effectiveness) Cost Per Unit of Reduction
1. Police officer	$20,000.00	5	50	$4,000.00
2. Speed Limit and School Signs	$500.00	1	10	$500.00
3. Traffic Controls	$1,500.00	4	40	$375.00
4. Safety Education	$5,000.00	2	20	$2,500.00
5. Bumps	$1,000.00	4	40	$250.00

tion teachers, and bumps galore. This is not how the world works, however. With a multitude of other programs competing for the public dollar it is not possible to mount a total, all-fronts assault on every problem. So a choice has to be made from among the alternative approaches for solving the problem. Cost effectiveness tells us how much each alternative must spend to reduce a problem by a specific amount. In Table 13.2, column 4 shows the cost effectiveness of our several programs for reducing injuries to pedestrians from automobiles. The first three columns treat each program in terms of the effort, effectiveness, and impact criteria and indicate the mixing process that leads to cost effectiveness data. The table assumes that there is an average of 10 children struck every year and that information on the alternatives is available as a result of their use in other areas.

Although this is a rather simplified scheme, it contains the essence of program evaluation. It gives the cost of each program, their accomplishments, the extent to which they reduce the problem, and the cost per accident prevented for each alternative. One suspects that decision makers, in this case, would feel much better if they had such a chart in place of, or in addition to, parents picketing for a traffic light, teachers demanding a public safety course, newspapers calling for a traffic cop, and a city council crying for economy.

This method of laying out alternatives also can be used to determine the choices involved in adding one or another program to an existing set of programs. It tells how much it will cost to purchase the additional impacts offered by the supplemental alternatives. (See Table 13.3.) For instance, if you already have a traffic light program, the injury rate has been reduced by 40 percent at a cost of $375 dollars per unit of

TABLE 13.3 ALTERNATIVES FOR FURTHER
REDUCING THE NUMBER OF PEDESTRIANS HIT BY CARS

Alternative I "Almost All"	Cost Per Year	Accidents Prevented	% of Problem Resolved	Cost Per Unit of Reduction
Existing Programs				
Speed Limits/School Signs	$500.00	1	10	$500.00
Traffic Control Devices	$1,500.00	4	40	$375.00
Total Existing Programs	$2,000.00	5	50	$400.00
New Program Bumps	$1,000.00	4	40	$250.00
Totals Alternative I	$3,000.00	9	90	$333.33
Alternative II "All"				
Existing Programs				
Speed Limits/School Signs	$500.00	1	10	$500.00
Traffic Contol Devices	$1,500.00	4	40	$375.00
Total Existing Programs	$2,000.00	5	50	$400.00
New Program				
Police Officer	$20,000.00	5	50	$4,000.00
Totals Alternative II	$22,000.00	10	100	$2,200.00

Cost of Preventing the Last Traffic Accident *$19,000* ($22,000 − $3,000)

reduction. Speed limit and school signs have also been installed, further reducing the problem by 10 percent at a unit cost of $500. If you are now authorized to add one more program, you have a choice between bumps that will prevent four of the five accidents still occurring, and a police officer who will prevent them all. Preventing all the accidents or almost all the accidents is one way of looking at this choice. However, the cost effectiveness approach compels us to consider the difference in *cost* between "all" and "almost all."

As you can see, this sort of design really makes the choices stark. We can eliminate all but one of the injuries for $333.33 apiece. However, preventing all 10 of the yearly injuries will cost us $2200 for each. Nor is that all; if we atrribute all of the additional costs of Alternative II to the final accident that it seeks to prevent, the cost of preventing the last accident is $19,000.

With this, we have just stepped into the realm of economics and a technique called marginal analysis. With *marginal analysis,* economists seek to determine the point at which program benefits begin to fall short of the program expenditures. While precise calculations often are impossible, especially in the public sector, it is possible to distinguish roughly between expenditure increments that have marginal utility and those that do not. The above example is such a case. With Alternative I, assuming that all the accident victims end up in the hospital, it makes perfect sense to spend $333.33 to keep each out. The way hospital costs are these days, it would cost about that much for the ambulance, emergency room, and the first day's stay. Therefore, the program mix that prevents the first nine accidents provides benefits—hospital and legal cost avoided; pain and suffering reduced—that are greater than the cost of the program. The expenditure for the bumps—Alternative I—has marginal utility. However, Alternative II, in preventing the last accident, creates program costs that undoubtedly exceed the benefits that are provided as a result.* The expenditures to prevent the last accident have marginal disutility. They are the straw that breaks the camel's back. The entire program no longer "pays." The rational decision maker in business will not make that final expenditure that changes profits to losses. In analyzing government programs, where the bottom line is not so clear, evaluators try to quantify costs and benefits as much as possible to discover the point where a dollar spent begins bringing back $0.99.

Process Evaluation   Suchman's last category, process evaluation, is essentially a reverse of the procedures followed above. Let us assume that we have a fabulously wealthy community. It uses all of the programs above to fulfill the objective of safety in the area surrounding the school. It has police, bumps, traffic lights, stop signs, speed limits, warning signs, and a safety education program. Of course, no one gets hit by cars. The question here is not how to do better. What evaluation would seek to find is the part that each program element plays in giving our wealthy town a perfect safety record. To find out, the evaluator might look for situations in other cities where each of the components had been recently added to the traffic safety program. The evaluator would then compare pedestrian safety statistics from before and after the program addition to determine what impact it had. The result of this study might be program impact figures similar to those in Table 13.1. If so, the evaluator could inform the townsfolk that they had 160 percent of the coverage necessary to produce zero accidents; or, to put it another way, over one-third of the traffic safety expenditures were accomplishing absolutely nothing.

---

*This example merely illustrates the use of cost effectiveness techniques to evaluate problem solving alternatives. In reality, the accident problem, small in scope and clearly understood, would hopefully be approached with a 100 percent solution in mind. Mangled children are not acceptable products of conscious public policy. However, cost effectiveness analysis can also point the way to the least expensive 100 percent solution that, in this case, might be achieved by adding a safety education course instead of a police officer.

EVALUATION DESIGN:
THE REAL MEETS THE IDEAL

As should be apparent from the previous examples, comparison is the essence of appraising program results. For evaluation to be useful, outcomes of the program or policy must be compared with something else in order to reveal the effect of the program. The basis for comparison may be the outcome of an alternative policy or of the same program at an earlier time. The comparison of planned variations among projects within an existing program may help to identify important characteristics and potential improvements. A comparison of similar programs, if feasible, may provide some of the same information.

Choice of a comparative approach depends both upon the questions to be asked and the availability of data. This is not only a procedural matter; it also involves questions of access to and the comparability of data and restrictions on its collection and use if confidentiality is involved. These problems may be more severe than many evaluators, auditors, and examiners realize.

Even where data are accessible, collecting it and working it into usable form is likely to present difficulties. All the information that is needed is not likely to be neatly packaged in census tract information. It may be necessary to draw upon several data sources, including municipal records, academic research, and the records of insurance companies and other private institutions. Where an important environmental factor has not been the subject of previous treatment, it may be necessary for the evaluators to draw up their own questionnaires or other survey devices and gather the information themselves. Furthermore, these untreated factors may include citizens' attitudes and motivations or other social and psychological phenomena that present great measurement difficulties.

Nonetheless, if the evaluators have obtained funding, avoided cooptation by the management, cultivated agency contacts, defined objectives, set up criteria to measure attainment, chosen an analytical approach, and are aware of data deficiencies, suicide would appear to be the only alternative to proceeding with the evaluation. Having satisfied everybody else, it becomes time for the evaluators to satisfy themselves.

"We must be clear in our own minds what proof consists of, and we must, if possible, provide dramatic examples of the advantages of relying on something more than plausibility," notes Samuel Stouffer. "And the heart of our problem lies in study design *in advance,* such that the evidence is not capable of a dozen alternative interpretations."[32]

A *design* is merely the way in which evaluators are going to compare phenomena. Basically, the methods of comparing proceed from those that give analysts a clear picture of relative performance to those that give analysts a fair idea and on to those that merely give a hint. As long as conscientious evaluators are aware of the level of confidence that they can expect from their design, it does not matter which design they use although one would naturally want to use the best, if possible.

The best way evaluators can determine whether their programs are having an effect is the experimental method. The experimental method seeks purity. It says, take a person or thing; subject it to the prescribed treatment and *nothing but;* observe the change. At the same time evaluators should take an identical person or thing; *do not* subject it to *any* treatment; observe the change. If the subjects are identical, and nothing except the evaluators' program intervened between subject selection and observation, the difference in the change between the treated and the untreated subjects is due to the program. In order to explore the logic behind a thoroughgoing research design, let us assume that we have quintuplets identical in all respects. First, two of the quintuplets are subject to the following experiment in order to determine the effectiveness of a program to increase reading skills.

EXPERIMENT A

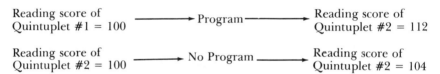

Reading score of
Quintuplet #1 = 100   ⟶ Program ⟶   Reading score of
Quintuplet #2 = 112

Reading score of
Quintuplet #2 = 100   ⟶ No Program ⟶   Reading score of
Quintuplet #2 = 104

Therefore: Score change of Quintuplet #1 (12) minus score change of Quintuplet #2 (4) = Program effect (8 point increase in reading score)

As should be evident, certain questions arise because of the disparity between the progress of Quintuplet #1 and the progress of Quintuplet #2. On the surface, it appears as if the program has been responsible for the 12-point reading score increase chalked up by Quintuplet #1. However, Quintuplet #2 also has registered a 4-point increase. Thus, the evaluators' first task is to find out the cause of the 4-point increase common to both quintuplets. The first target might be the reading test given to Quintuplets #1 and #2 prior to their exposure to the program. Familiarity with the test format, rather than the effectiveness of the program, may have been partially responsible for the improved reading scores. So, the evaluators run:

EXPERIMENT B

No reading test for
Quintuplet #3   ⟶ Program ⟶   Reading score of
Quintuplet #3 = 110

Then, the evaluators compare Quintuplet #3's reading score to the postprogram reading score of Quintuplet #1 in Experiment A.

Therefore: Postprogram reading score of Quintuplet #1 (112) minus the postprogram reading score of Quintuplet #3 (110) = Test familiarity impact (2 test points)

Experiment B indicates that 2 points of Quintuplet #1's 12-point increase in reading skills in Experiment A were due to Quintuplet #1's familiarity with the type of examination used to determine reading ability. (This also accounts for 2 points of Quintuplet #2's improvement in Experiment A.) Experiment B does not end the search for nonprogram factors that contributed to Quintuplet #1's reading improvement. During the program period, the quintuplets may have learned a little bit without the program; without taking the first test; without anything. So, the evaluators run:

EXPERIMENT C

No reading test for
Quintuplet #4 ⟶ No program ⟶ Reading score of
Quintuplet #4 = 102

Then, the evaluators compare Quintuplet #4's reading score with the preprogram reading score of Quintuplet #1 in Experiment A.

Therefore: Reading score of Quintuplet #4 (102) minus the preprogram reading score of Quintuplet #1 (100) = Normal learning impact (2 test points)

With the normal learning impact and the test familiarity impact factored in, it appears that the program increases reading skills by 8 points. However, the program's actual impact may be even less. A Hawthorne effect may be at work; that is, Quintuplet #1 responded, in part, to the attention he received rather than the program's substance. So, the evaluators subject Quintuplet #5 to an impressive-looking program that is, however, completely irrelevant to the problem. Thus:

EXPERIMENT D

Reading score of
Quintuplet #5 = 100 ⟶ Placebo ⟶ Reading score of
Quintuplet #5 = 106

Therefore: Score change of Quintuplet #5 (6 points) minus the test familiarity impact (2 points) and the normal learning impact (2 points) = Hawthorne impact (2 test points)

By comparing Experiments A, B, C and D, evaluators determine that 2 points of Quintuplet #1's reading improvement were attributable to the Hawthorne effect; 2 points of the improvement were attributable to Quintuplet #1's familiarity with the reading tests; and 2 points of Quintuplet #1's improvement would have occurred in any event. This analysis is in sharp contrast to the measurement favored by some program administrators: namely, the undiluted improvement of program participants. As we saw in the above example, the difference between such administrative claims and evaluative findings can be substantial.

This type of experiment usually is not feasible for program evaluation, but it gives you the idea. The evaluators want to insure to the fullest extent possible that the program and nonprogram comparison groups were as similar as possible before the program treatment. They want to separate program from nonprogram effects. To do this, they adopt several real-world devices to simulate identical program-nonprogram participants and to identify the extent to which the evaluation results can be said to be free of outside influence.

One real-world answer to preexisting differences is randomization. Random selection and assignment, if the population pool is large enough, cancels out individual differences, thus fulfilling the experimental design's requirement that the affected group and the group not affected possess similar characteristics. For this reason, the potential participants in an experiment must be *randomly* assigned so that each one has the same chance of ending up in either the treatment or nontreatment group before the program begins. Unless this is achieved, there is no assurance that the results are attributable to the program.

For example, unless randomly assigned, enrollees in a job skills program may be better educated, more skilled, and more eager for work than are nonenrollees. This biases any comparison of the response or performance of the two groups because their motivations and other characteristics were not the same.

In evaluating social programs, however, random selection may be neither right nor possible. Denying entry to a methadone program to a randomly chosen group of drug addicts so they can be compared with others on the program would be wrong. In evaluating primary school education in the United States, finding a significantly large group of unexposed school-age children would likely be impossible. Even if such a group was discovered, their prompt exposure to primary education would be required by law. Where "pure" experimentation is unethical, impossible, or impractical, other "quasi-experimental techniques" are applied. Nonrandom comparison groups is one such technique.

With nonrandom comparison groups, the *control group* is made as similar to the experimental group as possible by matching individuals with the same sex, age, racial, or socioeconomic characteristics. For example, the patients in a methadone maintenance program might be compared with addicts who refuse to participate in the program. Through an analysis of law enforcement records, the groups could be matched in terms of average age, length of addiction, number of arrests, types of crimes. Education and work experience might also be matched along with the other characteristics suggested above. The differences in results between the two groups are attributable, as in experimental designs, to the results of the program. However, without random assignment there is greater danger that the observed results are attributable to nonprogram influences. Other difficulties with the method include potential bias resulting from self-selection by participants—addicts who shun rehabilitation may be so hard-core and trouble-prone that they will make any comparison group look good, regardless of program.

The quintuplet design and randomization, or matching, represent the social scientists' attempt to exclude as many complicating factors as possible from the study of the effects of a phenomenon. Obviously, in most evaluations of ongoing government programs, excluding most of the complicating factors would be a mighty achievement. Programs change as they are being studied. Clients are subject to a multitude of other influences while they are program participants. The world changes, and as you will recall from the March of Dimes response to the disappearance of polio (Chapter 4), the program can shift to a whole new arena of results and subjects. In such a dynamic process, few things hold still long enough to be measured with the accuracy that an experimental design would hope to achieve. However, this does not diminish the importance of evaluation research as a tool.

Comparing different programs that attack the same problems; following up on program participants over time; and studying the impact of program changes on beneficiaries before and after the program all provide information on how the program is working. If the degree to which extraneous factors may distort the results is recognized, all such evaluations have utility to the public decision maker.

PUTTING EVALUATION TO WORK

In the examples used in this chapter, evaluation was an action tool. It showed what a program was, or was not, achieving. It factored out the components of a program and identified their relative contribution to the overall effort. Any administrator who does not see the potential in having such information on a regular basis is not looking very hard. Evaluation is a feedback device. It takes the "pulse" of the administrative environment in an analytical manner. Thus, "evaluation findings can be used to modify current operations and plan future programs and policies."[33]

Even if administrators are comatose, or resist strongly because they see the evaluation results as damaging, the evaluators are still receiving fairly hard data on program impact. Evaluators, unless they do not care or realize that they have done a shoddy job, are not likely to let the results of their work and analysis disappear quietly into the bureaucratic maze. Nor are conscientious analysts likely to consult the "prevailing mood" in drawing up the conclusions of the evaluation. If they have followed Stouffer's advice and set up a plan of evaluation that they feel will produce reliable results, the results are not a function of forces outside of the study plan. The conclusions flow from a carefully designed tool of investigation that was dedicated to finding out, not fitting in.

Thus, analysts should be constrained only by the possibility of defects in their study designs when making recommendations based on the evaluation. If the evaluation shows that a particular program or strategy is useless, elimination or radical change, rather than slight modification, should be the recommendation. If a program is shown to be good, its expansion or multiplication should be strongly urged. After all, evaluation itself would have to be evaluated as useless if it did not lead to program decisions. In this process, evaluators are not out of line if they try to translate their findings into "effective operating policy so as to improve the performance of agency programs."[34]

CONCLUSION

We will conclude this chapter with several recommendations made by program evaluators, including those who have evaluated program evaluation, concerning things that can be done to make evaluation a more useful tool in the hands of government administrators.

> Statements of desired program results should be incorporated in authorizing legislation.
> Authorizing legislation should require evaluation and provide funding for it.
> Congress should make full use of the evaluations that result.
> Specialized evaluation units should be a full-time component of the central staff of federal agencies.
> The evaluation staff should receive the support of the agency executive and sufficient time to conduct analysis.[35]

Although there has been an increasing emphasis on evaluation of government programs, a full realization of the state of affairs called for above is still in the future. However, it can be said with some assurance that program evaluation is more than a passing fad. Finding out whether a program works, and why and how it does or does not, is a job that many present and future public employees will find themselves doing.

KEY TERMS AND CONCEPTS

Control group	Effectiveness
Cost effectiveness	Effort
Criteria	Evaluation

NOTES

1. These characteristics are adapted from Carol Weiss, *Evaluation Research: Methods of Assessing Program Effectiveness* (Englewood Cliffs, N.J.: Prentice-Hall, 1972), p. 5.
2. Ibid., p. 5.
3. Ibid., p. 5.
4. Ibid., p. 5.
5. Allen Schick, "The Road to PPB: The Stages of Budget Reform," in *Planning Programming Budgeting: A Systems Approach to Management,* eds. Fremont J. Lyden and Ernest G. Miller (Chicago: Rand McNally, 1972), p. 19.
6. Ibid., p. 24.
7. Ibid., p. 19.
8. Ibid.
9. Joseph S. Wholey, et al., *Federal Evaluation Policy: Analyzing the Effects of Public Programs* (Washington D.C.: Urban Institute, 1975), p. 15.
10. Walter Williams and John W. Evans, "The Politics of Evaluation: The Case of Head Start," in Lyden and Miller, *Planning Programming Budgeting,* p. 380.
11. Wholey, et al., *Federal Evaluation Policy,* p. 53.
12. Public Law, 93–344.
13. Quoted in *The Dimension of Public Administration,* 2nd ed., ed. Joseph A. Uveges, Jr. (Boston: Holbrook Press, Inc., 1975), p. 408.
14. Wholey, et al., *Federal Evaluation Policy,* p. 11.
15. Weiss, *Evaluation Research,* p. 2.
16. Wholey, et al., *Federal Evaluation Policy,* p. 19.
17. Weiss, *Evaluation Research,* p. 7.
18. Ibid., p. 11.
19. Wholey, et al., *Federal Evaluation Policy,* p. 23.
20. *New York State Environmental Conservation Law* (St. Paul: West, 1977), p. 18.
21. Ibid., p. 31.
22. Ibid., p. 15.
23. Harry P. Hatry, "Criteria for Evaluation in Planning State and Local Programs," in Lyden and Miller, *Planning Programming Budgeting.*
24. Ibid., p. 206.
25. Ibid.
26. Lewis Mumford, "The Sky Line," *New Yorker,* 1 December 1962.
27. Ibid.
28. Robert Caro, *The Power Broker* (New York: Knopf, 1974), pp. 966–978.
29. Patricia Cayo Sexton, *Spanish Harlem: Anatomy of Poverty* (New York: Harper & Row, 1965), p. 38.
30. Wholey et al., *Federal Evaluation Policy,* p. 33.
31. Edward A. Suchman, *Evaluative Research: Principles and Practices in Public Service and Social Action Programs* (New York: Russell Sage Foundation, 1968), quoted in Wholey, et al., *Federal Evaluation Policy,* p. 94.

32. Samuel A. Stouffer, "Some Observations on Study Design," in *Handbook of Research Design and Social Measurement*, 2nd ed., ed. Delbert C. Miller (New York: McKay, 1970), p. 30.
33. Wholey et al., *Federal Evaluation Policy*, p. 34.
34. Williams and Evans, quoted in ibid., p. 46.
35. Wholey et al., *Federal Evaluation Policy*, pp. 35, 57, 68, 84–85.

BIBLIOGRAPHY

Agnew, Neil, and Pyke, Sandra W. *The Science Game: An Introduction to Research in the Behavioral Sciences.* Englewood Cliffs, N.J.: Prentice-Hall, 1969.

American Institutes for Research. *Evaluative Research Strategies and Methods.* Pittsburgh: 1970.

Bauer, Raymond, ed. *Social Indicators.* Cambridge: MIT Press, 1966.

Beyer, Glenn H. *Housing and Society.* New York: Macmillan, 1965.

Boston Urban Observatory. *The Impact of Housing Inspectional Services on Housing Maintenance in the City of Boston: A Preliminary Evaluation.* Boston: University Urban Institute, 1971.

Brewer, Gary D. *Politicians, Bureaucrats and the Consultant: A Critique of Urban Problem Solving.* New York: Basic Books, 1973.

Cherney, Paul R., ed. *Making Evaluation Research Useful.* Columbia: American City Corporation, 1971.

Dorfman, Robert, ed. *Measuring Benefits of Government Investments.* Washington, D.C.: Brookings, 1965.

Dror, Yehezkel. *Ventures in Policy Sciences.* New York: Elsevier, 1971.

Fellin, Phillip; Tripoldi, Tony; and Meyer, Henry J., eds. *Exemplars of Social Research.* Itasca, Ill.: Peacock, 1969.

Fried, Joseph P. *Housing Crises USA.* New York: Praeger, 1971.

Hudson Institute, Inc. *The Future of American Poverty: Some Basic Issues in Evaluating Alternative Anti-Poverty Measures.* Croton-on-Hudson: Hudson Institute, 1968.

McKean, R. N. *Efficiency in Government Through Systems Analysis.* New York: Wiley, 1968.

Miller, Delbert C. *Handbook of Research Design and Social Measurement.* 2nd ed. New York: McKay, 1970.

Mishan, E. J. *Economics for Social Decisions: Elements of Cost Benefit Analysis.* New York: Praeger, 1972.

Moynihan, Daniel P. *Maximum Feasible Misunderstanding: Community Action in the War on Poverty.* New York: Free Press, 1969.

Muth, R. F. *Cities and Housing.* Chicago: University of Chicago Press, 1969.

O'Toole, Richard, ed. *The Organization, Management and Tactics of Social Research.* Cambridge: Schenkman Publishing Co., 1970.

Pressman, Jeffrey L., and Wildavsky, Aaron B. *Implementation: How Great Expectations in Washington Are Dashed in Oakland.* Berkeley: University of California Press, 1973.

Rothenberg, Jerome. *Economic Evaluation of Urban Renewal.* Washington, D.C.: Brookings, 1967.

Sexton, Patricia Cayo. *Spanish Harlem: Anatomy of Poverty.* New York: Harper & Row, 1965.

Suchman, Edward A. *Evaluative Research: Principles and Practice in Public Service and Social Action Programs.* New York: Russell Sage Foundation, 1967.

Summers, Anita A., and Wolfe, Barbara L. *Which School Resources Help Learning?: Efficiency and Equity in Philadelphia Public Schools.* Philadelphia: Federal Reserve Bank, 1975.

————. *Urban Renewal: The Record and the Controversy.* Cambridge: MIT Press, 1966.

Weiss, Carol H. *Organizational Constraints on Evaluation Research.* New York: Bureau of Applied Social Research, 1971.

————. *Evaluating Action Programs: Readings in Social Action and Education.* Boston: Allyn and Bacon, 1972.

————. *Evaluation Research: Methods of Assessing Program Effectiveness.* Englewood Cliffs, N.J.: Prentice-Hall, 1972.

Wholey, Joseph S., et al. *Federal Evaluation Policy.* Washington, D.C.: Urban Institute, 1970.

In addition to the sources cited in the notes and bibliography, the following *Public Administration Review (PAR)* articles are a convenient starting point for a more detailed exploration of the material in this chapter.

Brown, Richard and Ray D. Pethtel. "A Matter of Facts: State Legislative Performance Auditing," *PAR* 34, no. 4 (July/Aug. 1974): 318–326.

Gastil, Raymond D. "Social Indicators and the Quality of Life," *PAR* 30, no. 6 (Nov./Dec. 1970): 596–601.

Hatry, Harry P. "Issues in Productivity Measurement for Local Government," *PAR* 32, no. 6 (Nov./Dec. 1972): 776–784.

Hatry, Harry P. "The Status of Productivity Measurement in the Public Sector," *PAR* 38, no. 1 (Jan./Feb. 1978): 28–33.

Havens, Harry S. "MBO and Program Evaluation, or Whatever Happened to PPBS," *PAR* 36, no. 1 (Jan./Feb. 1967): 40–45.

Horst, Pamela, Joe N. Nay, John W. Scanlon and Joseph Wholey. "Program Management and the Federal Evaluator," *PAR* 34, no. 4 (July/Aug. 1974): 300–307.

Lewis, Frank L. and Frank G. Zarb. "Federal Program Evaluation from the OMB Perspective," *PAR* 34, no. 4 (July/Aug. 1974): 308–317.

Lucy, William H., Dennis Gilbert and Guthrie S. Birkhead. "Equity in Local Service Distribution," *PAR* 37, no. 6 (Nov./Dec. 1977): 687–697.

Marvin, Keith E. and James L. Hedrick. "GAO Helps Congress Evaluate Programs," *PAR* 34, no. 4 (July/Aug. 1974): 327–332.

Meltsner, Arnold J. "Political Feasibility and Policy Analysis," *PAR* 32, no. 6 (Nov./Dec. 1972): 859–867.

Morehouse, Thomas A. "Program Evaluation: Social Research Versus Public Policy," *PAR* 32, no. 6 (Nov./Dec. 1972): 868–874.

Newland, Chester A. "Policy/Program Objectives and Federal Management: The Search for Government Effectiveness," *PAR* 36, no. 1 (Jan./Feb. 1976): 20–27.

Poland, Orville F. "Program Evaluation and Administrative Theory," *PAR* 34, no. 4 (July/Aug. 1974): 333–338.

Prather, James E. and Frank K. Gibson. "The Failure of Social Programs," *PAR* 37, no. 5 (Sept./Oct. 1977): 556–564.

Savas, E. S. "An Empirical Study of Competition in Municipal Service Delivery," *PAR* 37, no. 6 (Nov./Dec. 1977): 718–724.

Schneider, Mark. "The 'Quality of Life' and Social Indicators Research," *PAR* 36, no. 3 (May/June 1976): 278–286.

Skogan, Wesley G. "Efficiency and Effectiveness in Big City Police Departments," *PAR* 36, no. 3 (May/June 1976): 278–286.

Stanley, David T.   "How Safe the Streets, How Good the Grant," *PAR* 34, no. 4 (July/Aug. 1974): 380–389.

White, Orion, Jr. and Bruce L. Gates.   "Statistical Theory and Equity in the Delivery of Social Services," *PAR* 34, no. 1 (Jan./Feb. 1974): 43–51.

Wholey, Joseph S.   "The Role of Evaluation and the Evaluator in Improving Public Programs: The Bad News, the Good News and a Bi-Centennial Challenge," *PAR* 36, no. 6 (Nov./Dec. 1976): 679–683.

Wildavsky, Aaron.   "The Self-Evaluating Organization," *PAR* 32, no. 5 (Sept./ Oct. 1972): 509–520.

RELEVANT PERIODICALS
Annals of Economic & Social Measurement
Applied Economics
Evaluation Quarterly
Journal of Sociology and Social Welfare
Policy Sciences
Public Management
Public Policy
Review of Economics and Statistics
Social Research
Social Science Research
Sociology & Social Research

RELEVANT CASE STUDIES
(Cases marked ICCH are available from the Intercollegiate Case Clearing House, Soldier Field, Boston, Mass. 02163.)

Allison, G. T. and M. H. Moore.   *The Fourth Platoon,* [ICCH]

Christenson, C. J.   *Disease Control Programs,* [ICCH]

Lovelock, C. H. and J. S. Kahn.   *911 Emergency Number in New York,* (A)(B),* [ICCH]

Lynn, L. E., Jr. and W. B. Marcus.   *Locks and Dams 26,* (A)(B)(C),* [ICCH]

Silvers, J. B. and S. Epstein.   *Salt and Water* (A): *Benefit Cost Analysis of Kidney Disease Treatment,* [ICCH]

Taylor, G. M.   *Streetlights,* [ICCH]

Taylor, G. M.   *Swimming Pools,* [ICCH]

*Letters indicate that the case is presented in several installments.

CHAPTER 14

COMPUTERS AND GOVERNMENT ADMINISTRATION

INTRODUCTION

As we have emphasized, high-level government officials, whether federal, state, or local, make decisions that have systemic impacts. Whether executives rely on intuition or have highly sophisticated analytical tools, an understanding of the reverberating effects of their decisions is often the key to successful and effective leadership. However, not everyone is a mayor, governor, president, or an executive staff assistant. In fact, most government executives are involved in carrying on the day-to-day business of the bureaucracy. While government managers should not be insensitive to the wide-ranging and long-term impacts of their decisions, their primary function is turning out a product or service and doing it with efficiency and effectiveness. To do this, government managers are turning with increasing frequency to computers, not as an analytical tool but as a management tool. It is this use of the computer that we shall address in this chapter.

MORE DATA PROCESSING FOR MORE DATA

Computers are big business. In 1976, $30 billion were spent for computer equipment, personnel, and related services in the United States. In that year, the computer industry's biggest customer, with nearly 10,000 systems in place, was the federal government.[1] State, county, and local governments, taken together, were not far behind and advancing rapidly. There seems little doubt that government will account for much of the 20 percent annual growth rate projected for the computer industry through the 1980s. Indeed, public expenditure may increase at a faster rate than private ones since, in many cases, the computer appears to be the only solution to the administrative problems confronting government.

Much of the demand for computerized relief stems from the enormous volume of information generated by modern society. Government, for better or worse, is the prime processor and storer of much of this information. Births, deaths, marriages and divorces, educational records, social security records, tax information, data on land sales, property evaluations, court records, and license applications for a bewildering variety of trades and activities, all speak to government's recordkeeping activities and, at that, are but a partial listing of the bookkeeping functions carried on by federal, state, and local governments.

These information requirements increase as new programs are formulated or as populations increase. Medicare as of 1975 had reached over 24 million elderly out of a potential clientele that is even larger. Even without the institution of new programs, many "Sunbelt" localities are undergoing population increases that rapidly expand the amount of information to be recorded on existing data bases. Consider the situation that confronted one western county. The home of fewer than 200,000 people in 1940, it had over a million by 1970 with a growth rate of 45,000 per year. The county, having early implemented data processing in the 1950s, was running not one, but two, medium-size computers on an around the clock basis by the 1960s. However, this capability proved insufficient, giving rise to a system's-wide plan to integrate duplicative data bases such as those pertaining to fire department and building department inspections of the housing stock. The disturbing aspect of this tale is that, among local jurisdictions, this county was an early convert to data processing. Yet, even with a superior data processing capacity and experienced personnel, information overloads arose. The county's solution—systems improvement—was an option keyed to an existing and sophisticated computer operation. Other jurisdictions, with less adequate computer resources, often must cope with processing overloads by shifting service delivery personnel to handle information requirements.

The United States has been christened by many as "the information society." This description, accurate now, will become even more apt in the future. Institutions oblivious to "the information society" are in jeopardy. Without some high-speed and space-reducing methods of information storage and retrieval, many governments may gradually choke to death on their steadily increasing diet of facts and figures. Jurisdictions that turn to the computer do so with the realization that, even now, more effective service delivery demands an attentiveness to minimizing housekeeping costs. A note of urgency is added by the revenue crunch faced by many states, counties, and municipalities. For the foreseeable future, increased revenues cannot be relied upon to resolve the housekeeping-service delivery dilemma. As one observer notes:

> Municipal costs are increasing much faster than the revenues needed to pay for them. All across the nation, increasing financial demands are squeezing key municipal services. Expectations and demands for services have grown, often rapidly: costs of providing even current levels of services have risen, the citizens' resistance to higher taxes has stiffened.[2]

The Machine's Capabilities: Imagined and Real

Thus, it is with compulsion, and no small degree of uncertainty, that governments turn to the computer—a tool that, in the public's eye, is a "composite of demonic and godly characteristics and capabilities."[3] On TV, in film, and most prolifically, in the science fiction novel, this characterization is borne out. Ordinary mortals are turned into supermen via "bionic" modifications. Electronic devices implanted in their brains transform unwitting individuals into run-amok psychopaths. Computerized robots are portrayed both as servants of humans and, when out of control, as a virtually unstoppable enemy because they never tire, have great strength, possess an infallible logic, and act without emotion. Fictional computers entrusted with military tasks are prone to break off from supervision and embark on adventures such as taking over the world or starting World War III. In Stanley Kubrick's classic film, *2001: A Space Odyssey,* the spaceship's computer was so intelligent and sophisticated that it suffered a nervous breakdown, replete with paranoia and delusions of grandeur, leading it to wrest control from the plotting, weak, and intellectually infantile human beings on board. Indeed, the relationship between humans and computer is becoming as pervasive a fictional theme as was the interplay between humans and organizations through the twentieth century. One senses that Kafka, if alive today, would place Josef K. on the "2001" spaceship to be killed by the efficiency-minded computer HAL.

Despite all of this, the computer is not perverse, devious, or omnipotent. It is a hunk of metal, glass, rubber, and plastic. It is an inanimate object that can be activated only by humans. The information that it possesses is only such information as has been placed within it. The manipulations that it performs with stored data progress according to instructions that are external to the system. It is a mechanical tool and, unlike the movie versions, it does only what it is told to do. In this sense, computer systems differ radically from the "probabilistic" social systems discussed previously. Social systems are probabilistic because there is no way of predicting *exactly* the effect that a given manipulation, such as a

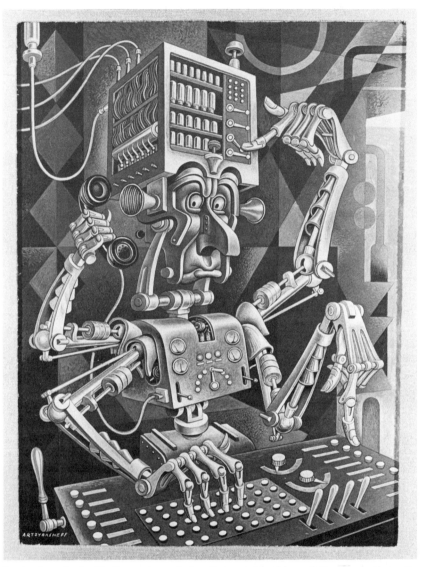

Boris Artzybasheff, Executive of the Future. In this artist's conception, the future executive is mechanized, computerized and vaguely bewildered. Actually, the properly utilized computer should make more managerial time available for dealing with people problems and public policy. (Courtesy of the Syracuse University Art Collection)

program in an urban area, will have on the whole. Changes imposed on social systems have unanticipated consequences, both unintended benefits and costs, because the response of the system to change can not be fully determined.

A computer system, on the other hand, is "deterministic." It is fully controlled by an external source. A computer can never say, as might a court clerk, "The judge isn't using the information I am sending to him, so the next time he asks for it, he won't get it." Inputs into a computer system are only those that are given to it by its environment, and its outputs are only those that are demanded by the environment. This is why "garbage in, garbage out" is an apt comment when the computer puts out a useless product. It is the environment that errs when computers perform poorly.

Even though computers are systems that do what they are told, they can be told to do highly complicated tasks, and can accomplish them quickly and correctly. The urban modeling that was discussed in Chapter 12 uses computers to ferret out highly complex interrelationships through an intricate series of statistical and mathematical procedures. The Apollo program saw what was undoubtedly the most massive, complex, and sophisticated computer application to date. While humans knew the techniques of landing on the moon and could calculate and correct the position of the lunar module in transit, it was the computer that had the capacity to assimilate flight data and display the necessary course corrections at electronic speeds. Once the computer had been implanted with the logic of the Apollo scientists it could apply that logic with astounding speed and unerring accuracy.

Roadblocks to Implementation

Despite the fact that computers are capable of applying programmed logic to a given set of facts, the use of computers by governments often ignores this fact. Computers, instead, are looked at as electronic file cabinets with extremely fast messengers. As one observer writes, "In most states, the capabilities of the computer are used primarily in ways that implicitly view the computer as an army of green eye-shaded clerks."[4] In effect, computers are often told by governments to swallow and regurgitate. This is quite an underutilization of a tool that has the capacity to process information to a decision—if only someone would supply it with decision rules—or interrelate and combine a number of data bases—if only someone would take the time to introduce it to other data bases. There are several reasons for this lack of innovation and coordination in government's use of computer systems. Some of the factors are:

> fragmentation in government services.
>
> a two-way misunderstanding in which government managers know little about computers and computer managers know little about government.
>
> a rapidly changing technology whose full utilization requires equipment, programming, and personnel innovation.

an executive reluctance to invest in costly computer equipment at the expense of protecting or adding to existing personnel or forgoing more visible, vote-generating capital expenditures.

a legislative reluctance to "throw good money after bad" in the wake of early failures in advanced computer applications.

Each of these bars to the innovative use of the computer will be considered in more detail below.

Fragmentation in Government Services The retarded development of computer applications in government bears the stamp of institutionalization. Personnel socialized to guard jealously every organizational resource often do not relate to the possibility of sharing their computer domains. Thus, several agencies might each have a computer system operating at undercapacity. Further, much of the information stored in the separate systems might be redundant. Fire inspection and housing inspection reports on a given building, for instance, may differ in only one or two particulars. However, the introspective view often prevalent in organizations does not foster the kind of cooperation necessary to combine or compare such data. It has been the experience of one of the authors that, even where data integration procedures are instituted, an agency's inhibitions about sharing its information can blockade complete implementation. The efforts in question involved a joint federal, state, and local effort to generate a computerized, regional master list of consumer complaints from the raw, uncomputerized complaint data in the participating agencies. However, from one agency known to receive a large volume of complaints, only a trickle of complaint data was forwarded. Whether the agency was unwilling to devote the time and materials to compile the data in a form suitable for computer entry or it was reluctant to reveal its investigatory targets was not determined. The latter reason, however, often was used to turn away direct requests for information from other agencies. In any event, whether it seeks to hoard manpower or information, the inward-looking agency is always a potential bar to the full realization of the computerized information-sharing capacity of government.

Poor Communications Between Executive and Computer Personnel The second bar to the effective utilization of computer capacity is the disparity in language and attitude between government executives and computer personnel. Computers are complex machines. They have to be talked to in foreign languages such as COBOL or FORTRAN. Unfortunately, many computer personnel speak in a strange dialect as well. Having staff that "signs off on the CRT to the CPU" is enough to convince many agency executives to leave them alone since understanding what is going on seems impossible. The whole business might seem more approachable if the executive had the English translation of that sentence, which is "I shut off the TV screen that's connected to the computer." Of course, if the administrators keep their distance and provide little feedback, there is little reason for the computer staff to respond with innovative ideas. Thus, they continue to do what they have always done. Moreover, computer personnel operate in a world that is factual and deterministic—there is a right way and a wrong way. They have little affinity for the administrator's world of negotiation and compromise—the middle way. Bridging the gulf in attitudes and language requires increased, perhaps even forced, interaction. As administrators and computer personnel better understand each other, the utility of the computer to government operations should increase.

Failure to Innovate   Computer operations can become outdated in three ways: antiquated equipment, antiquated procedures, or antiquated personnel. While antiquity does not always equal inadequacy, it often does.

Data processing equipment is particularly susceptible to sclerosis. *Computer hardware*—central processing units, terminals, sorters, and other physical equipment—has come quite a distance in the past 30 years. The first electronic computer, ENIAC (Electronic Numerical Integrator and Calculator) at the University of Pennsylvania, was a massive hodgepodge of vacuum tubes and wires that took up a large room. For all its bulk, it was incapable of performing some of the feats that today's higher-priced pocket calculators accomplish with the push of a button. The simple circuitry that replaced the fragile, bulky, and energy-gulping vacuum tube has successively miniaturized and microminiaturized computer parts. The result is smaller machines that do more, do it better and faster, and cost less to operate. Thus, outdated equipment, a common occurrence among governments, can be inadequate for present needs and costly to operate. The lackluster performance that often results can turn legislative and executive policy makers against the expansion or modernization of computer operations.

The procedures for utilizing the computer have not been dormant while the machines have undergone their rapid evolution. Computer utilization procedures—referred to as *software* in contrast with the machinery—are programming and other activities performed by people in instructing the machine as to task performance. Innovations in this field have more than kept pace with machine evolution. The software industry now sells prepackaged computer programs to users. Thus, an organization might purchase a program for inventory control, materials routing, or accounting from a software company that would make the adjustments necessary to account for the particular needs of the purchasing firm. Getting the most out of data processing equipment requires that an organization keep abreast of developments in the software field. Without software, the computer is not a system. It is an inanimate object of no use to anyone. With outdated or inadequate software, a jurisdiction's computer equipment is likely underutilized.

As computer systems evolve, which they do rather quickly, having reached their "third generation" in 25 years of commercial use, the adaptation of governments' computer personnel looms as a problem. Switching to a new generation computer, or a larger machine of the same generation, can mean a new language or a new set of procedures. The application of new software components can have the same effect. However, if the governmental jurisdiction has rigidly drawn personnel specifications, the flexibility to match quickly existing personnel to the new computer applications may be lacking. "Going by the book," union interventions on behalf of members resisting job reformulation, and tenure protections may all combine to delay innovation in government computer operations. Recounting his experiences implementing new computer software in government settings, IBM executive F. Terry Baker writes: "People's job descriptions or their particular organizational structure sometimes make it difficult to create a new type of job, one that differs somewhat from any kind of existing job in the organization."[5]

Compounding the personnel problem is the fact that private sector data processing managers and programmers usually are paid more than their government counterparts. Thus, attracting and holding highly qualified computer personnel is difficult. Most do not consider the public sector. Others might use a short stint in government for experience and experimentation before going on to private employment. Data processing personnel that remain for longer periods may lack the initiative and innovative approach that would utilize the government's computer capacity to its fullest.

The net result of the personnel, equipment, and software deficiencies in the public sector is "a costly disaster."[6] This situation, moreover, tends to reinforce the executive and legislative bias against investments in computerized management information systems.

Low Political Returns for Executives   The fourth problem in the implementation of computer systems in state and local governments is the tendency to respond to a reduction in operating income with capital expenditure cuts rather than personnel cuts. Thus, the executive who is responsible for budget cuts, in deciding between people and things, focuses on the latter. Looking down the list of maintenance and equipment expenditures in most budgets, even the eye of the untrained observer is likely to come to rest on computer services. Developmental costs alone can run to the hundreds of thousands of dollars and that is before a single piece of equipment is purchased. Capital expenditures on equipment can be millions of dollars. Moreover, the computer as a capital project fails to provide public executives with many of the high-impact, image-enhancing benefits that they have come to associate with vast capital investments. The computer investment will not, for instance, create "3,000 jobs in the construction industry over the next three years." On the contrary, it will arrive already built and, very likely, from out of state besides. (When New York's lottery commission contracted out computer support activities to a Georgia firm, there was a storm of protest.)[7] The workers who will benefit from its installation will be white-collar technicians, an amorphous group that does not stand very high on the political executives' list of people to be reckoned with. The computer is also not a very visible capital investment. It will be hidden away in an office; there will be no ribbons to cut; very few voters are likely to point to the computer and say, "This is what the mayor did for us," particularly if the computer is one that harasses citizens about their parking tickets.

Even as a money saver, the computer will not pay back its high, initial costs for a number of years. The political executive can point only to estimated savings—and likely be accused by opponents of lying—while the actual savings will accrue to some future executive. In short, selling public decision makers on low-visibility benefits that may not occur for several years can be extremely difficult in an administrative environment that is largely concerned with demands that are short term and call for external, rather than internal, government impacts.

Legislative Resistance In their oversight capacity vis-à-vis the budget, the eyes of the legislators are likely to come to rest on computer expenditure items. They are costly and, therefore, prominent. Furthermore, they threaten personnel. Computer expenditures cannot be used to hire additional workers. Computer systems may also eliminate existing jobs. Present and potential employees are constituents and, perhaps, political appointees. The power base of legislators is enhanced by such employment and any proposal that might reduce it is likely to be viewed with suspicion. The resumption of the highly computerized New York State Lottery, for example, was delayed by a dispute over personnel issues, a dispute that involved maintaining a proper mix of legislative (Republican) and gubernatorial (Democratic) appointees to the agency.[8]

In its general oversight capacity, the legislature is likely to become aware of problems in existing computer facilities. The indiscriminate exchange of computerized information about citizens among agencies may cause, in addition to legislation prohibiting the practice, a general legislative skepticism toward computer applications. Large-scale disasters—for example, a New York City computer system designed to administer rent control equitably broke down so badly that an almost complete reversion to manual processing was required—can elicit outright hostility.[9] In most instances, legislators are likely to demand a clear explanation of the benefits of computerization. The manager who is an advocate of data processing had best be prepared to provide this information.

Overcoming the Obstacles

The foregoing is quite a formidable array of obstacles to the implementation of data processing systems. One way for managers to meet these challenges is to set their defenses in advance. Unfortunately, some common defenses are not very convincing. If managers view a computer application as a toy or something that they have to have to keep up with other jurisdictions, they may not be able to justify its acquisition to bosses and legislators who are slashing the budget. If they swallow whole the pitch of some computer salesperson, the managers' superficial understanding of the costs and benefits involved is likely to become painfully evident under questioning. Furthermore, neither approach—and they are all too common—is indicative of managers who are doing what they are supposed to do; that is, carefully analyze the information and processing needs of their particular agencies and choose from among alternative data processing systems the one that is best suited to their needs. If managers follow this latter course, it will, among other things, compel them to deal extensively with their computer personnel; broaden their knowledge of computer applications; and strengthen their hand in dealing with superiors and legislators. The questionnaire on the following page is one way of evaluating proposed data processing systems and, in completed form, represents a strong defense of the system chosen.

In this questionnaire, the proposed computer system is reviewed by organizational supporters and detractors. Additionally, the system's impact on services is estimated and its value to management considered. Although computers are the focus of this questionnaire, this general evaluative approach may be applied to many operational changes contemplated by the public manager.

The first four questions tend to highlight the benefits of the proposed system. They address the most visible and immediate impacts and thus afford proponents the opportunity to make a case for the system. Usually, there is enough evidence or advocacy to present a convincing initial brief. Most organizations have at least one unit or function that exhibits high costs, low productivity, and operational confusion: symptoms ripe for data processing therapy. Furthermore, even the well-run organization is beset by salespersons offering the latest computer techniques for making satisfactory operations more satisfactory. Thus, the

---

EVALUATION AND ANALYSIS OF AN ELECTRONIC
DATA PROCESSING SYSTEM IMPACT

	Yes	No
1. Will it reduce costs? How Much?	———	———
2. Will it improve internal operation in some way? State specific tangible improvements we can expect—simple, understandable, meaningful, and measurable.	———	———
3. Will it increase productivity in certain areas of activity? Where?	———	———
4. How can we measure this increased productivity? Give this in operational terms, such as number of jobs per day, reduced time to get jobs done, faster response to inquiries, reduced time to develop new computer applications, etc., in quantitative terms.		
5. Will the operational methods of any departments change (e.g., purchasing, accounts payable, etc.)? Describe briefly which departments will experience change in mode of operation, and the nature of the change.		
6. Have these departments and all affected users been involved in the plans for these changes, and have they agreed to these new modes of operation?	———	———
7. Have you laid out plans with all affected users for making the transition to new modes of operation, and costed them out?	———	———
8. Will it increase service delivery?	———	———
9. Will it improve the quality of our services? State specific tangible improvements we can expect—things we can check on to see if they are improved.	———	———
10. Will it make top management's job any easier? How?		

---

adherents of computerization, usually managers close to the problems or the salespersons, are armed with facts and figures showing that the system will dramatically reverse poor performance and skyrocket acceptable performance. They present their evidence in answer to the first four questions.

Of course, staunch advocates of computers should not unilaterally provide the organization's guiding vision. Nor should there be an uncritical acceptance of the prescription advanced by managers primarily concerned with solving the problems of their own units. Thus, questions 5, 6, and 7 expand the scope of the inquiry. With the question "Will the operational methods of any department change?" the investigation enters territory where hostile witnesses may be found. Moreover, these witnesses have standing since the computer's effects are felt across the organization. As Michael Greenblatt has reported, when data processing activity increased in the central office of the Massachusetts Welfare Department so did the clerical responsibilities of caseworkers. Existing forms were expanded, new ones were introduced. Printouts of "ineligibles" and "reclassifications" bombarded harried caseworkers. Short-term deadlines attached to the printouts required that caseworkers give high priority to dealing with the listed individuals. Campaigns were launched against clients receiving unemployment compensation, those with post office boxes, and any recipient from whom a letter had rebounded with the notation "undeliverable." The result was a demoralized staff that felt overburdened by the clerical fallout from a front office that was mesmerized by computers.[10]

The Massachusetts experience illustrates that a computer installation often compels a large part of the organization to adjust to its rhythm. Thus, question 6, "Have these departments and all affected users been involved in the plans for these changes, and have they agreed to the new mode of operation?" seeks to determine the attitude of managers whose units will feel the effects of the proposed system. Of course, some unit heads will dream up dire consequences simply to forestall change. However, when a multimillion-dollar investment that will transform the organization is being considered, the time spent weeding out the spurious objections from the substantive ones is worthwhile. If there are negative side effects, the good executive will want to know about them in advance, not after it is too late.

Question 7 completes the debit ledger by determining the costs associated with the introduction and operation of the proposed computer system for the entire organization. These costs are then compared to the estimated savings. If the long- and short-term costs exceed the promised benefits, the proposed system should be rejected.

Questions 8 and 9 attempt to gauge the impact of computerization on the quantity and quality of services provided by the organization. By factoring in service delivery, it can be determined, for instance, whether excess clerks will be replaced by field personnel. If possible, the manager wants to avoid the situation reported by Greenblatt where time previously spent on providing services was devoted to preparing paper meals for the ravenous computer. Proposals that housekeeping savings be used to create more housekeeping tasks should be looked upon with skepticism. Services should be the first beneficiary of savings generated by streamlined internal operations.

If it is shown that the proposed system enhances task performance, benefits the organization as a whole, and improves service delivery, the decision makers should be ecstatic. They have a good data processing system, one that they should buy. However, executives should still ask the final question, "Will it make top management's job any easier?" What they should be looking for is a management information system: a means for determining where problems are coming from or will be coming from. For instance, a computer system becomes a top management tool if it can project an increase in the demand for a certain service or give an early warning that a unit's productivity is slacking off. Such a system aids in decision making as well as operations and fully exploits the capabilities of the computer.

MANAGEMENT INFORMATION SYSTEMS

A fully utilized *management information system (MIS)* enhances operational control, tactical control, and strategic planning: three key determinants of managerial effectiveness. A brief look at MIS applications in these areas illustrates what a well-designed system can do for managers.

Operational control is organizational pulse taking. With or without computers, managers periodically check the organization's health. A management information system facilitates operational control by allowing the decision makers to keep their fingers on the pulse of the organization. MIS monitors the organization's vital signs—productivity, profits, absenteeism, turnover—on a continuing basis. If deviations occur, MIS detects them and reports to management, permitting an early probe of the factors underlying the change. Thus, malignancies, such as a dissaffected workforce, can be treated, and benign growths, such as productivity drops during work reassignments, can be allowed to cure themselves. MIS for operational control, thus, aids managers by augmenting their knowledge of the organization and alerting them to possible malfunctions.

MIS facilitates tactical control by keeping an inventory of organizational resources. By providing detailed information on equipment, personnel, and operating conditions, it increases the manager's ability to realign the organization to meet sudden environmental demands. For instance, if a plane crashes, MIS could help a hospital administrator rapidly identify and dispatch the ambulances closest to the crash site. Staff doctors and nurses experienced in treating burn victims could be identified and assembled. All support personnel in the receiving hospitals, except those necessary for the maintenance of the existing patient population, could be assigned to the crash victim units. As a tactical control tool, then, MIS serves decision makers by providing a detailed picture of the organization's capabilities.

When used for strategic planning, MIS monitors the organizational environment. Often, operational control indicators indirectly monitor the environment. Lower profits, for instance, may be traced to consumer dissatisfaction, not poor operations. However, if the computer capacity exists, MIS should monitor the environment directly so that the organization can adjust *before* negative impacts are felt. In planning school construction, for example, an estimate of the quantity and location of the future demand for education is useful. Demographic trends adjacent to the planned site might show an aging population or an increase in an ethnic group committed to parochial education. Such information can help avoid the construction of underutilized facilities. MIS for strategic planning, then, assists managers by increasing their knowledge of the environment and advising them of probable changes in it.

A management information system can perform yeoman services for organizations. Through MIS, the managers can better understand what their organizations do, what they can do, and what they should do. A computer, however, is not a management information system. Neither is raw data, even if available by the ton. The organization that wants MIS must be able to exploit its computer equipment and information resources. This task, as we will see, is not always easy.

Why Information Systems Cannot Get Promoted

Organizations are fond of the name "management information system." It bespeaks an organization sophisticated and innovative enough to have achieved computer mastery. Unfortunately, many systems christened with the name "management information" are not worthy. Management is neglected. What is left are "information systems" of dubious value to managers. Instead of useful information, such systems inundate managers with a deluge of disorganized data. This often results in the computer's permanent demotion to the clerical ranks.

Often, when management information systems fail to live up to their name, the computer is partly at fault. A marvelous and expensive machine, it demands to be put to use. In a headlong rush to comply with this demand, many organizations throw anything and everything into the computer. Thus, as Herbert Simon has pointed out, what goes in is usually information that is easy to find and already in a form suitable for computer entry.[11] The data that fit these requirements tend to be internal organizational data. Relevant or irrelevant, huge amounts of data are shoveled into the computer system. The result is a management information system that presents an internal picture when, in fact, most top managerial decisions require an analysis of external events. Furthermore, the internal picture may be too detailed. Few top executives have the time to go through a three-inch thick printout that presents more folding difficulties than a roadmap and continually falls off the desk. Thus, even for operational decisions, the executive may fall back to more familiar and less unwieldy ground.

Government has an additional problem in attempting to exploit the potential of the computer; namely, unlimited fuel. If it is data that computer systems require, there is likely no better place to look than in government. Here, data exist in abundance and, there is little doubt, overabundance. "Red tape" is not merely the utterance of some cynic standing on a street corner. Entire buildings are used to house the papers of a single ex-president. And for every document the former chief executive removes, there are probably several carbon copies housed within the bureaucracy. Furthermore, few government documents stand alone. Other papers and memoranda go before them and they, in turn, breed additional documents. The government's routine recordkeeping and reporting procedures are of such magnitude that there is almost always, somewhere, a government or legislative commission whose purpose is to recommend ways of reducing government paperwork. Recently, a middle-level federal manager revealed to one of the authors that "I process approximately 70 files a day, 350 a week, for a total of about 17,000 per year. The total number of papers proverbially shuffled amounts to more than 100,000 per year or 500 per day, the equivalent of a large novel."

The government, then, has food a plenty for data processing systems. The question is whether the food is nutritious or if it is just a bunch of empty calories. The question is somewhat central from an administrative standpoint since a computer system is too expensive to be fed junk. However, government's approach to a computer system is often one of feeding it everything and connecting it to everyone. For example, one observer reports, "an intense preoccupation with the instantaneous reporting of criminal activity and driving violations so that every arm of the law becomes part of a network of intelligence, from the governor of the state down to the local dog catcher."[12]

Those who take the approach of universal inputs and reporting are sorely missing the point of systems management. Dumping current procedures into the computer without analysis does nothing more than electrify them. Current practices may well be outmoded, redundant, or inappropriate. The least that a switch to computer processing should accomplish is a weeding out of bad procedures before they become institutionalized, possibly forever, in an electronic memory.

The central idea is to put into the computer data that mean something. The data that government collects, while voluminous, are often not related to various program objectives. This deficiency often draws biting criticisms. Columnist Elizabeth Drew's is typical:

> If the purpose of an adult basic education program is to teach people how to read and write, the Office of Education might reasonably be expected to know how many people thereby actually learned how to read and write, but it does not.[13]

If this sort of statement came only from a columnist, as in the usual government characterization of "sniping columnist," we might be inclined to discount it. However, in this case, the Department of Health, Education and Welfare chimes in with an echo rather than a retort. "The nation has not a comprehensive set of statistics reflecting social progress or retrogression. There is no government procedure for stocktaking of the social health of the nation."[14] The key word in this statement is "comprehensive." Usually, raw material is available; government has a plentiful supply of both statistical and specific data.

Statistical records are those that are divorced from the identity of the persons or things to which they relate. Census data, financial data, and all types of "per capita" and "per ten thousand" data are statistical records. Specific records identify the person or object to which the information relates. Information on traffic violations, social security records, credit reports, and monthly credit card bills are all computerized data banks that have individuals as their focus. The county or municipal property tax roster, certificate of occupancy files, and building inspection reports are all data bases that concern themselves with individual structures.

It is the creative combination of statistical and specific records that undergirds a management information system. The mix and match will be determined by the individual agency's needs. Planning boards and engineering departments may want "to have available detailed demographic patterns and trends. Particularly for technological services, where the capital investments often have long design and lead times and even longer lives, good projections are essential."[15] Other agencies may want detailed and specific information on a single aspect of the environment. Individual water consumption, electricity use, or the traffic on a single street may be part of a data processing system so that charges can be assessed against homeowners or modifications can be made in traffic control procedures. Such data processing utilizations apply to individual agencies. They assist management and contribute to organizational efficiency. However, for the full realization of the computer's potential, it is often necessary to look beyond the agency's borders. For instance, computerized billing by the water authority, and by the utility commission, may save untold clerical work hours, but a combined bill and a single meter reader would save the jurisdiction still more.

Thus, the failure to integrate data bases can substantially wipe out the computers' advantages through duplication. Also, further gains can remain unrealized if data are so fragmented that they cannot be used as a decision tool. For instance, trends in water and utility consumption, if analyzed, might aid in the more effective planning of future facilities. This cannot be done if the data are viewed only as billing information. To understand and manage information effectively, the subsystems in which parts of the data are stored must be interrelated. To achieve utility in planning and evaluation as well as in day-to-day operations, meaningless and redundant information must be eliminated and relevant data combined into a yardstick to measure performance and progress.

TYPES OF COMPUTER APPLICATIONS

Computers do several things that modern organizations find extremely useful. Leaving aside specific applications for a moment, the computer is organizationally valuable because it:

Processes large amounts of data very quickly.
Can recover stored information very quickly.
Can integrate a number of data sources.
Can remember decision rules and apply them.

The first two applications are the most familiar. Quick processing and information recovery characterized most of the early business and government uses of computer systems. Even today, the bulk of computer activity still revolves around the administrative tasks of billing, payroll, and file maintenance. The use of computers for integration, trend analysis, and decision making, although more recent, is expanding. Private business is a prime customer with integrated financial systems, computerized marketing forecasts, and automated manufacturing processes with internalized decision rules to regulate production levels. Government has been somewhat slow, however, in adapting the computer to such uses. As one critic noted:

> In most states, computers are confined to administrative systems without becoming a part of the operational activities of major state agencies. . . . They store the results of such decisions as patient or inmate assignment, without storing the underlying logic so that people could be automatically routed.[16]

Despite this gloomy picture, governments have undertaken increasingly more sophisticated applications of computer technology.

Some will be described below and there appear to be more on the horizon. We will now treat each of the general applications described above in somewhat more detail.

Quantity Processing   If there is a sound that we have come to associate with computers, it is the incessant staccato of electronic type, backgrounded by the low grating of the racing cartridge, and punctuated every second or so by the sharp sound of paper snapping upward. Usually, when the computer stops making noise, there are thousands of checks, bills, or license renewal applications ready to bring joy, sorrow, or annoyance to their recipients.

This type of computer application is carried out by *batch processing systems.* They are characterized by quantity production at high speed. Usually associated with bills and payrolls, and accompanied by determined, disturbing, and continuous noise, such systems are often referred to as *"number crunching" machines.* Their usefulness in many government activities is apparent. A single government document can go to millions of individuals. License and registration renewal applications, income tax forms and refund checks, and payrolls for some 15 million public employees represent clerical tasks that are primarily performed by computer. One shudders to think of the impact on government services should these processes ever revert to the domain of the individual clerk and typist. However, this is unlikely. Indeed, we are approaching the day when almost all routine government documents will bear the familiar type of the industrious, "number crunching" computer.

Quick Information Retrieval   It is getting harder to be a swindler these days. More and more retail businesses are acquiring the capability of determining immediately one's integrity, financial and otherwise. This on the spot investigation of checking account and credit card status is made possible by a hookup to any of several computer systems that provide credit information on an individual. Having been presented your check or credit card, the clerk activates the electronic screen behind the counter, enters your identity number, and receives a near instantaneous report of your balance. Further, the silver screen may contain such historical data as "card stolen," "history of overdrafts," "frequent late payments." Such minute information can cause one varying degrees of embarrassment.

It is generally not the store that maintains the credit reporting system. Rather, the electronic credit files are maintained by companies that sell access to retail subscribers. The terminal at the checkout counter connects, via regular telephone channels, to a central computer that may be several thousand miles away. In another, slower variation, retail subscribers, although not having terminals within the store, may call the central credit file where a clerk will summon up the individual's file and deliver a status report over the phone. Regardless of the method of access, these information-providing computers are referred to as *inquiry systems.*

In government, instantaneous access to information on individuals has been chiefly associated with law enforcement organizations. A number of statewide, computer telecommunication systems have been implemented to aid police in apprehending felons. A police officer can radio the license number of a vehicle under surveillance to a dispatcher and in a matter of seconds know whether the vehicle has been reported stolen or used to commit a serious crime. In addition to FBI, state, and local police data on vehicles, these systems contain information on stolen parts and equipment, boats, firearms, stocks, bonds or other securities, and wanted or missing persons. These data are continuously updated. In some traffic courts, clerks post hearing results to the individual's computer file almost as soon as a decision has been rendered. Consider the poor soul who, convicted of one traffic violation at 10 o'clock, has to answer a second ticket at 11 o'clock. The second hearing may be in another part of the building before a different hearing officer and clerk. Nonetheless, the remorseless computer will include the hour-old conviction when the hearing officer summons up the driver's record on the cathode screen.

Systems that permit modification of the computerized file by the person at the remote terminal are called *inquiry and on-line updating systems.* Their advantages in judicial or quasi-judicial settings are apparent. Recordkeeping, always a problematic part of court operations, can be streamlined. However, the security of inquiry and on-line updating systems is a major consideration. With keyboard access and knowledge of the code that allows systems use, unsavory characters could redo their court records, or scofflaws could dismiss all of their outstanding traffic violations. Thus, elaborate and expensive precautions against unauthorized access are built into such systems.

In one application of quick retrieval technology, the city of Charlotte, North Carolina, has a computerized *data base*—a data bank or group of files so keyed and related as to be the base for a management information system—that treats every building within the municipality from a fire-fighting perspective. Each building profile includes:

> building occupancy by time of day (total—children—elderly—invalids).
> available water.
> location and main size of primary and secondary hydrants.
> location of sprinkler and standpipe connections.
> locations and type of shutoffs—vertical openings.
> location and nature of hazardous materials.
> structural hazards.
> security systems.[17]

When a fire is reported, the dispatcher enters the address into the computer that then displays the above information. The dispatcher then relays the information to the companies en route or on the scene. What is saved here is "sizing up" time. The firefighters can have an idea of what they are up against before arriving on the scene.

In the Sheriff's Department of Hillsborough County, Florida, computerized inquiry systems appear to have reached a new state of refinement.[18] In what may well turn out to be a prototype, patrol cars in Hillsborough County have been equipped with computer terminals that allow police officers direct access to data bases.

Besides providing near-instantaneous relay of requested information, the system eliminates the dispatcher time previously spent on being the intermediary between the patrol car and the computer. Furthermore, the procedure reduces the amount of radio air time spent on voice transmissions. If you have ever eavesdropped on a patrol car, you will know that the relay of messages is fairly constant. Especially during high-activity periods, police bands are either near or at capacity. In fact, the familiar code (10–4; 2–11 in progress at 950 Main) reflects the need to shorten messages to make the most out of limited air time. In Hillsborough County, the signals that relay the request punched in by the police officer and return the desired information occupy the airways for only a second or two. Yet it can fill up the patrol car screen with data that might take a dispatcher 30 seconds to recite. Other dispatcher–patrol car interactions, such as the acknowledgment of the receipt of a message, can be accomplished by the pressing of a single key, thus saving additional air time for emergency transmissions.

Personnel records are another area where the computerized information retrieval systems can be useful. Finding the right person for the right job can be an almost impossible task if, as in the federal government, the pool of talent is composed of over 3 million individuals. The federal government has already computerized much of its employee data, and for positions such as the mid-level career executive, data on applicants are computerized as well. Thus an agency might want a person with a master's degree in social work, with five years of work experience, and fluency in Spanish. By feeding these specifications into the data base of applicants, a list of candidates meeting these requirements can be obtained. Reproduced below are some of the 75 data points that comprise the computerized record of employees in Great Britain's civil service. The potential for using these data in recruitment, assignment, and the planning of future personnel needs is apparent.

Information Integration   Information processing and data retrieval systems are, from the perspective of an overall management information system, merely components. They may perform very effi-

CENTRAL PERSONAL RECORD—CONTENT[19]

PRISM Standard Element No.	Element Name
	Basic Details
100	National Insurance number/Civil Service identity number
101	Surname—recorded date
102	Surname
103	Initials—recorded date
104	Initials
105	Date of birth
106	Sex
107	Marital status—recorded date
108	Marital status
112	Hours of work (part-time staff)—date
113	Hours of work (part-time staff)
114	Registered disabled
115	Employment status or type of appointment—date
116	Employment status or type of appointment
	Civil Service Career
200	Civil Service—date of entry
201	Civil Service—grade on entry
202	Civil Service—method of entry
203	Civil Service—source of entry
204	Department—date of entry
205	Department
206	Department—method of entry
207	Grade—date of entry
208	Grade
209	Grade—method of entry
210	Grade—seniority date
211	Professional/scientific discipline—date of entry
212	Professional/scientific discipline
213	Occupational group or class—method of entry
214	Temporary promotion—date
215	Temporary promotion—grade
216	Responsibility allowance—date
217	Responsibility allowance—amount
	Academic and Professional Qualifications
300	Qualification—type
301	Qualification—awarding institution
302	Qualification—level of attainment—overall
303	Qualification—subject
304	Qualification—year of award, or year of cessation/reinstatement of membership of a professional institution

ciently, but they stand alone. To be utilized to their fullest, the interrelationships of the data bases to each other must be discovered and the data bases integrated. For instance, a "paper crunching" payroll system relates not only to finance but to personnel. If the payroll department and the personnel department have separate computer systems, there will be redundant aspects in each—salary levels, grade, pension payments, etc. To maximize the public's computer investment, it is necessary to insure that systems talk to each other so that considerable time is not spent "reinventing the wheel."

The electronic cash registers that are appearing in many stores are the most visible examples of integrated data base computer systems. The cash register is, in fact, a computer terminal. It has linkages to the accounting, inventory, and buying subsystems of the store's computer. When you purchase an item, the computerized cash account (or in the case of charges, an accounts receivable ledger) is automatically credited. The item purchased, entered via code number through the cash register terminal, is automatically subtracted from inventory. If your purchase has caused the stock of the item to fall below a predetermined level, a reorder form will be generated by the computer. Thus, a significant amount of clerical time is saved; there is no accountant to post figures; no clerk to record manually reductions from inventory; no buyer time consumed filling out a purchase order. There are also clear advantages in terms of communications time saved and communications dysfunctions avoided. The buyer does not have to instruct a stock clerk to take inventory. Nor does the buyer have to worry that the clerk might count the wrong item or make up a figure out of laziness. Therefore, the chances of a buyer decision based on wrong information is substantially reduced.

The *"universal product code"* is the latest addition to the computerization of retail sales. The ubiquitous square of black bars and numbers that now appears on most food products automates yet another relationship in the retail store. Between product presentation for purchase and register entry there stands a cashier. Mistakes can occur at this point. The cashier may misread the price or the product code. A clerk may have stamped the wrong price on the item. The customer may be an inventive sort who applies his own price stickers. The universal product code eliminates these possibilities via a light beam passed over the code by the cashier. The computer reads the product's "name" and automatically rings up the price stored in its memory. The computer will also perform the accounting, inventory, and purchasing chores described above. One thing that stands in the way of the implementation of universal product codes is the requirement of most government jurisdictions that prices be marked on individual items. However, since most of the machinery necessary for implementation is already in place, one suspects that, sooner or later, that machinery will be used.

Government integration efforts in electronic data processing are at a much earlier stage, although progress is evident. The state of Louisiana effectively operates an automated management system based on federal-aid programs to the state and its political subdivisions (parishes). The system coordinates, on an annual basis, applications for federal aid by the parishes or the state operating agencies; monitors spending on all federal grants; and manages the budgets of governmental units.[20]

Financial management and, to a lesser extent, physical planning functions have achieved the highest degree of data base integration on the state, county, and municipal level. For instance, some jurisdictions have integrated the computer systems that record cash outflows—disbursements, interest repayments—and inflows—taxes, fees, and fines—so that an up to the minute net balance is known. Thus, such balances can be invested overnight or over the weekend, with the resulting interest accruing to the jurisdiction. However, much remains to be done, particularly in the sharing of information bases among the various government levels and among neighboring jurisdictions. California, through its Intergovernmental Board on Electronic Data Processing, and Pennsylvania, through its Interagency Municipal Information Systems Advisory Committee, are two states that are laying a groundwork for the effective integration of data bases among governments.[21]

Decision-Making Aid Computers are decision tools. They can be used to bring executives information upon which decisions can be made, or they can internalize decision logic and make decisions on their own. Even a simple payroll system contains a decision logic that the computer applies automatically. It has been programmed with the decision rules concerning the taxes to be withheld from various salary amounts at a given number of dependents. Additionally, it is implanted with guidelines for deciding social security withholding, pension contributions, and other deductions. However, the payroll computer deals with a world where there is little complexity. The rules change infrequently, usually once a year when tax withholding rates go up or down. The rules are simply a matter of a few percentage calculations. Contrast this with a decision situation where there are several fires occurring simultaneously. The severity of each is not clear, and life or death may depend on dispatching the right equipment to the right fires in a minimum of time. It is probable in such situations that the computer would be most useful in providing the dispatcher with up to the minute information and suggested assignments for a given situation. It might also completely assume some of the subdecisions, such as equipment paths to the assigned fire.

In industry, the computer has had highly sophisticated applications as a decision tool. The routing of the rolling stock on some of the nation's railways is done by computers in response to demand locations, available capacity, the location of available capacity, destination, origin paths, and a host of other factors. Automated factories are run by computers implanted with the production logic determined by systems analysts. Computers are being increasingly used to make eligibility determinations for car insurance and bank loans. These determinations are not only applied to individuals but are also used to set basic area-wide rates in response to past indicators such as loans in default or claims generated.

Routing considerations are central to many government services. Some, in fact, are almost exclusively concerned with routing. Air traffic controllers, for instance, are responsible for preserving a given amount of air space for every commercial flight within the United States. The high density of air traffic makes safe spacing a difficult, complex, and nerve-wracking job. The daily number of flights in and out of Chicago's O'Hare Airport, the country's largest, can approach 2000. The vast number of flights combined with high speeds provide the context for two commercial jet liners colliding at speeds close to 1000 miles per hour. These conditions force a heavy reliance on computer assistance both on the ground and in the plane. Computers on the plane, called command and control systems, contain course and speed settings. Information on air speed, altitude, and course headings feeds back to the computer that then makes any corrections necessary to maintain the programmed flight path. On the ground, the air traffic is monitored by computers to determine if flights are astray. Deviations are reported to the controllers so that the flight can be brought back on course. In the wake of several mid-air near misses, even more elaborate control and warning devices are being instituted to further insure air traffic safety.

Routing is also important to municipal service delivery. Service impacts can be diluted by poor assignment procedures. For instance, if sanitation trucks cannot get curbside, there are significant increases in pickup costs. Although many cities have several "no parking" hours each week to allow for mechanical street sweeping, garbage pickup schedules may not account for this curbside access. A computerized routing schedule that would maximize the coincidence of no parking hours and garbage pickup hours would certainly enhance the service delivery picture in such areas.

Police activity becomes very dependent on effective routing procedures as well, particularly on weekends when the incidence of activity requiring police attention exceeds the capacity of the units available.

(First come, first served is a fairly meaningless concept when the waiting list is composed of twisted ankles and massive coronaries. Similarly, kids drinking wine in a hallway may stay for quite a while as the police work through a roster of assaults, robberies, and other high-priority events.) A computerized system for logging and assigning priorities to emergency service requests could relieve part of the burden on dispatch units and lead to more effective coverage of the service area.

A similar condition obtains in fire dispatching. When fires are numerous, the closest company often cannot be dispatched to a new alarm because it is tied up with an earlier one. In such cases, dispatch policy seeks to ensure a rapid response from the more distant units. Equity is also a consideration in the dispatching scheme. When fires occur more often in certain districts, it is important to spread the workload to lighten the burden of the company most frequently assigned on the basis of geographic proximity.

In dispatching fire-fighting equipment, workload distribution and the assignment of priorities to events (one alarm, two alarms) are joined by a need for expeditious response. Of the local uniformed services, fire protection is probably the most emergency-oriented. Every alarm is, potentially, a major conflagration. Furthermore, fire grows quickly. Under the right conditions, it can spread in six directions at once. In such a case, a fire starting in a five-foot pile of trash need only spread outward by five feet to increase its overall size 27 times. In fire protection, minutes can make the difference between a burnt room and a devastated house or be the time that separates life and death. Thus, the operative word in fire protection is speed. Speed to the scene of a fire. Speed in setting up hoses and other apparatus to combat the blaze. Speed in ascertaining the amount of equipment needed so that the manpower on the scene may be augmented if insufficient or dispatched to other occurrences if there is an excess. With speed of response as a primary test of effectiveness for fire protection, the computer becomes the best management tool to help direct this municipal service.

A major computer application in the delivery of fire services is San Francisco's SAFER (System for the Assignment of Fire Equipment and Resources). At its heart are two computers that

> contain a geographic description of the entire city, plus a complete set of assignment rules. In addition, the computers store routing information to every alarm box location from the nearest fire station, along with temporary street closures and hazard information.[22]

This is a computer that makes decisions according to preprogrammed rules. The job of the dispatcher is to enter in the address of the reported fire. The computer then assigns apparatus. Dispatchers have the option of rejecting the computer assignment and making their own.

As the computer assigns companies to the fire, a teletype in the individual firehouses prints out routing instructions to the location. The computer then removes the assigned company from the list of available units. On a status display board in the department's command center, the status of all the firehouses and every piece of equipment is indicated. Besides being an operational tool, SAFER is also an analytical one. It keeps historical records of all dispatched calls. Periodically, these aggregate records are analyzed to discern patterns that might require a shift in assignment rules. Also, trends in the incidence of fires can identify areas where prevention programs might be emphasized or even provide a basis for determining the location of future firehouses.

Applications such as SAFER illustrate the potential of management information systems. Up to the minute information on environmental demands, resource deployment, and systems capacity can only heighten the probability that operating decisions will be correct. Moreover, as the computer assumes routine but time-consuming decisions, executives have more time to devote to major problems. Thus, fully utilized, the computer enhances management, operations, and services while freeing human resources that can be applied to improve further the organization's product. Future public administrators should be aware of such benefits because, in most cases, they can be extracted if the full potential of the computer is tapped.

THE PROBLEMS WITH COMPUTERS

The computer is not the answer to all the problems that exist in public and private organizations. Indeed, even as it benefits society, computerization extracts costs. Computers make the world a little more impersonal and a little less private. They are a handy weapon for administrators who, out of fear, distrust, or disdain, want to keep a close eye on the citizenry. The unrestrained sharing of computerized information by public and private organizations can occasionally result in the trampling of individual rights. Finally, there is the possibility that, as the computer takes over our work, we may wrongly bequeath it our judgment as well. This is the view of Joseph Weizenbaum, who writes:

> It is common for the soldier, say the bomber pilot, to operate at an enormous psychological distance from his victims. Modern technological rationalizations of war, diplomacy, politics and commerce, such as computer games, have an even more insidious effect on the making of policy. Not only have the policymakers abdicated their decision-making responsibility to a technology they do not understand . . . but responsibility has altogether evaporated. No human is any longer responsible for "what the machine says."[23]

This is a somewhat philosophical view, but it is one that should not be taken lightly. The computer has shown its ability to waylay those who should know better: namely, managers. Transfixed by the machine's marvelous capabilities for internal control, many forget that the computer's function is to automate processes to allow more managerial attention to be devoted to organizational purpose. As an observer of the computer's penchant for clouding the executive mind writes, "The computer, its operations, controls and data base induces the administrator to look at the managerial objective of his world when he should be involved with the political, social and economic meaning of what he does."[24]

The cultural impact on a society that is fast becoming computerized is also the subject of considerable speculation. There is a definite trend toward everybody and everything being treated as a number. Social security numbers are being used as identifiers by the military services, schools, employers, and numerous others. It is, in fact, quite close to becoming the "universal identity number" that some see as a characteristic of the totalitarian state. More and more correspondence from organizations reminds us to include our "reference number" on all future letters, which can give one the feeling that they do not care much whether we put our name or not. More and more advertising brochures, charitable solicitations, and overdue parking ticket reminders arrive in the mail printed in computer type that indicates that no human being in the world even knows that the document was sent. We even know of a housing development, the home of 60,000 people that covers some 25 streets, where most residents have to think about the street name if the cab driver does not understand when told to go to "Building 26B." When everything loses its character and we become numbers living in numbers, the result may be, as Weizenbaum suggests:

> There is the psychological impact on individuals living in a society in which anonymous, hence, irresponsible, forces formulate the large questions of the day and circumscribe the range of possible answers. It cannot be surprising that large numbers of perceptive individuals living in such a society experience a kind of impotence and fall victim to a mindless rage.[25]

Although we would hope that all public administrators would retain a bit of the philosopher in them as they progress through their government careers, not all the issues that surround computer applications are philosophical ones. Two issues that have been the subject of recent legislation are the access to computerized information on individuals and the methods of rectifying the damage caused by a computer that has made a mistake. Confidentiality and responsibility by organizations are involved in both.

Privacy   Many computers collect information on people. This we know. Most of us can assume, if we have a driver's license, that there is a computerized record somewhere of our name, address, age, height, weight, and driving record. Accepting the existence of such a computer file is not difficult. However, when a part of that file becomes a mailing list sold to an organization that then proceeds to clutter up our mail boxes with junk, we are likely to be more than a little bothered. What has happened is that someone, in this case the state agency selling the mailing list, has intruded on our privacy. According to Ruth Davis, privacy "is the right of an individual to decide what information about himself he wishes to share with others."[26]

Some of our privacy is willingly relinquished. The collection of certain data is legitimized by rules that the society has agreed upon. Most do not view eye tests required by the motor vehicle bureau or venereal disease tests required by the marriage bureau as a trespass upon their private lives. Further, in return for some goods and services, we sell a portion of our privacy. In applying for a car loan, a mortgage, or life insurance, we are likely to provide financial and physical information in some detail. However, the information is a required part of the cost of the product. What does upset people is that the privacy thus relinquished often is passed on by the original holder. Its confidentiality is breached. It becomes common currency among organizations. This often happens despite legislative safeguards against such expropriation. The Census Bureau and the Internal Revenue Service both collect information pursuant to constitutional dictums and laws passed by Congress. However, in both instances, the authorizing statutes explicitly provide for the confidentiality of such data. Thus, all Americans are required to report all of their income and its sources even if they happen to be gangsters. In theory, at least, an income tax form stating an occupation of narcotics dealer should instigate no investigation other than to determine if proper taxes were paid. Despite this, political operatives in both Republican and Democratic administrations had access to opponents' tax files and used them to launch punitive investigations. As a result, victims sued, charging that politics, rather than tax profiles, motivated the investigations.

While the IRS leaked in only one direction, upward to the White House, other government agencies, notably in law enforcement, can spray computerized data in all directions. The passage below describes the path that computerized arrest records could take through the society in the 1970s.

> "Rap sheets" maintained by local, state and federal police were available to a variety of criminal justice and non-criminal justice agencies. . . . The

> Identification Division of the FBI ... operated without formal rules and routinely made its files available to organizations outside the criminal justice community, ranging from the United States Civil Service Commission to state and local organizations, such as bar admission committees or taxicab license boards, and some private employers.[27]

Moreover, some criminal-justice officials hold that acquittals should not affect the mobility of arrest records. Law enforcement, a former FBI director asserted, was enhanced by such exchanges.[28] A federal judge had a different perspective. Describing the FBI's information system as "out of effective control," Judge Gerhard Gesell awarded damages to an individual whose arrest record received wide distribution despite the fact that charges had been quickly dropped for lack of evidence.[29]

The response of Congress to the free flow of confidential information on individuals was the *Privacy Act of 1974.* It was one of a number of state and federal statutes that permitted a greater degree of citizen access to the files and deliberations of government bodies. Known as "Sunshine Laws," they have been directed at everything from the "opening" of "closed" legislative hearings to the public availability of complaints against regulated business. Specifically, the Privacy Act provided that information on individuals gathered by the federal government could be used only by the collecting agency and only for the purposes for which it was collected, except where the individual consented in writing to other uses. The circulation of law enforcement files was substantially exempted from these requirements. This has led to criticisms that the Privacy Act has overlooked the biggest offender. Nonetheless, the law provides some protection against a government official's summoning up your file for lack of anything better to read or in a random search for political ammunition.

Correcting Errors   In the 1970s, several laws gave citizens and consumers more leverage with respect to their computerized files. The Sunshine Laws made files obtainable and the Fair Credit and Reporting Act made some files correctable.

Although Sunshine Laws are not aimed specifically at computerized files and emphasize access rather than error correction, many misrepresented citizens, by waving their newly acquired file in public or in court, have secured apologetic retractions from public organizations. When errors in computerized files were addressed, it was by the Fair Credit and Reporting Act. In the early 1970s, when consumer consciousness was high, the conflict between customer and computer was highlighted. Innocent consumers were being placed on credit market blacklists. It was retail businesses, credit reporting firms, and collection agencies, networked by computer, that blacklisted consumers as the capstone of a harassment campaign featuring computerized letters and bills. Consumerists were quick to dramatize the situation and legislatures reacted by granting consumers corrective access to credit files.

It should be noted that the causes of credit file inaccuracy remain largely unaddressed by legislation. As a result, some credit companies still expand their profitable information supply via cursory "investigations" in which fact, hearsay, and slander can be indiscriminately vacuumed up and computerized. Some retailers, unconvinced of the computer's brainlessness, treat the machine as infallible and treat indignant complainants like petty swindlers. At the clerical level, conditions conducive to the rejection of just complaints remain. For the lazy clerk ensconced at the computer console, or the harried employee expected to answer many complaint letters a day, summoning up the computer file is preferable to instituting a search for the original documents. Similar attitudes and motivations occasionally surface in government. When they do, legal threats usually back up the belief in computer omniscience or the view that only scofflaws protest parking fines.

Whether the adversary is business or government, the scenario for the righteous consumer-citizens is the same. They hurl indignant protests against a stone wall of organizational obstinacy while up to their necks in a flood of tactless letters demanding money. At this point, the advances made by the private sector in integrating data bases often compounds the individual's predicament. Credit companies maintain relations with retail subscribers and information is exchanged on "deadbeats." Thus, consumers battling the local department store may find themselves hung on the retail world's version of the post office wall. Other businesses will refuse to extend them credit. When this happens, the Federal Fair Credit and Reporting Act permits the consumer to obtain, from the central credit company, a copy of the report upon which credit denial was based. The individual can then request the removal of erroneous information. If the company feels that removal is unjustified, it must insert the consumer's version of the disputed information. Several states, such as Minnesota, New York, and California have similar laws.

The remedies provided by fair credit laws will not help every individual locked in combat with an organization. If the organization does not resort to the retail credit grapevine, credit access is useless. Moreover, the law is neutralized if complainants are unaware of it or lack the time, money, and knowledge needed to apply it. When legal redress is too expensive, too complex, or closed off, the tactical skill and organizational know-how of the consumer-citizen can be the key to victory. Wise consumers aim their complaints high on the organizational hierarchy. They multiply the corrective impact of direct hit on target by demon-

3436 Corsa Avenue
Bronx, N.Y. 10469
September 23, 1975

Commissioner Michael Lazar
Parking Violations Bureau
40 Worth Street
New York, N.Y. 10013

Dear Sir:

Attached you will find a chronology of the correspondence
between various segments of your agency and this writer.
Copies of the documents identified in this chronology are
also attached.

Please be advised that I intend no further correspondence with
your agency. On June 4, 1975 this writer did file a proper and
timely plea of "not guilty." As a result of this plea, on July
14, 1975, the summons issued to this writer, and the violation
cited herein, was dismissed. Your subsequent communications,
which indicate that you would like to re-try me for a violation
dismissed pursuant to a not guilty plea, are moot, without legal
justification and border on harassment.

While I shall not communicate further with the Parking Violations
Bureau, I do intend to contact my attorney, the American Civil
Liberties Union and other organizations whose interest lies in
computer misuse, improper dunning, double jeopardy and administrative abuse, should I receive further harassment from you. Also,
if further harassed I intend to inform the Municipal Assistance
Corporation, the new Deputy Mayor for Finance, and the various
emergency management boards of the incredible and costly actions
on your part which have been duplicative, contradictory, misdirected, priorityless and stupid.

Very truly yours,

Janice O'Hara

Janice O'Hara

Enc.

A Letter of this Genre Usually Is Effective in Shifting One's Dialogue with the
Public Agency from the Computer to the Commissioner (or someone equally
organic who can resolve the complaint).

strating an awareness of the organization's environment and a willingness to upset it. When applicable, the law can be used to bolster the
individual's show of force. The letter above is a good example of how
to talk back to the organization and its computer. The response—swift,
high-level, and entirely satisfactory—is reproduced on the next page:

NEW YORK CITY
TRANSPORTATION ADMINISTRATION
PARKING VIOLATIONS BUREAU

475 Park Avenue South   New York, N.Y. 10016   (212) 481 1403

Michael J. Lazar
Administrator

Elbert C. Hinkson
Director

OCT 7 1975

T-PVB-ECH-26063

Ms. Janice O'Hara
3436 Corsa Avenue
Bronx, N.Y.   10469

Re: Summons No. 516380211
Date Issued: 6/3/75
Plate No. 201XDE

Dear Ms. O'Hara:

This is in answer to your letter dated September 23, 1975.

On behalf of the Bureau, please accept my apologies for any inconvenience you may have suffered because of a clerical error in that the above captioned summons was dismissed on July 14th and the computer did not reflect this dismissal. We recognize the erroneous letter submitted to you dated September 12, 1975, with the attached summons indicating valid verifiable defense denied.

I am confident that you will not receive further notices regarding the above captioned summons as by now the computer has recorded the dismissal.

Very truly yours,

Michael J. Lazar
Administrator

Sweet Satisfaction! Although It Is a Trivial Encounter for the Organization, the Vindicated Complainant Often Cannot Help Feeling like David Standing over the Fallen Goliath.

As you can see, jousting with the organization need not be a quixotic adventure. Letters addressed by name to organization heads can breach the executive sanctum. Once there, complaints are reviewed by a staff sensitive to mistakes, particularly those that threaten environmental relationships. The subsequent "investigate and report" order issued by executive staff generates rapid and detailed probes rather than routine inquiries to the computer. For the complaining individual, the result is usually vindication.

Whether legislative, judicial, or personal, efforts to correct computer-connected abuse are aimed at a larger target. According to Goldstein and Nolan, Privacy Acts and Fair Credit and Reporting Acts are a "direct effort to increase the power of individuals in their dealings with large organizations, which often seem remote, domineering and unconcerned about individuals."[30] Whether organizational disdain is apparent or real, accidental or purposeful, the computer can act as a barrier to individuals and as a readily accessible repository of harmful information about them. When this happens, rebuffed individuals should strike at the organization's sensitive parts; courts should penalize organizations that bully and injure innocent people; and legislature should even the odds if individuals are consistently outgunned. Above all, the public administrator should seek to prevent such problems from arising by guarding against organizational introspection and xenophobia.

CONCLUSION

In this brief review of computer applications in organizations, we have seen that they can accomplish much. We have also seen that computers can be applied in ways that prevent their maximum utilization by organizations and decision makers. Computer technology can also have subtle, but pervasive, societywide impacts, and its misuse can inflict hurt on individuals. We will close this chapter with a rather provocative statement. It is not intended as an editorial. Indeed, both of the authors are proponents of computer applications. However, it is never a bad idea to leave one's audience thinking. It is a way of insuring that learning and growth continue after the lesson is finished. Thus, as food for thought we offer an observation by Joseph Weizenbaum. "Sensible men correctly perceive that large data banks and enormous networks of computers threaten man. But they leave it to technology to formulate the corresponding question. While a simple man might ask, 'Is it good?', technology asks, 'What electronic wizardry will make them safe?' "[31]

KEY TERMS AND CONCEPTS

Batch processing systems
Computer hardware
Computer software
Data base integration
Inquiry systems
Inquiry and on-line updating
   systems

Management information system
  (MIS)
Operational control
Privacy Act of 1974
Strategic planning
Tactical control

NOTES

1. *Data Management,* 14, no. 2 (February 1976): 39.
2. Edward H. Blum, *The Community Information Utility and Municipal Services* (Santa Monica, Calif.: Rand Corporation, 1972).
3. Edward A. Tomeski, "Building Human Factors into Computer Applications: The Computer Profession Must Overcome a 'Jackass Fallacy'!", in *Computer Systems and Public Administrators,* eds. Richard A. Bassler and Norman L. Enger (Alexandria, Va.: College Readings Inc., 1976), p. 140.
4. Harold Hovey, "Some Perspectives on Data Processing in State Government," in Bassler and Enger, *Computer Systems,* p. 9.
5. F. Terry Baker, "The Pros and Cons of Structured Programming," in ibid., p. 194.
6. Hovey, "Some Perspectives on Data Processing," p. 10.
7. *New York Times,* 14 May 1976, section 2, p. 1.
8. *New York Times,* 28 March 1976, p. 35.
9. *New York Times,* 11 June 1972, section 8, p. 1.
10. Michael Greenblatt, *The Welfare Office: Notes from the Underground,* (Syracuse: Inter-University Case Program, 1977).
11. Herbert A. Simon, *Administrative Behavior,* 3rd ed. (New York: Free Press, 1976), p. 301.
12. Abe Gottlieb, "The Computer and the Job Undone," in *Computers in Public Administration: An International Perspective,* ed. Samuel J. Bernstein (Elmsford, N.Y.: Pergamon Press, 1976), p. 45.
13. Drew quoted in Abe Gottlieb, "Information Systems and Social Change," in Bassler and Engler, *Computer Systems,* p. 23.
14. Ibid.
15. Blum, *Community Information Utility,* p. 9.
16. Hovey, "Some Perspectives on Data Processing," p. 9.
17. T. F. Gardner and Dick Passine, "An Automated Fire Support System," in Bassler and Enger, *Computer Systems,* pp. 260–263.
18. John F. Kirk, Jr., "Getting the Message: Telecommunication in the Patrol Car," in ibid., pp. 53–57.
19. C. P. H. Marks, "Computer Based Personnel Information Systems," in Bernstein, *Computers in Public Administration,* pp. 130–131.
20. Samuel J. Bernstein, "Computer Applications in State and Local Government: A Survey of Accomplishments," in Bernstein, *Computers in Public Administration,* p. 428.
21. Ibid., p. 428.
22. Robert E. Rose, "A Computerized Command and Control System," in Bassler and Enger, *Computer Systems,* p. 51.
23. Joseph Weizenbaum, "On the Impact of the Computer on Society," in Bernstein, *Computers in Public Administration,* p. 465.
24. Gottlieb, "Information Systems and Social Change," p. 21.
25. Weizenbaum, "Impact of Computer."
26. Ruth M. Davis, "Privacy and Security in Data Systems," *Computers and People* 23, no. 9 (Sept. 1974): 22.
27. Mark H. Gitenstein, "The Right to Privacy Is American," in Bassler and Enger, *Computer Systems,* p. 76.
28. Clarence D. Kelly, "(The Right to Privacy Is American...) But So Is the Right to Law and Order," in ibid., pp. 77–81.

29. Gitenstein, "Right to Privacy."
30. Robert C. Goldstein and Richard L. Nolan, "Personal Privacy versus the Corporate Computer," in Bassler and Enger, *Computer Systems,* p. 68.
31. Weizenbaum, "Impact of Computer," p. 461.

BIBLIOGRAPHY

Abrams, Peter, and Corvine, Walter. *Basic Data Processing.* 2nd ed. San Francisco: Rhinehart, 1971.

Bassler, Richard A., and Enger, Norman L., eds. *Computer Systems and Public Administrators.* Alexandria: College Readings, 1976.

Bemer, R. W., ed. *Computers and Crisis: How Computers Are Shaping Our Future.* Philadelphia: Auerbach, 1972.

Bernstein, Samuel J. *Computers in Public Administration: An International Perspective.* Elmsford, N.Y.: Pergamon, 1976.

Brink, Victor Z. *Computers and Management: The Executive Viewpoint.* Englewood Cliffs, N.J.: Prentice-Hall, 1971.

Burck, Gilbert, ed. *Computer Age and Its Potential for Management.* New York: Harper & Row, 1968.

Chapin, Ned. *Computers: A Systems Approach.* New York: Van Nostrand Reinhold, 1971.

Chartrand, L. L. *Computers in the Service of Society.* Elmsford, N.Y.: Pergamon Press, 1972.

Cowan, Paul; Egleson, Nick; and Hentoff, Nat. *State Secrets.* New York: Holt, Rinehart & Winston, 1972.

Dukes, C. W. *Computerizing Personnel Resource Data.* New York: American Management Association, 1971.

Feingold, Carl. *Introduction to Data Processing.* Dubuque, Iowa: Brown, 1971.

Fitz, Harry H. *The Computer Challenge to Urban Planners and State Administrators.* Washington, D.C.: Sparton, 1965.

Foy, Nancy. *Computer Management: A Common Sense Approach.* Philadelphia: Auerbach, 1972.

George, F. H. *Computers, Science and Society.* Buffalo, N.Y.: Prometheus, 1972.

Goldstine, Herman H. *The Computer from Pascal to Von Neumann.* Princeton, N.J.: Princeton University Press, 1972.

Kelly, Joseph F. *Computerized Management Information Systems.* New York: Macmillan, 1970.

Miller, Arthur R. *The Assault on Privacy: Computers, Data Banks and Dossiers.* Ann Arbor: The University of Michigan Press, 1971.

Oettinger, Anthony G. *Run, Computer, Run.* Cambridge: Harvard University Press, 1969.

Pylyshyn, Zenon W. *Perspectives on the Computer Revolution.* Englewood Cliffs, N.J.: Prentice-Hall, 1970.

Rodgers, William. *Think: A Biography of the Watsons and IBM.* New York: Stein and Day, 1969.

Sanders, D. H. *Computers and Management.* New York: McGraw-Hill, 1970.

Simon, H. A. *The Science of the Artificial.* Cambridge: MIT Press, 1969.

Tyran, Michael. *Computerized Accounting Methods and Controls.* Englewood Cliffs, N.J.: Prentice-Hall, 1972.

Westin, Alan F., with Baker, Michael A. *Databanks in a Free Society.* New York: Quadrangle, 1972.

In addition to the sources cited in the notes and bibliography, the following *Public Administration Review (PAR)* articles are a convenient starting point for a more detailed exploration of the material in this chapter.

Danziger, James N. "Computers, Social Government and the Litany to EDP," *PAR* 37, no. 1 (Jan./Feb. 1977): 28–37.

DeBalogh, Frank G. "Public Administrators and 'The Privacy Thing': A Time to Speak Out," *PAR* 32, no. 5 (Sept./Oct. 1972): 526–530.

Downs, Anthony. "A Realistic Look at the Final Pay-offs from Urban Data Systems," *PAR* 27, no. 5 (Sept./Oct. 1967): 204–210.

Henry, Nicholas L. "Knowledge Management: A New Concern for Public Administration," *PAR* 34, no. 3 (May/June 1974): 189–195.

Kraemer, Kenneth L. "Local Government, Information Systems and Technology Transfer: Evaluating Some Assertions About Computer Application Transfer," *PAR* 37, no. 4 (July/Aug. 1977): 368–382.

Kraemer, Kenneth L. "The Evaluation of Information Systems for Urban Administration," *PAR* 29, no. 4 (July/Aug. 1969): 389–402.

Magazine, Alan H. and Beatrice G. Shields. "The Paperwork Forest: Can State and Local Governments Find a Way Out," *PAR* 37, no. 6 (Nov./Dec. 1977): 725–729.

Mindlin, Albert. "Confidentiality and Local Information Systems," *PAR* 28, no. 6 (Nov./Dec. 1968): 509–518.

Quinn, Robert E. "The Impacts of a Computerized Information System on the Integration and Coordination of Human Services," *PAR* 36, no. 2 (March/April 1976): 166–174.

Relyea, Harold C. "Opening Government to Public Scrutiny: A Decade of Federal Efforts," *PAR* 35, no. 1 (Jan./Feb. 1975): 3–9.

Richter, Anders. "The Existentialist Executive," *PAR* 30, no. 4 (July/Aug. 1970): 415–422.

Roman, Daniel D. "Technology Assessment: Perspective from the Managerial Position," *PAR* 33, no. 5 (Sept./Oct. 1973): 393–400.

Saloshin, Robert L. "The Freedom of Information Act: A Governmental Perspective," *PAR* 35, no. 1 (Jan./Feb. 1975): 10–13.

Simon, Herbert A. "Applying Information Technology to Organization Design," *PAR* 33, no. 3 (May/June 1973): 268–278.

Tabb, William K. "Data Retrieval Systems, the University, and State Decision Making," *PAR* 31, no. 4 (July/Aug. 1971): 327–333.

RELEVANT PERIODICALS

Automation
Business Automation
Business Week
Computer Decisions
Computerworld
Data Management
Datamation
Infosystems
Journal of Systems Management
Law and Computer Technology
Public Automation
Technology Review

RELEVANT CASE STUDIES
(Cases marked ICCH are available from the Intercollegiate Case Clearing House, Soldier Field, Boston, Mass. 02163; cases marked ICP are available from the Inter-University Case Program, Box 229, Syracuse, N.Y. 13210.)

Bell, J. R. and L. B. Steedman. *Personnel Problems in Converting to Automation,* [ICP]
Greenblatt, M. *The Welfare Office: Notes from the Underground,* [ICP]
Raymond, T. C. and F. W. McFarland. *Chicago Police Force,* (A),* [ICCH]

*Letters indicate that the case is presented in several installments.

INDEX